Judging the Constitution

·—Judging the —————·
CONSTITUTION

CRITICAL ESSAYS ON JUDICIAL LAWMAKING

Edited by

Michael W. McCann
University of Washington

Gerald L. Houseman
Indiana University, Fort Wayne

Scott, Foresman/Little, Brown Series in Political Science
SCOTT, FORESMAN AND COMPANY
Glenview, Illinois   Boston   London

Library of Congress Cataloging-in-Publication Data

Judging the Constitution.

(Scott, Foresman/Little, Brown series in
political science)
    Includes index.
    1. United States—Constitutional law.   I. McCann,
Michael W., 1952–   II. Houseman, Gerald L.
III. Series.
KF4550.A2J83   1989   342.73   88–18590
ISBN 0–673–39897–8   347.302

    2 3 4 5 6 7 8 9 10—MVN—95 94 93 92 91 90 89

Printed in the United States of America

Acknowledgments

Quote on p. 23 from Stuart Taylor Jr., "Speeches Provide Insight into Judge Kennedy's Philosophy," *The New York Times,* December 1, 1987. Copyright © 1987 by The New York Times
Company. Reprinted by permission.

Quote on p. 43 from Stuart Taylor Jr., "Court, 5–4, Votes to Restudy Rights in Minority Suits,"
The New York Times, April 26, 1988. Copyright © 1988 by The New York Times Company.
Reprinted by permission.

Portions of Chapter 4 are from "The Critical Legal Studies Movement," 96 *Harvard Law Review,*
January 1983, pp. 563–675. Copyright © 1983 by the Harvard Law Review Association. Reprinted with permission.

Portions of Chapter 11 adapted from "Unpacking Patriarchy" in *A Less Than Perfect Union*
edited by Jules Lobel. Copyright © 1988 by Jules Lobel. Reprinted by permission of Monthly
Review Foundation.

Dedicated to our families ————————— .

Preface

This book project was conceived in the fall of 1986 from our common interest in several different but overlapping developments. First, it quickly was becoming clear to us that officially sponsored Bicentennial events would do little to generate serious reflection regarding our nation's constitutional legacy. Second, we agreed that the evolving Critical Legal Studies movement had succeeded in catalyzing much interesting intellectual inquiry regarding many aspects of our legal system, but we also recognized that only a few of these scholars focused their study directly on constitutional issues. Finally, we sensed that much similar critical analysis on constitutional lawmaking was emanating from social science departments, but we were frustrated that most of this work was scattered about in academic journals or conference papers that were known only to a limited audience. Hence, there seemed to exist both demand for and supply of scholarship for the collection of critical, progressively oriented perspectives regarding judicial constructions of the Constitution that this book has become.

From the start, this book has been a collective endeavor in every way. The actual shape and substance of the project emerged from discussions between the two of us over many months. From there, many minds have been enlisted in a host of important ways, and our accumulated debts have been many. First, we must thank the specific authors of chapters in the collection for their cooperation and contributions. All these scholars developed new papers, or adapted previous work, specifically for this volume. Moreover, these original drafts were subjected to numerous interventions and requests for changes—sometimes involving as many as five stages of review and revision—from us, the co-editors. These requests for further work were accepted in all cases with admirable professionalism, commitment to the project, and even good cheer—and almost always in expeditious fashion. And, of course, we in turn have learned through these exchanges much more about the nature of lawmaking and constitutionalism than could ever be conveyed in the essays alone.

Second, we would like to thank those who have shared their ideas and judgments on various aspects of the project, from overall design to choices of contributing authors to the content of specific papers. This includes again the extraordinary services rendered by several of our authors, including most importantly Stuart Scheingold, Lief Carter, and Bill Haltom. We also owe considerable debt to the outside reviewers selected by the publisher, among them especially to Austin Sarat, whose extensive commentary at different stages was invaluable.

We also enthusiastically acknowledge our great appreciation for the efforts made by John Covell, our editor at Scott, Foresman/Little, Brown. He responded to our initial proposal quickly and enthusiastically; he pushed us at every point to rigorous rethinking of our goals; he solicited critical commentary from numerous outside reviewers; and he supported us when we and his supporters doubted the project. Much of what is best about this volume grew from John's suggestions, and he has shown great patience with our inability to fully incorporate or realize other equally sound ideas.

Finally, we want to thank our families, who supported us spiritually and materially as we gave far more of our time to this project than we initially thought would be necessary. We hope that it was worth the sacrifices.

Given the strong supporting cast noted above, we admit that there is no plausible excuse for errors or deficiencies in this volume. We thus have agreed in advance simply to blame each other for those flaws in the book that surely will be identified by some of our readers.

Michael McCann
Gerald Houseman

Contents

————— .

Introduction: Constitutionalism and Critical Scholarship

MICHAEL W. McCANN AND GERALD L. HOUSEMAN

The bicentennial celebration of the U.S. Constitution was a bust. Despite the well-meaning efforts of many individuals and groups, the planned events simply failed to generate much enthusiasm.

Such public indifference to constitutional birthday parties is not entirely new or surprising, but specific events in 1987 especially seemed to dampen the celebratory spirit.[1] For one thing, the crass commercialization of the commemoration manifest in tacky television spots, printings of the legal text on cereal boxes, and glitzy ceremonies hardly encouraged reverence among the citizenry. Moreover, the growing list of investigations, indictments, and convictions that riddled the Reagan administration surely nurtured pessimism about claims that our constitutional government is either accountable to the people or bound by the rule of law. Finally, the controversy generated by the nomination and defeat of Robert Bork as Supreme Court justice revealed an all too human reality behind the prevailing myths celebrating an apolitical judicial interpretation of constitutional truths. Judge Bork's impassioned arguments for limiting legal constructions to those consistent with the intentions of the constitutional framers supported mainstream ideals, to be sure. However, his lengthy televised testimony tended to raise more questions than it answered about the actual nature of legal constraints on judicial decision makers, the substantive agenda behind arguments for judicial restraint, and the politically charged character of modern judicial lawmaking activity generally.[2]

This book has developed from the conviction that our constitutional legacy is better served by frank inquiry into these questions than by the formal rituals and patriotic platitudes recycled in most bicentennial events. Specifically, this collection of original essays offers a variety of critical views concerning the character and implications of constitutional lawmaking by the Supreme Court in contemporary American public life. These inquiries are "critical" in several senses. First, most of these authors share the assumption that constitutional lawmaking is an important dimension of our political legacy. In particular, they assume that inherited constitutional discourses play significant roles in structuring, reforming, and legitimating—that is, in "constituting"—both the organizational forms and substantive values that dominate our political system. At the same time, the essays in this collection express parallel critical judgments that prevailing judicial constructions of the Constitution are highly problematic at best, radically deficient at worst, and in any case in need of fundamental reconceptualization. For some authors, the legacy is incomplete or requires only minor adjustments; others urge more systematic transformation. All agree, however, that the status quo is unacceptable and that change within and through the courts can be a resource for the achievement of greater justice and freedom in our society.

THE CRITICAL TRADITION AND LEGAL SCHOLARSHIP

The critical understandings and spirit expressed in this book build upon a long tradition of debate and dissent concerning American constitutionalism. After all, the very idea of a written constitution that exists independent of government itself was a radical departure from inherited European traditions. The actual constitutional document was forged out of considerable debate and disagreement at the Philadelphia Convention and was subjected to even greater criticism, abuse, and rejection by a great many early Americans. Moreover, even many of those who approved the document defended it as a limited instrument deserving neither "sanctimonious reverence" nor immunity from revision by future generations of citizens. As Thomas Jefferson and others argued, a truly democratic nation has both a right and an obligation to "reconstitute" itself continually through principled organizational changes informed by past experience, new challenges, and changing circumstances.[3]

Equally important is the fact that frequent invocations of natural law and natural rights traditions have provided an enduring source of critical dissent and creative departure *within* routine judicial practices of constitutional lawmaking. Indeed, our entire constitutional system from the beginning has displayed a curious mix of formal routines and pragmatic instrumentalism, which has allowed almost ceaseless adjustment in response to changing social conditions and values. For every affirmation of Chief Justice John Marshall's claim that "Courts are the mere instruments of the law, and can will nothing," there are abundant testimonies to the contrary.[4] Some judges have echoed William O. Douglas's comment that he simply favored the underdog whenever possible, while many others have instead cast their votes consistently for the privileged—yet few can contest that such political factors have considerable impact on lawmaking activity.

It was not until early in the twentieth century, however, that critical recognition of these factors was openly voiced, systematically developed at the level of theory, and linked to progressive conceptions of social change in which the political character of judicial lawmaking was acknowledged. The vanguard of this movement, the so-called "legal realists," played a pivotal role, above all in challenging the formalist and conceptualist pretenses that long had guided law school teaching and scholarship.[5] At the level of method, the realists drew heavily on pioneers of sociological jurisprudence such as Roscoe Pound, Louis D. Brandeis, and Benjamin N. Cardozo to debunk the canon that reasoning from rules and precedents alone determines judicial decision making in some mechanical and nondiscretionary manner. Focusing on what judges "do" rather than on what they "say," realist leaders such as Oliver Wendell Holmes, Karl Llewellyn, and Jerome Frank worked to demonstrate that formal judicial opinions thus are not objective or neutral in any meaningful sense but typically are only rationalizations for judgments reflecting a host of largely arbitrary personal, social, and political factors. Such assumptions further led the realists to provide compelling critiques of the prevailing formal doctrinal logics themselves and to demystify the social relations they governed. In particular, scholars such as Morris Cohen and Robert Hale focused their critical attacks on the prevailing private law logic, which served to insulate capitalist property relations from democratic public control. There can be little doubt, moreover, that these critical contributions were politically as well as academically motivated. In particular, most realist scholars and activists aimed not so much to undermine the traditional authority of judges and law as to encourage and justify more flexible, pragmatic, and responsible judicial action consistent with New Deal liberal social engineering commitments and statist obligations.[6]

The 1930s witnessed a parallel development in more radical Left legal activism as well. Not content merely to theorize about law or to assume a role in the liberal state, many lawyers took up difficult and often futile cases for oppressed citizens in arenas of civil rights, free speech, tenants' rights, unorganized farmworker, and organized labor union (especially CIO) struggles. Some activists worked on their own from both within and without law schools, but most were affiliated with groups such as the National Association for the Advancement of Colored People (NAACP), The Civil Rights Congress, the American Labor Party, the American Civil Liberties Union (ACLU), various labor unions, and especially the National Lawyers Guild.[7] Often working within climates of hostility, intimidation, and even violent opposition, such lawyers worked courageously to build the foundations of precedent and debate that still undergird civil rights, civil liberties, labor, and administrative law today.

Although highly influential, the views of realists and leftists did not succeed in supplanting traditional understandings of law in the academy or the profession. Indeed, during the postwar years a variety of postrealist schools attempted to strike a middle ground and managed to salvage at least some semblance of older formalist convictions about the inherent continuity, neutrality, and objectivity of legal constraints on judicial lawmakers. In most cases, they achieved this by emphasizing the integrity of the judicial process rather than substantive content.[8] But the collapse of the New Deal consensus and the explosion of challenges to government-supported injustices during the 1960s again exposed the illusory nature of such claims to legal objectivity.

This in turn sparked several new turns in critical legal thought. On the one hand was the founding of the Law and Society movement in 1964. Reformist in its political bent and guided by the dual social science models of behavioralism and realist-inspired political jurisprudence, this movement expanded serious scholarly inquiry into the interpenetration of legal practice and the broader society within which it takes place.[9] On the other hand, another group of advocates revived perspectives far more radical in substance if notably less disciplined in method. Deriving to a great extent from New Left origins and centered to a large degree in the National Lawyers Guild, such activists painted a far grimmer picture of liberal law as the very cornerstone and source of legitimation for an essentially repressive classist, racist, and patriarchal state.[10] Much as during the New Deal era, both developments in legal scholarship were paralleled by, and closely connected to, expanding ranks of activist lawyers. These new legions of radical and "public interest" lawyers identified with a wide range of progressive political commitments and played a crucial role in offering legal assistance to the primary social struggles of the period—the civil rights, welfare reform, anti-war, feminist, consumer, and environmental movements.[11]

Once again, these trends produced countertrends and new attempts at synthesis. The most important of the former has been the conservative Law and Economics movement. Centered at the University of Chicago, this movement has been the source of many books, articles, and briefs that have influenced both judicial policy and judicial appointments (including Richard Posner on the Seventh Circuit) in the Reagan era. Its twin intellectual foundations have been the ethical conservatism of Straussian political philosophy and neoclassical economics. Beginning from the premise that wealth maximization is a cardinal human desire, the movement's leading theorists have advocated ambitious schemes for limiting legal interventions into marketplace exchanges to those which support the marketplace itself. In short, it is argued that microeconomic calculations of optimal efficiency in allocating social goods offer a compelling objective foundation for constraining otherwise discretionary legal decisions about citizen rights claims. Although this position has been widely criticized with regard to its underlying assumptions about human rationality and its frankly inegalitarian normative biases, such simple schemes for normative restructuring of law have greatly influenced both legal practice and scholarship in recent years.[12]

Not surprisingly, this resurgence of conservative jurisprudence provided impetus to yet another emerging left-oriented movement, that of the Critical Legal Studies movement (the crits).[13] CLS developed from a 1977 meeting of various political activists and sympathizers from the 1960s who convened to pool thoughts on mainstream legal ideas, legal education, and legal practice. Although they undeniably owed much to both the Law and

Society movement and earlier radical views, the crits quickly charted a path of their own. At the level of method, much of their work has pointed toward a more sophisticated version of realist demystification, demonstrating the inherent indeterminacy of law as a constraint on judicial practice. Invoking the technique of so-called "trashing," crit scholars have showed how legal decisions often contradict their stated premises, exclude consideration of plausible alternatives, or lack justifiable or coherent ethical premises at all. Unlike most realists, however, most crits do not assume that legal practice is wholly arbitrary or without pattern. Rather, CLS scholars have tended to emphasize the existence of persistent ideological biases built into the structures of legal action, which thus must be "deconstructed" to reveal their contradictory or objectionable character as well as to offer alternative legal constructions.[14]

At the substantive level, crits again have tended to follow the realist lead in attacking privileged legal principles, such as the distinction between public and private spheres in corporate capitalist society. From this general perspective, they have aimed their critical fire at a host of traditional legal arrangements in the areas of criminal law, tort doctrine, contract theory, and free speech policy. The key difference, however, is that the crits share few of the illusions about New Deal liberalism that guided the realists and instead draw on a host of more radical, New Left–inspired normative perspectives— including neo-Marxist, feminist, and populist stances—in criticizing existing areas of liberal public law and pointing toward new directions of progressive legal activity. Indeed, critical evaluations of the variously cooptive, contradictory, and depoliticizing character of many modern welfare state legal forms— such as labor relations law, welfare administration, social regulatory practice, and antidiscrimination policy—have been a staple contribution of CLS scholarship and practical activism.

CONTEMPORARY CONSTITUTIONAL CRITICISM: A THEMATIC OVERVIEW

The essays on constitutional lawmaking in this book owe much to all of these dissenting traditions in American legal history and, not surprisingly, mostly to CLS. All of the authors here express much the same critical temperament as the crits. All owe the same debt to earlier realist, radical, and Law and Society contributions. Moreover, all of the authors reflect a faith in law as a resource for democratic social change—an attitude that again parallels that of the crits.

Some important differences also deserve mention, however. First, most CLS works have focused on the politics and history of private and statutory law rather than on the primary concern of this book, that of constitutional law. This book thus can be understood as an effort to help fill an important gap in the corpus of contemporary critical discourse about law.

Moreover, this collection offers analyses by authors who are not only formally unaffiliated with the crits but who also draw far more from social science and political philosophy backgrounds than from law schools and who do not consider themselves to be part of a unified movement at all. Thus, both the methodological and substantive perspectives in this book range more widely than do crit studies. Finally, this book includes several essays that directly challenge some views most commonly associated with the crits. Rogers M. Smith's provocative critique regarding some strains of CLS thought ("After Criticism") is the most direct example of such a challenge, but more subtle departures are apparent elsewhere as well.

Given the relative independence of authors in this book, it seems worthwhile in this introduction to provide some further general observations about the particular themes and perspectives common to most of these essays. These essays tend to follow the realists and crits in assuming that rules and principles—whether rooted in the written text, the framers' intent, standing precedents, or ethical arguments—neither determine constitutional lawmaking in any mechanical sense nor impart to it any universal claims of ethical objectivity. Rather, as the initial chapters by Lief Carter and John Gilliom and Judith A. Baer contend, judicial decisions are understood as inherently creative and highly discretionary activities of legal construction influenced by a diverse range of factors; thus, law is seen as an essentially plastic medium subject to numerous internal tensions, conflicts, and change over time. As such, one concern of many contributors to this collection is simply to explore the often contradictory, inconsistent, or simply undesirable aspects of those legal constraints crafted by judges over time in different areas of constitutional concern.

Contrary to the realists and some strands of CLS, however, most authors here still assume that normal constitutional lawmaking practices remain substantively "bounded" or constrained in important ways. These loose constraints derive from both the internal conventions of learned legal practice (the modes of argument, procedural rituals, and professional norms that constitute legal "ways of being and doing" in the world) and external contextual or institutional factors (including sensitivity to specialized audiences—such as other government actors, law scholars, and the media—as well as to more general mainstream cultural values). Such constraints, it is assumed, impose at least some general structure of familiar logics and meanings that contain diversity and conflict within constitutional lawmaking discourses over time. One important implication of this principle, as Carter and Gilliom's essay points out, is that the legitimacy of judicial lawmaking derives not from any singular correctness of "right" decisions but rather primarily from the ability of judges to make at least plausible arguments justifying their often controversial and contestable decisions in terms of familiar legal conventions.

It further follows that not only are individual decisions assailable in terms of their own legal premises and logics, but also that the broader conventional constraints of logic, principle, and language within which law is formulated deserve direct critical analysis as well. Here the focus of authors in this collection converges closely with many crits in emphasizing larger "ideological" biases of law. Like the crits, many of the authors in the following pages seek to expose the often unarticulated premises, to examine their contradictions and limitations, to demonstrate their exclusion of alternative understandings, and to evaluate critically their implications for addressing fundamental social problems. In particular, many authors focus on the general but indeterminate role of traditional "liberal" ideas that continue to justify constitutional indifference to, or protection for, the racial, gender, and class inequalities that pervade American society.[15]

Although this common critical perspective toward mainstream liberalism unites this collection and parallels CLS studies, we want to emphasize that the range of substantive ethical and political values that inform these analyses is rather broad. Some essays here draw on neo-Marxist (Radin, McCann), feminist (Rhode, Copelon), populist (Brigham, Shockley, Simpson) and progressive reform (Scheingold, Adler) traditions that are influential among the crits, it is true. But these essays also reflect other vibrant critical traditions in contemporary scholarship not readily identified with CLS. For example, Rogers M. Smith's frank advocacy of reconstituted liberal theory and Donald A. Downs's provocative challenge to libertarian values are good examples of arguments with which many crits probably would disagree. Conversely, Lief Carter and John Gilliom, Judith A. Baer, William Haltom, and Ronald Kahn provide conceptual frameworks, raise questions, and offer insights that are compatible with a host of potentially competing ethical orientations. But even though the potential political implications of these essays are diverse or indeterminate, we believe that all of them make important contributions that deserve attention from legal scholars and activists alike.

Finally, we have already noted that, while they are critical of the status quo, all of the authors echo the CLS hope that legal criticism and advocacy can offer important resources to campaigns for progressive social change. Some differences of emphasis again should be noted, however. First, many of the essays here arguably are more self-conscious about the promises and limits of attempts to mobilize liberal legal principles as a lever for political transformation than often is the case in much of CLS scholarship. Moreover, as Stuart Scheingold's thoughtful discussion well exemplifies, many of these essays (especially by the social scientists) reflect somewhat less optimism about the potential of legal institutions and lawyers to achieve significant change in American public life than is expressed by many reform-minded scholars in law schools. In sum, most of the authors included in this book reflect the view that taking judicial constructions of constitutional law seriously requires frank recognition of the important limits to law as a force within society.

THE ORGANIZATION AND USE OF THIS BOOK

The organization of this book is quite simple and straightforward. Part One contains four chapters that address the character of constitutional lawmaking in general terms. The first two of these focus on the inherently discretionary and creative character of judicial decision making; the other two address issues concerning the uses of law and legal criticism as a resource for social change. Part Two through Part Five include chapters on various key areas of modern constitutional debate—including separation of powers, property regulation, equal protection, and freedom of speech, press, and religious practice. The authors of these chapters attempt to summarize the evolution of major decisions, to discuss their historical social significance, and to critically analyze and evaluate their implications for the legal structuring of American life in their respective areas of concern.

We have aimed for a sophisticated level of analysis throughout; as such, the authors have presumed at least some familiarity with both the general character and specific doctrinal areas of constitutional law. At the same time, most discussions focus on broad political issues, questions, and implications surrounding contemporary constitutional lawmaking rather than on doctrinal intricacies. The result is that the analyses should be of interest to a broad range of scholars, students, and citizens not ordinarily interested in the technical aspects of law. We hope that this latter characteristic renders the book a useful text for a wide range of advanced undergraduate and graduate classes in legal philosophy, law and public policy, and political theory as well as in U.S. constitutional law.

NOTES

1. On the first bicentennial celebration, see Michael Kammen, *A Machine That Would Go of Itself: The Constitution in American Culture* (New York: Vintage, 1987).
2. For critical evaluation of Judge Bork's substantive arguments about the character of legitimate constitutional lawmaking, see Judith A. Baer's chapter in this book, "The Fruitless Search for Original Intent."
3. For example, see Jefferson's letter to Samuel Kercheval, in Adrienne Koch and William Peden, eds., *The Life and Selected Writings of Thomas Jefferson* (New York: Modern Library, 1944), pp. 673–676.
4. Marshall in *Osborn v. Bank of the United States,* 9 Wheat. 738 (1824).
5. See Wilfred W. Rumble, Jr., *American Legal Realism* (Ithaca, N.Y.: Cornell University Press, 1968); Karl Llewellyn, *The Bramble Bush: On Our Law and Its Study* (New York: Oceana, 1951); Jerome Frank, *Law and the Modern Mind* (New York: Coward-McCann, 1930). For an excellent brief overview of the various critical trends in jurisprudence referred to in this introduction, see Harry M. Stumpf, *American Judicial Politics* (San Diego: Harcourt Brace Jovanovich, 1988), Chapter 1.

6. On the frankly political impulses behind Realist jurisprudence, see Jerold S. Auerbach, *Unequal Justice: Lawyers and Social Change in America* (New York: Oxford University Press, 1976), Chs. 5–7; Peter Irons, *The New Deal Lawyers* (Princeton, N.J.: Princeton University Press, 1982).

7. Ibid. See also Marlise James, *The People's Lawyers* (New York: Holt, Rinehart and Winston, 1973).

8. See, for example: Henry M. Hart, Jr. and Albert M. Sachs, *The Legal Process: Basic Problems in the Making and Application of Law* (Cambridge: Harvard Law School, 1958); Alexander Bickel, *The Least Dangerous Branch: The Supreme Court at the Bar of Politics* (Indianapolis: Bobbs-Merrill, 1962); John Hart Ely, *Democracy and Distrust: A Theory of Judicial Review* (Cambridge: Harvard University Press, 1980). For comment, see Lawrence Tribe, "The Puzzling Persistence of Process-Based Constitutional Theories," *Yale Law Journal* 89 (1980), pp. 1063–1080; Richard Parker, "The Past of Constitutional Theory—and Its Future," *Ohio State Law Journal* 42 (1981), pp. 223–259.

9. See Lawrence M. Friedman, "The Law and Society Movement," *Stanford Law Review* 38 (February 1986), pp. 763–780; Harry P. Stumpf et al., "Whither Political Jurisprudence: A Symposium," *Western Political Quarterly* 36, No. 4 (1983).

10. See Robert Lefcourt, ed., *Law Against the People: Essays to Demystify Law, Order and the Courts* (New York: Vintage, 1971).

11. On radical lawyers, see Jonathan Black, ed., *Radical Lawyers: Their Role in the Movement and in the Courts* (New York: Avon, 1971); James, *The People's Lawyers*. On public interest lawyers, see Joel F. Handler et al., *Lawyers and the Pursuit of Legal Rights* (New York: Academic Press, 1978); Michael W. McCann, *Taking Reform Seriously: Perspectives on Public Interest Liberalism* (Ithaca: Cornell University Press, 1986).

12. Classic examples of the movement orientation include Richard Posner, *Economic Analysis of the Law*, 3rd ed. (Boston: Little, Brown, 1986); Richard Epstein, *Takings: Private Property and the Power of Eminent Domain* (Cambridge: Harvard University Press, 1985). For criticism, see Duncan Kennedy and Frank Michelman, "Are Property and Contract Efficient?" *Hofstra Law Review* (1980) pp. 711–769; and Margaret Jane Radin's chapter, "The Constitution and the Liberal Conception of Property," in this book.

13. For the link between CLS and Law and Economics, see Mark Kelman, *A Guide to Critical Legal Studies* (Cambridge: Harvard University Press, 1987), especially Chapter 6.

14. On the crits generally, see Kelman, *A Guide to Critical Legal Studies;* Roberto M. Unger, *The Critical Legal Studies Movement* (Cambridge: Harvard University Press, 1986). For a critical analysis, see Rogers M. Smith's chapter, "After Criticism: An Analysis of the Critical Legal Studies Movement," in this book.

15. On liberal ideology and constitutionalism, see Stuart A. Scheingold, *The Politics of Rights: Lawyers, Public Policy, and Political Change* (New Haven: Yale University Press, 1974). See especially the chapters by Scheingold, Smith, Radin, McCann, and Copelon in this book.

Part 1 ———————————————— ·
Contemporary Constitutional Theory

We begin this volume with four chapters addressing the general features and roles of constitutional lawmaking in modern society. The authors of the first two chapters focus their analysis upon debates regarding the distinctive character of constitutional policy making. In the first chapter, Lief Carter and John Gilliom call into question the foundationalist logic underlying traditional theories of legal interpretation. Drawing on the insights of postmodern philosophers, they argue instead for a nondeterministic approach to understanding constitutional lawmaking as a dynamic historical process of creative discourse among authoritative legal actors. Furthermore, the authors synthesize aspects of both the tradition-bound "insider" and the critical "outsider" versions of discourse theory to make the case that constitutional lawmaking is best judged according to aesthetic criteria of conversational goodness rather than by conventional ethical or rule-bound standards of legal legitimacy. Judith A. Baer's analysis parallels that of Carter and Gilliom in important regards, but Baer focuses critical attention directly on the inadequacies of recently revived arguments urging judicial restraint through fidelity to the original intentions of the constitutional framers. She not only outlines the manifold problems at stake in deriving clear guidance from historical records but also draws on modern language philosophy to raise important epistemological questions about the character of subjective intentionality itself. She thus concludes that, although appeals to original intent are a routine and often effective mode of judicial rhetoric, such claims can be employed to justify a wide range of conflicting policy positions and cannot insulate lawmaking from either broad judicial discretion or political factors also at work in other policy forums. Although different in thematic focus and philosophical debt, both chapters clearly reflect parallel new directions in the analysis of constitutional lawmaking.

The remaining two chapters in this section shift the focus of attention away from discrete decision makers and decisions to the broader social context of ideas, norms, and cultural forms that shape, and in turn are shaped by, constitutional lawmaking activity. Stuart Scheingold addresses these issues by focusing on the complex relationship between law and social change. Charting a prudent course between optimistic liberals and pessimistic radicals, he argues that law has proved to be a valuable but intrinsically problematic and limited resource for progressive social reform activists. Scheingold draws primarily on the experience of the civil rights movement to exemplify his argument. The general terms of his position of placing qualified faith in the progressive potential of legal advocacy are reflected in most of the subsequent chapters of this book. Rogers M. Smith's bold essay sheds light on the subject by focusing critical attention specifically on those modes of progressive scholarly criticism and practical legal activity advocated in recent years by the Critical Legal Studies movement. Although generally sympathetic to many of their policy goals, Smith contends that the deconstructionist critical method adopted by the crits is less novel than their substantive commitment to an ethic of "radical freedom," which he finds conceptually problematic and ultimately undesirable as a foundation for democratic change. Smith's more mainstream liberal ethical position is not necessarily representative of other authors in this collection, many of whom tend either to side more clearly with the crits or to stand somewhere between these contending positions. However, the general debate that he outlines raises fundamental methodological and substantive issues that concern virtually all critical constitutional analysts and legal reform activists.

The Constitution and Problems of Legitimacy

1 ——— ·

From Foundation to Discourse: Trends in Contemporary Constitutional Philosophy

LIEF CARTER AND JOHN GILLIOM

> While consciousness, language, and social conditions are replete with
> contradictions, they shape each other so as to make it possible for people to
> live with moral dilemmas, and with chronic failure to resolve the dilemmas
> and contradictions.
>
> ———*Murray Edelman*

INTRODUCTION: THE RULE OF LAW

We commonly think of law, and of all command, as a process that achieves
some end—order, peace, and cooperation, for example—by imposing clearly
stated limits on choices and actions. Laws, by definition, rule. The Constitution, the "supreme law of the land," structures and limits the power of
government and therefore should constrain the choices of judges and administrators who enforce it. Writing in defense of judicial review in *Marbury v.
Madison,* Chief Justice John Marshall asked, "Why does a judge swear to
discharge his duties agreeably to the constitution of the United States, if that
constitution forms no rule for his government?"[1]

It is hard to imagine law being law if it does not rule, if it does not
prescribe general policies of social action and specific limitations on how to
apply these prescriptions in concrete cases. For Marshall, if the Constitution
"forms no rule for his government" that binds judges, then the judicial oath
is "worse than a solemn mockery."[2] The Constitution's limits on government
power thus create a double demand. Law must not only constrain political
preferences, personal discretion, and whims in both primary legislative and
administrative decisions; it must constrain and guide the judicial evaluations
of these decisions as well.

Constitutional philosophers, and legal philosophers more generally, have for many centuries labored to determine proper tests and standards for defining when this double demand has been successfully met—when law has ruled and judges have thereby avoided solemn mockery. Yet legal philosophers at the bicentennial of the U.S. Constitution seem farther than ever from a consensus on such standards. Philosophical standards for identifying correct or simply good legal decisions range widely, from the unchanging jurisprudence of original intent espoused by Robert Bork, through James Boyd White's description of a poetic and changing Constitution, to the Critical Legal Studies complaint that law and the philosophical standards that justify it are too often a front for perpetuating the interests of the powerful.

The extent of this philosophical diversity may simply reflect the diversity of opinion that characterizes pluralistic American politics. Political diversity may have so thoroughly invaded the academy that we will live with philosophical diversity indefinitely. However, in this chapter, we tentatively suggest another explanation for such diversity. Prominent elements in modern, or "postmodern," social and moral philosophy cast great doubt on the capacity of law to rule in the ways John Marshall supposed. Murray Edelman's epigraph at the beginning of this chapter captures the essence of the problem. Law helps our language, our consciousness of self, and our experience of social conditions to shape each other, but that interactive shaping does not solve problems and contradictions in judicial choices. Legal philosophy may not yet have caught up with these developments; its diversity may be a product of having camps in an old and a new world.

In this chapter, we examine how constitutional philosophy has reacted to this shift in the world of social and moral philosophy that legal philosophy inhabits. This shift, best documented in Richard Rorty's *Philosophy and the Mirror of Nature*, abandons philosophy's search for the foundations of knowledge.[3] It abandons the conviction that the analysis of mental activities and representations of the world or literary texts permit philosophers to distinguish accurate and objective knowledge from inaccurate and subjective knowledge. The shift abandons a philosophy of "knowledge as accurate representation, made possible by special mental processes and intelligible through a general theory of representation," in favor of a philosophy that illuminates and edifies the indeterminate project of public debate and decision making.[4]

This reemphasis poses a major problem for legal theory, for it abandons as untenable the very liberal philosophical positions on which the definition of legal justice in the United States depends. Constitutional philosophy still yearns to retain the epistemological foundations of the old order because it is so difficult to imagine how law can rule without a theory that distinguishes accurate from inaccurate knowledge. In this chapter, however, we suggest that discursive postfoundational views of law can preserve the capacity of law to do justice and the capacity of constitutional philosophy to articulate standards of good law without debating which epistemology of legal interpretation is best. Law and philosophy, as well as religion and theology, may each contribute to a shared understanding and community without forcing agreement on principles or consensus on policy. In making such an argument, we will recognize and incorporate the critiques of feminists, genealogists, and others on the Left who argue that many of us should explicitly reject "common ways of understanding" that are built upon the problematic terms of constitutional law. Our discussion will conclude with an argument for a version of discursive philosophy that substitutes aesthetic standards for epistemic standards of goodness. We will briefly show that legal philosophers of many sorts defend their cases in aesthetic terms and will argue that the search for social justice in the discursive framework involves not finding the correct answer but speaking, writing, and acting in ways that preserve the faith and commitment of a diverse citizenry to seek understanding in common ways.

In short, a paradigm shift from foundation to discourse in legal philosophy may be reconstructing its terms and thereby narrowing the diversity of the field. But speculating on the possibility of increased philosophical consensus poses two hazards. First, a discursive model of politics and law helps explain why diversity always persists—that is, why we cannot agree on foundations. Discourse itself may thrive on diversity, disagreement, and debate, and the competing and highly diverse claims to have discovered philosophical standards of legality may persist because they drive good discourse. Diversity and difference may not diminish in fact, then, but simply will no longer pose formidable problems for either legal practice or legal philosophy. Second, from the discursive perspective, whether this shift prevails will depend not on the superior truthfulness of any one paradigm but on the discursive and unpredictable politics of the academy itself. Thus we may see a return to foundationalism; as Rorty noted, a new genius may come along whose power reunites the field on foundational terms.[5] The shift we discuss, then, is a possibility; it is a trend but not yet an accomplishment.

FOUNDATION AND DISCOURSE

In classical liberal philosophy, law rules by expressing the polity's conclusions about values and policies. Law's statements need not express absolute truths; in most versions of liberalism a wider and imperfect political process creates legal rules. But law itself expresses, both by the contents of its rules and the legal system's methods of enforcing them, settled and clear statements about the conduct of group life. Thus John Locke, in his "Letter Concerning Toleration," speaks of the "duty of the civil magistrate, by the impartial execution of equal laws, to secure unto all the people in general and to every one of his subjects in particular the just possession of their things belonging to this life." From this perspective, the rule of law, created and structured by constitutions, maintains political order by defining clearly what property entitlements and other rights people justly possess in particular cases and contexts. Rational citizens express their choices through an objective social contract that, given the "natural" morality of consent, they will obey.

This liberal view of law is foundational.[6] It assumes that law creates and communicates firm and clear principles and conditions that allow people to make personal decisions securely. Law, in this view, speaks with a clarity that allows citizens to predict the consequences of their actions with confidence. The foundationalist basis of the "rule of law" ideal assumes that texts, interpretive methods, and underlying political values are or can be made clear enough for philosophers to derive conclusive answers to such questions as:

> What is a legal right?
> What is the proper separation of legislative and executive power?
> What is the proper scope of judicial review?
> Does the due process clause create a right of privacy so as to prevent governmental interference with contraception and abortion choices?
> Did the Supreme Court in a given case properly interpret and apply the intent of the framers of the text in question and the principles the framers believed?
> What balance should be drawn between preserving the state and preserving the dignity of individuals?

The discursive approach, by contrast, holds that these familiar foundational questions only pose dilemmas and contradictions that law cannot solve. It begins from the assumption that the foundational standards of legal and constitutional goodness—whether derived from the meaning of texts, agreement on interpretive methods, or a political consensus on desirable social policies and moral values—are not and never have been fixed or firm enough to provide a philosophical standard for assessing the goodness of legal decisions. Two hundred years of constitutional experience give us no evidence that either the courts or those who philosophize about them have answered these questions or generated consensus on approximate methods for answering them. As any first-year student of constitutional law can tell us, John Marshall's own tortured reasoning in *Marbury* belies his assertion that law rules government.[7]

Law as discourse thus attends to characteristics of law other than the correctness of its methods and answers. The word *discourse* derives from the Latin *discursus,* which originally meant "running back and forth" and later connoted "conversation." The discourse approach preserves its claim to evaluate legal goodness by evaluating law's openness, its dialogic, back-and-forth quality. The discourse approach involves evaluating the quality of communication and conversation inside the legal system among lawyers, judges, and citizens as well as the extent to which law's autonomous and professionalized language may enhance or impair its capacity to respond to social claims made upon it from outside. The discursive approach thus asks such questions as:

In what ways do judicial constructions of law and the Constitution
enhance or frustrate the reader's capacity to respond and to
judge the decision?

Does democracy discourage or encourage the articulation of
innovative legal claims by compelling those in power to defend
their choices in language that is widely shared and "popular"?

How well does a given opinion tell a story? To what extent does
law's goodness depend on telling stories that are coherent and
that heighten our awareness of the moral character of our
personal experiences?

To what extent is law responsive to the diversity of viewpoints and
stories from all sectors of the larger society?

Two illustrations may put some life into these abstractions. First, consider the modern Supreme Court's decisions in *Goldman v. Weinberger*.[8] In
this case an Air Force psychologist, an Orthodox Jew, testified for the defense
in a court-martial while wearing his yarmulke. He had worn it for several
years on duty in the service without incident, but a regulation forbade everyone except for military police from wearing headgear indoors. The opposing
counsel in the court-martial had filed a complaint, and Goldman's commander had ordered him not to wear his yarmulke indoors. When Goldman
announced that he would take legal action, the commander changed his positive recommendation for extending Goldman's tour of service to a negative
one. Goldman took the First Amendment issue to the Supreme Court, where
he lost 5–4.

A foundationalist evaluation of *Goldman* might defend the majority
opinion in terms of a theory of the judicial role in politics: Judicial restraint
is a desirable policy and this decision wisely defers to what Justice William
Rehnquist has called "the considered professional judgement" of the military.
An alternative foundational defense might concur with the asserted need for
military uniformity. A foundational attack on the *Goldman* majority could, as
Justices William Brennan and Thurgood Marshall did in dissent, insist that
religious liberty, which heads the Bill of Rights, deserves prima facie protection and that our law contains ample precedent for exempting those of sin-
cere religious beliefs from general legal obligations, such as saluting the flag
or even providing their children with formal education.[9] All of these foundational responses are similar in their insistence that they represent a definitive rule—the right answer to the question.

A discursive evaluation of *Goldman*, in contrast, would accept the
premise that these foundational arguments shape legal rhetoric but would
deny the conclusion that such rhetoric converts into a philosophically viable
critical position. For each argument there is a set of legally plausible counter-
arguments. In short, precedents requiring uniformity compete with those
requiring exemptions. In a discursive critique, one would not ask whether
the free exercise clause exempts Orthodox Jews from the Air Force's headgear

policy; instead, one would examine how the majority opinion, by employing a rhetoric that implicates the best-imagined characteristics of the military— its discipline, its professionalism, and its impartiality—avoids engaging the more open rhetoric of religious rights and liberties. The majority's rhetoric invests the Court with a quasimilitary authority of its own, an authority to declare rather than to justify results. Also, in their dissenting opinions, Justices Sandra Day O'Connor and Harry A. Blackmun objected that the military did not in fact provide evidence in trial to support its professional judgment. Indeed, the only expert testimony at trial claimed that such exceptions would enhance soldier morale. These dissents complain that the military failed a conversational test and therefore failed to meet discursive standards of good law.

Thus far the argument might seem no more than a familiar restatement of the conclusions of legal realism, conclusions now a half-century old. But that observation misses the point. The realists and more recent discourse theorists share a skepticism about the textual determinism urged by formalists, but the realists' reductionist tendency to discount almost entirely the role of ideas, logic, and language in shaping law blunted the critical edge of their work. The realist attempt to simply replace textual determinism with psychological, sociological, and political forms of determinism altered the direction of analysis without fully displacing the lingering formalist faith in foundationalism as a basis of constitutional theory. This failure to fully criticize and replace foundationalist premises has contributed to the persistence of foundational "grand theory" in constitutional philosophy. Hence, our second illustration of the foundation/discourse distinction comes from scholarship itself. Perhaps the most widely publicized grand theory is that of Robert Bork,[10] whose conservative originalist jurisprudence is carefully scrutinized in Judith A. Baer's chapter in this book. But other, more liberal scholars, such as Ronald Dworkin and Sotirios Barber, who endorse dignitarian as opposed to statist views of the Constitution, also employ foundationalist methods.

Dworkin's familiar grand theory in particular acknowledges much of the indeterminacy in social choice that modern philosophy describes. In 1985 he wrote: "We are not a community tied together by a concrete moral settlement, by shared opinions about the details of what justice and fairness and a decent and valuable life require. . . . We debate about justice and fairness."[11] Yet Dworkin has still sought to preserve the ideal of theoretically determinate and objective constitutional law. In his earlier writings, Dworkin posed an omnicompetent Hercules who could, by comprehending the moral, social, and political elements that together make up our law, find right answers to hard legal questions.[12] Mortal humans can imagine the existence in theory of one best fit among the elements of law that will dictate the right answer. Though they will not achieve truth, they are bound to strive for it. Dworkin thus liberated legal theory from interpretivism limited to legal texts and the intentions behind them. According to this view, a judge is entitled to adopt a moral principle in place of the plain or intentionalist meaning of a legal statement if the moral principle affords a better accommodation of the political and social elements in the legal culture. The law thus, over time, fulfills the promise of ethical certainty.

In a variety of writings in the late 1970s and early 1980s, Dworkin defended his Herculean theory by suggesting that we all accept an imperfect version of it in our personal experience.[13] We would, for example, find that if we were part of a team writing a serial or chain novel, the author of the first chapter would have almost complete discretion. The accumulation of events and revealed traits of the characters that emerged in ensuing chapters, however, would increasingly constrain the authors of subsequent chapters, and the final chapter might almost write itself. Given the long accumulation of legal materials in our culture, judicial discretion is (or ought to be) tightly constrained by the demands of context.

More recently, in his widely reviewed book, *Law's Empire,* Dworkin refined his theory by positing what he calls "law as integrity."[14] Integrity is not merely the sum of fairness and equity in making and implementing policy choices through law. Integrity also requires government to link its actions in different cases and circumstances to a single coherent set of principles. It is our commitment to integrity, he suggests, that prevents us from even considering the adoption of such political compromises as checkerboard statutes. A checkerboard law would, for example, allow the right to an abortion only to women born in even- or odd-numbered years. Such a statute would seem no less acceptable than any of the thousands of compromises we observe in politics every year. Yet the checkerboard statute cannot be made to fit with the principle that people be treated with equal concern and respect. Thus we learn that integrity and "fittedness" exist in addition to justice and fairness as a measure of legal goodness.[15]

But Dworkin's works, particularly his most recent, *Law's Empire,* have thus far failed to persuade and generate an academic following. From the discursive perspective, which describes legal and academic communities alike, Dworkin's high stature in the academy depends not on his correctness but on his powers as a conversationalist. Dworkin enhances our faith and trust in academic life because he sharpens our individual understanding, not because he persuades us to agree with him. John Stick, for example, writes that Dworkin's arguments are "never conclusive" and that he "criticizes an extreme version of the position not his own and then concludes that his own position must be correct, without justifying his suppression of the excluded middle." Yet Stick concludes—and exemplifies a discursive orientation—by praising how Dworkin's suggestions will "continue to feed the dialogue. . . . *Law's Empire* can be recommended as a true philosopher's delight" because philosophers enjoy "a suggestive although flawed and incomplete argument much more than a sound but trivial one."[16]

The preceding discussion of Dworkin and his critic reveals some central elements of the contemporary struggle. Dworkin himself seems to be trying to move beyond foundationalism but ends up with only a modified, less narrowly deterministic foundationalism based on a perceived consensus on liberal values. Stick, in his review, reveals a more complete transition to discursive orientation. He does not attempt to replace Dworkin's foundation with another; rather, he acknowledges the flaws, points out some of Dworkin's conversational shortcomings, tells of his feelings about a good, interesting, and provocative discursive exchange, and moves on. Thus we do not witness a shift from a foundational theory of law as a liberal consensus on public values to another foundational theory of law as discourse. Constitutional philosophy is itself becoming more discursive and less committed to discovering "correct" philosophical positions.

In the next sections of this chapter, we will sketch this apparent withering of foundationalism in legal theory and map more precisely the emerging alternatives. Before doing so, however, let us acknowledge several caveats, questions, and issues that we raise but cannot fully address in this context. First, we do not address directly the extent to which these philosophical materials can or ought to "make a difference" in the ways judges and lawyers speak and act. Although judicial examples are used, here we are primarily concerned with conversations that professors have with each other and shifts in the direction of academic discourse. As will be evident in our final section, however, it would be wrong to conclude that a treatment of the philosophical study of law is unrelated to the questions of what makes "good" law and legitimate authority.

Second, our position implies a dichotomy between the ideal types of foundation and discourse, which is undeniably a rhetorical oversimplification. All "talk" requires at least temporary and socially constructed linguistic foundations, and all foundational arguments contribute to communities of discourse at the same time they challenge them. Instead, our position emphasizes that we can safely abandon the hope of philosophical agreement on foundations without sacrificing the hope that philosophical discourse can generate fruitful criticisms of law's processes and outcomes and thereby create attractive and sharable visions of a better legal order.

Third, we shall see within discursive jurisprudence substantial differences in opinion concerning the degree to which language and rhetoric constrain communities from articulating and advancing new, uncertain, and potentially threatening ideas. The writings of James Boyd White, which celebrate much in our law, suggest that law's poetic and nonlinear rhetoric enhances the ability of judges and other lawmakers to articulate and sustain significant innovations. By contrast, the more radical scholarship of CLS thinkers, the genealogists, and of many authors included in this book is less sanguine precisely because it sees legal rhetoric as screening us from painful truths of social injustice that demand dramatic innovation. Allan Hutchinson has suggested that grand theory in legal scholarship produces the same unfortunate blindness and that the academic affection for getting the "right theory" of constitutional protection of human dignity reduces sensitivity and diverts ameliorative responses away from the hard fact that inner-city poverty and squalor crush human dignity on a daily basis.[17] We do not claim to resolve that dilemma here; however, at the outset we assert that all of the many discursive perspectives seem to make the achievement of enhanced dignity and respect of citizens a necessary precondition, and therefore a goal, of good lawmaking.

BACKGROUND TO THE SHIFT IN CONSTITUTIONAL PHILOSOPHY

Three developments in the evolution of Western political thought have propelled modern jurisprudence in discursive directions: liberalism, pragmatism, and the influence of contemporary European critical thought on social and moral philosophy.

Liberalism contains a paradoxical blend of foundational and discursive elements and represents, from the discursive perspective at least, the beginnings of a transition. It is liberalism that kept one foot in the old world and put the other in a new world. Liberalism's emphasis on the foundation of the rule of law can be traced back to the Judeo-Christian sense of the covenantal relationship between man and God. The covenantal relationship—"keep my commandments and I will protect you as my chosen people"—was transformed through Lockean liberalism into the social contract. This contractual view of social order requires *knowing the law,* whether rooted in God's commandments or in the conditions of the social contract suggested by Locke. Both orthodox Judaism and the liberal state generate extensive legal systems designed to determine the tone and permanent meaning of the covenant between God and man and the contract between ruler and citizen.

But liberalism arose in a political context dominated by centuries of warfare. The autocratic character of feudal political structures and the Church concentrated power in the hands of territorial rivals sufficient to allow each to coerce from its subjects the resources necessary to wage war for the advantage of the powerful. These conflicts were fueled and justified by the claim that Christianity could have only one correct application to earthly affairs. Liberalism, in conjunction with the Protestant rebellion against the authority of the Church, proposed to deal with these problems not merely by creating government accountable to citizens and limited by respect for their rights; it also liberated people's consciences. In Protestant theology each person remains free to seek God and interpret scripture in his or her own way, free from the control of the dictates of the Church. Liberal political theory, by valuing freedom of conscience and free and open debate, thus sowed the seeds of modern pluralism.

Hence liberalism's paradox. The old version constituted a contractarian state made possible through a general commitment to the rule of law and to specific authoritative texts that limit government power. At the same time, the new version posits a citizenry free to disagree about the terms of group life. For these more liberated aspects of liberalism, binding texts, including the Bible and constitutions alike, cannot have a fixed, final, certain authoritative meaning imposed by institutions. This aspect of liberalism discourages constructing a foundational epistemology for reaching textual certainty in religious or social affairs, for doing so disenfranchises dissenters. Foundationalism, and the concomitant belief in our ability to correctly read determinative texts,[18] however, reintroduces the authoritarian quality of the old order from which liberalism sought to escape. Classical liberalism did not perceive this paradox because it coincided with the growth during the Enlightenment of the belief—stimulated by the great voyages of discovery—that citizens inhabited a scientifically knowable objective world. In an age of discovering continents, new microscopic species, a heliocentric solar system, and so on, it became plausible to imagine the objective discoverability of human rights and of effective political systems whose correctness would become clear as long as truth remained free to combat error.

The conviction that our social and political order mirrors a discoverable natural order has given way to a pragmatic strain in modern liberalism, however. This second development in Western thought challenges the discoverability of scientific and political foundations. Richard Rorty, who describes himself as a "new pragmatist" and a "modern Deweyan," notes two conditions that undercut foundationalism. First, it is not possible to create criteria for settling arguments that are themselves beyond argument. All such criteria are truth claims about which people will disagree. For Rorty and many others, therefore, "'theory'—when defined as 'an attempt to govern interpretation in general'—has got to go."[19] Attempts to generate foundational criteria for determining the goodness of an argument from the terms of the argument itself produce a vicious circle. The search for criteria outside discourse leads into an infinite philosophical regress.[20]

Second, pragmatism stresses that neither the physical nor the social worlds are static. They are, rather, constituted by our relationship with them and therefore are dynamic, multiple, and constantly changing. Hence pragmatism, which is often misrepresented (most recently in Dworkin's *Law's Empire*) as a philosophy of exploiting the world for selfish ends, displaces the epistemic search for truth with a view of communal discourse in which the meaning of individual experiences is shared and negotiated. For Dewey and Rorty, democracy entails conversations that edify and illuminate more than they resolve or define. Pragmatists stress the openness of communications systems and deemphasize both the possibility and the desirability of analytical finality. By itself, this posture entails no specific outcome or substantive logic. For example, Justice Arthur Kennedy may prove as conservative as the defeated nominee Robert Bork, but Kennedy clearly displayed more pragmatic tendencies when he said, "My philosophy has always been that as to some fundamental constitutional questions it is best not to insist on definitive answers. . . . The constitutional system works best if there remain twilight zones of uncertainty and tension between the component parts of government."[21]

The "new pragmatism" of Rorty is perhaps the most optimistic of the postfoundational perspectives. Other contemporary approaches agree with his views on the importance of rejecting foundationalist elements in favor of discursive theories of ideology and language but take a more critical path on other issues. Rorty, taking the stance of what we call an "insider," eschews a focus on politics, power, and domination in discussing the nature and role of the social conversation. But the more critical "outsiders"—genealogists, neo-Marxists, and feminists, among others—analyze discourses as modes of power and domination that systematically exclude and subjugate various groups and perspectives.

Michel Foucault and the expanding group of scholars that share his genealogical project, for example, concur with Rorty in rejecting foundationalism and the idea of moral objectivity. But the genealogists go on to offer some of the most startling and total rejections of Rorty's complacency and optimism regarding the inclusiveness of cultural "conversations," the character of human agency and ability for rational choice, and the very possibility of consensus and legitimate authority.[22]

While Rorty tends to see discourses as idiosyncratic products of different lives and experiences and sees conversations as gentle exchanges that can lead to edification and consensus, Foucault sees the elements of language and knowledge as a terrain of battle in which enclosed discourses struggle to subjugate and exclude others. Thus, where Rorty uses metaphors of conversation, edification, and playfulness to characterize cultural discourse, Foucault uses images of domination, imprisonment, and warfare. Foucault's concept of power-knowledge suggests that discourses emerge as integral parts of broad matrices of power in societies. For Foucault, discourses are systems of rules and language that both constitute and subjugate; modes of thought and subjectivity that do not fit the rules of the dominant discourse face either subjugation or existence as external forms of resistance.[23]

The genealogists' very definition of power is quite different from traditional liberal or pragmatic views. For the former, relations of power are more important in shaping people than people are in shaping relations of power. Where liberals and pragmatists see power as something that is instrumentally and intentionally used by conscious agents seeking to make someone act or cease to act in a certain way, Foucault sees power in any society as a diffuse and circulating element that is not controlled by agents and that is more important in *positively shaping* our ways of doing and being than for its negative restrictions on action.[24] Directly refuting Rorty's peaceful conversational salon, Foucault has described power not as something that can be cleansed from a situation or held in check; rather, it is relational, circulating, and manifest at all levels of society, and it both shapes and is reflected in all forms of communication and interaction. From this concept we can begin to see the challenges that would arise from a Foucauldian perspective. Gentle conversation between competing discourses is unimaginable; consensus is impossible because agreement actually involves domination, which in turn always produces a resistance. In short, Foucault's analysis has tended to reject altogether the notions of pursuing meaningful social change through normal political institutions and of pursuing "legitimate" governance.

The genealogical movement has paralleled and supported a number of recent developments in neo-Marxism and other critical orientations. Inspired by Antonio Gramsci's reworking of Marxist themes and by the influences of Nietzsche and Foucault on language philosophy, some neo-Marxists have attempted to direct theory away from the instrumentalist, deterministic, and rigidly foundationalist terms of Old Left criticism and advocacy. The emphasis of the neo-Marxists has instead been on ideology and other forms of hegemony that are viewed as sustaining domination and hierarchy in society.[25] At times sounding much like Foucault, many neo-Marxists emphasize that ideas and knowledge—and the elements of discourse—are relatively autonomous forces that shape and constitute the human subject and power relations. In general, however, the neo-Marxists differ from Foucault insofar as they tie ideology to class divisions in society and maintain a focus on a groups-specific agency—class or state—in the process of domination. Despite this continued focus on material relations and class divisions, however, many neo-Marxists have moved beyond simple determinism to address the dialectical and "articulated" relations between structure and superstructure. Similarly, the traditional focus on the state as a locus of power is often deemphasized relative to the study of more informal, subtle, and microlevel sites of power in society in ways that, again, parallel genealogical analysis.

Numerous feminist scholars, likewise, are producing influential and insightful "outsider" views that to some extent draw on and reflect tensions between the Foucauldian and Marxist perspectives. Many feminist theorists tend to share the latter's emphasis on ideology and knowledge as noninstrumental forms of relational power; their focus, in particular, is on the role of discursive elements in excluding women and feminist perspectives from formal participation and in maintaining pervasive informal structures of patriarchal domination. Most feminists, like many Marxists, also tend to differ from Foucault in placing greater emphasis on the possibilities of agency and the potential of the modern subject to improve society. Thus, Kathy Ferguson, in *The Feminist Case Against Bureaucracy*, argues that the historical position of women in the public and private political economy has produced a female subject that is different from and resistant to the predominant patterns of patriarchy and bureaucratization.[26] While Ferguson avoids making foundational claims in her work, it should be noted that some feminists and Marxists alike, for both strategic and epistemological reasons, tend to posit new forms of foundationalism; but even these theorists are careful to reject the deterministic and objectivist pretenses of older foundational claims.[27]

Whatever the variations among these outsiders, therefore, they combine to form a critical element to discourse theory that shows a number of important differences from the Rorty-Dewey tradition of insider pragmatism. All forms of discourse theory share a common skepticism over the objective or predetermined character of social reality, moral meaning, and texts, but the outsider and insider discourse theorists see social and political issues differently. Where insiders emphasize the open-ended, unconstrained, inclusive, and roughly egalitarian character of dynamic cultural conversations among free subjects, the critical outsiders emphasize diffuse structural constraints, discursive continuity, exclusive biases, and the hierarchical implications of power-knowledge relations among socially constituted subjects. Hence, where insiders laud the virtues of incremental pragmatism in advancing individual claims through the ongoing conversation, the outsiders emphasize the importance of challenging the conversations themselves. Such challenges can involve efforts to reconstitute the material relations and participating subjects or may use marginal resistance and shock techniques intended primarily to disturb the ongoing discourse. The outsiders reject the joiners' mentality of hope for accord and faith in compromise; their goal is not to assure citizens amidst the disagreements of modernity, as Rorty does, but to stir discontent and anger about the impoverishment of social relations structured by the limits of the dominant discourse. They feel that the institutional process of creating consensus is necessarily repressive. Legal institutions, for example, impose power by standardizing and simplifying language, ideas, and knowledge itself. The institutionalized limitations on language and the reductionist tendencies in all politics confine, narrow, and control our capacity to define ourselves. Thus, the law's point of view is *not* the point of view of all—much less an objective claim of right—and hence the radical philosopher's task in seeking liberation is to shock institutions into loosening their grip on language and discourse. In William Connolly's words, radical criticism replaces "epistemology with poetics, striving thereby to ventilate and illuminate the connections which govern us."[28]

The next two sections of this chapter trace some applications of recent discourse theories to constitutional philosophy. Although dualism itself artificially constrains discourse, we posit that modern discursive constitutional writings tend to emphasize either a pragmatist, "inside" approach or a critical, "outside" approach. The insiders, for whom "theory has got to go," look primarily to praise or criticize the quality of legal conversation and discourse as we now experience it. We should note at the outset that insider perspectives are not necessarily conservative; indeed, they are often progressive or reformist in content. The distinctive feature is only that insiders look to traditional ideals, values, and modes of argument as the basis of change and tend to want such change to be incremental in character. Outsiders, on the other hand, attempt to expose law's systematic biases and restrictions on conversation and argue that law's appearance as an objective natural order perpetuates the same static configurations of power it helps create. The very solidity and rootedness of convention, therefore, make external shocks and challenges necessary to any efforts to promote social freedom and justice.

INSIDE LAW: PRAGMATISM AND CONVERSATION

The insights of discourse theories developed by Rorty, language philosophers, and other postmodern thinkers undoubtedly have had a liberating effect on the study of law—much like that which Kuhnian theories of paradigms and scientific revolution have had on the study of science. The parallel changes in studies of science and law are not strictly coincidental; as we argued above, classical liberalism preserved many of the foundational habits of theology because the age of scientific discovery in the natural world raised hopes of discovering foundational solutions to secular political problems. To put the point in discursive terms, we might say that classical liberalism arose in a community of discourse that presupposed an objective and knowable world.[29] Today, confidence in the capacity of science to discover objective truths has given way to a more pragmatic conviction that science can collect and describe data in ways that, at best, might disconfirm specific theories and the paradigms behind them. Owing to the influence of Kuhn and others, science today is more comfortable—though clearly not entirely contented— with a discursive model as an accurate description of itself.

In a similar manner, a number of recent postmodern scholars have invoked discourse theory to offer a more accurate description of how the conversational character of law enables it to operate effectively. The specific achievement of these "new pragmatists" has been to discredit the foundationalist fetish for legal certitude by reconceptualizing our understanding of legitimacy. Increasingly, the discussion of legitimacy is expressed in terms that both recognize and celebrate the reality of disagreement, diversity, and conflict in authoritative lawmaking activity. We will provide two examples of recent scholarship that contribute to such an understanding. The first, represented by the work of Rogers M. Smith, develops the discursive side of liberalism's paradox;[30] the second inside approach, headed by James Boyd White, explores the character of legal discourse itself.

Given the failure of moral foundationalism, Smith, who speaks for himself in this book (see Chapter 4), claims that we can nevertheless evaluate constitutional decisions in terms of the extent to which they arise out of conditions of rational discourse.[31] Smith defends his rational discourse model experientially and pragmatically. His ideal holds that legal policy must derive from "prevailing community standards to define the boundaries of permissible conduct." But his ideal does lead "the community to ask, through various deliberative processes . . . what conduct is part of reflective self-direction and maintains the capacity for self-governance in the actor and others."[32] Smith believes that the competing constitutional visions and the compromises among them that the law has generated follow from a deeper, imperfect, but genuine commitment to rational discourse.

Rational discourse of the sort that interests Smith occurs within and is shaped by political institutions. He therefore proposes a "new institutionalism" in public law research. In this view, politics is not simply a matter of performing a social calculus for summing up preferences and distributing wealth accordingly. Political institutions do not merely aggregate and mediate. Rather, institutions, including the judiciary, independently influence events because institutions are themselves communities of discourse whose values and rhetoric have an authoritative history sustained internally and independently of the external configuration of political preferences.[33]

Smith urges his readers to describe more thoroughly the discursive historical matrix in which legal policy—such as equal protection and affirmative action policies—evolves in order to see more precisely how varying characteristics of institutional discourse shape political decisions and the subsequent distribution of resources. But Smith endorses neither raw empiricism nor moral complacency. We can in turn set these specific descriptions against a broader view of political processes and values. We can decide on

> our moral positions via reasoned judgements about the conceptions of the human self, its worth, and its enhancement that seem most persuasive. Our "deliberate reflections and choices" on these matters should be guided . . . by the light of our experience of "fundamental characteristics of the human condition" and its possibilities, and of history's lessons about how different ideals have worked out in practice.[34]

Smith thus believes that we can compare the state of, say, affirmative action policy at a given time against an independent history of human experiences with equality and inequality, advantage and disadvantage and that, through "reasoned judgements," rational discourse, and "deliberate reflection," we can arrive at persuasive conclusions. In his book *Liberalism and American Constitutional Law,* he explained at some length how liberalism itself identifies the rational, reasoned, and reflective elements of sound political and legal discourse. For Smith, the alternative political visions revealed in history and experience endorse a form of democratic decision making in which institutions and decisions treat citizens' judgments and standards about the nature of rights and liberties as authoritative. In his view, no institution or official should possess the power to declare authoritative principles and enforce them on all. He thus offered the hope that by taking its own liberal premises seriously, law can be a critical progressive and reformist force in political life.[35]

Smith has viewed political institutions and the language that constructs them as sufficiently stable, continuous, and internally homogenous to permit persuasive descriptions and conclusions. But do these assumptions fit our institutional experience? Do public law, political science, the Supreme Court, or the constitutional law bar, each a community of discourse, display the institutional stability and homogeneity that Smith assumed? Experience may suggest otherwise. After all, the interplay of individual convictions and values, the imprint of diverse personal histories, the dynamics of accommodation and cooperation in work groups, the tactics for self-advancement, and the unpredictable accidents of life all push toward diversity, heterogeneity, and contingency at the level of institutional life where Smith posits stability. These institutional conditions would, if true, prevent both the academy and political institutions from developing or responding to specific doctrines and ideas in any extended systematic way. William Haltom's chapter in this book (see Chapter 5) illustrates one version of the problem; after 200 years the Supreme Court has yet to create a clearly defined and consistently applied understanding of the seemingly straightforward concept of the separation of powers. Nevertheless, Smith may carry the day. He may persuade us to adopt ideal models of rational discourse and discover ways of applying them to constitutional lawmaking. But insiders who hear a cacophony of voices beneath the formal politics of institutions may prefer to turn to a more explicitly conversational legal perspective, with all its inclusiveness, to find evaluative standards of law's goodness.

James Boyd White adopts something close to this latter view in describing legal activity as poetics. As he sees it, we experience law's goodness, and particularly the goodness of judicial opinions, in terms of the ways we read them and interact with their styles and messages. The quality of this interaction for White depends on the literary and poetic element in legal and judicial writing. In White's conversational view of law, the experience of conversation—by parties to litigation and by those who read and, thus, indirectly converse with the authors of opinions—provides the material for judging law's goodness. The conversational view of law in effect shifts the essential nature of justice away from the interpretation of texts and empirical descriptions of institutional histories and practices and toward the experience of people. White applies to law a formal and stylized version of the conversations of daily life, which are extended exchanges of messages and whose conclusions, if any, depend on what is said and how. Conversation presumes openness of mind, willingness to listen, candor, and trust. The essence of formal conversation is that the outcome cannot be specified in advance. The goodness of a conversation depends less on the answers it generates than on the quality of the debate.

There is nothing mysterious about this theory of law as conversation. Law is conversational in many ways. Legal procedures, rules of evidence, and customs of advocacy all claim to preserve law's openness; the common law system is adversarial; trials and appeals are dialectical. Oral arguments, briefs, voir dire of potential jurors, examination and cross-examination—however formal, stylized, and hierarchical—nevertheless can be viewed as conversations. Moreover, law schools socialize future lawyers and judges not to discover correct textual interpretation but to create positions and arguments that serve their clients' interests. Judges cannot know good results except through conversation. The opportunity to appeal judgment in significant cases underscores the imperfections of all conversations. In short, we cannot trust any single conversation to produce the best outcome. Apellate judges serve on teams and converse with each other in chambers and in the draft opinions they circulate, and their final opinions converse both with other opinions in the case with the outside world of the litigants, lawyers, scholars, and students who read them.

Within constitutional doctrine, Footnote Four of *U.S. vs. Carolene Products,* that staple of conventional postwar jurisprudence, could be seen as expanding the promise of legal conversation by emphasizing the importance of giving political voice to insular minorities and victims of prejudice.[36] So could the philosophy of the "sober second look," advocated by Alexander Bickel and Guido Calabresi and written explicitly into the Canadian constitution.[37] The sober second look doctrine in effect imposes a rebuttable presumption of unconstitutionality on a statute or practice. It invites legislative reconsideration of the issue in light of facts and arguments articulated in litigation, but reconsideration may rebut the presumption of unconstitutionality.

White's conversational argument does not generate substantive legal interpretations of textual clauses and, unlike Smith, White proposes no unified conclusions about constitutional policy. Nevertheless, he sets philosophically evaluative standards of good legal practice in the following ways.

1. Law, like scripture and liturgy, creates boundaries—topical and rhetorical limits—that are prerequisites for any conversation. Thus, according to White, a constitution creates "the fundamental terms of a new kind of conversation; for it creates a set of speakers, defines the occasion for and topics of their speech, and is itself a text that may be referred to as authoritative."[38]

2. Law's literary character—its use of irony, ambiguity, contrast, and similar poetic devices—at the same time keeps law open. The indeterminate, multivoiced character of law preserves the capacity for people with competing interests to tell their stories.[39] The law's indeterminacy is a blessing, not a curse, because law never arrives at policy positions final enough to prevent those affected from conversing about what law ought to be. In a similar tone, Martha Minow, writing about the difficulty of reconciling competing claims of legal rights through rights doctrine, stated, "Rights can be understood as a kind of communal discourse that reconfirms the difficult commitment to live together even while engaging in conflicts and struggles."[40]

3. To the extent that law becomes a multivoiced conversation, it helps make us part of a common world. Law's language, according to White, helps unify political experience and provide a nondoctrinal base for law's authority:

> The language of the law, in hands trained this way, can be at its heart what Owen Barfield calls a poetic language, not a theoretical one—a language that works by association and connotation, by allusion and reference, by the way words are put together to make a whole. In this way it can maintain connections with the terms and processes of ordinary life and ordinary language. This in fact is a source of much of its political authority and significance.[41]

4. Conversation creates an affective or psychological bridge between our desire for justice and an acknowledgment of law's imperfections. Conversation is a mechanism that allows the losers to trust that results with which they disagree are honest mistakes rather than exercises of raw power. As Philip Soper has argued, law does so by assuring losers of "the right to discourse, a right to insist on the bona fides of belief in the only form in which sincerity can be tested: communication, dialogue, exchange, debate."[42]

5. We have suggested that conversational models of law do not depend on extended foundational conclusions about correct doctrinal or policy outcomes. Nevertheless, especially for White, law as conversation necessarily honors and preserves the values of equal respect and dignity advocated by the more grandly foundational and epistemic theories of Dworkin and Barber. The good legal hearing achieves a "performed equality among the speakers. . . . This, as we learned from Thucydides, is the essential premise of the social practice of argument."[43] In short, law's conversation, if taken seriously, can equalize voices. In this view, the deficiencies of legal standardization, such as those analyzed in trial court processes by Bennett and Feldman,[44] do not disprove White's point. Rather, they confirm in their deplorability that White's conversational standards constitute a critical perspective that allows us to evaluate law philosophically.

However different, the views of Smith and White are not contradictory. Smith seeks to evaluate constitutional policy and therefore focuses on the institutional processes of discourse that generate policy. White assesses adjudication and believes that we can understand the conversational process of the law as a valuable political phenomenon independent of institutional arrangements, theories of law, and the efficacy or desirability of law's policy outcomes. Lon Fuller, whose jurisprudence anticipates White's, put the point this way: "[T]he process of adjudication can itself be a moral force in men's lives, and . . . this moral force is not necessarily derived from some other higher principles such as established law or government."[45] For White and Smith, effective legal discourse is closed enough to enable the search for common understanding yet is inherently open and dynamic enough to be a potentially responsive and progressive forum for change and social justice. Law, on its own terms, can "heal itself."

OUTSIDE LAW: CHALLENGING AND TRANSFORMING LEGAL DISCOURSE

The insider models of discursive law that we have just described, to borrow Connolly's felicitous phrase, "gravitate . . . toward an ontology of concord. That is, each assumes that when properly constituted and situated the individual or collective subject achieves harmony with itself and with the other elements of social life."[46] Connolly was describing denominators common to competing grand ethical theories such as those of MacIntyre and Dworkin, but the conclusion applies equally well to approaches to legal analysis based on rational discourse and poetic conversation.

Applications of critical outsider discourse theory to legal analysis have produced quite different conclusions. From the outsider perspective, neither grand theory nor pragmatic experience of law's alleged conversational process is able to promote social harmony, justice, or freedom. To the contrary, it is our very experience with law in action that reveals how its inherently conservative rhetoric cushions and disguises even as it constitutes the power that maintains or, perhaps, *is* the status quo. According to outsiders, insider justifications of law divert us from the evidence that constitutional policy as the Supreme Court declares it rarely translates into social betterment. For example, in his critique of *Law's Empire,* Allan Hutchinson noted twenty-six statistical statements concerning the nature of racial inequality. For example: "Chance of an American being in state prison on any given day: 1 in 800. Chance of a black male American being in a state prison on any given day: 1 in 33." He then wrote:

> Of course, this stark listing of data does not refute or conclusively confound Dworkin's claims. However, it does present a formidable challenge and counterpoint to the typical lawyer's empirical naivete (or arrogance) that Dworkin's extravagant statements reflect. With almost no supporting evidence, lawyers make the most sweeping and smug claims for the instrumental impact and efficacy of adjudication; when the courts speak, the world not only sits up and listens, but changes in line with judicial expectations. The small amount of evidence available strongly suggests the contrary view that litigation and adjudication are of marginal importance to global change.[47]

The gap between aspiration and reality in law and society propels outside critics to challenge the habits of both the legal profession and the academy through both analytical critiques and tactics intended to shock and surprise. Grant the misfit between the aspirations—be they equitable distributions of wealth and dignity or the creation of a rational legislative democracy—and the reality of an American polity split by material and political inequality, and the insider legal models of rational discourse and poetic conversation seem less like the naive pipe dreams of academics than the ugly enemies of the aspirations themselves. Moreover, outsiders might tell us that whereas the image of a peaceful conversation is nice, judicial action at all levels seeks primarily to justify the use of political force to hurt someone—a point both Robert Bork and the late Robert Cover made with some force of their own.

Critical discourse theorists of law can point to existing work by students of political jurisprudence showing that the courts are populated by judges who are selected or appointed by the very political coalitions that are linked to the maintenance and enjoyment of the inequalities of the system. The conversational process of pragmatic jurisprudence does not generate independent criteria for determining the agenda of topics addressed; instead, the political process of selecting topics shapes the conversation that follows. In light of this recognition, the virtually total discretion of the Supreme Court over its docket means that the choice of topics to be discussed is in the hands of a powerful few. The agenda is left, in short, to political forces that are themselves hidden from reflective review and are motivated to avoid confronting difficult aspirational matters. As E. E. Schattschneider has pointed out, those in a position to set the terms and issues of debate have gone a long way toward winning it.[48]

Moreover, critical discourse theorists draw on institutional studies to challenge the very idea that law is conversational in practice. Case loads and related pressures of assembly line justice artificially limit, routinize, stylize, and thus conventionalize legal discourse. As we pointed out in the earlier review of outsider orientations, what actually happens is more like dictation than conversation. The often hidden premises of law, the necessary reductionism and limitations, and the more mundane issues of case load and other daily pressures simply negate the image of law as an open conversation. As for the idea that the law is a conversation between equals, numerous studies have indicated that the inequality of resources available to litigants results in a highly imbalanced distribution of power among the voices before the law.[49]

Courts may, then, exist not to open up discourse but to close it and give a constitutional stamp of approval to actions taken. Judges justify power by saying that of all the plausible alternatives, "*this one* is law and destroy or try to destroy the rest."[50] To justify imposing the hurt that legal decisions necessarily entail, judges must claim that the hurt is inevitable and final. In other words, Justice Rehnquist's majority opinion in *Goldman,* far from displaying an unfortunate lapse from the conversational ethic of constitutional law, is archetypal. Courts themselves tend consistently to behave like the military; they tend to enforce for the sake of enforcement the appearance of uniformity and to maintain an appearance of impartiality. Courts must be final, not correct, and finality requires that we trust the judiciary's "considered professional judgment," just as Rehnquist trusted without conversation the judgment of the Air Force regarding Captain Goldman's yarmulke.

Recent critical discourse theorists have moved beyond earlier studies of judicial politics in focusing their attention on the very structures and substance of legal discourse itself. For these outsiders, the legal discourse is seen as constituting and legitimating the prevailing power relations of domination, exclusion, and hierarchy within society. In short, recent critical work extends the argument raised in the preceding paragraphs—that the very practice of law by definition serves to reproduce and support modes of existence that are antithetical to liberation and social justice.

The contributions of Foucauldian, or genealogical, scholars to constitutional law per se have been rather sparse and mixed. Some have employed genealogical tools to show how the legal discourse subjugates aspects of the self that do not fit the legal model. For example, in reviewing Susan Estrich's *Real Rape*, Kim Lane Scheppele argues:

> Women and men *do* have very different perceptions of experience, but in the context of law one set of perceptions is hidden. Michel Foucault speaks of subjugated knowledges to describe such buried views. What remains—the perceptions acknowledged, recognized, *seen* in law—is the socially constructed "objective" point of view against which both men's and women's actions are judged by both men and women. That point of view *is* the law. But it is not the point of view at all.[51]

Others working from this perspective tend to eschew a focused treatment of the law. In *Beyond the Public/Private Division: Law, Power and 'the Family,'* Nikolas Rose argues that a focus on law erroneously posits the state as the predominant source of power, promotes the misperception of power as primarily instrumental, and mystifies law by making it seem totalizing and coherent.[52] Furthermore, academic analysis of the law, by focusing our attention on the sovereign state, serves to mask the more diffuse and important forms of power in the local institutions of, for example, the family, the school, the workplace, and the asylum.[53]

Neo-Marxists and other leftists, by contrast, have provided an extensive body of critical insights to the analysis of legal discourse in recent decades. In particular, the work of such figures as E. P. Thompson, Stuart Hall, and Douglas Hay, to name a few, has contributed to the development of highly sophisticated theories that regard law as constitutive ideological structures that uphold enduring class divisions within capitalist society. From this perspective, the focus is not necessarily on the instrumental use of law by economic elites, or on the ways that legal discourse masks or distorts other social forms. Rather, analysis centers on the role of law and concepts of rights, citizenship, and the legal subject in political struggle and subjectivity in contemporary society.[54] Such Marxian analysis of legal ideology proceeds by deconstructing dominant forms in order to show their implicitly capitalist or bourgeois-liberal origins, then goes on to explore the role of these forms in constituting society and the modern subject and to show how this ideology deflects or negates attempts by lower classes to redress their grievances through the legal system. In this book, the chapters by Margaret J. Radin,

Stuart Scheingold, and Michael McCann include discussions that further illuminate the contemporary dimensions and directions of neo-Marxist critique as applied specifically to constitutional lawmaking.

Because of the importance of both legal rights and recent Supreme Court decisions to the political interests of women, feminist academics have provided an especially rich body of contributions to the study of legal discourse. Where Marxian critique would tend to focus on processes of exclusion and hegemony on a primarily economic axis, feminist critiques shift a similar set of questions to the gender dimension. Often—as in the works of Deborah L. Rhode and Rhonda Copelon in this book—such analyses demonstrate not only the legal restriction of women from enjoyment of basic constitutional rights but also reveal how the basic patriarchal underpinnings of the liberal legal model effectively exclude more liberating and communal understandings such as those emerging from the feminist movement. Clearly more hopeful about the possibilities for effective change than many genealogists, some critical feminists have argued that the expression of the alternative subjectivity and experiences of women can both advance the position of women and contribute to the liberation of law and society in broader senses.[55] Elizabeth Schneider exemplifies many outsiders' recognition of both the potentials and basic limitations of the legal discourse in addressing the rise of a feminist reconceptualization of rights.

> Both the right to equality and the right to reproductive choice are rights derived from the contexts of political struggle and feminist organization. Both rights emerged from a radical feminist vision that equality was not limited to formal legal treatment or assimilation of women into male roles, but rather required the radical restructuring of society. The expression of these visions began with the formulation of rights claims in the courts. Yet even though these visions have neither been nor could be achieved in the courts, their introduction through rights claims started the "conversation" in society at large about women's roles and women's subordination under law.[56]

Finally, all of these strands of radical discourse analysis have influenced the most visible group of legal scholars drawing on discourse models, the Critical Legal Studies movement, discussed at length in Rogers M. Smith's chapter in this book. But rather than offering one more analysis of these well-publicized and familiar critical perspectives or reiterating arguments that appear elsewhere in this book, we turn to a unique, surprising, and less-publicized example of outsider analysis. This example involves the claim that constitutional discourse should, but so far has failed to, draw directly on its Judeo-Christian heritage. Two books by Milner Ball provide an outside critique of law that seeks to shift discourse by surprise.[57] Influenced by what might seem an unmanageable combination of theology, legal studies, and postmodern philosophy, Ball reminds us that law is a system of metaphors for dealing with the world and then directly challenges modern law's basic metaphors. Following Rorty and White, Ball tells us that courts are theaters and that law tells stories. But unlike White, Ball insists that law must tell a certain specific story. Ball's sentimental and at times deliberately disjointed style is startling, but even more startling is his claim that the Constitution commands the legal system to tell a specific and continually unfolding story of continuous human encounter with a Creator and Redeemer.[58]

Ball's message holds that from Genesis forward, texts, principles, and commands do not hold the authoritative center we give them in legal theory today. They are, rather, the backdrop against which the ongoing story of creation and redemption is played out. Ball suggests that constitutional discourse ought to be fundamentally shaped by the essential quality of Judeo-Christian stories. This position does not urge adoption of any foundational moral or theological orthodoxy; its focus, rather, is on the continual sense of communal commitment and rebirth that lies in the authoritative story telling of the biblical tradition. For Ball, law's authority grows from the fact that the Constitution, like Genesis, the Exodus, and the New Testament, begins a political story. The Constitution's "beginningness" is the promise that holds our story together.

Ball's work is itself highly discursive and claims to build on the discursive character of religion manifest in authoritative story telling. Authoritative story telling recognizes that the teller can assert powerful metaphors, which, if successful, can shift the listener's consciousness of a situation; it also recognizes that a good story is essential to building or maintaining the authority itself.[59] The stories that Ball urges on us bring to life the commitment to community, a sense of continual beginning and regeneration, and the promises of the more noble and empowering aspects of constitutional history. Courts, then, tell specific stories that connect present with past; but each case, each judicial encounter with the story, should replicate the beginning of an effort to create a polity. Judges should approach each case as an opportunity to begin rather than end a search for justice.

As is essential to most critical outsider perspectives, Ball condemns the exclusiveness of the law as it is and argues that the promise and rebirth of the constitutional story demands the inclusion of alternative voices—the "powerless minorities" in American politics. Each instance of this inclusion, he suggests, represents both a continuation of the story and promise that began, whatever its flaws, in Philadelphia as well as the beginning of a new story and promise.

Neither Ball nor his message are "outsiders" to many aspects of our culture—and clearly he is neither Marxist, feminist, nor genealogist. But the emphasis on the Judeo-Christian heritage and the turn away from search-ending principles to regenerative stories is clearly outside the legal mainstream and progressively egalitarian in substance. Moreover, Ball's style and rhetoric startles in many ways. He rejects the elegantly elaborate comparison of legal and religious sources that we would expect from within the world of legal discourse. (Sanford Levinson's *Constitutional Faith* provides such comparisons.[60]) He makes no academic case or elaborate defense of the compatibility of his vision with First Amendment establishment doctrine. Rather, he presents a style of argument he implicitly recommends for the law itself, a rhetoric that surprises by claiming to speak not objective truth but inspirational, authoritative words. In this view, Justice Rehnquist fails in *Goldman* because he makes no effort to tell a moving story—no moral claims, no sense of human dilemma, no effort to bring to life the heritage of the community. Rather, he depersonalizes the issues so as to convert the case from a human story into a social science speculation on organizational dynamics. Ball's language, in contrast, provides an ethic of inclusiveness, solidarity, and the extension of rights. In using such language, he attempts to create in us—and it is the nature of authority that we may accept or reject it—a new and promising vision of the constitutional conversation. And he often reminds his readers of the radical open-endedness of the search, as in the final words of *Lying Down Together:* "I hope that you invent your own, better way to talk about these things and do them. It will be better if you and law are made more responsive to your neighbor, those victimized by the system as it now is."[61]

AESTHETICS, DEMOCRATIC AUTHORITY, AND CONSTITUTIONAL DISCOURSE

We have described a transition from John Marshall's notion of the Constitution as ruling government to Lon Fuller's notion of law as a moral force independent of its epistemic foundations, doctrinal assertions, and conclusions in specific cases. Current convictions about philosophy as well as the political psychology of decision making explain why we no longer believe in a Constitution that rules. A complex mixture of prefigurative social forces and idiosyncratic preferences shape judicial choices and decisions. Judges and philosophers alike experience the "realities" of their worlds in ways that are at once similarly constituted yet separate and unique. Neither legal doctrines nor foundational philosophical concepts behind legal doctrines will generate consensus or ensure continuity.

There is currently disagreement over whether "good constitutional law" or other forms of moral authority are even a possibility in the present philosophical context. For some, the implications of the genealogical tradition and other critical schools spell an end to the social concept of consensus and legitimacy altogether. Moreover, we recognize that revolution or the construction of autonomous communities may be the only means available to overcome existing hierarchy and domination. But we take to heart William Connolly's advice that in an age marked by "the politics of ambiguity," the promise inherent in the struggle toward legitimate authority outweighs the dangers of creating new forms of domination in the process. In short, "Authority is an indispensible and dangerous practice."[62]

In addressing the dilemma of constitutional authority in the postfoundational era, the authors have feet in both the insider and outsider camps. We tend to be outsiders in that we reject prevailing forms of judicial argument and agree with Ball and others that the constitutional discourse must strive for greater inclusiveness and responsiveness to the needs and aspirations of those who have been excluded. But, on the other hand, we tend to be insiders in that we entertain at least the possibility of good constitutional lawmaking and believe that it can, or must, be done with at least some of the tools at hand. These tensions may show that our insider-outsider dichotomization is, as most such constructions are, a bit over-simplified; virtually anyone involved in critical legal analysis must be an insider and an outsider both. Many of the other authors of this book express the angst of those who waver on the insider-outsider lines; they see and address the exclusive and dominating aspects of the law but retain the hope of salvaging the promise of law—partly for lack of better options—and are drawn to participation in the constitutional discourse.

Although it may appear to some, then, that we are insiders urging a continuation of a largely unchanged process of constitutional lawmaking, we argue that the discursive approach can create a different form of authority. And, as Connolly argues, a new form of authority is essential: "[T]he mode of authority appropriate to modernity involves an appreciation of its ambiguous character. . . . [A]n appreciation of ambiguity must be installed in the institutional matrix of society if authority is to assume its appropriate place in modern life."[63]

Our version of discursive philosophy—which we label an "aesthetic" model—thus accepts ambiguity but nevertheless retains a conviction that law can be a moral force. That is, law remains a potential tool for advancing a justice that involves the capacity of communicative relationships among members of a community to maintain a faith in and a commitment to continuing that very community. However critical, discursive justice involves the attempt to preserve a commitment to staying in conversation and debate through reassuring community members of the integrity, the trustworthiness, and the virtue of the participants in the dialogue. Judicial and academic writers alike thus perform justly to the extent that their performances convincingly provide such reassurance—reassurance that the writer's world is enough like our own that we may realistically hope to act upon joint commitment. This hope depends in turn on trusting the integrity of authorities who, except for their writing, are strangers to us.

G. Edward White recently criticized the jurisprudence of Justice William O. Douglas on these grounds when he charged the latter with breaking the discursive rules of the legal community: "Douglas, who seemed to operate on the premise that ideology counted for more than doctrine or institutional role, had his reputation suffer accordingly."[64] The doctrines that Douglas disdained were part of an inside, shared world of legal discourse that constituted and preserved the integrity, trustworthiness, impartiality, and openness of the members of that world. By substituting his own ideology without regard for the rhetoric that bound lawyers and judges together, and by assuming that individual piety mattered more than collective trust, Douglas presented himself not so much as legally wrong but as untrustworthy, and hence, according to White, he was less able to persuade others to take his ideas seriously.

It is by now a truism that doctrine's substance alone does not determine the outcome a judge reaches or the position an academic philosopher takes. Rather, the rhetoric of doctrine steers philosophical argument and the legal justification of power toward formulating beliefs and positions that an audience can perceive in sharable ways. Given this rejection of doctrine's role in determining good judicial performance or legal philosophy, we turn in this section to specifying some aesthetic characteristics that are essential in evaluating performance. We will suggest that these basic characteristics can help explain how legal and academic rhetoric can strengthen the integrity of and thereby strengthen commitment to legal and philosophical communities. As such, the aesthetic vision of justice elevates the idea of a conversation between performer and audience from an imperfect description of existing law to a normative standard for evaluating legal activity.

All performances seek to excite and motivate responses from those who experience them; how and why performances succeed or fail to engage the audience depends on their aesthetic qualities. In general, the aesthetically effective performance fits its component parts together in such a way that it creates, for those who experience it, images that seem, on their own terms, coherent and complete. The achieved image, that which seems complete in itself, need not always please or win approval. Pleasure and approval matter, but they are not decisive. As a case in point, someone may not "enjoy" classical opera but nonetheless may respect the integrity and fullness of a good performance. Another person may not enjoy the Talking Heads but nonetheless may respect the integrity and aesthetic value of their performance. Although these two people would not be likely to attend all the same concerts, they may enjoy debating the merits of various forms of music, unite in their appreciation of much good music, and feel themselves to be members of a community that enjoys music. Similarly, a majority and dissenting opinion in a case may be both aesthetically satisfying and frustrating. We may, as did John Stick in his reaction to *Law's Empire*, delight in the creation of a vision against which we wish, perhaps passionately, to argue. We can respect a performer and his or her performance at the same time that we disagree with its conclusions.

This recognition shifts our search for standards in law and legal philosophy from the persuasiveness of static epistemology and determinant proof toward the aesthetic integrity and political inclusiveness of discourse. The good constitutional opinion, judged on aesthetic terms, would, for example, seek to create complete and coherent images regarding the appropriate and fair distribution of resources and power. Remembering that the audience will feel deprived by the substantive implications of the distribution, we see that the aesthetic vision of form is inseparable from a concern for content. Although the discussion here centers on the form of the performance—that is, opinions and academic critiques—we emphasize the clear implications for legal substance as well: (1) that few groups will or should maintain faith in communal conversation when promises are broken, and (2) that standards of aesthetic performance should not mask the fact that faith and authority cannot be built on a base of continuous abuse, neglect, and deprivation.

In the pages that follow we elaborate on two other specific aspects of aesthetics in legal discourse. First, we discuss the frequency with which the persuasiveness of legal and philosophical arguments is based on the claim that they create the "best fit" among the materials in the legal and political worlds that we share. Second, we note how legal and philosophical writers resort to "sentiment" to facilitate and strengthen their arguments.

"BEST FIT" AND CONSTITUTIONAL VISION

No theme emerges more clearly from a wide range of contemporary legal philosophical works than does an author's request that we believe the conclusions because his or her rhetoric has shaped our shared world in coherent ways. Although this pattern appears in both foundational and discursive philosophies, contemporary philosophers rarely claim that a foundational conclusion is morally convincing. Rather, they claim that the materials their analysis deems relevant fit together better than any other imaginable configuration. In this sense, insider discourse theorists aspire to fittedness as an end in itself, as part and parcel of legitimate, community-building lawmaking. Given the aforementioned concordant tendencies of insider views, it is clear that they expect their world to make sense and, therefore, consider fittedness to be a sign of goodness.

This claim to persuade on the basis of the coherence of one's vision in modern legal philosophy parallels the Kuhnian view of scientific discourse, in which natural science tests the fittedness of data and observation within existing paradigms. Paradigms fail when the effort to retain the internal fit becomes too cumbersome and inelegant.[65] The claim of fittedness rises in all corners of the law. We have already seen extensive examples of fittedness claims in Ronald Dworkin's idea of legal integrity, in Rogers M. Smith's case for "rational discourse,"[66] and in James Boyd White's argument for "coherence of vision."[67] Sotirios Barber, as a further example, believes that the Constitution, given its aspirational preamble and its setting in a new and hopeful territory, is internally coherent only if we treat it as a statement of political aspirations. We must "interpret and apply its provisions in light of our best understanding of an ideal state of affairs adumbrated by those provisions. At the center of this constitutionally ideal state of affairs is a typical citizen, who is governed by an attitude that places the highest social or political value on the activity of reasoning about how one ought to live." Barber's sense of what fits best with the aspirations of the Constitution leads directly and without the aid of complex philosophical agreement to reject "such unconstitutional attitudes as racism, sexism, self-righteousness, zealotry, wilfulness, acquisitiveness, and moral skepticism."[68]

Fittedness arguments are perhaps most clearly exemplified by Richard Fallon, who has recently applied structural aesthetic criteria to constitutional argument by lawyers and judges. He has shown that good legal argument abides by standards of "constructivist coherence" and "commensurability." Fallon's rather conventional analysis leads him to focus on the integrity of writers and speakers. He acknowledges that lawyers on competing sides of cases can and usually do satisfy the standard of commensurability, and that commensurability is not therefore a final test of correctness of the result. For Fallon the ethics of doing justice reside in the virtue of individual judges. The obligation of justice is consistency: A judge who fits constitutional language, history, and values together in a certain way to justify his or her result in case X must not violate that fit in justifying the result in case Y.[69] Again, the process of creating commensurability in law does not itself verify the superiority of one result over another. Rather, it reassures us of the integrity and trustworthiness of strangers who hold power over us.

Insiders tend to make their fits with elements already present within law; Ball and other outsiders, conversely, focus much of their attention on challenging the structural incoherence of law—its arbitrariness and its failure to implement the ideals of equality and dignity that its doctrines presuppose. In Ball's case, the protest centers on the disconnection between law's authority and its commitment to continue the story that forms the basis of our culture. From a critical perspective, the ideal of fittedness is useful in two ways: (1) as a mode of criticism for contending that ideas/decisions handed down do not fit well with precedents or tradition, and (2) as a source of positive suggestions for promoting new directions for policy that might fit better with old ideals and values. Tactics of critical deconstruction that reveal a lack of fit and tactics of reconstruction that promise a better fit have been central to much of the work of the Critical Legal Studies movement as well as that of feminists, neo-Marxists, and other progressive critical analysts. All seek to show how discourse now lacks fit, especially regarding promises of equality, citizenship, and dignity, and that it can be redefined in ways that would make for a better fit between aspiration and reality in American politics.

Assuming the pervasiveness of the claim of "best fit" in modern philosophical argument, what is its significance for legal philosophy? It may reflect the ascendance of pluralistic ethics against authoritarian justifications for the use of power. The argument of one who claims to have found correct moral and political principles and structures is final; it implicitly requires us to agree or disobey. The best fit/coherence argument, by contrast, is inherently more egalitarian than are foundationalist approaches; its adherents reject the idea that there is a final, ultimately conclusive fit and thus admit its disconfirmability. The best fit argument invites us to reply—whether cooperatively or confrontationally—with a better fit of our own, and in doing so empowers us to stay in the discursive community even as we may seek to radically alter it.

JUSTICE AND SENTIMENT

We noted earlier that foundational philosophy leads either to an infinite analytical regress or to a logical vicious circle. By "sentiment," we refer to the commitment from author to reader to avoid the infinite regress into which the analytical search for foundations leads. Through sentiment, the writer invites readers to join his or her circle and to agree to limit the terms of argument. Without such limits it is impossible to create the boundary, or frame, that limits the materials the performer must fit coherently together to a workable number. The appeal of sentiment is thus a leap of faith toward maintaining commitments to and faith in dialogue; it takes over where rational argument alone fails.

Sentiment in legal writing—and it occurs in judicial opinions more overtly than in academic writing—asks us to join the writer on an affective plane. Some writing proceeds by inserting an occasionally loaded word— "community," "convention," "dignity," "liberty," "harmony," "struggle," and so on. In other instances—Ball and White come to mind—the author speaks in a consistently sentimental style. Rorty himself used such phrases as "that sense of community which only impassioned conversation makes possible," and "we should side with the Romantics and do our best to aestheticize society, to keep it safe for the poets in the hope that the poets will eventually make it safe for everybody else."[70]

It should be clear from these examples that sentiment, like fittedness, is a characteristic of both insider and outsider work. Indeed, radical critics may rely on sentiment even more than outsiders. Consider Unger's "solidarity is the social face of love,"[71] and Ball's consistent appeals to our sense of faith and community. If we momentarily overlook the substance of these claims, then the sentimental nature of their rhetorical use becomes clear. Sentiment is necessary in all legal philosophy, but it is more acceptable and prominent in discursive than in foundational writing because the meaning of justice itself differs between the two approaches. In discursive philosophy, justice exists when a litigant, perhaps a loser, experiences law's operation as fair, or when a reader of a judicial opinion experiences a vivid image of a social order in which she can engage. In such cases, justice necessarily merges rational analysis with sentiment—affective feelings of neighborliness, trustworthiness, and stability.[72]

An especially familiar example of the use of sentiment as well as a claim of best fit is found in Justice Robert H. Jackson's decision in *West Virginia State Board of Education v. Barnette*. This decision, made in the middle of World War II, overturned local regulations compelling Jehovah's Witnesses to salute the flag in public schools.[73] The Witnesses expressed conviction that the salute violated the biblical injunction against worshipping graven images. In order to be persuasive, Jackson's opinion needed to rebut the recent and much criticized *Gobitis* precedent and Justice Felix Frankfurter's belief that the electoral process would generate a more effective debate on the issues than could litigation. Jackson also needed to distinguish older precedents, particularly *Davis v. Beason,* which denied the fundamental freedoms of free political expression to Mormons in the name of national self-interest.[74] Jackson used sentiment to accomplish both results. Regarding *Gobitis,* he stated, "The very purpose of a Bill of Rights was to withdraw certain subjects from the vicissitudes of political controversy. . . . One's right to life, liberty and property, to free speech, a free press, freedom of worship . . . [may] not be submitted to vote, depend on the outcome of no elections."[75]

A more celebrated passage disposed of *Davis v. Beason:*

> If there is any fixed star in our constitutional constellation, it is that no official, high or petty, can prescribe what shall be orthodox in politics, nationalism, religion, or other matters of opinion or force citizens to confess by word or act their faith therein. If there are any circumstances which permit an exception, they do not now occur to us.[76]

Both passages use sentiment to transcend difficult jurisprudential problems, namely, the distinction between belief and action and the nature of symbolic action. Having thus framed the boundary of his argument to exclude the need to fit these concerns into his analysis, Jackson freed himself to hold that compulsory flag salute cannot be made coherent—either in the context of the historical commitment to freedom of conscience on which the nation was founded or in light of the wartime commitment to battle enemies advocating state-controlled and compelled patriotism.

One final and more contemporary example brings to life the interaction of fittedness and the need of judicial performers to foster the sentiment necessary for the maintenance of conversation. In dissenting from the Supreme Court's recent decision to reconsider key aspects of civil rights laws as set down in *Runyon v. McCrary,* Justice John Paul Stevens criticized the majority for its lack of concern with fitting established patterns of discourse. He noted that the majority was making a "spontaneous decision" and had "cast itself adrift from the constraints imposed by the adversary process." Turning to issues of sentiment, trust, and the broader fittedness of law, Stevens feared that the decision endangered "the public's perception of the court as an impartial adjudicator" and "the faith of victims of racial discrimination in a stable construction of the civil rights laws."[77]

CONCLUSION

Writers committed to discursive constitutional philosophy have a hard time writing definitive conclusions. We nevertheless believe that the aesthetic-discursive approach provides a better and more coherent fit between actual constitutional discourse and the wisdom of contemporary philosophy and that it can contribute to the construction of a more true and inclusive form of community. Returning to the example with which this chapter began, we thus do not claim the power to prove whether Orthodox Jews have a constitutional right to an exception from military headgear policy. But we do know that Justice Rehnquist's majority opinion in *Goldman* failed aesthetically. The dialogical character of our legal system exists and is encouraged precisely because we mistrust blind reliance on "independent professional judgment." Rehnquist failed to fit together his justification in this case with the justification that allowed him to decide at all.

In closing, we should recall some of the warnings of the more critical "outsiders" discussed earlier. Genealogists, clearly, would note that the idea of the performance includes a skilled and dominant figure on stage and would wonder whether the aesthetic model is not simply a new set of clothes for old forms of centralized power and discourse. Furthermore, the concepts of "fittedness" and "sentiment" may mean little more than, respectively, a replication of old patterns of discourse and the sparking of new "self-discipline" in the modern legal subject. William Connolly's fears about Richard Rorty's discourse merit attention here; the performance or conversation in a given culture, with a given language, and with given distributions of power and resources, runs the risk of doing little more than "mirroring" the established tendencies of that culture.[78] Similarly, Nancy C. M. Hartsock has argued that women and other outsiders cannot afford to give up the search for foundations when the latter are so crucial in establishing identity, critical voice, and power. Indeed, to her it seems somewhat suspect that philosophy is trying to abandon foundations and definition just at the time when women and other formerly powerless groups finally begin to develop their own foundational standpoints.[79]

For others, the aesthetic trend we have described may seem to negate the possibility of developing any interesting constitutional standards that are distinctively legal. Those who feel some discomfort with aesthetic talk often voice the criticism that art is inherently incompatible with law, that art confers freedom and discretion whereas law limits it. They might point out that Hitler's art swayed a people no less than Churchill's, or that in the name of art Georges Perec wrote a novel, *La Disprition,* whose orienting aesthetic was no more significant than that the letter "e" never appeared in it.[80]

The yearning for foundational standards of legal evaluation is thoroughly understandable, but the opponents of aesthetic standards should not overlook two points. First, whether or not this particular effort to cope with postfoundational law and politics is successful, the broader condition of postfoundationalism remains, and theories based on yearnings for definition will become increasingly less able to convince. It is essential to separate discomfort with what Paul Feyerabend called the "spectre of relativism" from critical dissatisfaction with attempts to deal with the implications of that "spectre."[81] Second, the connections between aesthetic theories and observable political phenomena should not be ignored. Grant that we exist in highly pluralistic economic, social, and ideological conditions and then any foundational claim carries a strong authoritarian character in implying that millions of people should change their minds and accept its terms. In such conditions political allegiance and order may depend on the structural integrity and sentimental power of dynamic political debate as much or more than it depends on agreement over policy preferences. If discursively informed constitutional lawmaking can achieve some continuing level of trust in the common commitments to a just and open polity amid disagreement and difference, then discursive standards of legal goodness may help build a more laudable form of community law than did liberalism's mythical rule of law.

NOTES

1. *Marbury v. Madison,* 5 U.S. 137 at 180 (1803).
2. Ibid.
3. Richard Rorty, *Philosophy and the Mirror of Nature* (Princeton: Princeton University Press, 1979).
4. Ibid., p. 6.
5. Ibid., p. 393.
6. Ibid., pp. 139–148.
7. See Lief Carter, *Contemporary Constitutional Lawmaking* (Elmsford, N.Y.: Pergamon Press, 1985), Chapter 2.
8. *Goldman v. Weinberger* 106 S. Ct. 1310 (1986).
9. *West Virginia State Board of Education v. Barnette,* 319 U.S. 624 (1943) and *Wisconsin v. Yoder,* 406 U.S. 205 (1972).
10. Robert Bork, "Neutral Principles and Some First Amendment Problems," *Indiana Law Journal* 47 (1971), p. 1.
11. Ronald Dworkin, "Law's Ambitions for Itself," *Virginia Law Review* 71 (1985), p. 173. Quotation is on p. 187.
12. Ronald Dworkin, *Taking Rights Seriously* (Cambridge: Harvard University Press, 1978); and "No Right Answer?" *New York University Law Review* 53 (1978), p. 1.

13. Dworkin's "intent" is presumably best expressed in his essays, some of which he reworked, collected in *A Matter of Principle* (Cambridge: Harvard University Press, 1985). For a critical evaluation of Dworkin's use of aesthetic theory, see Jessica Lane, "The Poetics of Legal Interpretation," *Columbia Law Review* 87 (1987), p. 197.

14. Ronald Dworkin, *Law's Empire* (Cambridge: Harvard University Press, 1986).

15. Ibid., pp. 164–186. Dworkin's grand theory presumably applies to all formal legal systems. Although it calls for integrating the legal with the political and the cultural, and therefore appears "culturally relative," its rational analytical structure is a universal one. Should law as Hercules, integrity, or consistency serve as a universal standard of justice among the Sioux, or in Pago Pago? Dworkin seems to say so, but the literature in legal anthropology would strongly disconfirm it. Thus Lane, in "The Poetics of Legal Interpretation," wrote: "Rationality alone, then, cannot do the work that he requires of it" (p. 204). And see Jeffrey Abramson, "Ronald Dworkin and the Convergence of Law and Political Philosophy," *Texas Law Review* 65 (1987), p. 1201.

16. John Stick, "Literary Imperialism: Assessing the Results of Dworkin's Interpretive Turn in *Law's Empire*," *UCLA Law Review* 34 (1986), pp. 428–429.

17. Allan Hutchinson, "Indiana Dworkin and *Law's Empire*," *Yale Law Journal* 96 (1987), p. 637.

18. Richard Bernstein, *Beyond Objectivism and Relativism* (Philadelphia: University of Pennsylvania Press, 1985), pp. 34–37.

19. Richard Rorty, "Philosophy Without Principles," in W. J. T. Mitchell, ed., *Against Theory* (Chicago: University of Chicago Press, 1985), p. 132.

20. William Connolly, *Politics and Ambiguity* (Madison: University of Wisconsin Press, 1987), p. 116.

21. Arthur Kennedy, quoted in "Speeches Provide Detailed Insight into Judge Kennedy's Philosophy," *New York Times* (December 1, 1987), sec. 1, p. 13.

22. Michel Foucault, *Discipline and Punish* (New York: Vintage, 1979); Michel Foucault, *Power-Knowledge* (New York: Pantheon, 1981); Hubert L. Dreyfus and Paul Rabinow, *Michel Foucault, Beyond Structuralism and Hermeneutics* (Chicago: University of Chicago Press, 1983); Barry Smart, *Michel Foucault* (New York: Tavistock, 1985).

23. Foucault, *Power-Knowledge*, pp. 90–92.

24. Nikolas Rose, "Beyond the Public/Private Division: Law, Power and 'the Family,'" manuscript for *Journal of Law and Society* 14 (Spring 1987), pp. 61–76.

25. Antonio Gramsci, *Selections from the Prison Notebooks* (New York: International, 1971); Stuart Hall et al., *Policing the Crisis* (London: Macmillan, 1978); Alan Hunt, "The Ideology of Law: Advances and Problems in Recent Applications of the Concept of Ideology to the Analysis of Law," *Law and Society Review* 19, no. 1 (1985), pp. 11–37; Edward Thompson, *Whigs and Hunters: The Origin of the Black Act* (New York: Pantheon, 1975); Raymond Williams, *Marxism and Literature* (Oxford: Oxford University Press, 1977).

26. Kathy Ferguson, *The Feminist Case Against Bureaucracy* (Philadelphia: Temple University Press, 1984).

27. See, for example, Nancy C. M. Hartsock, *Money, Sex, and Power* (Boston: Northeastern University Press, 1983).

28. Connolly, *Politics and Ambiguity*, p. 125.

29. Rorty, *Philosophy Without Principles*.

30. Rogers M. Smith, *Liberalism and American Constitutional Law* (Cambridge: Harvard University Press, 1985); and "Political Jurisprudence, the 'New Institutionalism,' and the Future of Public Law," *American Political Science Review* 82 (1988). For another example of legal scholarship that has been influenced by the work of Richard Rorty, see Lief Carter, *Contemporary Constitutional Lawmaking* (New York: Pergamon, 1985).
31. See also Bruce Ackerman, *Reconstructing American Law* (Cambridge: Harvard University Press, 1984).
32. Smith, *Liberalism*, p. 226.
33. Smith, "Political Jurisprudence," pp. 89–91.
34. Rogers M. Smith, "The New Institutionalism and Normative Theory: A Reply to Sotirios Barber," as yet unpublished paper (1988), pp. 2–3.
35. Smith, *Liberalism*, pp. 200–220.
36. *United States v. Carolene Products Co.*, 304 U.S. 144 (1938).
37. Guido Calabresi, "Between Brennan and Bork: The Role of the Court in Protecting Fundamental Rights," *Georgia Law Review*, forthcoming.
38. James Boyd White, *When Words Lose Their Meaning* (Chicago: University of Chicago Press, 1984), p. 245 (This book is a collection of White's essays); and *Hercules' Bow* (Madison: University of Wisconsin Press, 1985).
39. James Boyd White, "Thinking About Our Language," *Yale Law Journal* 96 (1987).
40. Martha Minow, "Interpreting Rights: An Essay for Robert Cover," *Yale Law Journal* 96 (1987), p. 1911.
41. James Boyd White, "The Judicial Opinion and the Poem: Ways of Reading, Ways of Life," *Michigan Law Review* 82 (1984), pp. 1674–1675 and 1685–1686.
42. Philip Soper, *A Theory of Law* (Cambridge: Harvard University Press, 1984), p. 134.
43. White, *When Words Lose Their Meaning*, p. 266.
44. W. Lance Bennett and Martha Feldman, *Reconstructing Reality in the Courtroom* (New Brunswick: Rutgers University Press, 1981).
45. Lon Fuller, quoted in Peter Teachout, "The Soul of the Fugue: An Essay on Reading Fuller," *Minnesota Law Review* 70 (1986). Compare Richard Weisberg, "Law, Literature, and Cardozo's Judicial Poetics," *Cardozo Law Review* 1 (1979); and *The Failure of the Word* (New Haven: Yale University Press, 1984).
46. Connolly, *Politics and Ambiguity*, p. 10.
47. Hutchinson, "Indiana Dworkin," p. 664.
48. E. E. Schattschneider, *The Semi-Sovereign People* (New York: Holt, Rinehart and Winston, 1960).
49. Marc Galanter, "Why the Haves Come Out Ahead," *Law and Society Review* (1974), pp. 95–151. See also Michael McCann, *Taking Reform Seriously* (Ithaca: Cornell University Press, 1986).
50. Robert Cover, "Forward: Nomos and Narrative," *Harvard Law Review* 97 (1983), p. 53.
51. Kim Lane Scheppele, "The Re-Vision of Rape Law," *Chicago Law Review* 54 (1987), pp. 1111–1112.
52. Rose, "Beyond the Public/Private Division"; Peter Fitzpatrick, "Law and Societies," *Osgoode Hall Law Journal* 22, no. 1 (1984), pp. 115–138.
53. Rose, "Beyond the Public/Private Division."

54. Karl Klare, "Law-Making as Praxis," *Telos* 40 (1979), pp. 123–135; Isaac Balbus, "Commodity Form and Legal Form: An Essay on the 'Relative Autonomy' of Law," *Law and Society Review* 11 (1977), pp. 571 ff.; Mark Tushnet, "A Marxist Analysis of American Law," *Marxist Perspectives,* no. 1 (Spring 1978); Andrew Fraser, "The Legal Theory We Need Now," *Socialist Review,* nos. 40–41 (July–October 1978); Douglas Hay, "Property, Authority, and the Criminal Law," in Douglas Hay et al., eds. *Albion's Fatal Tree* (New York: Pantheon, 1975).

55. See Ferguson, *The Feminist Case.*

56. Elizabeth M. Schneider, "The Dialectics of Rights and Politics: Perspectives from the Women's Movement," *New York University Law Review* 61 (1986), p. 589. For a review of feminist works on the law, see Catherine Mackinnon, "Feminism, Marxism, Method and the State: Toward a Feminist Jurisprudence," *Signs: Journal of Women, Culture and Society* 8 (Summer 1983), p. 635; Diane Polan, "Toward a Theory of Law and Patriarchy," in D. Kairys, ed., *The Politics of Law* (New York: Pantheon, 1982), p. 83; Wendy Williams, "The Crisis in Equality Theory: Maternity, Sexuality, and Women," *Women's Rights Law Report* 7 (1982), p. 175.

57. Milner Ball, *The Promise of American Law: A Theological, Humanistic View of Legal Process* (Athens: University of Georgia Press, 1981); and *Lying Down Together: Law, Metaphor and Theology* (Madison: University of Wisconsin Press, 1985).

58. Ball's *Lying Down Together,* an extended meditation on the need to shift law's fundamental metaphor from "bulwark" to "medium," so violated Peter Teachout's sense of acceptable philosophical argument that he wrote a forty-page satirical review of the book in the style of Thomas Reed Powell. See "Sentimental Metaphors," *UCLA Law Review* 34 (1986).

59. John Scharr, "Legitimacy in the Modern State," Philip Green and Sanford Levinson, eds., *Power and Community* (New York: Vintage, 1970).

60. Sanford Levinson, *Constitutional Faith* (Princeton: Princeton University Press, 1988).

61. Ball, *Lying Down,* p. 138.

62. Connolly, *Politics and Ambiguity,* p. 127.

63. Ibid., p. 128.

64. G. Edward White, "The Anti-Judge: William O. Douglas and the Ambiguities of Individuality," *Virginia Law Review* 74 (1988), p. 84.

65. Thus Philip Kitcher's *Abusing Science: The Case Against Creationism* (Cambridge: MIT Press, 1982) compares evolution science favorably to creation science on standards of aesthetic coherence, symmetry, parsimony, and fit. See also Scott Kleiner, "Darwin's and Wallace's Revolutionary Research Programme," *The British Journal for the Philosophy of Science* 36 (1985), pp. 367–392.

66. Smith, *Liberalism,* p. 227, emphasis added, and p. 230. Smith here rolled two assertions about the integrity of his vision into one: All interpretation best fits this pattern, and this interpretive pattern itself seeks coherent visions of American law and politics.

67. White, "The Judicial Opinion and the Poem," p. 1679.

68. Sotirios Barber, *On What the Constitution Means* (Baltimore: Johns Hopkins University Press, 1984), p. vii.

69. Richard H. Fallon, "A Constructivist Coherence Theory of Constitutional Interpretation," *Harvard Law Review* 100 (1987).

70. Richard Rorty, "The Historiography of Philosophy: Four Genres," in Richard

Rorty and J. B. Schneewind, eds., *Philosophy in History* (Cambridge: Cambridge University Press, 1984), p. 74; "The Contingency of Community," *London Review of Books* (July 24, 1986), p. 14.

71. Roberto Mangabeira Unger, *Law in Modern Society* (New York: Free Press, 1976), p. 206.

72. Robert Ellickson's field research indicates that the Coase Theorem, which undergirds much law and economics analysis, does not describe political experience. For example, the norms of neighborliness powerfully inhibit resorting to lawsuits to settle economic damage caused by straying animals. See "Of Coase and Cattle," *Stanford Law Review* 38 (1986), pp. 680–684.

73. *West Virginia State Board of Education v. Barnette,* 369 U.S. 624 (1943).

74. *Davis v. Beason,* 133 U.S. 333 (1890).

75. *West Virginia v. Barnette,* 369 U.S. 624 (1943) at 638.

76. Ibid.

77. "Court, 5–4, Votes to Restudy Rights in Minority Suits," *New York Times* (April 26, 1988), p. 11.

78. Connolly, *Politics and Ambiguity,* p. 120.

79. Nancy C. M. Hartsock, "Rethinking Modernism: Minority vs. Majority Theories," *Cultural Critique,* no. 7 (Fall 1987), pp. 187–206.

80. See Sven Birkerts, "House of Games," *The New Republic* (February 8, 1988), pp. 38–40.

81. Paul Feyerabend, *Science in a Free Society* (London: Verso, 1978), pp. 79–86.

2 ——— ·
The Fruitless Search for Original Intent

JUDITH A. BAER

Neither judicial activism nor critical reaction to it is new. The branch of the national government that Alexander Hamilton described as the "least dangerous" of the three has been a far from silent partner.[1] The Supreme Court has based many controversial rulings on interpretations of the Constitution that have no obvious support in history, text, or authority. The supporters of judicial activism have been many,[2] but others have urged judicial restraint, moderation, and fidelity to text, majority opinion, and the intent of the framers.[3]

Some of the Court's critics have been defeated and disgruntled interested parties. Given the many decisions of the past fifty years recognizing the rights of criminal suspects, it is hardly surprising to find an attorney general among the proponents of judicial restraint. But a recent incumbent of that office, Edwin Meese III, has linked self-interest to constitutional theory. His address on July 9, 1985, to the American Bar Association approached a common prosecutorial theme in a new way. His call for "disincorporation"—a reversal of decisions making parts of the Bill of Rights binding on the states—repudiated sixty years of judicial doctrine concerning the basic rights of minorities and limitations on governmental power. Meese's suggested alternative was a "jurisprudence of original intention," which would "resurrect the original meaning of constitutional provisions and statutes as the only reliable guide for judgment."[4] In the late summer of 1987, a predecessor of Meese's, Robert Bork, was forced to defend his similar views as President Ronald Reagan's nominee to the Supreme Court. The Senate's defeat of this nomination indicates that the controversy over appropriate modes of constitutional interpretation is not only alive but is vigorous and vehement.

Meese's argument is easy to dismiss. His criticism of the Court for departing in 1925 from its ruling in 1833 that the Bill of Rights did not apply to the states ignores an intervening event of some importance: the ratification of the Fourteenth Amendment in 1888.[5] But Meesian jurisprudence has not been ignored. Those who share Meese's political views have embraced his argument. These points have been made more persuasively by other judicial conservatives, including Bork. This contemporary version of judicial originalism can be useful if we allow it to stimulate new thought about constitutional theory.

Meese's address advanced two premises. First, it maintains that there is only one correct way to interpret the Constitution: according to its original meaning. Second, it declares that a particular interpretation of that meaning is correct. Meese and Bork are not the only adherents to the first premise. As we shall see, a small but persistent minority of American constitutionalists, by no means all conservative, have held the view that the framers' intent must dictate interpretation. Although "disincorporation" is new, the practice of basing interpretation of specific provisions on a reading of original intent is not.

We can examine—and, I submit, reject—the premise that original intent is the sole guide to interpretation. But jurisprudence must not stop here. Beyond Meese's explicit premise lies two unstated premises that have gone unrecognized in most discussions of interpretation. To rely on original intention implies that the original intention is knowable. Behind that assumption lies, finally—perhaps as one of those facts too obvious to need mentioning—the assumption that such a thing as original intention exists.

My examination of the available primary sources about the original Constitution and the Fourteenth Amendment—including some sources largely untapped until now—leads to the conclusion that we must reject the first unstated premise. Simply put, we cannot know original intention. I then examine the most complex and difficult of these premises: the assumption that original intention even exists. I conclude, from my analyses of the process of constitution making and of insights from language philosophy, that this last question is unanswerable. The assumption that any original intention exists is highly problematic in philosophical and epistemological terms.

I conclude that the difficulties interpreters have encountered with the explicit premises arise from the problematic nature of the implicit ones. Jurisprudence of original intention, and its specific applications, founder not only because of human error but, more importantly, because we can neither discover original intention nor know that it exists. And this observation, finally, will lead us to speculate about why, if the search for original intent is fruitless, conservatives now find the notion so appealing.

IS ORIGINAL MEANING THE ACCEPTED
SOLE DETERMINANT OF INTERPRETATION?

Reliance on original meaning has a perennial appeal because it provides a partial answer to a perennial question: "How and whence do nine lawyers, holding lifetime appointments, devise or derive principles which they are prepared to impose upon a democratic society?"[6] Meese is not the first jurist to praise reliance on intent as preventing a "jurisprudence of idiosyncrasy."[7] The argument has gone, roughly, as follows: If judges only impose principles that the framers meant to impose, then the judges are exercising appropriate self-restraint rather than imposing their own views on society.

At present, this argument is mainly the preserve of those labeled "judicial conservatives." Raoul Berger, for example, relies on legislative history to support a narrow, if not crabbed, interpretation of the Fourteenth Amendment.[8] Judge Bork has written: "It is necessary to establish the proposition that the framers' intentions with respect to freedoms are the sole legitimate premise from which constitutional analysis may proceed. . . . That abstinence from giving his own desires free play, that continuing and self-conscious renunciation of power, that is the morality of the jurist."[9] But this sort of jurisprudence has not always been confined to conservatives. Justice Hugo Black used original intention to argue a position antithetical to Meese's: that the Fourteenth Amendment bound the states to the first eight.[10] We can thus establish one point at the start: Reliance on the framers does not produce consistent results, nor, despite Bork's and Meese's claims, does it seem to prevent a jurisprudence of idiosyncrasy.

These uses of the same method to produce contradictory results may help explain why few jurists, however conservative, have accepted intent as the sole determinant of interpretation. Judges as diverse as Oliver Wendell Holmes, Felix Frankfurter, John Marshall Harlan II, Earl Warren, and William Brennan have held the view that Chief Justice Warren put most concisely: [History is] "at best . . . inconclusive."[11] Courts have practiced what these judges have preached. Warren's statement came in a unanimous decision interpreting the Fourteenth Amendment to outlaw a practice that had been common at the time the amendment was adopted. Two rulings in the next decade went even further in departing from the apparent dictates of the past. *McLaughlin v. Florida* and *Loving v. Virginia* struck down laws forbidding interracial cohabitation and marriage—subjects that some members of the Thirty-ninth Congress had explicitly said lay outside the scope of the law.[12] The school prayer decision of the 1960s and the sexual equality cases of the 1970s indicate continued reliance on modes of interpretation other than a search for intention.

But judges who reject a Meesian jurisprudence do not necessarily ignore legislative history. The Court decided *Brown v. Board of Education* only after ordering reargument on the issue of intent. Three decades later, judges continue to resort to the documents. Chief Justice William Rehnquist has acknowledged that "Where the framers of the Constitution have used general language, they have given latitude to those who will later interpret the instrument to make that language applicable to cases that the framers might not have foreseen."[13] But Rehnquist argued in a dissent in *Trimble v. Gordon* that courts should limit the reach of the equal protection clause to "cases where the framers obviously meant it to apply, classifications based on race or national origin, the first cousin of race."[14]

Nevertheless, most judges have concluded that, usually, history is inconclusive. Segregated public schools did exist in the 1860s, but, within ten years after ratification, Congress was debating whether the amendment empowered it to end the practice. History is even less conclusive in those common situations where judges must apply law to a problem that never occurred to the legislators. The case against simplistic historicism was made by Brennan in the 1963 school prayer cases (*Abington School District v. Schempp*):

> Whatever Jefferson or Madison would have thought of Bible reading or the recital of the Lord's Prayer in what few public schools existed in their day, our use of the history of their time must limit itself to broad purposes, not specific practices. By such a standard . . . the devotional exercises carried on in the Baltimore and Abington schools offend the First Amendment because they sufficiently threaten in our day those substantive evils the fear of which called forth the Establishment Clause of the First Amendment.[15]

CAN WE DISCOVER ORIGINAL INTENTION?

The state of constitutional interpretation provides small comfort to the jurist who regards original meaning as either a source of certainty or a corrective to idiosyncrasy. Most interpretations of original meanings have been challenged. The historian Alfred Kelly criticized several Court opinions as biased historical research of the "law-office variety."[16] The only change that has occurred in the years since Kelly wrote is that several more interpretations are available for criticism. The rule seems to be that for every interpretation there is at least an equal, if not excessive, and opposite counterinterpretation. For example, Hugo Black's "incorporation" thesis met Charles Fairman's charge that "history is overwhelmingly against him"—a thesis that provoked its own critics.[17] Raoul Berger's reading of the Fourteenth Amendment must contend with a persistent counterargument that the amendment was a lavish, open-ended guarantee of individual rights.[18] Nearly every essay from the bench has provoked criticism from the academy.[19]

The discovery of inconsistencies and contradictions in readings of legislative history does not, however, doom the enterprise to failure. Individual efforts may have failed because of biased and inadequate research. In order to assess the possibility of a jurisprudence of original intention and to see whether better use can be made of the evidence, it is necessary to examine the sources on which interpreters have relied.

The search for original intention requires interpreters to investigate the sources on the adoption and ratification of the Constitution and of subsequent amendments. Contemporary records of these events are expansive enough to lead the scholar into unrealistic expectations. Enough primary source material exists to occupy several researchers for an entire professional career. These records appear to hold at least as much information about original intent as anyone would want. But this appearance is deceptive. The records are "mainly unofficial and decidedly incomplete."[20]

The documents on the Philadelphia Convention have been easily accessible since 1911 in a four-volume work edited by Max Farrand. These volumes contain the terse official journal, notes taken by several delegates, correspondence, and other relevant materials. Although the sets of notes do contain enough agreement to assure the reader that all the note takers attended the same meetings, the "Rashomon effect," which confounds all research, is present here: There are variations and contradictions in the accounts. According to Farrand, the delegates regarded James Madison as the convention's semiofficial scribe; they often gave him copies of their speeches.[21] But their thoughtfulness to him and to us only replaces the Rashomon problem with what we might call the *Congressional Record* problem: How do we know that the speakers did not edit their remarks? An additional problem with Madison's notes is that they are almost certainly summaries rather than transcripts. Participants are recorded as having said about one-tenth as much as would actually have been uttered by speakers at normal speed during the hours of debate at the Convention.[22]

Some state ratification records have been available since Jonathan Elliott's five volumes of debates were published between 1830 and 1845. Researchers at the University of Wisconsin are now carrying out a multivolume project of collecting and publishing primary source materials relating to ratification. Slowed by the deaths of two successive editors, this project has so far resulted in only two volumes, one for pre-Convention sources and one for Pennsylvania.[23]

Elliott's records fill two massive tomes, but their authenticity is doubtful. Only six states—Massachusetts, North and South Carolina, Virginia, Pennsylvania, and New York—have what look like complete records of debate. Fragments exist for New Hampshire, Connecticut, and Maryland, which leaves four states unrepresented. Elliott himself recognized this problem: "The Editor is sensible, from the daily experience of newspaper accounts of the present time, that the sentiments [these records] contain may, in some instances, have been inaccurately taken down and, in others, probably, too faintly sketched, fully to gratify the inquisitive politician."[24] The Wisconsin project is as rich a collection as a scholar could hope for. But collecting more documents does not solve the problem of subjectivity, nor is any collection, however large, ever complete. And the more the material, the greater the likelihood that parts of it will be mutually contradictory or inconsistent.

There exists for the Fourteenth Amendment, by contrast, one source that is lacking for the original Constitution: an apparently complete official record of the first debates. Not only may this record be found in the official journal—as is the case for all amendments since the Eleventh—but it has also been anthologized along with the debates on all Reconstruction legislation in a volume edited by Alfred Avins.[25] We do not, as yet, know whether members could edit their remarks back in 1866. Even if we could be sure that the record is complete, explorations of this amendment's legislative history are distressingly incomplete. Almost without exception, scholars have ignored the state legislatures.[26] Indeed, the state records on the Fourteenth Amendment are one of the last untapped sources about original intent.

If intent were the sole guide to interpretation, this gap in our knowledge would be intolerable. "If one claims that the intent of the framers is *the* critical element in constitutional construction, one cannot refuse to do the labor needed to uncover that intent."[27] Even those who look to original meaning to guide rather than to control ought to learn as much about ratification as they can. The states are equal partners with Congress in amending the Constitution. Legislators' votes depend, at least in part, on what they think an amendment means. As legislators' intentions are a crucial part of the amending process, any information we can get about these interpretations will be valuable.

Such a project looms in advance as huge and intimidating. The Fourteenth Amendment was passed by Congress on June 13, 1866, and declared ratified on July 27, 1868. At that later date, there were thirty-seven present or former states, all with bicameral legislatures.[28] All seventy-four of these had considered the amendment at least once during that time period. By 1870, twenty-six houses had reconsidered it. New Jersey and Ohio rescinded their ratification. So did Oregon, but not until September 1868, which made that rescission nugatory.[29] All ten "insurrectionary" states rejected the amendment between November 1866 and February 1867. In March, Congress passed the first Reconstruction Act, which made ratification a condition of readmission for these states. Congress continued to impose this condition even after three-fourths of the states had ratified, and all ten states eventually complied. One hundred sets of debates, therefore, demand analysis.

The task becomes far less formidable once one begins. The labor consists of getting access to the records, not in reading them.[30] The state journals are similar to the official record of the Philadelphia Convention; that is, the record is nearly barren. No complete official record of debate in any house survives. The fullest records, from Massachusetts and Indiana, are not official. The Boston *Daily Advertiser* published versions of both the House and Senate debates early in 1867; but these are newspaper accounts, subject to the usual constraints of space and readability. Indiana has a volume called *Brevier's Legislative Reports,* but the volume's subtitle reference to *Short-Hand Sketches* is its own warning. The fact that one speech, which the editor's notes say lasted for forty-five minutes, is summarized in one paragraph does not reassure the reader about the record's completeness or accuracy.[31]

Documents from thirty-three states contain official governors' messages to the legislators mentioning the Fourteenth Amendment.[32] Twenty-two legislatures referred the amendment to one or more committees; some reports or fragments were reprinted, including a few minority reports. Several journals contain only a governor's message, the dates the amendment came up, and the final vote. The documents are an unsystematic hodgepodge.

The sparseness of this record is no surprise. Few, if any, state legislatures hired stenographers in the 1860s. After all, the legislatures met for only a few months in each session. Still, the lack of official documents forces the researcher to explore other sources. There are several possibilities. Students of the congressional history of the Fourteenth Amendment have enlarged the field to include debates on the Thirteenth and Fifteenth Amendments and on the Reconstruction statutes. This approach does not work with the states, however, because their records on the antislavery and voting rights amendments are no better than those on the Fourteenth Amendment. In addition, newspaper accounts and personal papers might fill in some gaps.

To the jurisprude of original intention, such materials can offer little help. Newspaper stories and individual accounts must be used guardedly for interpretive purposes. The former consist of journalists' subjective renderings of events as filtered through editors; they must fit into available space—and in the mid-nineteenth century, the typical daily paper was four pages long. Worse still, we have no independent check on the reliability of these stories. Letters and diaries are equally subjective and partial accounts. Basing interpretation even partly upon something that a North Carolina senator wrote to his wife in 1867, or on the lead story in the Providence *Daily Post* the day after the vote in Rhode Island's lower house, would be a dubious enterprise indeed. But for the student of history, these records may be all that exist.[33]

The lack of information about the state debates on the Fourteenth Amendment forces the jurist to interpret in ignorance. What frustrates the scholar most is not the possibility that no discussions occurred—there were too many days of debate for silence to have been likely—but the probability that important debates went unrecorded. Things were said, but we cannot discover what they were. Part of our constitutional history is irretrievable.

The gaps in the records do not provide an excuse for neglecting what we can retrieve. The documents about the amendment that are available may well inform us about the thoughts of some framers. Until we examine the evidence, we do not know what it contains; scattered, disparate, and incomplete as the records are, they demand attention.[34] These documents indicate—although they certainly do not prove—that supporters and opponents shared a general, vaguely defined understanding of the Fourteenth Amendment. They agreed that it would deprive the states of significant powers and establish federal supremacy and that Section 1 was not a narrow guarantee of rights but a broad recognition of them. Governor Oliver Morton of Indiana, a consistent supporter and lavish interpreter of the amendment, told the legislature:

The power which I claim for Congress is vast and generous, and should be exercised with deliberation, and only in cases of clear necessity, as it touches directly upon the general theory and structure of Government, yet it unquestionably exists. . . . As a question of natural right, it is hard to say that suffrage is not a natural right, when upon its exercise may depend the possession and enjoyment of all other acknowledged natural rights. It is hard to say that a man has a right to life, liberty, and the pursuit of happiness, and yet has no natural right to a voice in the government by which these other rights will be protected.[35]

Opponents tended to share Morton's understanding of the amendment—and that was the trouble. Opponents rejected the principles of the Declaration of Independence; they shared neither Morton's trust of Congress nor his views on the need to enable the national government to protect individual rights. The fear that Congress and the federal courts would encroach upon states' powers was widespread. Maryland's joint committee, for example, said of the enforcement powers in Section 5: "The proposition . . . is virtually to enable Congress to abolish the state governments."[36] Some opponents stressed their fear of judicial rather than legislative interference with state autonomy. In Massachusetts, one of the last northern states to ratify, a representative warned that "all rights, civil and criminal, would be transferred from the courts of the states to the courts of the nation."[37]

The records contain no evidence that supporters tried to allay opponents' fears. What the documents provide is evidence that supporters of the amendment construed it at least as broadly as opponents did. The records provide more support for broad readings than for narrow ones. The lieutenant governor of Connecticut, the first state to ratify, put it this way:

How to wisely profit by the experience of the past, and so to amend our national organic law as to give it unity of purpose, harmony with the Declaration of Independence, and efficiency adequately to protect the rights of each and every citizen, without encroaching upon those reserved to the states and to individuals, is the great question before our country.[38]

Remarks like these echoed several speeches by Members of Congress who had argued that the amendment either gave constitutional status to the principles of the Declaration or recognized that, as the abolitionists had argued for thirty years before the war, the Constitution had always contained those principles.[39]

Furthermore, the legislatures often dealt in the type of "grand symbolism" that Alfred Kelly found in the congressional debates.[40] The pervasive use of such imprecise rhetoric can forestall any effort to apply these records to specific issues. Charles Fairman's assertion that the states provide no explicit support for the incorporation thesis is correct. But, perhaps fatally for the prospects of ever resolving that particular controversy, neither do the state records provide solid grounds for rejecting Hugo Black's thesis in favor of Edwin Meese's ideas. The records simply do not address the question. The materials concerning incorporation remain what they have always been— speeches by the floor leaders, Senator Jacob Howard of Michigan and Representative John Bingham of Ohio, and the arguments against it. The probable truth, which the state records support but hardly prove, is that Section 1 was written to include the guarantees of the Bill of Rights but was not limited to them.[41]

Drawing any conclusions about whom the amendment was meant to protect is no easier than determining precisely what rights were included. The state records reveal general agreement that the former slaves were the amendment's primary beneficiaries. The states disagreed, however, on what sort of guarantee was to be provided and how it might be extended.

For example, one familiar interpretation of the equal protection clause now viewed as a narrow reading is the doctrine, now propounded by William Rehnquist, that the clause applies only to discrimination based on race or national origin. This doctrine existed in the 1860s, but at that time, some lawmakers found this interpretation far from narrow. Florida's governor refused to support an amendment that, in his view, would give Congress "the power to legislate in all cases touching the life, liberty, or property of every individual in the Union, of whatever race or color."[42] Similar views were expressed in the northern states. Members of Indiana's lower house filed a minority report accusing Congress of "forcing into our political system the odious doctrine of negro equality."[43] But not everyone who thought the amendment was aimed at racial inequalities feared its scope. For a Massachusetts legislator, "This was taken solely for the reason of obtaining protection for the colored people of the South; the white men who do not need this article and do not like it, sacrifice some of their rights for the purpose of aiding the blacks."[44]

These examples lend support to the "race only" interpretation, though hardly for all of Rehnquist's restrictive equal protection theory. Those quotations, with their emphasis on protection for blacks, challenge the chief justice's consistent opposition to reverse discrimination.[45] At any rate, they are only scattered remarks from a few states. Other documents contain interpretations that go beyond race. In Arkansas' second session with the amendment, Governor Isaac Murphy declared that "every human being in the State will feel confidence that his life, liberty, character, and property are fully and equally protected. Class rule, class monopoly, and class oppression, will no more be known."[46] "Class" had been a favorite word of Senate floor leader Jacob Howard in Congress. He had said that the Fourteenth Amendment "abolishes all class legislation in the states."[47] But neither Howard nor anyone else had a clear notion of what "class" was; all the examples were racial ones.[48]

The Arkansas records quote no further explanations from either the governor or the legislators, but their concept does not seem to have been limited to race. There is no evidence of consensus on what, if anything, other than race was included in the concept of class.

About as much historical support exists for Rehnquist's limited "race only" interpretation of Section 1 as exists for Black's limited "incorporation" doctrine. Black's reading appears very broad to us as, no doubt, Rehnquist's reading would have seemed all too broad to some opponents of the amendment. But Black subsequently made it clear that he saw his interpretation as a narrow one: The amendment protected the rights listed in the first eight amendments *and nothing else*.[49] Both Black's and Rehnquist's interpretations make some sense, have some support, and provide intelligible rules that can guide decisions. But each also ignores some evidence that suggests it excludes too much. Thus, both conclusions are built on flawed, incomplete interpretations.

Furthermore, both of these doctrines are *activist* ones. This fact has long been clear with respect to Black, but it needs emphasis with respect to Rehnquist. The *Trimble* doctrine, followed consistently, will restrain judges. But the doctrine is an active, autonomous, and far from incontrovertible judicial choice. Like the incorporation doctrine, the "race only" thesis is persuasive only if we assume that *any* narrow, limited interpretation is good precisely because it is narrow and limited. This assumption, which is not Black's, Rehnquist's, Meese's, Bork's, or any other jurist's, is just as subjective, activist, and vulnerable as any other constitutional doctrine. And, whatever else it is, it is certainly not a jurisprudence of original intention.

The state records on the Fourteenth Amendment are simply too sparse to reveal most of what was said or written. Those parts of the record that are retrievable do not support any inference of an original intention. The records neither prove nor disprove any thesis about original intent. They give us no information that the reader of the *Congressional Globe* does not already have. Historians might profitably explore newspaper accounts and archives in individual states in order to better "imagine the past."[50] Such a reconstructed past could help guide and enrich constitutional interpretation by outlining shared understandings and the terms of debate. But there is simply not enough information to dictate the narrow interpretation urged by conservative defenders of an intent. We cannot rely on intent if we do not know what it was. I contend that we do not know, and we will never know.

No historical record is perfect and complete. An individual account, even James Madison's, is an account of what one person perceived, not of what happened in its totality. The subjectivity of memory confounds all investigation. It makes eyewitness testimony unreliable, as students of criminal law know. The Rashomon effect exists even when the recollections of all witnesses are honest—an assumption that no investigator can safely make. Historians have long been aware of this problem; they teach undergraduates in basic introductory courses that the first rule of historical research is a distrust of evidence. It may be unfortunate that few interpretations of legislative history have come from historians. Most of these authors have been judges, lawyers, or political scientists, all of whom may often be inattentive to the historian's first premise.

But suppose a complete, accurate, and unedited record of debate did exist? We could certainly preserve such documentation of any future constitutional change. Even a complete record, however, can never be a record of original intention. What is present is what was said, not what was meant. People do not, after all, say everything that is on their minds. A thought may go unexpressed because the thinker anticipates harmful consequences from such utterance. Lawmakers try to get provisions ratified or rejected, not to interpret them. They may be less than fully candid about their own interpretations. For instance, do we really know that no member of Congress believed that the Fourteenth Amendment legalized racial intermarriage? Are we willing to draw that conclusion from the apparent fact that no member *said* that he believed so? Excellent reasons existed in 1866 for not advancing that interpretation. On the other hand, we must resist the temptation to conclude that, "They saw it, but were prudent enough to disavow it." We cannot prove that possibility either.

Another reason that thoughts may go unexpressed is that some things are so obvious in a given time and place that they do not need to be said. Assumptions too basic to need to be verbalized are often the most important beliefs in any culture. What is said in public debates is only what is safe enough to say and questionable enough to need saying. Indeed, a typical record gives no inkling of what some lawmakers thought at all. The debates that survive are dominated by a few vocal individuals. The majority's reticence, however welcome to colleagues at the time, constitutes yet another gap in our knowledge.[51] As Felix Frankfurter once remarked, Congress votes on a law, not on the speeches.[52]

So no jurisprudence of original intention is possible, because original intention is undiscoverable. We can and should go to the primary sources to learn about the origins of the Constitution, but the past is something we can only learn about and learn from, not learn per se. The records are too incomplete, and the nature of lawmaking too imprecise, to enable us to discover original meaning.

The conclusion is inescapable: Constitutional interpretation is the product of *choices* made here and now. Evidence of original intention is so inadequate and contradictory that any use of it demands active decisions on the part of the interpreter. A theory of original intention is a theory of what the interpreter believes original intention to be. For a theorist to claim anything else is intellectually dishonest and self-deluding.

DOES ORIGINAL INTENTION EXIST?

To speak of original intention implies the existence of an understanding shared by the lawmakers. But even a single deliberative body, like the Philadelphia Convention, may lack a shared understanding.[53] And when we include among the framers, as we must, the members of the state conventions, we imply that fourteen separate deliberative bodies shared an interpretation. In the case of an amendment, the authors do not even belong to one legislative body. Congress has two houses that act separately. The Fourteenth Amendment was ratified by twenty-eight bicameral state legislatures. A literal quest for original intent, then, presumes the existence of an understanding shared by no fewer than fifty-eight deliberative bodies in twenty-nine cities over a two-year period. This presumption is dubious on its face.

Inevitably, the interpreter is left with what all these groups had in common: the words of the provisions that they enacted. But much of the meaning of those words lies not within the framers' minds but in the words themselves, and the meaning of the words varies according to the context and the user. Philosophers of language often remind us that neither speakers nor words determine meaning alone. As Ludwig Wittgenstein wrote, "According as we assume one definition or another [of Moses] the proposition 'Moses does not exist' acquires a different sense, and so does every other proposition about Moses. . . . And this can be expressed like this: I use the name 'N' without a *fixed* meaning."[54]

If we use words without "fixed meaning," it is difficult to see how an "original meaning," in Meese's sense, can exist. If these observations are true about the names of specific individuals and objects, they are even more apt for abstract concepts like "privileges and immunities" and "equal protection"—the sort of concepts that are prevalent in constitutions. We do not know exactly what any person, let alone any group of persons, means or meant by words or concepts used in a document. The connection between language and thought is too tenuous and problematic to permit categorical statements about original intention.

Another passage from Wittgenstein illuminates this connection. "Someone says to me, 'Show the children a game.' I teach them gaming with dice, and the other says, 'I didn't mean that sort of game.' Must the exclusion of the game with dice have come to his mind when he gave me this order?"[55] One reason that this rhetorical question has a negative answer comes from a presumed shared understanding of appropriate juvenile activities—a shared understanding that is inseparable from value judgments and social conventions. Lief Carter has pointed out that we can envision a different understanding: Consider, for example, a father who hires a Las Vegas croupier to teach his child. "The context—Las Vegas versus living room—makes all the difference."[56] We can imagine still other situations: What about the sort of games described by the practitioners of "transactional analysis?"[57] The problem for constitutional interpretation is that we do not know what the context is, whether it is akin to the psychotherapist, the Las Vegas tourist, or the Oxford philosopher.

Hans-Georg Gadamer has examined the specific problem of legal hermeneutics:

> The criterion of understanding is clearly not in the actual words of the order, but solely in the understanding of the situation and the responsibilities of the person who obeys. . . . The comic situation in which orders are carried out literally, but not according to their meaning, is well known. Thus there is no doubt that the recipient of an order must perform a definite creative act of understanding its meaning.[58]

As interpreters of oral and written communication, we perform such definite creative acts all the time. Consider, for example, the following familiar question: "How did you expect me to know if you didn't tell me?" The common failure of this particular exercise in self-defense, designed to get the speaker out of whatever interpersonal difficulty made it necessary, reveals that we *do* expect people to know things that have not been spelled out for them. An illustration of this phenomenon is the familiar situation in which a friend tells you something. She may say, "This is confidential" and mean it—or not. Or, if she does not tell you to keep the information confidential, you may know very well that she expects you to do so. Conversely, it is entirely possible that she hopes you will share this particular piece of knowledge widely within your circle of mutual acquaintances. Creative interpretation within a shared context is a common occurrence in everyday life; and it is no different in general for activities of lawmaking.

Another common situation will provide further illustration of this point. We often have the opportunity to read records of the minutes or proceedings of a meeting of some sort—of our university senate, for example, or of a private association. It is often possible to guess, from the typically bland and truncated accounts, what objections were made to specific proposals and even by whom they were made. Such guesses are possible because the context within which the deliberations took place is one that is known to us and in which we ourselves often must operate. The act of interpretation proceeds from and relies upon shared understanding.

To interpret the original intent of constitutional provisions is an act far more difficult than any of these everyday interpretations. The jurisprude of original intention has the task of performing a "definite creative act of understanding" the meaning of speakers and writers who lived a long time ago and who are not available to us for questioning about what they meant. The context in which they operated—a context in which shared understandings of morals, conventions, and political principles existed—is not ours. However much we study the history of those times, we cannot reconstruct that context. Such study is "imagining the past," because imagining it is all we can do. When we interpret the orders of past generations, a shared understanding may not exist.

The question that provides the heading for this section thus is unanswerable: We cannot determine whether original intention exists. Philosophy of language theories reinforce the rejection of the premise that original intent is knowable. Whether it exists or not, original intent cannot help the interpreter if we cannot discover it. The problem is that the language of law, like all language, fails to create meaning by itself; legal language presumes a shared political context. Our interpretation of the legal language of the past can only apply the understandings of our time to the language of another time. Such interpretation is always in part a guess; and it is an *individual* guess, stemming from the interpreter's mind. All constitutional interpretations pick and choose among the possible constructions of the constitutional text.

Timothy O'Neill has analyzed the limited way in which jurists interpret the equal protection clause; for instance, to protect individual rights, but never group rights.[59] Nothing in the language of the clause itself, however, demands such a choice. We choose particular readings out of the infinity of possible readings available to us because of preconceived notions we bring to adjudication. A similarly autonomous choice has been the transformation of "equal protection" (in the text) and "class legislation" (in the debates) to so bland and neutral a concept as "discrimination."[60] It is often true in constitutional interpretation that "you can't get there from here," or from a particular possible interpretation to any likely decision. We do not approach a case like *Lynch v. Donnelly* by questioning the decision of a local religious majority to offend a minority through a public display; nor did any judge see any relationship in *Rostker v. Goldberg* between the continued refusal to ratify the Equal Rights Amendment and a law limiting draft registration to males.[61] There is no reason why we should not approach either of these cases in these ways, certainly no reason embodied in constitutional text or history; we just do not do so because of political choices *we* have made. These choices are in no way dictated by original meaning; we make them and are responsible for them. I believe that purported reliance on original meaning is no more than a smokescreen for individual choice. Honesty demands that we drop the pretense and take responsibility for these choices, guided by the wisdom of past generations but not locked into their mistakes.

WHY DOES A JURISPRUDENCE OF
ORIGINAL INTENT APPEAL TO CONSERVATIVES?

We do not need recourse to language philosophy to show that our evidence of original intention is inadequate and the notion of collective original intention problematic. Anyone who reads the available sources must become aware of these difficulties. As the sources invite—and have borne—diverse and contradictory interpretations, it is not immediately apparent why original intent has recently become the almost exclusive preserve of conservatives. What makes this mode of interpretation so appealing to jurists with particular political views?

The choice of the term "jurists" rather than "people" is deliberate. The Senate's rejection of the Bork nomination calls into question any assumption that the doctrine of original intent is selling very well with the electorate. Several senators obviously concluded that they had better not assume the doctrine's popularity. But the conservatives' electoral success in 1980 and 1984 may well have encouraged Meese to believe that original intent would appeal to voters.

For conservatives, original intent is the current version of that staple of politics; the answer that is simple, obvious, and wrong. Meese's notion of original intention is very simple indeed. His speech does not recommend, or even encourage, research on the original documents. It presents the view that any practice current at the time a provision was adopted, or unknown to and therefore not addressed by the framers, cannot be forbidden by the Constitution. The more one learns about constitutional history, the less tenable that simplistic notion of intent becomes. But part of the conservative thesis is not only tenable but incontrovertible. It is true that a number of practices, like school prayer, that have been invalidated by the Court were common in the early days. The shared political understandings of those early days *were* more conservative and regressive than modern ideas. A 1987 speech by Thurgood Marshall reinforced this point. Marshall pointed out that the Constitution was adopted at a time when neither blacks nor women were regarded as complete human beings. There exists, therefore, an argument for the conservative position that is superficially appealing. The argument invites the listener to react rather than to question—and that, of course, is what successful politicians ask voters to do.

Another appealing feature of originalist jurisprudence is that original intent is virtually the only mode of interpretation that can consistently be made to support the conservative position. The flexible mode urged by Brennan in *Schempp* can, of course, support conservative as well as liberal jurisprudence; indeed, a version of that argument is not unknown in conservative decisions. But the difficulty is that such an approach supports conservative and liberal arguments equally well; it gives the former no advantage. An appeal to public opinion would work for issues like capital punishment but would not work for the abortion issue, where the polls indicate that a majority supports the Court's decisions. Emphasis on adherence to precedent would all too often lead to results exactly the opposite of what conservatives want. All that is left is their particular notion of original intention.

This notion is not only simplistic; it is also curiously skewed. Judge Bork's words quoted earlier are revealing: He spoke of the framers' intentions *with respect to freedoms.*[62] But why should the framers' intentions not be equally controlling with respect to governmental powers? With few exceptions, Meese, too, has concentrated his criticisms on decisions that have involved protection of individual rights. Controlling the courts' powers to protect the individual—or, more precisely, getting the courts to control themselves in this regard—seems far more important to contemporary judicial conservatives than a judicial self-restraint, which would curb the courts' endorsement of growth in governmental power. The suspicion begins to grow that what the new judicial conservatives really want is not to curb the courts but to curb individual freedom. Original intent, in its Meesian sense, becomes an easy way to achieve this objective.

Perhaps it should not surprise us that a call for judicial restraint with respect to freedoms comes from the present chief prosecutor and one of his predecessors—but this fact should certainly make us suspect conservative motives. The more closely we look at the new call for a focus on original intent, the less it resembles dispassionate jurisprudence and the more it partakes of a self-serving, partisan agenda. Self-conscious renunciation of power becomes an unstated, and therefore highly suspect, endorsement of the government against the individual. This "jurisprudence of original intention" does not deserve to be called jurisprudence at all; it is occupational interest masquerading as philosophy. Meese is not a student of jurisprudence; he is a prosecutor telling judges what to do.

CONCLUSION: THE FUTURE OF CONSTITUTIONAL INTERPRETATION

No effort to discover the literal original meaning of law has succeeded. No interpreter has avoided the accusation of using historical evidence to give constitutional status to personal opinion, nor has any produced a perfect literal reading. These failures have their roots not in human imperfections and biases—though the latter are abundant at present—but in the inherent impossibility of a jurisprudence of original intention. The inadequacy of the records, the mechanics of constitution making, and the complexities of language all ensure that there can be no reliance on original meaning.

Even if a reliable notion of original intent did or could exist, moreover, a jurisprudence of original intention would be disastrous. The successful battle to prevent the confirmation of Judge Bork suggests that senators and their constituents have come to realize what most judges have held all along: General principles, not specific opinions or practices, must be our guide. John Marshall's insistence that "it is a *constitution* we are expounding"[63] is a reminder that constitutions, meant to endure for generations, are written in general, flexible language so that they may bear general, flexible interpretations: They are not meant to be legal codes where every point is spelled out. Constitutional principles are vague guides and, thus, sources of conflict. They may constrain and focus conflict, but they do not dictate outcomes.

Legal indeterminacy is more than a necessity: It is also a *positive* factor in a constitutional system. Dynamic rather than static interpretations of concepts such as "due process" and "equal protection" allow future generations to respond to new ideas of justice arguably superior to those possessed by the framers. In his bicentennial speech, Thurgood Marshall reminded his audience of facts of which we should not need reminding: The authors of the Constitution had a profoundly regressive understanding of equality. To lock future generations into an "original meaning" fixed at that point in the history of thought and knowledge is to repeat the errors of the past.

Judges who interpret the constitutional text to include postconstitutional values are not simply writing into law their own opinions. The ideas judges use will, of course, be theirs, since judges, like the rest of us, have only their own minds to think with. But a person's "own" ideas do not spring newborn from his or her mind. Ideas are drawn from the currency of discourse present in the surrounding society or available from the past. A jurisprudence that goes beyond past ideas to include newer ones incorporates the values not only of the framers but also of the intervening generations and of the present. Any or all of these ideas may be wrong, unjust, or incomplete. But surely that risk is preferable to a limited approach that ensures that the errors of the past will be frozen into law beyond correction.

The advocates of judicial restraint have a standard rebuttal to this argument: The principles of popular government require that such changes be made by the people's representatives, through constitutional amendment, rather than by judges. But this common objection is far from persuasive. The amending process, useful as it is, is cumbersome and skewed in favor of rejection rather than adoption. Indeed, it is possible that the events leading up to the Civil War indicate that the likely alternative to judicial flexibility is not peaceful constitutional change. As Joseph Tussman and others have argued, judicial activism may be an effective alternative to revolution and violence that advances justice.[64]

A still more important point here is that the government designed by the framers is not one of pure democracy or majority rule; a *constitutional* government places some issues outside of majority control and gives powers of interpretation to officials neither elected nor accountable.[65] Since the judge's task is to ensure that laws conform to the spirit and constraint of our constitutional tradition, it is not clear why renunciation of power in doing that job might be considered appropriate. Those who advocate limited approaches to adjudication commonly rely on the countermajoritarian aspects of judicial power; but why should that factor restrain judges who were never expected to reinforce majority rule in the first place?

Since constitutional language is indeterminate and judges interpret constitutional language, judges must give meaning to indeterminate language by using their powers of interpretation and must be freed from forced obedience to original intent or any other dictated mode. The values of indeterminacy do not mean either that intent is irrelevant to decision making or that judging is wholly subjective. Knowledge of legislative history is surely preferable to ignorance. Although the words of the framers cannot control interpretation, they can be one of many sources of guidance. Indeed, there are rich insights in the original debate records as well as in the proceedings on the Fourteenth Amendment. For example, the knowledge that Illinois ordered copies of the governor's plea for ratification of the amendment to be printed in German and Swedish as well as in English may never decide any judge's vote on any case, but, at the very least, the information catches the reader's attention in 1988.[66] The interpreter trying to assess the relevance of the Thirty-ninth Congress' views on racial intermarriage to current constitutional doctrine will benefit from noticing a curious fact: Whenever opponents raised the issue, the hypothetical couple consisted of a black man and a white woman.[67] Certainly, any sources that provide insights like these merit study. Furthermore, the study of original sources enables progressive jurists to meet conservatives on their own ground and to dispute readings of history while insisting that intent cannot control judging. Only the student of the original sources will know how inadequate are the existing interpretations of intent.

Ultimately we must reject the claims made by jurisprudes of original intention. Such an approach does not keep the individual judge out of the decision; the jurist's "definite creative act" of interpretation cannot occur without the use of his or her own mind. "There is in each of us a stream of tendency, whether you call it philosophy or not, which gives coherence and direction to thought and action," wrote Benjamin N. Cardozo long ago.[68] This philosophy guides any interpretation, of whatever mode. Where the record dictates no obvious results, interpretation is impossible without some guidance from the individual stream. Reliance on original intention can no more eliminate subjectivity from judging than can any other approach. It is impossible to remove the personal element from constitutional interpretation.

We must accept the fact that personal preferences will influence adjudication. Judging is not *only* enacting one's views into law, but judging is impossible *without* doing so. Automatic deference to decisions made by other governmental officials would seem to be the only alternative to subjectivity. However attractive that alternative might be to governmental officials, it seems a cure worse than the disease. In fact, such deference would only be another manifestation of the disease; it would be a choice as subjective as any other.

This inherent subjectivity can become idiosyncrasy; judicial power, like any other power, is subject to abuse. But the judicial despot who wants to use the law to enact personal opinions can use legislative history as badly as he or she can use any other approach. Such a judge will be stopped only by the institutional factors that restrain judges.

These factors are, of course, rather stricter restraints than those that limit prosecutors, to pick an example at random. An appellate court judge has to get a majority of his or her colleagues to agree with the chosen opinion. Courts do not have to enforce their own rulings. And presidents have latitude (though not license) to choose judges whose views conform to their own to fill vacancies on the federal courts. A judge who bends original intent or any other doctrine to personal purposes is rather less frightening than a prosecutor who is similarly inclined.

Although judging is partly subjective, it goes beyond the merely subjective. More goes into decision making than judges' own ideas. After all, jurists are unlikely to have preconceived preferences on every issue that they must decide. Even when they do have such ideas, new knowledge and interaction with other ideas may influence their stream of tendency. One's philosophy shapes study but need not control it. Legislative history, community values, and a consideration of the Constitution's broad purposes are among the influences available to guide decisions. The judge with imperial ambitions can misuse any of these authorities. The thoughtful jurist, however, will benefit from studying historical sources to help shape a jurisprudence of disciplined creativity. The sources available to the conscientious judge—a critical audience of officials, lawyers, and citizens; readings in philosophy and history; colloquy among judges themselves—are almost without limit. The conventions and political context of Court performance are strong incentives to this end of disciplined, principled creativity. That end, not futile renunciation of power or the shackling of the mind to originalism or any other mode of interpretation, is the goal to be sought.

NOTES

Versions of this article were presented at the Social Sciences Colloquium, University of California, Irvine, February 13, 1987; the annual meeting of the Western Political Science Association, Anaheim, California, March 27, 1987; and the interim meeting of the International Political Science Association Committee on Comparative Judicial Research, Rotterdam, the Netherlands, August 10, 1987. I am indebted to Michael McCann, Walter Murphy, and Karen O'Connor, for their detailed and valuable criticisms of earlier drafts, and to the California State Polytechnic University, Pomona, for supporting this research through its Faculty Development Programs.

1. *Federalist* 78.
2. For example, Judith A. Baer, *Equality Under the Constitution: Reclaiming the Fourteenth Amendment* (Ithaca, N.Y.: Cornell University Press, 1983); Sotirios A. Barber, *On What the Constitution Means* (Baltimore: The Johns Hopkins University Press, 1984); Lief H. Carter, *Reason in Law,* 2nd ed. (Boston: Little, Brown, 1984); Ronald Dworkin, *Taking Rights Seriously* (Cambridge: Harvard

University Press, 1977); William F. Harris II, "Binding Word and Polity," *American Political Science Review* 76 (March 1982), pp. 34–45; Timothy O'Neill, "The Language of Equality in Constitutional Order," *American Political Science Review* 75 (September 1981), pp. 626–635; Michael Perry, *The Constitution, the Courts, and Human Rights* (New Haven: Yale University Press, 1982); Laurence H. Tribe, *Constitutional Choices* (Cambridge: Harvard University Press, 1985).

3. For example, Alexander M. Bickel, *The Morality of Consent* (New Haven: Yale University Press, 1975); Robert H. Bork, *Tradition and Morality in Constitutional Law* (Washington, D.C.: American Enterprise Institute, 1984); Archibald Cox, *The Court and the Constitution* (Boston: Houghton Mifflin, 1987); John Hart Ely, *Democracy and Distrust* (Cambridge: Harvard University Press, 1980); Leslie F. Goldstein, "Judicial Review and Democratic Theory," *Western Political Quarterly* 40 (September 1987), pp. 391–412.

4. Edwin Meese III, Address to the American Bar Association, July 9, 1985, pp. 15–17.

5. Ibid., p. 13; *Barron v. Baltimore,* 7 Peters 243 (1833).

6. Alexander M. Bickel, *The Least Dangerous Branch: The Supreme Court at the Bar of Politics* (Indianapolis: Bobbs-Merrill, 1962), p. 235. Although Bickel did word the question in this way, reliance on original intent was not his answer.

7. Meese, Address, p. 6.

8. Raoul Berger, *Government by Judiciary: The Transformation of the Fourteenth Amendment* (Cambridge: Harvard University Press, 1977).

9. Bork, *Tradition*, pp. 10–11.

10. *Adamson v. California,* 332 U.S. 46, 105–107 (1947).

11. *Brown v. Board of Education,* 347 U.S. 483, 489 (1954).

12. *McLaughlin v. Florida,* 374 U.S. 184 (1964); *Loving v. Virginia,* 388 U.S. 1 (1967).

13. William Rehnquist, "The Notion of a Living Constitution," *Texas Law Review* 54 (May 1976), pp. 693–706, 694.

14. *Trimble v. Gordon,* 430 U.S. 762, 777 (1977).

15. *Abington School District v. Schempp,* 376 U.S. 203, 241 (1963).

16. Alfred Kelly, "Clio and the Court: An Illicit Love Affair," *Supreme Court Review* (1965), pp. 119–58, 122.

17. Charles Fairman, "Does the Fourteenth Amendment Incorporate the Bill of Rights? The Original Understanding," *Stanford Law Review* 2 (December 1949), pp. 5–139, 139. See Judith A. Baer, "Does the Bill of Rights Apply to the States? The Disincorporation Debate," *Utah Law Review* (November 1987); Kelly, "Clio"; William W. Crosskey, "Charles Fairman, 'Legislative History,' and the Constitutional Limitations on State Authority," *University of Chicago Law Review* 27 (Autumn 1954), pp. 1–143.

18. Baer, *Equality,* Chapter 4; Michael Kent Curtis, *No State Shall Abridge* (Durham, N.C.: Duke University Press, 1986); Richard Kluger, *Simple Justice* (New York: Alfred A. Knopf, 1975); Jacobus Ten Broek, *Equal Under Law,* rev. ed. (London: Collier Books, 1965).

19. For example, see Black's "incorporation" thesis, *Adamson v. California;* Fairman's critique, "Does the Fourteenth Amendment Incorporate the Bill of Rights?"; Berger, *Government by Judiciary;* Baer, *Equality;* and Curtis, *No State Shall Abridge.* Arthur Goldberg's argument that the Ninth Amendment provided au-

thority for a right of privacy, in *Griswold v. Connecticut,* 381 U.S. 479, 481–524 (1965) was disputed by Kelly, "Clio," pp. 149–155. John Marshall Harlan II's thesis that Section 1 of the Fourteenth Amendment was irrelevant to voting rights, in *Carrington v. Rash,* 380 U.S. 89, 97–100 (1965) was countered by William W. Van Alstyne, "The Fourteenth Amendment, the 'Right' to Vote, and the Understanding of the Thirty-ninth Congress," *Supreme Court Review* (1965), pp. 33–118. Potter Stewart's reading of the Civil Rights Act of 1866, *Jones v. Mayer,* 392 U.S. 409, 420–436 (1968), received similar treatment from Gerhard Casper, "Jones v. Mayer: Clio, Bemused and Confused Muse," *Supreme Court Review* (1968), pp. 89–132.

20. William Anderson, "The Intent of the Framers: A Note on Constitutional Interpretation," *American Political Science Review* 49 (June 1955), pp. 340–352, 341.

21. Max Farrand, *The Records of the Federal Convention,* rev. ed. (New Haven: Yale University Press, 1937), vol. 1, p. xvi.

22. This point was made by Professor Arval Morris at the Conference on Judicial Interpretation of the Constitution, American Studies Center, Washington, D.C., June 12, 1987.

23. Merrill Jensen, ed., *The Documentary History of the Ratification of the Constitution,* 2 vols. (Madison: State Historical Society of Wisconsin, 1976).

24. Jonathan Elliott, *The Debates in the Several State Conventions on the Adoption of the Federal Constitution* (Philadelphia: J. B. Lippincott, 1941), Book 1, p. iii. (Original work published 1830–1845.)

25. Alfred Avins, *The Reconstruction Amendments' Debates* (Richmond: Virginia Commission on Constitutional Government, 1967).

26. The exception is Fairman, "Does the Fourteenth Amendment Incorporate the Bill of Rights?" whose investigation was limited to information relevant to the "incorporation" question.

27. Walter F. Murphy, "Constitutional Interpretation: The Art of the Historian, Magician, or Statesman?" *Yale Law Journal* 87 (July 1978), pp. 1752–1771, 1768. Emphasis in original.

28. The following union states ratified the amendment: Maine, New Hampshire, Vermont, Massachusetts, Rhode Island, Connecticut, New York, Pennsylvania, New Jersey, West Virginia, Ohio, Indiana, Illinois, Michigan, Missouri, Minnesota, Kansas, Wisconsin, Oregon, Nevada, and Iowa. Three union states, Delaware, Maryland, and Kentucky, rejected it; California never voted on it. Nebraska (which then had a bicameral legislature) was not admitted until after the war; it ratified the amendment in 1867. Of the eleven Confederate states, Tennessee was readmitted in 1866, after it ratified. The other ten states—North Carolina, South Carolina, Virginia, Georgia, Florida, Alabama, Mississippi, Louisiana, Arkansas, and Texas—rejected the amendment in late 1866 or early 1867 and ratified it between 1868 and 1870.

29. The question of whether a state may rescind ratification of a constitutional amendment has never been resolved.

30. Most state records are available either in the Library of Congress or at the University of North Carolina at Chapel Hill, or in both libraries. Only one state, Rhode Island, never made copies of its records, necessitating a trip to the state archives in Providence.

31. *Brevier's Legislative Reports,* 1867, p. 46.

32. Governors have no official part in the ratification of constitutional amendments. In taking an advisory role, however, these governors had a national role model: The president has no official role, either, but Andrew Johnson's opposition was vigorous.

33. Some state studies did appear early in the twentieth century, written by students of William A. Dunning. However, these studies are limited to the South and marred by pro-Southern, antiblack bias. See J. G. Randall and David Donald, *The Civil War and Reconstruction*, 2nd ed. (Boston: D. C. Heath and Company, 1961), pp. 779–781. A study of newspapers and archives for all the states would be beyond this article's scope. In my studies of North Carolina and Rhode Island, one Confederate and one Union state (see n. 35), I found scattered stories in a few newspapers. For Rhode Island, the Providence *Daily Post* is helpful. Archives in neither state contain useful personal papers. The fact that only 11 of the nearly 300 North Carolina legislators between 1866 and 1868 have any extant papers will not surprise the experienced researcher, nor will the failure of those 11 legislators to stress the Fourteenth Amendment in their letters home. The most complete account comes from the papers of Leander Gash, who represented six western counties in the senate (P.C. 384, North Carolina Archives, Raleigh).

34. The present article developed out of an ongoing study on the ratification of the Fourteenth Amendment. An article is now being prepared for publication.

35. Senate Journal, January 11, 1867, pp. 44–45. In the U.S. Senate, Oliver Morton became a strong supporter of the proposed Civil Rights Act of 1874, which became, in a milder version, the Act of 1875. See Avins, *The Reconstruction*, p. 683.

36. Senate Journal, Document X, p. 14. See also Governor's Message, Document A, pp. 21–22; New Jersey, Minutes of Assembly, 1866, September 11, pp. 18–20; North Carolina Senate Journal, 1866, p. 96; South Carolina House Journal, 1866, Regular Session, p. 34; Florida House Journal, 1866, pp. 211–212; Mississippi Senate Journal, 1866–1867, p. 7; Texas House Journal, 1866, p. 578.

37. Boston *Daily Advertiser* (March 14, 1867), p. 4. See also Alabama Senate Journal, 1866–1867, Appendix, pp. 78–79.

38. Senate Journal, 1866, pp. 27–28.

39. Baer, *Equality*, Ch. 4; Howard Jay Graham, *Everyman's Constitution* (Madison: State Historical Society of Wisconsin, 1968), Chs. 1, 2, 4, 5, 7, 14; Kluger, *Simple Justice;* Ten Broek, *Equal Under Law.*

40. Kelly, "Clio," p. 134.

41. Baer, *Equality*, pp. 94–102; Kelly, "Clio," pp. 132–134.

42. House Journal, 1866, p. 12. See also South Carolina House Journal, 1866, Regular Session, p. 33; Maryland Senate Journal, 1867, Document A, pp. 24–25.

43. House Journal, 1867, p. 102.

44. Boston *Daily Advertiser* (March 14, 1867), p. 4. See also Kansas House Journal, 1867, pp. 64–65; Nevada Senate Journal, 1867, pp. 9–10; Tennessee Senate Journal, Called Session, 1868, p. 8; Vermont Senate Journal, 1866, p. 28.

45. See *Trimble v. Gordon;* Rehnquist's dissenting opinion in *Steelworkers v. Weber,* 443 U.S. 193, 219–222 (1979); and his votes, without opinion, in *Regents of*

the University of California v. Bakke, 438 U.S. 265 (1978); *Fullilove v. Klutznick,* 448 U.S. 448 (1980).

46. Assembly Journal, p. 20.
47. Avins, *The Reconstruction,* p. 220.
48. Ibid., pp. 212, 220, 231; Baer, *Equality,* pp. 88–94.
49. *Griswold v. Connecticut,* 381 U.S. 479, 509–513 (1965).
50. Alexander M. Bickel, *The Supreme Court and the Idea of Progress* (New York: Harper and Row, 1969), p. 13.
51. Anderson, "Intent."
52. Walter F. Murphy and C. Herman Pritchett, eds., *Courts, Judges, and Politics,* 4th ed. (New York: Random House, 1986), p. 486.
53. Anderson, "The Intent of the Framers," pp. 340–348.
54. Ludwig Wittgenstein, *Philosophical Investigations,* 3rd ed. (New York: Macmillan, 1951), vol. 1, p. 79. Emphasis in original.
55. Ibid., p. 33.
56. Carter, *Reason in Law,* p. 108.
57. See, for example, Eric Berne, *Games People Play* (New York: Grove Press, 1964).
58. Hans-Georg Gadamer, *Truth and Method,* 2nd ed., translation edited by Garrett Barden and John Cumming (New York: The Seabury Press, 1975), pp. 298–299.
59. O'Neill, "Language of Equality."
60. Baer, *Equality,* Ch. 5.
61. *Lynch v. Donnelly,* 465 U.S. 668 (1984); *Rostker v. Goldberg,* 453 U.S. 57 (1981).
62. Bork, *Tradition,* pp. 10–11.
63. *McCulloch v. Maryland,* 4 Wheaton 316, 407 (1819).
64. Joseph Tussman, *Obligation and the Body Politic* (New York: Oxford University Press, 1960).
65. See Walter F. Murphy, James E. Fleming, and William F. Harris II, *American Constitutional Interpretation* (Mineola, N.Y.: Foundations Press, 1986), Ch. 2.
66. House Journal, 1867, p. 41.
67. See, e.g., Avins, *The Reconstruction,* pp. 108, 141, 170.
68. Benjamin N. Cardozo, *The Nature of the Judicial Process* (New Haven: Yale University Press, 1921), p. 12.

anchored in the control of economic resources and who use this economic power to advance their own interests, inter alia, by way of the constitutional and legal structures, which allow them to call upon both coercive and consensual capabilities.[9] The coercive face of these structures is the most familiar: A failure to obey authoritative rules leads to official sanctions. But to rely solely, or even principally, on coercion would be costly in terms of both resources and authority. Instead, compliance draws its most basic strength from our belief in the necessity and the beneficence of law. According to this hegemonic understanding, then, those who accept the democratic view of law are dupes, and insofar as they call upon rights on behalf of social change, they become complicit in the domination of society's "have-nots."[10]

These concepts can be made more concrete by considering alternative interpretations of the civil rights experience. These interpretations hinge on two basic questions: (1) Have blacks in America been liberated? and (2) Has constitutional litigation been an effective agent of liberation? From the democratic perspective, *Brown v. Board of Education* and subsequent cases, brought largely through the auspices of the NAACP Legal Defense Fund, were the quintessential instruments of black liberation. In short, this view answers both questions posed in an affirmative way: Blacks have been liberated and that liberation has been accomplished largely through the courts. The hegemonic view leads to a diametrically different conclusion: The courts have not only failed to liberate black people; they have actually contributed to black oppression.

The case for a constitutionally engendered liberation rests on the rights that have accrued to black people and on the instrumental role of courts in securing those rights.[11] These achievements are too familiar to require anything but cursory reference to litigative victories in school desegregation, voting rights, equal access to places of public accommodation, and more controversially, affirmative action in professional schools, hiring, and promotion. It is further argued that the political branches of government at both the state and national levels consistently turned deaf ears to the claims of blacks until the Supreme Court initiated change with *Brown v. Board* in 1954, and that the Court has pretty consistently been out in front on civil rights issues. This fact, however, does not preclude second thoughts over the slow pace and erratic course of liberation. But from the democratic perspective, the bottom line remains that the judicial system has proven to be the most reliable ally of black Americans. The results of judicial activism are readily visible for all to see in hotels and restaurants, in politics and in business, and in integrated classrooms in all sections of the country and at all levels of education. With the courts' help, blacks have, in short, gained full and equal citizenship.

The counterargument made by proponents of a hegemonic view is that the courts have been ineffectual at best and counterproductive at worst with respect to the liberation of black Americans. At its core, this argument rests on the judgment that American blacks are far from liberated. They are still disproportionately represented in a growing underclass in America that is self-perpetuating and living in appalling and hopeless circumstances.[12] In other words, no real progress has been made, because the courts, whether as a result of bad faith or only misplaced faith in the law, have elevated form over substance. Whatever rights have been won are seen as empty and mis-leading promises. Litigative victories have simply imprisoned blacks within a cage of formal equality and have failed to address the social and economic disadvantages of black Americans.[13] What good, according to this way of thinking, does it do to give blacks equal access to a housing market they cannot afford or to an employment market for which they are unprepared? The situation created is often likened to a footrace in which some of the competitors have broken legs. In such a situation, it is absurd to think the race is fair just because all of the runners must run the same distance and start at the same time. With constitutional rights so implicated in the repression of blacks, it stands to reason that the Constitution should be thought of in terms of domination rather than liberation. Such is the obvious message of the hegemonic view.

It might be said that this controversy is really not about the nature of the Constitution but rather about the nature of liberation. From one per-spective, liberation is equal citizenship—equality before the law. From the other perspective, liberation requires a redistribution of material resources—a transformation of the economic status of American blacks. But just beneath the surface and giving meaning to these competing conceptions of liberation are the democratic and hegemonic views of the Constitution. If, after all, one believes in the liberating capabilities of constitutional rights, then these con-stitutional entitlements are both a necessary and a sufficient condition for social justice. Conversely, insofar as the Constitution is perceived as a way of mystifying the relationships of domination and submission, to use the law is to become implicated in those relationships.

THE POLITICS OF RIGHTS

There is, however, another way of looking at both the civil rights experience and what it signifies about the character of American law. Rights, like the law itself, do cut both ways—serving at some times and under some circum-stances to reinforce privilege and at other times to provide the cutting edge of change. This ambivalence means that rights in the abstract cannot be thought of as either allies or enemies of progressive tendencies but rather as an arena for struggle.[14]

The core ambivalence of rights is doctrinal. A right once proclaimed is available to protect the interests of rich and poor, black and white, demo-crat and fascist. The ACLU, the most consistent voice of rights in the United States, provides ample testimony to the political "neutrality" of rights. Thus, innovative lawyers who work to expand the protections provided by rights may unwittingly be developing tools that will be used by their opponents. Broadly speaking, the growth of right-wing "public interest" law suggests how and to what extent rights can be turned against progressive trends.[15]

But given consistent neutrality, a politics of rights would be relatively unproblematic. After all, the opportunities afforded by rights would add only marginally to the resources already available to the privileged segments of society while adding substantially to the resources at the disposal of the disadvantaged and the dispossessed. Moreover, this net gain would be enhanced by the intrinsic social value of the liberal democratic rights embodied in the Constitution. Although something of a two-edged sword, neutral rights would have considerable liberating potential, providing a necessary if not a sufficient condition of liberation.

The problem is that rights are not simply neutral. The rights written into the Constitution as well as their interpretation and implementation are shaped by the prevailing balance of political, economic, social, institutional, and cultural forces. One need look no further than the diversion of the benefits of the Fourteenth Amendment from blacks to business.[16] Of course, the history of the Fourteenth Amendment and of the Constitution itself also reveals progressive interpretations both before and after *Brown*—albeit in episodic and unpredictable fashion. The implementation issue is more murky, but there are surely significant discontinuities between the declaration of rights and their implementation as social policy. Still more fundamentally, the practice of rights is itself inextricably linked to the prevailing liberal democratic hegemony, thus imposing significant limitations on what can be expected, even in the most receptive political climate, from a politics of rights.

To some extent, thinking of the law in terms of a politics of rights is a kind of middle way between the democratic and hegemonic views. But there is more to it than that. In the first place, the politics of rights must stand on its own—it must provide a distinctive and coherent understanding of legal process, albeit with a decidedly hegemonic spin. In addition, the politics of rights provides a frame of reference for exploring the opportunities and pitfalls of deploying rights on behalf of progressive change and thereby sheds light on the political character of American law. In making a case for this politics of rights perspective, I shall reverse the order of the previous discussion—that is, I will begin with the civil rights experience and conclude with generalizations on that experience.

REINTERPRETING THE CIVIL RIGHTS EXPERIENCE

My interpretation of the civil rights experience can be broken down into three propositions.

> *1.* Constitutional litigation has contributed to a chain of events that has had a profound impact on American blacks.
>
> *2.* The role of constitutional litigation in these changes has been

indirect and its basic impact unintended and even unwelcome—at least to the litigators.

3. The impact of constitutional litigation has been liberating for significant numbers of blacks but not for black Americans as such. Moreover, the litigative strategy shares equally in the credit for liberating individual blacks and in the blame for failing to liberate blacks as a people.

The larger truth is that litigative strategies are constrained by and derivative of the prevailing liberal democratic hegemony that has, in effect, been reaffirmed and reinvigorated by the civil rights experience.

There is no denying that a variety of opportunities have opened up for blacks in the period since *Brown v. Board of Education,* particularly in the south, where apartheid was an unequivocal fact of life. Things have also changed for the better elsewhere in the country. Blacks have gained significant access to the political process, especially in urban areas where black majorities, for example, frequently elect black mayors. More broadly, blacks are increasingly found among elected officials and in the corporate world. Although significant de facto segregation remains in schools, housing, employment, and places of public accommodation, it is not so pervasive nor so unyielding as it once was and there is a substantial black presence for all to see.[17]

The role of litigation in effecting these changes is, however, much more elusive than may appear at first glance. Insofar as these things can be established with any confidence, a strong case can be made that legislation rather than litigation did the trick. Only after the passage of the Civil Rights Act of 1964 did any real changes begin to occur.[18] It is, therefore, reasonable to conclude that even so seminal a decision as *Brown v. Board* was, in itself, unable to bring about substantial change.

The civil rights experience, thus, unequivocally discredits at least the more naive versions of a well-entrenched American credo—what I have referred to elsewhere as the "myth of rights." According to the myth of rights, politics in America "is conducted in accordance with patterns of rights and obligations established under law."[19] In other words, the myth of rights attributes decisive authority to the Constitution as well as to the legislative and judicial decisions emanating from it. According to this vision, there is, in short, a close and largely unproblematic linkage between judicial stimulus and political response. But the "massive resistance," which was the immediate response to the *Brown* decision, and the massive evasions, which have been the more enduring and elusive legacy of *Brown,* clearly demonstrate that judicial decisions are not really politically decisive.

But what about a more sophisticated version of the myth of rights that posits an *indirectly* legalistic vision of the American political process? According to this view, the fruits of constitutional litigation, while indirect, rest on the legitimating capabilities of judicial decisions, especially those of the Supreme Court. Charles Black was one of the first to make explicit and systematic the widely shared view that Supreme Court decisions exercise a special kind of moral suasion among the American people.[20] A parallel argument was made at about the same time by Black's more conservative colleague at the Yale Law School, Alexander Bickel, who claimed that properly framed Supreme Court decisions are capable of generating a special form of *constitutional politics* based on a principled constitutional colloquy among the branches and levels of government.[21] From this Bickelian perspective, the most important function of the Court's desegregation decisions was to awaken the conscience of the public and the politicians, thus contributing significantly, albeit indirectly, to the legislative achievements of the civil rights movement.

There is, however, no reason to believe that *Brown* and its progeny were able to draw on a reservoir of good will and respect for the law to change people's minds. On the contrary, the evidence suggests that minds were not changed—certainly not the minds of the southern political leadership that organized and orchestrated the campaign of massive resistance.[22] Perhaps fence sitters were swayed, but it is difficult to believe that opponents were persuaded. Nor did blacks and their allies have their eyes opened by *Brown*. Judicial decisions were simply unable to legitimate desegregation and thus generate support for or disarm the opponents of a racially integrated society.

These problems do not imply that litigation was irrelevant, but rather that its role has been catalytic and contingent rather than participatory and straightforward. As I see it, the courts' major contribution has been largely unintended. Indeed, I would go one step further and argue that there is an inverse relationship between what the courts intended to do and what they have actually accomplished. At the heart of this argument is the idea that the courts' most significant contribution to racial justice in America has been a kind of dual demystification of the equal protection doctrine and of the political efficacy of rights. Although the former was intended, the latter was unintended and unwelcome but of considerably more political salience.

For almost a century, constitutional interpretation of the Fourteenth Amendment mystified racial relations in the United States by concealing exploitation and domination beneath a veil of fairness and consent. Demystification began when the Supreme Court abandoned the separate but equal doctrine in *Brown v. Board*. But doctrinal demystification contributed only modestly and somewhat perversely, as I will argue shortly, to the reduction of racial discrimination in the United States. Indeed, it could be argued that a byproduct of *de*mystification of particular rights was the *re*mystification of rights in general in that civil rights litigation seemed to demonstrate the self-correcting capabilities of legal and constitutional processes.

The second, the more important, and the unequivocally unintended aspect of demystification was the demonstration that rights cannot neutralize entrenched power. The massive resistance that greeted the *Brown* decision made only too clear how modest was the impact of rights on social and political practice. But as it became apparent that the Supreme Court civil rights decisions were insufficient to alter governmental and nongovernmental action, the struggle for racial justice was politicized. Because Americans tended to believe in the myth of rights, *Brown* and its progeny evoked hopes among civil rights supporters and evoked fears among opponents. These hopes and fears altered the political climate and, ultimately, the balance of political forces.

Thus, judicial decisions served more as mobilizing devices contributing to the broadening of American pluralism than as authoritative agents of change. Although preferences were not changed by the law, expectations were. People believed that changes would take place, and in this sense belief in the law had both long- and short-term consequences that significantly altered the political situation. In the short term, the massive resistance to *Brown* and subsequent decisions overwhelmed the law, which helps to account for the lack of progress. But the ugly face of massive resistance, dramatized nightly on the television news, created a backlash among blacks, their supporters, and eventually among the undecided. It was this backlash— among those whose hopes for integration were being frustrated and among formerly unengaged Americans who were angered by the failure to enforce Supreme Court decisions—that generated the civil rights movement and finally motivated the so-called political branches of the government to support enforcement.[23]

Accordingly, it was not the decisions themselves but the political mobilization spawned by *resistance* to the decisions that brought positive results. And not only were these results indirect and unexpected, they were also unwelcome to most civil rights lawyers who resisted politicization. As a result, the NAACP became alienated from the mainstream of the civil rights activism, which identified most clearly with civil disobedience and the nonviolent peaceful protests led by the Rev. Martin Luther King, Jr.[24]

This interpretation suggests that the courts have sufficient power to politicize—to provoke a crisis—but not to effect social change on their own. The crisis of massive resistance was resolved in a racially progressive fashion because demystification revealed that the courts had failed to deliver on their desegregative promises and, *more importantly,* because desegregation was widely accepted as a just ideal in our society. It is, of course, true that this value was latent rather than manifest and that it seldom received more than lip service prior to *Brown.* But I would argue, albeit speculatively, that the hypocritical response of Americans to racial injustice is a good example of the old adage that hypocrisy is the tribute vice pays to virtue. Thus, in the aftermath of the Supreme Court's declaration that segregation is inherently unequal, it became increasingly difficult to conceal from ourselves any longer the powerful currents of injustice that characterized the treatment of blacks in America.

If this analysis is correct, we are currently in perilous times with respect to the courts and racial discrimination. I do not refer to the increasingly conservative composition of the courts, which is better seen as a symptom than a cause and may even be a blessing in disguise. These days it seems unlikely that political crises precipitated by judicial decisions responsive to black claimants will be resolved in a manner consistent with the claimants' goals. On the contrary, there is reason to believe that the backlash of such decisions is likely to turn the tide against racial justice and, thus, overwhelm any modest concrete gains that may have resulted from the decisions themselves.

Without the power to change our beliefs, the courts can only focus our attention on accepted values and on departures from those values. Politicization "worked" on behalf of desegregation because there was no competing ideal; instead, there was only the cynical defense of entrenched privilege. That is not the case, however, with issues like busing and affirmative action, where there are competing values as well as competing interests.[25] Clearly, white males who are individually blameless tend to be disadvantaged by affirmative action programs, and busing programs burden children and restrict parental prerogatives to translate upward social mobility into improved public educational opportunities. The constitutional politics of affirmative action and of busing are thus more contingent, and less likely to evoke a consensual response, than the politics of desegregation.

In this more complex political arena, the courts could easily do more harm than good. Declarations of rights to affirmative action or to busing, if and when they emerge, may provide bargaining leverage useful in political and bureaucratic negotiations and may even lead to some limited direct benefits for individuals. Insofar as these declarations of rights provoke political crises, however, the prognosis is not very promising. In defending affirmative action and/or busing schemes, the courts are no longer identifying themselves with widely accepted, if latent, values. They are not, in short, in a position to take advantage of the benefits of demystification. Politicization under these circumstances seems more likely to generate a backlash that would reinforce the status quo than to promote the extension of racial equality.

There is yet another important observation about the quality of the changes that were promoted, albeit catalytically and indirectly, by civil rights activism. American culture has become infinitely more receptive to black achievement. Blacks can and do succeed in virtually all realms of American life, and the fruits of success can be enjoyed in a nonsegregated society. No doubt, upwardly mobile blacks face barriers, subtle and not so subtle, that are unknown to whites and are denied advantages that whites can take for granted. If, however, this were the whole story, it would be appropriate to think in terms of liberation.

The cutting edge of the hegemonic critique is concerned not with the upwardly mobile but with the growing underclass, which is disproportionately composed of blacks who are really unable to take advantage of the employment, housing, and political opportunities that are, in principle, available to them.[26] To make matters worse, the net effect of civil rights activism has probably been to syphon off significant numbers of the most dynamic blacks from the community. Although many blacks have remained committed to the community, the same cultural changes and individual strengths that make upward mobility possible tend to channel blacks, like other Americans, toward personal achievement rather than community solidarity. Thus, when one considers the black community as such, the civil rights gains must be seen as a distinctly mixed blessing and as a testimonial to the hegemonic tendencies of a politics of rights.[27]

Moreover, as Michael McCann clearly demonstrates in his chapter in this book, the hegemonic outcome is implicit in the watered-down equal opportunity principles that have guided and constrained the Supreme Court interpretation of constitutional equality. The Court has confined dereach of the Fourteenth Amendment to *individuals* deprived of their rights by *state action* and to remedies that restore the *neutrality* of the state. Consistent applications of these constraints has meant that the structural causes of inequality are concealed beyond the reach of constitutional litigation.

> The result has been not only that the Constitution remains indifferent to the deprivations and needs of the American underclass generally, but that constitutional remedies for past discriminatory acts contributing to racial, ethnic, gender, and other forms of social injustice also have been limited by this refusal to address the structural character of class inequality.[28]

In other words, the authoritative ideology of constitutional equality is geared, as McCann put it, to the "logic of the marketplace"—to rewarding those best suited to compete but with only a half-hearted effort to equalize the competitive baseline. Thus, the reach of the politics of rights is limited not only by political obstacles to implementation and impact but also by the "individualistic, exchange-oriented" nature of constitutional equality.[29]

THE SOFT HEGEMONY OF CONSTITUTIONAL RIGHTS

The reinterpreted civil rights experience clearly reveals both the hegemonic properties of American public law and the softness of that hegemony. The traditional liberal democratic guarantees embodied in the Bill of Rights provide necessary, but not sufficient, protections against state and corporate power. A society structured according to the values of the Bill of Rights is to a significant degree an open and responsive society that minimizes overt repression. Moreover, should something go wrong, the rights themselves provide, indeed invite, opportunities for resistance to a significant range of injustices. Nor is it necessary to have vast resources in order to deploy rights against political repression.

The message of civil rights is, however, a good deal more equivocal with respect to the effectiveness of a politics of rights as an instrument of social change. A politics of rights is constrained, in the first place, by the liberal capitalist values of the U.S. Constitution; by the individualistic mechanisms for claiming and implementing those rights; and by the limited political power of judicial institutions.[30] Of course, the civil rights experience has also demonstrated the contribution that a politics of rights can make to the mobilization of social movements.[31] There is, however, reason to believe that the mobilizing success of the politics of rights may be only selectively replicable, and as I have argued above, even with successful mobilization, political outcomes are contingent. Indeed, the legalistic tendencies of a politics of rights may work at cross purposes with effective political action.

I will address each of these drawbacks of a politics of rights in this concluding section. Nonetheless, it would be wrong to neglect or dismiss the politics of rights as an arena of struggle—in part, because of the lack of alternatives. But it is also true that in a polity that takes rights seriously, they can provide both ideological and institutional leverage that social movements cannot afford to ignore.

THE DRAWBACKS OF A POLITICS OF RIGHTS

Constitutional rights are suspect agents of social change because of their integral association with the prevailing hegemonic values of individualism, private property, the market, and liberal democracy. A "realist" view of judicial decision making might suggest that these limits are figments of the legal imagination and that they are regularly and easily swept aside by Supreme Court justices inclined to do so. But it is as naive to think of justices as free agents as it is to think of them as the impersonal voices of determinate constitutional norms. As a number of chapters in this book indicate, judges work within the constraints of an interpretive community and a web of institutional practices that define the limits of constitutional innovation.[32]

Certainly, as McCann has demonstrated, the interpretation of the Fourteenth Amendment has been constrained by the constitutional ethos of an individualistic understanding of equal opportunity.[33] By the same token, constitutional solicitude for private property has thwarted efforts to extend the protections accorded by the Bill of Rights to welfare or economic rights.[34] It is, moreover, true that rights attach to individuals, qua individuals, and must be asserted in order to be realized. Accordingly, rights work best for assertive and upwardly mobile individuals—hardly those most in need of assistance.

Of course, the civil rights experience suggests that gaining rights can transform the quiescent into the assertive. The mobilizing capabilities of rights rest, however, on a premise that, when carefully examined, leads to questions about the replicability of the civil rights experience. Mobilization depends on an acceptance of at least a portion of the myth of rights—that is, the belief that American politics is and should be responsive to the patterns of rights and obligations authoritatively established by the Constitution. Only insofar as people believe that their rights can be redeemed will their hopes and expectations be nurtured by a litigative victory that grants a public good previously denied.[35]

The problem is that marginalized members of the society do not take the myth of rights seriously because they think of the law in terms of domination rather than liberation. As Richard Abel explained it: "They experience law only as constraint, not power, and therefore are reactive and fatalistic. When they cannot avoid the law, they seek to minimize their losses, pursuing short-term, expediential aims."[36] Kristin Bumiller's research on victims of discrimination sheds considerable light on this distrust of the law. Because of their dependent status as employees, tenants, students, welfare recipients, and the like, Bumiller's respondents were unwilling to take legal action to claim their rights. Mobilizing the law opened them to hostility, reprisals, and defeat. The legal arena was also perceived as diminishing rather than empowering; it served only to confirm their status as victims, and it required them to speak for themselves in a setting where they felt incompetent and which they deemed too "cut and dry" to be responsive to their real needs.[37] Better, then, to suppress anger and not "make waves"—otherwise "I'd be angry all the time."[38] Claiming rights was, in short, contrary to the "ethic of survival" because legal intervention and legal discourse could not "overcome power differentials"—but, on the contrary, "reinforced . . . the bonds of victimhood."[39]

The myth of rights seems, in short, to have a much stronger grip on middle-class and working-class Americans than among the dispossessed or the underclass. Legal victories may energize and console attorneys but not their threatened and marginalized clients.[40] Parallel concerns can be posed about each stage of the politics of rights. Clearly, interests salient to the most assertive and well-organized elements of the society will have advantages in raising resources to launch campaigns of constitutional litigation and in pressing for implementation of successful class action suits. Thus, the politics of rights will, generally speaking, prove more successful for consumers, environmentalists, feminists, the disabled, and even the mentally ill than for the homeless.[41] Once again the civil rights experience is instructive, insofar as it seems to have empowered the most upwardly mobile among black Americans. Moreover, in thus rewarding and nurturing competitive individualism, rights reaffirm rather than challenge hegemonic values. And as I have already argued, politicization of rights will backfire unless the values being advanced resonate well with the general public—in other words, unless they are hegemonic values.

There is also reason to believe that a politics of rights will not be able to transcend its legalistic roots. The complex litigation that provides the impetus for a politics of rights is, of course, the terrain of lawyers and provides no meaningful role for grass-roots activists. Perforce lawyers will conduct the litigation, and their influence will be decisive in choosing justifiable objectives. In the abstract, lawyers may be perfectly willing to view their leadership roles as transitional. In the real world of social movements, however, the transition from a top-down organization controlled by legal professionals to a grass-roots social movement is likely to be highly problematic at best. As McCann points out: "Legal advocacy may be an attractive resource for power to reform-minded professional lawyers and lobbyists, but it generally is not for most citizens lacking equal resources of time, money, skill, experience, and ongoing organizational support."[42] In other words, the forms and resources of the organization will generate inertial forces that will work against restructuring. Legal professionals are also likely to resist challenges to their leadership. In part, this resistance will stem from a simple reluctance to yield power, but it will also stem from lawyers' distrust, due to their training and socialization, of grass-roots politics—particularly of the confrontational variety.[43]

A more fundamental drawback is the tendency of litigative politics to shrink the field of political action and to cause divisiveness. Litigation tends to focus on conflicts between identifiable parties over particular violations of rights and rules. Consider, for example, the conflict involving Native American sport and commercial fishing interests over dwindling salmon resources in the Pacific Northwest. By focusing on nineteenth century treaty rights, litigation has, as Rita Bruun has demonstrated, precluded consideration of the crippling impact of logging and land development on salmon spawning. Adversary forms have thus divided the mutually victimized fishing interests while insulating the victimizers—that is, the loggers and the land developers.[44] More broadly, insofar as the extension of rights has "multiplied greatly *the number of access points*," there are opportunities, indeed incentives, for social movements to fragment around go-it-alone tactics.[45]

The drawbacks of a politics of rights are, in sum, extensive. Prevailing hegemonic values embodied in constitutional structures and goals constrain the objectives that can realistically be pursued through litigation. Moreover, litigation is distinctly more useful for discrete challenges to repressive practices than for promoting programmatic political change. Finally, the mobilizing opportunities that are at the heart of a politics of rights are, when subjected to careful scrutiny, suspect on two grounds. First, constitutional and legal symbols are not likely to be particularly useful for rallying those most in need. Second, with litigation at its core, mobilization tends to be divisive insofar as its principal long-term consequence is merely to broaden the pluralist political arena. The net effect is to pit have-not segments of the society against one another in a zero sum struggle over scarce resources. With all that said, there are opportunities as well as drawbacks to a politics of rights.

THE OPPORTUNITIES OF A POLITICS OF RIGHTS

Although the transformative opportunities provided by a politics of rights are modest at best, rights are political resources that progressive political movements cannot really afford to ignore. The hegemonic properties of the Constitution are incontestable but so too is the softness of that hegemony. What E. P. Thompson has written about the law in general is equally applicable to our Constitution:

> On the one hand, it is true that the law did mediate existent class relations to the advantage of rulers. . . . On the other hand, the law mediated these class relations through legal forms, which imposed, again and again, inhibitions upon the actions of the rulers. For there is a very large difference, which twentieth-century experience ought to have made clear even to the most exalted thinkers, between arbitrary extra-legal power and the rule of law.[46]

At the very least, rights are useful for challenging repressive practices, and in an era with unparalleled opportunities for abuse of power, these defensive capabilities are of real significance.

The soft hegemony of constitutional rights provides both cultural and institutional opportunities for social movements. Culturally, the promises of the Bill of Rights and of progressive legislation, whatever their limitations may be, offer considerable cultural space for liberating activism. These promises resonate broadly and powerfully with political leaders and the more influential members of the public and may be stretched by creative interpretation—albeit within the protean boundaries of the interpretive community. As such, the gap between promise and delivery is not simply an invitation to seek litigative remedies but also a cultural space for politicization. Institutionally, litigation offers direct and authoritative access to the agencies of the state. Although litigation leverage may not determine institutional outcomes, it does provide resources for prodding quiescent agencies to act and for bringing pressure against abuses of power. Moreover, innovative practices worked out in connection with institutional reform litigation have attenuated the divisive and fragmenting constraints of litigative strategies.[47]

Taken together, these institutional and cultural resources can contribute to progressive reforms. Surely this conclusion is the ultimate message of civil rights litigation—however indirect and contingent its impact may have been. Similarly, recent research on criminal process in California indicates that, evasion and opposition notwithstanding, Warren Court decisions on defendants' rights have in effect legalized the ethos of policing.[48] Litigation has also contributed to much the same kind of change in the circumstances of Native Americans, the handicapped, and the mentally ill and has played a parallel role on behalf of consumer and environmental interests.[49] The model of change operative in these cases has yet to be adumbrated, but at the core of this politics of rights is surely the push of institutional pressure and the pull of cultural persuasion.

A politics of rights, therefore, calls upon activist lawyers to function as cultural mediators and, more problematically, as political entrepreneurs. Activist lawyers are in a unique position to bear witness to, to dramatize, to nurture, and to universalize grievances. Legal practice provides lawyers with a three-dimensional understanding of the grim realities of everyday life at the bottom of the society. The language of the law enables lawyers to reframe client problems in terms of the broad standards of American law and culture and, thus, to convey the plight of the have-nots in terms that maximize the likelihood for a sympathetic response culturally as well as legally. Lawyers have less to offer as political entrepreneurs, but a politics of rights does require that they sort out the promising from the less promising opportunities for political mobilization and for other forms of political action.

Within obvious limits, then, the soft hegemony of constitutional rights offers opportunities for meaningful, if not fundamental, social change. There are, to be sure, tactical and strategic pitfalls in pursuing these opportunities. Tactically, it is important to know when a politics of rights may prove self-defeating and to act accordingly. The strategic problem is more intractable; namely, that the long-term consequence of a successful pursuit of the politics of rights is to reinforce the prevailing hegemony. But these long-term drawbacks can hardly take precedence over the immediate opportunities afforded by a politics of rights to improve the lot of marginalized Americans.

NOTES

I am very grateful to Martin Krygier and Michael McCann, who in quite different ways served as intellectual midwives for this chapter. Those two, along with Dan Lev and some anonymous reviewers, also provided careful critiques of preliminary drafts.

1. Alexis de Tocqueville, *Democracy in America,* vol. 1 (New York: Vintage Books, 1959), p. 290.
2. Joel F. Handler, *Social Movements and the Legal System* (New York: Academic Press, 1978); Charles A. Johnson and Bradley C. Cannon, *Judicial Policies: Implementation and Impact* (Washington, D.C.: Congressional Quarterly Press, 1984); Arthur Selwyn Miller, *The Supreme Court and American Capitalism* (New York: The Free Press, 1968).
3. Alexander M. Bickel, *The Least Dangerous Branch: The Supreme Court at the Bar of Politics* (New York: Bobbs-Merrill, 1962); Owen M. Fiss, "Forward: The Forms of Justice," *Harvard Law Review* 93 (1979), pp. 1–58; Lawrence M. Friedman, *Total Justice* (New York: Russell Sage Foundation, 1985), Chapter 5; James Willard Hurst, *Law and the Conditions of Freedom in Nineteenth-Century United States* (Madison: University of Wisconsin Press, 1956).
4. Robert G. McCloskey, *The American Supreme Court* (Chicago: University of Chicago Press, 1960), pp. 12–13.
5. Martin Shapiro, "The Constitution and Economic Rights," in M. Judd Harmon, ed., *Essays on the Constitution of the United States* (Port Washington, N.Y.: Ken-

nikat Press, 1978), pp. 74–98. But see John Brigham, "Constitutional Property: The Double Standard and Beyond," Chapter 7 in this book.

6. The spirit of this expansive interpretation of rights is most closely associated with work of the Warren Court and its supporters. See, for example, Anthony Lewis, *Gideon's Trumpet* (New York: Random House, 1964). For a more academic analysis, see Walter F. Murphy, "The Art of Constitutional Interpretation," in Harmon, *Essays on the Constitution,* pp. 130–159; Michael J. Perry, *The Constitution, the Courts, and Human Rights* (New Haven: Yale University Press, 1982). More generally, see Ronald Dworkin, *Taking Rights Seriously* (Cambridge: Harvard University Press, 1978).

7. Christopher Wolfe, "A Theory of U.S. Constitutional Interpretation," *Journal of Politics* 43 (1981), pp. 292–316; Bruce Fein, "Selecting a Supreme Court Justice Devoted to Judicial Restraint," *Benchmark* 1 (November–December 1984), pp. 1–12; Robert Bork, "The Constitution, Original Intent, and Economic Rights," *San Diego Law Review* 23 (1986), pp. 823–832; Raoul Berger, *Government by Judiciary: The Transformation of the Fourteenth Amendment* (Cambridge: Harvard University Press, 1977); Donald L. Horwitz, *The Courts and Social Policy* (Washington: Brookings Institution, 1977); Nathan Glazer, "Towards an Imperial Judiciary?" *The Public Interest* 41 (1975), pp. 104–123; Edwin Meese III, "The Battle for the Constitution: The Attorney General Responds to His Critics," *Policy Review* 35 (1986), pp. 32–35.

8. Bickel, *The Least Dangerous Branch;* John Hart Ely, *Democracy and Distrust* (Cambridge: Harvard University Press, 1980).

9. Charles A. Beard, *An Economic Interpretation of the Constitution of the United States* (New York: The Free Press, 1965); Stanley Diamond, "The Rule of Law Versus the Order of Custom," in Robert Paul Wolff, ed., *The Rule of Law* (New York: Simon and Schuster, 1971), pp. 115–144; Robert Lefcourt, "Law Against the People," in Robert Lefcourt, ed., *Law Against the People* (New York: Vintage Books, 1971), pp. 21–37; Kenneth Cloke, "The Economic Basis of Law and State," In Lefcourt, ed., *Law Against the People,* pp. 68–80.

10. This theme is prominent in David Kairys, ed., *The Politics of Law: A Progressive Critique* (New York: Pantheon Books, 1982). See, for example, the essays by Edward Greer, "Antonio Gramsci and 'Legal Hegemony,'" pp. 304–309; Alan D. Freeman, "Antidiscrimination Law: A Critical Review," pp. 96–116; Peter Gabel and Jay M. Feinman, "Contract Law as Ideology," pp. 172–184. See also Karl E. Klare, "Judicial Deradicalization of the Waganer Act and the Origins of Modern Legal Consciousness, 1937–1941," *Minnesota Law Review* 62 (1978), pp. 265–339; Peter Gabel, "Reification in Legal Reasoning," in Piers Beirne and Richard Quinney, eds., *Marxism and Law* (New York: John Wiley, 1982), pp. 262–278; and Richard Quinney, *Class, State, and Crime,* 2nd ed. (New York: Longman, 1980).

11. Richard Kluger, *Simple Justice: The History of Brown v. Board of Education and Black America's Struggle for Equality* (New York: Alfred A. Knopf, 1976); Archibald Cox, *The Role of the Supreme Court in American Government* (New York: Oxford University Press, 1976), Chapter 3; Jack Greenberg, "The Supreme Court, Civil Rights and Civil Dissonance," *Yale Law Journal* 77 (1968), pp. 1520–1544.

12. William Julius Wilson, *The Truly Disadvantaged: The Inner City, the Underclass, and Public Policy* (Chicago: University of Chicago Press, 1987).

13. Freeman, "Antidiscrimination Law"; Howard Moore, Jr., "Brown v Board of Education: The Court's Relationship to Black Liberation," in Lefcourt, ed., *Law Against the People,* pp. 55–64; Lewis Steele, "Nine Men in Black Who Think White," *New York Times Magazine* (October 13, 1968), pp. 56–57, 112–122.

14. Alan Hunt, "The Politics of Law and Justice," *Law and Politics* 4 (1981). In a similar vein, Michael E. Tigar and Madeleine R. Levy called for a jurisprudence of insurgency in *Law and the Rise of Capitalism* (New York: Monthly Review Press, 1977), pp. 310–330. See also Franz Neumann, "The Changing Function of Law in Modern Societies," in Herbert Marcuse, ed., *The Democratic and the Authoritarian State* (Glencoe, Ill.: The Free Press, 1957), pp. 22–66; Ed Sparer, "Fundamental Human Rights, Legal Entitlements, and the Social Struggle: A Friendly Critique of the Critical Legal Studies Movement," *Stanford Law Review* 36 (1984), pp. 509–574.

15. Karen O'Connor and Lee Epstein, "Rebalancing the Scales of Justice: Assessment of Public Interest Law," unpublished paper prepared for delivery at the 1983 annual meeting of the Law and Society Association, June 1983.

16. Arnold M. Paul, *Conservative Crisis and the Rule of Law: Attitudes of the Bar and Bench, 1887–1895* (New York: Harper & Row, 1969).

17. Charles S. Bullock III and Charles M. Lamb, *Implementation of Civil Rights Policy* (Monterey, Calif.: Brooks/Cole, 1984); Edward Dorn, *Rules and Racial Equality* (New Haven: Yale University Press, 1979); Harrell R. Rodgers, Jr., and Charles S. Bullock III, *Law and Social Change: Civil Rights Laws and Their Consequences* (New York: McGraw-Hill, 1972).

18. Gerald N. Rosenberg, "The Courts, Congress and Civil Rights: Comparing Institutional Capabilities," unpublished paper prepared for delivery at the 1983 annual meeting of the American Political Science Association, September 1–4, 1983.

19. Stuart A. Scheingold, *The Politics of Rights: Lawyers, Public Policy, and Political Change* (New Haven: Yale University Press, 1974), p. 13.

20. Charles L. Black, Jr., *The People and the Court: Judicial Review in a Democracy* (Englewood Cliffs, N.J.: Prentice-Hall, 1960).

21. Bickel, *The Least Dangerous Branch,* Chapter 6.

22. On the united opposition of southern Congress persons to *Brown,* see "The Southern Manifesto: Declaration of Constitutional Principles," in Hubert H. Humphrey, ed., *School Desegregation: Documents and Commentaries* (New York: Thomas Y. Crowell, 1964), pp. 32–35. On the discriminatory legislation passed by the legislatures of the southern states in response to *Brown,* see Richard Bardolph, ed., *The Civil Rights Record: Black Americans and the Law, 1849–1970* (New York: Thomas Y. Crowell, 1970), pp. 373–393. For a summary of the evasive responses to *Brown,* see G. Theodore Mitau, *Decade of Decision: The Supreme Court and the Constitutional Revolution, 1954–1964* (New York: Charles Scribner's Sons, 1967), pp. 60–78.

23. Frances Fox Piven and Richard A. Cloward made a similar argument, which traced the roots of black mobilization to changing economic conditions, in *Poor People's Movements: Why They Succeed, How They Fail* (New York: Vintage Books, 1979), Chapter 4. See also Scheingold, *The Politics of Rights,* Chapter 9.

24. On the disenchantment of blacks with the moderate legal strategies of the NAACP, see Martin Luther King, Jr., *Where Do We Go from Here: Chaos or Community?* (Boston: Beacon Press, 1968), pp. 10–11, 130; Stokely Carmichael and

Charles V. Hamilton, *Black Power: The Politics of Liberation in America* (New York: Vintage, 1967), pp. 154–155. Research on black attitudes in the mid-1960s indicated strong support for both the NAACP and for Martin Luther King, Jr. Although blacks became somewhat more radical about means, they continued to be moderate as to ends—as illustrated by considerable distrust of the Black Muslims and their most prominent leader, Malcolm X. See Gary T. Marx, *Protest and Prejudice: A Study of Belief in the Black Community* (New York: Harper & Row, 1967), pp. 25–28.

25. Thomas J. Cottle, *Busing* (Boston: Beacon Press, 1976); Nathan Glazer, *Affirmative Discrimination* (New York: Basic Books, 1978); Allan P. Sindler, *Bakke, DeFunis, and Minority Admissions: The Quest for Equal Opportunity* (New York: Longman, 1978); Thomas Sowell, *Civil Rights: Rhetoric or Reality?* (New York: Morrow, 1984).

26. Wilson, *The Truly Disadvantaged.*

27. Manning Marable, *From the Grassroots: Social and Political Essays Towards Afro-American Liberation* (Boston: South End Press, 1980), pp. 224–227.

28. Michael W. McCann, "Equal Protection for Social Inequality: Race and Class in Constitutional Ideology," Chapter 9 in this book.

29. Ibid. See also Freeman, "Antidiscrimination Law."

30. Scheingold, *The Politics of Rights,* Chapters 7 and 8.

31. Ibid., Chapter 9.

32. Fiss, "Objectivity"; John Brigham, *The Cult of the Court* (Philadelphia: Temple University Press, 1987), pp. 51–62.

33. McCann, "Equal Protection."

34. Scheingold, *The Politics of Rights,* pp. 104–107.

35. Ibid., Chapter 9.

36. Richard L. Abel, "Law Without Politics: Legal Aid Under Advanced Capitalism," *U.C.L.A. Law Review* 32 (1985), p. 521.

37. Kristin Bumiller, "Victims in the Shadow of the Law: A Critique of the Model of Legal Protection," *Signs* 12 (Spring 1987), p. 436.

38. Ibid., p. 430.

39. Ibid., p. 438.

40. Abel, "Law Without Politics," pp. 604–606.

41. Susan M. Olson, "The Political Evolution of Interest Group Litigation," in Richard A. L. Gambitta, Marlynn L. May, and James C. Foster, *Governing Through Courts* (Beverly Hills: Sage Publications, 1981), pp. 239–254; Neal Milner, "The Dilemmas of Legal Mobilization: Ideologies and Strategies of Mental Patient Liberation Groups," *Law and Policy* 8 (January 1986), pp. 105–129. Consider also the growth of the consumer movement in connection with the activities of Ralph Nader and the lawyers associated with him.

42. Michael W. McCann, *Taking Reform Seriously: Perspectives in Public Interest Liberalism* (Ithaca, N.Y.: Cornell University Press, 1986), p. 200.

43. Scheingold, *The Politics of Rights,* p. 141.

44. Rita Bruun, "The Boldt Decision: Legal Victory, Political Defeat," *Law and Policy* 4 (1982), pp. 271–298.

45. McCann, *Taking Reform Seriously,* pp. 225–226.

46. E. P. Thompson, *Whigs and Hunters: The Origins of the Black Act* (New York: Pantheon, 1975), pp. 264–265.

47. Abram Chayes, "The Role of the Judge in Public Law Litigation," *Harvard Law Review* 89 (May 1976), pp. 1281–1316; Fiss, "Forward." But see also Nikolas Rose, "Unreasonable Rights: Mental Illness and the Limits of the Law," *Journal of Law and Society* 12 (1985), p. 199; David L. Kirp and Gary Babcock, "Judge and Company: Court-Appointed Masters, School Desegregation, and Institutional Reform," *Alabama Law Review* 32 (1981), pp. 313–397; Robert F. Nagel, "Controlling the Structural Injunction," *Harvard Journal of Law and Public Policy* 7 (1984), p. 395.
48. Priscilla Fay Slocum, *Judicial Reform of the California Criminal Justice System Through the Exclusionary Rule,* unpublished Ph.D. dissertation, University of California at Los Angeles, 1986.
49. See footnote 41, *supra.*

4 ———— ·
After Criticism: An Analysis of the Critical Legal Studies Movement

ROGERS M. SMITH

One of the aims of this book, which has been initiated by and largely popu-lated with political scientists, is to revitalize the study of law within that discipline. Its title, however, will inevitably evoke interest from the much-publicized Conference on Critical Legal Studies, populated mostly by law professors; and so the question arises concerning the relationship, if any, between these two groups. The study of public law has in fact been part of both these academic professions in American universities since they emerged in the late nineteenth century, and its center of gravity has oscillated between them, sometimes accompanied by undignified grumbles on both sides.[1] Readers may well wonder whether this anthology originated in renewed faith that political science gives distinctive, perhaps better, perspectives on consti-tutional issues.

This chapter is not an attempt to assert that position.[2] The revival of public law studies in political science, if indeed one can be said to be taking place, is too incipient for its characteristics to be well defined. Political science is in any case such a diffuse and diverse discipline that its practitioners inevi-tably offer many different methodological and political orientations. A num-ber of the contributors to this book, including myself, have been stimulated and assisted by CLS arguments, though the extent to which we concur with CLS perspectives varies considerably.

My purpose here is simply to identify some important characteristics common to the (also diverse) work of a few leading CLS writers and to indicate my own fundamental agreements and disagreements on those points. Insofar as they are not purely idiosyncratic, my arguments certainly must be labeled products of a "political science" perspective: I am entirely innocent of formal legal education, having instead acquired three degrees in political science through the studies of the history of political ideas and of institutional, behavioral, and historical works on U.S. government, which dominates the training of many political scientists who write on public law. I also believe that the normative perspective I defend is part of a turn thus far visible mostly among political scientists—a turn away from "neutral" neo-Kantian and pluralist liberal theories toward more purposive conceptions of liberalism that can guide reforms in current practices.[3] Although some of my arguments are shaped by the ways political scientists have viewed the world, the positions advanced here are my own, not those of the other contributors, much less political scientists generally.

The chapter focuses on three positions supported by noted CLS scholars: (1) the claim that conventional legal texts and doctrines display incorrigible logical indeterminacies and contradictions; (2) the claim that American law embodies "liberal legalism" and that it both directly and subtly serves the relations of unjust domination that characterize an advanced capitalist liberal society; and (3) the claim that normatively valuable arguments must move us toward the realization of a radical conception of human freedom, one which calls us to make all aspects of our lives ever more vulnerable to our collective deconstruction and reconstruction. I suggest that the first two claims, properly understood, contain some important truths but that they have no necessary connection with the left-oriented political positions many critical legal scholars expect them to advance. The distinctive substance of CLS views derives essentially from their third claim, the desirability of a quite demanding notion of freedom. That claim is more visible in the work of some CLS authors than that of others, but it is responsible, I contend, for their characteristic critical normative posture. I argue instead for a different substantive conception of human liberty. Although the radical sense of freedom that these writers employ can generate useful critical efforts aimed against genuine oppression, ultimately it represents an attitude of profound resentment toward the human condition as we experience it. The danger is that such resentment can support nihilistic pessimism, gloomy conservatism, or a despairing frivolity as easily as it can support constructive change.

THE CLAIMS OF THE CRITICAL LEGAL STUDIES MOVEMENT

The Conference on Critical Legal Studies began in the late 1970s as a self-conscious movement among diverse left-leaning legal scholars (now widely referred to as "crits"). All of these scholars had been nurtured on the epic narrative of modern American legal training; that is, the story of how legal realist perspectives rose up in the 1930s to smash the *Lochner* era's reactionary constitutional doctrines of "natural" economic rights, which courts used to invalidate reform legislation via a facade of apolitical, formalistic, deductive reasoning.[4] Many CLS affiliates were also influenced by the New Left of the 1960s and by exciting Warren Court decisions. The Supreme Court's partial acceptance of Charles Reich's famous "New Property" argument in *Goldberg v. Kelly,* for example, suggested that New Left objectives might be furthered through constitutional law.[5]

CLS scholars were, however, correspondingly impatient with the dominant consequences of legal realism's debunking of higher law theories and with the nonpolitical character of judicial decision making. The established academic heirs of realism seemed daunted by the willful judicial subjectivity that their critiques of "objective" values appeared to license. As a result, the postrealist legal establishment most often defended judicial deference to "democratic" legislatures and defended constitutional activism only to preserve relatively frictionless and representative political and legal processes, or to protect fairly traditional "consensus" values. To the budding critical legal scholars, those positions supported unduly limited reforms when they were not frankly conservative.[6]

Nor were these scholars attracted to the "Old Left" Marxism often visible in the established leftist lawyers' group, the National Lawyers Guild. The rigid determinism and materialism of more traditional "vulgar Marxist" outlooks not only seemed intellectually unconvincing; they also appeared to be incompatible with the aspirations for more spontaneous, participatory politics and cultural flourishing that the New Left had stressed. For similar reasons, many CLS scholars were dissatisfied with the Law and Society Association and the "political jurisprudence" that had become the mainstream in political science after many of its public law specialists, veterans of the war on *Lochner's* natural law, embraced the "behavioral revolution" of the 1950s. Such political scientists paid less and less attention to the subtleties of judicial opinions and began to accept without much anxiety or recrimination the fact that judges routinely exploited the law's indeterminacies and contradictions to produce results satisfying powerful political interests. In so doing, adherents of "political jurisprudence" minimized the significance of legal discourse and embroidered their discipline's pluralist model of interest group politics in a manner that the critical legal scholars again found to be conservative and unduly reductionist.[7]

Consequently, CLS writers have sought to portray the immersion of law in politics in ways that fully reveal its incoherencies, its false pretensions to neutrality, and its often repressive character. But they have tried to do so without rendering legal discourse *merely* epiphenomenal to competing interest groups or capitalist imperatives, and they have given some indication of how truly significant assaults on the status quo might yet be advanced through law. To further this quest they have drawn on the heirs of the Deweyite leftist liberal pragmatists, who inspired many legal realists, such as Richard Rorty. But they have also relied on the deconstructionist literary school of Jacques Derrida and Stanley Fish, whose critique of objective interpretations is rooted in Nietzsche's perspectivism; on the analysis of hegemonic ideologies stemming from Antonio Gramsci and embraced by most leading neo-Marxists; and on the notions of freedom advanced by "modernist" perspectives, chiefly nineteenth-century romanticism and twentieth-century existentialism, as articulated especially by the movement's most powerful philosophic voice, Roberto Mangabeira Unger.[8]

Early writings by CLS-affiliated scholars such as Morton Horwitz, Duncan Kennedy, Mark Tushnet, and Unger himself tended to be predominantly critical legal histories and, to a lesser extent, critiques of contemporary doctrines.[9] The dominant theme was to show how decisions on legal doctrines were battlegrounds that not only instantiated the conflicts, contradictions, and tendencies of ruling political ideologies but also could shape dominant social and political structures as well as mirror them. In recent years contemporary critiques have become more prevalent, and they have more often been addressed to constitutional issues.[10] Various CLS writers have also begun to define affirmative philosophical and political positions of their own, though Unger's efforts remain indisputably the most comprehensive.[11] Collectively, these works more or less persistently advance the three claims noted above concerning the law's indeterminacy, its subservience to the ruling interests in our liberal capitalist society, and the desirability of a richer, postliberal sense of human freedom. Not all these writers understand these claims in the same way, however, so I will review each claim in more detail before turning to my own criticisms.

LAW'S INDETERMINACY

Virtually all critical legal scholars agree that the bulk of existing Anglo-American legal rules are endlessly "flippable," so full of logical indeterminacies and contradictions that they can be manipulated to justify virtually any result. But many also agree that the law is *too* determinate, that its prevailing structures of values, empirical premises, and modes of reasoning dull normative sensitivities, distort empirical perceptions, and stunt the imaginative quest for alternatives.[12] How can critical legal scholars advance both these claims? The answer lies in their insistence that law is *logically* indeterminate. The issues of what the "facts" of a given situation are, what rules and precedents apply to them, and what those rules and precedents require, are, in our complex legal system with its multiple jurisdictions, legal sources, and values, sufficiently ambiguous that most lawyers can find grounds logically supportive of wildly disparate results.

CLS writers differ on how far to go with this argument. Some buttress it with the deconstructionism of contemporary critical literary theory, which argues that not only Anglo-American law but also all human languages can be shown to display such indeterminacy and contradictory implications.[13] Indeed, the more radical literary critics suggest that, at bottom, all human discourse reveals a pervasive contradiction: It purports to tell us something about the objective world yet proves on analysis to be only a self-referential set of signs and symbols that can never affirm a connection to an order outside of itself.[14] Only a few crits, however, seem willing to carry deconstructionism or their own critiques to the point of simply dismissing "the power of objective reason" and "the possibility of transparent communication."[15]

Most CLS writers argue more mildly that determinate legal rules are possible and that our legal system is not wholly indeterminate, merely "far more indeterminate than traditional theorists realize it is."[16] And most crits believe that even logically ambiguous rules are often given predictable meaning in practice through institutionalized routines and customs, patterns of thought and belief, and "ideologies" or "social visions" that prevail in our legal and political culture. Although a given rule might be logically consistent with a result radically different from those dominant customs and political values, judges can be expected to choose among the much narrower range of arguably logical results that conform to or reinforce such practices and values.[17]

In the eyes of these critics, this predictability is, however, no defense for existing legal rules. The legal system still *claims* that logic mandates the predictable results when, in reality, it simply does not. Instead, according to this view, results flow from dominant ways of thinking and believing that reflect the political balance of power in society. When we falsely reify the prevailing structures of thought into logical mandates, we usually protect the existing power structure while closing our minds to the possibility of more imaginative and normatively superior alternatives. The point of relentlessly exposing the absence of logical closure in existing law is to rip away some of the legitimating cloaks for what are really political decisions and to make it possible to roam more widely in the quest for answers.

"LIBERAL LEGALISM"

The CLS's first claim leads into the second—the insistence that law currently provides a spurious legitimacy as well as a concrete structure of implementation and enforcement for the powerful political interests in our advanced capitalist society.[18] Precisely because indeterminate legal rules gain practical meaning from the broader political culture, our law works out in various areas the internal contradictions and the repressive potential of the various brands of liberalism that have achieved virtual hegemony in Anglo-American political discourse. Nowhere is this process more true than in constitutional law, which initially helped structure the new American regime and which continues to be an arena of potentially significant political conflict.[19] Perhaps the greatest of these internal contradictions is that our liberal constitutional law professes to be neutral, above petty partisan politics, concerned to treat all equally, respectfully, with fairness and due process.[20] In fact it systematically abets the economic and political power of some ruling groups while neglecting the poor, the weak, and the culturally marginal.

Again, critical legal scholars differ on what this claim of "liberal legalism" really means. Most began, after all, by rejecting traditional Marxist treatments that depict law as the thinly disguised expression of capitalist class interests. The Marxist view makes conflicts in the courtrooms and legal academies appear quite peripheral to the power struggles between the high bourgeoisie and the proletariat that determine historical development. Most CLS works stress instead that the outcome of legal disputes, while always part of broader political struggles, can play a "relatively autonomous" role in shaping which interests will prevail and how those interests will be institutionalized. This role is not simply dictated by who wins in the adjacent arenas of workplaces and battlefields, much less by polls and legislative assemblies.[21]

But how autonomous is "relatively autonomous," and how significant is the shaping role of legal decisions? Here crits vary considerably. Mark Tushnet remains close to traditional Marxist perspectives, arguing that:

> We can still expect the law to embrace positions that are required by the interests of the ruling class as a whole, even if they are inconsistent with the interests of individual members of that class. The law remains linked to the relations of production directly through the political perception of advanced segments of the ruling class and indirectly through the political principles that are ultimately rooted in those relations.[22]

Robert Gordon defends a more sharply non-Marxist view, holding that "causal relations between changes in legal and social forms" are "radically undetermined." Law is a "product of political conflict," but legal ideologies are "relatively autonomous" from other political arenas to a greater degree than even neo-Marxism acknowledges. Such ideologies have their own peculiar internal character and tensions; participants in the legal culture often respond to these characteristics and reach decisions that in turn may "shape the content of the immediate self-interest of social groups" as much as they reflect any ideology.[23] When traditional property conceptions are persuasively argued to support constitutional welfare rights, for example, large numbers of persons may come to identify their economic interests with welfare benefits (not, e.g., new labor agreements or public ownership) to a degree that would not have seemed rational otherwise. Roberto Unger, too, has been critical of all claims that legal rules are merely epiphenomenal to a distinctive type of social structure governed by predictable internal dynamics, even though he seems alternately more or less optimistic about how much change can be wrought via legal victories.[24]

But even those critical scholars who, like Unger, have become dissatisfied with gross categories like "capitalism" and "liberal legalism" nonetheless insist fervently that the political and economic institutions, practices, and structures of thought that constitute the "formative contexts of the present day impose unnecessary and unjustifiable constraints" on human freedom as they understand it.[25] If existing law is not simply the reflex of economically rooted domination that older Marxists held it to be, all crits agree that it is much more a vehicle of oppression than an instrument of meaningful empowerment. That belief leads us to their third claim, concerning what constitutes genuine human freedom.

RADICAL FREEDOM

The basic sense of freedom shared by the leading CLS writers is traceable, as Unger has argued, to the understanding of the human self, its possibilities, and its predicaments dominant in what Unger labeled "modernist" thought, particularly nineteenth-century romanticism and twentieth-century existentialism.[26] In his important work *The Longing for Total Revolution,* Bernard Yack argued that such post-Kantian outlooks, of both the Right and Left, have generally embraced two views that, at least initially, seem mutually reinforcing. These views portray human personality as receiving its content from various external social contexts and define human freedom in terms of our ability to gain control of those contexts and subject them to our conscious direction. The most powerful modernist thinkers have contended uncompromisingly that only insofar as we actually master the contexts that shape our selves can we be said to be free. Measured by this demanding standard of freedom, classical liberalism falls far short, for it is held to provide only a limited, ersatz collective self-governance in the "political" realm. It treats the worst forms of domination in our gender, familial, and economic relations as "private" and hence largely untouchable, thus propagating rationalizations for those social contexts that shackle our minds along with our conduct.[27]

Yet modern social theory's ongoing elaboration has only multiplied the long list of external contexts that influence our lives. It may seem absurd to think that people might ever be able to constantly and collectively recreate and regulate the totality of these contexts. Critical social theorists have therefore tried repeatedly to find some social subsphere that holds the key to mastering the character of the rest of the societal "superstructure." For early romantic theorists this sphere was art, philosophy, or religion; for Marx, more plausibly and momentously, it was material production.

Some critical theorists still hope we can really find some pivotal lever that can bring all the social forces that now dominate us under our conscious collective determination, thereby humanizing our world and making true freedom possible for the first time in history.[28] Some critical legal scholars take their insistence on the relatively autonomous role of law in creating social relationships to the verge of claiming that legal ideology may be this lever. Even Unger stressed that legally defined rights are architectonic; law "helps draw the boundaries of all of the other social stations and institutional havens."[29]

The failure of Marxism to realize the promise of a revolutionary transformation to this sort of comprehensive, radical freedom has, however, given pause to most contemporary heirs of the modern critical theory tradition.[30] Perhaps no such transformative lever can be found. Hence, many critical legal scholars have been deeply troubled by what Duncan Kennedy once termed the "fundamental contradiction" of the human condition (a formulation he now disavows). There seems to be no way to harmonize self and "other," to reconcile the self's conflicting aspirations to be part of a community and at the same time to stand alone. To achieve the total collective self-determination that our socially situated selves require to be free, it seems that we have to accept communal constraints on our immediate personal autonomy; yet these constraints simultaneously render us unfree.[31]

Roberto Unger similarly treats this "irresolvable conflict" between "self-expression and attachment to other people" as perhaps the most crucial one we confront, as it is "in reality a tension between the conflicting demands of self-assertion themselves." But he believes these demands can be harmonized to a far greater degree than we have yet realized. His genuinely stirring hope has helped sustain a similar faith in many CLS members.[32]

Unger accepts the "shaped character of social life," the notion that human beings "habitually move" within finite, particular sets of social and mental structures, or "formative contexts."[33] He also has repeatedly insisted that no "formative institutional and imaginative contexts," past or present, represent the fulfillment of our nature or our freedom. While we "are our fundamental practices," we "are also the permanent possibility of revising of them." None of these practices "describe or determine exhaustively our capabilities of human connection." All are "partial and provisional." Neither individually nor collectively do they "do justice to a being whose most remarkable quality is precisely the power to overcome and revise, with time, every social or mental structure in which he moves."[34] Yet his belief in the "power of the self eternally to transcend the limited imaginative and social worlds that it constructs" does not lead Unger to accept the utter "irreconcilability of freedom and structure," or of autonomy and social contexts, that Duncan Kennedy's formulation of the "fundamental contradiction" suggests.[35]

Unger argues instead that "social worlds . . . differ in the degree as well as the character and severity of their constraining quality" and asserts that it is worthwhile to search for "less conditional and confining forms of social life." He has explicitly assaulted extreme modernist existentialists for failing to see that "enduring social and mental orders may differ" in this way, with some much more open to frequent transformation and recreation. Thus modernists are driven to see freedom *simply* as "rebellion against whatever is partial and factitious in the established social and mental structures," so that freedom becomes no more than recurring "temporary acts of context smashing." Unger has wisely denounced this sense of freedom, this striving for independence "from any instituted form of social life," as "unattainable," "empty," and "anguishing." He recognized that it ends in "a desperate self-concern" on the part of those unable to connect their notion of authentic personal freedom with any concrete form of collective existence. Unger asserted instead that "freedom, to be real, must exist in lasting forms of social life."[36]

At the same time, Unger has admitted that his own position is "closer" to existentialist and modernist views than to traditional Aristotelian or Christian ones. The latter views hold some conception of an ultimate natural or divinely ordered "context" that permanently structures the capacities, opportunities, and purposes that constitute our lives. Unger stated that he builds on, but radicalizes, the "great secular doctrines of emancipation," liberalism, socialism, and communism, creating a kind of "superliberalism." As freedom means provisionally accepting some social structures, institutions, and forms of thought, we must strive to politicize and democratize all aspects of life. To fulfill our context-transcending selves, we must establish contexts that allow us, indeed inspire us, to "reimagine" and "remake" them "as much as possible." Our "institutional order" must both secure people "against oppression and deprivation" and multiply "their opportunities and reasons for engagement in conflict over the basic terms of social life."

Unger's hope is for the ultimate "effacement of the contrast between revolutionary struggles over the established order and routine deals within it," through the ongoing establishment, transformation, and recreation of a social life that makes available "the instruments of its own revision." And their exercise should be "constant": While we are not to see freedom just as context smashing, neither should we see any social form that encourages us to rest satisfied with it as consistent with true empowerment. Such social institutions or contexts still do injustice to "a self that discovers the divergence between its own transcending capabilities and the limitations of the structures in which it lives and then struggles by every means at its disposal to narrow this gap." One should therefore reject the efforts to preserve stability and to guide democratic decision making away from certain choices that have traditionally driven liberal constitutionalism.[37]

SOME CRITICISMS OF LAW'S CRITICAL CRITICS

These CLS arguments have had considerable success in broadening, politicizing, and thereby reinvigorating legal discourse. Their descriptive contentions have much force and cannot be ignored by contemporary legal analysts. The degree to which these characterizations support their sweeping indictments of current American law and the liberal perspectives it embodies finally depends, however, on how fully we accept the postliberal conception of freedom best articulated by Unger. Without that substantive commitment, the movement's other claims contribute something to political wisdom but very little to a genuinely radical politics.

THE INDETERMINACY OF INDETERMINACY

The claim that the law often falls far short of full logical determinacy when we look to it for resolution of particular situations seems simply true. As noted above, this claim has been a routine premise of most empirical legal research in political science for years; whatever the limitations of that research, it has uncovered no reason to doubt that lawyers can and do manipulate rules and precedents to reach a wide range of results. Those manipulations are not all equally logical, but many are sufficiently so to sustain the claim of considerable logical indeterminacy.

The politics of the political scientists engaged in such research tends, however, to be predominantly liberal pluralist or conservative, which shows that there is no necessary connection between the claim of indeterminacy and any particular political outlook. Indeed, the deconstructionists' argument that interpretations reveal only the perspective of the interpreter has its roots in Friedrich Nietzsche's claim that there is only perspective here, as does the structuralist and contextualist contention that a "subject's" perspective really only instantiates the socially and biologically rooted structures that constitute it. Nietzsche, of course, linked those contentions with a radically inegalitarian esteem for the self-exalting *übermensch* who dominates others, in sharp contrast to the egalitarian, communitarian sentiments of most CLS members.[38] And the fate of legal realism, which first popularized such claims of indeterminacy, confirms that the calls for "ad hoc, contextualized judgments" based on "experience, emotion, introspection, and conversation" (advanced by CLS analysts of indeterminacy like Joseph Singer) can lead to a rather complacent and pragmatic "balancing" approach to law as easily as to significant change.[39] Similarly, Richard Rorty, whose defenses of pragmatism are often cited by CLS authors, and Lief Carter, whose "aesthetic jurisprudence" is the leading defense of CLS perspectives in political science, each appear to espouse substantive political values not so far from Ronald Dworkin's.[40] The point is too obvious to belabor further: The implications of legal indeterminacy are, unsurprisingly, politically indeterminate.

Accepting the law's logical indeterminacy does require some sensible modifications in the way certain defenses of the "rule of law" are made, but extensive modifications are not needed. Dworkin's writings on jurisprudence, for example, can plausibly be read as concurring fully with the CLS claim that legal rules gain determinacy only from the broader political practices, customs, and values of our political culture. Dworkin's contribution has in fact been to call us to accept our reliance on these often tacit sources of legal meaning as a perfectly appropriate aspect of legal reasoning and to elaborate them more systematically and explicitly as much as possible. Dworkin has at times suggested that our readings of the broader political culture can produce a determinate "right answer" for particular cases,[41] but CLS writers have derided these suggestions as reintroducing the illusions of legal formalism.[42] Dworkin has also regularly acknowledged that, out of ambiguous and diverse materials, judges must construct a vision of the polity and the values to which they appeal and that they must rely at crucial junctures on their own "controversial judgments" about which available principles are more worthwhile than others. Thus, he recognizes that judicial perspectives and decisions will always legitimately be politically disputable.[43]

The suggestion that one position may nonetheless be the "right" reading of our political culture does not in practice distinguish this picture of legal decision making from the ones most CLS writers advance. There may be a theoretical difference between claiming that one's political vision, as derived from one's evaluations of our culture's political experiences and traditions, is substantively better than other visions, and claiming that it is the interpretation that presents our legal culture at its best. But despite the polemics between liberal and radical legal theorists, that difference, if it exists, is hardly so great as to make either the integrity or the survival of our legal system hinge upon which view prevails.

The real difference between liberals like Dworkin (and myself) and CLS theorists like Unger is not over whether the law is logically indeterminate and thus becomes meaningful only through the coloration provided by broader political practices and norms. The crucial dispute is over whether our broader legal and political culture can plausibly be held to be more or less conformable to a coherent and substantively desirable political theory or vision. Liberals contend that a new theory affirming many features of the American political system and calling, by and large, for only gradual reforms could plausibly be constructed out of the nation's political, legal, and cultural traditions, though these theorists differ on what that theory should be and which features of existing arrangements should be preserved and which ones should be altered.[44] Unger wrote scornfully of all notions that existing legal materials "display, though always imperfectly, an intelligible moral order." He contended that if a defensible normative theory of any kind could be found, "it would be a sheer miracle for its implications to coincide with a large portion of the received doctrinal understandings." Unger assumed instead that no matter "what the content of this background theory, it is, if taken seriously and pursued to its ultimate conclusions, unlikely to prove compatible with a broad range of the received understandings."[45]

But why is it so improbable that we could develop a background theory supporting much, though by no means all, of existing legal practices and rules, at least for the present? After all, Unger *agreed* that the logically indeterminate legal rules in most contemporary "rich North Atlantic countries" gain intelligibility and determinacy from a "social vision," or at least a set of cognate social visions, which he, like most CLS writers, has identified with liberal political theory and a liberal political culture.[46] Why is it unlikely that a persuasive version of liberal theory could be developed that would affirm much in modern liberal societies while pointing out nonrevolutionary paths of further improvement?

The answer is that, in Unger's view, liberal thought, like contemporary legal systems, is full of irreconcilable "conflicting tendencies" that point to certain "alternative schemes of human association." Indeed, he has suggested at times that the "counterprinciples" that are visible in current law could support "internal" lines of development that would ultimately reach a "convergence" with his "visionary insight." The constitutional doctrine of equal protection, for example, contains elements that could quite naturally be expanded into a means to "disrupt those forms of division and hierarchy" that are otherwise sheltered from "transformative conflicts." Hence, on analysis, our current liberal law may lead not to some Lockean, Kantian, or pragmatic liberalism but to Unger's own "superliberalism." To an agnostic, however, this unexpected "convergence" must surely appear far more miraculous than the possible harmony between a defensible liberal theory and current law that Unger has derided; and in fact Unger has admitted that "persuasive arguments can be offered" for moving current law in directions other than his own.[47]

His contentions—that all efforts to achieve coherence within the bounds of liberal thought can be deemed hopeless in advance and that legal doctrines should instead be guided toward his own social vision—therefore rest on his normative case for the superiority of his own conception of freedom. If some form of moderate liberalism could be shown to be substantively justifiable, it would in all likelihood provide considerable support for the American constitutional system despite the realities of legal indeterminacy. Hence, it is the substantive inadequacy of moderate liberal conceptions of freedom, not legal indeterminacy, that Unger and like-minded writers must establish in order to make their case for sweeping change.

LIBERAL LEGALISM'S DOMINATION

CLS claims that Anglo-American law embodies liberal political ideas and that it both structures and reflects the power relations of advanced capitalist liberal societies are in themselves largely uncontroversial. It is hard to imagine why analysts of any persuasion would expect law somehow to be essentially independent of the prevailing values and power structures of its society. To what degree and in what ways law has a "relatively autonomous" role in fostering, not simply mirroring, that structure is less clear, but even CLS writers themselves have no settled position on this perplexing point. The provocative claim of the CLS scholars is that liberal ideas are analytically incoherent and serve only to mask what are in fact indefensible power relationships. To sustain that claim, it is obviously not enough to assert that liberal ideas are often manifested in law. CLS writers must also show: (1) that no philosophic articulation of liberal values is coherent; (2) that these philosophic deficiencies are visible in liberal notions as popularly deployed within legal discourse; (3) that these conceptually inadequate notions do operate empirically to buttress certain social structures in significant ways; and (4) that those structures are demonstrably oppressive.

Much CLS scholarship appears to take on these tasks, but critical assaults so far have produced more smoke and noise than any decisive breaches in liberal defenses. The problem is that too many CLS writers focus almost exclusively on the second task, that of showing that the specific doctrines and conceptions employed in particular areas of law really do manifest characteristically liberal precepts and patterns of reasoning. CLS writers take for granted the successful completion of the first task, that of showing the philosophical incoherence of liberal ideas, and they engage in no serious empirical or normative execution of the latter two tasks, those of demonstrating that legal notions serve to mask and maintain power relations and that those power relations are unjustifiable.

One reason very few CLS members have critiqued major works of liberal theory in detail is that they regard those works as having been adequately refuted by other scholars. C. B. Macpherson's *Political Theory of Possessive Individualism,* now a quarter of a century old, is most often cited to characterize classical liberalism (e.g., Mark Tushnet's fine book on the law of slavery defines liberalism exclusively by reference to Macpherson). Michael Sandel is cited to refute the neo-Kantian liberalism of John Rawls and Ronald Dworkin. Sometimes these critiques are buttressed by citation of European critical theorists, such as Theodor Adorno and Max Horkheimer's *Dialectic of Enlightenment,* and often Roberto Unger's first two books are invoked.[48]

These are all significant works, but many of their central tenets look much less sustainable today in light of recent scholarship on classical liberalism, much of it by scholars with left-leaning political orientations. CLS writers rarely discuss these studies. Works on Locke by political theorists such as John Dunn, Neal Wood, and Richard Ashcraft indicate that Macpherson and Unger (and Leo Strauss) were wrong to assimilate this moderate but still revolutionary Whig to the illiberal, politically absolutist Thomas Hobbes and designate the latter as the paradigmatic liberal theorist. Even more importantly, Macpherson's claim that Lockean thought was inherently supportive of class oppression because it treated workers as "subrational" beings who were not persons has been decisively rebutted.[49] It is certainly true nonetheless that liberal precepts have often functioned historically to provide ideological rationalizations for harsh capitalist institutions. Yet that fact alone does not prove that liberal values would be worthless in constructing more adequate defenses of other aspects of contemporary liberal societies or in providing critical guidance toward institutional reforms, for liberal values, historically, have also played those roles.[50]

Sandel's critique of Rawlsian liberalism does not make the CLS case either, for it does not seriously engage the significantly different versions of liberal ideas that have historically been most influential in American law, and at any rate it appears to lend at least as much support to neoconservatives as to radicals.[51] Adorno and Horkheimer's stimulating essay and Unger's sketches of Enlightenment philosophy skillfully critique genuine strains in liberal thought.[52] But it would take a fully documented scholarly work in the history of ideas to show that these strains have been dominant in Anglo-American liberalism (a questionable proposition). These writings do not purport to be such studies and cannot properly be cited to that effect. Since CLS writers have done little else, the case for the philosophical hopelessness of all imaginable versions of liberalism remains far more an article of faith than an achievement of the movement.

Because CLS members so frequently employ Macpherson's crude picture of liberal theory in identifying liberal patterns of thought in law, it is not clear that they have done justice to the complex countercurrents in American legal and political thought. Too often the "deep structure" of American political culture is portrayed as little more than a hegemonic, monolithic, largely unchanging albeit self-contradictory "liberalism." This view neglects the non-liberal traditions of discourse in America as well as the variations and the transformations in American liberalism over time.[53] But the best recent CLS writings increasingly avoid these pitfalls, so here I will stress the movement's failings in regard to its attempts to prove that the ideas of "liberal legalism" have played a crucial role in reinforcing, if not in creating, structures of domination that appear illicit in light of feasible alternatives. Much CLS writing remains focused on judicial opinions, often on those of appellate judges. Frequently, broad historical studies are invoked to suggest that certain doctrinal moves decisively abetted the political success of specific social groups or classes. But the evidence for such claims remains suggestive at best. Morton Horwitz's influential discussion of how decisions in the Jacksonian age aided emerging entrepreneurial interests, for example, provides little more than an analysis of judicial decisions, historical observations on what groups came to wield power, and speculations on the necessity of the former for the latter. Horwitz may be right, but nothing approaching sustained historical or empirical demonstration of those speculations is provided.[54]

In fairness, few mainstream scholars in history or political science have made much progress in determining the extent to which legal ideas contribute to the existing structures of power. The "relative autonomy" and actual significance of judicial decisions in shaping and maintaining such relations is an issue of sufficient importance, and before the CLS efforts were begun, these matters received insufficient attention from sophisticated researchers. CLS scholars have done a service in bringing the issue more explicitly to the fore of research agendas, even if nothing very authoritative has yet been achieved. Their decisive task, however, is to show that the power arrangements promoted by the law have actually been indefensible. Horwitz's work provides another example in which this assertion seems to be assumed yet is not really argued. To be sure, I hold no brief for the power relations of the Jacksonian era as an enduring model, but it is not clear what plausible paths of development would have surpassed its genuine accomplishments in expanding political rights and economic resources. Normative criticisms require both some empirical showing of what was possible and a substantive standard for what is desirable.

One reason some CLS writers have not tried to show evidence for the notion that liberal legal conceptions serve the evils of existing political systems is that they take for granted a quasi-Marxist portrait of capitalist liberal systems as inherently exploitative and oppressive. Hence, if law serves liberal capitalism, then by definition it serves repression and exploitation. But this assumption can stand only if we accept a quite reductionist Marxist portrait of the inherent internal dynamics of capitalism conceived as a well-defined social formation. As noted previously, CLS writers have increasingly felt compelled to abandon all faith in the real-world existence of such "supposedly integrated social worlds." Instead, scholars like Roberto Unger and Robert Gordon have stressed the complex connections between law and political conflicts without relying on any "metastructural" premises about the processes "inherent" in "capitalism" as a fixed type of social system. As Gordon acknowledged, there is little difference between his methodology and that of mainstream historians of ideas, like Louis Hartz, who generally have not believed that liberalism's historic connections to capitalism made meaningful liberal reforms impossible. Hence, once again this approach does nothing by itself to vindicate CLS claims about the necessarily repressive functions of liberal ideas in law.[55]

The critical scholars' case can only be sustained, then, if we are persuaded that their basic sense of human liberty is normatively compelling and that this basic liberty would have demanded different decisions in the course of American political development. To be sure, persons with a range of normative commitments might well find the CLS's descriptive characterizations of American constitutional law disturbing, but the alternative courses such persons might esteem, in the past and present, would range widely. Although the issue of what could and should have been done in the past is always complex, I will concede that the CLS sense of freedom is radical enough to make the undesirability of many legal rules rather likely once we accept it. But that point only confirms that the degree to which the movement's work supports their radical posture turns on the validity of their postliberal conception of freedom.

THE TYRANNY OF RADICAL FREEDOM

The basic problem with the sense of freedom that Roberto Unger and most CLS writers defend and deploy, explicitly or implicitly, is that it in fact is not significantly distinguishable from the radical modernist conception that Unger himself correctly argued to be hopeless, demoralizing, and self-defeating. Unger strove for a more balanced and sensible understanding of freedom— one that recognizes not only human capacities to transcend and transform particular contexts but also our longings for "an assurance of being at home in the world," for "real human communities," and "secure forms of associa- tion," stabilized by "continuing loyalties" and "a provisional order, even a daily routine."[56] Correspondingly, he has rejected both the "conservative re- form" politics, which he attributed to liberals, and the "textbook revolution" of traditional radicals in favor of something different and intermediate, a politics of "revolutionary reform."[57]

Unger's desire to correct modernism in this way is, I believe, pro- foundly right. But he cannot bring himself to pursue the attempt fully, for it would bring him embarrassingly close to a contemporary form of the mod- erate Enlightenment liberalism he wishes to overcome. I believe (and to a degree, Unger would concur) that despite the negative role this liberalism has often played, historically it has been the most enduringly effective vehicle of genuine "revolutionary reform."[58] Today its workings are, however, too slow and too solicitous of existing interests for Unger's tastes. Hence, instead of providing a balanced conception, Unger offered theoretical portraits of freedom that are overwhelmingly tilted in favor of near-anarchical context destabilization with virtually no discussion of why we might properly bolster certain sorts of lasting structures. And precisely because his theoretical con- ception of freedom requires disruption of so many established social institu- tions, his specific legal and political proposals tilt the opposite way, toward the dangerously commanding, centralized elite rule that the post-Marxist left was supposed to avoid. Because of Unger's intellectual integrity and genuine dedication to democracy, he has retreated from those dangers whenever they have loomed large; but the one-sided view of freedom he employs repeatedly brings him back to their brink.

A Liberal View of the Self and Its Aspirations

These contentions can be brought into sharp relief by first exploring what Unger acknowledged but failed to develop—the reasons why an ade- quate conception of freedom must include support for "lasting forms of so- cial life."[59] Up to a point, Unger's view of human personalities is persuasive. I believe he was correct to portray our "selves" as beings who derive their "standards of sense and value" from "historically given and flawed human communities," although people have usually ascribed those standards to un- changing natural and divine moral orders.[60] I also agree that, as we acquire the minimal cognitive capacities that are involved in the learning of language in a community, we feel ourselves to have the ability to deliberate on our formative social contexts and to consider alternatives; so we sense our poten- tial to work some consciously determined changes in our world, usually small but sometimes great. This sense of our selves may be in some manner an illusion incident to the deterministic chemical processes of our physical brains and bodies, but it is nonetheless an enduring characteristic of our condition as we experience it. And I believe, along with Unger but even more with the moderate liberalism of the Enlightenment, that we should view our capacities to comprehend, deliberate upon, and direct our conduct, both through internal self-direction and through our interactions with others and with the physical world, as giving us moral agency, while their responsible exercise gives us moral dignity.[61]

But what constitutes the responsible exercise of our capacities? Or, to put it more Socratically, how should we live? Although we may not feel we have certain access to divine or natural answers to this fundamental question, still we cannot help but answer. It seems wisest to do so through conscious choices based on consideration of what appear to be the most central aspects of our experience. Among those aspects are the multifaceted capacities to question and alter our social worlds, as just noted; but among them, too, are equally multifaceted forms of finitude. We generally believe we understand some things about ourselves, our communities, and our physical world and that we can beneficially remake them in some ways in order to lead different, more satisfying lives. But we also know there is much of importance that we do not understand and much inside and outside of ourselves that we cannot as yet change or control. Indeed, we believe there are some things we will never be able to change or control. Although we may learn and become many things in our lives, we cannot learn and become all things; we cannot change our pasts; we cannot pursue some choices without permanently foreclosing others; and we cannot prevent death from ending our potential for further changes and from leaving our lives defined much more by what we did than what we might have done.

It is these latter aspects of our condition, the realities of our finitude and mortality, that Unger unduly minimized. Because I believe he was right to value the capacities for critical reflection that make it plausible to assign our conduct moral significance, I believe he was also right to denigrate all social and political forms that stunt those capacities. Moreover, he was right to call us to seek institutions that enhance our powers for both personal and collective democratic, deliberative self-direction. Indeed, I have contended that the pursuit of such empowerment, which may be termed "rational liberty," should be taken as the central goal of a liberal polity and of the U.S. Constitution.[62] But the realization of rational liberty cannot simply involve "an ever greater jumbling up" of all our social relations and attachments "in a state of heightened plasticity," always vulnerable to "aggravated conflict" and struggle over their fundamental terms.[63] Upon reflection, we simply do not find that our social contexts only limit us. We also find that some social contexts are integral to our senses of who we are and what we most value. These contexts may involve our families, our churches, our fellow workers or political partisans, our communities of intellectual inquiry or artistic creation, or some combination of these and other social settings. But virtually all people find that certain social relations and pursuits are what they most care about, and those cares define their dreams.

If we come to accept the moral importance of preserving our capacities to understand, question, and change, as Unger's ideal and "rational liberty" both do, we will reject or modify any memberships or social relations that threaten to damage those capacities.[64] But we will usually find that even aspirations pursued in social contexts that are not dangerous in this way still require forms that are relatively enduring. And since we cannot change the past or endlessly start again, it is frequently of vital importance to us to shelter, to a significant degree, the memberships and pursuits we value most from destabilizing conflicts. Otherwise we face the prospect of looking back at the end of our lives on a long series of false starts, aborted efforts, broken ties, and ragged, incomplete pieces of thwarted dreams.

That is a life of frustration and disappointment, not freedom. Such a choice would be worth making only if all our available attachments did not deserve to be sustained. Despite life's travails and the injustices of our institutions, few people abhor their experience of human existence so much. Instead, we find a good deal in ourselves and our social worlds to cherish and preserve. No doubt if we were to recreate our condition from scratch, much in these social worlds would be different. But we cannot do so, and the fact is that current structures do embody much of what the real persons alive today value and wish to further. Since we cannot help but be conscious of how precarious and vulnerable those aspects of our lives are, it is only sensible to wish to give them considerable protection if we can.

Consequently, a polity embodying a balanced conception of human liberty would not seek to radicalize Jefferson's call for revolution every twenty years, as Unger sought to do. It would instead adopt a more Madisonian emphasis on the maintenance of alterable but relatively enduring political and social structures within which personal freedom, thus understood, can flourish—an emphasis that forms the heart of American constitutionalism at its best. The balance of such a system, to be sure, should not be a static equilibrium. The commitment to preserving and promoting freedom means that such a polity must prevent social contexts and communities from suppressing human capacities for understanding and reflection and from foreclosing all practical possibilities for peaceful change. Such a polity may also properly seek to enhance these dimensions of our lives by educating all, helping all to acquire ample material resources, and by favoring forms of social organization that encourage informed, deliberative personal and political self-governance by their members; any necessary trade-offs among these aims should be made in ways that maximize the aspirations of the greatest number without nullifying core freedoms of any minority.[65] In the long run the pursuit of these difficult goals is likely to produce quite sweeping transformations.

But out of concern to enhance its own durability, a moderate liberal polity should not outlaw or otherwise assault economic, social, and political associations that make their own transformation relatively cumbersome but still practical. If freedom meant that all duties owed to each other by members of families and communities could easily be abandoned, that fundamental religious tenets could lightly be tossed aside, that all property claims of innovators and recipients of public entitlements could instantly be extinguished, no one should be faulted for rejecting it. Only if we recognize that the reflective self-direction of persons is usually assisted by such lasting arrangements will we have a conception of freedom that deserves to be what Unger termed a "regulative ideal."[66]

The CLS View of the Self and Its Institutional Realization

It is, of course, almost certainly true that many CLS writers would differ in some ways from Unger's views on the self, freedom, and in particular the institutions that best fulfill them. But only Unger has provided us with fully elaborated positions on these points in writings that claim to speak for the movement and are often cited by its adherents as authoritative. Hence it is proper to focus on him in characterizing the ways CLS views contrast with the liberal views just sketched.

As noted, Unger did recognize and attempt to accommodate these moderating concerns, explicitly disavowing the extreme modernist identification of freedom simply with context-smashing.[67] Duncan Kennedy, too, has abandoned his proclamation of the "fundamental contradiction" between individuality and social attachments that modernist thought produces.[68] Neither, however, has really overcome the root difficulty of modern critical social theory. Such theory, again, portrays the human self as constituted by diverse social contexts, and it portrays freedom as the self's mastery of all those contexts. Thus, as Kennedy previously argued, "the very structures against which we rebel" provide us "the stuff of our selves."[69]

Yet to speak of a self that rebels against the structures that constitute it comes close to implying that this self can act wholly autonomously of its memberships; so does the call for us to place our "selves" in full control of their contexts. Such an ontologically independent self cannot be reconciled with an unqualified modernist view of the self as contextually constituted. Perhaps a Platonic idea of man or a Christian concept of the soul could serve as this asocial self, but critical theorists have not defended any such conception. Their explicit descriptive thrust has been against these "ghostly" notions, but their normative pronouncements repeatedly imply something like them.

A more tenable position is that although we may have no "self" that can step wholly outside of all its social contexts to manipulate them on behalf of its own empowerment, our cognitive capacities do enable us to criticize any particular context by drawing on other facets of our experience. Thus, each context can eventually be made open to questioning and revision. Many CLS writers might contend that this sort of image of the self is what they really have in mind. But this image does not fit Unger's superliberalism nearly so well as the moderate liberalism just described, in which freedom is considered to be the ongoing realization of relatively enduring ways of life and social attachments, combined with the periodic questioning and alteration those ways of life must permit.[70]

Despite his occasional hedges, Unger has continued to imply, like most critical theorists, that we do have some "real" selves that can stand outside and seek "greater individual and collective mastery" of all our "social settings," or at least that we are most real when we are distancing ourselves from them. He distinguished sharply between one's "self" and one's "character," or one's established "limited repertory of dealings with others," and called us to free ourselves from "the tyranny of character" in order to express "the kind of being we really are," a "self that can always violate the generative rules of its own mental or social constructs."[71] This self finds "true satisfaction" only when engaged "in an activity that enables people to fight back . . . against the established settings of their lives." Only via such "struggle" can one be "fully a person."[72]

Unger was careful to indicate that we thus free ourselves "only partially," that we remain to some degree "defined by the current forms" of our existence, and he certainly has never suggested how the self as he conceived of it could do or be otherwise. But he gave explicit moral approval, if not indeed moral significance, *only* to exercises of our "most remarkable quality," our power to "revise, with time, every social or mental structure" in our lives. We hear much about "the dignity of a context-transcending agent" and "a context-revising self" but never about the moral worth of a "context-embracing" or "context-sustaining" self. Even when attempting explicitly balanced formulations, his focus has been entirely on avoiding constraints, not on affirming one's memberships and obligations. He calls for an "institutional order" that "secures people in their vital immunity against oppression and deprivation" while multiplying "reasons for engagement in conflict." The security promised comes not at all from belonging and from fulfilling our duties but rather comes entirely from escaping external burdens. Unger admitted that "people have also always put their sense of basic security in the maintenance of particular social roles, jobs, and ways of life." But he sternly admonished us that "Any attempt to indulge this conception of security would prove incompatible with the institutions of the empowered democracy and with the personal and social ideals that inspire them." People "should wean themselves away" from all their desires to be secure in such attachments.[73]

In *Passion,* his essay on the personal dimensions of his social vision, Unger did briefly claim that someone committed to his conception of freedom would take his "attachments for real" and cling to "established relations." He also noted that viewing a marriage as "indissoluble" might enable "husband and wife to accept and experience conflict without fearing . . . separation." But these contentions fit uneasily with his repeated calls for "structure-denying" structures that greatly increase our "opportunities and reasons" for conflict over their "basic" terms: Our opportunities obviously are limited when separation is not on the near horizon of possibilities. And indeed Unger quickly emphasized that everything must still always be viewed as "up for grabs." His person's *most* affirmative sentiment toward his social relations is "You haven't seen anything yet"—hardly a ringing endorsement of what those relations have meant thus far.[74]

It is also revealing that Unger's discussion of fundamental personal relations in *Passion* said little directly about the parent-child relationship, the human relationship where a significant measure of enduring stability is most clearly required for human well-being and empowerment.[75] Unger's chief explicit comment expressed his typical emphasis on the optional character of existing family arrangements. He wrote that children need "empathetic response" but that there "is no clear limit to the forms that the empathetic response may take or to the people who may provide it. The assignment to the father, the mother, or others, of fixed responsibilities in providing this response merely reflects a particular version of family life in a particular society."[76]

This passage is ambiguous: It is not clear whether it is simply the bearers of "fixed responsibilities" for child rearing who may be altered or if "fixed responsibilities" in general represent an optional type of arrangement. In either case Unger's position poses difficulties. It is obviously true that child care arrangements can be varied, and perhaps in a society long characterized by collective child rearing, parenthood would not need to imply any special responsibility for a child. But many would question whether such arrangements could ever provide the substantial, ongoing, secure attention from a relatively few particular others that seems necessary to nurture a young child's potential for healthy consciousness.[77] The number of conscientious child-rearing professionals would have to be large.

At any rate, in most if not all existing societies the parent-child relationship is so pervasively defined as vital that few children escape significant, often damaging psychological consequences if a parent refuses to honor that relationship (a responsibility that does place weighty constraints on the "plasticity" of the parent's life). Hence, any less than gradual effort to alter the relatively enduring quality of parent-child relationships is almost certain to cripple youthful capacities for self-understanding and interactions with others, which Unger must wish to strengthen. Indeed, it is highly questionable whether this relationship can ever be made significantly less "fixed" or made vulnerable to frequent revisions without fostering widespread psychic instability. Our society's unintended experiments in that direction in the inner cities are hardly encouraging. It is certainly proper to foster greater sharing of responsibilities for sustained, attentive child rearing, especially by fathers, instead of assigning this role solely to biological mothers. But it is not likely that genuine freedom would be furthered by making the duties of parenthood open to rapid fundamental transformations.

Since he does not address the issue of parents and children very fully, it cannot be said that Unger would wholly reject that conclusion. Yet despite his sporadic qualifications, Unger has often acknowledged the truth: The "heart" of his "gospel of plasticity" is purely "the power of the self eternally to transcend" its contexts, not our powers to affirm as well as to transform. He admitted that his institutional program "downplays" the "continuance of particular loyalties to individuals and groups." Unger believes that human attachments will prove more fulfilling when they have no taint of subjugation to rigid social forms; but his focus is on developing capabilities for "individual and collective self-assertion," not "lasting, secure forms of association." He has explained that he "presupposes that over the long run the practical, moral, and cognitive advantages to be won by disentrenching formative contexts outweigh . . . the benefits" of any other course, including further sustaining or entrenching some such contexts. Thus, his program is to "favor the recurrence of the transforming passions" and "the breaking open of structure to politics" in order to fulfill a conception of the self as "relentlessly negative," never accepting, always struggling against all the "limitations" it experiences. As all enduring relations involve some confinement, from this standpoint they must all ultimately be obstacles—precisely the modernist stance of repugnance toward all contexts that Unger claimed to want to modify.[78] But such modification requires more affirmation of the value of stable personal relations and social structures than he could bring himself to endorse. Though he wishes, like Nietzsche, to transcend human *ressentiment,* our rebellion against our existential limitations, the spirit of Unger's work bespeaks more his avowed longing for the "heart's revenge."[79]

Unger has recently released a three-volume counterpart to *Passion* that develops the implications of his position for legal, political, and economic institutions, building on his 1983 essay, "The Critical Legal Studies Movement." I cannot discuss his program in depth, but it shows plainly that the bias in favor of undue context destruction, now by governmental action, has repeatedly infected Unger's political and social prescriptions. His imagination and insight are such that his proposals can nonetheless stimulate thinking on constructive reforms, but only if that infection is combatted by antibodies of concern for legitimate existing ties.

In these works Unger has developed a bold program of "empowered democracy" that includes extensive governmental and economic reorganization as well as transformation of the legal "system of rights." In regard to government, Unger has sought to prevent state powers from becoming dangerously entrenched while granting them sufficient scope to act in behalf of citizens' welfare and liberties—the classic dilemma of liberal constitutional theory. But because Unger found liberal solutions too pale, rigid, and weak, in need of dramatic expansion, he called for further multiplications of the branches and powers of government while granting his new agencies overlapping, hence checking, functions. Like liberal American political scientists since Woodrow Wilson, Unger also leans toward a parliamentary system of party government, although he would prefer one more democratic and more empowered than existing models.

Specifically, Unger would establish, first, a kind of "Democratic Communications" branch or agency, which would be entitled to intervene in all economic and social institutions and "change their operations, by veto or affirmative initiative" and to ensure that the "means of communication, information, and expertise" was not confined to elites within those institutions, which would limit their members' capacities for meaningful collective deliberations. He also would favor another, still more powerful new branch, which might be termed a "Subjugation Reconstruction" agency. Chosen by the other branches, existing "parties of opinion," and the "universal electorate" and armed with "radical extensions" of the contemporary judiciary's power to issue "complex, collective injunctions," this agency would "destabilize," administer, and reconstruct any social institutions that threatened to become stultifyingly hierarchical or oppressive toward their current or potential constituents. The actions of both agencies would be subject to review by the parliament or an electoral referendum. The efficacy of the much more broadly representative parliament would be aided by having within it a smaller council, representing the parties in office, which would initiate programs and supervise their execution in cooperation with the cabinet.[80]

This program combines and radicalizes most of the leading, and often incompatible, modern liberal institutional innovations: the growth of administrative agencies; more party-directed and extensive legislative authority; and expanded injunctive powers. Its promise to fulfill Unger's fundamental aim of rendering all existing institutions more open to revision should be obvious. Yet, as Unger has developed it so far, its potential for sweeping social intervention and ferocious intragovernmental clashes are far more clear than the means of truly democratic participation and control. Unger has admitted these dangers but asserted that the overriding authority of the parliament, or the electorate at referendum, would forestall them.[81] One must still wonder: could the electorate effectively combat an incumbent central parliamentary council that used the massive interventionist weapons of the agencies it helped appoint to "restructure" all established and developing opposition organizations? Perhaps. But that outcome of the plan is debatable, while its sweeping expansions of central governmental powers are not.

In regard to the organization of the economy, Unger originally advocated the pooling of social capital into a "rotating capital fund," which would be controlled by "central agencies of government." These agencies would extend monies to selected enterprises on the government's terms, in pursuit of economic and social aims that would be matters of "ongoing political controversy."[82] That system clearly raised the dangers of inefficiency and, especially, of domination by a centralized elite, which has plagued existing state-directed economies. In his new work Unger modified his plan significantly, indicating that central governmental officials, "the party in office and the supporting representative assemblies," should allocate resources to "a variety of semi-independent investment funds" specializing in different sectors of the economy. Much "like contemporary central banks," these funds would be staffed by governmentally appointed officials as well as members elected from these sectors, and interest would be paid on the social capital they received. Capital would then be auctioned or rationed to teams of "workers, technicians, and entrepreneurs," in return for interest and under terms that accorded with broad objectives set by the central government. These capital takers would interact with each other in a market system.[83]

I believe that Unger's effort to focus economic reforms on the control of capital rather than on worker control alone, is commendable, and his new proposals are suggestive for further inquiry. But it is difficult to avoid the suspicion that in practice his semi-independent investment funds would indeed be "much like" modern central banks, permitted considerable discretion, and that funds would usually be used for those investments that promised to be most productive. If so, the status quo would not be greatly altered. Indeed, the program's new semigovernmental financial elites might prove to be the greatest beneficiaries of this "empowered democracy."

In 1983, Unger described four kinds of rights that critical lawyers should seek to establish in order to transform the legal system: immunity rights, including welfare and political entitlements; destabilization rights, or claims to disrupt established institutions and practices; market rights, or very "conditional and provisional claims to available portions of social capital"; and solidarity rights, or legal entitlements for various forms of "communal life."[84] In that essay, he elaborated only on "destabilization rights," which he called "the most obscure and original" of his four types of rights and the one that "best reveals the ruling intentions of the entire program"—a choice that in itself indicated how provisions for disruption were given priority over concerns to shelter and cultivate the forms of association people might value most.[85]

Unger's brief treatment of "immunity" and "solidarity" rights in his new work does nothing to shift that emphasis. Under "immunity rights," he offered no "political and civic freedoms" beyond those currently provided in most liberal democracies. Unger argued only that his "empowered" democratic governmental institutions will make such rights to participate more meaningful. He would promise welfare entitlements to "nourishment, housing, health care, and education" at levels "proportional to the wealth of society," but as this "proportional" judgment is to be made democratically, again there is no assurance that these rights would go beyond current provisions in western welfare states. And Unger explicitly refused to provide any sort of "immunity" protection for jobs, social roles, or ways of life, because these would limit the plasticity that he wishes to promote. He did give some recognition to social attachments via "solidarity rights," which are to honor implicit obligations that have developed in sustained interactions between people, but this recognition is grudging indeed. Unger prefers such rights to be "enforced, when they are enforced at all, by more informal means of mediation," not the judiciary, and he suggested that "many solidarity rights may best remain unenforceable, as a statement of an ideal." Clearly, Unger's sympathies are all with the "destabilization" rights that his "Subjugation Reconstruction" agency would enforce and the "market rights" that really represent an assault on traditional "consolidated" property rights. His main message concerning "immunity" and "solidarity" rights is that these should not be used as vehicles for preserving, as opposed to challenging, existing social structures.[86]

In sketching these rights, moreover, Unger made clear that his "superliberalism" would not remedy, and instead would deliberately exacerbate, some of the most widely lamented features of modern liberal polities: the disintegrative forces that hamper the development of any common life and the tendencies of public arenas to display only conflicts between transient, self-seeking interest groups, who fail to define or realize any shared purposes with their fellow citizens to benefit the community as a whole. Unger actually boasted that his destabilizing program would simply "make social life resemble more closely what politics . . . are already largely like in the liberal democracies: a series of conflicts and deals among more or less transitory and fragmentary groups."[87] Of course, freedom cannot mean much more if its core is the constant breaking away from any structures that show signs of becoming "frozen." This social vision is disappointing, however, if we view freedom as more plausibly located in the balance between protecting the relations and pursuits we most love and ensuring that our loves do not blind us into accepting self-diminishing forms of subservience.

I believe the recent turn toward more purposive versions of liberalism has been motivated largely by the conviction that such a balanced sense of freedom has often been the central political value of liberal societies, including the U.S. constitutional system, but that modern liberals like Rawls and Dworkin have failed to recognize and defend this conception adequately, preferring instead to pretend to be "neutral" on the question of the good life (a claim Unger rightly assaulted). Contemporary "purposive" liberals suggest that a society seeking to advance this balanced liberal freedom more self-consciously and purposefully than existing liberal societies would be more likely to have flourishing and spiritually rich communities within it than would Unger's association of temporary interest groups.[88]

Furthermore, the ongoing quest to actualize that balance could itself serve as a sustaining, morally meaningful shared social purpose. The quest to empower oppressed persons while maintaining some governmental and social order has, in fact, often played this role in America's best hours, such as the Revolution, the Civil War, the New Deal, and the modern civil rights movement. Those periods show that the pursuit of such balanced freedom, or rational liberty, should not generate only the "conservative reform" that Unger assigned to liberals.[89] Because the commitment to achieve this sense of liberty calls us periodically to rethink the adequacy of our basic memberships and to seek to ensure that they really are preserving if not heightening our understanding and self-direction, it will often point to reforms in existing ways of life. Indeed, under some circumstances where social arrangements are clearly repressive and threaten to become so permanently, this commitment will demand quite fundamental changes—peaceful gradual change if possible but immediate force if necessary, as demonstrated by the examples of the partial but significant liberations wrought by colonial American revolutionaries and Abraham Lincoln's north.

In the contemporary United States, I believe, many legal, political, social, and economic institutions can be peacefully altered in ways that would meaningfully advance our capacities for reflective self-direction. Such changes might involve more deliberative and democratic forms of government, including control over decisions regarding the allocation of social capital; more flexible and equitably shared labors of commercial employment and child rearing; and greater worker participation in the management of large corporations. These sorts of significant changes could be sought, however, without ever attempting to permanently efface the contrast between revolutionary struggles and routine politics. Because this moderate liberal understanding of freedom recognizes that empowering people involves not only helping them to escape oppression but also to fulfill their fondest enduring aspirations, it most often points to a politics of lawful, gradual reform. The critical legal scholars are not the first to deride that politics as a program of cowardly, unprincipled compromises, incapable of producing genuine freedom. But if we genuinely care for the actual persons living today and in the foreseeable future, whose decisions and commitments are intimately bound to the communities in which they live, we may come to see that a program of gradual reform is usually the best way to realize the most defensible and humane conception of freedom attainable in the only world we have.

It can be argued that this endorsement of gradual reform comes all too easily to the already privileged and that, in any case, radical postures are often necessary to achieve even modest improvements. At times these claims may be simply true. As I have tried to indicate throughout, I believe that the critiques of inherited descriptions of law provided by the critical legal scholars are not inherently radical but do contribute to clearer thinking about law and that the genuinely radical proposals offered by thinkers like Unger do usefully expand the horizons of existing discourse.

Yet there are costs to insistently radical rhetoric. Although by itself the Conference on Critical Legal Studies hardly poses great dangers, it would be shortsighted to assume, after a century of major revolutions and wars, that no one in the many countries where radical intellectual movements are heard will ever take calls for revolutionary change seriously, perhaps more seriously than those issuing the calls. And this century's leading revolutionaries, drawn more often from the disaffected intelligentsia than from the economically or racially oppressed, have arguably been as destructive of social worlds— churches, local communities, ethnic and kinship groups—valued by the people they claimed to serve as they have been empowering. It is unclear whether revolution was the only available route to the changes human freedom demanded in Russia, China, Cuba, and elsewhere; and often, as Unger observed, "despotic government" resulted instead.[90]

In any case, as Unger has also acknowledged, the situation in the contemporary "industrialized West" is different, for "brutal tyrannies do not exist" there.[91] In such contexts, although radical demands can at times be tactically useful, persistent condemnation of virtually all existing structures may only have the effect of alienating or demoralizing potential supporters of meaningful reforms. I believe that a more enduring, widely acceptable, and hence more successful spirit of constructive change can result from a commitment to the more balanced sense of freedom that liberalism offers.

To be sure, the critical legal scholars are right to insist on these controversial political positions on the issues of the good or goods we can hope to achieve in our collective life and the means to their attainment. It is not an outlook required by the very idea of the rule of law, nor one that some hypothetical choice situation reveals to be neutral—yet just—toward the aspirations of all citizens. As in the case for Unger's superliberalism, the case for this moderate liberalism's ability to provide a defensible moral vision, which affirms much of the current American political and legal system while continuing to suggest improvements, rests above all on the persuasiveness of its substantive understanding of freedom. That fact should be acknowledged by liberals without reservation, for despite the insightful criticisms of the critical legal scholars, the wisdom of this sense of freedom remains secure.

NOTES

1. In the early days of the professionalization process, political scientists such as John W. Burgess and Edward S. Corwin offered perhaps the most advanced graduate training in public law. During the white-hot constitutional controversies of the New Deal era, public law loomed large in the attention of academics in both fields. In the postwar era, however, public law was the subfield most thoroughly captured by the "behavioral revolution" in political science, while academic lawyers found ways to continue to focus on doctrinal argument despite the success-

ful onslaughts of legal realism against the traditional modes of doing so. Younger public law scholars in political science can generally be described as "postbehavioral" just as CLS members are "postrealist," but an even greater range of outlooks in political science (including my own) can fit under that umbrella label.

2. This chapter is an expansion of an earlier essay, entitled "All Critters Great and Small: Critical Legal Studies and Political Theory," that was intended to prompt discussion of CLS work among political scientists via the section in the newsletter of the American Political Science Association entitled "Law, Courts, and Judicial Process Section" (Summer 1986, pp. 1–9). That piece had a more lighthearted tone, inspired by the exuberance visible in many CLS works. Sadly, the ugly acrimony over tenure for CLS-affiliated scholars at major law schools makes that tone no longer appropriate. Instead, I must stress that despite my various substantive disagreements, I believe that the scholarly contributions of the critical legal scholars have been on balance not only academically "legitimate" but of significant value.

3. For examples and discussion of this turn in contemporary liberal theory by liberal political and constitutional theorists with significant differences in their philosophic foundations and substantive commitments, see S. A. Barber, *On What the Constitution Means* (Baltimore: Johns Hopkins University Press, 1984); W. Galston, "Defending Liberalism," *American Political Science Review* 76 (1982), pp. 621–629; W. Galston, "Liberal Virtues," paper delivered at the 1987 annual convention of the American Political Science Association, September 3–6; R. M. Smith, *Liberalism and American Constitutional Law* (Cambridge: Harvard University Press, 1985); J. Raz, *The Morality of Freedom* (Oxford: Clarendon Press, 1986); T. Spragens, "Reconstructing Liberal Theory: Reason and Liberal Culture," in Alfonso Damico, ed., *Liberals on Liberalism* (Totowa, N.J.: Rowman and Littlefield, 1986); S. Macedo, "Liberal Foundations of America's Constitutional Community," paper delivered at the 1987 annual convention of the American Political Science Association, September 3–6.

4. I. Shapiro, *The Evolution of Rights in Liberal Theory* (Cambridge: Cambridge University Press, 1986), pp. 91–92.

5. R. W. Gordon, "New Developments in Legal Theory," in David Kairys, ed., *The Politics of Law* (New York: Pantheon Books, 1982), pp. 282–284; J. H. Schlegel, "Notes Toward an Intimate, Opinionated, and Affectionate History of the Conference on Critical Legal Studies," *Stanford Law Review* 36 (1984), p. 406; L. B. Schwartz, "With Gun and Camera Through Darkest CLS-land," *Stanford Law Review* 36 (1984), pp. 15–16.

6. E. Mensch, "The History of Mainstream Legal Thought," in Kairys, ed., *The Politics of Law*, pp. 29–37; A. C. Hutchinson and P. J. Monahan, "Law, Rights and the Critical Legal Scholars: The Unfolding Drama of American Legal Thought," *Stanford Law Review* 36 (1984), pp. 204–205; M. V. Tushnet, "Critical Legal Studies and Constitutional Law: An Essay in Deconstruction," *Stanford Law Review* 36 (1984), p. 628.

7. Gordon, "New Developments," pp. 282, 284–286; "Critical Legal Histories," *Stanford Law Review* 36 (1984), pp. 69–70, 74–85, 85–86; T. C. Heller, "Structuralism and Critique," *Stanford Law Review* 36 (1984), p. 200; Tushnet, "Critical Legal Studies and Constitutional Law," pp. 625–627, 630; R. M. Unger,

Social Theory: Its Situation and Its Task (Cambridge: Cambridge University Press, 1987), pp. 9–10, 96–120, 130–134; *False Necessity: Anti-Necessitarian Social Theory in the Service of Radical Democracy* (Cambridge: Cambridge University Press, 1987), pp. 14–19.

8. Gordon, "New Developments," pp. 304–309; R. M. Unger, "The Critical Legal Studies Movement," *Harvard Law Review* 96 (1983), pp. 660–662; *Passion: An Essay on Personality* (New York: Free Press, 1984), pp. 79–81; *Social Theory*, pp. 219, 223, 228, 238; J. W. Singer, "The Player and the Cards: Nihilism and Legal Theory," *Yale Law Journal* 94 (1984), p. 7; Tushnet, "Critical Legal Studies and Constitutional Law," p. 629; C. Dalton, "An Essay in the Deconstruction of Contract Doctrine," *Yale Law Journal* 94 (1985), pp. 1007–1009.

9. R. M. Unger, *Knowledge and Politics* (New York: Free Press, 1975); *Law in Modern Society: Toward a Criticism of Social Theory* (New York: Free Press, 1976); D. Kennedy, "Form and Substance in Private Law Adjudication," *Harvard Law Review* 89 (1976), pp. 1685–1778; "The Structure of Blackstone's *Commentaries*," *Buffalo Law Review* 28 (1979), pp. 205–382; M. J. Horwitz, *The Transformation of American Law* (Cambridge: Harvard University Press, 1977); M. V. Tushnet, *The American Law of Slavery, 1810–1860* (Princeton: Princeton University Press, 1981).

10. A. D. Freeman, "Antidiscrimination Law: A Critical Review," in Kairys, ed., *The Politics of Law;* N. Taub and E. M. Schneider, "Perspectives on Women's Subordination and the Role of Law," in Kairys, ed., *The Politics of Law;* Tushnet, "Critical Legal Studies and Constitutional Law."

11. Mark Tushnet has argued that description, not normative argument, is "the heart of the Critical enterprise," which would indicate that the earlier descriptive phrase is more central than current constructive philosophical efforts (Tushnet, "Critical Legal Studies and Constitutional Law," p. 630). I contend here instead that CLS descriptive efforts only acquire their distinctive critical bite from normative commitments to a certain sort of understanding of freedom. For example, Tushnet ends the very essay in which he claims description is central to the CLS enterprise by dryly mocking the view that Marx's descriptions of capitalism do not imply condemnation of that system as unjust (pp. 646–647).

12. Unger, "The Critical Legal Studies Movement," pp. 619, 660, 669; *False Necessity*, pp. 452–453; Singer, "The Player and the Cards," pp. 14–15, 21–25.

13. Tushnet, "Critical Legal Studies and Constitutional Law"; Dalton, "An Essay in the Deconstruction of Contract Doctrine."

14. J. Derrida, *On Grammatology* (Baltimore: Johns Hopkins University Press, 1976).

15. Dalton, "An Essay in the Deconstruction of Contract Doctrine," p. 1008.

16. In "The Player and the Cards," pp. 13–14, Singer acknowledged that "traditional theorists" have seen some indeterminacy in law, but he never indicated just how much *more* indeterminate critical theorists think it is. I argue below that the real contrast is not on whether the law is indeterminate—the best writers in both groups believe the law gains tolerable determinacy from the broader structures of thought and belief in the political/legal culture—but over whether those broader structures are substantively defensible.

17. Unger, "The Critical Legal Studies Movement," pp. 570, 578–579; Singer, "The Player and the Cards," pp. 21–24; Dalton, "An Essay in the Deconstruc-

tion of Contract Doctrine," pp. 1009–1010, 1110. Because of the inconsistency and indeterminacy she sees in broader social structures and values, Clare Dalton argued for a relatively weak version of this claim, contending only that prevalent social notions of, for example, gender roles are "another source of influence" (Dalton, p. 1110).

18. K. E. Klare, "Critical Theory and Labor Relations Law," in Kairys, ed., *The Politics of Law*, p. 66; Unger, "The Critical Legal Studies Movement," p. 563; Singer, "The Player and the Cards," p. 6.
19. Freeman, "Antidiscrimination Law"; Tushnet, "Critical Legal Studies and Constitutional Law," pp. 636–646.
20. Unger, *False Necessity*, p. 345.
21. Gordon, "New Developments," p. 286.
22. Tushnet, *The American Law of Slavery*, p. 30.
23. Gordon, "Critical Legal Histories," p. 101.
24. Unger, "The Critical Legal Studies Movement," pp. 563, 614–615, 648, 664, 666; *False Necessity*, pp. 2–3, 551, 554–556.
25. Unger, "The Critical Legal Studies Movement," pp. 650, 664; *Social Theory*, pp. 101–113.
26. Unger, "The Critical Legal Studies Movement," pp. 660–662; *Passion*, pp. 22–23, 69; *Social Theory*, p. 12; *False Necessity*, pp. 9, 13–14.
27. B. Yack, *The Longing for Total Revolution* (Princeton: Princeton University Press, 1986), pp. 124, 365; Unger, *False Necessity*, pp. 518–519.
28. Yack, *The Longing for Total Revolution*, pp. 29–31, 366–367.
29. Unger, "The Critical Legal Studies Movement," pp. 667, 673.
30. Unger, *Social Theory*, pp. 2, 13; *False Necessity*, p. 39.
31. Kennedy, "The Structure of Blackstone's *Commentaries*," pp. 205, 211–212; P. Brest, "The Fundamental Rights Controversy: The Essential Contradictions of Normative Constitutional Scholarship," *Yale Law Journal* 90 (1981), p. 1108; Hutchinson and Monahan, "Law, Rights and the Critical Legal Scholars," p. 208; Gordon, "Critical Legal Histories," p. 114.
32. Unger, "The Critical Legal Studies Movement," pp. 623, 650; *Passion*, pp. 21, 135, 193, 211; *False Necessity*, pp. 9, 40, 351–352.
33. Unger, "The Critical Legal Studies Movement," pp. 584, 663, 665.
34. Ibid., pp. 584–585, 666; *Passion*, pp. 7, 21, 193, 211; *False Necessity*, p. 351.
35. Unger, "The Critical Legal Studies Movement," pp. 587, 662.
36. Ibid., pp. 660–662; *Passion*, pp. 9, 63, 73–75; *Social Theory*, pp. 12–13; *False Necessity*, pp. 11–14, 283, 347, 510.
37. Unger, "The Critical Legal Studies Movement," pp. 584, 592, 602, 662, 673; *Passion*, pp. 11, 193, 259–260, 311; *Social Theory*, pp. 1, 5–8, 45–48; *False Necessity*, pp. 32, 283, 348, 586–689.
38. W. Kaufmann, ed., *Basic Writings of Nietzsche* (New York: Vintage Books, 1968), pp. 201–204, 213–214, 220–221, 225, 554–555; F. Nietzsche, *The Will to Power* (New York: Vintage Books, 1968), pp. 148–150, 266–267, 274–276, 304–305.
39. Singer, "The Player and the Cards," pp. 53, 56.
40. R. Rorty, "Postmodernist Bourgeois Liberalism," *The Journal of Philosophy* 80 (1983), pp. 583–589; L. H. Carter, *Contemporary Constitutional Lawmaking* (Elmsford, N.Y.: Pergamon Press, 1985).

41. R. Dworkin, *Taking Rights Seriously* (Cambridge: Harvard University Press, 1977), pp. 279–290; *A Matter of Principle* (Cambridge: Harvard University Press, 1985), pp. 119–145.

42. P. Gabel, book review of R. Dworkin, *Taking Rights Seriously*, in *Harvard Law Review* 91 (1977), pp. 302–315; Mensch, "The History of Mainstream Legal Thought," pp. 18–19; Unger, "The Critical Legal Studies Movement," pp. 574–576.

43. Dworkin, *Taking Rights Seriously*, pp. 117, 123–128; *A Matter of Principle*, pp. 146, 164–166; *Law's Empire* (Cambridge: Harvard University Press, 1986), p. 163.

44. Dworkin, *A Matter of Principle*, pp. 144–145; Smith, *Liberalism*.

45. Unger, "The Critical Legal Studies Movement," pp. 565, 567, 571.

46. Unger, *Knowledge and Politics*, pp. 100–103; *Law in Modern Society*, pp. 166–181; "The Critical Legal Studies Movement," pp. 578–579.

47. Unger, "The Critical Legal Studies Movement," pp. 585, 587, 612–615, 648.

48. See Kennedy, "The Structure of Blackstone's *Commentaries*," p. 205; Tushnet, *The American Law of Slavery*, pp. 32–33, 236; Mensch, "The History of Mainstream Legal Thought," p. 19; Singer, "The Player and the Cards," pp. 37, 38, 41.

49. J. Dunn, *The Political Thought of John Locke* (Cambridge: Cambridge University Press, 1969), pp. 233–236, 253–255; Shapiro, *The Evolution of Rights*, pp. 137–139; R. Ashcraft, *Locke's Two Treatises of Government* (London: Allen and Unwin, 1987), pp. 251–259; N. Wood, *The Politics of Locke's Philosophy* (Berkeley: University of California Press, 1983), pp. 113–116.

50. Shapiro, *The Evolution of Rights*, pp. 302–304.

51. M. Sandel, *Liberalism and the Limits of Justice* (Cambridge: Cambridge University Press, 1982).

52. T. Adorno and M. Horkheimer, *Dialectic of Enlightenment* (London: Verso Press, 1979); Unger, *Knowledge and Politics; Law in Modern Society*.

53. Unger, *Law In Modern Society*, pp. 8–9; Mensch, "The History of Mainstream Legal Thought," pp. 22–23.

54. Horwitz, *The Transformation of American Law*.

55. Unger, "The Critical Legal Studies Movement," p. 664; *False Necessity*, p. 18; Gordon, "Critical Legal Histories," pp. 101–102.

56. Unger, *Passion*, pp. 63, 107; *False Necessity*, pp. 283, 462.

57. Unger, "The Critical Legal Studies Movement," pp. 666–667, 672; *False Necessity*, p. 253.

58. Unger, *False Necessity*, pp. 292–293, 588.

59. Unger, "The Critical Legal Studies Movement," p. 661.

60. Unger, *Passion*, pp. 68, 81, 87; *False Necessity*, p. 351. I am agnostic on the veracity of such descriptions and do not dismiss efforts to affirm their validity, but it seems only right to conclude that thus far the social origins of all known human standards are more firmly documented than their eternal character.

61. Smith, *Liberalism*, pp. 205–207; Unger, *False Necessity*, pp. 5, 595.

62. Smith, *Liberalism*, pp. 200–201.

63. Unger, *Passion*, pp. 188, 250, 288; *False Necessity*, pp. 293, 514–515.

64. Smith, *Liberalism*, p. 223.

65. Of course these general principles, while providing some normative guidance,

still leave many questions unanswered. For an initial effort to resolve some of those questions, including questions concerning what constitute "core freedoms," see Smith, *Liberalism*, pp. 213–259.

66. Unger, *Passion*, p. 265.
67. Unger, *Social Theory*, pp. 12–13.
68. D. Kennedy, with P. Gabel, "Roll Over Beethoven," *Stanford Law Review* 36 (1984), p. 15.
69. Kennedy, "The Structure of Blackstone's *Commentaries*," pp. 211–212.
70. Views of the self as diversely but inextricably socially situated acknowledge that at any particular time we must embrace some of the structures of thought and attachment that give purpose to our lives, even though we may later reconsider them from the vantage point of our other beliefs and memberships. We might well think it vitally important to engage in such periodic deliberation on our various contexts, especially those memberships and pursuits we have most persistently treated as central to us. But few will believe we can ever hope to bring all our formative contexts under our constant conscious control, and few are likely even to think that true freedom consists in approaching that state. Recognizing that there are no unqualifyingly felicitous, comprehensively empowering paths available to us and that all choices involve giving up some things to gain others, most persons will probably feel that they are best realizing their freedom when they commit themselves deeply to the ways of life that they have in times of reflection deemed most crucial to them, so long as they are confident that their commitments will not prevent them from periodically rethinking and revising as seems advisable.
71. These passages emphasize how distant Unger's view really is from an Aristotelian moral perspective, since they make it *improper* to seek to attain and preserve a "good character." See Aristotle, *Nichomachean Ethics*, book 2.
72. Unger, "The Critical Legal Studies Movement," p. 602; *Passion*, pp. 89, 98–99, 188; *Social Theory*, pp. 11, 29, 30; *False Necessity*, pp. 27, 36, 279, 348, 363.
73. Unger, "The Critical Legal Studies Movement," pp. 585, 651; *Passion*, pp. 36, 211; *False Necessity*, pp. 13, 364, 513, 524.
74. Unger, *Passion*, pp. 211, 259–260, 267; *Social Theory*, p. 46; *False Necessity*, pp. 449, 572.
75. Unger's biographical sketch in *Passion* indicates that he has "directed a governmental organization that assists homeless and needy children" in Brazil, a commendable endeavor that is consistent with the greater reliance on public institutions for child care that his program seems to imply.
76. Unger, *Passion*, p. 152.
77. On this point, J. Harvie Wilkinson III and G. Edward White cited anthropologist Margaret Mead, hardly a hidebound traditionalist: "There needs to be a place where children will know that they belong, where they have an unquestioned right to be, where there will always be responsible adults to welcome them and care for them. . . . So far in human history . . . societies have not found a way to rear children without the ties of parents to children or children to parents" (Wilkinson and White, "Constitutional Protection for Personal Lifestyles," *Cornell Law Review* 62 (1977), p. 623, n. 276).
78. Duncan Kennedy remains even more plainly in the modernist mode: He aspires only to achieve brief moments of felt insight and community, which he roguishly

described as experiences of "intersubjective zap." The reduction of the movement's radical social vision to the quest for such personal experiences comes perilously close to the "desperate self-concern" Unger rightly called "the most common perversion of cultural-revolutionary practice" (Unger, "The Critical Legal Studies Movement," pp. 661–662; Kennedy, "Roll Over Beethoven," p. 4).

79. Unger, "The Critical Legal Studies Movement," pp. 587, 651, 660–662; *Passion*, p. 265; *False Necessity*, pp. 279, 297, 364–365, 462; *Plasticity into Power: Comparative-Historical Studies on the Institutional Conditions of Economic and Military Success* (Cambridge: Cambridge University Press, 1987), p. 2.

80. Unger, "The Critical Legal Studies Movement," pp. 592–593, 614; *False Necessity*, pp. 449–461, 532–533.

81. Unger, *False Necessity*, pp. 453, 456–467.

82. Unger, "The Critical Legal Studies Movement," pp. 595–596.

83. Unger, *False Necessity*, pp. 491–500.

84. Unger, "The Critical Legal Studies Movement," pp. 399–600.

85. Ibid., p. 602.

86. Unger, *False Necessity*, pp. 522, 524, 526, 528–529, 532, 537–539.

87. Unger, "The Critical Legal Studies Movement," p. 602.

88. Raz, *The Morality of Freedom*, pp. 319–320, 418–424; Smith, *Liberalism*, pp. 214–215, 223–224; "The Irony of Liberal Citizenship in America," paper delivered at the Claremont Institute's Fourth Annual Bicentennial Conference, "What Constitution Have I? Freemen and Immigrants Under the New Order," February 13, 1987.

89. These periods are clear, if still partial, victories for rational liberty values because they provided, on balance, increased capacities for political and economic deliberative self-direction for the members of the American polity, taken as a whole. It is true that the aspirations of Loyalists, slave owners, some businessmen, and segregationists were thwarted by these developments, but their desires were for forms of life that unquestionably denied basic elements of rational self-direction to others (i.e., freedom from slavery, political representation, and economic subsistence). Hence, the frustration of these aspirations must be judged to further, not to violate, rational liberty goals.

90. Unger, *False Necessity*, p. 25.

91. Unger, "The Critical Legal Studies Movement," p. 671.

Part 2 ——————————— .
Separate Powers in the Modern State

One of the most important principles of constitutional theory from the original debates among the nation's founders and throughout the history of judicial review has been the commitment to a government of divided authority. The basic constitutional text itself outlines a national state divided into three separate branches (with a dual legislature), each with its own constituent sources of accountability and organizational autonomy but all connected by a complex distribution of shared responsibilities and overlapping claims to authority in the public policy-making process. From the beginning, this framework of checks and balances has been decidedly ambiguous in its contributions to democratic government. On the one hand, the overall design has aimed, and often served, to limit concentrations of state power that might threaten vested minority interests and rights. On the other hand, this division of authority has worked most often to impede the direct expression of popular majorities through the legislative branches while favoring unilateral action by more centralized executive authority. Thus, it is not surprising that Supreme Court exercise of judicial review in mediating interbranch disputes has played, for the most part, an important role in contributing to both patterns of institutional development.

The two chapters in this section explore judicial complicity in promoting the latter trend in particular. William Haltom focuses on two recent disputes between legislative and executive branches that significantly affect modern domestic policy making. Employing a rhetorical framework that clearly recalls Carter and Gilliom's aesthetic analysis, Haltom demonstrates that the formalistic modes of justification employed by a core faction on the Court have been inconsistent, misleading, and inadequate to resolve the disputes at stake. Haltom's analysis not only aims to demonstrate the logical deficiencies of poor judicial performances, however; he also contends that these recent constitutional constructions have both confounded and mystified the inability of the contemporary federal government to address the most fundamental challenges of economic (budgetary) and social (immigration) management. By contrast, David Gray Adler argues that the Supreme Court's role in mediating disputes over foreign policy making has been generally consistent and clear but that the policy implications of this pattern have been equally lamentable. Specifically, he demonstrates that decisions of the past fifty years have systematically authorized a kind of presidential power in foreign policy affairs that is inherently undemocratic in terms of both formal procedure and substantive content. He contends that such complicity in the rise of an imperial president not only defies the textual language and logic of early American constitutional thought, but more important, it thwarts the fundamental capacity for an effective government that serves the causes of international freedom and justice.

5 ——— ·
Separating Powers: Dialectical Sense and Positive Nonsense

WILLIAM HALTOM

> . . . We might note a distinction between positive and dialectical terms—
> the former being terms that do not require an opposite to define them, the
> latter being terms that do require an opposite. "Apple," for instance, is a
> positive term, in that we do not require, to understand it, the concept of a
> "counter-apple." But a term like "freedom" is dialectical, in that we cannot
> locate its meaning without reference to some concept of enslavement,
> confinement, or restriction. . . .
>   Our courts consider the Constitution in accordance with theories of
> positive law—yet actually the Constitution is a dialectical instrument; and
> one cannot properly interpret the course of judicial decisions unless he treats
> our "guaranties of Constitutional rights" not as positive terms but as
> dialectical ones.
>
> <div align="right">———<i>Kenneth Burke,</i>
Philosophy of Literary Form, <i>pp. 109–110</i></div>

Twentieth-century courts have interpreted the separation-of-powers doctrine
as a general, flexible design for countervailing interdependence among
branches of the U.S. government. They have rejected the utter heterogeneity
of legislative, executive, and judicial functions that judges of the previous
century purported to find in the Constitution. Recent applications of the
separation-of-powers doctrine, however, revive the myth of neatly cabined
powers. Consistent majorities on the Burger Court relied on positive readings of constitutional language, rejecting decades of more dialectical readings
that adapted the constitutional system to the responsibilities of the federal
government. I lament this recent yen to dodge difficult political and economic judgments through positive readings. In this chapter, I contend that
positive readings impoverish judicial justifications by denying or obscuring
the discretion that the justices possess.

Throughout this chapter, I assume an analytic distinction between "reading" and "interpreting" the Constitution. Judges read the Constitution by defining the meaning of its text; they interpret the Constitution by applying it to specific circumstances. I argue that a poor reading of the separation-of-powers concept has impaired interpretation of the Constitution in recent landmarks.[1] First, a positive reading induced the Court to interpretations so ad hoc that defenses of decisions only three years apart contradict one another. Second, that reading forced the justices to revive helpful fictions and expedient labeling to manage the complexities raised by the separation-of-powers issue in modern politics. My concern is not with the holdings in these cases but with the opinions with which the majorities defended their holdings. Because inadequate justifications shape subsequent legal reasoning as opinions age into doctrines, I will inventory the reasons why future majorities must correct the course of the Burger Court before an aberration settles into law.

POSITIVE AND DIALECTICAL READINGS

Along with Burke, I assume that there are two fundamentally different ways of reading any text: positive and dialectical. Positive readers regard the Constitution as a set of self-defined terms that require, at most, occasional supplementation from context. The concepts of the Constitution denote for positive readers intersubjective, uncontroversial criteria for judging governmental actions and arrangements.[2] But presuming that constitutional concepts are so clearly defined sacrifices some richness and flexibility in favor of order and predictability. Dialectical readers, in contrast, treat the Constitution as a set of evaluative terms that are so internally complex or persistently ambiguous that their application is subjective and often controversial.[3] The dialectical reader does not expect to derive from the Constitution determinations of issues but merely to identify the authoritative, substantive dimensions along which controversies rage for those who treat terms dialectically.[4]

The Constitution requires both positive and dialectical readings. Some passages virtually defy dialectical readings. Numbers need no opposites to define them, so minimal ages for national offices, for example, demand positive readings. These are rules that literalists can love, for no judgment is involved and decisions are quite predictable. Other passages, however, pivot on adjectives and adverbs that demand dialectical readings. One cannot declare that a law has been "faithfully" executed or that a state's government is indeed "republican" in form without examining a range of opposites and thus a range of dimensions. Some passages yield to both kinds of readings. The Fifth Amendment proscribes being "subject for the same offense to be twice put in jeopardy of life or limb." The Court has read the number positively[5] but has read the "life or limb" clause dialectically to denote nontrivial criminal cases.[6]

Thus, the Constitution cannot be simply positive or exclusively dialectical; it must be both. The Constitution serves as a positive guide when "settledness" outweighs substance, when less would be gained from flexibility than from determinacy. However, when conflicts cannot be resolved in advance or even anticipated in detail, when correct outcomes cannot be forecast but incorrect outcomes can, or when the process of conflict itself ennobles or legitimizes, the Constitution does not issue rules but channels conflicts along anticipated, consensual dimensions.

Because the Constitution may be read both positively and dialectically, readings tend to condition interpretations. Those who prefer positive readings presume that the text forces interpretations on the interpreters and invoke "the formal style" of reasoning in which the facts of cases are subsumed under headings supplied by settled, authoritative language.[7] By precluding interpretive options, positive readings aid interpreters in claiming that they exercise no discretion but simply effect the preordained judgments of the Constitution. Even formalistic positive readings needn't spoil the effect, because, arguably, absurd results are compelling evidence that interpreters used no discretion (or even common sense) but only followed the dictates of the Constitution.

In contrast, dialectical readers can hardly deny discretion because their reading of the text yields only authorized continua along which they must "place" the case. Dialectical interpretations involve multidimensional judgments whenever a terse, general constitution must be applied to complex circumstances.[8] Dialectical interpreters must justify the use of discretion by making sense of the Constitution in each case. That, in turn, requires them to adapt text and cases to one another, a burden that positive formalists spare themselves by pretending that the meaning of the text is unambiguous and uncontroversial.

In sum, positive and dialectical readings offer interpreters different choices; the jurisprudential choice is between formalism and candor in opinions. Positive readings mask discretion better than dialectical readings but only by denying the contestability of constitutional concepts and the craft of constitutional interpretation.[9] The values and objects that shaped the constitutional terms and still inform constitutional disputes disappear when positive readers mistake the terms of the Constitution for ends in themselves. Dialectical readers trumpet discretion and, in so doing, admit that interpretation often depends on subjective judgments. However, that very candor permits judges to acknowledge competing values and to balance them openly. The political choice is between mystification and responsibility. Positive readings yield simple rubrics that tempt jurists to reductionism. Interpretation reduced to labeling obscures the substantive consequences and empirical complexities of cases and perhaps protects the justices from criticism, but such approaches certainly deprive the polity of constitutional insight, argument, and dialogue worthy of major conflicts and problems. Dialectical readings provide no such haven. In assessing degrees of resemblance between specific conflicts and constitutional opposites, interpreters relying on dialectical readings must at least refer to complications and consequences. To put the matter conversely: Purposes underlying the text, difficulties in applying the text to cases, and the consequences of alternative interpretations all may inform dialectical readings but cannot inform positive readings.

SEPARATION OF POWERS

Elliptical references to the separation of powers in the U.S. Constitution and the malleability of the concept both as popular myth and term of legal art give interpreters opportunities to render it positively or dialectically. There are two levels at which questions arise: (1) Macrolevel questions concern the meaning of separation of powers as a structural design implicit in the Constitution; and (2) Microlevel questions concern the definitions of legislative, executive, and judicial powers as assigned in Articles I–III of the Constitution.

On the macrolevel, those who choose positive readings insist that separated powers are exclusive (no categories overlap) and exhaustive (no powers fall outside all three categories), lest interpretation be seen as embellishment of a text that is not self-defining. If separated powers did overlap, they could be assigned to the appropriate institutions and actors only by balancing that would require interpreters to have some leeway or discretion. Hence, positive readers must assume that powers are exclusive. If legitimate powers of the federal government elude classification in one of the three categories, then the text of the Constitution is insufficient and "gap filling" is necessary. Hence, a positive reading and the primacy of textual arguments that such readings assume can be sustained only if overlaps and gaps are wished away.

Assuming that powers are exclusive and exhaustive camouflages the substantive choices that the interpreters must make. Acknowledging gaps and overlaps at the macrolevel compels the dialectical interpreter to defend judgments about the degrees of interdependence that are acceptable. From the dialectical perspective, the separation of powers can be understood only through its opposite, the integration of powers.[10] In order to "locate" a case along the continuum between separation and integration, the interpreter must notice specific facts of the case, general facts of modern U.S. politics, and the myriad perspectives on separation of powers fostered by widely accepted modes of constitutional interpretation and argument.[11] A dialectical Court could not dwell above the fray but would have to admit that reading and interpretation require discretion and judgment that must be defended.

In the cases discussed below, I contend that the Burger Court denied political choices, obvious facts, and the actual workings of the modern state. Perhaps assuming exclusivity and exhaustiveness misled the justices into their holdings. Perhaps the justices reached their holdings first and grasped at exclusivity and exhaustiveness as the only means to ground their holdings in the Constitution. Either way, positive readings of the separation-of-powers doctrine at the macrolevel were associated with willful or accidental misrepresentations.[12]

On the microlevel matters are even simpler. Positive readers define "legislative," "executive," and "judicial" without reference to one another. As the Constitution provides no explicit definitions of these categories, their definitions demand dialectical thinking.[13] A power can be "judicial" only in contrast to the nonjudicial. For example, certain cases are deemed to involve "political questions" because the specific issues of the case or the general nature of the interests at stake are not suitable for judicial decision. Positive readers, who take each of the terms of jurisdiction to be unproblematic, incontestable, and self-defined, may merely announce holdings as if the application of the terms were obvious, but no sophisticated citizen would believe such nonsense. In the cases discussed below, majorities used tactical labeling of actors and powers to suit their holdings. Their ad hoc definitions of purportedly self-defining terms at the microlevel divorced the separation-of-powers doctrine from constitutional design and contemporary politics alike. This approach reduced the doctrine to the status of a senseless impediment to responsible, adaptive governance and, in my opinion, resulted in embarrassment to the Court as the majorities applied the terms inconsistently.

POSITIVE READINGS OF THE SEPARATION-OF-POWERS DOCTRINE

The simplicity of a positive rendering of the separation-of-powers doctrine allures the ingenuous and the disingenuous alike, but that may be its sole virtue. A positive reading runs afoul of the letter and spirit of the Constitution, the intentions of its framers, the general purpose behind the doctrine itself, twentieth-century precedents, and prudent adaptations of political arrangements; thus, political practices and statutory devices premised on the convergence of all of these modes of interpretation violate interpretations based on positive readings at both the macrolevel and the microlevel. The Court can profess—like Claude Rains in *Casablanca*—to be shocked to discover that violations are rampant, but the performance will be unpersuasive. Dialectical views, less useful for denying discretion, will usually be more persuasive, at least for relatively sophisticated audiences, because they are informed by the variety of legitimate sources of constitutional insight that positive readings ignore.[14] Indeed, review of those sources makes it clear that the routine mode of argument undermines the positive reading.

First, the Constitution unequivocally mixes governmental functions to force mutual interdependence and influence among branches and actors.[15] Such overlapping powers present no problems for dialectical readers, who depend on oppositions between powers to define the continuum on which one power blends into another. If, like positive readers, we take the separation of powers to be exclusive, the Constitution flagrantly violates the principle. Positive readers admit the exceptions that the text specifies but fail to see in the exceptions any overall design, purpose, or "spirit." Thus, a positive reading obscures the letter and spirit of the text and trades a coherent constitutional system for easy-to-follow directions that deny judicial responsibility for decisions.

Second, the intentions of the most famous proponents of separation foredoom the positive reading. At the macrolevel, Montesquieu argued against the union of two or more whole powers,[16] not against incidental overlaps and gaps among the powers. James Madison argued in *Federalist* 47 that total separation was unnecessary, and in 48, that a degree of mixing was necessary to make separation of powers practicable.[17] Both thinkers defended the separation of powers by specifying the opposite to be avoided—a dialectical writing that warrants dialectical reading. At the microlevel, in *Federalist* 37 Madison argued that the legislative, executive, and judicial powers were often impossible to differentiate. Thus, when positive readers insist that powers are well defined and heterogeneous, they are contradicting two major authors of the separation-of-powers doctrine in the Constitution.

Third, a positive reading also contradicts the "structure" of the separation-of-powers doctrine as presented in the Constitution. Positive readings treat the separation as an end, but it was designed as a means to prevent usurpations and to promote efficiency.[18] Formalistic reasoning and the positivistic assumption of utter heterogeneity of powers results in enforcing separation for the sake of separation, exacerbating democratic deadlock,[19] and encouraging growth of powers in that least defined of the three categories, the executive branch. By treating any overlap as a violation of principle, the Burger Court augmented executive powers, thereby threatening the tyranny that separation was designed to avoid.[20] Oddly enough, avoidance of the appearance of choice has thus led to unacknowledged, unjustified choices in fact.

Fourth, a positive reading flouts twentieth-century precedents. In order to retard the growth of national government, courts in the nineteenth century cast aside text, spirit, and framers' intent and reshaped the separation-of-powers doctrine into the very principle that Madison explicitly eschewed.[21] Judicial notice of the practical necessities of governance then drove courts away from this distortion of the doctrine. The proliferation of independent bureaucratic entities forced judges to acknowledge that powers could often be shared for greater efficiency.[22] Judicial validations of delegations of legislative authority made shared powers apparent and the positive view anachronistic. Many observers adopted the more dialectical rendering of "separated institutions sharing powers."[23] The view that powers were exclusive and exhaustive yielded to the view that powers overlapped and that some administrative powers were quasi-legislative, quasi-executive, and quasi-judicial. To disguise discretion, positive readers deny the evolution and current state of the U.S. government.

The text, spirit, and structure of the Constitution, the intentions of its framers, modern constitutional case law, and the realities of the administrative state all argue, then, for at least a modestly dialectical interpretation of the separation-of-powers doctrine. The Burger Court stoutly resisted a dialectical reading in favor of positive readings that yielded formalistic interpretations[24] contradicting the origins, purposes, and evolution of the principle of separation of powers.

I have shown the enervation of interpretation that positive readings of the separation-of-powers doctrine can be expected to work. Now I shall concentrate on the baneful effects of a positive reading on interpretation in recent practice. First, I will show that, at the macrolevel, the positive view led to dubious categorizations of facts in *Bowsher v. Synar*. I contend that separation of powers as conceived by the majority in that case could not accommodate the routine complexities of independent agents in the modern administrative state. Something had to give. The accuracy of the Court's description of the comptroller general and his duties under the law suffered, owing to the sclerotic interpretation of the separation-of-powers principle, brought on by a positive reading. Then I will show, at the microlevel, that the majority's insistence on exclusivity and exhaustiveness led them into incredible definitions of "legislative," "executive," and "judicial" in both *Bowsher* and in *Immigration and Naturalization Service v. Chadha* (hereinafter referred to as *INS v. Chadha*). Taken together, these two recent separation-of-powers cases reveal the distortions necessary to reshape the polity to suit constitutional terms whose adaptability has been sacrificed for an image of constitutional determinacy.

JUDICIAL SHIBBOLETH AT THE MACROLEVEL

The Burger Court invalidated Congress's preferred means for enforcing budgetary restraints in *Bowsher v. Synar*. The practical consequences of the Court's voiding of section 251 of the Balanced Budget and Emergency Deficit Control Act (1985)[25] (commonly called the Gramm-Rudman-Hollings Act and so called below) remain unclear, but the importance of budget deficits would seem to have demanded that the Court validate any but a clear violation of the Constitution.[26] Given the propensity of the other branches for electoral rationality and fiscal irresponsibility, the last thing the republic needed from the Court was more blame-avoidance. The budget problems at hand called for a sensible, prudent, impartial assessment of Gramm-Rudman-Hollings. Instead, Chief Justice Warren Burger's opinion for the Court created a violation of the separation-of-powers doctrine through a positive reading of the Constitution.[27] The opinion, a frantic response, characterized a perceived fiscal crisis as a dangerous accretion of power "in constitutional terms," neatly inverting admissions of congressional impotence that had sired the law.[28] In short, voodoo constitutionalism invalidated the elected branch's remedy for voodoo economics.

Bowsher v. Synar raised a novel problem. Section 251 of Gramm-Rudman-Hollings required the comptroller general to specify reductions in spending to meet deficit targets should Congress fail to approximate those targets. The comptroller general would compute reductions by reviewing the estimates of the Office of Management and Budget (OMB) and the Congressional Budget Office (CBO). The president would then order the comptroller general's reductions unless the Congress made cuts to eliminate the excess deficits. Representative Mike Synar and others challenged Section 251 as an unconstitutional assignment of executive functions to a legislative agent (the comptroller general, Chester Bowsher). The challenge prevailed in a three-judge district court, and Bowsher, the Senate, and the Speaker appealed to the U.S. Supreme Court.

Figure 5.1 depicts the major features of opinions in *Bowsher*.[29] Five justices agreed with the line of logic indicated by the arrows in the middle of the figure. First, they assumed that neither Congress nor agents under the "coercive influence" of Congress could execute laws.[30] Then they argued that the comptroller general was in fact under the coercive influence of Congress, while his responsibilities under Section 251 were clearly executive.[31] In sum, the majority fashioned a proscription out of the separation-of-powers doctrine, fitted Section 251 within the proscription, and then found it unconstitutional.

Closer inspection of Figure 5.1 reveals why Justice Byron White in dissent rejected this argument as "distressingly formalistic."[32] Burger assumed the uncontroversial proposition that Congress cannot execute its own laws, but in elaborating his meaning he slipped into the more problematic assumption that the separation-of-powers doctrine defines the powers of the federal government exclusively and exhaustively. Restating the majority's argument as a formal syllogism shows why Burger's assumptions were necessary:

1. The powers of the federal government are *exclusive* and *exhaustive*.
2. *Hence,* every agent must belong to one and only one of three branches.
3. Bowsher is not a member of the *judicial branch*.
4. Bowsher is subservient to the *legislative branch*.
5. A member of the *executive branch* cannot be subservient to the *legislature*.
6. *Thus,* Bowsher *must* belong to the *legislative branch*.

Although this syllogism may be formally adequate, its premises are seriously suspect, as an analysis of Burger's support for them will show.

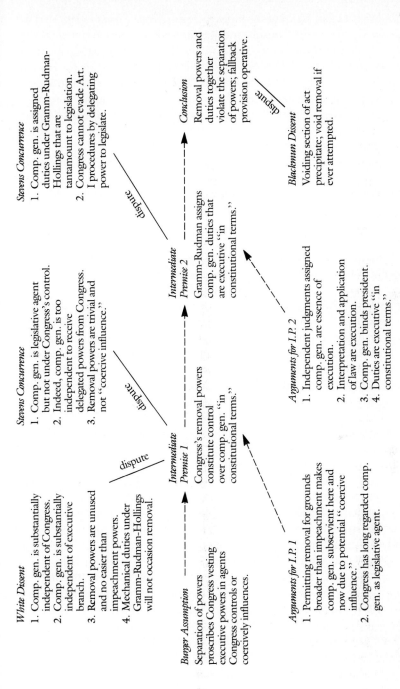

Figure 5.1
Bowsher v. Synar (1986)

Burger began by quoting himself from *INS v. Chadha* (1983): "We noted recently that '[t]he Constitution sought to divide the delegated powers of the new Federal Government into three defined categories, Legislative, Executive, and Judicial.'" This positive reading, a starting point for *Bowsher* and *Chadha* alike, is plainly mythological. The Constitution itself does not define the categories; it leaves their definitions to readers and interpreters.[33] Indeed, the absence of definitions seems itself to warrant a dialectical approach, as the three categories are defined only by their mutual opposition in the first three articles of the Constitution.

Burger supported his fictional account by misusing both Madison and Montesquieu in a single quotation, as one must do if one is to secure their putative agreement with reasoning that they themselves rejected. Although Madison did quote Montesquieu with approval in *Federalist* 47 ("there can be no liberty where the legislative and executive powers are united in the same person, or body of magistrates"), both thinkers clearly meant that *whole* powers ought not to be vested in any singularity. This quoted wisdom is hyperbolic in the context of *Bowsher,* and the proposition that Burger used it to advance is refuted by Madison himself in *Federalist* 47 and by the structure of checks and balances as presented in the Constitution.[34] Burger then rendered "checks and balances" to suit his version of separation of powers: "The Framers provided a vigorous legislative branch and a separate and wholly independent executive branch."[35] The legislature and the executive cannot be wholly independent of each other, even in theory, because complete independence would render one incapable of checking the other. Burger's list of instances of this independence actually illustrated the separation of institutions and the sharing of powers.[36]

This naive, reductionist account of separation of powers at the macro-level framed the majority opinion. If the separation-of-powers doctrine admits of intersections between legislative agents and executive duties, the majority would be compelled to show that Gramm-Rudman-Hollings had effected some more substantial union of legislation and execution in the comptroller general. Such a showing would be onerous and probably impossible. Even assuming utterly separated powers, the majority were singularly unpersuasive in arguing that the comptroller general was an agent under the direct control of Congress (see Intermediate Premise 1 in Figure 5.1).

Having declared that any congressional removal powers, beyond impeachment powers, constituted illicit control "in constitutional terms," Burger and the majority had only to show that it was possible for Congress to remove the comptroller general for reasons less restrictive than impeachment. Congress had never exercised this removal power nor even threatened to do so, but such a hypothetical threat constituted "here and now" subservience and created "coercive influence" in constitutional terms, according to the majority.

We must take the phrase "in constitutional terms" seriously, for it signals the majority's awareness that only through restricting discussion to a conceptual field under the justices' control could "coercion" be detected. In dissent, Justice White settled for ordinary descriptions of the comptroller general's roles, which place him at the periphery of the legislative branch. Justice White noted (1) that the comptroller general, despite his technical location in the legislative branch, had been substantially independent of the Congress for decades;[37] (2) that Congress had provided for theoretically more extensive removal powers to maintain the comptroller general's independence from the executive;[38] (3) that removal had never been threatened or used; and (4) that the essentially mechanical duties demanded by Gramm-Rudman-Hollings augured no occasion for the threat or use of removal. The chief justice's "bout" with Justice White illustrates how the majority opinion cast Bowsher as subservient to Congress by invoking "constitutional terms" even as White's dissenting opinion cast him as largely independent of the Congress by invoking commonplaces about the modern comptroller general.

In "Round 1," the chief justice claimed that the susceptibility of the comptroller general to removal at the initiative of Congress was the "crucial factor"[39] demonstrating his subservience. Burger reasoned that, because Congress could remove the comptroller general on grounds broader than the "high crimes and misdemeanors" required for ordinary impeachment, the comptroller general was not independent of Congress.[40] In dissent Justice White noted *degrees* of independence ignored by the majority. He showed that the comptroller was hardly at either pole of the "subservient/independent" continuum but was too independent of the will of Congress to be called an agent of the legislature.[41] As agents independent of all three branches often perform tasks akin to those performed by one or more branches, White believed that *Bowsher* necessitated only judicial notice of political actuality. He thus asserted as accepted fact what the majority could not conceive "in constitutional terms."

In their next round, Burger and White pondered directly this problem of realism versus "constitutional terms." The chief justice cited Congress's reasons for broadening removal under the Budget and Accounting Act of 1921—Congress wanted control without unwieldy impeachment. White parried this discussion of original intentions by noting that the process in practice prevented easy control of the comptroller by any branch (something not allowed if we assume exhaustiveness).

In "Round 3," White referred to sixty-five years of experience and to the highly technical duties assigned the comptroller general under Gramm-Rudman-Hollings to establish that removal has never been likely and would not be likely in the current case.[42] Burger eluded the historical record by once again invoking the field he preferred:

> The separated powers of our government cannot be permitted to turn on judicial assessment of whether an officer exercising executive power is on good terms with Congress. . . . *In constitutional terms,* the removal powers over the Comptroller General's office dictate that he will be subservient to Congress.[43]

The majority were unconcerned that removal was a hypothetical threat. They repeated that the comptroller general was subservient to Congress "in constitutional terms." The substitution of argot for argument could hardly be more blatant.

These clashes make clear the difference that the mode of reading can make. The experts agree that the comptroller general combines legislative, executive, and judicial attributes.[44] Although dialectical readers accept this as just one instance of the de facto mixing of powers in the modern administrative state, positive readers cannot. At the macrolevel, the opposite of separation of powers is the consolidation of powers in a single agent or agency. Gramm-Rudman-Hollings did not consolidate powers beyond the level already inherent in the office. Only a reading that demands that powers be exclusive and exhaustive could justify finding a violation of the separation-of-powers doctrine at the macrolevel. The majority's "constitutional terms" created an unnecessary, unpersuasive violation.

When courts justify themselves by denying what attentive citizens believe to be the case, they encourage suspicions that the Court operates in a formal universe uninformed by ordinary experience. In *Bowsher,* the Court cried wolf without a discernible or even foreseeable threat, imagining a threat that existed—that could exist—only "in constitutional terms." When "constitutional terms" are formal anachronisms, the cynical are not wholly wrong to call constitutional language the tool of judicial renegades free to manipulate maxims and symbols as they please.[45] The majority demeaned the judiciary even as they abetted the decline of congressional competence and enlarged the powers of the executive branch.

In sum, the positive reading used in *Bowsher* reduced a richly dialectical principle to a rigidly positive formula. The majority denied the doctrine's genesis and evolution for the sake of denying judicial discretion. They stripped the separation-of-powers doctrine of most of its content and all of its sense at the macrolevel. What remained was form without meaning. Contortion of the Constitution is not always necessary to exercise choices while denying their existence, however. Sometimes tactical tailoring of constitutional categories at the microlevel suffices.

TACTICAL CATEGORIZATIONS OF POWERS AT THE MICROLEVEL

Having caricatured the comptroller general as thrall to Congress, the *Bowsher* majority proclaimed the duties assigned him under Gramm-Rudman-Hollings as executive duties, completing their creation of a violation of the separation-of-powers doctrine. The absence of definitions of "legislative," "executive," and "judicial" in the Constitution eased the majority's task. The majority located the comptroller general in the legislative branch and his tasks under Gramm-Rudman-Hollings as an executive power. They created a constitutional conflict via convenient categorization. So superficial and ad hoc was this labeling in *Bowsher* that Justices John Paul Stevens and Byron White were able to contest it logically, effortlessly, and persuasively (see Figure 5.1). In *Chadha* the absence of standards and the facility of tactical categorization were even more obvious: Justices in that case assigned the "legislative veto" to three categories! In both cases, then, positive readings authorized unconvincing labeling as a substitute for judgment.

In *Bowsher,* Chief Justice Burger and Justice White agreed that the powers assigned the comptroller general were executive. The majority first noted that the comptroller general would exercise independent judgment in collating the estimates produced by the directors of the CBO and the OMB. "Interpreting a law enacted by Congress to implement the legislative mandate is the very essence of 'execution' of law."[46] The majority then supplemented this facile, overinclusive definition with a non sequitur:

> Under Section 251, the Comptroller General must exercise judgment concerning facts that affect the application of the Act. He must also interpret the provisions of the Act to determine precisely what budgetary calculations are required. Decisions of that kind are typically made by officers charged with executing a statute.[47]

Decisions of that kind are also made by justices of the Supreme Court who, to determine the constitutionality of the Gramm-Rudman-Hollings Act, must exercise judgment concerning facts (such as the nature of the calculations that the comptroller general must make). The majority opinion fails to differentiate between execution and adjudication before pronouncing Bowsher's duties "executive" in constitutional terms.

Having failed to separate the executive duties from the judicial ones, the majority compounded difficulties by confounding executive and legislative powers. The majority maintained that Gramm-Rudman-Hollings conferred executive powers because it gave Bowsher "the ultimate authority to determine the budget cuts to be made. Indeed, the Comptroller General commands the President himself to carry out, without the slightest variation, . . . the directive of the Comptroller General as to budget reductions."[48] Far from showing that the duties were executive, this reasoning supports Justices John P. Stevens and Thurgood Marshall in claiming that the duties conferred on Bowsher were legislative. The ultimate authority to determine budget cuts ("the power of the purse") is usually reckoned a congressional power. The ability to bind the president is surely more characteristic of the legislature than of the executive branch (which, after all, is supposed to answer to the president).

If Burger's definition of Bowsher's responsibilities under Gramm-Rudman-Hollings fails to convince, the fault is not entirely his. The executive branch is the residual category in the separation of powers, the least-defined class that seems to accumulate what does not fit neatly under legislative or judicial powers. Legislative and judicial powers have distinctive functions, rituals, and standards. The function of the legislature is to make laws. The Congress makes laws according to its own established practices, rules, and routines and in accordance with such constitutional standards as bicameral passage and presentation to the president. Courts judge cases (function) in keeping with procedures that judges and legislators have devised (rituals) and subject to Article III of the Constitution (standards). The executive branch, in contrast, fulfills a mélange of functions, follows routines far less institutionalized and far more idiosyncratic, and obeys constitutional standards even more ambiguous than those for Congress and the federal courts. Rigorous insistence on the exclusivity and exhaustiveness of the three powers incorporates a bias against the two relatively defined branches in favor of the least-defined branch, the executive. This bias is the nexus between macrolevel and microlevel questions concerning the separation of powers.

In his concurrence, Justice Stevens showed that the majority's microlevel confusions resulted from positive readings of the separation-of-powers doctrine at the macrolevel. He criticized Burger (and White) for relying on the utter heterogeneity of legislative and executive powers:[49]

> One reason that the exercise of legislative, executive, and judicial powers cannot be categorically distributed among three mutually exclusive branches of government is that governmental power cannot always be readily characterized with only one of those three labels. On the contrary, as our cases demonstrate, a particular function, like a chameleon, will often take on the aspect of the office to which it is assigned. For this reason, "[w]hen any Branch acts, it is presumptively exercising the power the Constitution has delegated to it."

Stevens further noted that in *Chadha* Justice Lewis Powell found that the legislative veto involved "judicial" decision making, the attorney general found deportation decisions inherently "executive," and the Court ruled the veto "legislative."[50] Having reminded readers of this unappealing disarray in doctrine, he then noted the *Bowsher* majority's obvious difficulty: If Section 251 of Gramm-Rudman-Hollings was invalidated, the "fallback" provisions therein would reassign the comptroller's duties to Congress. If the duties were executive, as Burger and White maintained, how could Congress fulfill them?

Having exposed the speciousness of assuming the exclusivity of powers, Stevens then showed that the exercise of legislative powers by agents independent of both Congress and the executive branch was common and had been accepted by courts.[51] Stevens thus attacked the majority's assumption of the exhaustiveness of the three powers specified in the Constitution:[52]

> Thus, I do not agree that the Comptroller General's responsibilities under the Gramm-Rudman-Hollings Act must be termed "executive powers," or even that our inquiry is much advanced by using that

term. For, whatever the label given the functions to be performed by the Comptroller General . . . or by the Congress . . . the District Court had no difficulty in concluding that Congress could delegate the performance of those functions to another branch of the Government. If the delegation to a stranger is permissible, why may not Congress delegate the same responsibilities to one of its own agents?

In just a few pages, then, Stevens unraveled the logic of the majority and exposed the inadequacies of the exclusivity and exhaustiveness principles in answering macrolevel questions. Stevens and Marshall concurred in the decision only because they believed that Congress had allowed the comptroller general to legislate without procedures mandated by Article I of the Constitution. In effect, they saw in *Bowsher* a reprise of *INS v. Chadha.*

In *INS v. Chadha*, the Court had to decide whether the House of Representatives could constitutionally disapprove a suspension of deportation. Jagdish Rai Chadha had overstayed his visa and sought to suspend his deportation on grounds specified by the Immigration and Nationality Act.[53] In accordance with the ruling of an INS immigration judge, the attorney general suspended Chadha's deportation. The House of Representatives disapproved the suspensions of Chadha and others, exercising that "legislative veto" that Congress had reserved to either house in passing the act.[54] Chadha challenged the constitutionality of this legislative veto, and the Supreme Court overlooked ample opportunities to decline to decide the case.[55] The Court upheld Chadha's challenge and soon issued summary decisions that invalidated other legislative vetoes,[56] threatened hundreds of legal provisions, deprived Congress of a very useful tool that it had used for half a century, and shifted even more powers from Congress to the executive branch.

Figure 5.2 displays the major features of the opinions in *Chadha*. As Stevens would note in *Bowsher,* a crux of *Chadha* was the "nature" of the House's veto of the attorney general's decision. Chief Justice Burger pronounced the one-house veto "legislative." Justice Powell (and the administrative law judge who had heard the case earlier) labeled it "judicial." Justice White thought it most closely resembled the "quasi-legislative" discretion that executive or independent bureaucrats typically exercised. I focus on this confusion in the *Chadha* case as a key example of the difficulties to which positive interpretation led at the microlevel, notwithstanding the "clarity" that Burger claimed to characterize the separation of powers and the definitions of each of the powers.[57]

In *Chadha* Chief Justice Burger asserted that legislative powers were constitutionally defined and functionally identifiable.[58] The legislative veto was a legislative act because it was "essentially legislative" in purpose and effect.[59] The House's veto, Burger maintained, had the purpose and effect of "altering the legal rights, duties, and relations of persons, including the Attorney General, Executive Branch officials and Chadha, all outside the legislative branch."[60] The one-house veto was also legislative in effect because it

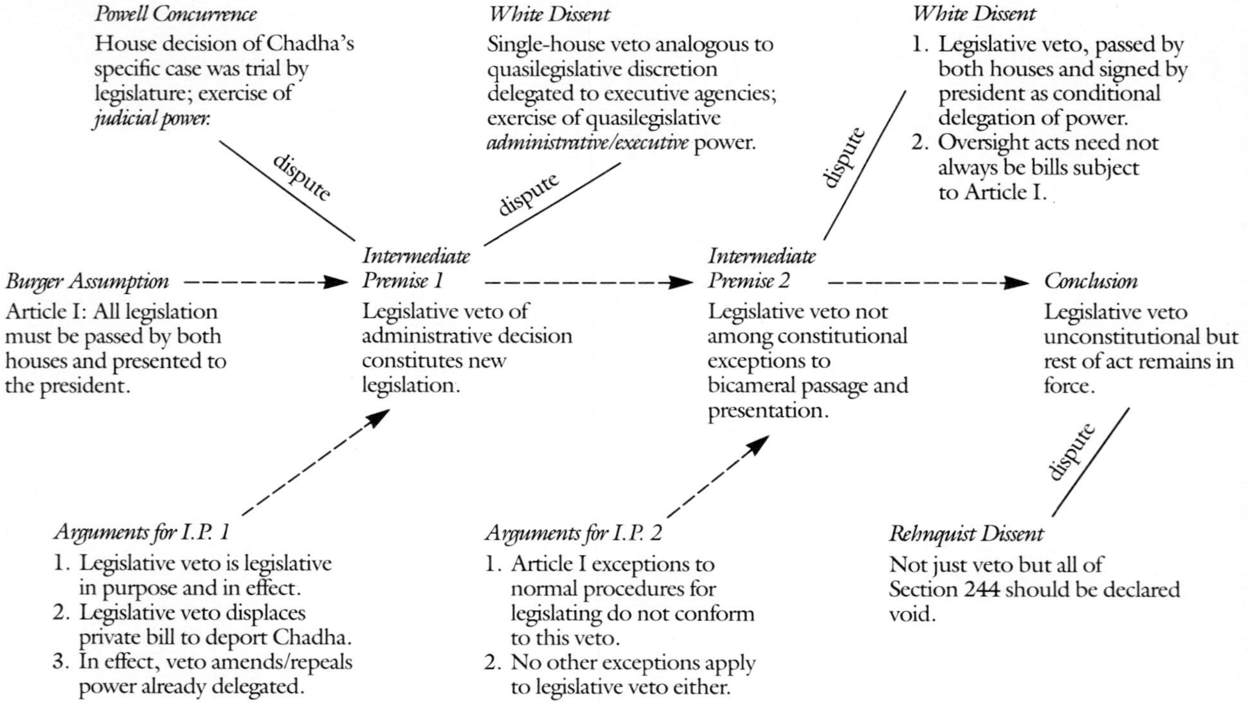
Powell Concurrence
House decision of Chadha's specific case was trial by legislature; exercise of *judicial power.*
dispute
White Dissent
Single-house veto analogous to quasilegislative discretion delegated to executive agencies; exercise of quasilegislative *administrative/executive* power.
dispute
White Dissent
1. Legislative veto, passed by both houses and signed by president as conditional delegation of power.
2. Oversight acts need not always be bills subject to Article I.
dispute
Burger Assumption
Article I: All legislation must be passed by both houses and presented to the president.
Intermediate Premise 1
Legislative veto of administrative decision constitutes new legislation.
Intermediate Premise 2
Legislative veto not among constitutional exceptions to bicameral passage and presentation.
Conclusion
Legislative veto unconstitutional but rest of act remains in force.
dispute
Arguments for I.P. 1
1. Legislative veto is legislative in purpose and in effect.
2. Legislative veto displaces private bill to deport Chadha.
3. In effect, veto amends/repeals power already delegated.
Arguments for I.P. 2
1. Article I exceptions to normal procedures for legislating do not conform to this veto.
2. No other exceptions apply to legislative veto either.
Rehnquist Dissent
Not just veto but all of Section 244 should be declared void.

Figure 5.2
INS v. Chadha (1983)

supplanted a private bill ordering deportation and amended the original delegation of power to the attorney general.[61] We see here a classic exercise of a positive reading at the microlevel—the majority defined "the legislative" without reference to other powers.

Indeed, had the other powers entered the majority's thinking they might have noticed that their rendering of "legislative" hardly excluded ordinary actions by executives and judges.[62] All kinds of authority may alter legal rights, duties, and relations, supplant legislation otherwise necessary, and amend previous laws and delegations. It is difficult to imagine an exercise of power or authority that might not accomplish each of the purposes or effects adduced by Burger as the essence of legislative action. More embarrassing, by the definitions that Burger forwarded in *Chadha,* Bowsher's tasks under Gramm-Rudman-Hollings must be classified as "essentially legislative" rather than executive, exactly the opposite of Burger's reasoning in the latter case.

Such arbitrary labeling typifies problems that positive readings of constitutional language occasion. At the microlevel the problem is obvious. If the justices cannot even agree among themselves which category a specific act fits into, then the categories must be essentially contested to some degree. All of this contradicts the positive assumption that terms are self-defining. Even if the microlevel problem were addressed, a macrolevel problem would persist. The most obvious conclusion from the justices' disagreements would be that the powers must overlap to some degree. Thus, Burger, Powell, and White are not wrong to see that the legislative veto is legislation, adjudication, or administration, respectively. It is all three to some degree. They simply disagree about the relative "placement" of the legislative veto. From this perspective, the justices' disagreement makes sense. Unfortunately, we can make sense of the dilemma only by acknowledging that the three powers are not exclusive. To see how cognizance of two different overlaps led Justices Powell and White away from the nonsense of the majority, we will examine their views in *Chadha* more closely.

Justice Powell's concurring opinion showed that the majority's criteria failed to differentiate legislative from judicial acts. Powell invoked neither the majority's mythological version of separation of powers (macrolevel) nor their ad hoc usage of "legislative" (microlevel). He noted instead that the founders had "vested the executive, legislative, and judicial powers in separate branches"[63] but avoided the assumption of exclusivity. He claimed that the imprecise boundaries between the separated branches could be discerned through common sense and prudence. According to Powell, the Court ought to invalidate violations of the separation-of-powers doctrine only when one branch clearly exercises powers "central to another branch."[64] Powell then concluded that the House had in fact decided Chadha's fate as if it were a court and that the legislative veto in this case usurped a core function of the judicial branch.[65] Powell's "core/periphery" analysis deserves careful scrutiny, for it shows the advantages of a dialectical reading of the separation-of-powers doctrine.

Powell categorized the legislative veto by admitting that it fell into an overlap between legislative and judicial powers. He then ventured that the action was only modestly legislative but centrally judicial. This balancing reflects a dialectical view of the separated powers. Having rejected the heterogeneity of powers, Powell candidly admitted that the legislative must be balanced against the judicial to determine where between those two the legislative veto in Chadha's case lay.

Powell displayed a dialectical understanding of the separation-of-powers doctrine on the macrolevel as well. Allowing that the majority's definition of legislative essence might be useful, Powell noted that "reasonable minds may disagree over the character of an act, and the more helpful inquiry, in my view, is whether the act in question raises the dangers the Framers sought to avoid."[66] That is, Powell understood the separation of powers on the macrolevel not as some ideal, or as an impracticable heterogeneity of powers and branches, but rather as a negation of that consolidation of core functions that Montesquieu, Madison, and others had dreaded.[67] He defined separation of powers by differentiating it from its opposite, the integration of powers.

Powell's concurrence connected specific legal issues to the facts of Chadha's case, existing practices in U.S. politics, and actual rights and powers at stake. At the microlevel, Powell made a very traditional and dialectical distinction between legislatures and courts: Legislatures propound general, prospective rules that courts apply to specific cases.[68] On the basis of that distinction, he found this specific legislative veto to be more judicial than legislative. Moving to the macrolevel, he showed how legislative adjudication generated exactly the evils against which the framers had erected the checks and balances:[69]

> In deciding whether Chadha deserves to be deported, Congress is not subject to any internal constraints that prevent it from arbitrarily depriving him of the right to remain in this country. Unlike the judiciary or an administrative agency, Congress is not bound by established substantive rules. Nor is it subject to the procedural safeguards . . . present when a court or an agency adjudicates individual rights. The only effective constraint on Congress' power is political, but Congress is most accountable politically when it prescribes rules of general applicability. When it decides rights of specific persons, those rights are subject to "the tyranny of a shifting majority."

Powell's dialectical approach compelled him to weigh the substantive issues at stake in order to differentiate judicial from legislative or executive functions. His characterization of political theory and practice is not the only conclusion a justice might reach, but at least he strove to accommodate his "constitutional terms" to actualities.

In contrast to Powell's discussion of the legislative-judicial overlap, Justice White in dissent focused on the legislative-executive overlap. In terms of the macrolevel, Powell denied exclusivity, while White denied exhaustiveness. White recounted judicial validation of delegations of authority to executive agents, independent regulators, and even private citizens.[70] Such legislative powers could be exercised by independent agents or executive agencies but not by Congress?[71] White was pointing to a flaw in the majority's opinion. In the absence of the legislative veto, the attorney general would decide Chadha's fate. The majority denied Congress "legislative" powers that would now repose in a member of the executive branch. That result would seem to violate the exclusivity on which the majority depended. White defined the House's veto not as a legislative act but as oversight of the execution of the original act ensuring "faithful" execution.[72] The legislative veto operated in this case, White concluded, as "a necessary check on the unavoidably expanding power of the agencies . . . in exercising authority delegated by Congress."[73] In White's view the legislative veto was neither an essentially legislative action nor an essentially judicial one. It could hardly be called executive action simpliciter. Instead, White conceived of the legislative veto as oversight of the administrative state and as a function largely outside of those core functions separated by the Constitution. He challenged the majority's proposition that the three defined powers exhausted the possibilities for the federal government in the twentieth century and opined that burgeoning bureaucracy threatened freedoms more than an allegedly imperious Congress.

This discussion of microlevel problems in both *Bowsher* and *Chadha* reiterates an obvious point: "Legislative," "executive," and "judicial" are not self-defining or unambiguous. The less obvious point here is that a positive reading of the separation-of-powers doctrine requires what we know to be impossible—a comprehensive trichotomy of discrete powers of federal government. Because Burger and his majorities in both opinions were prepared to assume exclusivity and exhaustiveness, they were compelled to assert that every actor and act can reliably be classified under one and only one constitutional rubric. Abandoning the nonsensical assertion of exclusivity, Powell could candidly and plausibly balance the judicial and the legislative roles in *Chadha*. White balanced the administrative and the legislative roles in *Chadha* because he abandoned the assertion of exhaustiveness, just as Stevens and Marshall could candidly classify the comptroller general and his tasks under Gramm-Rudman-Hollings in *Bowsher* because they refused to treat the three categories as the only possibilities.

CONCLUSIONS

If the solvency of the nation and the efficiency of its government were uninvolved, the disarray that *Bowsher* and *Chadha* signal might simply amuse us, like a magic show. The material validity of premises in judicial opinions has often been doubtful, but the tactics in these two opinions must stun and amaze those audiences who discover the Court's rationale. First, there is the sleight of hand. In *Bowsher* the majority declared the comptroller general to be a servant of Congress, overlooking the actual history and present status of the office and the demeanor of its current holder and focusing instead on congressional intent in 1921 and the hypothetical possibility of removal. It is difficult to ignore the historical and actual role of the comptroller general in favor of what was envisioned and what might someday be. After a wave of the majority's hands and chants of "constitutional terms," however, the actual vanished and the imaginary became real. For its next trick, the Court wheeled out its "Incredible Constitutional Boxes." Disciples of Procrustes rushed about the judicial stage dicing and splicing political phenomena to make them fit into different categories. This dangerous trick is not for ordinary students of the Constitution, for the elasticity of constitutional concepts necessary for the tricks to succeed threatens to render "constitutional reasoning" an oxymoron. The majority fit the comptroller general into the legislative box. Justices Stevens, Marshall, and White made Bowsher appear in the independent box that the majority had wished away. Then the majority, this time joined by Justice White, forced the comptroller general's tasks into the executive box. Stevens and Marshall pulled the same tasks out of the legislative box. Three years previously, this same team of magicians had pulled off even more dizzying feats. The majority showed that the one-house veto precisely fit the essentially legislative box, but when Justice Powell balanced the legislative and judicial boxes, a legislative veto reappeared in the judicial box. Concentrating on all three constitutional boxes, Justice White pronounced the incantation "quasi-legislative executive decision-making" and levitated the legislative veto above all three boxes.

This prestidigitation cannot amuse students and critics of the Court. When constitutional arguments are indistinguishable from parlor tricks, illusions become an important part of the medium of constitutional discourse. What was once deliberate and tactical can become unconscious and unavoidable if the justices' assumptions and premises are accepted uncritically. That is why I reprove the Burger majorities for their justifications rather than their holdings. Moreover, audiences duped by cleverness are unlikely to experience any constitutional elevation of mind or heart. Rather, the justices through misdirection confirm the suspicions of cynics that constitutional arguments are tricks played on the unwary.

Beyond encouraging cynicism, the Court has encouraged accumulation of power in the executive branch. I have shown that the macrolevel and microlevels of separation of powers are connected. I argued that an insistence that the powers are separated exclusively and exhaustively (the macrolevel) makes the executive category a catchall, because the legislative and judicial powers are relatively well defined (the microlevel). The very vagueness of the executive category, then, makes it relatively flexible when a positive reading and formalism deprive the legislative and judicial categories of elasticity. Voiding the legislative veto and upsetting Gramm-Rudman-Hollings may not threaten the republic seriously for long. The vitiation of legislative and judicial powers and expansion of executive power, however, may be far more ominous.

These difficulties are even more tragic because the Burger opinions fail in the only conceivable mission we can identify for them—denial of the discretion that the justices, and every other educated American, know they have. Justices of the Supreme Court of the United States are supposed to be masters of the art of fitting rules to cases in satisfying ways. When the Constitution, precedent, and logic do not discipline perception, when legal categories do not channel cognition, the discretion available to judges is too evident for mechanical jurisprudence to work. What makes *Bowsher* and *Chadha* not comic but tragic is that the majorities in both cases appear to have tried to fend off the ubiquitous specter of judicial discretion. In their headlong flight from obvious discretion, they have made their discretion obvious.

We can only speculate why the majorities chose such weak justifications. First, we suspect expediency behind the purple curtain: Current practices and rules have so diverged from the civics textbook verities and invite so many complex constitutional judgments that formalistic simplifications offer the justices respite from excruciating choices and arguments. Positive readings and formalistic reasoning, as I have shown, are not very persuasive, but they do allow for ad hoc labeling that does not commit the Court to a long-term doctrine. Second, I agree with Professor Jesse H. Choper that the Court is least adept at direct battle with coordinate branches.[74] Well might a cautious Court protect itself in separation issues through formalism and apparent literalism.

A majority of the Burger Court have insisted that the separation-of-powers doctrine be read as exclusive and exhaustive. This insistence, as I have shown, is not grounded in the text of the Constitution, in the intentions of its framers, in the evolution of case law and doctrine, or in the modern administrative state but can be explained in terms of its utility for denying discretion. Such self-defense may be understandable, but it is not clearly necessary and is clearly disingenuous at best. This chapter showed why the Court must become confused and the law disheveled if interpreters persist in reading the separation-of-powers doctrine formalistically. The positive rendering of the doctrine abandons established modes of constitutional interpretation for a civics textbook world of neatly compartmentalized powers. Such a world exists only in very basic textbooks. In the world of adults, the positive, formalistic view is intellectually dishonest, jurisprudentially self-defeating, politically disruptive, and philosophically nonsensical.

NOTES

1. The landmarks are *INS v. Chadha,* 103 S. Ct. 2784 (1983) and *Bowsher v. Synar,* 92 L. Ed. 2d 583 (1986). Five justices endorsed or failed to oppose positive readings in both cases. Chief Justice Warren Burger wrote the opinions of the Court in *Bowsher* and *Chadha.* Justices William Brennan and Sandra Day O'Connor joined both majority opinions. Justice Harry Blackmun dissented from *Bowsher* because he believed that Section 251 need not be declared unconstitutional, but he did not disagree with the positive readings of the separation-of-powers doctrine in either case. Justice William Rehnquist dissented from the severability of the legislative veto from the rest of the act in *Chadha* but did not dispute the positive readings of the majority in either case. Justice Lewis Powell concurred in *Chadha* and joined the majority opinion in *Bowsher.* Justices John P. Stevens and Thurgood Marshall endorsed the majority opinion in *Chadha* but offered concurring analysis based on a more dialectical reading in *Bowsher.* Only Justice Byron White avoided the positive reading in both cases. Since Justice Antonin Scalia pioneered much of Burger's analysis in deciding *Bowsher* in the D.C. Circuit Court of Appeals, and Justice Anthony Kennedy did the same in deciding *Chadha* in the Ninth Circuit Court of Appeals, we expect the Rehnquist Court to track the positive reading and formalistic interpretation characteristic of the Burger majorities.
2. For example, Justice Hugo Black read the Constitution in an unabashedly positive manner much of the time. See Mark Silverstein, *Constitutional Faiths* (Cornell University Press, 1984), Chapter 3; Philip Bobbitt, *Constitutional Fate* (New York: Oxford University Press, 1982), pp. 26–36.
3. W. B. Gallie, "Essentially Contested Concepts," in Max Black, ed., *The Importance of Language* (Englewood Cliffs: Prentice-Hall, 1962), pp. 120–146. Burke notes that the dialectical reader defines terms by their opposites, but constitutional terms need not be merely unidimensional so multiple opposites may be necessary to specify the continua presumed by terms. (See also note 10.)
4. See William E. Connolly, *The Terms of Political Discourse* (Lexington, Mass.: D. C. Heath, 1974), Chapter 1.
5. *Benton v. Maryland,* 395 U.S. 784 (1969).
6. *Benton v. Maryland* and *Robinson v. Neil,* 489 U.S. 505 (1973).
7. On the "formal style" see Karl Llewellyn, *The Common Law Tradition* (Boston: Little, Brown, 1960), pp. 38–40; Vernon K. Dibble, "What Is and What Ought to Be: A Comparison of Certain Characteristics of the Ideological and Legal Styles of Thought," *American Journal of Sociology* 79, no. 3 (November 1973), pp. 511–549; Roberto Mangabeira Unger, *Law in Modern Society* (New York: The Free Press, 1976), p. 194; Frank I. Michelman, "Foreword: Traces of Self-Government," *Harvard Law Review* 100, no. 1 (November 1986), p. 8, n. 20.
8. For example, "due process" never remains a positive, procedural term for long but recurrently assumes more dialectical usages that account for the multiplex relations among individuals with rights and governments with powers. In using "due process," candid interpreters admit to discretion, for virtually every law will survive merely procedural readings of the due process clause.
9. Indeed, Cardozo excluded such purely mechanical reasoning from "serious busi-

ness" of the judge! See Benjamin N. Cardozo, *The Nature of the Judicial Process* (New Haven: Yale University Press, 1921), p. 21.

10. I speak of a single continuum here only for convenience. I do not assume that separation of powers is so simple that only one opposite is necessary to define it. Indeed, I assume throughout this chapter that at least two dimensions are necessary at both macro- and microlevels. At the macrolevel, the continua can be defined by the relative exclusivity and exhaustiveness of powers. At the microlevel, a trilateral opposition among legislative, executive, and judicial powers that cannot conveniently be conceived in a single dimension can be assumed.

11. On modes of constitutional interpretation and argument, see Bobbitt, *Constitutional Fate*, Book 1; Craig R. Ducat, *Modes of Constitutional Interpretation* (St. Paul, Minn.: West Publishing Co., 1978); William F. Harris II, "Bonding Word and Polity: The Logic of American Constitutionalism," *American Political Science Review* 76, no. 1 (March 1982), pp. 34–45; and Richard H. Fallon II, "A Constructivist Coherence Theory of Constitutional Interpretation," *Harvard Law Review* 100, no. 6 (April 1987) pp. 1189–1286.

12. See E. Donald Elliot, "INS v. Chadha: The Administrative Constitution, The Constitution, and the Legislative Veto," in Philip B. Kurland, Gerhard Casper, and Dennis J. Hutchinson, eds., *Supreme Court Review 1983* (Chicago: University of Chicago Press, 1984), pp. 126, 138–139, 145.

13. "Experience has instructed us that no skill in the science of government has yet been able to discriminate and define, with sufficient certainty, its three great provinces—the legislative, executive, and judiciary; or even the privileges and powers of the different legislative branches. Questions daily occur in the course of practice which prove the obscurity which reigns in these subjects, and which puzzle the greatest adepts in political science." James Madison, *Federalist* 37 (New York: New American Library, 1961), p. 228.

14. I assume that interpretations that demonstrate a coherence of all or most accepted means of interpreting the Constitution are more persuasive to most audiences than interpretations that flout such a coherence. See Fallon, "A Constructivist Coherence Theory."

15. On this point see Forrest McDonald, *Novus Ordo Seclorum* (Lawrence: University Press of Kansas, 1985), p. 258.

16. The classic expression of these views is Madison, *Federalist* 47, pp. 302–303. See also Arthur T. Vanderbilt, *The Doctrine of Separation of Powers and Its Present-Day Significance* (Lincoln: University of Nebraska Press, 1953), p. 45. For a misstatement of these ideas that supports a positive reading, see Chief Justice Burger's opinion in *Bowsher v. Synar*, at 593.

17. "(U)nless these departments be so far connected and blended as to give each a constitutional control over the others, the degree of separation which the maxim requires, as essential to a free government, can never in practice be duly maintained." Madison, *Federalist* 48, p. 308.

18. L. Peter Schultz, "The Separation of Powers and Foreign Affairs," in Robert A. Goldwin and Art Kaufman, eds., *Separation of Powers—Does It Still Work?* pp. 121–127; Ann Stuart Anderson, "A 1787 Perspective on Separation of Powers," in Goldwin and Kaufman, eds., *Separation of Powers*, pp. 143–151; and Cass R. Sunstein, "Constitutionalism After the New Deal," *Harvard Law Review* 101,

no. 2 (December 1987), p. 432. To cite these two ends to which separation of powers was means is not, of course, to claim that such ends definitively settle matters. The usurpations thwarted by separation could be legislative predations on other branches or liberties (the admitted motive for separation) and/or the exercise of majority rule contrary to the interests of the propertied (a possible ulterior motive for separation). See Charles A. Beard, *An Economic Interpretation of the Constitution of the United States* (New York: Free Press, 1935), pp. 154–161. In like manner the efficiency end could be used by both sides in the conflict over the legislative veto. See Barbara Hinkson Craig, *Chadha: The Story of an Epic Constitutional Struggle* (New York: Oxford University Press, 1988), pp. 58–66.

19. James MacGregor Burns, *The Deadlock of Democracy* (Englewood Cliffs, N.J.: Prentice-Hall, 1963).

20. Indeed, congressional reliance on legislative vetoes was premised on the felt need to redress accumulation of powers in the executive. See Craig, *Chadha*, pp. 39–50.

21. The Court denied what must impress any reader of the Constitution when it declared that the document "blocked out with singular precision, and in bold lines, in its three primary Articles, the allotment of power to the executive, the legislative, and judicial departments of the government." *Kilbourn v. Thompson*, 26 L. Ed. 377 (1881) at 387. Separation of powers is hardly expressed precisely or boldly. Even Chief Justice Burger, in *Bowsher* and *Chadha*, settled for calling the categories "defined," *INS v. Chadha*, 46 U.S. 919 (1983) at 951, although he could support that claim only by relaxing the normal standards of definition. See similar formalistic stratagems in *Kendall v. U.S.*, 37 P.U. 54 (1838) at 610, and *Mississippi v. Johnson*, 4 Wall 475 (1866) at 500–501.

22. For example, in *Humphrey's Executor v. U.S.*, 295 U.S. 602 (1935), the Court escaped its own analyses in *U.S. v. Myers*, 272 U.S. 52 (1927), and *Springer v. Philippine Islands*, 277 U.S. 189 (1928), by declaring that Federal Trade Commissioners exercised "quasi-legislative" yet "quasi-judicial" powers. This signaled the limits of treating the separated powers as mutually exclusive and exhaustive.

23. Richard E. Neustadt, *Presidential Power* (New York: John Wiley & Sons, 1976), p. 101. This formulation is dialectical because it admits that the powers that branches exercise are nonexclusive although the branches are exclusive. Once the separation-of-powers doctrine is so conceived, interpreters must "triangulate" among the branches by differentiating among opposites by degrees. In the positive view, the legislative, executive, and judicial powers meet only at a border that is walled and patrolled to keep the branches separated. The dialectical approach views the meeting of powers as a gradation, more a shoreline than a wall.

24. See "Leading Cases," *Harvard Law Review* 100, no. 1 (November 1986), p. 221; Laurence Tribe, *Constitutional Choices* (Cambridge: Harvard University Press, 1985), pp. 66–83; Elliot, "INS v. Chadha," pp. 144–145; Sunstein, "Constitutionalism," pp. 493–494.

25. Budget and Emergency Deficit Control Act, 2 USCS Sections 901 et seq. (1985).

26. On the causes and significance of budgetary politics, see Joel Krieger, *Reagan, Thatcher and the Politics of Decline* (New York: Oxford University Press, 1986);

David Stockman, *The Triumph of Politics* (New York: Avon, 1986); William Greider, *The Education of David Stockman* (New York: Dutton, 1982).

27. *Bowsher v. Synar,* at 610–611.

28. On the inability of Congress to discipline its own spending, see David R. Mayhew, *Congress: The Electoral Connection* (New Haven: Yale University Press, 1974); Morris P. Fiorina, *Congress: Keystone of the Washington Establishment* (New Haven: Yale University Press, 1977).

29. We portray opinions along the lines of the "layout" of arguments pioneered by Stephen Toulmin in *The Uses of Argument* (Cambridge: Cambridge University Press, 1958), Chapter 3. We use neither Toulmin's labels nor all of his features.

30. *Bowsher v. Synar,* at 594–597.

31. Ibid., at 597–601.

32. Ibid., at 617.

33. See the very first sentences of Articles I, II, and III of the U.S. Constitution.

34. In *Federalist* 47 (pp. 302–303), Madison presumed that overlaps between powers presented no problem: "From these facts, by which Montesquieu was guided, it may clearly be inferred that . . . he did not mean that these departments ought to have no partial agency in, or no control over, the acts of each other. His meaning, as his own words import, and still more conclusively as illustrated by the example in his eye, can amount to no more than this, that where the whole power of one department is exercised by the same hands which possess the whole power of another department, the fundamental principles of a free constitution are subverted." If Burger and the majority had taken seriously the very "sacred text" to which they appealed in *Bowsher,* they could not plausibly have maintained that the trivial overlap that they discerned in Gramm-Rudman-Hollings resembled the integration of whole powers that Madison and Montesquieu feared and that the framers made provision against.

35. *Bowsher v. Synar,* at 593.

36. Ibid., at 594.

37. On the independence of the comptroller general, see Frederick C. Mosher, *The GAO* (Boulder, Colo.: Westview, 1979), especially Chapter 7, and *A Tale of Two Agencies* (Baton Rouge: Louisiana State University Press, 1986); Joseph Pois, *Watchdog on the Potomac* (Washington, D.C.: University Press of America, 1979); and Richard E. Brown, *The GAO—Untapped Source of Congressional Power* (Knoxville: University of Tennessee Press, 1970).

38. Making an agent independent of the executive branch does not make him or her more a member of another branch unless one assumes that powers are separated exclusively and exhaustively.

39. *Bowsher v. Synar,* at 597–598.

40. Ibid., at 597–600.

41. Ibid., at 624.

42. Ibid., at 626–627.

43. Ibid., at 599 (emphasis added).

44. See Brown, *The GAO,* p. 5.

45. Compare Thurman Arnold, *Symbols of Government* (New Haven: Yale University Press, 1935) and David Shapiro, "In Defense of Judicial Candor," *Harvard Law Review* 100, no. 4 (February 1987), pp. 737–745.

46. *Bowsher v. Synar,* at 600. Note that this essence fits adjudication as well as execution of the law.
47. Ibid.
48. Ibid., at 601.
49. Stevens argued that the claim that Gramm-Rudman-Hollings delegated the comptroller general executive powers "rests on the unstated and unsound premise that there is a definite line that distinguishes executive power from legislative power." *Bowsher v. Synar,* at 610. That is, Stevens and Marshall attacked the exclusivity of powers on which the majority's argument depends.
50. Ibid., at 611.
51. Ibid., at 612–613.
52. Ibid., at 613.
53. Immigration and Nationality Act, 8 U.S.C. Section 1254 (a)(1)(1976). For a thorough recap of the facts of the case, see Craig, *Chadha.*
54. Immigration and Nationality Act, 8 U.S.C. Section 1254 (c)(2)(1976).
55. See Elliot, "INS v. Chadha," pp. 129–131.
56. *Pacific Gas Consumers Group v. Consumer Energy Council of America,* 463 U.S. 1216 (1983); *United States Senate v. Consumer Energy Council of America,* 463 U.S. 1216 (1983).
57. In so arguing we reject Professor Craig's contention that expounding the Constitution literally must lead to invalidation of the legislative veto. Craig, *Chadha,* pp. 93–101. Positive and dialectical readings represent distinguishable "literal" approaches. Positive readings, while they are nonsensical, can lead to invalidation of the legislative veto. Dialectical readings can justify validation or invalidation of the legislative veto, as the concurring and dissenting opinions in *Chadha* demonstrate.
58. *INS v. Chadha.*
59. Laurence Tribe argues that finding and marshaling "essences" in constitutional reasoning about separation of powers endangers sound analysis. See Tribe, *Constitutional Choices,* p. 76. Needless to add, the positive view lends itself to reasoning from and about "essences," because the positive view assumes that qualities can be defined without reference to opposites.
60. "Congress has acted and its action has altered Chadha's status." *INS v. Chadha,* at 2785. Notice that, again, all of these "proofs" of legislation were also true of the Court's decision in *Chadha.* Was the Court's decision essentially legislative?
61. Ibid., at 2785.
62. See Elliot, "INS v. Chadha," pp. 134–135, for flaws in the majority's definition of "legislative." Unger, *Law and Modern Society,* pp. 192–195, shows that in positive states each of the branches necessarily performs all three sorts of tasks.
63. *INS v. Chadha,* at 2789.
64. Ibid., at 2790.
65. "Although the parallel is not entirely complete, the effect on Chadha's personal rights would not have been different in principle had he been acquitted of a federal crime and thereafter found by one house of Congress to have been guilty." Ibid., at 2791, n. 8.
66. Ibid., at 2791, n. 7.
67. Justice Powell's opinion does not discuss how much danger this legislative veto posed of integrating *whole* powers—the specific evil Montesquieu and Madison

sought to forfend. Presumably he could have argued that integration of powers proceeds by stages and thus even small steps constitute constitutional violations.

68. "The House did not make a general rule; rather it made its own determination that six specific persons did not comply with certain statutory criteria. It thus undertook the type of decision that traditionally has been left to other branches." *INS v. Chadha,* at 2791–2792.

69. Ibid., at 2792.

70. Ibid., at 2801.

71. Ibid., at 2802. Compare Stevens' concurrence in *Bowsher.*

72. Ibid., at 2810.

73. Ibid.

74. Jesse H. Choper, *Judicial Review and the National Political Process* (Chicago: University of Chicago Press, 1980).

6 ——— ·
Foreign Policy and the Separation of Powers: The Influence of the Judiciary

DAVID GRAY ADLER

The unmistakable trend toward executive domination of U.S. foreign affairs in the past fifty years represents a dramatic departure from the basic scheme of the Constitution.[1] The constitutional blueprint assigns to Congress senior status in a partnership with the president for the purpose of conducting foreign policy. It also makes Congress the sole and exclusive repository of the ultimate foreign relations power—the authority to initiate war. The president is vested with only modest authority in this realm and is clearly only of secondary importance. In light of this constitutional design, commentators have wondered at the causes and sources of this radical shift in foreign affairs powers from Congress to the president.[2] Although a satisfactory explanation is perhaps elusive, it is nevertheless clear that the growth of presidential power in foreign relations has fed considerably on judicial decisions that are doubtful and fragile. It is, of course, beyond the scope of this chapter to attempt an exhaustive explanation, which has so far escaped the efforts of others. The aim here is to examine the judiciary's contribution to executive hegemony in this area as manifested in its rulings regarding executive agreements, travel abroad, the war power, and treaty termination.

In the second section of this chapter, I provide a brief explanation of the policy preferences underlying the Constitutional Convention's allocation of foreign affairs powers and argue that those values are as relevant and compelling today as they were two centuries ago. In the third section, I contend that a wide gap has developed in the past fifty years between constitutional theory and governmental practice in the conduct of foreign policy. The courts have greatly facilitated the growth of presidential power in this area in three interconnected but somewhat different ways: (1) adhering to the teaching of the sole-organ doctrine as propounded in the 1936 case of *United States v. Curtiss-Wright Export Corporation*;[3] (2) invoking the political question doc-

154

trine; and (3) inferring congressional approval of presidential action by virtue of its inaction or silence. I then offer an explanation of the Court's willingness to increase presidential foreign affairs powers well beyond constitutional boundaries. For a variety of reasons, the Court views its role in this area as a support function for policies already established. In this regard the judiciary has become an arm of the executive branch. Finally, I conclude with the argument that in order to maintain the integrity of the Constitution, the Court must police constitutional boundaries so as to ensure that fundamental alterations in our governmental system will occur only through the process of constitutional amendment. It is impermissible for the judicial branch to abdicate its function "to say what the law is."[4]

THE CONSTITUTION AND THE CONDUCT OF FOREIGN POLICY

The Constitution envisions the conduct of foreign policy as a partnership between the president and Congress. Perhaps surprisingly, Congress is assigned the role of senior partner. This assignment reflects, first, the overwhelming preference of both the framers at the Constitutional Convention and the ratifiers in the various state conventions for collective decision making in foreign as well as in domestic affairs and, second, their equally adamant opposition to unilateral executive control of U.S. foreign policy. This constitutional arrangement is evidenced by specific, unambiguous textual language, almost undisputed arguments by framers and ratifiers, and by logical-structural inferences from the doctrine of separation of powers.[5] This design, moreover, is compelling and relevant for twentieth-century America for at least three reasons. First, separation-of-powers issues are perennial, for they require consideration of the proper repository of power. Contemporary questions about the allocation of power between the president and Congress in foreign affairs are largely the same as those addressed two centuries ago. Second, the logic of collective decision making in the realm of foreign relations is as sound today as it was in the founding period. Third, although it is true that the world and the role of the United States in international relations have changed considerably over the past 200 years, it is nevertheless the case that most questions of foreign affairs involve routine policy formulation and do not place a premium on immediate responsive action. A slightly more detailed understanding of the constitutional landscape and the values that characterize it would prove beneficial to both the courts, which must forge policy in light of this background, and liberal activists, who would find history friendly to their critiques of judicial decisions in the area of foreign affairs.

The preference for collective, rather than individual, decision making runs throughout those provisions of the Constitution that govern the conduct of foreign policy. Congress derives broad and exclusive powers from

Article I to regulate foreign commerce and to initiate all hostilities on behalf of the United States, including full-blown, total war. As Article II indicates, the president shares the treaty-making power and the power to appoint ambassadors with the Senate. Only two powers in foreign relations are assigned exclusively to the president. He is commander in chief, but he acts in this capacity by and under the authority of Congress. As Alexander Hamilton and James Iredell argued, the president, in this capacity, is merely first admiral, or general of the armed forces, after war has been authorized by Congress or in the event of a sudden attack against the United States.[6] And the president also has the power to receive ambassadors. Hamilton, James Madison, and Thomas Jefferson agreed that this clerk-like function was purely ceremonial in character. Although this function has come to entail recognition of states at international law, which carries with it certain legal implications, this founding trio contended that the duty of recognizing states was more conveniently placed in the hands of the executive than in the legislature.[7] This list exhausts the textual grant of authority with respect to foreign affairs jurisdiction. The president's constitutional authority pales in comparison to that of Congress.

This preference for shared decision making is stated strongly in the construction of the treaty power: "He shall have Power, by and with the Advice and Consent of the Senate, to make Treaties, provided two-thirds of the Senators present concur." The compelling simplicity and clarity of the "plain words" of this clause hardly leave room for doubt as to its meaning.[8] Given the absence of any other clause that so much as intimates a presidential power to make agreements with foreign nations, it is to be supposed, as Hamilton argued, that the treaty power constitutes the principal vehicle for conducting U.S. foreign relations.[9] In fact, there was no hint at the Constitutional Convention of an exclusive presidential power to make foreign policy. To the contrary, all the arguments of the framers and ratifiers were to the effect that the Senate and president, which Hamilton and Madison described as a "fourth branch of government" in their capacity as treaty maker,[10] "are to manage all our concerns with foreign nations."[11] While a number of factors contributed to this decision,[12] the pervasive fear of unbridled executive power loomed largest.[13] Hamilton's statement in *Federalist* 75 fairly represents these sentiments:

> The history of human conduct does not warrant that exalted opinion of human nature which would make it wise in a nation to commit interests of so delicate and momentous a kind, as those which concern its intercourse with the rest of the world, to the sole disposal of a magistrate created and circumstanced as would be a President of the United States.[14]

The widespread fear of executive power that precluded allowing presidential control of foreign policy also greatly influenced the Convention's design of the war clause. Article I, section 8, paragraph 11 states: "The Congress shall have Power . . . To declare war." The plain meaning of the clause is buttressed by the fact of unanimous agreement among both framers and ratifiers that Congress was granted the sole and exclusive authority to initiate war. The war-making power, which was viewed as a legislative power by Madison and Wilson, among others, was specifically withheld from the president; he was given only the authority to repel sudden attacks.[15] James Wilson, second only to Madison as an architect of the Constitution, summed up the values and concerns underlying the war clause for the Pennsylvania Ratifying Convention:

> This system will not hurry us into war; it is calculated to guard against it. It will not be in the power of a single man, or a single body of men, to involve us in such distress; for the important power of declaring war is vested in the legislature at large. This declaration must be made with the concurrence of the House of Representatives; from this circumstance we may draw a certain conclusion that nothing but our national interest can draw us into war.[16]

No member of the Constitutional Convention and no member of any state ratifying convention ever attributed a different meaning to the war clause.[17]

This undisputed interpretation draws further support from early judicial decisions, the views of eminent treatise writers, and from nineteenth-century practice. I have discussed these factors elsewhere;[18] here the barest review must suffice. The meaning of the war clause was put beyond doubt by several early judicial decisions. No court since has departed from this early view. In 1800, in *Bas v. Tingy,* the Supreme Court held that it is for Congress alone to declare either an "imperfect" (limited) war or a "perfect" (general) war. In 1801, in *Talbot v. Seeman,* Chief Justice John Marshall, a member of the Virginia Ratifying Convention, stated that the "Whole powers of war [are] by the Constitution of the United States, vested in Congress. . . ." In *Little v. Barreme,* decided in 1804, Marshall held that President John Adams' instructions to seize ships were in conflict with an act of Congress and were therefore illegal.[19] In 1806, in *United States v. Smith,* the question of whether the president may initiate hostilities was decided by Justice William Paterson, riding circuit, who wrote for himself and District Judge Tallmadge: "Does he [the president] possess the power of making war? That power is exclusively vested in Congress. . . . It is the exclusive province of Congress to change a state of peace into a state of war."[20] In the *Prize Cases* in 1863, the Court considered for the first time the power of the president to respond to sudden attacks. Justice Robert C. Grier delivered the opinion of the Court:

> By the Constitution, Congress alone has the power to declare a natural or foreign war. . . .
> If a war be made by invasion of a foreign nation, the President is not only authorized but bound to resist force, by force. He does not initiate the war, but is bound to accept the challenge without

waiting for any special legislative authority. And whether the hostile party be a foreign invader, or States organized in rebellion, it is none the less a war, although the declaration of it be "unilateral."[21]

These judicial decisions established the constitutional fact that it is for Congress alone to initiate hostilities, whether in the form of general or limited war; the president, in his capacity as commander in chief, is granted only the power to repel sudden attacks against the United States.[22]

The Convention's attachment to collective judgment and its decision to create a structure of shared power in foreign affairs provided, in the words of Wilson, "a security to the people," for it was a cardinal tenet of republican ideology that the conjoined wisdom of many is superior to that of one.[23] The emphasis on group decision making came, of course, at the expense of unilateral executive authority. But this hardly posed a difficult choice, for among the framers and ratifiers, there was a pervasive distrust of executive power, a deeply held suspicion that dated to colonial times.[24] As a result of this aversion to executive authority, the Convention placed control of foreign policy beyond the unilateral capacity of the president. Furthermore, as Madison said, it "defined and confined" the authority of the president so that a power not granted could not be assumed.[25]

The structure of shared powers in foreign relations serves to deter the abuse of power, misguided policies, irrational action, and unaccountable behavior.[26] As a fundamental structural matter, the emphasis on joint policy making permits the airing of sundry political, social, and economic values and concerns. In any event, this structure wisely ensures that the ultimate policies will not merely reflect the private preferences or the short-term political interests of the president.[27]

Of course this arrangement has come under fire in the postwar period on a number of policy grounds. Some have argued, for example, that fundamental political and technological changes in the character of international relations and the position of the United States in the world have rendered obsolete an eighteenth-century document designed for a peripheral, small state in the European system of diplomatic relations. Moreover, it has been asserted that quick action and a single, authoritative voice are necessary to deal with an increasingly complex, interdependent, and technologically linked world capable of massive destruction in a very short period of time. Extollers of presidential dominance also have contended that only the president has the qualitative information, the expertise, and the capacity to act with the necessary dispatch to conduct U.S. foreign policy.[28]

These policy arguments have been reviewed, and discredited, elsewhere;[29] space limitations here permit only a brief commentary. Above all else, the implications of U.S. power and action in the twentieth century have brought about an even greater need for institutional accountability and collective judgment than existed two hundred years ago. The devastating, incomprehensible destruction of nuclear war and the possible extermination of the human race demonstrate the need for joint participation, as opposed to the opinion of one person, in the decision to initiate war. Moreover, most of the disputes at stake between the executive and legislative branches in foreign affairs, including the issues discussed in this chapter, have virtually nothing to do with the need for rapid response to crisis. Rather, they are concerned only with routine policy formulation and execution, a classic example of the authority exercised under the separation-of-powers doctrine. But these functions have been fused by the executive branch and have become increasingly unilateral, secretive, insulated from public debate, and hence unaccountable. In the wake of Vietnam, Watergate, and the Iran-*contra* scandal, unilateral executive behavior has become ever more difficult to defend. Scholarly appraisals have exploded arguments about intrinsic executive expertise and wisdom in foreign affairs and the alleged superiority of information available to the president.[30] Moreover, the inattentiveness of presidents to important details and the effects of "groupthink" that have dramatized and exacerbated the relative inexperience of various presidents in international relations have also devalued the extollers' arguments. Finally, foreign policies, like domestic policies, are a reflection of values. Against the strength of democratic principles, recent occupants of the White House have failed to demonstrate the superiority of their values in comparison to those of the American people and their representatives in Congress.

The assumption of foreign relations powers by recent presidents represents a fundamental alteration of the Constitution that is both imprudent and dangerous. We turn now to an examination of the judiciary's contribution to executive hegemony in foreign affairs.

THE JUDICIARY AND FOREIGN AFFAIRS

THE INFLUENCE OF CURTISS-WRIGHT

There can be little doubt that the opinion in *United States v. Curtiss-Wright Export Corp.* in 1936 has been the Court's principal contribution to the growth of executive power over foreign affairs. Its declaration that the president is the "sole organ of foreign affairs" is a powerful, albeit unfortunate, legacy of the case. Even when the sole-organ doctrine has not been invoked by name, its spirit, indeed its talismanic aura, has provided a common thread in a pattern of cases that have exalted presidential power above constitutional norms.

The domination of *Curtiss-Wright* is reflected in the fact that it is quite likely the most frequently cited case involving the allocation of foreign affairs powers.[31] It possesses uncommon significance in spite of the fact that it raised merely the narrow question of the constitutionality of a joint resolution that authorized the president to halt the sale of arms to Bolivia and Paraguay, then involved in armed conflict in the Chaco, in order to help stop the fighting. In an opinion by Justice George Sutherland, the Court upheld the delegation against the charge that it was unduly broad. If Justice Sutherland had confined his remarks to the delegation issue, *Curtiss-Wright* would have been overshadowed by *Panama Refining Co. v. Ryan*[32] and would never have even surfaced in the tables of contents of undergraduate casebooks. But Sutherland strayed from the issue and, in some ill-considered dicta, imparted an unhappy legacy—the chimerical idea that authority in foreign affairs was essentially an executive power, which he explained "as the very delicate, plenary, and exclusive power of the President as the sole organ of the federal government in the field of international relations—a power which does not require as a basis for its exercise an act of Congress."[33]

Let us consider the historical context from which Sutherland ripped the sole-organ doctrine. In short, Sutherland greatly expanded on Congressman John Marshall's speech in 1800 in which he noted that, "The President is the sole organ of the nation in its external relations. . . . Of consequence, the demand of a foreign nation can only be made on him."[34] Marshall was defending the decision of President John Adams to surrender to British officials a British deserter, Jonathan Robbins, in accordance with the Jay Treaty. The Robbins affair involved a demand upon the United States, according to Marshall, and it required a response from the president on behalf of the American people. At no point in his speech did Marshall argue that the president's exclusive authority to communicate with foreign nations included a power to formulate or develop policy. Professor Edward S. Corwin properly concluded: "Clearly, what Marshall had foremost in mind was simply the President's role as instrument of communication with other governments."[35] This point of procedure had been acknowledged in 1793 by then Secretary of State Thomas Jefferson.[36] And this view had not been challenged. Thus, it was Sutherland who infused a purely communicative role with a substantive policy-making function and thereby manufactured a great power out of the Marshallian sole-organ doctrine. To have done this, as Allan McDougal and David Riesman observed, was to confuse the "organ" with the "organ grinder"[37] and effectively undermine the constitutional design for cooperation in the conduct of foreign relations.

Curtiss-Wright, then, was a radical, path-breaking case. Despite the fact that it was a product of Justice Sutherland's imagination, and despite the fact that its rhetoric has been dismissed as "dictum,"[38] it has nevertheless enjoyed a long life—now more than fifty years—because the Court has trotted out the sole-organ doctrine whenever it has required a rationale to support a constitutionally doubtful presidential action in foreign affairs. On such occasions, and they have been numerous, the ghost of *Curtiss-Wright* has been made to walk again. Even the most cursory review of the cases in which it has been invoked makes clear that the essence of this "spirit" is great "def-

erence to executive judgment in this vast external realm" of foreign relations.[39]

This deference is perhaps attributable to the effects of "court-
positivism." By this doctrine, the Court's decisions are treated "as a given, to
be explained, manipulated, and systematized, but criticized only within narrow limits."[40] This doctrine culminates in the view that the Constitution
means what the justices say it means; the tendency, therefore, is to treat as
"oracles" the few cases that have dotted an otherwise barren constitutional
landscape. Professor Gerhard Casper has described it thus: "It has also the
paradoxical effect of assigning a disproportionate importance to the few 'legal' precedents that do exist. Absent the continuous consideration and reconsideration of rules and principles, a few oracles have led to the emergence of
a constitutional mythology that does not bear close analysis."[41] For all its
shortcomings, *Curtiss-Wright* has assumed the status of an oracle. As we shall
see, it has led the judiciary to defer to "executive judgment" in cases involving
executive agreements, travel abroad, treaty termination, and the war power.
Of course these judicial decisions have not totally relied on *Curtiss-Wright*.
They have also drawn on the political question doctrine and on the silence
and inaction of Congress. But the spirit of *Curtiss-Wright* pervades these
techniques.

EXECUTIVE AGREEMENTS

Perhaps it is no exaggeration to observe that since *Curtiss-Wright*, presidents
have utilized executive agreements as the primary means of dominating the
conduct of foreign policy.[42] This practice, which has resulted in a flood of
unilateral presidential agreements, obviously precludes a role for the Senate;
therefore, it subverts the basic constitutional scheme established in Philadelphia. The structural design of the treaty clause, as I have already shown, was
to preclude the president from entering the field of foreign relations without
the participation of the Senate, and fear of the abuse of power dissuaded the
framers from vesting the executive with such unilateral authority.[43]

There was apparently no doubt among the framers and ratifiers that
the treaty-making power was omnicompetent in foreign affairs; its authority
covered the field. As explained by Hamilton:

> From the *best opportunity of knowing the fact,* I aver, that it was under-
> stood by *all* to be the intent of the provision to give that power the
> most ample latitude—to render it competent to all the stipulations
> which the exigencies of national affairs might require; competent to
> the making of treaties of alliance, treaties of commerce, treaties of
> peace, and *every other species of convention* usual among nations. . . .
> And it was emphatically for this reason that it was so carefully
> guarded; the cooperation of two-thirds of the Senate with the Presi-
> dent, being required to make any treaty whatever.[44]

The text of the Constitution makes no mention of executive agreements. Moreover, there was no reference to them in the Constitutional Convention or in the state ratifying conventions. The *Federalist* papers are silent on the subject as well. There is, then, no support in the architecture of the Constitution for the use of executive agreements. Yet their usage, since 1936, has flourished; presidents claim independent constitutional power to make them,[45] and the judiciary has sustained such presidential claims of authority. What is the source of the president's power to make executive agreements?

An examination of the leading cases involving executive agreements discloses judicial reliance on two constitutional grounds: the sole-organ doctrine and the recognition power of the president. Neither claim is tenable, in my view. In *United States v. Belmont,* Justice Sutherland wrote the opinion for the Court upholding the validity of an executive agreement that President Franklin D. Roosevelt negotiated with the Soviet Union in 1933 involving the assignment of assets in both countries. The Court took judicial notice of the fact that the Litvinov Assignment—an agreement on property claims between Franklin Roosevelt and Maxim Litvinov—was executed in conjunction with the 1933 recognition of the Soviet government and said that the pact derived its force from both the president's status as sole organ and his power to recognize foreign governments. Justice Sutherland stated that Senate consultation was not required.

We have already exposed the infirmities of Justice Sutherland's sole-organ doctrine. It fares no better in the *Belmont* setting. Moreover, his invocation of the president's "recognition power," which is derived from his duty under Article II, section 3, to "receive Ambassadors and other public ministers," is puzzling. It appears that there was no disagreement during the founding period among Hamilton, Madison, and Jefferson, who shared the understanding that the recognition clause conferred upon the president merely a ceremonial function that does not include any "discretion" to reject foreign ministers.[46] Writing what Madison considered the "original gloss" on the meaning of the clause, Hamilton explained in *Federalist* 69 that the authority

> to receive ambassadors and other public ministers . . . is more a matter of dignity than authority. It is a circumstance which will be without consequence in the administration of government; and it was far more convenient that it should be arranged in this manner, than there should be a necessity of convening the legislature, or one of its branches, upon every arrival of a foreign minister, though it were merely to take the place of a departed predecessor.[47]

By any measure, Hamilton was talking about the effectuation of a diplomatic function. As Professor Louis Henkin has observed, "receiving ambassadors" seems "a function rather than a 'power,' a ceremony which in many countries is performed by a figurehead." Indeed, the distinction between a power and a function cannot be stressed too strongly. Henkin has justly remarked that "while making treaties and appointing ambassadors are described as 'powers' of the president, receiving ambassadors is included in section 3, which does not speak in terms of power but lists things the President 'shall' or 'may do.'"[48]

Given the apparent refusal of the Convention to convert the recognition clause into a well of discretionary power, and its refusal to clothe the president with the treaty-making power so that he might, alone, conduct foreign policy, *Belmont* certainly represents an "extreme extension" of presidential power in foreign relations.[49] This extension clearly contravenes not only the structure of the treaty power but also the policy reasons that predetermined that structure. Justice Sutherland did not discuss any of these points in *Belmont*.

The Court again considered the validity of the Litvinov Assignment in 1942 in *United States v. Pink*. Virtually echoing the opinion in *Belmont*, Justice William O. Douglas invoked the sole-organ doctrine as well as the recognition power as authorization for the executive agreement. However, there was no need for Justice Douglas to attempt to sustain the assignment on purely presidential powers, for he had said that "the executive policy had been 'tacitly' recognized by congressional appointment of commissioners to determine American claims against the Soviet fund."[50] It would appear, however, that Chief Justice Harlan Stone's dissent, in which Justice Owen Roberts concurred, exposed the real question in the case: "We are referred to no authority which would sustain such an exercise of power as is said to have been exerted here by mere assignment unratified by the Senate."[51]

Clearly, *Belmont* and *Pink*, in drawing upon *Curtiss-Wright*, can be seen as facilitating the trend toward presidential control of U.S. foreign policy, at least with respect to the use of executive agreements. And beginning in 1937, a virtual torrent of such agreements was unleashed—at the expense of the Senate and its constitutional role in making treaties. This trend, which continues to this day, as seen in *Dames and Moore v. Reagan*, constitutes a fundamental and extraordinary shift of power from Congress to the president.

In *Dames and Moore*, which clearly represented "a political decision by a political court,"[52] the High Tribunal was at pains to sustain the constitutionality of President Jimmy Carter's executive agreement with Iran that secured the release of American hostages. In his opinion for the Court, then Justice (now Chief) William Rehnquist found *statutory authorization* for much of the agreement but none for a critical leg—the suspension of all claims pending against Iran in U.S. courts.[53] Undaunted, Justice Rehnquist held that Congress had "tacitly" approved the president's pact. Apparently, it had evinced its support in two ways. First, Rehnquist located two statutes, the "general tenor" of which, he said, had delegated broad discretionary power to the president. He conceded, however, that neither statute by itself provided sufficient authority for the agreement.[54] Second, he asserted that, by virtue of its silence, Congress had acquiesced in the agreement. The Court concluded that the absence of explicit delegation did not imply congressional disapproval but merely showed that Congress had not anticipated such a situation.[55]

To be sure, the doctrine of "tacit" delegation based on congressional acquiescence has its place in American jurisprudence. But it is an acquiescence of a particular kind; it is based on a settled congressional understanding of an administrative construction of a statute. In other words, suppose an administrative agency adopts an erroneous interpretation of a statute. If Congress reenacts the statute with knowledge of the administrative interpretation, it is said to incorporate that interpretation and to give statutory standing to what was previously unlawful.[56] In effect, it ratifies and adopts that construction. We find a signal decision in this tradition. In the nineteenth century, Congress passed a number of statutes that made available public lands for private occupation. However, on hundreds of occasions, without statutory authority, the president withdrew some land from the right of entry. In 1915, in *United States v. Midwest Oil Co.*, the Court upheld President William Taft's withdrawal in 1909 of certain lands from the appropriation of oil rights offered to the public by an act passed in 1897. The Court, consistent with the doctrine of tacit delegation, might have held that the Act of 1897, passed as it was with the knowledge of earlier executive withdrawals, silently included the practice. However, it stated that the "long-continued practice, known to and acquiesced in by Congress," had gained the "implied consent of Congress."[57] There is, of course, no merit to the argument that an executive abuse of power acquires legal status if Congress does not correct it. In a parallel case, the Supreme Court held that a well-established, well-known and long-continued practice of granting suspended sentences did not justify the federal courts in following this practice when the statute did not authorize it.[58] Nevertheless, the case is one of statutory interpretation. It treated congressional acquiescence as statutory authorization, not as a gloss on the Constitution.

Justice Rehnquist invoked *Midwest Oil* as precedential authority for his theory that Congress may exhibit acquiescence regarding presidential practices through silence. Of course, *Midwest Oil* is inapposite to *Dames and Moore*. With respect to the former, the Court recognized that Congress had passed a number of statutes with full knowledge of prior presidential action. Those statutes provided the requisite ratification of an administrative action. There was no such ratification in *Dames and Moore*. Indeed, even Rehnquist conceded that Congress had not passed a single statute to authorize the executive agreement in the Iranian hostage crisis. Finally, Congress did not even evince the "tacit" consent that it had in *Pink*, by virtue of its appointment of negotiators. There was no such congressional support in *Dames and Moore*.

What remained for Rehnquist at this point was to glean congressional support from congressional silence. This enterprise is a very problematic one; indeed, the Court has stated that it is "treacherous to find in congressional silence the adoption of a controlling rule of law."[59] A failure to object does not necessarily mean that Congress approves of the action. There may be numerous reasons why Congress may not act, even though a majority of the body may disagree with the president. Professor Gewirtz has written:

> When Congress is faced with an executive policy that is in place and functioning, Congress often acquiesces in the executive's action for reasons which have nothing to do with the majority's preferences on the policy issues involved. . . . In such a situation, Congress may not want to be viewed as disruptive; or Congresspersons may not want to embarrass the President; or Congress may want to score political points by attacking the executive's action rather than accepting political responsibility for some action itself; or Congresspersons may be busy running for reelection or tending to constituents' individual problems; or Congress may be lazy and prefer another recess.[60]

The implications of Justice Rehnquist's reasoning are staggering. Ineluctably, the "doctrine of silence" would sanction "an almost total transfer of legislative power to the executive, so long as Congress does not object."[61] Justice Rehnquist's argument is not new, of course, for it is but a page torn from Theodore Roosevelt's "stewardship theory" of the presidency. As explained by Roosevelt:

> I declined to adopt this view that what was imperatively necessary for the nation could not be done by the President, unless he could find some specific authorization to do it. I did not usurp power but I did greatly broaden the use of executive power. In other words, I acted for the common well being of all our people whenever and in whatever measure was necessary, unless prevented by direct constitutional or legislative prohibition.[62]

Roosevelt's view, like Rehnquist's, "means that the President is free to undertake any folly, provided it is so gross that it has not occurred to Congress to forbid it."[63]

At bottom, perhaps *Dames and Moore v. Reagan* should not be understood as having sustained a purely executive agreement; after all, Justice Rehnquist ruled that the president enjoyed congressional authorization through tacit delegation. But my contention is that he has misapplied that doctrine. As applied, it is a prescription for the exercise of arbitrary presidential power in foreign affairs.

TRAVEL CASES

For the past thirty years, the Supreme Court has steadily increased the power of the president to restrict the right of U.S. citizens to travel abroad. Since the peak of the Court's respect for the wishes of citizens to visit foreign lands, as exhibited in its 1958 holding in *Kent v. Dulles*[64] that the right to travel is guaranteed by the due process clause of the Fifth Amendment, the Court has managed to "find" exceptions to that right by bowing to painfully plastic invocations of national security needs. Its vulnerability to the spirit of *Curtiss-Wright*—"deference to the judgment of the executive"—and its willingness to find, on the flimsiest of pretexts, congressional "approval" of State Department passport policies, has created an environment in which the administration is the sole judge of its policies. In just a handful of cases, the Court has transmuted what has been regarded as a congressional lawmaking function—to determine what, if any, restrictions are to be imposed in foreign travel—into a discretionary executive policy-making tool of great scope. In light of this fundamental shift of power, Justice Brennan has been moved to remark: "The reach of the Secretary's [of State] discretion is potentially staggering."[65]

The first national passport legislation passed in 1858 vested the exclusive authority to issue passports in the executive branch. Congress codified the language of this act in the Passport Act of 1926. The Act did not grant specific authority to the secretary of state to refuse or revoke passports because, at that time, Congress did not require passports for international travel by U.S. citizens except during periods of war or national emergency. (The general passport requirement became law in 1952 with passage of the Immigration and Nationality Act.)[66] However, the Court held in *Kent v. Dulles* that in the 1926 Passport Act Congress had adopted earlier the prior administrative practice of the State Department. Apparently, the secretary of state had authority to resolve questions of the allegiance of a passport applicant, which meant verifying his or her citizenship as well as investigating the applicant's criminal activity. In the latter case the secretary could deny passports to those violating U.S. law or seeking to escape the law. As I have observed, the adoption of an administrative practice by statute constitutes a legalization of the practice.

The Court has ruled on only a few cases challenging the validity of State Department regulations developed under the Passport Act. In *Kent v. Dulles,* the first major case concerning this issue, the secretary of state denied the passport applications of two Communists under a department regulation that prohibited the issuance of passports to Communist party members or to persons going abroad to engage in activities enhancing the Communist movement. The Court invalidated the regulation, per Justice Douglas, who ruled that the freedom to travel is a "liberty" protected by the Fifth Amendment and, moreover, that any regulation of the freedom to travel must be made pursuant to the congressional lawmaking function and must therefore be narrowly construed. Since the secretary lacked express authority to deny passports, only an administrative practice clearly adopted by Congress would imply a delegation of its lawmaking function. The Court found that neither the established administrative practice nor the specific delegation to the secretary were sufficient to deny a passport merely because of one's beliefs and associations.[67]

The bubble burst seven years later in *Zemel v. Rusk,* in which the Court, per Chief Justice Earl Warren, sustained the administration's total ban on travel to Cuba.[68] The Court applied the standard developed in *Kent* and claimed to have discovered a substantial and consistent State Department practice of restricting travel to named geographic areas, both in wartime and peacetime, sufficient to warrant a conclusion that Congress was aware of the secretary's policy and thus implicitly approved of such restrictions. The substance and "consistency" of such a practice is doubtful. Justice Arthur Goldberg, in a dissenting opinion, revealed that these "precedents" occurred during the proximity of war and were thus immaterial because they fell within the war power of the executive.[69]

The *Zemel* Court also dismissed the Fifth Amendment challenge, reasoning that if the government can restrict travel within the United States for safety and welfare purposes, then surely the State Department could similarly restrict travel to Cuba for the same reasons. Chief Justice Warren, invoking *Curtiss-Wright,* said that "the weightiest considerations of national security" permit these travel restraints without violating due process.[70]

Justice Hugo Black filed a strong dissenting opinion and took Warren to task for permitting the executive branch to make laws:

> Since Article I, however, vests "All legislative Powers" in the Congress, and no language in the Constitution purports to vest any such power in the President, it necessarily follows, if the Constitution is to control, that the President is completely devoid of power to make laws regulating passports or anything else. And he has no more power to make laws by labeling them regulations than to do so by calling them laws. Like my brother Goldberg, I cannot accept the Government's argument that the President has "inherent" power to make regulations governing the issuance and use of passports.[71]

The *Kent-Zemel* standard, which required a consistent pattern of actual enforcement in order to establish the requisite congressional approval, was for all intents and purposes overruled in *Haig v. Agee.*[72] In this case, the Court recognized enforcement as one method of establishing congressional awareness and approval of the regulation. But it also stated, in terms echoing *Dames and Moore v. Reagan,* that courts could also find approval from nothing more than congressional silence about a long-standing administrative practice. Chief Justice Warren Burger concluded that Congress had implicitly adopted the administrative construction because it had not made any changes in the executive's basic rule-making power when it passed the Immigration and Nationality Act of 1952, or when it amended the Passport Act in 1978. Chief Justice Burger observed that Congress must have been aware of the "longstanding and officially promulgated view" of the State Department that the president could revoke passports for reasons of national security. There is, of course, no such official policy, and the cases advanced by Burger are not supportive.[73]

Haig v. Agee produced a new standard for establishing congressional approval: That Congress allows the State Department to construct its own regulations provides sufficient basis to assume implicit congressional approval of a passport regulation. The Court in *Kent* had rejected a similar assertion by the government, holding that only an established departmental practice can convince the Court that Congress is sufficiently aware of the claimed authority. But the Court in the *Haig* decision would not even require frequent instances of enforcement in order to build a track record. Even if no enforcement occurred, the validity of the executive's authority would not be destroyed, nor would lack of enforcement preclude congressional awareness of the Department's construction.

That the Court could assume this position is all the more incredible in view of the fact that in 1978 Congress amended the Passport Act so as to deprive the president of all discretion with respect to the issuance of passports except to those countries with which the United States is at war or where there is imminent danger to Americans.[74] Yet in the face of this statute the Court asserted the superiority of national security claims, stating that "it is obvious and unarguable that no government interest is more compelling than the security of the nation." Therefore, said the Court, the government may regulate foreign travel within the limits of due process. But the guarantees of due process demand nothing more than the offer of a prompt revocation administrative hearing and a statement of reasons for the action.[75]

Given the Court's view in *Haig* that the executive branch need merely assert a construction of its own regulation in order to satisfy the need for congressional awareness, it is little wonder that Justice Brennan would view the State Department's discretion as "potentially staggering." Perhaps his use of the word "potentially" was optimistic. The discretion already is "staggering."

THE POLITICAL QUESTION DOCTRINE

The political question doctrine, the "principle under which the courts defer the determination of an issue to the political branches of government," stems primarily from the Court's concern for the separation of powers and its own role within that scheme.[76] But there is a continuing debate about the scope of the doctrine, the essence of which involves two very different theories.

Chief Justice John Marshall espoused the "classical" view in *Cohens v. Virginia* (1821), stating that the courts "have no more right to decline the exercise of jurisdiction which is given, than to usurp that which is not given." Similarly, Professor Herbert Wechsler has said that the existence of a political question in any particular issue is determined by "whether the Constitution has committed to another agency of government the autonomous determination of the issue."[77] Accordingly, a court must first decide the threshold separation-of-powers issue before it can invoke the political question doctrine.[78] A second theory, the "prudential" view, holds that courts should weigh the consequences that a particular case might have on the judiciary before addressing the merits of the claim.[79]

The invocation of the political question doctrine has been a major means by which the judiciary has strengthened the role of the president in the conduct of foreign affairs. This section examines the judicial application of the doctrine in the areas of war making and treaty termination. First we turn to *Goldwater v. Carter* (1979), in which Rehnquist, writing for a plurality, stretched the doctrine beyond its previous limits.

TREATY TERMINATION

In *Goldwater v. Carter*, Senator Barry Goldwater challenged President Carter's unilateral termination of the 1954 Mutual Defense Treaty with Taiwan.[80] In an opinion by Rehnquist (Burger, Stewart, and Stevens concurring), it was held that the issue of treaty termination represented a nonjusticiable political question precisely because it involved "the authority of the President in the conduct of foreign relations and the extent to which the senate or congress is authorized to negate the action of the President."[81]

The plurality's decision clearly is unfounded. In the words of Justice William Brennan's dissent, the quartet "profoundly" misapprehended "the political question doctrine as it applies to foreign relations." Indeed, in the opinion of Justice Lewis Powell, who concurred in the dismissal of the case, but on grounds of ripeness, the foursome's "reliance upon the political question doctrine" was "inconsistent with our precedents."[82]

In his notable opinion in *Baker v. Carr*, Justice Brennan drew order from the confusion surrounding the political question doctrine. After a discussion of the previous cases, he set forth six alternative tests for identifying the political questions:

> Prominent on the surface of any case held to involve a political question is found a textually demonstrable constitutional commitment of the issue to a coordinate political department; or a lack of judicially discoverable and manageable standards for resolving it; of the impossibility of deciding without an initial policy determination of a kind clearly for non-judicial discretion; or the impossibility of a court's undertaking independent resolution without expressing lack of respect due coordinate branches of government; or an unusual need for unquestioning adherence to a political decision already made; or the potentiality of embarrassment from multifarious pronouncements by various departments on one question.[83]

The issue of treaty termination does not conform to any of these analytical components of the political question doctrine. Justice Brennan's first test—a textual commitment—has been justly characterized by Wechsler as the governing principle of the doctrine. He stated that "all the doctrine can defensibly imply is that the courts are called upon to judge whether the constitution has committed to another agency of government the autonomous determination of the issue raised."[84] There is, of course, no textual commitment of the authority to terminate treaties, for the Constitution is silent on the point. Thus *Goldwater* certainly could not be labeled a political question case on this ground. Nor is there "a lack of judicially discoverable and manageable standards" for resolving the issue. For example, the Court might have examined the logic of the treaty power's structure and drawn the inference that the authority to terminate treaties belongs to the treaty power. Support for this symmetrical construction was expressed by Justices Joseph Story and Benjamin Cardozo, two of our most eminent jurists. Or the Court might have studied the historical practice of treaty termination, which would have revealed three alternatives: termination by the president and Senate jointly, by congressional directive, or by independent presidential action. Any one of these inquiries would have disclosed "manageable standards."[85] Neither Brennan's third test, which prohibits a nonjudicial policy determination, nor his fourth, which precludes resolution of the issue if it would require the judiciary to exhibit insufficient respect toward a coordinate branch of government, is applicable here. Surely the courts may not undertake an initial policy determination to make or terminate a treaty, for this type of action is nonjudicial. But deciding whether the appropriate political branch has made that determination is clearly justiciable.[86] Moreover, the Court does not commit such a social solecism if it determines that the president has transgressed constitutional bounds. As Chief Justice John Marshall stated in *Marbury v. Madison,* "to what purpose are powers limited, and to what purpose is that limitation committed to writing, if these limits may, at any time, be passed by those intended to be restrained?" Whatever risk exists of insufficient respect toward the president, the overriding concern must attach to the integrity of the Constitution and its framework of limited government. "It is far more important," observed Justice Douglas, "to be respectful to the Constitution than to a coordinate branch of the government."[87] Brennan's fifth criterion is "an unusual need for unquestioned adherence to a political decision already made." Although it is not clear which cases might satisfy this criterion, outside of, perhaps, a declaration of war, it is hard to imagine that this test could encompass the termination of a treaty. The last reason cited by Brennan was "the potential embarrassment from multifarious pronouncements by various departments on one question." Probably Brennan had in mind *Luther v. Borden,* in which the Court was asked to decide which of two rival governments was the legitimate republican government in Rhode Island.[88] That case represented the possibility of six pronouncements by six departments on one question. In *Goldwater,* however, we do not find "multifarious pronouncements"; indeed, only the president acted, and that action was challenged as unconstitutional. If the Court had ruled that President Carter's termination of the Taiwan Treaty was invalid, that fact no doubt would have been embarrassing to some and annoying to Peking, but it would not have produced the chaos Justice Brennan had in mind.

For Justice Rehnquist the issue of treaty termination was a nonjusticiable political question merely because it raised the question of the allocation of power between the president and Congress in the realm of foreign affairs. Rehnquist thus ignored Justice Brennan's sagacious observation in *Baker v. Carr* that "it is error to suppose that every case or controversy which touches foreign relations lies beyond judicial cognizance."[89] Justice Rehnquist's obeisance to the president in the conduct of foreign policy recalls the folly of *Curtiss-Wright,* the proposition that the president is sole organ in foreign affairs. Whatever authority the president has in the formulation of international policy, he is not the Pied Piper, and the other branches of government and the American public are not the children of Hamlin. Such a storybook view of presidential power cannot be reconciled with constitutional restrictions. To be sure, the allocation of power in the Constitution is not always clear. But when there is question as to the repository of authority, determination of the matter is left to the courts. Justice Rehnquist's view that each of the branches "has resources available to protect its interests" would, as Raoul Berger has remarked, "return us to settlement of differences by Kentucky feud."[90] Rehnquist's adoration for this sort of legal Darwinism would not save us from a covetous or usufructuary executive, but a court committed to the Constitution might.

In an astute study of the political question doctrine, Professor Fritz Scharpf concluded that "the political question . . . had no place when the court was presented with conflicting claims of competence among the departments of the federal government."[91] That was the view of the Court in *Powell v. McCormack,* where it declared that its principal duty was to decide "whether the action of [another] branch exceeds whatever authority has been committed." In *Goldwater,* however, the Court abdicated that duty. Despite Justice Powell's reminder that in the past the Court had been willing to determine "whether one branch of our government has impinged upon the power of another,"[92] the Court declined to answer a very straightforward question in *Goldwater:* In which department of government does the Constitution vest the authority to terminate treaties?

As a practical matter, the Court's action, or rather its inaction, left the termination of the Mutual Defense Treaty intact. Although the plurality opinion in *Goldwater* did not establish a legal precedent, it will nevertheless establish a foundation, however shaky, for future unilateral presidential treaty terminations.[93] This result will have the unfortunate effect of placing the exclusive authority to terminate defense, commercial, economic, and arms control agreements, among others, in the hands of the president.

POLITICAL QUESTIONS AND THE WAR POWER

Since 1950, the United States has been involved in a series of unilateral executive wars. Presidential usurpation of the war power has become a commonplace. This practice obviously violates the policy objectives of the war clause. Those present at the Constitutional Convention, fearful that one man might rush the nation into war, vested in Congress the exclusive power to initiate hostilities. Apparently oblivious to the common sense underlying this allocation of power, the judiciary remains a coconspirator in this gross disjuncture between law and practice.

Indeed, its invocation of the political question doctrine has been a major means by which the judiciary has strengthened the role of the president in the conduct of foreign policy. Throughout the Vietnam War, lower courts routinely invoked the doctrine in response to challenges to the constitutionality of that war, and many observers viewed this unwillingness to address the merits of the claims as a sign of judicial approval of administration policy.[94] This reticence certainly did not dissuade the president from continuing the war effort. Aside from the problematical inferences drawn from the silence of the courts, the Vietnam War—like the Korean War before it and the later war in Grenada—did not receive congressional authorization, which the Constitution requires.[95] The fact that various presidents initiated war without congressional authorization created a constitutional crisis that might have been resolved by the judiciary. But it was not and, as a consequence, the United States has suffered a string of presidential wars from Korea to Libya. This fact constitutes a fundamental shift of power from Congress to the president. In a few cases challenging President Ronald Reagan's military adventures in Grenada, Nicaragua, and El Salvador, lower courts have refused to rule on the merits. As might be expected, they have held that these cases constituted nonjusticiable, political questions. Judicial reluctance to enforce constitutional boundaries in the area of foreign policy has threatened, in Jefferson's phrase, to convert the "chains of the Constitution" into "ropes of sand." The effect has been to encourage the tendencies of the "imperial presidency." It is no surprise, therefore, that recent presidents have come to view the military of the United States as a private army at their beck and call to fulfill the goals of a foreign policy agenda. This shift threatens the foundation of our republican form of government as well as our tradition of constitutionalism.[96]

The nation's need for a judicial branch that will unflinchingly "say what the law is," therefore, is of greatest importance. The law, as we have seen, was articulated in a number of cases at the dawn of the Republic: Only Congress may constitutionally initiate war. Viewed in this light, the unwillingness of the judiciary to declare the Vietnam War unconstitutional clearly illustrates the fact that the judicial branch of government abdicated its institutional duties. There is no need here to review the judiciary's treatment of the cases challenging the legality of that war, for such reviews can be found elsewhere.[97] Suffice it to say that although no court affirmed the legality of the unilateral presidential war, only one court declared the war illegal. At the district and circuit court levels, judges routinely declared the issues nonjusticiable. The Supreme Court routinely denied certiorari.

Recent lower court decisions have, in the tradition of the Vietnam War rulings, dismissed challenges to President Reagan's military adventures as nonjusticiable political questions. The leading case in this respect is *Crockett v. Reagan*. In this case, Congressman George Crockett of Michigan and twenty-eight other members of Congress challenged President Reagan's failure to comply with the 1973 War Powers Resolution's reporting and termination requirements in regard to the administration's military involvement in El Salvador.[98] They claimed that the introduction of armed forces into hostilities or imminent hostilities triggered the Resolution's cut-off mechanism. The plaintiffs claimed that advisers had suffered casualties, operated in combat areas, had been attacked, and while fighting side-by-side with government troops, were drawing "hostile fire pay." Plaintiffs sought, inter alia, a declaratory judgment that the Resolution's sixty-day cut-off provision had been triggered as well as an injunctive relief directing that the military forces be withdrawn from El Salvador.

The case was dismissed on the ground that the fact finding necessary to determine whether a section 4 (a) (1) report was required to be filed would be too difficult. In dismissing the case as a political question, the district court concluded that deciding whether the situation in El Salvador involved hostilities or imminent hostilities would require the resolution of disputed questions of fact that were beyond judicial competence. The tribunal indicated that if the facts were clarified, a court should proceed to trigger the resolution's cut-off provision. It distinguished between Vietnam, where "it would be absurd for [a court] to decline to find that the United States forces had been introduced into hostilities," and El Salvador, where "a small number of American military personnel . . . apparently have suffered no casualties." That response may appear to be a reasonable concern about the problem of fact finding, which can be difficult. However, it puts the court on a slippery slope: How large a military commitment is required before the cut-off provision of the resolution can be triggered?

In the end, the court was influenced by the fact that Congress had taken no action on the question. This fact led the court to dismiss the case by virtue of the doctrine of equitable discretion, which mandates dismissal of congressional claims where members have an effective in-House remedy for their alleged injuries.[99]

Although there certainly is merit to the idea that the courts should avoid interfering with a coordinate department's consideration of an issue, there is, nevertheless, a higher concern—that is, maintaining the integrity of the Constitution. As it stands, if a minority in either the House or the Senate is unable to move its chamber to act against an alleged presidential usurpation, the minority cannot find relief in the courts. This problem is especially important in the case of war making, where members of Congress have been deprived of their right to vote on the wisdom of declaring war. The doctrine should not be applied to also deprive them of a private right of action under the Constitution.[100] But that is what the *Crockett* decision did. The upshot is that the judiciary expects Congress to force the president to file a report that will trigger the cut-off provision of the resolution. While it is reasonable for a court to expect Congress to assert its powers, it is, nevertheless, the duty of the judiciary to enforce the law.

In *Sanchez-Espinoza v. Reagan*, then Circuit Court Judge (now Justice) Antonin Scalia held that the case, brought by twelve members of Congress on issues arising from U.S. actions in Nicaragua, was controlled by *Crockett*.[101] Judge Benjamin Ginsburg, in a concurring opinion, dismissed the war clause claim as not ripe for review: "The Judicial Branch should not decide issues affecting the allocation of power between the President and Congress until they reach a constitutional impasse." Moreover,

> Congress has formidable weapons at its disposal—the power of the purse and investigative resources far beyond those available in the Third Branch. But no gauntlet has been thrown down here by a majority of the Members of Congress. On the contrary, Congress expressly allowed the President to spend federal funds to support paramilitary operations in Nicaragua and "if the Congress chooses not to confront the President, it is not our task to do so."[102]

The last sentence, drawn from Justice Powell's concurring opinion in *Goldwater v. Carter*, sets an ominous tone for constitutional government. The judges take an oath to uphold the Constitution; thus, if Congress is reticent in the face of presidential usurpation of power, it is the duty of the Court to "say what the law is." If Congress abdicates its responsibilities, and the Court shirks its duty, what is left in the way of governmental institutions to bring an errant president to heel? Who will act to maintain the integrity of the Constitution?

JUDICIAL DEFERENCE TO THE EXECUTIVE

As we have seen, the Court has been willing, even eager, to manipulate the Constitution and statutory law in order to justify executive action in the realm of foreign affairs. The Court's reflexive use of law to legitimate the international politics of the president, and its concomitant paralytic refusal to invoke its paramount prerogative of invalidation, have for all intents and purposes served to elevate the president's authority in these matters above constitutional norms.[103] In short, the Court has become a shill for the executive in foreign affairs.

The judiciary's subservience to the executive and its determination to clothe him with powers that are not tethered to the Constitution evokes questions about its motives. Why has the judicial branch been so loath to find usurpation of power? Why has it evinced no disposition to frustrate the tremendous growth of power in the executive, especially in the field of foreign relations? A complete explication is beyond the reach of this chapter. The explanatory factors adequate to such a task are like pieces of a puzzle that cannot at this juncture be fitted properly. No more is hoped for here than to succeed in placing most of the pieces on the table.

It is quite likely that the Court views its function as supporting governmental policy once it has been established. Invariably, this perspective translates into support for presidential conduct of U.S. foreign relations. Certainly, any attempt to adduce an explanation would have to include the fact that the Court believes the president has plenary powers in the area of foreign policy that give him a broad discretionary authority to identify and define national interests and national security. Second, the Court seems to believe that it lacks competence, expertise, equipment, and guidelines for resolution of foreign affairs cases. Third, the Court fears the embarrassment, chaos, and confusion that may attend the exercise of judicial review against a presidential act. These factors have conduced to make the judiciary an arm of the executive in the conduct of foreign policy. As such we ought not be surprised by the institutional loyalty it has shown toward the president.

There can be little doubt that *Curtiss-Wright* has overwhelmed the foreign relations law of the United States. The Court's penchant for precedent, even flimsy precedent, drives it almost inexorably back to *Curtiss-Wright,* the source of the view that the president exercises plenary authority over foreign affairs. The effect of court-positivism has given this case an oracular status that will not likely be diminished. Indeed, from *Belmont* and *Pink* to *Zemel* and *Haig,* the Court has regularly evinced its support of the president's dominant role. As an attribute of his authority, the president has virtually unlimited discretion to identify and define U.S. national security interests. And the Court has shown an exaggerated deference to the president's perception in this area, as manifested in *Zemel v. Rusk,* and again in *Haig v. Agee,* in which the Court withdrew all checks on the executive's power to regulate travel where national security interests are concerned. Of course, it is of no moment to the judiciary that the sole-organ doctrine has been savaged by constitutional scholars as utterly without foundation and support in Anglo-American legal history. Apparently, Thomas Reed Powell used to tell his students at Harvard Law School, "Just because Mr. Justice Sutherland writes clearly, you must not suppose that he thinks clearly."[104]

The Court's obeisance to the president cannot be explained solely in terms of its subscription to the sole-organ doctrine. Fifty years ago, Professor Louis Jaffe was at pains to understand the Court's almost "unreasoning sense of incompetency" in foreign relations cases.[105] This sense of incompetency—which becomes, in the judges' minds, "no competency"—should be considered in the broader context of the Court's view that the president is superior in every aspect of policy making. Thus, the president has superior information, expertise, foreign relations machinery, diplomatic skills, and a better understanding of the national interest. In short, the judges place more faith in the executive process of weighing values and measuring the gains and losses of policies than they do in the judicial process. Clearly, this mindset is evident in a number of the cases that we have reviewed, ranging from *Curtiss-Wright,* in which Justice Sutherland supported the president's lofty status with the claim of superior information,[106] to the unwillingness to rule on the issue of unilateral presidential war making. It is also reflected in the political question doctrine, as for instance in the test involving a lack of "judicially discoverable and manageable standards."

Given this backdrop—the judiciary's insecurity and lack of confidence—and the fact that the Court, usually, can only check acts *after* they have occurred, the fact of judicial deference becomes somewhat more comprehensible. There is, therefore, something of an urge to "go along" with the established policy. In reality, this trend provides a support function for the executive, as Congress rarely acts first. But, this act of filial piety also can work tragedy, as it did in the internment of Japanese-Americans in World War II.

Finally, the Court has not been willing to ignore the political realities of the international realm. The contortions of Justice Rehnquist in *Dames and Moore,* the stretching and twisting to find congressional authorization for President Carter's agreement with Iran, reflected his understanding of realpolitik and the complexities of international negotiation. If the Court had ruled against the Iranian pact, chaos and confusion would have resulted and a carefully crafted diplomatic package would have been unraveled. A similar fate awaited President Roosevelt in both *Belmont* and *Pink* if the Court had not contrived authority for the executive acts involved in those cases. Clearly, embarrassment is a weighty concern for the Court, as are its desires to promote order and tranquillity and avoid confusion and stress.

For all of these reasons, and perhaps others, the Court is inclined to take a very narrow view of its role in foreign affairs cases. The reasoning underlying this conception leads it to grant considerable respect, latitude, and discretion to other departments when it can, and in foreign affairs cases, as we have observed, it always follows this approach. In short, the Court believes it should not interfere with the policy-making organ, the president, but should give him virtually untrammeled authority. With this line of thought we have come full circle, for we have returned to the argument of *Curtiss-Wright.*

CONCLUSION: POLICING CONSTITUTIONAL BOUNDARIES

The growth of executive foreign affairs powers in the past fifty years has been tremendous. Although given only modest authority by the Constitution, the president's powers have become so great as to provide him with a virtual "monopoly"[107] over foreign relations. The judicial contribution to presidential hegemony is reprehensible. Beginning with *Curtiss-Wright,* the courts have steadily fed the springs of presidential power. They have done so by showing great deference to the executive, sometimes by virtue of the political question doctrine and other times by blanket disregard of congressional intentions. Whatever the method, the judiciary has played a pivotal role in the trend toward executive domination of foreign affairs. Its obeisance to the president betrays the wisdom of the deep-seated suspicion with which the framers and ratifiers viewed executive discretion—an animus so powerful that it led them, virtually without dissent, to place the conduct of foreign policy beyond the presidency and in the more trusted hands of Congress. That decision, of course, also reflected their commitment to the republican principle of collective decision making, a process they believed would produce foreign policy consistent with the national interests.

Acting as an arm of the executive branch, the Court has done much to undermine collective decision making and shared powers in foreign affairs at the expense of its duty to police constitutional boundaries. As Justice Robert Jackson said, "some arbiter is almost indispensable when power is . . . balanced between different branches, as the legislative and executive. . . . Each unit cannot be left to judge the limits of its own powers." [108] By policing constitutional boundaries, the Court would not only maintain the integrity of the Constitution, it also would protect the entire political community against usurpation. A political community like the United States expects that the allocation of governmental power by the Constitution will be maintained—barring, that is, fundamental changes through the amendatory process. Change through that method assures the sovereign people a voice in the system by which they are governed. But a radical departure from the constitutional blueprint that the people ratified deprives them of such a voice. When the written Constitution is violated by usurpation of power, the people may wonder about the utility of limiting powers "if these limits may, at any time, be passed by those intended to be restrained." John Marshall, speaking as a member of the Virginia Ratifying Convention, had an answer: "To what quarter will you look for protection from an infringement on the Constitution, if you will not give the power to the judiciary? There is no other body that can afford such a protection." [109]

In recent years, the judiciary has failed to provide protection against executive usurpation of legislative power in foreign affairs; indeed, it has sanctioned it. As a result, the doctrine of shared powers has been virtually emasculated. If Marshall was right, and he very likely was, then the Constitution and the Republic are imperiled.

NOTES

I am grateful to the editors and to the anonymous reviewers for many helpful suggestions. Research for this article was made possible by a grant from the Idaho State University Research Committee. I am grateful for its assistance.

1. For a discussion of this trend from a sharply critical perspective, see David Gray Adler, *The Constitution and the Termination of Treaties* (New York: Garland Publishing, Inc., 1986); Adler, "The Constitution and Presidential Warmaking: The Enduring Debate," *Political Science Quarterly* 103 (Spring 1988), p. 1; Raoul Berger, *Executive Privilege: A Constitutional Myth* (Cambridge: Harvard University Press, 1974); Arthur Schlesinger, Jr., *The Imperial Presidency* (Boston: Houghton Mifflin, 1973); Francis D. Wormuth and Edwin B. Firmage, *To Chain the Dog of War: The War Power of Congress in History and Law* (Dallas: Southern Methodist University, 1986).

2. For differing explanations, see Ira Katznelson and Kenneth Prewitt, "Constitutionalism, Class, and the Limits of Choice in U.S. Foreign Policy," in Richard Fagen, ed., *Capitalism and the State in U.S.–Latin American Relations* (Palo Alto: Stanford University Press, 1979); Theodore Lowi, *The Personal President: Power Invested, Promise Unfulfilled* (Ithaca: Cornell University Press, 1985); Philip Kurland, *Watergate and the Constitution* (Chicago: University of Chicago Press, 1978); Leslie Gelb and Richard Betts, *The Irony of Vietnam: The System Worked* (Washington, D.C.: Brookings, 1979). See also authors cited in note 1.

3. *United States v. Curtiss-Wright Export Corporation,* 299 U.S. 304 (1936).

4. *Marbury v. Madison,* 5 U.S. 137 (1803).

5. See Adler, *Termination,* pp. 84–148.

6. For a discussion of the commander-in-chief clause, see Adler, "Warmaking," pp. 8–13; Berger, *Executive Privilege,* pp. 60–64.

7. See Hamilton's explanation in *Federalist* 69, in Edward M. Earle, ed. (New York: Modern Library, 1937), p. 451. Madison's remarks may be found in *The Letters of Pacificus and Helvidius,* Richard Loss, ed. (Delmar, N.Y.: Scholar's Facsimile, 1976), pp. 76–77.

8. Such a straightforward, textualist approach provides a basis which, in the words of Professor Philip Bobbitt, is "readily apprehendable by the people at large, namely, giving common-language meanings to constitutional provisions." Philip Bobbitt, *Constitutional Fate* (Oxford: Oxford University Press, 1982), p. 31. The significance of the plain meaning of words should not be underestimated, for as Justice Joseph Story observed, "Constitutions . . . are instruments of a practical nature, founded on the common business of human life, adapted to common wants, designed for common use, and fitted for common understanding. The people make them; the people adopt them; the people must be supposed to read them . . .; and cannot be presumed to admit in them any recondite meaning." Quoted in Bobbitt, *Constitutional Fate,* pp. 25–26.

9. Hamilton, *Federalist* 75.

10. Adler, *Termination,* p. 93.

11. Hamilton made this point in the New York Ratifying Convention. Jonathan Elliot, *Debates in the Several State Conventions on the Adoption of the Federal Constitution,* vol. 2, 2nd ed. (Washington, D.C.: J. Elliot, 1836), p. 305. For similar remarks see pp. 291, 323. Senator Rufus King, a framer, stated in Congress in 1818 that, "To the validity of all . . . proceedings in the management of foreign affairs; the constitutional advice and consent of the Senate are indispensable." Annals of Congress (1818), 31:106–107. See also Adler, *Termination,* pp. 84–148.

12. For example, it was argued in the Constitutional Convention that the various

political, economic, and security interests of the states could be protected *only* if each state had an equal voice in the treaty-making process. See Adler, *Termination*, pp. 84–88.

13. In the North Carolina Ratifying Convention, William Davie, who had been a framer, said "that jealousy of executive power which has shown itself so strongly in all the American governments, would not admit" of lodging the treaty powers in the president alone. Elliot, *Debates*, vol. 4, p. 120. In order to allay fears that the Convention had created an embryonic monarchy, Hamilton launched into a minute analysis of presidential power, in *Federalist* 69, and noted that nothing was "to be feared" from an executive "with the confined authorities of the President." *Federalist* 69, p. 448. "Fear of a return of Executive authority like that exercised by the Royal Governors or by the King had been ever present in the States from the beginning of the Revolution." Charles Warren, *The Making of the Constitution* (Cambridge: Harvard University Press, 1947), p. 173.

14. Hamilton, *Federalist* 75, p. 487.

15. When the framers were discussing the repository of the war power, they considered a proposal to give the national executive the executive powers of the continental congress. But there was concern expressed that this power would include the power of war, which would make the executive a monarchy. James Wilson sought to reassure such concerns: "Making peace and war are generally determined by writers on the Laws of Nations to be legislative powers." He added that "the Prerogatives of the British Monarchy" are not "a proper guide in defining the executive powers. Some of the prerogatives were of a legislative nature. Among others that of war & peace." Max Farrand, *The Records of the Federal Convention of 1787,* vol. 1 (New Haven: Yale University Press, 1911), pp. 73–74, 65–66. Madison agreed with Wilson (see p. 70). For discussion of the allocation of the war power and the president's authority to repel attacks against the United States, see Adler, "Warmaking," pp. 3–13.

16. Elliot, *Debates*, vol. 2, p. 528.

17. For statements in the state ratifying conventions see Adler, "Warmaking," p. 5. For example, James Iredell stated in North Carolina: "The President has not the power of declaring war by his own authority. . . . Those powers are vested in other hands. The power of declaring war is expressly given to Congress." And Charles Pinckney, a delegate in Philadelphia, told the South Carolina Ratifying Convention that "the President's powers did not permit him to declare war." Elliot, *Debates*, vol. 4, pp. 107, 108, 287. Hamilton, moreover, had stated flatly that the "declaring of war . . . by the Constitution . . . would appertain to the legislature." *Federalist* 69, p. 448.

18. See Adler, "Warmaking," pp. 3–29.

19. *Little v. Barreme,* 4 Dall. 37, 40–42, 43, 45–46 (1800); 1 Cranch 1, 28 (1801); 2 Cranch 170, 177–78 (1804).

20. *United States v. Smith,* 27 F. Cas. 1192, 1230 (No. 16342) (C.C.D.N.Y. 1806).

21. *Prize Cases,* 67 U.S. 635, 668 (1863).

22. Some academics and various presidents—Truman, Johnson, Nixon, Ford, Carter, and Reagan—have invoked the commander-in-chief clause as a source of independent presidential war-making authority. There is no merit to these claims. The Supreme Court never has held that this clause is a fountain of warmaking power for the president, and there is no foundation for this view in either

the Constitutional Convention or the state ratifying conventions. See Adler, "Warmaking," pp. 8–13, 28–29.

23. Elliot, *Debates,* vol. 2, p. 507. In the First Congress, Roger Sherman, who had been a delegate in Philadelphia, argued in defense of the shared powers arrangement in foreign affairs and stated: "The more wisdom there is employed, the greater security there is that the public business will be well done." Annals of Congress (1789), 1:1085. This statement echoed the sentiment expressed by Benjamin Franklin at the close of the Constitutional Convention, when he urged the delegates to set aside their remaining differences in favor of the collective judgment. Farrand, *Records,* vol. 2, pp. 641–643. For discussion of republicanism, see generally, Gordon S. Wood, *The Creation of the American Republic, 1776–1787* (New York: W. W. Norton, 1968), pp. 1–124.

24. Dread of executive power surfaced again and again in the various conventions; see Farrand, *Records,* vol. 1, pp. 66, 83, 90, 101, 113, 119, 153, 425; vol. 2, pp. 35–36, 101, 278, 513, 632, 640; Elliot, *Debates,* vol. 3, pp. 58, 60; vol. 4, p. 311. This fear had been common among the colonists. Edward S. Corwin, *The President: Office and Powers,* 3rd ed. (New York: New York University Press, 1948), p. 4.

25. Farrand, *Records,* vol. 1, p. 70. The Convention believed the enumeration of presidential powers was essential. See Berger, *Executive Privilege,* pp. 49–59.

26. Gelb and Betts, *The Irony of Vietnam,* p. 363; Mulford Q. Sibley, "Can Foreign Policy Be Democratic?" in Robert Goldwin and Harry Clor, eds., *Readings in American Foreign Policy,* 2nd ed. (New York: Oxford University Press, 1971), pp. 20–28. See generally, Robert Dahl, *Congress and Foreign Policy* (New York: Harcourt, Brace, 1950); Adler, *Termination,* pp. 344–355.

27. Dahl, *Congress,* p. 181; Francis D. Wormuth, "The Presidency as an Ideal Type," in D. Nelson and R. Sklar, eds., *Essays in Law and Politics* (Port Washington, N.Y.: Kennikat Press, 1978), pp. 200–201.

28. See, e.g., Eugene Rostow, "Great Cases Make Bad Law: The War Powers Act," *Texas Law Review* 50 (May 1972), p. 833; William Rogers, "Congress, the President, and War Powers," *California Law Review* 59 (September 1971), p. 1194.

29. See, generally, Schlesinger, *Imperial Presidency;* Wormuth and Firmage, *Dog of War;* Berger, *Executive Privilege;* Adler, *Termination,* pp. 344–362.

30. This view, as Schlesinger observed, "went down in flames in Vietnam." Schlesinger, *Imperial Presidency,* p. 282.

31. For some of the evidence, see Charles Lofgren, "United States v. Curtiss-Wright Export Corporation: An Historical Reassessment," *Yale Law Journal* 83 (1973), pp. 1, 3–5.

32. *Panama Refining Co. v. Ryan,* 293 U.S. 388 (1935).

33. *United States v. Curtiss-Wright Export Corporation,* at 328.

34. Annals of Congress (1800), 10:613–614.

35. Corwin, *The President,* p. 216.

36. *Writings of Thomas Jefferson,* vol. 6 (Ford ed., 1895), p. 451.

37. Quoted in Raoul Berger, "The President's Unilateral Termination of the Taiwan Treaty," *Northwestern University Law Review* 75 (1980), p. 591.

38. In *Youngstown Sheet and Tube Co. v. Sawyer,* Justice Robert Jackson dismissed Sutherland's theory as "dictum." 343 U.S. 579, 635–636 n. 2 (1952). The

Court has repudiated the theory several times. See, e.g., *Reid v. Covert,* 324 U.S. 1 (1957). For discussion of the sole organ doctrine, see Adler, "Warmaking," pp. 29–35; Lofgren, "Curtiss-Wright"; Berger, *Executive Privilege,* pp. 100–108.

39. See, e.g., *Regan v. Wald,* 468 U.S. 243 (1984); *Haig v. Agee,* 453 U.S. 280 (1981); *Dames and Moore v. Reagan,* 453 U.S. 654 (1981); *Goldwater v. Carter,* 444 U.S. 996 (1979); *Zemel v. Rusk,* 381 U.S. 1 (1965); *United States v. Pink,* 315 U.S. 552 (1942); *United States v. Belmont,* 301 U.S. 324 (1937).

40. The term, I think, was coined by H. Jefferson Powell, "Book Review," *Northwestern Law Review* 80 (1986), pp. 1128, 1136.

41. Gerhard Casper, "Constitutional Constraints on the Conduct of Foreign and Defense Policy: A Nonjudicial Model," *Chicago Law Review* 43 (1976), pp. 463, 475. With respect to the conduct of foreign policy and its relationship to the Constitution, Casper observed that the "relative scarcity of case law in the field has made it easier for judges to engage in unchecked flights of fancy, which in turn have facilitated the creation of a constitutional mythology. In that mythology, the role of Zeus is usually assigned to the President" (p. 477).

42. "The Office of Legal Adviser of the State Department reports 368 treaties and 5,590 other international agreements concluded by the United States between January 1, 1946, and April 1, 1972." Louis Henkin, *Foreign Affairs and the Constitution* (Mineola, N.Y.: Foundation Press, 1972), p. 420, n. 1. See also Raoul Berger, "The Presidential Monopoly of Foreign Relations," *University of Michigan Law Review* 71 (1972), p. 1.

43. William Davie, a framer from North Carolina, stated that "jealousy of executive power" would not permit a grant of treaty power to the president alone. Elliot, *Debates,* vol. 4, p. 120.

44. Hamilton, *Federalist* 75, pp. 486–487.

45. For a fine discussion of the constitutionality of executive agreements, see Berger, *Executive Privilege,* pp. 140–163.

46. I am presently engaged in an examination of the origins and scope of the president's recognition power. See "Constitutional Principle and Governmental Practice in Foreign Affairs: The President's Recognition Power," paper delivered to the annual meeting of the Western Political Science Association, March 10–12, 1988.

47. Hamilton, *Federalist* 69, at 451.

48. Henkin, *Foreign Affairs,* p. 41.

49. Hamilton stated that "the history of human conduct does not warrant" the commitment of "interests of so delicate and momentous a kind . . . to the sole disposal" of the president. *Federalist* 75, p. 487.

50. Berger, *Executive Privilege,* p. 160.

51. *United States v. Pink,* at 249.

52. Arthur S. Miller, "Dames & Moore v. Reagan: A Political Decision by a Political Court," *U.C.L.A. Law Review* 29 (1982), pp. 1104, 1107.

53. *Dames and Moore v. Reagan,* at 673–677.

54. Ibid., at 677–678.

55. Ibid., at 678–679. It has been held that unchallenged historical practice is no longer sufficient evidence of constitutionality. *United States v. Woodley,* 726 F. 2d 1328 (9th Cir. 1983), rehearing granted, 732 F. 2d 111 (9th Cir. 1984).

56. See, e.g., *United States v. Arrendondo,* 6 Pet. 691, 713–714 (1832); *United States v. Alexander,* 12 Wall. 127, 180 (1871); *United States v. Safety Car Heating and Lighting Co.,* 297 U.S. 88, 95 (1936).

57. *United States v. Midwest Oil Co.,* 236 U.S. 459, 474, 478 (1915).

58. *Ex parte United States,* 242 U.S. 27 (1916).

59. *Girouard v. United States,* 328 U.S. 61, 69 (1946). See also *Scripps Howard Radio v. FCC,* 316 U.S. 4, 11 (1942).

60. Gewirtz, "The Courts, Congress and Executive Policy-Making: Notes on Three Doctrines," *Law and Contemporary Problems* 40 (1976), pp. 46, 79.

61. Chemerinsky, "Controlling Inherent Presidential Power: Providing a Framework for Judicial Review," *Southern California Law Review* 56 (1983), pp. 863, 889.

62. Theodore Roosevelt, quoted in William Howard Taft, *Our Chief Magistrate and His Powers* (New York: Columbia University Press, 1925), p. 144.

63. F. D. Wormuth, "The Nixon Theory of the War Power: A Critique," *California Law Review* 60 (1972), pp. 623, 678.

64. *Kent v. Dulles,* 357 U.S. 116 (1958).

65. *Haig v. Agee,* at 319.

66. *Zemel v. Rusk,* at 31–32.

67. *Kent v. Dulles,* at 117–119, 124–125, 128, 130.

68. *Zemel v. Rusk,* at 15–16.

69. Ibid., at 17–18, 27–40.

70. Ibid., at 15–16.

71. Ibid., at 20.

72. *Haig v. Agee,* 101 S. Ct. 2766 (1981).

73. Ibid., at 2778–2779. For example, although the Court relied on *Zemel,* the *Zemel* Court had asserted a consistent history of imposing area travel restrictions both before the passage of the Passport Act of 1926 and afterward. That practice, or at least the claim of a practice, and not the State Department's construction of its own regulation, permitted the Court to sustain the travel ban to Cuba.

74. Passport Act, 92 Stat. 963, 22 U.S.C. sec. 211a (Supp. III. 1979).

75. *Haig v. Agee,* at 2782–2783.

76. Edwin B. Firmage, "The War Powers and the Political Question Doctrine," *Colorado Law Review* 49 (1977), pp. 65, 66; *Powell v. McCormack,* 395 U.S. 486, 518–522 (1969); *Baker v. Carr,* 369 U.S. 210 (1962).

77. *Cohens v. Virginia,* 19 U.S. 264, 403 (1821); Herbert Wechsler, "Toward Neutral Principles of Constitutional Law," *Harvard Law Review* 73 (1959), pp. 1, 7–8.

78. *Powell v. McCormack,* 395 U.S., at 521; *Baker v. Carr,* 369 U.S., at 210–211.

79. See, e.g., Alexander Bickel, *The Least Dangerous Branch* (New Haven: Yale University Press, 1962); Philippa Strum, *The Supreme Court and Political Questions: A Study in Judicial Evasion* (University of Alabama Press, 1974).

80. *Goldwater v. Carter,* 100 S. Ct. 533 (1979). Mutual Defense Treaty, December 2, 1954, United States–Republic of China, U.S.T. 6:433. Article X of the Treaty provided that it "shall remain in force indefinitely. Either Party may terminate it one year after notice has been given to the other Party" (437). For details of the case and the history and law regarding treaty termination, see Adler, *Termination.*

81. *Goldwater v. Carter,* at 536.

82. Ibid., at 534, 539.

83. *Baker v. Carr,* at 210.
84. Wechsler, "Neutral Principles," p. 7.
85. See Adler, *Termination,* pp. 84–237 for a discussion of these points.
86. Justice Brennan said as much in his dissenting opinion: "The issue of decision-making authority must be resolved as a matter of constitutional law, not political discretion; accordingly, it falls within the competence of the courts." *Goldwater v. Carter,* at 539. Moreover, Justice Powell stated: "We are asked to decide whether the president may terminate a treaty under the constitution without congressional approval. Resolution of the question may not be easy, but it requires us to apply normal principles of interpretation to the constitutional provisions at issue." Ibid., at 535.
87. *Marbury v. Madison,* 1 Cranch 137, 177 (1803); *Massachusetts v. Laird,* 400 U.S. 886, 894 (1970).
88. *Luther v. Borden,* 7 How. 1 (1849).
89. *Goldwater v. Carter,* at 536; Baker v. Carr, at 211.
90. Berger, "Taiwan," p. 625.
91. Frank Scharpf, "Judicial Review and the Political Question: A Functional Analysis," *Yale Law Journal* 75 (1966), p. 585.
92. *Powell v. McCormack,* at 521, 536; *Goldwater v. Carter,* at 535.
93. In *United States v. Pink,* the Court observed that an equally divided vote on the controlling "principle of law involved prevents [the case] from being an authoritative determination for other cases." (203, 216). In fact, the Goldwater case was vacated by the Court. Nevertheless, it already has been invoked as authority in *Beacon Products v. Reagan,* 633 F. Supp. 1191 (D. Mass. 1986).
94. See generally, Ratner and Cole, "The Force of Law: Judicial Enforcement of the War Powers Resolution," *Loyola of Los Angeles Law Review* 17 (1984), p. 715; Casper, "Constraints," p. 471, n. 30.
95. See notes 15–22; Adler, "Warmaking," pp. 1–29.
96. "The manner of the exercise of the war powers determines not only the nation's freedom from external danger, but also the respect which the national government has for law and for constitutional limitations on the exercise of power." Wormuth and Firmage, *Dogs of War,* p. 66.
97. See, e.g., Ratner and Cole, "The Force of Law."
98. *Crockett v. Reagan,* 558 F. Supp. 893 (D.D.C. 1982), aff'd per curiam, 720 F. 2d 1355 (D.C. Cir. 1983). Pub. L. No. 93–148, 87 Stat. 55 (codified at 50 U.S.C., sec. 1541–1548 (1976)).
99. *Crockett v. Reagan,* at 898–899; *Riegle v. FOMC,* 656 F. 2d at 873, 879 (D.C. Cir. 1981), cert. denied, 454 U.S. 1882 (1981).
100. See *Davis v. Passman,* 422 U.S. 228, 242 (1972).
101. *Sanchez-Espinoza v. Reagan,* 770 F. 2d 202, 204, 210 (1985).
102. Ibid., at 210, 211, quoting Justice Lewis Powell's opinion in *Goldwater v. Carter,* at 534.
103. See the development of this theme in Arthur S. Miller, "Reason of State and the Emergent Constitution of Control," *Minnesota Law Review* 64 (1980), p. 585.
104. Thomas Reed Powell, quoted in Schlesinger, *Imperial Presidency,* p. 103.
105. Louis Jaffe, *Judicial Aspects of Foreign Relations* (New York: McGraw-Hill, 1933), p. 223.

106. Schlesinger, *Imperial Presidency,* p. 102.
107. Berger, *Executive Privilege,* p. 117.
108. Robert Jackson, *The Struggle for Judicial Supremacy* (New York: Knopf, 1949), p. 9. Madison wrote that neither of the two departments "can pretend to an exclusive or superior right of setting the boundaries between their respective powers." *Federalist* 49, p. 328.
109. *Marbury v. Madison,* at 176; Elliot, *Debates,* vol. 3, p. 554.

Part 3
Property Rights and Economic Regulation

One of the most important goals guiding the original design of our limited and fragmented constitutional government was to secure the rights of private property owners from democratic control. Indeed, James Madison stated in *Federalist* 10 that the "first object of government . . . (was) the protection of the different and unequal faculties of acquiring property." This commitment has informed and motivated the primary activity of Supreme Court judicial review for most of American history. The depth of the commitment quickly became clear in Marshall court rulings during the early period of capitalist market development and reached its high point in the evolution of "substantive due process" and "dual federalism" doctrines limiting state control of corporatizing capitalist enterprises during the half century prior to the New Deal. The chapters in this section demonstrate that the debate over the constitutional foundations of property-based entitlements and the role of state authority in managing economic relations is still highly charged and has significant implications today.

John Brigham's overview of the subject challenges the accumulated weight of most contemporary scholarship, which suggests that the post–New Deal "double-standard" doctrine has signaled the High Court's withdrawal from economic policy making. His analysis demonstrates not only that the Court continues to play an active role in determining the boundaries between property rights and government authority but also that prevailing distinctions between old and new property prerogatives remain highly biased toward preserving class inequalities in modern society. Margaret J. Radin focuses more directly on the terms of the contemporary debate about entitlements to due process and compensation at work in Fifth Amendment "takings" doctrine. Building from criticism directed at classical liberal anti-statist property ideals, she offers a highly original normative theory of property built around postliberal notions of personhood and community. Specifically, she argues for developing a constitutional hierarchy of property rights that elevates protections for personal autonomy and security above those related to market exchanges of commoditized goods. Together, these chapters contribute to our understandings about both the biases of recent decisions and the possibilities for transforming the elements of traditional legal discourse into effective resources for progressive social change.

7 ——— ·
Constitutional Property:
The Double Standard and Beyond

JOHN BRIGHAM

For the past fifty years,[1] doctrinal and conceptual developments concerning the constitutional property right have been difficult to discern because of a judicial practice known as the "double standard." This standard has held that the Supreme Court should pay particular attention to fundamental political rights while avoiding review of economic rights. Political rights were thought to include things like the right to vote and the right to freedom of expression; economic rights incorporated the old liberty of contract protections and other creative uses of constitutional due process. Property, viewed as an economic right, has been subjected to this standard.

Thus, property has received little systematic attention from the Supreme Court for half a century. Those who depend on the Court for discussion of fundamental rights or for grounds on which to base their own analysis of constitutional property have been left to wander aimlessly, except for a few cautionary comments.[2] The double standard, though it is a widely recognized practice, may profitably be discussed in terms of its institutional significance,[3] and because it now appears to be changing.[4] The institutional significance and the change can be seen in decisions about the economy and in some provocative property cases. The justices seem to be paying more attention to economic issues than in the past, and the change in the double-standard practice coincides with an ideological shift on the current Supreme Court, to which Ronald Reagan and Ed Meese have appointed a significant group of relatively young and quite conservative judges. Institutionally, changes on the Court may presage a shift from the double standard to a new basis for judicial authority.

Because of these developments there is reason to suspect that the Court is renewing its interest in economic matters, as when it protected the powerful in the guise of a now discredited orientation to economic rights.

The shift will probably not appear exactly like the earlier version, but it will no doubt bear some relation. Once considered the ultimate vested right, property is sensitive to changes in constitutional jurisprudence and seems to coincide with particularly significant doctrinal developments. This chapter will examine constitutional property, particularly the contemporary institutional and political manifestations of a conservative economic policy reminiscent of the *Lochner*[5] era. The consequence appears to be a new double standard in which institutional decisions about property are removed from the domain of civil rights and cast into the market. I conclude with a description of how this trend will affect constitutional politics.

THE DOUBLE STANDARD

The double standard is a practice that has come to delineate the boundary between the Court and the Constitution; that is, this standard sets the terms on which the justices deal with constitutional questions. According to this practice, the Court defers to legislative bodies when it reviews a law passed by Congress or a state legislature on economic matters. Such laws include those which the Court learned to be wary of during the New Deal struggles as well as claims arising from state efforts to aid workers or children and those concerning consumers against corporate interests.[6] According to the double standard, when faced with state regulation over this sort of economic interest, the justices merely ask that there be a reasonable basis for the law. The Court, since 1937, as a matter of convention has justified its more probing attention to noneconomic issues as necessary when the political process has closed off initiatives lodged through conventional forums. This has amounted to the latest claim by the justices for an institutional distinctiveness in American government.[7]

Although the practice may be described in various ways, its meaning and institutional implications have been clear to most observers of the Supreme Court. According to Henry Abraham, "what the post-1937 judiciary did was to assume as constitutional all legislation in the proprietarian sector . . . but to regard with a suspicious eye legislative and executive experimentation with other basic freedoms,"[8] that is, those associated with the Bill of Rights. To constitutional scholar Gerald Gunther,[9] "The modern Court has turned away due process challenges to economic regulation with a broad 'hands off' approach," and "Only on a few occasions have some Justices expressed doubts about the Court's stance of extreme deference to economic regulation."[10] These observers, the justices, and others knowledgeable in the lore of the institution have made it clear that the practice has played a significant role.

The practice of deferring on economic questions as a basis for judicial review was a consequence of the New Deal struggle over the orientation of the Supreme Court. Retreating from a perceived strict supervision of the economy in *West Coast Hotel Co. v. Parrish*[11] in 1937, Justice Owen Roberts, the exemplar of a disposition in jurisprudence that has come to be termed "mechanical," switched his vote and saved the Court from institutional reconstruction.[12] The decision upheld a Washington state minimum-wage law for women and children. This stance by the justices was the first time, following the Franklin D. Roosevelt Court-packing threat, that the Supreme Court upheld such a statute, and as the chronicle of the emerging standard goes, "Gradually the Court embarked upon a policy of paying close attention to any legislative and executive attempt to curb basic rights and liberties in the 'noneconomic' sphere."[13]

The standard took shape in *United States v. Carolene Products*. This 1938 case contained Justice Harlan Stone's crucial footnote 4, which would later be used to support intensified judicial supervision of noneconomic public policy. The Stone note claimed a special justification for judicial intervention where: (1) legislation appears on its face to be within a specific prohibition of the Constitution; (2) legislation "restricts those political processes which can ordinarily be expected to bring about repeal of undesirable legislation" like voting, or political assembly; and (3) legislation that is prejudicial to discrete and insular minorities.[14]

Robert G. McCloskey, in one of the first attempts to examine the double standard that has become a particularly influential commentary for political science scholars, said that later decisions—such as *Day-Brite Lighting v. Missouri* in 1952 and *Williamson v. Lee Optical* in 1955—made it "pellucid" that no claim of a deprivation in the domain of substantive economic rights would be sustained by the Supreme Court.[15] The Court never repudiated jurisdiction over economic questions in clear and unequivocal terms, and McCloskey described the process as ad hoc and believed that it "set unforeseen limits on" constitutional adjudication.[16] Rather, the justices of the liberal courts, from those of Franklin Roosevelt's time to Earl Warren, built a basis for interpretation and judicial review out of a footnote. McCloskey subjected the doctrine of economic due process, which had been buried by the double standard, to an "exhumation and reburial." He wrote that the double standard "seems to have been a kind of reflex, arising out of indignation against the excesses of the Old Court, and resting on the vague, uncritical idea that 'personal rights' are 'O.K.' but economic rights are 'Not O.K.'"[17] The standard is clearly linked to state interventions that limited the prerogatives of corporate powers. Although the pre-1937 Court had intervened vigorously in struggles over early twentieth-century regulation, the post-1937 Court was described by Willard Hurst, the dean of American legal historians, as practically withdrawing "from the function of judicial review affecting statutory regulation of private market dealing."[18]

The distinction between economic and political matters carried by the double standard fits well with the basic proposition of modern liberalism. The double standard is the institutional commitment to this distinction.

However strained its logic and forced the distinction may be when describing fundamental rights, which quite often have economic correlates—as in the right to counsel or the right to have an abortion, for example—the Court has relied on the distinction between politics and economics and thus has offered a form of interpretation basic to liberal thought. In this and various other forms, such as in the distinction between law and markets, state and society, or even public and private, the distinction between politics and economics has become a characteristic of constitutional thought.[19]

In this sense, the institutional practice of a double standard is a specific manifestation of a larger cultural phenomenon, and like that aspect of culture, the double standard structures political practice. Back in 1937, and now in 1987, we hear the claim that the Constitution, read with the proper institutional gaze, can hold back the tides of arbitrary politics and subjective interest. Yet our experience is that politics is the most significant factor influencing the emergence of such practices, and that the practices[20] in turn are a significant influence on politics. Civil rights in the age of the double standard expanded right up to the economic boundary[21] but seldom crossed it.

The federal courts "as an engine of liberal social policy reform,"[22] for all their intrusions into the political realm,[23] have seldom pushed beyond the liberal wall of moderate political reform. The judges have become entangled with school committees, as they did in Boston, and they have occasionally dictated to budget officers, as they did in Michigan, but the intrusion has been characterized by respect for the liberal standard protecting economic interests without quite taking these interests into account.[24] Although there have been redistributive effects from these interventions, such as equalization standards for school districts with different economic resources, the real pressure for redistribution has always come from outside the courts. The poor people's movements of the 1960s and the 1970s and labor's struggle to establish community property interests in the workplace today are both examples of this type of pressure.[25]

The nature of this process is not revealed by the study of precedent, impact, or behavior but requires attention to the communities that constitute institutions—in this case the Court and the Constitution. The institutional perspective on the double standard and its links to property rights offers an interpretation that incorporates its ties to communities. Some of the focus necessarily shifts to the forces behind the text as the source of a new double standard and the basis for an expanded property right based on legitimate expectations.

We observers and scholars of the law have all learned to be realists when addressing judicial decisions, and now, in an age of interpretation, we aspire to understand better the significance of communities in determining what makes sense for judges to say. We know that judges have learned the law's codes and rituals first as lawyers. Although his or her breakfast may determine a judge's tolerance or disposition, it cannot determine the parameters of sensible discourse. For discourse, communities are needed, groups who know the issues and can contribute to the debates. These communities, in turn, are influenced by the ways they come to address political issues and describe political interests. Property issues are seriously contested by communities around the law. Conversely, we are beginning to think more carefully about the significance for these communities of what judges say. It is not enough to acknowledge the world outside the authority of the state; we need to know the extent to which it is actually autonomous and the extent to which the state influences choices that might seem to be beyond the reach of the law. Political strategies in the feminist antipornography movement might provide one example of these distinctions, for instance. In this sense, we can suspect that the meaning of property as it comes to be interpreted in the appellate courts will have some impact on how people in various movements talk about property.

A focus on the practice of the double standard, and the resulting widespread conception that the Supreme Court withdrew from the arena of economic matters, misses some important developments that have occurred over the past half century. In this period a jurisprudence arose around the "takings clause" of the Fifth Amendment, which, although it had significant implications for civil liberties, was seldom considered to be an aspect of that important realm. Under the takings provisions, property rights continued to be protected by the courts as exceptions to the double standard until more recent developments emerged in the civil liberties field to provide support. But one effect of the double standard noted by political scientists[26] has been to prevent these developments from being incorporated into constitutional jurisprudence. That is, those who have collected the opinions and commented on the doctrines, such as Gerald Gunther, Henry Abraham, and Sheldon Goldman,[27] have generally deferred to the institutional practice as outlined in footnote 4. In most constitutional law texts, there is no section on property. The issue, where it is treated, is considered a matter of substantive due process.[28] I will now review some of the traditions in constitutional property law with an eye to assessing how it has developed since the New Deal.

OLD PROPERTY UNDER THE CONSTITUTION

Mechanisms to protect economic interests appear throughout the Constitution. Article I establishes federal power to regulate commerce, coin money, and punish pirates while limiting state power to "impair the obligation of contract."[29] Article IV guarantees a republic form of government, and Article VI provides for payment of debts against the United States. And as commentators for nearly the past 200 years have pointed out, there was considerable attention paid to economics by the founding generation.

The term property, however, is used in the original Constitution only in the Fifth Amendment, which provides that no citizen shall "be deprived of life, liberty, or property without due process of law; nor shall private property be taken for public use without just compensation." The early Supreme Court protected economic interests without developing the meaning of constitutional property by referring to the various other constitutional provisions. In the 1810 case of *Fletcher v. Peck,* Chief Justice John Marshall relied on the contract clause to prevent governmental whim from denying legitimate expectations.[30] Before the Civil War, interests that ranged from status in the community to franchises to do business constituted contested forms of property.[31]

Due process protection emerged after the Civil War when property began to be viewed in terms of its value in the market (exchange value) rather than in terms of its utility (or use) value.[32] This right was much more appropriate to an expanding industrial order, and the Fifth and Fourteenth Amendments became the keys to constitutional protection for property. Thus, before judicial attention turned away from regulation of the economy in 1937, a conception of constitutional property had developed that remained significant for a very long period owing to the limited number of constitutional pronouncements on economic issues.

Justice Oliver Wendell Holmes, Jr., set a conceptual framework for property in the modern Constitution just as he did for so many other aspects of constitutional law. In the 1922 case of *Pennsylvania Coal v. Mahon,*[33] he addressed a situation where a coal mine had been dug beneath land to which a Pennsylvania coal-mining company held subsurface rights. Mahon, who lived in a house above the mine, tried to stop the tunneling on the basis of a state statute prohibiting such activity. Giving new life to the Fifth Amendment's just-compensation clause, Holmes referred to the traditional "bundle of rights" in the common law definition of property. This metaphor protected constitutional property by modifying the takings provision to allow property to be protected even though full legal title to it had not changed hands. Holmes wrote in *Mahon* that "a strong public desire to improve the public condition is not enough to warrant achieving the desire by a shorter cut than the constitutional way of paying for the change."[34] The Pennsylvania statute, the Court held, had "taken" mine property.[35] Since 1922, Holmes's concept of a "bundle" has called attention to the intangible rights in property and has provided the framework for a movement away from *things* and toward expectations.[36]

"Takings" jurisprudence during the half-century reign of the double standard was used very infrequently in judicial intervention and has only recently begun to find a place in a larger discussion of constitutional law. In his treatise on constitutional law, Laurence Tribe described the protection of the Fifth Amendment's takings clause in terms of a model of "settled expectations," a distinctive form of constitutional adjudication. For Tribe, the Constitution places "restraints on government power" that vest rights in property on the grounds "that certain settled expectations . . . should be secure against governmental disruption, at least without appropriate compensation."[37] Review of Supreme Court decisions since 1789 reveals that property protection grounded in the Constitution depends on expectations that have been settled or legitimated in some fashion, as by title, grant, or the decision of a court, rather than mere possession of tangible things.[38]

Adjudication of "takings" questions is often concerned with what the state owes the property owner for appropriation or restriction of uses; that is, what constitutes adequate compensation.[39] Interest by the Supreme Court in these questions in the past decade is one manifestation of a growing orientation to economic issues. The contemporary doctrine of settled expectations was developed in *Penn Central Transportation Company v. New York*.[40] The case involved restrictions placed by the City of New York on development of historic landmarks. The constitutional form of the dispute addressed by the Supreme Court was whether these restrictions, as applied to the train station, constituted a "taking." Writing for the majority, Justice William Brennan admitted an inability to develop any set formula for determining when "economic injuries caused by public action must be compensated." Moreover, he indicated that, although takings are more readily found where there is a "physical invasion" by government, the broader understanding is that a taking may simply interfere with interests "sufficiently bound up with the reasonable expectation of the claimant." Thus these reasonable expectations would, according to Brennan, constitute 'property' for Fifth Amendment purposes."[41] The Court held that Penn Central would not lose sufficient profits to constitute a violation of legitimate expectations. Although the regulation did not amount to a constitutional taking, the analysis by the Court had subordinated state power over historic preservation to a reasonable expectation of profit.

Commenting on the 1983 term, conservative Judge Frank Easterbrook said that the Supreme Court's major cases, *Hawaii Housing Authority v. Midkiff* and *Ruckelshaus v. Monsanto Co.*, responded to the double standard by placing takings largely outside the realm of judicial review. He wrote that they treated "governmental expropriation of property as simply another form of socioeconomic regulation."[42] But the more significant consequence of these decisions may have been that the Court and the commentators took a close look at a very political expropriation case in *Hawaii* while relying on the more modern standard of civil libertarian deference to private over public in *Monsanto*, a case that dealt with disclosure of trade secrets by the Environmental Protection Agency (EPA) in the process of reviewing health and safety issues. The *Hawaii* case, involving a large-scale redistribution of title to end the concentration of land in the hands of a few in the islands, was upheld by the Supreme Court. Thus, the practice of the double standard still appears in constitutional discourse even as the justices display an evident interest in economic matters.

NEW PROPERTY UNDER THE CONSTITUTION

A comparison of the takings decisions to cases dealing with modern state entitlement during the past fifty years calls attention to the continuing "bias" in favor of constitutionally-protected property interests as well as to a new meaning for the double standard. The courts have said a great deal about which expectations are legitimate or "settled," but they have not based that judgment on market considerations.[43] In spite of some ideas to the contrary among those who see a theorist behind the constitutional system, John Locke is not residing in the U.S. Constitution. In the common law until this century, much was made of a distinction between individual "rights" surrounding the old property and "privileges" adhering in government largess. The traditional example is cited from an opinion by Holmes, written when he was a judge in Massachusetts, that concerns the case of a policeman who had been fined for criticizing his chief. "The petitioner may have a constitutional right to talk politics, but he has no constitutional right to be a policeman."[44] The distinction denied constitutional protection where a benefit or expectation arose from government largess.

The initial application of constitutional property status to public welfare benefits involved Social Security. As the Social Security program was set up along the lines of private insurance programs, few were surprised that property interests were evaluated. The program itself was held constitutional in 1937 against a substantive challenge to the authority of Congress to create the system.[45] The justices subsequently addressed the entitlement issue directly in terms of the right to benefits owed to the otherwise eligible family of Ephram Nestor, who had come to the United States from Bulgaria in 1913. Nestor became eligible for Social Security in 1955, and in 1956 he was deported for having been a member of the Communist party from 1933–1939.[46] Focusing on the nature of an entitlement to Social Security, the Supreme Court overruled the District Court in Washington, D.C., which had held that the benefits constituted "accrued property rights." Rather, according to a bare majority of the U.S. Supreme Court, the interests were a "noncontractual benefit" that could be withdrawn simply on the basis of a "rational justification." The majority opinion was written by Justice John Marshall Harlan, but dissents by Justices Hugo Black, William Douglas, William Brennan and Chief Justice Earl Warren went along with the D.C. court and indicated significant support for the property claim.

Justice Black's opinion is quite powerful. His straightforward prose lays out the nature of Nestor's right in the tradition of American rights to property rather than in terms of the evils of Communism. Based on Nestor's continuous residency in the United States for forty-three years and membership in the Communist party when it was neither illegal nor a statutory grounds for deportation,[47] Black saw a taking of property "without just compensation"[48] as an ex post facto law and a bill of attainder that he understood as part of the anti-Communist hysteria in the country at the time. To Justice Black, the majority was telling contributors to the Social Security system "that despite their employer's payments the Government . . . is merely giving them something for nothing and can stop doing so when it pleases."[49] Black's reading of the law, he said, was that it was Congress's intent that the elderly *not* think the government was giving them "something for nothing." He went on to chide the majority for suggesting that "a decision requiring the Social Security system to keep faith would deprive it of flexibility."[50] He acknowledged that Congress has the power to alter and amend the Social Security Act and that the legislators could decide to stop covering new people or choose not to increase obligations to elderly contributors, but it could not disappoint "the just expectations of the contributors to the fund."[51]

Constitutional protection for new entitlements grew in the United States and in the Supreme Court during the 1960s and early 1970s. In 1961, the Court held that when public employment was terminated, only an unusually important government need could outweigh the right to a prior hearing.[52] A few years later, Charles Reich called the body of entitlements that are guaranteed in the welfare state "the New Property" and set off a series of developments advancing the status of this form of property. He argued that the welfare state had altered the status of individuals and that benefits like unemployment compensation, public assistance, and insurance for the elderly urgently "need the concept of right."[53] A few years later, Justice Brennan noted that "It may be realistic today to regard welfare entitlements as more like 'property' than a 'gratuity.'"[54] He cited Reich's view on property, noting that "Much of the wealth in this country takes the form of rights which do not fall within traditional common law concepts of property." Unemployment compensation, tax exemptions, and employment security were on Justice Brennan's list.

Given the long-standing recognition of a property right to intangible expectations, what is "new" about property to which people are entitled by statute as part of the social service commitment of the modern state is the particular interest, the intangible or tangible thing that is expected. Social Security is a relatively recent expectation, as is Aid to Families with Dependent Children (AFDC) and its new 1988 successor (the Moynihan Act). Licenses to run nuclear reactors are "new" in much the same way. The application of the constitutional property right, however, in historical practice grew out of licenses for economic activity and a great variety of grants from the government. These licenses and grants were some of the first subjects of constitutional protection as property. The Supreme Court in the past fifteen years has allowed termination of federal disability benefits without a prior hearing, for instance, while granting that benefits provided by the government were a "statutorily created property interest protected by the Fifth Amendment."[55]

The new concept of property, having emerged under the double standard at a time of diminished concern for traditional economic interests and increased sensitivity to civil liberties in the Supreme Court, has contributed to the status of some traditional kinds of property. Justices and legal scholars have drawn on civil libertarian values to expand protection of property in land and disposable wealth.[56] A number of cases in the early 1980s reflected such concerns for personal or civil libertarian values—for example, in protecting the claim to a job of a handicapped shipping clerk,[57] the integrity of a small apartment house owner (as opposed to the big cable company),[58] and the programs of a Mennonite religious community whose land was taken for nonpayment of taxes.[59] In each of these cases the property was more of the old variety than of the new—a common law right of action, a building, and land—but the appeal was in the tradition suggested by the double standard—attention to the interests of those with little power.[60] Thus, traditional civil liberties concerns have been linked to property in order to transcend the constraints of the double standard, and litigation of this sort has had a better chance of success.

Yet, in spite of a civil liberties consciousness, important differences evident in the treatment of property questions go beyond the distinction between "old" and "new" property. Some of these differences are largely a function of the class of wealth involved and, indirectly, the class of the property holder. The wealth or property that we know of as "capital" is more fully protected than property that involves the obligations of the modern state to those who work or are in need. This connection between property and class is inconsistent with constitutional principles. The challenge in the final section of this chapter is to describe the different interests behind the jurisprudence of property and to face the political imperative for developing claims to fairness for holders of entitlements whose class status does not afford them the privileged economic and social position that has buttressed the property claims of the wealthy.

THE NEW DOUBLE STANDARD

The renewed concern for the "old" property as outlined above and a new fundamentalism evident in the doctrine of original intent[61] indicate some movement away from the double standard. At the same time, the "new" property of a generation ago is being subjected to greater scrutiny from an increasingly conservative judiciary. Perhaps as a result of the persistence of the double standard in the minds of its traditional champions, however, commentators on the Supreme Court have not adequately noted the shift in judicial attention and its implications for doctrinal discussion of property and constitutional jurisprudence. In spite of the extensive attention given to the impact of the Court's recent decisions on the power of states to regulate property through zoning,[62] most casebooks categorize property cases involving the new notion of property under the old "substantive due process" rubric. This categorization could be due to the lack of a more explicit property framework beyond the double standard,[63] but in any case it appears that little attention is being paid to the fact that a jurisprudential transformation seems to be taking place.

Two major decisions of the 1986–1987 term of the Supreme Court portend ill for those who see the conservative swing in the judiciary as simply a reluctance on the part of the new right to extend the constitutional guarantees of the Warren Court era. In property cases, covered by the double standard until recently, the Lochnerizing[64] of the modern court has become difficult to conceal. In the *Nollan* case[65] in June 1987, in a 5–4 decision, the Court overturned a state court's ruling permitting California's Coastal Commission to require the buyers of an oceanfront lot in Ventura County to donate an easement as a condition for a zoning variance. The easement would have run parallel to the shore, permitting direct passage between two neighboring public beaches. The state's Coastal Commission had been established in 1972 as a comprehensive way to manage access to the Pacific Coast, which, as part of the state's constitution, had been mandated open to the public. In the *Church Property Case,*[66] through an opinion by the chief justice, the Supreme Court ruled, also in June 1987, that property owners are entitled to compensation for government regulations that deprive them of reasonable use of their land.

In the same year, the Supreme Court extended principles of reasonableness to entitlement holders in public employment[67] and in private employment where there were state entitlement provisions.[68] The majority in the public employee case relied on *Cleveland Board of Education v. Loudermill,*[69] a 1985 decision in which the Court claimed to have clarified its position relative to the power of legislative bodies to determine the amount of property to which an entitlement holder would be entitled—the so-called "bitter with the sweet" doctrine.[70] Chief Justice Rehnquist, who authored the original doctrine, dissented on public employee property. In another case, dealing with private employment, a majority of the Supreme Court upheld efforts by the State of Maine to protect its workers from plant closings. The justices allowed provisions for severance benefits for dispossessed workers to stand. Corporate interests had made a claim of unconstitutional taking and federal preemption in the area of welfare benefits and collective bargaining. The dissenters, however, Justices Byron White, William Rehnquist, Sandra Day O'Connor, and Antonin Scalia, are somewhat younger than the majority and may not have to brood for very long before they can write their opinions into law. These cases show a continuing willingness to consider substantive protections for some private forms of property, but public or social welfare property must struggle to be accorded due process.

In this regard it is appropriate to clarify the distinctive character of constitutional property, especially as it operates today under something of a new double standard. Property in this area of law is different from common law property and yet represents a liberal conception of property.[71] The new constitutional standard for property sets the terms for interpretation and introduces a pernicious form of class bias into constitutional practice. The new standard leaves property in entitlements only partially fulfilled, while concern about the civil liberties in traditional property rights expands protection in that area. Constitutional protection for entitlements is incomplete by comparison to the protections for traditional property rights. The latter are accorded the safeguard of due process and also the substantive protection of compensation when property is taken.

The traditional argument for compensation is that monetary payment to one suffering a loss helps distribute the costs resulting from public action. A property owner whose front yard is needed for a roadway expansion is not expected to make additional economic sacrifices to subsidize the common good. Public compensation to distribute the costs of takings is central to constitutional protection. By inference, then, entitlement holders with a legitimate expectation of benefits should be able to make the same claim—that is, that any losses due to a change in policy, after an expectation has been established, must be compensated, as a matter of right. This point is implied in Justice Black's discussion of "just expectations" in his dissent, along with Douglas, Brennan, and Warren, in *Flemming*.[72] The withdrawal of benefits was described as a taking of property—of Social Security benefits—without compensation. In this early entitlements case the lower court decision also revealed support for property protection of this sort.

For commentators like Bruce Ackerman, the absence of constitutional protection for statutory entitlements is due to a limited conception of property that is protected by the constitution as "private wealth."[73] According to this theory, the basis for the protected right has been trade and the ability to transfer interests, which is characteristic of some forms of statutory property—such as liquor licenses, taxi medallions, and development rights—but not others, such as welfare entitlements.[74] Compensation seems to symbolize the higher status accorded to property when the right is associated with the market. Although neither property rights nor the market could exist as we know it without the State, the tradition has been to protect commercial expectations more fully than private ones that have no commercial potential,[75] such as the expectations of parents with regard to benefits promised to their children.[76]

The puzzle about market, or commercial, considerations as they come into play in the constitutional context is that they have little to do with hard work or creativity and everything to do with expectations made legitimate in the law. Rights associated with the old type of property protect wealth by a standard of market opportunities. In *Penn Central Transportation Co. v. New York City*, the decision by the Supreme Court rested, at least in part, on how much the company could reasonably expect as a return on its property.[77] The Court's attention was on the legitimate expectation of return on corporate property when it held that the transportation company was not prevented from making substantial profits on its building.[78] If the city had interfered in such a way as to preclude the company from reaping a reasonable benefit from its land and building, New York City would have been required to compensate the transportation company.[79] This protection of future benefits has been broad ever since intangible interests came under the constitutional mantle.

In the 1986 decision in the case of *Connolly v. Pension Benefit Guaranty Corp.*,[80] Justice White discussed the takings issue in the context of statutorily created financial liability of employers for contributions to a pension plan beyond those for which they had contracted. The Court held that Congress could increase private liability in the interest of public welfare and social responsibility without being obligated to consider compensation.[81] Protection for property grounded in market considerations, or what White termed "investment backed" expectations, supported the idea that because the field of employee pension plans was already heavily regulated, employers had adequate warning that Congress could increase their liability.[82] This strange transposition of the takings logic suggests that the key to the interest protected by compensation is not commerce. Instead, the sovereign authority to protect the public welfare is consistently the primary consideration.

If the expectation of a particular grant is extended for a fixed period or according to certain conditions—such as Social Security survivor's benefits granted to children until they reach eighteen or, as used to be the case, twenty-two, if they went to college—a cut-off prior to that time is a violation of legitimate expectations. In this example, not only are there the expectations of the children who were promised benefits but also those of the parents who paid into the system. After eliminating these benefits in 1982, Congress heard testimony from Alice James of Chestertown, Maryland, whose husband had died leaving four near college-age children no longer eligible for benefits he had earned and expected while paying into the Social Security system.[83] Although she spoke of betrayal and disappointment, Mrs. James did not rely on the fundamental right in the Constitution and constitutional decisions protecting legitimate expectations. The double standard, by drawing attention away from the fundamental right to property, and the limits of legal vision, which fail to see compensation issues, have conspired to preclude this powerful claim from emerging in policy debates or constitutional adjudication.

CONCLUSION

Thus, in judicial interpretation of the Constitution, there are now two levels of property protection—one for the wealthy, whose property gives them power, and one for the poor, whose property is symptomatic of their powerlessness. Treatment of constitutional property in the era of the double standard has relied on distinctions between economics and politics and between politics and law that have masked this bias in constitutional property. The recent shift toward protecting the interests of property owners and the implicit drift from the double standard would seem to indicate that these undeveloped implications of a constitutional system need to be reconsidered. The core of such a consideration would investigate the interpretive basis for judicial authority and link forms of interpretation to movement practice. The challenge today is that a conservative jurisprudence is moving to supplant the double standard with a new doctrinal fundamentalism that is unsympathetic to traditions behind entitlement rights and hostile toward the claims to an equitable standard just outlined. The judicial conservatives invoke exogenous mechanisms like "the intent of the Framers"[84] or an economic calculus[85] to support interpretive decisions that are beginning to create a new double standard.

On this its fiftieth anniversary, we should take special note of the *Carolene Products* footnote and the past five decades of civil rights practice. We can say goodbye to process-based justifications and, taking the determinancy of interpretation seriously, we can begin to assess its implications for progressive rights struggles. Examining the new property from this perspective leads us to appreciate the materiality of the constitutional "word."[86] Constitutional discourse is dominated by the legal profession—those judges, lawyers, and law professors who participate in professional discussions of the institutions, doctrines, and processes of the law. This is not surprising on the surface but is very difficult to discern at another level because the legal community is both diverse and particularly adept at incorporation and synthesis. In addition, although the dominance of positivism in formalist jurisprudence has been said to mask the discursive force in the profession, the positivism in realist jurisprudence and interpretation assures a continuing screen. Lawyers present their activity as simply telling tales and spinning yarns, yet their community makes certain yarns particularly salient and gives certain storytellers significant advantage. Through this activity the established institutions of the law maintain a legal order grounded in familiar practices.[87]

By focusing on what the justices should or might do and by giving persistent attention to Supreme Court opinions, scholarship on constitutional property is limited in two respects. It is bound by a tradition that I have shown to be biased, and it is limited by the emerging coalition of justices, who many expect to have a similar bias. Yet the Constitution is much more than the justices say it is. Outside the Supreme Court, commentary on the property issue invites caution with regard to relying on "legal contrivances" to produce social change[88] and stirs concern that the real gains from a revival of property rights will be for the wealthy and not the newly entitled,[89] nor shall new conceptions of rights based on community interests be allowed to emerge.[90]

There is a constituted "nomos" or normative sphere, with circumscriptions, worlds that are lost, and new worlds that are ascending. In the field of constitutional property, this nomos has been dominated by the judiciary and mystified by the double standard.[91] But their interpretations are not necessarily conclusive. This chapter is part of an effort from outside the lawyers' community to interpret the law with attention to its political and institutional dimensions. New jurisprudential propositions must continue to depend on interpretive communities beyond the judges, at least beyond the federal judges. Instead, it may be state judges, legislators, or communities of citizens that will ultimately overcome the intolerable bias of juridical practices and thwart the imposition of a new double standard in how we treat entitlements.

NOTES

1. *United States v. Carolene Products Co.*, 304 U.S. 144 (1938), footnote 4, in part: "There may be narrower scope for operation of the presumption of constitutionality when legislation appears on its face to be within a specific prohibition of the Constitution, such as those of the first ten Amendments, which are deemed equally specific when held to be embraced within the 14th."
2. Robert McCloskey, "Economic Due Process and the Supreme Court: An Exhumation and Reburial," in Philip B. Kurland, ed., *The Supreme Court Review* (Chicago: University of Chicago Press, 1962); Martin Shapiro, "The Constitution and Economic Rights," in M. Judd Harmon, ed., *Essays on the Constitution of the United States* (Port Washington, N.Y.: Kennikat Press, 1978); Richard Funston, "The Double Standard of Constitutional Protection in the Era of the Welfare State," *Political Science Quarterly* 90 (1975), pp. 261–287.
3. Rogers Smith, "Political Jurisprudence, The 'New Institutionalism,' and the Future of Public Law," *American Political Science Review* 82 (1988), pp. 89–108.
4. Martin Shapiro, "The Supreme Court's 'Return' to Economic Regulation," *Studies in American Political Development* 1 (1986), p. 94.
5. *Lochner v. New York*, 198 U.S. 45 (1905), has come to stand for an earlier conservative period in American jurisprudence when federal judges and justices ruled against progressive social legislation dealing with issues like working conditions and the distribution of wealth.
6. Martin Shapiro, in an apt turn of phrase, called this "Republican" property. Shapiro, "The Supreme Court's Return," p. 94.
7. John Brigham, *The Cult of the Court* (Philadelphia: Temple University Press, 1987).
8. Henry Abraham, *Freedom and the Court* (New York: Oxford University Press, 1982), p. 15.
9. When Judge Robert Bork was questioned before the Senate Judiciary Committee in the fall of 1987 on his nomination to the Supreme Court, he often referred to Gunther's treatise, *Cases and Materials on Constitutional Law*, 10th ed. (New York: Foundation Press, 1980).
10. Ibid., p. 540.
11. *West Coast Hotel Co. v. Parrish*, 300 U.S. 379 (1937).

12. Gregory A. Caldeira, "Public Opinion and the U.S. Supreme Court: FDR's Court-packing Plan," *American Political Science Review* 81 (1987), pp. 1139–1154.
13. Abraham, *Freedom and the Court.*
14. *United States v. Carolene Products Co.,* footnote 4.
15. McCloskey, "Economic Due Process," p. 38.
16. Ibid., p. 34.
17. Ibid., p. 54.
18. J. Willard Hurst, "The Function of Courts in the United States: 1950–1980," *Law and Society Review* 15 (1980–1981), p. 456.
19. See generally Rogers M. Smith, *Liberalism and American Constitutional Law* (Cambridge: Harvard University Press, 1985); Funston, "The Double Standard," has an excellent discussion of this history.
20. Martha Minow, "Law Turning Outward," *TELOS* (forthcoming).
21. John Brigham, "Means Discrimination," *Law and Policy* (1985), pp. 169–187.
22. Joel Grossman, "Beyond the Willowbrook Wars: The Courts and Institutional Reform," *ABF Research Journal* (Winter 1987), pp. 249–259.
23. Richard Morgan, *Disabling America: The Rights Industry in Our Time* (New York: Basic Books, 1984).
24. J. R. Lucas, *The Common Ground.*
25. Frances Fox Piven and Richard Cloward, *Poor People's Movements* (New York: Pantheon, 1977); Staughton Lynd, "Communal Rights," *Texas Law Review* 62 (1984), p. 1417. See also E. Sparer, "Fundamental Human Rights, Legal Entitlements, and the Social Struggle," *Stanford Law Review* 36 (1984), p. 509.
26. Funston, "The Double Standard"; Shapiro, "The Supreme Court's Return."
27. Gunther, *Cases and Materials;* Abraham, *Freedom and the Court;* Goldman, *Constitutional Law and Supreme Court Decision Making,* 2nd ed. (New York: Harper and Row, 1986).
28. Sheldon Goldman, *Constitutional Law.*
29. See Benjamin F. Wright, Jr., *The Contract Clause of the Constitution* (Cambridge: Harvard University Press, 1938); C. Peter Magrath, *Yazoo: Law and Politics in the New Republic* (New York: W. W. Norton, 1966).
30. *Fletcher v. Peck,* 6 Cranch [10 U.S.] 87 (1810). The case involved fraudulent land sales by a state legislature and the implications for innocent secondary purchasers.
31. *Marbury v. Madison,* 1 Cranch [5 U.S.] 137 (1803); *Gibbons v. Ogden,* 9 Wheat. [22 U.S.] 1 (1824).
32. John R. Commons, *The Legal Foundations of Capitalism* (Madison: University of Wisconsin Press, 1924).
33. *Pennsylvania Coal v. Mahon,* 260 U.S. 393 (1922).
34. Ibid., at 416.
35. Ibid., at 414.
36. C. B. MacPherson, "A Political Theory of Property," in *Democratic Theory: Essays in Retrieval* (1973).
37. Tribe, *American Constitutional Law,* 2nd ed. (Mineola, N.Y.: Foundation Press), p. 256.
38. John Brigham, "Property and the Supreme Court: Do the Justices Make Sense?" *Polity* 16 (1984), p. 242.

39. See A. Dunham, *"Griggs v. Allegheny County* in Perspective: Thirty Years of Supreme Court Expropriation Law," *The Supreme Court Review* (1962), pp. 65–66.

40. *Penn Central Transportation Company v. New York,* 438 U.S. 104 (1978).

41. Ibid.

42. Frank Easterbrook, "Leading Cases of the 1983 Term," *Harvard Law Review* 98 (1984), p. 226.

43. John Brigham, *The Cult of the Court.*

44. *McAuliffe v. Mayor of New Bedford,* 155 U.S. 216 (1892).

45. *Stewart Machine Co. v. Davis,* 301 U.S. 548 (1937).

46. *Flemming v. Nestor,* 363 U.S. 603 (1960).

47. Ibid., at 621.

48. Ibid., at 622.

49. Ibid., at 623.

50. Ibid.

51. Ibid., at 624.

52. *Cafeteria and Restaurant Workers Union v. McElroy,* 367 U.S. 886 (1961).

53. *Goldberg v. Kelly,* 397 U.S. 254 (1970).

54. Ibid., p. 262.

55. *Mathews v. Eldridge,* 424 U.S. 319, 334 (1976).

56. Gunther, *Cases and Materials;* C. Edwin Baker, "Property and Its Relation to Constitutionally Protected Liberty," *University of Pennsylvania Law Review* 134 (1986), p. 741; Margaret Jane Radin, "Property and Personhood," *Stanford Law Review* 34 (1982), p. 957.

57. *Logan v. Zimmerman Brush Co.,* 455 U.S. 422 (1982).

58. *Loretto v. Teleprompter Manhattan CATV,* 458 U.S. 419 (1982).

59. *Mennonite Board of Missions v. Adams,* 462 U.S. 791 (1983).

60. See note 1, e.g., the attention to racial, religious, national, or other "discrete and insular minorities" in the Stone quotation.

61. See John Brigham, "The Politics of Constitutional Interpretation," *Law and Society Review* 21 (1988), pp. 801–805.

62. Eugene J. Morris, "Supreme Court Land Use Decisions Uncertain in Defining a 'Taking,'" *The National Law Journal* (September 7, 1987), p. 20; Robert Lindsey, "California's Open Beaches Feeling the Strain," *The New York Times* (August 9, 1987), p. 26.

63. Frederick Schauer, "1987 Supplement," to *Constitutional Law,* 11th ed. (Mineola, N.Y.: Foundation Press, 1987).

64. See note 5.

65. *Nollan v. California Coastal Commission,* 483 U.S. __ (1987).

66. *First English Evangelical Lutheran Church of Glendale v. County of Los Angeles,* no. 85-1199 (1987).

67. *Brock v. Roadway Express, Inc.,* 481 U.S. __ (1987).

68. *Fort Halifax Packing Co. v. Coyne,* 481 U.S. __ (1987); see also Phyllis Farley Rippey, "The Constitution and Community Property Rights," paper delivered at the American Political Science Association annual meeting, September 1987; and *Fall River Dyeing v. N.L.R.B.,* 481 U.S. __ (1987).

69. *Cleveland Board of Education v. Loudermill,* 470 U.S. 532 (1985); see also *Regents of the University of Michigan v. Ewing,* 474 U.S. 214 (1985).

70. *Arnett v. Kennedy,* 416 U.S. 134 (1974); see also Brigham, *The Cult of the Court,* p. 196; Frederick Schauer, *1987 Supplement* (Mineola, N.Y.: Foundation Press, 1987), p. 100.
71. Margaret Jane Radin, in "The Constitution and the Liberal Conception of Property," Chapter 8 in this volume, examines the liberal conception as it is articulated in neoconservative constitutional theory, particularly, Richard A. Epstein, *Takings: Private Property and the Power of Eminent Domain* (Chicago: University of Chicago Press, 1985).
72. *Flemming v. Nestor,* at 38–43.
73. *Mennonite Board of Missions v. Adams,* at 269. Little has been made out of the fact that the wording of the Fifth Amendment links compensation to "private property," but the potential for issues arising from the wording remains.
74. Ibid.
75. In *U.S. Trust Co. of New York v. New Jersey,* 431 U.S. 1 (1977), the Supreme Court struck down regulations impairing the claims of bond holders, while in *Atkins v. Parker,* 105 S. Ct. 2520 (1986), food stamp benefits were reduced with only general notice of a change in the regulation from the state.
76. See generally, "Statement of Alice James, Before a Joint Hearing of the Subcommittee on Postsecondary Education and the Subcommittee on Elementary, Secondary, and Vocational Education, Concerning Social Security Student Benefit Cuts," Washington, D.C., 97th Congress, 2nd Session, February 3, 1982.
77. *Penn Central Transportation Co. v. New York City,* at 104.
78. Ibid.
79. Shapiro, "The Supreme Court's 'Return.' "
80. *Connally v. Pension Benefit Guaranty Corp.* 106 S. Ct. 1018 (1986).
81. Ibid., at 1024–1028.
82. Ibid., at 1024–1027.
83. "Joint Hearing before the Subcommittee on Postsecondary Education."
84. Christopher Wolfe, *The Rise of Modern Judicial Review* (New York: Basic Books, 1986).
85. *Brock v. Roadway Express, Inc.*; Martha Minow, "Law Turning Outward."
86. David Silverman and Brian Torode, *The Material Word: Some Theories of Language and Its Limits* (London: Routledge and Kegan Paul, 1980). See also Martha Minow, "Interpreting Rights: An Essay for Robert Cover," (unpublished manuscript, 1987); Robert Cover, "Violence and the Word," *Yale Law Journal* 95 (1986), p. 1601.
87. Richard H. Fallon, Jr., "A Constructivist Coherence Theory of Constitutional Interpretation," *Harvard Law Review* 100 (1987) pp. 1189–1286; Robert Cover, "Foreword: Nomos and Narrative," *Harvard Law Review* 97 (1983), pp. 4–68.
88. M. W. McCann, "Resurrection and Reform: Perspectives on Property in the American Constitutional Tradition," *Politics and Society* 13 (1984).
89. W. Van Alstyne, "Cracks in the 'New Property': Adjudicative Due Process in the Administrative State," *Cornell Law Review* 62 (1977), p. 445.
90. Lynd, "Communal Rights"; Sparer, "Fundamental Human Rights."
91. Timothy J. O'Neill, "The Language of Equality in a Constitutional Order," *American Political Science Review* 75 (1981), pp. 626–635; Ira L. Strauber, "Transforming Political Rights into Legal Ones," *Polity* 16 (1983), pp. 72–96.

8 ——— ·
The Constitution and the Liberal Conception of Property

MARGARET JANE RADIN

The ideology of property has played a central role in liberal political theory from the time of John Locke to the present. Locke thought that a central purpose of government is to protect prepolitical property rights of individuals.[1] Republicans thought that individual property ownership is necessary to self-government because it underlies the requisite independence and stake in the community.[2] Lockean theory is reincarnated in modern conservative "liberals" such as Robert Nozick and Richard Epstein.[3] Republican theory is reincarnated in modern liberal "liberals" such as Cass Sunstein and Frank Michelman.[4]

Both of these strains of thought about the centrality of property in creating a polity were present at the framing of our Constitution, and property was accorded a central place in it. The Bill of Rights provides, in the Fifth Amendment, that persons may not be deprived of property without due process of law (the due process clause) and that private property shall not be taken for public use without just compensation (the eminent domain clause). Through the Fourteenth Amendment these protections become limitations on state and local governments as well as the federal government. The question for today, and for the future, is exactly what rights of individuals these clauses should be understood to recognize. To answer that question we must theorize about what conception of property is embodied in our Constitution.

The classical liberal conception of property embraces a number of broad aspects or indicia, sometimes condensed to three: the exclusive rights to possession, use, and disposition. In this chapter I consider the question whether this liberal conception should be understood to be embodied in our Constitution: To what extent should our Constitution be interpreted (and to what extent is it in fact interpreted) as protecting—or requiring—the liberal conception of property? My consideration will range through a glance at neoconservative theory; some observations on the Supreme Court's recent "takings" jurisprudence; some thoughts on commodification and the liberal conception of property; and preliminary suggestions about how the liberal indicia might be reconceived under a normative property theory based on postliberal notions of personhood and community.

A NEOCONSERVATIVE VIEW OF PROPERTY IN THE CONSTITUTION

A strain of neoconservative argument vigorously maintains that the liberal conception of property, lock, stock and barrel, is part of our Constitution. I will call it the Epstein strain, after its best-known recent advocate.[5] The Epstein strain holds that the Constitution immunizes against change those liberal indicia of property existing in the legal and political status quo. Moreover, in its radical side, the Epstein strain holds essentially that the Constitution requires us to change the status quo insofar as it does not embody the liberal indicia. The Epstein strain thus constitutionalizes a classical liberal conception of private property.

At least in the hands of Epstein himself, the process by which this constitutionalization takes place is through the meaning attributed to the word "property" in the eminent domain clause of the Fifth Amendment. Later I shall direct some criticism toward this form of constitutional interpretation. Now I shall just set out what the (constitutional) conception of property is, according to Epstein.

Epstein states—encapsulating the classical liberal view—that the conception of property includes the exclusive rights of possession, use, and disposition.[6] Elaborating on possession, he says that "the idea of property embraces the absolute right to exclude."[7] Elaborating on disposition, he stresses alienation. The most important liberal subcategory of disposition is the right of one owner to transfer entitlement to another. (Alienation in this sense underlies freedom of contract and hence is at the heart of the market order.)[8] Epstein maintains that "as a first approximation it appears that any restraint upon the power of an owner to alienate his own property should be regarded as impermissible."[9]

For Epstein, *any* legislative curtailment of one of these broad "exclusive rights" to possession, use, and disposition is a prima facie taking under the eminent domain clause. The only limitation appears to be a version of the harm principle: The concept or idea of property does not include the right to invade or harm the persons or property of others; rather, it includes the right to fend off those who attempt to invade you. (Epstein assumes that a bright line can be drawn between harm-causing, nuisance-like activities and normal activities.)[10] Once a government action is a prima facie taking, compensation is due, unless the action can be defended in one of two ways. Compensation is not required if the government action can be seen to result in "implicit in-kind compensation" (Epstein's version of the notion of reciprocity, in which those injured by regulations also receive offsetting benefits), or (possibly, in extreme cases) if the action has caused widespread and long-term reliance. Thus, for Epstein, taxation is a prima facie taking, and so are all required welfare contributions, including social security. Price control— and any other regulation of the free market—is a prima facie taking. In addition, all forms of zoning restrictions or restrictions on development, unless they are antinuisance measures, are prima facie takings.

RECENT TAKINGS JURISPRUDENCE: THE SIGNIFICANCE OF CONCEPTUAL SEVERANCE

Unlike Epstein, our Supreme Court has not fully constitutionalized (that is, found "in" the Constitution) the classical liberal conception of property. To what extent has the Court done so, and is there now a trend under way to constitutionalize the liberal conception further? As I shall briefly recount here, the Court has not done so to a very great extent. But perhaps Chief Justice William Rehnquist is spearheading such a trend.

In the 1979 case of *Kaiser Aetna v. United States,*[11] the Court decided that the government "took" private property when it asserted that a private marina, created when the corporate developer dredged a pond and removed a barrier beach separating it from the Pacific Ocean, was subject to public access through the navigation servitude of the United States. In his opinion for the majority, Rehnquist stated that certain "expectancies" are "embodied in the concept of 'property,'" which, "if sufficiently important," cannot be curtailed by the government without condemnation and compensation.[12]

What are these "expectancies"? In *Kaiser Aetna,* Rehnquist focused on the "'right to exclude,' so universally held to be a fundamental element of the property right."[13] In 1982, Justice Thurgood Marshall referred to this passage in *Kaiser Aetna* in his majority opinion in *Loretto v. Teleprompter Manhattan CATV Corp.*[14] In *Loretto,* the majority held that it was a taking for a statute to permit a cable television operator to install a cable on a building without the owner's permission (even if the operator paid the owner a nominal fee and indemnified her for damages). The *Loretto* opinion reiterated the liberal triad (possession, use, disposition)[15] but also focused on exclusion, declaring that "the power to exclude has traditionally been considered one of the most treasured strands in an owner's bundle of property rights."[16] (In referring to an owner's bundle of property rights the Court was adopting the modern conceptualization of property as an aggregate of rights rather than a unitary thing.[17]) *Loretto* was a flashback to earlier takings jurisprudence in which physical occupation was the talisman. (It reminds one of pre-*Katz* Fourth Amendment law in which the illegality of wiretapping depended upon whether the presence of the wires in the walls of the building was a trespass—i.e., invasion of a property right.)[18] In *Loretto* the Court said that "permanent physical occupation" of property is *per se* a taking, because it "effectively destroys *each*" of the rights in the liberal bundle.[19]

Thus the reinvigorated physical occupation test of *Loretto* became a *per se* rule exception, in the form of a *per se* rule, to the prevailing "multi-factor balancing test" of *Penn Central Transportation Co. v. New York City*.[20] In *Penn Central* the Court had decided that New York's landmark preservation law did not "take" Penn Central's property by prohibiting construction of an office tower on top of Grand Central Terminal. Under the balancing test, whether or not the government action can be characterized as a physical invasion is only one of the significant factors to be weighed. (Others include the economic impact of the regulation, and particularly whether it has interfered with "distinct investment-backed expectations"; whether the regulation is an exercise of the taxing power; whether it promotes public "health, safety, morals, or general welfare"; whether it is reasonably necessary to the effectuation of a substantial public purpose; and whether it may be characterized as for the purpose of permitting or facilitating "uniquely public functions.")

Loretto exacerbates the well-known paradox of takings jurisprudence: Why is it that owners may suffer large pecuniary losses—as in *Penn Central*, or for that matter in the classic *Euclid v. Ambler Co*.[21] case—without having a taking found and compensation declared necessary, whereas if the Court decides to characterize the government action as a physical occupation, a taking will be found even if the loss or inconvenience to the owner is minuscule?[22] As I have recounted, Epstein would resolve this paradox by making loss of expected monetary gain just as compensable as "physical invasion." Unlike Epstein, the Court still focuses on exclusion.

Does the Supreme Court's trend toward constitutionalization of the liberal conception of property extend past exclusion toward the aspect of alienability? For the Court to treat freedom of alienation as sacred would be radical indeed, because then any regulatory deviation from a laissez-faire regime would be a prima facie taking. So far, to the contrary, the Court has not even held that a complete market-inalienability—ban on sales—is necessarily a taking. In *Andrus v. Allard*,[23] with no dissent, the Court held that it was not a taking for Congress to declare eagle feathers and other bird artifacts nonsalable pursuant to a conservation statute.

The liberal aspect of alienability, though it is a pillar of the notion of private property in a capitalist society, has not received the solicitude accorded to the aspect of exclusive physical occupation. Neoconservative dismay over cases like *Andrus* has not yet moved the Court.[24] Yet it may have begun to move some of its members. In *Hodel v. Irving*, Chief Justice Rehnquist and Justices Antonin Scalia and Lewis Powell thought *Andrus* must now be limited "to its facts."[25] In *Hodel*, Justice Sandra Day O'Connor held for the court that another strand of the liberal bundle of rights, disposition at death, could not be abrogated, seemingly because its traditional importance is analogous with the right to exclude others that the Court had already made into a *per se* rule in *Kaiser Aetna*.[26]

At this point, however, even Chief Justice Rehnquist has not tried directly to constitutionalize alienability. He is certainly willing to push the notion of physical occupation to (or beyond) its extremes. In doing so, he may sweep in some aspects of alienability under the guise of physical occupation. In *Kaiser Aetna* Rehnquist had said that *nonexclusive* physical "invasion" (as when the government uses "only an easement" in one's property) requires just compensation.[27] He has since said that a regulation preventing a landlord from demolishing a rent-controlled apartment building "is" permanent physical occupation by the government, hence a taking requiring compensation.[28] The latter case, especially, is more readily understood as a restraint upon alienation: Under certain circumstances, the regulation withdrew the landlord's supposed right to rent or not to rent as it saw fit.

At a minimum, Rehnquist's statements go further than *Loretto,* which based its *per se* rule on the idea that physical occupation "effectively destroys *each*" of the rights in the liberal bundle. When "occupation" is nonexclusive or merely constructive, the government action does not effectively destroy all rights in the bundle; it merely curtails some of them. Thus, Rehnquist is closer to Epstein's position than is the Court as a whole, though he is still not as radical as Epstein. For Epstein, any curtailment of one of the liberal indicia is a prima facie taking, whereas for Rehnquist, it appears that the curtailment must be deemed significant.

In 1987 the Supreme Court held, per Chief Justice Rehnquist, that if regulatory legislation is ultimately determined to work a taking, compensation is due for the period from the imposition of the legislation until its judicial invalidation. In *First English Evangelical Lutheran Church of Glendale v. County of Los Angeles,*[29] the church was rendered temporarily unable to use its campground by an interim flood control ordinance that prohibited construction or reconstruction in a flood area pending County study of permanent flood control measures. Although there was some doubt, Rehnquist construed the church's complaint as alleging a taking. He then held, contrary to the rule prevailing in the California state courts, that if a taking is found, invalidation of the ordinance is not a constitutionally sufficient remedy. Rehnquist also declared that "temporary takings" are not "different in kind" from "permanent takings."[30] Formally speaking, this statement is dictum for the present case, because the courts had not yet passed on the church's taking claim. But it seems destined to come back as holding. Does the *Lutheran Church* case herald a turn toward more rigid constitutional protection of the liberal indicia of property?[31]

From the viewpoint of previous substantive law, if the decision rests on the *per se* rule against physical occupation, it seems to harbor a logical error.[32] The substantive decision that legislation is *per se* a taking, according to the majority view of *Loretto,* supposedly rests on the notion of "permanent" and complete physical occupation. By hypothesis, in a case like *Lutheran Church* the occupation is not permanent because it ceases when the ordinance is declared invalid. How can a taking in the requisite sense ever be found so as to raise the question whether California's remedy is constitutionally adequate?

If a taking *per se* cannot be found, we would be remanded to the balancing test on the underlying substantive issue of whether the government action "takes" property. If one were to accept this reasoning, all temporary takings would have to be decided under the much less stringent multifactor balancing test. To this argument Rehnquist might reply that temporary "occupations" rise to the level of *per se* constitutional injury, just as in his view do nonexclusive occupations (like the navigational servitude) or merely constructive occupations (like giving tenants tenure rights against landlords). In the important dictum quoted earlier, he seemed to make this reply by saying that temporary takings have the same constitutional status as permanent ones. This statement does seem to beg the question of how (if at all) the temporariness is to figure in the decision to call an action a taking. Moreover, the line of reasoning of this proposed reply seems capable of expanding to prohibit all government actions that alter entitlements in any way, thus arriving at the Epstein position. If Rehnquist limits it with a proviso to the effect that the alteration must be "significant," then we are back to some form of balancing test.

So Rehnquist might reply instead that the occupation in *Lutheran Church* was indeed permanent and complete—it was a permanent, complete taking of an estate for years. I will call this latter strategy "conceptual severance." It consists of delineating a property interest consisting of just what the government action has removed from the owner and then asserting that that particular whole thing has been taken. Thus, this strategy hypothetically or conceptually "severs" from the whole bundle of rights just those strands with which the regulation interferes and then hypothetically or conceptually construes those strands in the aggregate as a separate whole thing.

In the *Lutheran Church* case, Rehnquist did not stress conceptual severance, though he did analogize to the complete taking of a leasehold.[33] In *Penn Central,* however, Rehnquist in dissent explicitly relied on the conceptual severance strategy. He argued that depriving Penn Central of the right to develop an office building over Grand Central Terminal was a complete taking—of its air rights.[34] The whole thing taken, in other words, was a particular negative servitude precluding building into the air space above the existing building.

The Court as a whole has so far been less willing than Rehnquist to find takings by conceptual severance. The majority opinion in *Penn Central* declared that "'Taking' jurisprudence does not divide a single parcel into discrete segments and attempt to determine whether rights in a particular segment have been entirely abrogated"; rather, it focuses on "the parcel as a whole."[35] Nevertheless, *Loretto* moves away from that position: In order to find that placing a cable on a building "effectively destroys *each*" of the liberal rights, one must first decide that one is talking about fee simple absolute not in the building as a whole, but rather in the space occupied by the cable. And in the 1987 case of *Nollan v. California Coastal Commission*,[36] the Court (per Justice Scalia) again engaged in conceptual severance by construing a public access easement as a complete thing taken, separate from the parcel as a whole.

In *Nollan* the Court decided that even if, pursuant to California's Coastal Zone Conservation Act, the Coastal Commission could have denied entirely the Nollans' application to develop their beachfront property, the commission could not constitutionally adopt the seemingly less restrictive alternative of conditioning its grant of the permit upon the Nollans' dedication of a right of public access (which may indeed already have been owned by the public[37]) through their property beyond their seawall. Justice Scalia reasoned that the condition was not closely enough connected to the admittedly legitimate government purposes served by limiting beachfront development. He found conceptual severance to be the only rational way to construe the situation:

> To say that the appropriation of a public easement across a landowner's premises does not constitute the taking of a property interest but rather . . . 'a mere restriction on its use' [as the dissenters and the court below had done in applying the multifactor balancing test to the parcel as a whole] is to use words in a manner that deprives them of all their ordinary meaning.[38]

To the contrary, the Court has traditionally understood the ordinary meaning of property to be the owner's parcel as a whole. Thus, in order for the Court to find that "something" has been completely taken, the severance (i.e., the division of the fee into various discrete subpackages) must have existed prior to the government's action. In the famous *Pennsylvania Coal Co. v. Mahon*[39] case, legislation that de facto prevented coal mining "took" a coal company's mining rights, but mining rights were all that the company owned; whereas in the equally famous *Goldblatt v. Hempstead*[40] case, the would-be quarry operator owned the fee, and the loss of the quarry rights was not deemed a taking. This traditional reluctance to use conceptual severance is usually chalked up to crystallized expectations or ordinary language and culture.[41] That is, the appropriate understanding of what constitutes a "parcel as a whole" (and hence the owner's "property") depends upon previous real-life treatment of the resource, not the conceptual possibilities held available by property law.

Be that as it may, it is worth observing that as soon as one adopts conceptual severance, as it seems the Court did in *Loretto* and *Nollan,* there is an easy slippery slope to the radical Epstein position. Every curtailment of any of the liberal indicia of property, every regulation of any portion of an owner's "bundle of sticks," is a taking of the whole of that particular portion considered separately.[42] Price regulations "take" that particular servitude curtailing free alienability; building restrictions "take" a particular negative easement curtailing control over development, and so on.

Thus, one way to consider whether the *Lutheran Church* and *Nollan* cases presage greater constitutionalization of the liberal conception of property is to consider whether they will lead to more acceptance of conceptual severance. As we have seen, looking back on the Court's recent takings jurisprudence, a trend toward conceptual severance is already in progress. The interest taken by the legislation at issue in *Loretto* should—according to crystallized expectations, or our ordinary language and culture of property—be characterized not as a permanent, complete physical invasion of the owner's parcel but rather as an easement to run a cable. The interest taken by the government's action in *Kaiser Aetna* is likewise most readily characterizable as an easement or servitude. Moreover, the taking of easements or servitudes cannot be *ipso facto* a taking of an owner's entire parcel, as Justice Scalia seemed to assert in *Nollan,* for all curtailments of property rights can be conceptually characterized as easements or servitudes.

What we must now notice, however, is that even if there is a general trend toward conceptual severance, it relates only to the issue of *exclusion*. The Court's solicitude for exclusion may correspond to the picture, at the core of liberal ideology, of the individual's right to use property to express one's individual liberty, which means using property to fend off intruders into one's space. As Charles Reich put this ideological picture, property is supposed to provide "a small but sovereign island of one's own."[43] The boats of strangers physically entered the Kaiser Aetna corporation's water; the cables of another were physically placed on Loretto's building; other people walked on the beach owned by the Nollans. Ideologically, these are incursions into the owner's "island." In his *Penn Central* dissent, Rehnquist went beyond this ideological picture. By preventing Penn Central from using its air rights, New York had sent no physical object into the Penn Central corporation's space. Even though conservatives think it obvious that Rehnquist was right in *Penn Central,* the Court has not gone that far. The Court engages in conceptual severance only for curtailments of property rights that can be characterized as affirmative easements or servitudes, not for those that are negative.[44]

The idea that property is a "sovereign island" that can be used to defend one's arbitrary freedom of action seems to be an aspect of the liberal ideology of negative liberty. Inside your "sovereign island," your freedom consists in doing anything you want, no matter how irrational or antisocial, as long as you do not harm others (in whatever sense the harm principle is to be construed). It is true that negative servitudes also restrict an owner's arbitrary freedom of action: Penn Central's inability to build an office building indeed seems like a more serious restriction than Loretto's inability to rip the offending cable off her apartment building. Yet affirmative incursions seem to make more explicit and immediate the fact that the owner is not alone in control of a "sovereign island." The forced sharing of space brings home the forced coexistence with other people in the world and the forced sharing of decision-making power. Affirmative incursions, in other words, conflict more sharply than do negative restrictions with the ideology of individualism that underlies the liberal conception of liberty. Affirmative incursions give the lie, in a direct and immediate way, to Sir William Blackstone's declaration that property is "that sole and despotic dominion which one man claims and exercises over the external things of the world, in total exclusion of the right of any other individual in the universe."[45]

Thus, a commitment to negative liberty with a consequent constitutionalization of the "sovereign island" picture may be the reason for the centrality of the idea of "physical invasion" in the constitutional jurisprudence of property. If so, the Court has constitutionalized the "sovereign island" picture in a conservative and not very thoughtful way, applying it only to traditional property interests and not taking into account the difference in the ethical case for a "sovereign island" depending upon whether the property holder is a person or a corporation.[46]

Nevertheless, we should not fail to notice that there are vast reaches of the liberal conception of property that are not constitutionalized. Perhaps the most weighty aspect of the liberal conception of property is commodification, which involves exclusive management decisions and unfettered choice about exchange. These aspects of property relating to the laissez-faire market are not constitutionalized in the modern era. Since the rejection of *Lochner*,[47] the state is not forestalled from regulation of the terms and conditions under which things are produced and sold. Industrial health and safety regulations, environmental protection regulations, minimum-wage regulations, price control, and other restrictions on the laissez-faire market restrict the conditions under which things may be produced and exchanged but are not deemed "takings" of the owners' property rights.

CONCEPTUALISM VS. PRAGMATISM IN TAKINGS JURISPRUDENCE

In this section I briefly consider by what process of interpretation neoconservatives may find the rights to possession, use, and disposition, including alienation in a laissez-faire market, to be "in" the Constitution. For Epstein, who I believe to be rather typical in this regard, the process is clearly a kind of naive conceptualism.[48] (Perhaps his methodology should be called literalism or semantic reductionism.) It is the words of the document we are to obey, not the intent of the framers or the result of any kind of value inquiry. Epstein maintains that we can rely on objective timeless meaning and need not grapple with subjective historical mental states or evanescent values. He finds the meaning of the word "property" in the Fifth and Fourteenth Amendments to be obvious. He thinks that the meaning of the word should be incontestably obvious to everyone, and that articulated detailed rules that can mechanically decide individual cases are a part of that obvious meaning of the word "property." The entire classical liberal conception of property is the obvious, objective meaning of the word "property."

Why does Epstein not at least admit that the meaning of the word "property" can change over time? That possibility would raise for him the dilemma of whether, for purposes of understanding the Constitution, we should use the late eighteenth-century meaning or the meaning today. He avoids the dilemma by ambiguity, inconsistency, and fiat. He states first that "the community of understanding that lends meaning to the Constitution comes of necessity from outside the text, in the way these words are understood in ordinary discourse by persons who are educated in the normal social and cultural discourse of their own time";[49] then that "Blackstone's account of private property explains what the term means in the eminent domain clause";[50] then that "stable and unique meanings are possible in principle and usually obtainable in fact."[51] In spite of this inconsistency, Epstein's heart is with Blackstone.

In Epstein's scheme of constitutional inquiry, historical questions,[52] value questions,[53] and the problem of changing meanings over time are all ruled out.[54] It is unclear from Epstein's remarks on constitutional interpretation whether he thinks that Blackstone's view (or the "common law") is some philosophically "real" delineation of property, or whether he thinks that it simply happens to be empirically the case that we are monolithically socialized into a conventional Blackstonian view. Most of the time in the book he seems to be operating as if there is a "real" Platonic form of property: The "proposition which the eminent domain clause asserts" is that "there is some natural and unique set of entitlements that are protected under a system of private property."[55]

In contrast to Epstein's conceptualism, the Supreme Court has so far not based its limited constitutionalization of the liberal indicia on semantic assertions about the meaning of "property."[56] Takings jurisprudence has been criticized as notoriously ad hoc. Sometimes it seems simply conclusory, declaring that some action either is or is not "within the police power," therefore is not or is a taking. As Justice William Brennan candidly admitted in *Penn Central,* "This Court, quite simply, has been unable to develop any 'set formula' for determining when 'justice and fairness' require that economic injuries caused by public action be compensated by the government";[57] rather, whether a government action is a taking "depends largely 'upon the particular circumstances [in that] case.'"[58] The Court must engage in "essentially ad hoc, factual inquiries."[59]

Formalists think that if takings jurisprudence cannot be reduced to formal rules (a "set formula"—such as the *Loretto per se* rule) it must violate the rule of law.[60] Nevertheless, I think instead that this field is one where pragmatic judgment under a standard (an explicit balancing approach) is better. The pragmatic ethical issue defies reduction to formal rules. When the Court's takings jurisprudence has not been conclusory, it has usually attempted to address in a practical way an underlying issue of political and moral theory: Is it *fair* to make this particular person bear the cost of government action for the benefit of the community? Such is the burden of the *Penn Central* multifactor balancing test, created under the salutary influence of Frank Michelman's famous article.[61] For all but true believers in the Platonic form of property, squarely facing the ethical (political) issue in this way is far superior to any mediation through *per se* rules or conceptualism.

Yet now a *per se* exception to the multifactor balancing test has been declared for "permanent physical occupations"; now a majority has stated, albeit in dictum, that temporary takings are not different in kind from permanent takings; and now the "right to exclude" has been held to be embodied in the concept of property, and so fundamental that its loss must always give rise to compensation. So perhaps we have the beginning of a trend toward conceptualism, both on the grand level of seeing a Platonic form of property and on the strategic level of willingness to engage in conceptual severance. If so, the trend is just beginning.

COMMODIFICATION AND THE LIBERAL CONCEPTION OF PROPERTY

In this section I offer some further thoughts on the liberal conception of property. The classical liberal conception of property, with its aspects of total individual control and unfettered alienation, is the underpinning of the market society: private-property-plus-free contract.[62] In the liberal conception, property is paradigmatically fungible;[63] everything that is property is ipso facto tradeable in markets and has an objective market value. This conception of property expresses commodification: Property consists paradigmatically of market commodities.[64] Thus, those who hold that everything is propertizable—that all things human beings find scarce and of value can be thought of as property—embrace universal commodification. Those who hold that some things cannot be property conceive of a wall between market and nonmarket social realms, with the laissez-faire market realm being large, dominant, and the rule, and the nonmarket realm being small, subordinate, and the exception.[65] In either case there is no room in the classical liberal conception for things that are property and yet not commodified.

Condemnation with compensation at fair market value is, in our system, thought prima facie ethically and politically proper and is uncontroversially held to be "in" our Constitution. The eminent domain clause is thought to license taking of anything for public use if the owner is paid fair market value,[66] and the term "public use" has been interpreted as broadly as possible.[67] In assuming that compensation is an appropriate corrective measure, that it can be "just" or make owners whole, the idea of eminent domain assumes that all property is fungible—that is, that property by nature or by definition consists of commodities fully interchangeable with money. The notion of eminent domain constitutionalizes fungibility. It constitutionalizes an ethic of exchange value. In a sense this principle represents our strongest commitment to commodification and our strongest form of constitutionalization of the liberal conception of property.

Yet if we were really fully to constitutionalize the liberal conception of property, we would return to *Lochner.*[68] We would find unfettered freedom of contract (complete alienability) to be inherent in the idea of property and to be required by the Constitution, as indeed Epstein does.[69] The Court's rejection of *Lochner,* while maintaining an unfettered power of eminent domain, leaves us in an ambiguous, perhaps even paradoxical, situation with regard to the constitutional status of the liberal notion of fungibility (the ethic of exchange value). The unfettered power of eminent domain affirms fungibility even while the jurisprudence of takings denies it. Perhaps the philosophical rejection of *Lochner* will ultimately require some kinds of substantive due process limitations on the eminent domain power, so as to take into account the ethical and political status of property that is not—and ought not to be treated as—fungible. For example, as I suggested elsewhere, the government should not be allowed to take homes where it could just as well take parking lots.[70]

The Court's adherence to the notion that property protects individuals—the ideology of the "small but sovereign island of one's own"—is also ambiguous. This ideological commitment can be taken as part of the liberal conception of property, but it can also point beyond the liberal conception because it can be recharacterized as implicitly according more ethical importance to interests in property that are not fungible. If the "sovereign island" picture is revised to protect personal property—that which is normatively important to the freedom, identity, and contextuality of people[71]—it would operate to create a hierarchy of property rights. Property that is bound up with individuals in a normatively appropriate sense would enjoy greater constitutional solicitude than property conforming more closely to the market commodity paradigm. Then this revised ideological commitment would invite the Court to decide, pragmatically in the real world, in which cases property appropriately fosters individual freedom and development and in which cases it does not. The ideology of protection of the individual—if appropriately reconceived to avoid the traditional stress on negative liberty—would result in two important changes in our jurisprudence of property: (1) it would engender different constitutional statuses for personal and fungible property, and (2) it would undergird limits on the eminent domain power to take personal property, even if compensation is paid.

PRAGMATIC REINTERPRETATION BASED ON PERSONHOOD IN CONTEXT

Now a few thoughts on the ultimate large question: How *should* we think about what aspects of property are protected by the Constitution? As is clear from what I have said so far, I think that the Court should drop *per se* rules and conceptual severance. It should continue to ask the ethical question (which I call the Michelman question):[72] Is it fair to ask a citizen to bear these costs for the benefit of the community? To this it should add what I'll have to call the Radin question: What conception of human flourishing—of personhood in the context of community—are we fostering by sustaining or disallowing this legislation? The Radin question is explicitly a mixture of moral and political theory. It asks us to think not just about fairness to individuals but also about our vision of democratic community and about our understanding of the kind of community we are always in the process of creating. I shall elaborate my view here only slightly.[73]

Personal property marks out a category of things that become *justifiably* bound up with the person and (partly) constitutive of personhood. Thus, a normative view of personhood, and hence a normative view of human flourishing, is needed in order to identify which objects are appropriately personal. In my view a normative theory of community is inseparable from a normative theory of personhood. This is so because self-constitution takes place in relation to an environment, both of things and other people. This contextuality means that physical and social contexts are integral to the construction of personhood.

The relationship between personhood and context requires the pursuit of human flourishing to include commitments to create and maintain particular contexts of individual relationships both with things and with other people. Recognizing the need for such commitments requires turning away from traditional negative liberty toward a more positive view of freedom, in which the self-development of the individual is linked to proper social development, and in which proper self-development, as a requirement of personhood, can in principle limit an individual's desires for control over things and hence limit the traditional liberal conception of property. On the other hand, when we judge some category of things to be normatively appropriate to construction of personhood, then people's control over those things is worthy of greater protection than is afforded by the mere commitment of the eminent domain clause to pay the market value.

Why should we find this particular vision "in" the Constitution? In this chapter I am not attempting to set forth my theory of constitutional interpretation. Ultimately the answer to the question is that a constitution is only a constitution if we find "in" it our best conception of human flourishing in the context of political order; that is, it can be appropriately constitutive of us as a polity only if it embodies our commitments to notions of personhood and community. This view of constitutional interpretation treats our Constitution as a "normative hermeneutic object."[74] In this view both originalism and literalism are flawed hermeneutics; they are mythologies that have lost their ethical focus, their power to guide us as we attempt to maintain ourselves and our community.

Still, why should (or at least can) we find this vision "in" the Constitution without amending it? The ultimate answer is that on these particular issues our Constitution is sufficiently open-ended. The text we have commits us to protection of property, but not to the classical liberal conception of property. Property is a contested concept, and so is justice (as in the "just" compensation required for legitimate exercise of eminent domain). In arguing for my interpretations of those concepts as being the best now available to us, I think I am squarely within our tradition of constitutional argument.[75]

If we delve into our understanding of property, and the ideology of property, with our ethical commitments in mind—our ideals for ourselves of personhood and community—then liberal ideology can be usefully reinterpreted with the distinction between personal and fungible property in mind. In light of this reinterpretation, the liberal conception of property—hence the full panoply of liberal indicia—cannot be part of our Constitution. If commodification (fungibility) should be understood to be of lesser constitutional status than personal connection, then certain kinds of personal use are protected in a way that development rights or market alienability are not. How might this ideological reorientation be reflected in our constitutional practice?

Start with physical occupation. From the personhood point of view, physical invasion could not be the talisman the Court thinks it is. The relevant constitutional inquiry would include asking for what reason the resource is being "occupied." It would also include a normative inquiry: For what types of property interests is it ethically appropriate to permit and foster interconnection with persons? Use of property as one's residence is more closely connected to personhood than use as a garbage dump for one's factory. The connection between people and residences is recognizable by us as normatively appropriate.[76] Airplane overflight noise "takes" much more from a resident[77] than from a corporation that operates a noisy manufacturing business, or from its workers (the relevant hearers) if they must already wear ear protection. A cable on the roof of a building rented out as a fungible investment no more invades the owner's personhood than does a utility assessment.

Next consider disposition. If the government curtails transferability, from the personhood point of view it might make a difference whether only market transactions are foreclosed or if gifts are foreclosed too. Foreclosing market transactions works against commodification, whereas preventing gifts forecloses a different sort of human interaction, and one we might recognize as an essential element of our conception of human flourishing. Partial market-inalienability (restraint on alienation in markets) can be viewed as restriction of commodification, and sometimes respect for the interests of personhood can justify it. Here I think regulation of housing and labor are prime examples. Thus, labor regulation (collective bargaining, minimum wage, maximum hours, health and safety, unemployment insurance, etc.) and housing regulation (housing codes and other habitability rights, rent control, etc.) can be seen as an effort to foster workers' and tenants' personhood by recognizing the nonmarket personal significance of their work and homes.[78]

Other kinds of dispositions (abandonment, destruction) should also be examined not according to their conceptual description but rather according to their connection with personhood and community. Does a corporation have a property right to blow up its plant rather than sell to a worker cooperative at fair market value?[79] Would government action requiring such a sale be a taking? Such legislation should not be thought of as a taking, because the corporation's property is fungible. The corporation as a profit-maximizing entity should ethically be treated as indifferent between holding assets with fair market value of x dollars and possessing x dollars in currency or securities.

Government action that required resident homeowners to sell to a corporation, on the other hand, might be considered a taking or a violation of substantive due process. The liberal "property-rule entitlement"[80] normatively demanding that market alienation be a voluntary decision on the owner's part is more readily justifiable for personal property. This principle suggests that courts should not always allow governments to condemn property and then transfer it to a user adjudged to benefit the community. Even if doing so satisfies the insubstantial hurdle of "public use,"[81] in the case of personal property there should be some constitutional mechanism for keeping it in the hands of its holders except in dire cases. In other words, some kind of "compelling state interest" test for compensated takings of personal, but not fungible, property seems to be appropriate. In essence, we should recognize a substantive due process limitation on the eminent domain power.

The general claim here is that from the perspective of personhood and community interests, decisions that change the entitlement of personal property into a "liability rule" should be at least deeply suspect. For example, in *Poletown Neighborhood Council v. City of Detroit,* the Michigan Court upheld Detroit's condemnation of homes in a close-knit neighborhood at the request of General Motors, which wanted the parcel for a plant.[82] An analogous suspect case in "private" law is *Boomer v. Atlantic Cement Co.,* a class action for nuisance by homeowners against a cement company whose plant spewed out dust. In *Boomer* the court granted permanent damages but not an injunction, thus allowing the company to "condemn" a portion of the homeowners' property.[83]

The "use" prong of the liberal triad requires a detailed normative breakdown. If restrictions on use involve restrictions on choices internal to personal property holding—such as choices about association or life-style by residents—it is not difficult to find the restrictions at least suspect. In *Moore v. City of East Cleveland*,[84] the plurality found a substantive due process right to live in an extended family despite zoning restrictions. It is not surprising that Justice John Paul Stevens would have found a property right to the same effect. Because the zoning ordinance "cut[s] so deeply into a fundamental right normally associated with the ownership of residential property," Stevens thought it a taking of property without due process and without just compensation.[85]

Personhood interests, however, are not obviously implicated in restricting profits on investment or in restricting available options in changing from one investment to another. Predictably (from my point of view but not Epstein's), courts have not usually found takings where the government action did not prevent the owner from making a profit.[86] Price controls are not a taking unless "confiscatory"; Penn Central (according to its own accounting) was in the black with regard to Grand Central Terminal; banning conversion of rental units to condominiums does not prevent landlords from profiting.

Restricting original development (change from vacant land to residential or commercial use) is perhaps a more complex issue. An owner of vacant land does not have a personal connection to the money she hopes to reap from development. The question of restricting original development is more difficult if the owner of vacant land was planning to build a residence (to live in, not for sale) and has already become bound up with those plans. Then there is a personal connection to the land, and perhaps to the architect's design of the residence, though not yet to the residence itself. It seems that someone who buys land for a personal residence and then has residential use regulated away has a stronger claim than the speculator. But this issue depends upon whether we find it ethically appropriate that persons be closely connected with their residential plans for their property.

Those who invest in businesses or in the stock market understand that there is no right to a profit from investment, and land ownership as a fungible investment is similar when it comes to various vagaries of the market. The question is whether vagaries of government action are similar to other risks that investors face or different. Is how we answer this question simply a matter of acculturation, or does it rest on some kind of absolute principle?

The Michelman question would lead us to the conclusion that the risks associated with government interaction with us and our holdings are different in principle because they raise the possibility of systematic exploitation of the few by the representatives of the many. The Radin question has a slightly different focus. Do we want to think of our government as "them," as Leviathan, and ourselves as needing protection from exploitation, or do we want to think of our government as "us" and its disappointment of our hopes for profit from time to time as an acceptable responsibility of citizenship?

The reality of unequal power might lead to a conclusion that visionary communitarians will find ironic. Perhaps, in our nonideal world, would-be developers are in a better position to think of themselves and the government as closely connected, and hence it is more appropriate to expect them as citizens to endure disappointment of their hopes for profit sometimes. On the other hand, for most homeowners and welfare recipients, the public/private distinction better expresses their reality, and with them we should give more credence to the problem of systematic exploitation by Leviathan. Even admitting that the we/they picture of government should not be idealized or enshrined as a matter of principle, perhaps it is the right picture for now, at least for relatively powerless groups. Still, in order to make progress we should do two things: (1) we should not assume that political relations are Hobbesian in principle, and (2) we should make empowerment and enfranchisement part of the constitutional inquiry about property.[87]

Tenants are both a relatively disempowered group and a group claiming both a personal and community interest in maintaining continuity of residence. Hence the question of tenants' tenure rights is not difficult from my point of view, as long as the landlord's interest is fungible.[88] More difficult is the question of whether a landlord can permissibly be prevented from evicting tenants and moving in. If the landlord has never lived in the building, then her interest is not superior to a tenant's.[89] In any case, the systemic problem we face is not one in which the personhood interests of individual landlords are pitted against individual tenants, but rather one in which a class of residents is unable to count on continuity of residence and hence unable to form strong political communities, because of the asserted liberal property rights of a more powerful class of investors. The systemic situation is one in which individual self-development, as well as community formation and political expression, should take normative precedence over claims of fungible holders to maintain or extend their power.

Does this situation lead us to an ethical judgment that a landlord's interest (however she subjectively feels about it) is fungible? Some landlords live in one unit of a small building and rent out another, and it is not difficult to exempt them from such an ethical judgment. But there is a more general underlying question. To what extent are subjective feelings of personal connection relevant to our decision that property should be treated as personal? Elsewhere I have argued that even if one is self-constituted by the idea of power over others through control over commodified resources, this notion does not translate ethically into treatment of one's investment holdings as personal, because the "compleat capitalist" embodies an inferior conception of human flourishing, and one we should reject.[90]

But ethically more attractive subjective feelings are possible. Those who sell commodities (including commercial landlords) may have a more complex subjective experience than the caricature commodity holder (the pure self-interested profit maximizer). They may care about the buyers and their relationships with buyers, not just about their profits.[91] If this is so, should owners' subjective experience of incomplete commodification translate into greater control over their commodities—and hence translate into power over the buyers of them—than we would ethically accord to someone who corresponded to the caricature? I think that the question suggests its own answer. If such subjective experiences of interrelationships are rewarded with more power over others, the experience of sharing that we wish to recognize as ethically appropriate would itself be undermined. The nature of the experience is essentially that power over others is *not* the essence of one's property relations; instead, one wishes to treat others as equals and as persons even while selling things they need.

TOWARD A POSTLIBERAL UNDERSTANDING OF PROPERTY?

L. T. Hobhouse's old distinction between property "for use" and "for power"[92] can probably be made to do ethical work similar to my distinctions between fungible and personal property and between complete and incomplete commodification. So can reconstruction of the Marxist distinction between use value and exchange value.[93]

All of these ideas suggest a hierarchy of property rights related to its differing ethical significance. The fact that the discourse of property produces these recurring attempts to "disaggregate"[94] property into categories that further the ethical purposes of property and those that do not suggests that there are tensions within the broad liberal conception of property. More important, the fact that these ethical intuitions distinguishing between personal and fungible property are seen to be played out in constitutional practice to some extent—although sporadically and ambiguously—forms a strong countercurrent to the ideological commitment to the liberal conception of property. And in my view, the liberal commitments to equality of political power and respect for persons might extend these intuitions and their embodiment in practice, thus leading to a postliberal understanding of property.

NOTES

1. John Locke, "Second Treatise of Government," Chapter 9, in Peter Laslett, ed., *Two Treatises of Government* (Cambridge: Cambridge University Press, 1970).
2. See, e.g., James Harrington, "The Commonwealth of Oceana (1656)," in *The Oceana of James Harrington and His Other Works,* 4th ed. (London, 1771).
3. Robert Nozick, *Anarchy, State and Utopia* (New York: Basic Books, 1971); Richard A. Epstein, *Takings: Private Property and the Power of Eminent Domain* (Cambridge, Mass.: Harvard University Press, 1985), p. 304.
4. See, e.g., Frank Michelman, "Possession vs. Distribution in the Constitutional Idea of Property," *Iowa Law Review* 72 (1987), p. 1319. See also articles by Cass

Sunstein, Frank Michelman, and others, in a symposium on republicanism to be published in the *Yale Law Journal* (forthcoming).

5. See Epstein, *Takings*.

6. Ibid., pp. 58–62.

7. Ibid., p. 65.

8. See Epstein, *Takings*, at 74: "The right of disposition is a property right, in the same degree and manner as the right to exclusive possession. What a plaintiff demands is noninterference by the rest of the world in his dealings with any third party, X. . . . [A]t stake is the right to contract with X, which is good against the world."

9. Richard A. Epstein, "Why Restrain Alienation?" *Columbia Law Review* 85 (1985), pp. 970–971; *Takings*, pp. 252–253. ("The system of private property contains the right to dispose of acquired wealth"; hence the rationale that workers' compensation statutes are justified on the basis of unequal bargaining power is "*constitutionally* defective"); Epstein, "Past and Future: The Temporal Dimension in the Law of Property," *Washington University Law Quarterly* 64 (1986), pp. 667, 705. ("The only justification for restraints of private alienation is to prevent the infliction of external harms"); Epstein, "In Defense of the Contract at Will," *University of Chicago Law Review* 51 (1984), p. 947.

10. Epstein's critics have vigorously taken him to task for this and other philosophical camel-swallowing. See, e.g., Thomas C. Grey, "The Malthusian Constitution," *University of Miami Law Review* 41 (1986), p. 21.

11. *Kaiser Aetna v. United States*, 444 U.S. 164 (1979).

12. Ibid., at 179.

13. Ibid., at 179–180.

14. *Loretto v. Teleprompter Manhattan CATV*, 458 U.S. 419 (1982).

15. Ibid., at 435 (quoting *United States v. General Motors*, 323 U.S. 373, 378 (1945)).

16. Ibid., at 435.

17. Wesley Hohfeld, "Fundamental Legal Conceptions as Applied in Judicial Reasoning," *Yale Law Journal* 26 (1917), p. 710; Bruce A. Ackerman, *Private Property and the Constitution* (New Haven: Yale University Press, 1977).

18. See, e.g., *Olmstead v. United States*, 277 U.S. 438 (1928). In *Katz v. United States*, 389 U.S. 347, 351, the Court announced that "the Fourth Amendment protects people, not places."

19. *Loretto v. Teleprompter Manhattan CATV*, at 435.

20. *Penn Central Transportation Co. v. New York City*, 438 U.S. 104 (1978).

21. *Village of Euclid v. Ambler Realty Co.*, 272 U.S. 365 (1926). *Euclid* upheld the constitutionality of local zoning regulations; a 75% diminution in market value of Ambler Realty's 68 acres of vacant land was held not to be a taking.

22. For scholarly thoughts on this paradox, see Ackerman, *Private Property;* Frank I. Michelman, "Property, Utility and Fairness: Comments on the Ethical Foundations of 'Just Compensation' Law," *Harvard Law Review* 80 (1967), p. 1165; Margaret Jane Radin, "Property and Personhood," *Stanford Law Review* 34 (1982), p. 957.

23. *Andrus v. Allard*, 444 U.S. 51 (1979).

24. See, e.g., Epstein, *Takings* p. 76.

25. *Hodel v. Irving*, 107 S. Ct. 2076, 2085 (1987).

26. Ibid., at 2083.
27. *Kaiser Aetna v. United States*, at 180 (1979).
28. *Fresh Pond Shopping Center v. Callahan*, 464 U.S. 875 (1983).
29. *First English Evangelical Lutheran Church of Glendale v. Los Angeles County of Los Angeles*, 107 S. Ct. 2378 (1987).
30. Ibid., at 2388.
31. Justice William Brennan's solidarity with Chief Justice Rehnquist on the issue decided in *Lutheran Church* seems surprising. Joan C. Williams suggests that his push for compensation for "temporary" takings stems from his desire to preserve an avenue of redress against local governments for civil rights plaintiffs in 1983 actions. Joan C. Williams, "The Constitutional Vulnerability of American Local Government: The Politics of City Status in American Law," *Wisconsin Law Review* (1986), p. 83. If Williams is right, then the Justice seems likely to be disappointed. The Court's conservative majority, if it so desires, can find some basis upon which to distinguish property-holding plaintiffs from those who allege other kinds of injuries. After all, ironically enough, in pushing for the *Lutheran Church* rule, Justice Brennan has himself contributed to such a situation. After *Lutheran Church*, corporate developers can obtain damages from local governments who in good faith legislate in a way later found to be unconstitutional, whereas people whose homes are broken into or who are physically injured by police acting in good faith have no redress against government action later found to be illegal.
32. See *First English Evangelical Lutheran Church of Glendale v. Los Angeles County of Los Angeles*, at 2388–2389 (Stevens, J., dissenting).
33. Ibid., at 2388–2389.
34. *Penn Central Transportation Co. v. New York City*, at 142–143 (Rehnquist, J., dissenting). See also Rehnquist's dissent in *Keystone Bituminous Coal Ass'n v. De Benedictis*, 107 S. Ct. 1232 (1987).
35. *Penn Central Transportation Co. v. New York City*, at 130.
36. 107 S. Ct. 3141 (1987).
37. There was expert testimony that much of the access path was below the mean high tide line and thus within the public's right under California's public trust doctrine; there was also testimony that an access easement may have been acquired by the public in any case through its long use of the path. *Nollan v. California Coastal Commission*, at 3161.
38. *Nollan v. California Coastal Commission*, at 3145.
39. *Pennsylvania Coal Co. v. Mahon*, 260 U.S. 393 (1922).
40. *Goldblatt v. Hempstead*, 369 U.S. 590 (1962).
41. See Michelman, "Property, Utility and Fairness"; Ackerman, *Private Property*.
42. Thomas Grey has pointed out that mixing the modern Hohfeldian "bundle of sticks" image of property with earlier Lockean absolutism is intellectual apples and oranges. Thomas C. Grey, "The Malthusian Constitution," *University of Miami Law Review* 41 (1986), p. 21.
43. Charles Reich, "The New Property," *Yale Law Journal* 73 (1964), p. 733.
44. But the 1987 *Lutheran Church* case seems to be an exception to this proposition, because there the Church was prevented from doing something on its own land (i.e., it was temporarily prevented from building on a flood plain).

45. W. Blackstone, *Commentaries on the Laws of England*, Book 2, Chapter 1 (1765), p. 2.
46. In addition to my previous theorizing about this issue, see Meir Dan-Cohen, *Rights, Persons, and Organizations* (Berkeley and Los Angeles: University of California Press, 1986).
47. *Lochner v. U.S.*, 198 U.S. 45 (1905).
48. See Margaret Jane Radin, "The Consequences of Conceptualism," *University of Miami Law Review* 41 (1986), p. 239.
49. Epstein, *Takings*, p. 20.
50. Ibid., p. 23.
51. Ibid., p. 24.
52. Ibid., pp. 26–29.
53. Ibid., pp. 25–26.
54. Ibid., pp. 24–25.
55. Ibid., pp. 230–231.
56. But see text accompanying note 11 (Rehnquist's statement in *Kaiser Aetna* that certain "expectancies" are "embodied in the concept" of property).
57. *Penn Central Transportation Co. v. City of New York*, at 124.
58. Ibid.
59. Ibid.
60. Indeed, Frank Michelman finds the turn toward conceptual severance to be explainable solely by the search for standards that can be applied in conformity with the rule of law and therefore thinks that conceptual severance is not indicative of a conservative movement in the Court toward constitutionalizing the liberal conception of property. See Michelman, "Takings, 1987" (forthcoming in *Cornell Law Review*). For a review of the traditional ideology of the rule of law and an examination of its connection to formalism, see Margaret Jane Radin, "Reconsidering the Rule of Law" (forthcoming in *Boston University Law Review*).
61. Michelman, "Property, Utility and Fairness."
62. See Duncan Kennedy and Frank Michelman, "Are Property and Contract Efficient?" *Hofstra Law Review* 8 (1980), p. 485.
63. See Radin, "Property and Personhood," pp. 959–960.
64. See Margaret Jane Radin, "Market-Inalienability," *Harvard Law Review* 100 (1987), p. 1849.
65. See Margaret Jane Radin, "Justice and the Market Domain," forthcoming in J. Chapman, ed., *Markets and Justice* (NOMOS XXXI) (New York: N.Y.U. Press, forthcoming).
66. There is an interesting problem here lying in wait for those who think the body is property: Can the government condemn kidneys at fair market value? See Lori Andrews, "My Body, My Property," *16 Hastings Center Rep.* (October 1986), pp. 28, 36; Note, "Toward the Right of Commerciality: Recognizing Property Rights in the Commercial Value of Human Tissue," *UCLA Law Review* 34 (1986), p. 207.
67. In *Hawaii Housing Authority v. Midkiff*, 467 U.S. 229, 240 (1984) the Court declared the scope of public use to be "coterminous" with the scope of the police power, which means that any government activity deemed to further a legitimate government purpose is ipso facto a public use.

68. *Lochner v. United States,* 198 U.S. 45 (1905).
69. See Epstein, "Why Restrain Alienation?"
70. Radin, "Property and Personhood."
71. See Radin, "Market-Inalienability," pp. 1903–1906.
72. To be fair to the development of Michelman's thought, I should call this the "old" Michelman question. The "new" Michelman question asks whether self-government is enhanced or stifled by the regulation. See, e.g., Frank I. Michelman, "Property as a Constitutional Right," *Washington and Lee Law Review* 38 (1981), p. 1097.
73. My view is developed in more detail in "Property and Personhood"; "Residential Rent Control," *Philosophy and Public Affairs* 15 (1986), p. 350; and "Market-Inalienability."
74. Ronald R. Garet, "Comparative Normative Hermeneutics," *Southern California Law Review* 58 (1985), p. 35.
75. In fact, this makes me sound rather Dworkinian, for Ronald Dworkin has stressed the distinction between concepts and various competing conceptions of them, and the role of contested concepts in constitutional thought. See, e.g., Dworkin, *Taking Rights Seriously* (Cambridge, Mass.: Harvard University Press, 1978), pp. 134–136. I am certainly more Dworkinian than Epsteinian. But I won't attempt to catalogue my differences with Dworkin here.
76. See Radin, "Residential Rent Control"; "Market-Inalienability"; "Property and Personhood."
77. Thus, the Court could hold that extreme jet noise is a taking even if the planes do not invade the resident's air space, and still be able to distinguish this position from Rehnquist's position in his *Penn Central* dissent.
78. See Radin, "Market-Inalienability," pp. 1918–1921.
79. See Joseph William Singer, "The Reliance Interest in Property," *Stanford Law Review* 40 (1988), p. 611.
80. In the useful terminology of Guido Calabresi and A. Douglas Melamed, ownership is protected by a property rule if transfer must be voluntary, and it is protected only by a liability rule if the entitlement can be taken from the owner against her wishes upon payment of compensation set by the government or some other authoritative entity. See Calabresi and Melamed, "Property Rules, Liability Rules, and Inalienability: One View of the Cathedral," *Harvard Law Review* 85 (1972), p. 1089.
81. As long as efficiency or competition is thought to be served, the "public use" limitation on the eminent domain power does not prevent legislation from divesting *A*'s title and making provision for it to be vested in *B*. See *Hawaii Housing Authority v. Midkiff.* Nor is there anything wrong with this as long as *A*'s interest is properly treated as fungible and *B*'s may properly be treated as personal.
82. *Poletown Neighborhood Council v. City of Detroit,* 410 Mich. 616, 304 N.W.2d 455 (1981). An analysis that distinguishes *Midkiff* and *Poletown* on grounds I find plausible is presented in Note, "Leading Cases of the 1983 Term," *Harvard Law Review* 98 (1984), pp. 232–236.
83. *Boomer v. Atlantic Cement Co.,* 26 N.Y.2d 219, 257 N.E.2d 870 (1970).
84. *Moore v. City of East Cleveland,* 431 U.S. 494 (1977).
85. Ibid., at 520 (Stevens, J., concurring).

86. *Loretto* is wrongly decided in this regard. Conceptual severance and the *per se* rule for physical invasion allowed the Court to bypass this consideration.
87. Frank Michelman has begun this line of inquiry. See Michelman, "Property as a Constitutional Right"; "Possession v. Distribution in the Constitutional Idea of Property," *Iowa Law Review* 72 (1987), p. 1319. The Michelman question from the 1960s is more oriented to the we/they picture of government than the Michelman question of the 1980s.
88. I have also analyzed residential rent control as justifiable when necessary for continuity of residence in contexts where that would foster personhood and community. See Radin, "Residential Rent Control."
89. But what if the building is the landlord's ancestral home and she is still attached to it, but now the tenant has become attached to it too? This is the kind of hypothetical question that personhood theory cannot resolve very well. Yet it is perhaps one that we do not pragmatically face. Few people rent out their ancestral homes, especially in a context in which tenant tenure rights are coming to be recognized.
90. See Radin, "Residential Rent Control," pp. 364–365.
91. See Radin, "Justice and the Market Domain." But note that this argument does not apply to corporate landlords. I believe there is a strong case for treating corporate property as fungible. (See text accompanying notes 46 and 79.)
92. Leonard T. Hobhouse, "The Historical Evolution of Property, in Fact and in Idea," in *Property: Its Duties and Rights,* 2nd ed.
93. See, e.g., C. Edwin Baker, "Property and Its Relation to Constitutionally Protected Liberty," *University of Pennsylvania Law Review* 134 (1986), p. 741.
94. This term is Baker's, in "Property."

Part 4
Equal Protection

Constitutional scholars are fond of labeling Fourteenth Amendment equal protection decisions as the "new jurisprudence." This appellation reflects the undeniable fact that, after nearly one hundred years of relative judicial unconcern, equal protection restrictions on race, gender, and other forms of invidious state discrimination among persons, as well as affirmative protection on behalf of certain "fundamental rights" for all, have been accorded privileged constitutional status by courts in the post–New Deal era. Indeed, it seems in retrospect that the Supreme Court in *Brown v. Board of Education* set in motion some very important trends in U.S. constitutional law. The less-discussed truth behind these trends, however, is that the logic of equality from which they derive has remained limited to the traditional liberal terms of formal procedural access and fair treatment by state officials largely indifferent to concerns about continuing social inequality among citizens. Moreover, these minimal advances for long marginalized groups have been halted, and even undercut, by recent decisions of the Rehnquist Court.

The chapters in this section critically explore the logic of both these limited liberal advances and the conservative backlash in equality-related cases during recent decades. Michael McCann's initial chapter demonstrates that the individualistic, exchange-oriented, and socially "blind" terms of the prevailing equal protection logic generally tend to reproduce rather than to challenge the profound material inequalities of a market-oriented society. The result, he argues, is that the range of much-heralded entitlements for racial and ethnic minorities has generally been restricted to those correcting discrete acts of invidious state discrimination; moreover, concerns about the structural foundations of material class inequalities that oppress these and other groups have been specifically excluded. The chapters by Deborah L. Rhode and Rhonda Copelon extend critical analysis to the parallel gender-based hierarchies sustained by Supreme Court constructions of the Fourteenth Amendment. Rhode focuses on the inconsistent and ultimately inadequate attempts of the Court to develop a logic of justice that accounts for the social realities of gender difference. Copelon presses further to demonstrate the ways in which liberal equality ideals from the start have sanctified patriarchal domination in the socially constructed spheres of both private and public life. She illustrates this far-reaching critique by analyzing the highly tenuous and ill-founded logic of "privacy" rights that inform prevailing decisions concerning abortion and gay/lesbian rights.

9 ——— ·
Equal Protection for Social Inequality: Race and Class in Constitutional Ideology

MICHAEL W. McCANN

> Equality, as an abstraction, may be value neutral, but the Fourteenth Amendment is not.
> ———*Kenneth L. Karst*

> Every financial exaction which the State imposes on a uniform basis is more easily satisfied by the well-to-do than by the indigent. . . . The Equal Protection Clause does not impose on the States "an affirmative duty to lift the handicaps flowing from the differences in economic circumstances." To so construe it would be to read into the Constitution a philosophy of leveling that would be foreign to many of our basic concepts of the proper relations between government and society. . . . It is not required by the Equal Protection Clause to give to some whatever others can afford.
> ———*Justice Harlan,*
> (*Douglas v. California, 1963*)

Much of the commonly accepted wisdom among modern constitutional scholars turns on the alleged revolution in the defense of citizens' rights initiated by the Supreme Court during the post–New Deal era. According to most interpretations, the Court during the half-century prior to 1937 was animated by a misguided and undemocratic commitment to protecting the economic autonomy of corporate producers against both the interests and will of the American people. For most modern scholars, however, the Court eventually redeemed itself through conversion in the late 1930s. After a heated political struggle with President Franklin D. Roosevelt, the High Court was virtually reborn through its radical reversal of earlier priorities. Now that it was accepted that the "Constitution does not embody an economic theory," government regulation of long-sacred property rights was granted a "presumption of constitutionality"; the heroic President, backed

231

by a responsive Congress and technocratic executive corps, at last was freed to provide the economic leadership and social reform desired by the people. At the same time, the Court embraced a new role as guardian for long-ignored civil liberties and personal rights, such as free speech, due process for the accused, and, above all, equality of all citizens before the law. Whether for good or ill, the Constitution now was enlisted in defense of an "egalitarian revolution" against long-tolerated capitalist excesses in liberal postwar America.

Although undeniably true to a large degree, this simple narrative is misleading in important ways. On one hand, the alleged arbitrariness and irrationality of the old Court are often greatly exaggerated. After all, the justices' frequent invalidations of statist regulatory policies were well rooted in a tradition of constitutional protections for private property that stretches back to our nation's founding. Criticism concerning traditional free-market capitalist values may be warranted, but this criticism should not obscure the fact that the High Court's defense of these values in past eras for the most part flowed along with the prevailing currents of American law, culture, and politics.[1] On the other hand, the often controversial activism by the recent Court on behalf of personal and civil rights bears many similarities in form and substance to its earlier actions. Indeed, the parallels between the new "substantive equal protection" and the older substantive due process have been pointed out many times.[2] We need only to replace the modern language of fundamental rights and suspect classifications with that of older property rights, and the differences in judicial scrutiny of legislation during the two eras virtually disappear. Furthermore, as Martin Shapiro has well demonstrated, the recent judicial concern for civil and personal rights is no less "economic" in essence than the old conservative activism. Decisions protecting the free speech of dissident workers, tax exemptions for religious institutions, school busing programs, affirmative action in hiring of minorities and women, and due process for recipients of government subsidies all involve fundamental matters of financial expenditure and economic control.[3]

The aim of this chapter is to develop a more critical interpretation of modern equal protection doctrine. My contention is that recent Fourteenth Amendment jurisprudence parallels the older judicial activism not only in its substantive and economic character but also in its fundamental, if more subtle, embrace of ideas supporting uniquely capitalist forms of social organization against substantive egalitarian challenge. In some ways, of course, this claim is hardly a surprising or radical one; it would be more amazing if the governing judicial logic was alien to our prevailing structure of socioeconomic relations. Yet what is significant and often ignored by traditional legal scholarship is the complex character of this relationship between constitutional ideology and modern forms of capitalist social organization.[4] Specifically, while fully acknowledging that the modern shift in emphasis away from property rights to civil rights has opened up new opportunities for members of long-excluded social groups, I contend that the Court still adheres to the established constitutional tradition of limiting concern for systemic socioeconomic inequalities to an individualistic, exchange-oriented logic of public goods allocation. In other words, the recent expansion of equal protection for long-victimized citizens has taken those demands for justice in our modern bureaucratic system of state capitalism—which are no longer rendered sensible by the older constitutional language of autonomy-oriented property rights—and translated them into market-based distributive terms. The result has been not only that the Constitution remains indifferent to the deprivations and needs of the American underclass generally, but that constitutional remedies for past discriminatory acts contributing to racial, ethnic, and other forms of social injustice also have been limited by this refusal to address the structural character of class inequality. In short, contemporary constitutional discourse on equality has provided implicit ideological support for capitalist hierarchies in much the same terms and manner that was true of substantive due process doctrines in earlier years.

CAPITALISM AND CONSTITUTION: AN IDEOLOGICAL APPROACH

The basic arguments of this chapter are framed in terms of what is often called an ideological analysis of law—that is, an approach that focuses critical scrutiny on the intrinsic logic and implications of legal language. This approach to legal analysis has gained increasing attention during recent years from a variety of scholars, many of whom express little interest in class analysis. Since this chapter owes much to the basic insights of Marx concerning the relation of bourgeois law to capitalist social relations, however, we shall begin with his ideas before developing my own more eclectic, highly qualified revisionist understanding of legal ideology.

THE MARXIST PERSPECTIVE

Although a great deal of debate over the details continues to thrive, a general consensus about the structural characteristics intrinsic to bourgeois law has been developed by a number of modern Marxist thinkers.[5] In this view, law at once produces and reproduces core beliefs that legitimate the exploitive character of capitalist social relations in two general ways. First, and most obvious, the primary substantive doctrines of public and private law reflect and enforce the basic norms of capitalist ownership and exchange relations. This contention has been well supported by the commonplace recognition among scholars that the most important constitutional commitments—to individual private property, market competition, and limited state authority—derive from the more general liberal tradition that has long supported capitalist social relations in America.[6]

Equally important but less obvious, some Marxists have also argued that the liberal legal *form*—that is, the intrinsic logic of legal relations—parallels and supports the idealized form of capitalist social relations. The key concern for advocates of this view is the "mysterious" character of equal "citizenship" esteemed by bourgeois law. This insight derives from the fact that the legal equality of citizens in the public realm applies only to abstract representations of actual persons that are divorced from their diverse concrete needs and particular sensuous interests. In other words, the logic of legal exchange depends upon the artificial transformation of qualitatively different subjects into uniform and impersonal citizens through the universal political equivalent of recognized rights.[7] When we endorse that citizens should be treated equally before the law, we thus are affirming Marx's point that law "makes an abstraction of real Men" in denial of their actual social reality defined by birth, education, social rank, occupation, wealth, and so forth.[8]

What is noteworthy about this depersonalizing, abstract legal form of "citizenship" is its intrinsic parallel to the commodity form of market exchange that defines capitalist social relations as well.[9] Specifically, market-derived "exchange values" transform qualitatively distinct and incommensurable "use values" of discrete goods and services into the universal economic equivalent of money. Like the legal form, commodity exchange in the marketplace thus is rooted in an abstraction of meaning from the actual circumstances of persons laboring in the production of the object world. The result is that both formal legal and market exchange mutually reinforce the "blindness" of dominant institutions in state and society alike to the "real" or particularistic lives of the individuals who participate within them. Each "mystifies" the subjects who set collective life in motion by "extinguishing" the "memory" of their beings as discrete and context-bound social actors.[10]

The bourgeois legal form can be understood to mystify social reality in several significant ways. Most generally, the universal, abstract form of voluntary legal and market exchange—exemplified best in contract law—tends to mask, and hence to legitimate, in moralistic terms the actual instrumental, egoistic, and alienated behavior of individuals competing for exclusive wealth and power within the marketplace of capitalist society. As Marx put it,

> Where the political state has attained to its full development, man leads, not only in thought, in consciousness, but in reality, in life, a double existence. . . . He lives in the political community, where he regards himself as a communal being, and in civil society, where he acts simply as a private individual, treats other men as means, degrades himself to the role of a mere means, and becomes the mere plaything of alien powers.[11]

Moreover, the abstract formal equality presumed by legal and market exchange mystifies social life by obscuring the fundamental inequalities among concrete subjects. First, legal equality obscures that persons and groups are radically unequal in the skill, material resources, inherited advantages, and organizational power that they bring to the competitive exchange process. In short, the formal "neutrality" of equal treatment by the state for all citizens both facilitates and legitimates the de facto stratification of civil society into a dynamic division of individual winners and losers. To quote Marx, the right to legal "equality" is "a right of inequality in its content, like every other right."[12] Second, and more important, the individualistic exchange bias of liberal law obscures further the more fundamental structural class divisions between owners of production and workers. The bourgeois legal order performs the role of "depoliticizing" class relations by transforming challenges to the hierarchical social structure into discrete conflicts over individual rights to fair exchange and distribution of goods.[13] Finally, formal legal equality remains blind to the unequal abilities of citizens to satisfy basic needs, most of which derive from the structure of unequal class power. This point, of course, is demonstrated in Anatole France's oft-quoted quip that the law forbids the rich and poor alike from sleeping beneath bridges. And it is this basic denial of humanity that led Marx to his summary judgment that the heralded legal equality promised by political democracy is only a "political lion's skin" indifferent to pervasive social inequalities that impede realization of full citizenship for all persons.[14]

A REVISIONIST THEORY OF LEGAL IDEOLOGY

My analysis of legal ideology, both as a general concept and in its specific substantive manifestations, owes much to this critical tradition. Nevertheless, important confusions and problems within much Marxist analysis have led me to depart from this model in several regards. Indeed, one of the major dilemmas for Marxists is that Marx tended to use the concept of "ideology" in several different ways, referring sometimes to a class-specific system of beliefs imposed on others, sometimes to a general system of "illusory" and unscientific beliefs (false consciousness), and sometimes simply to the general social process of reproducing ideas and meaning.[15] Furthermore, each of these usages, and especially the first two, are fraught with conceptual fallacies, which will be explored briefly below.

My approach instead begins by adopting the more general definition of ideology posed by Clifford Geertz: a "symbolic framework in terms of which to formulate, think about, and react to political problems." In this view, the function of ideology is "to make an autonomous politics possible by providing the authoritative concepts that render it meaningful, the suasive images by means of which it can be sensibly grasped."[16] Such legal ideologies develop from constellations of "satellite ideas" bound together in coherent structures of meaning by specific artificial forms of judicial reasoning. These particular logics—manifest in reasoning from precedent, analogy, and example—provide something like a grammar that imparts sense to the symbols of legal discourse. And it is through the historical usage of legal symbols and ideas in such legal reasoning that the familiar narrative traditions that we identify as the law evolve into being.[17]

This approach thus emphasizes that law is an inherently creative and constructive enterprise; judicial discretion is both inevitable and desirable. "Judicial review . . . should speculate on mysteries. It must therefore be open-ended and future oriented," notes Lief Carter.[18] As such, this view agrees with instrumental Marxists and liberal realists that subjective factors of interest, opinion, and power are always at work in judicial policy formulation. But such a recognition of ineradicable subjectivity does not imply that interpretive freedom is absolute or that law is simply an arbitrary expression of will by the dominant class in society. "The interpreter is not free to assign any meaning he wishes to the text," Fiss points out regarding "normal" legal practice.[19] Rather, the idiosyncratic biases and prejudices of elite judges are constrained routinely by their dependence upon the inherited ideas, symbols, and other conventions of legal narrative as well as by institutional factors which shape the particular political contexts of judicial action.[20] It therefore is as misleading to characterize judicial opinions as mere post hoc rationalizations for decisions rendered on other grounds as it is to see law as an automatic, self-fulfilling prophecy. The fact is that what judges say they are doing at once reflects and shapes—is cause and constituent part of—what they are doing, whether the judges recognize this as such or not. The very act of justifying policy positions through constitutional language—that is, through inherited ideas and formal patterns of logic—constrains, structures, and informs those very policies themselves. This is why some scholars liken the ideological constraints of legal practice to other more tangible institutional structures that bind officials and citizens alike within society.[21]

Constitutional decisions usually do reflect a variety of arbitrary and subjective factors, then, but this subjectivity tends to be "bounded," more or less, by the constraints of an acknowledged tradition of authoritative legal discourse.[22] From this perspective, the operative criteria of legality and legitimacy thus are not the inherent rightness, certitude, or predictability of judicial opinions. Instead, what matters is that legal claims are plausible, coherent, and meaningful; they must fit or, as John Brigham says, "make sense" within the evolving tradition of constitutional discourse.[23] And it is this capacity to contain limited, if often intense and passionate, disagreements which explains why deeply divided court decisions, clear departures from precedent, and controversial rulings do not usually erode the legitimacy of courts and the legal systems generally. The interpretation of law as a dynamic "narrative" that some scholars propose is helpful in this regard. Part raconteur, part literary critic, and part analytic philosopher, each judge enjoys great discretion to choose how to continue particular stories through future events. But those choices will be convincing only to the degree that new developments build upon and address themes, ideas, sentiments, and logics established by previous decisions inscribed in the cumulative text.[24]

It is my view that this emphasis on the ideologically "bounded subjectivity" of legal discourse both supports and qualifies the Marxist model of "relatively autonomous" law in capitalist society. According to this theory, law does not simply reflect the narrow interests of the dominant capitalist class in specific disputes; rather, it is developed in fidelity to general principles of justice applicable to rich and poor alike. The crucial factor, however, is that those legal principles themselves are understood to support the larger structure of alienated, unequal, and exploitive social relations intrinsic to the capitalist system. Such formal legal logics tend to draw from, as well as to shape, the dominant ideological formations within the broader culture. They are reinforced more strictly by exclusivity of membership, social affiliation, and professional socialization (law school and practice), which sustain class-based and other social biases within the specialized "interpretive community" of elite legal actors.[25]

The danger with such a structuralist approach, however, is that it tends to overdetermine the complex causal relationships at stake. It is one thing to contend that the evolution of law as an authoritative resource for structuring social interaction and resolving disputes in capitalistic society has forged a marked closure of shared meanings, assumptions, and principles; in this sense, it is appropriate to note the common characteristics, elective affinity, or "homology" between capitalist social forms and liberal legal ideas.[26] But to agree with some Marxists that the bounded substance or form of the law merely "reflects," "mirrors," or "derives from" the exchange-based structure of capitalist society implies a gross simplification at odds with sound dialectical analysis.[27] Such a perspective denies the inherent contradictions and dynamic tensions within every legal order as well as between the legal order and the dominant forms of social organization at any point in time. Neither the liberal legal order nor capitalism itself are monolithic entities: The undeniable fact is that societies with similar historical capitalist structures have developed notably different cultural, political, and legal traditions, and vice versa. Likewise, changes in the primary forms of social relations often have given rise to real and unpredictable changes in legal principles and forms. It may be true that our legal order rarely develops in ways that fundamentally challenge capitalist structures of unequal class power, but there is still room in this legal order for considerable undetermined discretion about the forms of capitalism and legal norms. These may involve a whole host of both class- and nonclass-specific factors that emerge from a specific social context. In short, the Marxist model of economic causality tends to depoliticize and overdetermine law in much the same way as do traditional formalist or interpretivist theories. The structural relationships between legal ideology and capitalist social relations are important matters of analysis, yet they should be approached as variable, dynamic, and dialectical interactions between relatively independent and internally complex spheres of creative endeavor rather than reduced to simple terms of inevitability.[28]

Similar tendencies to reductionism are often manifest in the contrary claim by many Marxists that law does not reflect capitalist social relations so much as "mystify" and "distort" them in "illusory" terms that "obscure" the real facts to legal subjects. In the extreme version of this claim, the function of law is to legitimate social injustice by promoting "false consciousness." The virtue of this view is that it recognizes the gap between the orderly symbolic significations of legal language and the object world to which they refer. Yet, in doing so, it misleadingly conceptualizes "reality" and "representation" as static entities bound in fact by a single, predetermined true relationship. The implication is that legal ideology develops independently of the object world rather than through routinized social practices of legal reasoning constitutive of that world. It is true that legal discourse, like all specialized languages, does involve important dimensions of "structured bias" in its unique rendering of sensible meaning in American social life. Its ideological components "act as grids which select, sort, order, and reorder the elements of thought" in ways that at once both obscure and reveal, distort and clarify, our thinking.[29] But every mode of seeing is also a way of not seeing; every intellectual grid is selective, biased, and at least incomplete from a variety of perspectives. The proper question thus is not whether the resulting understandings are true or false in some absolute sense. Rather, the important analytical questions concern the ways in which legal ideologies are biased, the implications of such bias for understanding social relations, and the alternative perspectives that might make better or more just sense of those relations. And it is on these latter grounds of insight into legal bias that class-oriented interpretations, such as those urged by critical theorists and offered in the following pages, must demonstrate their value.[30]

We now turn to analysis regarding one dimension of such lingering structural bias in constitutional ideology—that of Fourteenth Amendment equal protection doctrine.

RACE AND THE EVOLUTION OF "EQUAL PROTECTION"

"All men are created equal," Thomas Jefferson proclaimed as the first of the "self-evident truths" inspiring the American Declaration of Independence. Jefferson's status as a slaveowner did not inhibit such pious proclamations, it seems, but the deep divisions within the new nation created by the slavery issue did deter the Republic's founders from including the language of equality within the text of the new Constitution.[31] Despite their recognition that the "most common and durable source" of factions dividing the nation was the competition for ownership of property (including slaves), the founders instead made the "protection of . . . those diverse and unequal faculties of acquiring property" the very "first object" of the new constitutional government.[32] This does not mean that the founders were indifferent toward the fundamental principle of legal equality for all. As federalist leader and inaugural Supreme Court Chief Justice John Jay put it, the Constitution implicitly granted "an equal right to all citizens to have, enjoy and to do, in peace, security, and without molestation, whatever the equal and constitutional laws of the country admit to be consistent with the public good." [33] But the implication is that, from the beginning, the dominant constitutional conception of equality would be one consistent with, and committed to, a society where competition for unequal ownership of property was the prevailing ethic.

It was not until after the violence and bloodshed of the Civil War, however, that this promise of equal protection was formally codified in the Constitution and extended to include those persons of color once shackled in slavery. Of the three constitutional amendments that legally sanctified the resulting legal emancipation, the Fourteenth Amendment promise to secure the "equal protection of the laws" for all persons has proved to be the most important and controversial one. This chapter is not the place to enter the debate concerning the framers' intended designs, but it is worth noting the one clear point agreed upon by all—that the framers sought to uphold and grant constitutional status to the Civil Rights Act of 1866. [34] What is significant about this act is that it made clear that the primary equality among free men, including the former slaves, is manifest in the right to own property and to be fairly judged in all matters concerning uses of that property. As the first section states,

> All persons born in the United States . . . are hereby declared to be citizens of the United States; and such citizens, of every race and color, shall have the same right . . . to make and enforce contracts, to sue, be parties, and give evidence, to inherit, purchase, lease, sell, hold, and convey real and personal property, and to full and equal benefit of all laws and proceedings for the security of person and property as is enjoyed by white citizens, and shall be subject to like punishment, pains, and penalties, and to none other, any law, statute, ordinance, regulation, or custom, to the contrary notwithstanding. [35]

As suggested by its coupling with due process for property owners in the same amendment, the logic of constitutional equality from the start was inextricably linked to capitalist exchange-based ideas of distributive social justice.

The implications of these new constitutional provisions were not spelled out in clear terms by their numerous authors, however, and hence were left to be worked out in subsequent judicial interpretations. The early trend in cases seemed to be promising, at times going beyond matters of marketplace freedom to rights of public citizenship. In 1880, for example, the Court invalidated a state law forbidding blacks from serving on juries in *Strauder v. West Virginia*. Any such discriminatory law is a "brand . . . of inferiority," the majority ruled, "and a stimulant to that race prejudice which is an impediment to securing to individuals of the race that equal justice which the law aims to secure to all others." But legal equality was soon subsumed by the marketplace logic of property rights. For example, the Court initially invoked the rights of property owners to invalidate antidiscrimination statutes as outside of the authority of the congressional commerce clause and just a few years later to uphold Jim Crow regulations requiring racial segregation in various aspects of public commercial exchange and transportation in the southern states.[36] Yet it was the evolving construction of the Fourteenth Amendment itself that quickly proved to hold the most durable limits to the struggle for equality by long-oppressed persons of color. To the central elements of these decisions we now turn.

STATE ACTION: THE LIMITS OF PUBLIC RIGHT

The first significant limitation upon the reach of the Fourteenth Amendment came down quickly in the *Civil Rights Cases* of 1883. These decisions found no constitutional support for the public accommodation sections of the 1875 Civil Rights Act prohibiting racial discrimination by operators of restaurants, inns, theatres, and public conveyances. The key argument by the eight-justice majority rested on the emerging principle limiting constitutional protection against racial discrimination only to the acts of state officials, thus excluding from legal concern the multifarious "social" acts of racial discrimination by institutions, groups, and individuals in the private market sector. Under the Fourteenth Amendment, Justice Joseph Bradley held, "it is state action of a particular character that is prohibited. Individual invasion of individual rights is not the subject-matter of the amendment. . . . It does not authorize Congress to create a code of municipal law for regulation of private rights." According to this view, the excluded blacks had suffered denial not of civil or political rights, but only of their "social" rights, for which there was no constitutional protection. Such is the "ordinary mode" of legal treatment for all full citizens, which prohibits the purported request of blacks to be "the special favorite of the laws" governing social life.[37] One could not find a better example of Marx's claim that liberal "political emancipation was at the same time an emancipation of civil society from politics and from even the semblance of a general content."[38]

The implications of this doctrine soon became apparent in cases upholding a variety of "private" discriminatory actions ranging from Ku Klux Klan racial violence to restrictive covenants among white property owners.[39] These same principles have continued to limit the reach of constitutional equal protection obligations even until today. It is true that such restrictions were significantly weakened by post–New Deal judicial interpretations, which extended state action classifications to private individuals and institutions that perform a "public function," that receive state financial aid, or that enlist other "significant" forms of state involvement.[40] Likewise, the more expansive commerce clause authorization of the 1964 Civil Rights Act extended statutory protections against racial discrimination to many areas of commercial and workplace activity as well. However, both legal routes to expanding state authority over the market have seen little progress in recent years and have even shown signs of significant retrenchment since the early 1970s. In a series of oft-ignored cases, the Burger Court departed from the liberal criteria of financial aid, regulatory entanglement, and public function that once bound social institutions to constitutional obligations.[41] What is more, the logic of limited state liability has been employed to restrict significantly the range of acceptable affirmative action policies where only patterns of societal discrimination can be found to explain racial inequalities. As Justice Lewis Powell put it in *Wygant v. Jackson Board of Education,* the "Court never has held that societal discrimination alone is sufficient to justify a . . . racially classified remedy."[42] In short, only injuries or deprivations imposed by the state are constitutionally suspect, and only a wrong by the state deserves remedy. The state action doctrine thus sustains an important conceptual line between public obligation and private freedom and gives greatest constitutional voice to the latter in ways that explicitly protect the autonomy of marketplace power in capitalist society.

STATE "NEUTRALITY" AS LIMITED LIABILITY

The second limiting tenet of the equal protection doctrine derives from the principle that state action under "the Constitution is neutral as to persons." As Marx put it, the state is bound to regard everyone abstractly as impersonal "citizens."[43] The promise of this commitment is that the state should treat all persons alike within the terms of classifications that are general, principled, and nonarbitrary in character. Undoubtedly, impersonal treatment from the state long ago offered an undeniable advance for a majority of white "common men" against the inherited inequalities of European aristocracy as well as eventually for racial and ethnic minorities, women, and other groups subordinated to unequal status by such men.

But the limitations of this position also were apparent from the start when, in the *Civil Rights Cases,* the High Court refused the demands of blacks to bar societal discrimination as a plea for status as "special favorites of the law." The infamous case of *Plessy v. Ferguson* (1896) even more dramatically displayed the exploitive possibilities of this new legal logic. In upholding the constitutionality of a Louisiana statute requiring separation of black and white travellers on an intrastate railroad line, the Court's interpretation of the Fourteenth Amendment concluded that segregationist policies did not inherently deny "equal protection" to persons of color. Drawing upon Justice Lemuel Shaw's distinction in *Roberts v. Boston* (1849) between the "principle" of equal protection and its differential "application," as well as the more recent holding in *Strauder v. West Virginia* (1880), the majority behind Justice Billings Brown denied that "the inferred separation of the two races stamps the colored race with a badge of inferiority." In other words, state discrimination *among* persons on the basis of color that does not deny the enjoyment of basic rights—to property ownership, political participation, mobility, and so on—does not add up to an invidious injury *against* persons as prohibited by the Constitution. Affirming the established difference between "political" and "social" equality, Brown explained that the Fourteenth Amendment "could not have been intended to abolish distinctions based on color" which arise from "the nature of things" in civil society. As long as the state did not initiate such distinctions, therefore, mere legal recognition of existing social practices does not offend its neutrality toward persons.[44]

This position concerning the implied neutrality of the state in the equal treatment of persons survived until *Brown v. Board of Education* declared in 1954 that "separate but equal" is a contradiction in terms. However significant this reversal of precedent, though, the *Brown* decision did not challenge the general principle of neutrality itself so much as redefine its specific obligations in terms more consistent with the post–New Deal liberal consensus. The unanimous Court called upon social science evidence to refute earlier assumptions that racial segregation does not inherently "brand" persons of color with a "stigma" of "inferiority" and the "badges of slavery." In fact, *Brown* and subsequent cases gave expression to the evolving position of the Court that all racially conscious discrimination is immediately "suspect" and thus "subject to the most searching scrutiny."[45] This scrutiny for invidious discrimination was aimed beyond the prima facie language of official statutes or actions to the very intentions and motives of their authors as well. In other words, while seemingly neutral on their face, various forms of discrimination among persons—job competence tests, for example—may be scrutinized to determine any covert manifestations of racial prejudice in either unequal administration or biased design of the rules or procedures. All in all, the emerging doctrine of equal protection declared that neutrality to persons requires a formal posture of nondiscrimination on the basis of race, color, and ethnicity except where there exists a compelling state interest. Recalling the dissent of Justice John Marshall Harlan in *Plessy,* Justice Robert Jackson spoke for the new majority in affirming that "Justice is blind and her daughter, the law, ought to at least be color-blind."[46]

The great deficiency in such a simple posture of color-blind neutrality is that it remains mostly amnesiac about the continuing impact of past state-supported discrimination that still burdens people of color throughout the land today. After years of requiring for the most part only termination of racist policies in schools and other public-sector enterprises, therefore, the Court began in the late 1960s to require more "affirmative" action to redress as well as to halt the biases of the past. As Chief Justice Warren Burger later put it, "the presumption must be made that past discriminatory systems have resulted in present economic inequalities" (*Fullilove v. Klutznick,* 1983).[47] But contrary to the claims of many critics of the Court, affirmative action mandates to remedy past wrongs aim more to realize than to abandon the principle of state neutrality by transcending the limits of the antidiscrimination ethic. The crucial point is that the mere fact of racially unequal impacts from state action does not establish a constitutional obligation to take remedial steps. Affirmative action is required, and allowed in most cases, *only* after "purposeful" (*dejure*) invidious racial discrimination has been shown, and then "the nature of the violation determines the scope of the remedy."[48] Thus, remedies must be closely tailored to particular aspects of official behavior within narrow allocational spheres for limited periods of time.

This logic has prevailed ever since the earliest cases. In the *Civil Rights Cases,* the Court narrowed the Fourteenth Amendment's authorization of "appropriate" congressional legislation for enforcement of equal protection entitlements to include only "corrective" measures for past acts of wrongful commission by state officials. The public accommodation provisions in question, by contrast, authorized "direct and primary" action aimed at social reorganization in cases where no explicit state wrongdoing was proven.[49] The same principle of remedial action has governed the logic of recent cases concerning school integration, employment preferences, statutory state contract awards, and other affirmative action policies. As the majority ruled in the path-breaking case *Swann et al. v. Charlotte-Mecklenburg Board of Education,* "Once a right and a violation have been shown, the scope of . . . equitable powers to remedy past wrongs is broad. . . . The task is to correct, by a balancing of individual and collective interests, the condition that offends the Constitution. [But] it is important to remember that judicial powers may be exercised only on the basis of a constitutional violation." This logic has been used repeatedly to restrict affirmative action obligations. In recent years, it has justified decisions limiting both mandatory and permissible voluntary remedies to ever narrower authoritative sectors (within rather than among school districts), to more specific aspects of allocational decisions (distinguishing seniority in promotion from seniority in firing), and to shorter periods of remedial obligation for official wrongdoers.[50]

In short, the logic of most affirmative action is hardly affirmative at all but instead aims only to restore state neutrality by requiring reflexive redress for all past incidents of racially nonneutral official action. As affirmative action policies are said to achieve a certain "wholeness" for wronged individuals, so do they promote a "sense of wholeness" to impersonal legal authority.[51] But such a commitment to "blind" justice has provided more justifications for constitutional indifference than actual remedies for long-developing social inequalities, much less positive guidelines for a more just restructuring of society. Even the most progressive efforts by some members of the Court to liberalize the standards of proof used to determine intentional state wrongdoing—by including "foreseeability" of consequences and discounting "remoteness in time"—have not departed from this basic legitimating logic of reflexive neutrality through remedial action.[52]

THE LEGAL SUBJECT: ABSTRACT INDIVIDUALISM

A third, and often misrepresented, principle stipulates that equal protection entitlements to impartial state treatment are limited to discrete individual subjects. This logic is manifest in the very words of the Fourteenth Amendment, which reads that "no state shall . . . deny to any person" the equal protection of the laws. The principle has been affirmed in numerous cases: "The rights created by the first section of the Fourteenth Amendment are, by its terms, guaranteed to the individual. The rights established are personal rights," a majority held in *Shelley v. Kraemer.*[53] Such an individualistic bias is hardly surprising, of course, given the commitment to private property rights at the heart of our constitutional tradition. Indeed, the evolving equal protection logic not only has respected the autonomy of the marketplace from government authority but has also incorporated the basic premises of competitive exchange relations among individuals *within* the logic of legal obligation that binds formal state actors and institutions. As John Schaar put it, the prevailing legal doctrine "is a precise symbolic expression of the liberal-bourgeois model of society, for it extends the marketplace mentality to all spheres of life. . . . Individualism, in Tocqueville's sense, is the reigning ethical principle."[54]

The most notable aspect of this individualist principle is its peculiarly restrictive manner of dealing with essentially structural social divisions. To begin with, the bias of the prevailing equal protection antidiscrimination logic is to place the focus of attention upon discrete violations by what Alan Freeman calls official "perpetrators." The result is that the criteria of legal injury are restricted not only to formally public spheres of activity but, more specifically, to verifiable transgressions by specific officials or laws on whom to pin the blame for injustice. According to Freeman, "It is a notion of racial discrimination as something that is caused by individuals, or individual institutions, producing discrete results that can be identified as discrimination and thereafter neutralized."[55] Although transcending the color-blind and amnesiac biases of older doctrines, the obligatory remedial actions thus still remain myopic and selective in memory regarding the complex, multifaceted structural dimensions of institutional racism, which transcend individual agency and control. The perpetrator perspective focuses on punishing the sins of official wrongdoers rather than addressing the needs of victimized groups and on redressing specific acts of discrimination rather than alleviating the pervasive citizen sufferings and injustices deriving from a history of racially specific deprivation. Moreover, by singling out specific laws and wrongdoers as offensive, the individualistic perpetrator perspective tends to promote the perception of racism as an anomalous disease curable by selective surgery and remedial therapies to restore an otherwise healthy body politic composed of "innocent" citizens. This type of logic was used in *Regents of University of California v. Bakke.* As Powell's pivotal position made clear, those members of the majority white race who are not guilty of discrete official wrongdoing are understood to be innocent victims; they are considered to be largely free of responsibility for the advantages derived from centuries of white domination simply because they themselves did not initiate it, and hence, are as equally entitled to nonpreferential treatment as are members of traditionally victimized minority groups. Despite universal agreement that "there has been serious racial discrimination in this country," leading judicial constructions of equal protection neither acknowledge original sins requiring collective penance nor promise redemption through new social relations.[56]

This approach has allowed some important benefits that Freeman discounts, it is true. Programs limited to remedying violations have extended at least minimal help for an indefinite time to many members of stigmatized groups who were not directly victimized by past acts of official wrongdoing. In the most extreme case, the use of racial (and other group-based) quotas to rectify imbalances resulting from past invidious discrimination has promised to provide benefits not only directly to select individual group members, but also indirectly to the larger group in the form of resource redistribution, group-specific role models and leadership, and a collective sense of esteem.[57] Nevertheless, Freeman's critical posture is still well founded. For one thing, the Court has ruled since *Bakke* that group-oriented quotas are contrary to the spirit of equal protection except where they are strictly remedial in intent, limited in duration, and flexible in implementation.[58] Moreover, contrary to claims by conservative critics, such limited quotas do not signify a mandate for broadly based redistribution of public resources. Although they have introduced a short-term group-oriented component in some selected institutional processes, such quotas still permit allocation of goods to members *within* those groups on largely competitive individualistic terms with predictably unequal results among group members and nonmembers alike. The result is that a small minority of victimized group members may enjoy improved access and position in the present system, but the large majority of members can expect no more than a marginal improvement in fortune from existing constitutional mandates.[59]

Finally, we should note that the alternative to group-oriented quotas endorsed most often in recent years is even more individualistic in character. Expressing preference for a program that "treats each applicant as an individual in the admissions process," Powell voiced the majority view in *Bakke* that it is only "the individual who is entitled to judicial protection against classifications based upon his racial or ethnic background because such distinctions impinge upon personal rights, rather than the individual only because of his membership in a particular group."[60] In this view, race may be considered as only one of many factors, and then only to the degree that it is presumed to have been an obstacle to citizen competition for position and power. Such a focus by a Court majority on the particular life circumstances of individuals may be more equitable and sensitive to citizen needs than suggested by Marx's analysis of bourgeois law. But at the same time this highly individualistic approach still excludes those elements of the structurally determined social context and historically disadvantaged group status that define important aspects of our social reality. Such a perspective reduces the complex systemic sources of inequality among citizens to idiosyncratic, random hardships discernable in discrete life histories. Law still largely respects a "pure, blank individuality," as Marx put it.[61]

Constitutional remedies thus are limited to mandates for more flexible and socially conscious discretionary processes of evaluation among claimants contending for scarce goods in specific public arenas. Coordinated policies of resource redistribution to mitigate continuing group-based sources of social deprivation or to meet citizen needs may be legislated, but none are required by the Fourteenth Amendment. The classical liberal union of faith in individual responsibility and antistatism has rarely found more clear expression.

MERITOCRACY AND THE MARKET LOGIC OF LAW

A key fact in regard to this issue is that the Court has not construed the equal protection doctrine as prohibiting all discrimination among citizens; it has ruled only that different types of discriminatory classification should receive different levels of review and thus variable degrees of presumed legal legitimacy. Most important for our purposes is that, although classifications made according to race and ethnicity have been subjected to rigorous review, those forms of differentiation that are related to alleged evaluations of citizen performance, skills, merit, and other market measures of worth typically have been subjected to a minimal standard of review requiring only a reasonable relation to a legitimate state interest. The result is that structural inequalities in both distribution of goods and institutional organization have been largely excluded from constitutional purview.

This problem has been well illustrated by recent legal challenges to competence tests as they are used in both public and private spheres. In *Washington v. Davis* (1976), for example, a majority of seven justices upheld a District of Columbia Police Department's standard personnel test (measuring verbal skills) administered to all applicants for positions as officers, even though the test disproportionately resulted in excluding blacks. The logic of the decision was clear: Absent clear proof of intent to discriminate on racial grounds, exclusion of persons on the basis of inability to demonstrate basic skills on ostensibly neutral performance tests meets the rationality test required by the traditional concept of equal protection.[62] This same meritocratic logic has governed constitutional cases involving professional school admissions and job advancement as well but perhaps has been most evident in cases involving the "more rigorous standard" of the Civil Rights Act. In *Griggs v. Duke Power Co.* (1971), the Court declared that a private employer's requirement of high school diploma and intelligence test scores for job applicants violated Title VII of the act. "What is required by Congress is the removal of artificial, arbitrary, and unnecessary barriers to employment when the barriers operate invidiously to discriminate on the basis of racial or other impermissible classifications." Merely unequal racial impacts may be permissible, however, where the criteria of discrimination are "substantially related to job performance." In other words, far from challenging the unequal impact or unexamined biases of meritocratic discrimination among citizens, the Court's rigorous scrutiny has simply held processes of applicant evaluation to their own rational standards of marketplace justification: "The touchstone is business necessity."[63]

Reflection on these points reveals much about the logic of neutrality implied by equal protection principles. Indeed, the fact that meritocratic or performance-based criteria generally are exempted from searching scrutiny calls attention to the underlying criteria determining "suspectness" itself. The most common reason given by experts on and off the Bench is that most suspect characteristics are "immutable" and "natural" in essence. Because they are "determined solely by the accident of birth," persons have no choice about them, and hence should not suffer before law because of them.[64] Although it is plausible in itself, though, this logic fails to explain why personal strength, beauty, and intelligence are not treated as suspect as well. Likewise, the frequent charge of past "stigmatization" alone is similarly insufficient because it fails to reveal why—except by degree—decisions penalizing persons for ugliness, stupidity, or clumsiness also are not "suspect." The additional point at stake in this logic is that stigmas attached to race, color, ethnicity, and religion focus on arbitrary personal traits rather than allegedly objective performances in social or marketplace interaction. Because discrimination on the basis of race is *not* related to one's ability to achieve, to one's display of creative talent, or to one's merit as defined by prevailing standards of social utility and moral worth in the social marketplace, the Court has deemed that it must be justified by a compelling state interest. In short, race discrimination is suspect because it focuses on the actor rather than on her acts, which are the allegedly just basis of legal discrimination among persons. As Justice Brennan argued for the plurality opinion in *Frontiero v. Richardson* (1973), what distinguishes race and ethnicity (and sex) "from such non-suspect statuses as intelligence and physical disability, and aligns it to the recognized suspect criteria, is that (it) . . . bears no relation to ability to perform or contribute to society."[65] Every justice on the High Court during the 1970s joined opinions invoking the same logic, although often with differing policy implications.[66] After centuries of struggle against stigmatizing myths, classifications based on race, ethnicity, and gender have been deemed "morally suspect" departures from the meritocratic marketplace logic of entitlement esteemed by liberal philosophy, American culture, and, at least indirectly, constitutional law.

It is true that compensatory policies giving preference to members of suspect classes have superseded considerations simply of individual citizen performance in allocating public goods. These policies underscore the important fact that judicial deference to state discretion in the use of ostensibly neutral performance-oriented or meritocratic standards to govern access and allocation has stopped far short of recognizing a basic constitutional right to such treatment. But affirmative action remedies at least implicitly still support the meritocratic logic of distribution. Not only are nonperformance-based remedial guidelines necessarily limited in scope and time, but they still allow a certain degree of meritocratic differentiation for members of groups accorded special preference. After all, most programs approved by the Court still require minimum standards of performance for all recipients of goods (such as job hiring and advancement or admission to higher education) and allocate goods unequally to members *within* victimized groups largely on grounds of performance-related ability or desert.[67] More important yet, most approved compensatory policies can be understood not to supersede merit considerations so much as to render them more rational in evaluating citizen talent and potential, which in many cases far exceed short-term performance but have been stifled by the impact of past illegitimate deprivations. In short, affirmative action programs that take the effects of past racial (or gender) discrimination into account ostensibly improve upon many traditional assessments of ability or merit and thus restore claims to the objectivity, utility, and fairness in allocating public goods.[68]

These developments represent an undeniable advance over older forms of overt racial, ethnic, and gender discrimination, but the deference extended to meritocratic justifications for differentiation are highly protective of status quo inequalities in at least three senses. First, as studies of employment and education patterns document, the invocation of performance-based standards often only masks decision processes that in practice are influenced profoundly (if subtly) by racial, ethnic, gender, and other forms of customary bias.[69] Second, the meritocratic emphasis on performance tends to reinforce the blindness to fundamental inequalities of citizens' social backgrounds and capacities for basic needs fulfillment in ways supportive of inherited stratification patterns. Finally, the sanctification of meritocratic distributive justice principles diverts egalitarian challenges away from the larger patterns of hierarchical organization and the exclusive power relationships themselves. In other words, equal protection disputes that are limited mostly to questions of who deserves access and allocation of goods within established structures of public institutions tend to "deconstitutionalize" substantive challenges to macrolevel decisions concerning the very deployment of resources among and within institutional spheres. We thus return to our basic starting point: The evolved logic of constitutional equality discourse, like that of older property rights doctrines, parallels and supports an individualistic, competitive logic of marketplace exchange relations that is profoundly inegalitarian at its core.

EQUAL PROTECTION AND UNEQUAL WEALTH

The expansion of the equal protection principle to arguments condemning invidious discrimination against members of racial and ethnic minorities competing in the economic and political marketplace—and eventually to arguments concerning "semi-suspect" classes such as women, aliens, and illegitimate children—has produced mixed results. It is true that opportunities for advancement within existing structures have been opened up to many individuals. In many sectors of public and private life, the increase in the racial and ethnic plurality of representation has been palpable.[70] Moreover, both official representatives and members of many once powerless groups have taken advantage of new political rights to support legislative statutes expanding both market access and various forms of state welfare relief for those still excluded from full social participation.

However, these legal changes in state distributive processes have not been redistributive in impact. Some members of these groups have prospered from the new legal doctrines, but the groups as a whole remain victimized by the unequal character of competition for position in modern public institutions as well as by the hierarchical structure of control and reward in those institutions beyond constitutional challenge. As a result, the gains in formal rights for racial and ethnic minorities, women, and other long-exploited groups have been thwarted by the dramatic but legally irrelevant reality of class division.[71] It thus is not surprising that many progressives—including both minority group leaders and liberal benefactors—have looked to the judiciary in recent decades to address more directly these economic dimensions of social inequality in America. Having explored the ideological evolution of equal protection in race disputes, we can now probe why this legal strategy likewise has provided few resources for addressing the fundamental material deprivations of citizens within the context of modern capitalism. My basic theme is simple: The same logic of equal protection that has limited constitutional redress for racial and ethnic groups (and women) to individual remedies for past state discrimination has excluded concern for class inequalities almost altogether.

"WEALTH DISCRIMINATION": A NONDOCTRINE?

On its face, the very fact of pervasive economic inequality and poverty might seem to suggest the need for close judicial scrutiny of all state legislation discriminating among people on the basis of wealth. As Frank Michelman argued in the late 1960s, "if money is power, then a class deliberately defined so as to include everyone who has less wealth or income than any person outside it may certainly be deemed [to] be especially susceptible to abuse by majoritarian process; and classification of 'the poor' as such, may, like classifications of racial minorities as such, be popularly understood as a badge of inferiority."[72] And so the Warren Court ruled in some cases that discrimination against persons on the basis of wealth alone is contrary to constitutional equal protection. In fact, a majority noted several times that "lines drawn on the basis of wealth or property . . . render a classification highly suspect."[73] Likewise, in the cases of *Williams v. Illinois* (1970) and *Tate v. Short* (1971), the Court invalidated state practices that converted monetary fines (for petty theft and traffic offenses, respectively) into prison terms for indigent persons who could not pay them. Equal protection, argued Justice Brennan, "requires that the statutory ceiling placed on imprisonment for any substantive offense be the same for all defendants irrespective of their economic status." Finally, the Court in *Turner v. Fouche* (1969) found that a "real property ownership" requirement for school board membership was "wholly irrelevant to achievement of a valid state objective" and hence a denial of equal protection.[74]

But such cases proved exceptions to the rule established later by the Burger Court denying "suspect" status and searching judicial scrutiny to those classifications made solely on the basis of wealth. At least as far back as 1973, a substantial majority ruled that the Court had "never held that wealth discrimination alone provides an adequate basis for invoking strict scrutiny." This position has been sustained by a majority in cases upholding a host of legislative wealth discriminations against the poor, from requirements of local referenda approval for low-income housing development to denials of state support for exercise of constitutionally protected rights to abortion.[75] "This Court has held repeatedly that poverty, standing alone, is not a suspect classification," ruled the majority in the latter case. Indeed, the Court most often has placed wealth-related discrimination cases at the opposite pole of equal protection scrutiny, requiring only the minimal standard of "mere rationality" to survive under the Constitution. This trend was made clear in *Dandridge v. Williams* (1970) where the Court refused to pass judgment on standards placing upper limits on benefits in the AFDC (Aid to Families with Dependent Children) program, thus discriminating against large families among the poor. In this policy area, the justices ruled, "a State does not violate Equal Protection merely because the classification made by its laws are imperfect. . . . It is enough that the State's action can be rationally based and free from invidious discrimination."[76] This rationality standard has not been entirely toothless, but the overall number and impact of such wealth discrimination cases benefiting the underclass have been insignificant.

The principle articulated here reflects in part the general logic of Fourteenth Amendment interpretation embraced by the Court in the post–New Deal era. Overthrowing the substantive due process doctrine that had protected private property from state regulation for nearly half a century, the Court in 1934 extended a general "presumption of constitutionality" to all forms of "economic" legislation. The only exceptions to the minimal standard of review were cases where "specific prohibitions of the Constitution" are involved; normal "democratic processes" are severely restricted; or a statute "was directed at particular religious . . . national . . . or racial minorities."[77] But this "double standard" of equal protection and due process has been marked by a convenient irony. By framing the new logic legitimating state regulation of producer property rights in terms of the abstractly neutral classification of economic issues, special judicial scrutiny of legislation adversely affecting the poor was inhibited along with that adversely affecting only the wealthy and powerful. In other words, the same doctrine of equality that precluded conservative judicial rulings invalidating laws to help workers and the poor also limited liberal Court action to prohibit discrimination against both groups, much less to mandate large-scale redistributive action on their behalf.[78] As Justice Potter Stewart wrote for a majority in *Dandridge v. Williams,* the reach of equal protection "in the main involved state regulation of business or industry. The administration of public welfare assistance, by contrast, involves the most basic economic needs of impoverished human beings (but) we can find no basis for applying a different constitutional standard." Despite occasional dissents from Justices Thurgood Marshall and William Brennan pointing out the obvious class distinctions between the "individual interests of the poor" and those of regulated businesses, a majority on the Court thus has consistently excluded the poor and other class victims from the suspect status accorded to racial/ethnic minorities and (in lesser degree) women. All in all, Stewart summarized, "the intractable economic, social, and even philosophical problems presented by public welfare assistance programs are not the business of the Court."[79]

Not surprisingly, this indifference to economic inequality is consistent with the prevailing individualistic, meritocratic logic of distribution laid out in previous pages. First of all, materially disadvantaged (unemployed, poor, etc.) citizens are understood to lack the attributes that define suspect-classified groups. Unlike racial minorities and women, for example, the poor have no obviously distinguishing "personal" characteristics such as those of skin color or physique. Moreover, it is often argued that material powerlessness is far more relative, variable, and diverse in degree than those traits of skin color and sex, thus resulting in experiences of deprivation far more variable and diverse in kind as well. The reason is that economic hardship—unlike race, ethnicity, or sex—is not an immutable or unalterable trait of nature entirely beyond the control of individuals. "Personal poverty . . . is not a permanent disability; its shackles may be escaped," Justice Marshall has pointed out.[80] In other words, the fundamental assumption is that relative poverty or wealth is primarily a product of justly arranged social relations that allow everyone considerable opportunity for personal mobility. All in all, the claim is that the poor (and unemployed) as a class of citizens simply lack the clear lines of demarcation, cohesion, and stability that can be claimed for the primary suspect classes. Hardly a "discrete and insular minority," the materially disadvantaged define "a large, diverse, and amorphous class," Justice

Powell contended in *San Antonio Independent School District v. Rodriguez* (1973). "The class is not saddled with such disabilities" of simple identification, or "subjected to such a history of purposeful unequal treatment, or relegated to such a position of powerlessness" as other groups so as to "command extraordinary protection from the majoritarian political process."[81] Even many of the most liberal arguments for overcoming the individualistic bias of equal protection through a "group-disadvantaging" principle offer little hope for addressing the problems of material inequality and deprivation; the reason given is that it is difficult to define an independent social identity for millions of economically marginalized citizens within modern society.[82]

These prevailing perspectives obscure the actual character of class inequality in America as much as they do that of race, ethnicity, and gender, of course. We need only recall, for example, that the Court has found little conflict between its individualistic pretenses and the rights of equal treatment granted to collectivized legal "persons" such as business corporations and labor organizations.[83] Moreover, the assumptions about economic mobility for workers and the poor are rooted more in fantasy than in fact. Widespread poverty, unemployment, and worker powerlessness are enduring aspects of our long-developing capitalist social legacy; they are as stable in character and degree as they are resistant to liberal reformist political tinkering. That poverty is relative and some individuals manage to escape its grasp does not alter the fact that most persons born into the underclass will never escape from it. The fact is that background inequalities of material wealth determine the actual life chances of citizens more than any other single factor in capitalist society.[84] More important, such a narrowly construed focus on distribution discounts challenges to the hierarchical structure of organization and control in capitalist society that sustains unemployment, worker powerlessness, and other forms of class inequality. Finally, it is difficult to accept that such deprivation is not a seriously stigmatizing status in a society that long has so closely identified a citizen's productive role and private wealth with personal virtue. As W. E. B. DuBois once put it, "to be a poor race is hard, but to be a poor race in the land of dollars is the very bottom of hardship."[85]

But the individualistic, quasi-formal ideology of opportunity adhered to by most justices nevertheless has kept the "antidiscrimination" principle at the heart of equal protection doctrine. This tradition is significant not only in that the poor do not constitute an identifiable social group of clear victims; a second reason is that the character of their victimage by state discrimination is quite consistent with basic constitutional values. We must remember that there is no right against discrimination per se, but only against specific forms of willful discrimination that "bear no relation to ability to perform or contribute to society" as measured by the standards of public purpose in legal statutes and individual "merit" in marketplace competition. The primary difference between suspect categories of race or ethnicity and of poverty is precisely that the latter are widely presumed to be a result of, as much as an obstacle to, individual social performance. "To the extent low income is related to low productivity—and it is to a large extent—poverty is not entirely unrelated to individual merit," argues Ralph Winter in an influential article defending the prevailing judicial doctrine. "One need not adopt productivity as the sole criterion of merit to say that poverty resulting from low productivity is far different from legal exclusion from public facilities because of one's race."[86]

The result is that state policies that have discriminatory impacts upon the poor are not "suspect" because they tend less to inhibit citizen access to social opportunity than to merely recognize the "natural" personal inequalities of ability, character, and motivation among citizens for which government, like the market, is not constitutionally obliged to remedy. After all, the "first object" of the Constitution has been to "protect the different and unequal faculties of acquiring property."[87] That some persons cannot afford basic services or suffer unequally from state policies is simply seen as one of the burdens for failing to contribute to society. Once again, such logic largely discounts the tremendous inequalities of acquired social advantage (inherited wealth, status, education, etc.) as well as the pervasive biases in the formulation and administration of meritocratic standards that determine most allocation of goods in our highly organized society. But his logic nevertheless prevails in our public ethics and law. Exposure to the judgment of market rationality is not only deemed unobjectionable in our culture, but we often regard it as the most fair, efficient, and neutral way to govern the public distribution of social goods among citizens.[88]

The final and most significant implication of prevailing doctrines is that, even were economic class deprivation considered a suspect category, it would still not require greater state redistribution of wealth. One reason is that the basic causes of economic inequality rarely can be traced to discrete acts of individual perpetrators or policies. "The 'wrong' of impoverishment . . . has victims but no specific perpetrators. Impoverishment is the residue of the whole set of transactions constituting the victim's economic life," Geoffery Hazard points out.[89] Even where official discrimination is demonstrated, it usually involves, at most, state inaction to help the poor rather than "causing" the evil of material deprivation itself. And without finding wrongful cause by a discrete policy or perpetrator, as we have seen, no "corrective" affirmative action is required under the Constitution. This principle is illustrated well by the Court's decision in *Warth v. Seldin* (1975) to uphold a zoning ordinance that excluded low-income housing development in Penfield, New York. Despite the fact that exclusionary zoning ordinances are a cornerstone of laws denying mobility to the poor, the Court could find "no actionable causal relationship between Penfield's zoning ordinance and plaintiff's asserted injury." It is not the city's fault, the Court implied, that the poor could not afford to live in existing Penfield homes. The plaintiff's exclusion "is the consequence of the economics of the area housing market rather than of respondent's assertedly legal acts." Because no specific wrong was imposed by the state, there was no violation of equal protection and no constitutional obligation to address the needs of the poor.[90]

This point only underlines the further fact that the most serious sources of discrimination take place in an allegedly private marketplace beyond the scope of direct "state action." Strict judicial scrutiny might possibly widen the reach of existing statutes prohibiting fraud, usury, breach of contract, and other abuses suffered widely by the poor in market transactions, it is true. But even the complete elimination of such illegal wrongs would fall far short of addressing the inherent structural sources of radical economic inequality and the hardships that it brings to many citizens in modern society. This fact was evidenced well in the case of *Flagg Bros., Inc., et al. v. Brooks et al.* (1978), where a majority of justices upheld the private actions of a warehouse company to sell the goods entrusted it for storage by a poor woman unable to pay her account. "Most rights secured by the Constitution are protected only against infringements by governments" into the marketplace, the majority ruled. "If the mere denial of judicial relief (for social hardship) is considered sufficient encouragement to make the State responsible for those private acts, all private deprivations of property would be converted into public acts whenever the State . . . denies relief sought by the putative property owner."[91] Despite the long history of state support for capitalism, our evolved constitutional logic largely ignores those systemic material inequalities that undermine chances for both individual improvement and basic material security for a large portion of the citizenry.

FUNDAMENTAL RIGHTS: THE LIMITS OF CONSTITUTIONAL "NEED"

The Court's relative timidity in extending searching scrutiny to wealth discrimination cases has not exhausted the relevance of Fourteenth Amendment equal protection for the poor. Although a majority of the Court has consistently held that official wealth discrimination alone does not constitute a suspect classification, those actions that deny indigent citizens the exercise of certain "fundamental rights" have been subjected to the strictest judicial scrutiny even where no purposeful (de jure) discrimination has been evidenced. Several specific rights have been deemed as "fundamental," including rights to political participation, to fair and full trial (both criminal and civil), to travel, and to family-related activities involving marriage, procreation, and abortion.[92]

Many progressive activists have seen this judicially constructed rights doctrine as an important resource that could be used to reduce inequalities of wealth through state subsidization of activities that are protected by such basic rights. Once again, however, the Court has held on to its formalistic logic and has refused to address the social deprivations that impede meaningful social opportunity and adequate need satisfaction among citizens in modern capitalist society. For one thing, the Burger Court in the 1970s refused to expand state subsidization responsibilities through invoking either well-established or new fundamental rights.[93] Even more significant have been the principled limits upon the types of rights considered fundamental under the Constitution. Most important, the Court has held that there exist no fundamental rights entitlements to a minimum subsistence income independent of that granted by legislative statute. This reasoning, we have seen already, formed the unequivocal logic justifying the majority's validation of an upper limit on AFDC benefits for families in *Dandridge v. Williams.* "The Equal Protection clause does not require that a State must choose between attacking every aspect of a problem or not attacking the problem at all. . . . The intractable economic, social, and even philosophical problems presented by welfare assistance programs are not the business of this Court," wrote Justice Stewart for the majority against dissents by Marshall and Brennan.[94] A majority repeated this logic in a 1972 decision upholding an Oregon statute permitting a landlord to bring action against tenants for possession of rental housing in specified circumstances. In *Lindsey v. Normet,* the Court rejected claims that the "need for decent shelter" and the "right to retain peaceful possession of one's home" are fundamental under the Constitution. "We do not denigrate the importance of decent, safe, and sanitary housing. But the Constitution does not provide judicial remedies for every social and economic ill."[95]

These decisions drew criticism from on and off the Bench, but they were not nearly as controversial as were those in two other areas of plausible rights construction. The first concerned public education. In a controversial 5–4 decision upholding a Texas financial program that at once limited and perpetuated unequal expenditures for students in different school districts with unequal tax revenue bases, the Court ruled that education is not a fundamental constitutional right (*Rodriguez*). As long as the program provided a minimally adequate education for all students, the Court reasoned, equal protection was not denied. This logic of "minimal" sufficiency did invalidate policies denying free public education to illegal alien children in *Plyler v. Doe* (1980), but it also later sustained the New York system of funding schools unequally through reliance upon local taxes (*Board of Education v. Nyquist,* 1983).[96] In perhaps no other cases have the biases of the Court's narrow antidiscrimination ethic, indifferent to facts of unequal citizen resources and social outcomes, been so apparent.

The second highly disputed area in which the Court has found no public obligation to help the poor has concerned funding for the individual exercise of fundamental rights to abortion. In *Maher v. Roe* (1977) the Court upheld a refusal by Connecticut to give Medicaid for nontherapeutic abortions even though it provided medicaid for childbirth. Such a policy, the majority ruled, involves no "suspect" class of discrimination and impinges upon no fundamental right. "The Connecticut regulation places no obstacles—absolute or otherwise—in the pregnant woman's path to an abortion." The 1980 decision in *Harris v. McRae* extended this position further by upholding the Hyde Amendment limiting federal funds for abortion to exceptional cases. "Regardless of whether the freedom of a woman to choose to terminate her pregnancy for health reasons (is exercised), it simply does not follow that a woman's freedom carries with it a constitutional entitlement to the financial resources to avail herself of the full range of protected choices," explained Justice Stewart.[97]

Numerous scholars have pointed out that this recently constructed doctrine of fundamental rights appears to depart from the terms of traditional equal protection principles developed in cases of racial, ethnic, and gender discrimination. The promise of this doctrine, it is argued, is less to eradicate stigmatizing discrimination against persons according to morally illegitimate criteria than to protect citizens from state-imposed hardship in those matters concerning the "basic necessities of life."[98] But what most commentators have ignored is precisely the common logic of formal state "neutrality" and meritocratic entitlement concepts, which link fundamental rights principles to other Fourteenth Amendment constructions. As with earlier substantive due process doctrine, the only fundamental rights recognized as basic constitutional necessities have been those traditional liberal entitlements of formal procedural *access* to, or *autonomy* from, the state. Specifically, rights to publicly subsidized access have been provided in those areas where the state has imposed its exclusive regulatory authority over civil society, including access to state legislative policy makers, criminal law enforcement, and civil enforcement of the marriage contract. Other basic rights to privacy, marriage, and travel, by contrast, aim to protect the private autonomy of citizens against regulatory action deemed beyond the legitimate scope of state authority. Indeed, contemporary fundamental rights to travel and privacy can be understood to offer in very limited form the same promise of individual autonomy in modern corporate society as did older property rights in pre-corporate America.[99]

But like that older doctrine, the fundamental rights ethic still provides no constitutional logic or language for redressing those material deprivations that derive from the structural inequalities of market society beyond those that have an exclusive state origin, much less for challenging the hierarchical organization of control and power itself. In each case, only a formal right of access to, or of private freedom against, public authority has been ensured, without regard for the guaranteed inequality of actual outcomes. The Court has not recognized any affirmative constitutional rights, either to egalitarian social restructuring or to minimum public provision for those "just wants" necessary for the development of citizens' productive potential and the satisfaction of their basic needs in modern society.[100]

Cases concerning rights to public funds for abortions clearly exemplify the point. The state is obliged to protect the "freedom to choose" implied by the fundamental right of privacy, the Court has ruled, but not to provide "financial resources" necessary for individuals to carry out their choices unless the state itself posed an "obstacle" to such action. "Although government may not place obstacles in the path of a woman's exercise of her freedom of choice, it need not remove those not of its own creation."[101] Legislatures may exercise their discretion to fund (or withdraw funds for) such actions. However, the Supreme Court has declined to recognize a constitutional right to the public redistribution of resources necessary to diminish inequalities of life chances among citizens, much less to equalize wealth, except where the state created the financial "necessity" in question. "Social importance," a majority on the Court has insisted repeatedly, "is not the critical determinant for subjecting state legislation to strict scrutiny."[102]

CONCLUSION

The primary aim of the preceding discussion has been to analyze the ideological character and content of our inherited constitutional discourse regarding equality. Building on the insights of critical social theory and contemporary language philosophy, this ideological approach has attempted to connect analysis of law, ethics, and society. The thesis developed from this approach is that constitutional "equality talk" systematically translates social conflicts emanating from the hierarchical structure of capitalist organization into the narrow terms of unfair discrimination against individuals competing for access to power and position in limited spheres of the state. In short, concern for class inequalities is reduced to the narrow terms of redressing specific official transgressions in the process of public goods exchange and distribution. The Court has interpreted the Fourteenth Amendment to allow legislated redistributive measures, but constitutional justice does not require such action. Not only is the Constitution largely silent about the needs and deprivations of the American underclass, therefore, but judicial remedies for pervasive racial, ethnic, gender, and other forms of discrimination have been limited as well. Hence, frequent claims that the modern equal protection doctrine supports no economic theory, or that it lacks any substantive content at all, are highly misleading.[103] Although they are hardly a mere reflection or mystification of material reality, the ideological biases of constitutional equality doctrine have served to support, legitimate, and structure the inequalities of modern capitalist social relations according to much the same logic as did property-oriented doctrines prior to the New Deal.

Despite this rather critical assessment regarding the limits and biases of constitutional construction by the High Court in recent decades, my aim is not to suggest that equal protection litigation is a hopeless enterprise for social reformers. For one thing, the Court's embrace of formal antidiscrimination principles and the expansion of affirmative action mandates undeniably have produced important, if limited, advances over earlier doctrines.

Moreover, as Stuart Scheingold has argued in this book, this legacy of progressive evolution well demonstrates the malleable, responsive, and relatively autonomous character of legal ideology, which should not be discounted by social activists in the future.[104] Law has provided a valuable resource for many political movements in modern America, and judicial battles both to protect past gains and to open up new possibilities will continue to play a key part in political struggles for greater equality. In particular, principled arguments by legal activists urging recognition of group rights, system-wide institutional policies that affirm egalitarian goals, and skepticism toward meritocratic justifications of market autonomy (as in comparable worth challenges, for example) all point toward plausible constructions of equal protection logic in positive directions. Given the increasingly conservative composition of our federal courts, however, it is likely that such strategic judicial challenges in the near future are still likely to play at best only a supporting role to those primary struggles waged on other politicized terrains of state and society.

NOTES

1. Arthur S. Miller, *The Supreme Court and American Capitalism* (New York: The Free Press, 1967); Edward S. Greenberg, "Class Rule Under the Constitution," in Robert J. Goldwyn and William Schambra, eds. (Washington, D.C.: American Enterprise Institute, 1983), pp. 22–48.
2. Wallace Mendelson, "From Warren to Burger: The Rise and Decline of Substantive Equal Protection," *American Political Science Review* 66 (1972), pp. 1226–1233. See also Gerald Gunther, "In Search of Evolving Doctrine on a Changing Court: A Model for the Newer Equal Protection," *Harvard Law Review* 86 (1972), pp. 1–48.
3. Martin Shapiro, "The Constitution and Economic Rights," in M. Judd Harmon, ed., *Essays on the Constitution of the United States* (Port Washington, N.Y.: Kennikat Press, 1978), pp. 88–89.
4. Exceptions to this claim include Frank Michelman, "On Protecting the Poor Through the Fourteenth Amendment," *Harvard Law Review* 83 (1969), pp. 7–69; William H. Clune, "The Supreme Court's Treatment of Wealth Discrimination Under the Fourteenth Amendment," *The Supreme Court Review* (1975), pp. 289–354; Alan D. Freeman, "Antidiscrimination Law: A Critical Review," in David Kairys, ed., *The Politics of Law: A Progressive Critique* (New York: Pantheon, 1978), pp. 92–116; John Brigham, "Wealth Discrimination: An Investigation into Constitutional Ideology," unpublished paper delivered at the Western Political Science Association annual meetings, 1984.
5. Marx's ideas on law are developed in both early ("On the Jewish Question") and late (*Capital*) writings. See Isaac Balbus, "Commodity Form and Legal Form: An Essay on the 'Relative Autonomy' of the Law," *Law and Society Review* 11 (1977), pp. 571–588; Andrew Fraser, "The Legal Theory We Need Now," *Socialist Review* 8 (1978), pp. 147–187; and the essays in Piers Beirne

and Richard Quinney, eds., *Marxism and Law* (New York: John Wiley and Sons, 1982).

6. Michael W. McCann, "Resurrection and Reform: Perspectives on Property in the American Constitutional Tradition," *Politics and Society* 13 (1984), pp. 143–176. The obvious text on the American "liberal tradition" is Louis Hartz, *The Liberal Tradition in America* (New York: Harcourt, Brace, and World, 1955).

7. Marx, "On the Jewish Question," in Robert C. Tucker, ed., *The Marx-Engels Reader* (New York: Norton, 1978), esp. pp. 42–46. For a non-Marxist view, see John C. Noonan, *The Persons and Masks of the Law* (Berkeley: University of California Press, 1978). On legal "masks," see also John Schaar, "Some Ways of Thinking About Equality," *Journal of Politics* 26 (1964), pp. 875–892.

8. Marx, "On the Jewish Question," p. 33.

9. Balbus, "Commodity Form."

10. Ibid. On law as "illusion," see Marx, "On the Jewish Question" and "The German Ideology," in Tucker, ed., *The Marx-Engels Reader,* pp. 146–200. For discussion, see Peter Gabel, "Reification and Legal Reasoning," in Beirne and Quinney, eds., *Marxism and Law,* pp. 262–278.

11. Marx, "On the Jewish Question," p. 34.

12. Marx, "Critique of the Gotha Program," in Tucker, ed. *The Marx-Engels Reader,* p. 530.

13. On the distortions of translating class division into the terms of exchange relations, see Nicos Poulantzas, *State, Power, Socialism* (London: Verso, 1980), esp. pp. 49–69.

14. Marx, "On the Jewish Question," p. 39.

15. The most comprehensive discussion of the subject is Colin Sumner, *Reading Ideologies: An Investigation into the Marxist Theory of Ideology and Law* (London: Academic Press, 1979). See Raymond Williams's excellent discussion on *Marxism and Literature* (Oxford: Oxford University Press, 1977), pp. 55–71; Alan Hunt, "The Ideology of Law: Advances and Problems in Recent Applications of the Concept of Ideology to the Analysis of Law," *Law and Society Review* 19 (1985), pp. 11–38.

16. Geertz, "Ideology as a Cultural System," in *The Interpretation of Cultures* (New York: Basic Books, 1973), pp. 222, 219.

17. John Brigham, *Civil Liberties and American Democracy* (Washington, D.C.: Congressional Quarterly Press, 1984); *Constitutional Language: An Interpretation of Judicial Decision Making* (Westport, Conn.: Greenwood Press, 1978); Owen Fiss, "Objectivity and Interpretation," *Stanford Law Review* 34 (1982), pp. 739–763; William Harris, "Bonding Word and Polity: The Logic of American Constitutionalism," *American Political Science Review* 76 (1982), pp. 34–45; Robert Cover, "Forword: Nomos and Narrative," *Harvard Law Review* 97 (1983), pp. 4–70.

18. Lief Carter, *Contemporary Constitutional Lawmaking* (New York: Pergamon, 1985), p. 94.

19. Fiss, "Objectivity and Interpretation," p. 744.

20. Brigham develops this point well in *Constitutional Language.*

21. See especially Harris, "Bonding Word and Polity"; and Cover, "Nomos and Narrative" for development of the *nomos* metaphor.

22. My idea of "bounded subjectivity" parallels but is less restrictive than Fiss's concept of "bounded objectivity." Fiss, "Objectivity and Interpretation."
23. Brigham, *Civil Liberties*, pp. 34–37.
24. Lief Carter develops most extensively the "aesthetic" approach to analyzing judicial performances, although he remains highly ambivalent about the issue of closure and continuity, in *Contemporary Constitutional Lawmaking*.
25. See Balbus, "Commodity Form." For critical overview, see Alan Hunt, "The Ideology of Law"; and Charles W. Grau, "Whatever Happened to Politics?" in Beirne and Quinney, *Marxism and Law*, pp. 196–209.
26. On "homology," see Balbus, "Commodity Form."
27. See Hunt, "The Ideology of Law," esp. pp. 16–20.
28. See Stuart Hall et al., *Policing the Crisis: Mugging, the State and Law and Order* (London: Macmillan, 1978). This book is a highly penetrating and comprehensive applied study in legal ideology. On the depoliticizing tendencies of structuralist analysis, see Grau, "Whatever Happened to Politics?"
29. See Williams, *Marxism and Literature*, pp. 55–71.
30. Hunt, "The Ideology of Law," p. 16.
31. On racism in the founding era generally, see Winthrop Jordan, *White Over Black: American Attitudes Toward the Negro* (Chapel Hill: University of North Carolina, 1968); David Brion Davis, *The Problem of Slavery in the Age of Revolution* (Ithaca: Cornell University Press, 1975).
32. James Madison, *Federalist 10* (New York: New American Library, 1961). See also John Adams, "Discourses on Davila," in George A. Peek, Jr., ed., *John Adams: His Political Writings* (New York: Bobbs Merrill, 1954), p. 193.
33. John Jay, quoted in J. R. Pole, *The Pursuit of Equality in America* (Berkeley: University of California Press, 1978), p. 118.
34. The debates about the intentions of the framers of the Fourteenth Amendment continue to rage on. See the chapter by Judith A. Baer in this book.
35. The most extensive treatment of this period is Harold M. Hyman and William M. Wiecek, *Equal Justice Under the Law* (New York: Harper and Row, 1982).
36. *Strauder v. West Virginia*, 100 U.S. 103 (1880); *Hall v. DeCuir*, 95 U.S. 485 (1878); *Louisville, New Orleans, and Texas Railway Co. v. Mississippi*, 133 U.S. 587 (1890). On law during this era, see C. Vann Woodward, *The Strange Career of Jim Crow* (New York: Oxford University Press, 1966); Richard Kluger, *Simple Justice: The History of Brown v. Board of Education and Black America's Struggle for Equality* (New York: Knopf, 1975).
37. *Civil Rights Cases*, 109 U.S. 3 (1883). See Kluger, *Simple Justice*, Chapter 3.
38. Marx, "On the Jewish Question," p. 45.
39. *United States v. Harris*, 106 U.S. 629 (1882); *Corrigan v. Buckley*, 271 U.S. 323 (1926).
40. *Marsh v. Alabama*, 326 U.S. 501 (1946); *Norwood v. Harrison*, 413 U.S. 455 (1973); *Burton v. Wilmington Parking Authority*, 365 U.S. 715 (1961).
41. Important cases signaling the retreat from finding "state action" include *Moose Lodge v. Irvis*, 407 U.S. 163 (1972); *Blum v. Yaretsky*, 457 U.S. 991 (1982); *Jackson v. Metropolitan Edison Co.*, 419 U.S. 345 (1974); *Rendell-Baker v. Kohn*, 457 U.S. 830 (1983).
42. *Wygant v. Jackson Board of Education*, 106 S.Ct. 1842 (1986). But see the dissents by Brennan, Marshall, and Blackmun.

43. Pole, *Pursuit of Equality,* pp. 287–292. For a similar but non-Marxist view of the "neutrality" mask, see Noonan, *The Persons and Masks of the Law.*

44. *Civil Rights Cases; Plessy v. Ferguson,* 163 U.S. 537, 543–544 (1896); *Strauder v. West Virginia.*

45. *Korematsu v. United States,* 323 U.S. 303 (1944).

46. The original source of this quote is attributed to counsel Albion Tourgee's brief in *Plessy.* See Harlan in *Plessy v. Ferguson,* at 537, 559.

47. *Fullilove v. Klutznick,* 448 U.S. 448, at 465 (1983).

48. *Swann et al. v. Charlotte-Mecklenburg Board of Education,* 420 U.S. 15 (1971).

49. *Civil Rights Cases;* see Kluger, *Simple Justice,* Chapter 3.

50. *Swann et al. v. Charlotte-Mecklenburg Board of Education,* at 15, 16; *Milliken v. Bradley,* 418 U.S. 717 (1974); *Pasadena Board of Education v. Spangler,* 427 U.S. 424 (1976); *Personnel Administrator v. Feeney,* 442 U.S. 256 (1979).

51. On the logic of wholeness, see Kenneth L. Karst, "Foreword: Equal Citizenship Under the Fourteenth Amendment," *Harvard Law Review* 91 (1977), p. 9.

52. See *Keyes v. School District,* 413 U.S. 189 (1973). *Personnel Administrator v. Feeney; City of Mobile v. Bolden,* 446 U.S. 55 (1980). Affirmative action has justified positive, reconstructive goals of promoting diversity (Powell in *Regents of University of California v. Bakke,* 438 U.S., at 272) or helping minority businesses (Stevens in *Fullilove v. Klutznick,* at 541–543, 552) only very rarely.

53. *Shelley v. Kraemer,* 334 U.S. 1, at 22 (1948).

54. Schaar, "Equality of Opportunity," p. 237. See also Carl Cohen, "Why Racial Preference Is Illegal and Immoral," *Commentary* (1979), pp. 42, 44; Philip Green, *The Pursuit of Inequality* (New York: Pantheon, 1978), pp. 165–265.

55. Freeman, "Antidiscrimination Law," pp. 98–99. See also Timothy O'Neil, "The Language of Equality in a Constitutional Order," *American Political Science Review* 75 (1981), pp. 626–635; Pole, *Pursuit of Equality,* pp. 112–147.

56. Freeman, "Antidiscrimination Law," p. 99; Green, *Pursuit of Inequality,* pp. 176–187.

57. See Edwin Dorn, *Rules and Racial Equality* (New Haven: Yale University Press, 1979), pp. 107–148.

58. *U.S. Steelworkers of America, AFL-CIO v. Weber,* 443 U.S. 193 (1978); *Fullilove v. Klutznick; Wygant v. Jackson Board of Education.*

59. Freeman, "Antidiscrimination Law," pp. 102–105. This point is the central thesis of Dorn, *Rules and Racial Equality.*

60. *Regents of University of California v. Bakke,* at 299, and 289–300 generally. See Cohen, "Why Racial Preference Is Immoral."

61. Marx, "Contribution to the Critique of Hegel's *Philosophy of Right,*" in Tucker, ed., *The Marx-Engels Reader,* p. 17.

62. *Washington et al. v. Davis et al.,* 426 U.S. 229 (1976).

63. *Griggs v. Duke Power Co.,* 401 U.S. 427. This meritocratic logic of this early Civil Rights Act case has been generally adhered to in dozens of cases involving federal pay equity (including "comparable worth") and job hiring.

64. Brennan for a plurality in *Frontiero v. Richardson,* 411 U.S. 677, 686 (1973). This is a sex discrimination case, but the logic is the same for race.

65. *Frontiero v. Richardson;* see also Stewart (dissenting) in *Fullilove v. Klutznick,* 65 L.Ed. 2d 902 (1980), at 954–955: "The color of a person's skin and the coun-

try of his origin are immutable facts that bear no relation to ability, disadvantage, moral culpability, or any other characteristics of constitutionally permissible interest to government." For discussion, see Green, *Pursuit of Inequality;* Daniel Bell, "On Meritocracy and Equality," *The Public Interest* (Fall 1972).

66. *Frontiero v. Richardson; Fullilove v. Klutznick.* See also *Regents of the University of California v. Bakke,* at 317. Cases involving illegitimacy invoke this same meritocratic logic: *Matthews v. Lucas,* 427 U.S. 495 (1976); *Weber v. Aetna Casualty and Surety Co.,* 406 U.S. 164 (1972).

67. See *Regents of the University of California v. Bakke,* at 317. For discussion, see McCann, "Equal Opportunity vs. Equal Results," in Stuart S. Nagel, ed., *Law and Policy Studies* (Greenwich, Conn.: JAI Research Annual, 1981).

68. See James S. Fishkin, *Justice, Equal Opportunity, and the Family* (New Haven: Yale University Press, 1983).

69. This point is developed in Green, *Pursuit of Inequality.*

70. See Civil Rights Commission, *Social Indicators of Equality for Minorities and Women* (Washington, D.C.: U.S. Government Printing Office, 1978); W. Julius Wilson, *The Truly Disadvantaged* (Chicago: University of Chicago Press, 1987).

71. The literature is extensive. On blacks, see Robert Hill, "The Illusion of Black Progress," *The Black Scholar* (October 1978), pp. 18–32. On women, see Suzanne Bianchi and Daphne Spain, *American Women: Three Decades of Change* (Washington, D.C.: Census Bureau, 1983).

72. Frank Michelman, "On Protecting the Poor Through the Fourteenth Amendment," *Harvard Law Review* 83 (1969), p. 21. For legal analysis, see William H. Clune, "The Supreme Court's Treatment of Wealth Discrimination Under the Fourteenth Amendment," *The Supreme Court Review* (1975), pp. 289–354. For economic analyses, see Paul Blumberg, *Inequality in an Age of Decline* (New York: Oxford University Press, 1981); Ken Auletta, *The Underclass* (New York: Random House, 1982).

73. *Harper v. Virginia Board of Elections,* 383 U.S. 663 (1966); *McDonald v. Board of Election Commissioners,* 394 U.S. 802 (1969).

74. *Williams v. Illinois,* 399 U.S. 235, at 244 (1970); *Tate v. Short,* 401 U.S. 395, at 398–399 (1971); *Turner v. Fouche,* 396 U.S. 346, at 362 (1969).

75. *San Antonio Independent School District v. Rodriguez,* 411 U.S. 29 (1969); *Maher v. Roe,* 432 U.S. 470–471 (1977); *James v. Valtierra,* 402 U.S. 137 (1971); *Harris v. McRae,* 448 U.S. 297 (1980).

76. *Dandridge v. Williams,* 397 U.S. 471, 483, 487 (1970).

77. *United States v. Carolene Products Co.,* 304 U.S. 144, 152 n.4 (1938). See Richard Funston, "The Double Standard of Constitutional Protection in the Era of the Welfare State," *Political Science Quarterly* 90 (1975), pp. 261–292.

78. For discussion of parallel developments in due process doctrine, see Michael W. McCann, "Resurrection and Reform."

79. *Dandridge v. Williams.*

80. *San Antonio Independent School District v. Rodriguez,* at 121–122, and Powell at 18–21. For justification, see Ralph Winter, "Poverty, Inequality, and the Equal Protection Clause," in Philip Kurland, ed., *The Supreme Court Review—1972* (Chicago: University of Chicago Press, 1972), pp. 41–102.

81. *San Antonio Independent School District v. Rodriguez,* at 28, and 18–28.

82. See Fiss, "Groups and the Equal Protection Clause," *Philosophy and Public Affairs* 5 (1976), p. 156.
83. See, for example, *Buckley v. Valeo*, 424 U.S. 1 (1976); *First National Bank v. Bellotti*, 435 U.S. 765 (1978). O'Neil makes this point in "Language of Equality," pp. 628–631.
84. See Fishkin, *Justice;* Wilson, *The Truly Disadvantaged;* Auletta, *The Underclass.*
85. See Clune's excellent discussion on these points in "The Supreme Court's Treatment of Wealth Discrimination," pp. 328–330.
86. Winter, "Poverty," pp. 98–99; Green, *Inequality,* p. 175. For a moral and historical critique of this prevailing logic within the law alone, see Judith A. Baer, *Equality Under the Constitution* (Ithaca: Cornell University Press, 1983).
87. Quoted from James Madison, *Federalist* 10. See McCann, "Resurrection and Reform."
88. See Green, *Pursuit of Inequality,* for a sustained argument on the illusions of "meritocratic" evaluation. See Fishkin, *Justice,* for a developed argument about the importance of "background inequalities" in American society.
89. Geoffery C. Hazard, Jr., "Social Justice Through Civil Justice," *Chicago Law Review* 36 (1969), pp. 699–712.
90. *Warth v. Seldin*, 422 U.S. 490, at 506 (1975).
91. *Flagg Bros. et al. v. Brooks et al.*, 436 U.S. 156, 165 (1978).
92. See J. Harvey Wilkinson, III, "The Supreme Court, the Equal Protection Clause, and the Three Faces of Constitutional Equality," *Virginia Law Review* 61 (1975), pp. 945–1118. Cases involving fundamental rights to citizen political participation include: *Harper v. Virginia Board of Elections; Kramer v. Union Free School District*, 395 U.S. 621 (1969); *Cipriano v. Huoma*, 395 U.S. 701 (1969); *Lubin v. Panish*, 415 U.S. 709 (1974); *Bullock v. Carter*, 405 U.S. 134 (1972). Landmark cases in criminal access include *Griffin v. Illinois*, 351 U.S. 12 (1956); *Douglas v. California*, 372 U.S. 353 (1963); *Gideon v. Wainwright*, 372 U.S. 335 (1963); and *Williams v. Illinois*. Cases affirming rights in civil cases include *Boddie v. Connecticut*, 401 U.S. 371 (1971); *Little v. Streater*, 452 U.S. 1 (1981); *Zablocki v. Redhail*, 434 U.S. 374 (1978). The right to travel is affirmed in *Shapiro v. Thompson*, 394 U.S. 618 (1969); *Doe v. Bolton*, 410 U.S. 179 (1973); *Memorial Hospital v. Maricopa County*, 415 U.S. 250 (1974).
93. For example, see *Ross v. Moffitt*, 417 U.S. 600 (1974); *United States v. Kras*, 409 U.S. 434 (1973); *Ortwein v. Schwab*, 410 U.S. 656 (1973); *McCarthy v. Philadelphia Civil Service Commission*, 424 U.S. 645 (1976); *Sosna v. Iowa*, 419 U.S. 393 (1975); *Vlandis v. Kline*, 412 U.S. 441 (1973).
94. *Dandridge v. Williams*, 486–487.
95. *Lindsey v. Dormet*, 405 U.S. 74 (1972).
96. *San Antonio Independent School District v. Rodriguez; Plyler v. Doe*, 457 U.S. 202 (1982).
97. *Maher v. Roe*, at 474; *Harris v. McRae*, 448 U.S. 316.
98. See Michael J. Perry, "Modern Equal Protection: A Conceptualization and Appraisal," *Columbia Law Review* 79 (1979), pp. 1023–1084.
99. This idea is developed in a provocative essay by Jennifer Nedelsky, "Law, Legitimacy, and the Liberal State," unpublished paper presented at the Canadian Political Science Association annual meeting, 1981.

100. *Maher v. Roe,* at 475. Michelman thus argues in "On Protecting the Poor" that fundamental rights should concern minimum needs, not equality.

101. *Harris v. McRae,* at 316.

102. *San Antonio Independent School District v. Rodriguez,* at 33–35.

103. For an argument that the equal protection doctrine lacks independent substantive content, see Peter Westen, "The Empty Idea of Equality," *Harvard Law Review* 95 (1982), pp. 537–596.

104. See Stuart Scheingold's chapter in this book.

10 ——·
Equal Protection: Gender and Justice
DEBORAH L. RHODE

For more than two and a half centuries, understandings about gender have significantly affected American legal doctrine. Yet only in the past two and a half decades has gender discrimination given rise to significant legal remedies. Until recently, American constitutional traditions excluded concerns about women, just as women themselves were largely excluded from the processes of constitutional decision making. Although subject to the Constitution's mandates, women were unacknowledged in its text, uninvited in its formulation, unsolicited for its ratification, and, before the past quarter-century, largely uninvolved in its official interpretation.

This chapter reviews the evolution of constitutional theories of gender equality. It begins with a brief history of women's subordinate status under traditional common law and their initial unsuccessful challenges to that status through appeal to equal protection principles. Analysis then centers on the development of antidiscrimination mandates during the 1970s and 1980s. What emerges from this review are certain recurrent difficulties in legal responses to gender difference. By tracing these difficulties, we may gain a better sense of the law's capacities and constraints in securing social change.

Traditional legal doctrine has been a means of both institutionalizing and undermining gender inequality. Over the past quarter-century, however, equal protection mandates have played an increasingly progressive role in challenging inequality. Despite this progress, certain patterns of gender subordination have remained. Women are still underrepresented in the highest positions of social, economic, and political power and overrepresented in the lowest positions. Limitations in the law's response to these patterns is an issue of practical and theoretical importance. Much of the difficulty in conventional doctrinal frameworks stems from a focus on gender difference rather than gender disadvantage. By exploring legal texts in cultural context, we may deepen our understanding of equality and the strategies for attaining it.

HISTORICAL PREMISES

Throughout the eighteenth and most of the nineteenth centuries, gender divided the landscape of American life. The prevailing assumption was that males should occupy the public sphere of commerce and politics and females the private sphere, and that law should reinforce that boundary. Thus, when the framers of America's founding documents spoke of men—of men "created equal" and "endowed with certain inalienable rights"—they were not using the term generically.[1] Rather, women were subject to a broad range of legal disabilities. Under early common law doctrines of marital unity, husband and wife were one, and as a practical matter, the "one" was the husband.[2] Married women lacked capacity to enter contracts, to hold property, to retain their own wages, or to engage in licensed occupations and professions. Whether married or single, women also lacked any rights of self-governance that would enable them to challenge their subordinate status.[3]

There were, to be sure, certain exceptions to these general common law constraints, based on special equitable principles and social customs. Given the limitations of existing research, the extent to which formal disabilities affected women's daily experience remains a matter of some controversy.[4] But the available records leave no doubt that legal restrictions contributed to a social order in which the sexes were more separate than equal.

By the mid-nineteenth century, these restrictions were becoming increasingly difficult to reconcile with broader social trends. A variety of forces coalesced to challenge the boundaries of women's separate sphere, including the growth of opportunities for female education, the decline in birthrates, and the rise in industrialization and demands for female labor. In addition, women's involvement in the abolitionist movement, and the disparity they experienced between the rhetoric of rights and the constraints of role helped lay the foundations for a feminist consciousness. These forces together helped inspire the first American women's rights conference (Seneca Falls, 1848) and fueled demands that women obtain the same constitutional guarantees as blacks.[5]

These demands gave rise to both political activism and legal challenges. Oddly enough, the Fourteenth Amendment, which is now the primary source of constitutional protection for women, met bitter opposition by many women's rights activists at the time of its drafting. Leading feminists such as Elizabeth Cady Stanton and Susan B. Anthony opposed the amendment both because its broad mandates of "equal protection of the law to all citizens" extended no explicit guarantees to women and because its enforcement provisions used the word "male" for the first time in the constitutional text. Stanton's prediction in 1866 was that "if the word male be inserted [in this amendment] it will take a century to get it out again."[6]

She was just about right, give or take a few years, but the delay was not for lack of effort. In the century after passage of the Fourteenth Amendment, the Supreme Court rejected challenges to gender discrimination in a wide range of contexts, including protective labor legislation, educational admission policies, jury selection procedures, voting rights, and eligibility requirements for certain occupations and professions. These decisions both reflected and reinforced certain broader societal concerns about women's participation in public pursuits. To many constituencies, any encouragement of feminist objectives could not help but undermine domestic tranquility, drive down male wages, coarsen female sensibilities, and invite those best equipped for motherhood to refuse its "sacred call."[7]

One of the clearest jurisprudential reflections of such concerns occurred as the American bar contemplated female intruders in its own separate sphere. Although women had occasionally served as attorneys during the Colonial era, that practice ceased after entry standards were formalized during the late eighteenth and early nineteenth centuries.[8] By the close of the Civil War, however, a few would-be practitioners began challenging their exclusion. The resulting legal opinions remain of interest as cultural texts. What is perhaps most striking is the utter unself-consciousness with which an exclusively male judiciary interpreted statutes adopted by exclusively male legislatures to determine issues of male exclusivity.

The most celebrated case involved Myra Bradwell's unsuccessful 1873 petition to the U.S. Supreme Court. In rejecting her claim, the Court's majority opinion relied on a dubious analogy to an earlier decision involving states' autonomy over vocational licensing. However, a concurring statement by three justices made clear that other concerns were also at work. According to these justices, women's difference justified differential treatment; the "natural and proper timidity and delicacy which belongs to the female sex evidently unfi[t] it for many of the occupations of civil life." Rather, the "Law of the Creator" decreed that woman's "paramount destiny" was to fulfill the "noble and benign offices of wife and mother."[9]

Similar divine inspiration was invoked in other late nineteenth-century legal texts. Many courts and commentators were equally able to discern "unwritten laws" that limited the females' nature to nurture. Yet such reasoning was highly selective. It was never clear why women's "purity," "delicacy," and "tender susceptibility" should bar them from prestigious professional activities but not from more indelicate labor in fields and factories.[10] This anomaly grew more apparent as the century drew to a close and as increasing numbers of women began obtaining higher education, securing paid employment, and engaging in political activities. By the 1920s, state legislatures had ratified a constitutional amendment guaranteeing women the vote and had largely withdrawn prohibitions on female professionals as well as restrictions on married women's property rights.

As in other contexts, however, equality in formal entitlements did not make for equality in actual practice. Gender discrimination by employers and educational institutions remained common for most of the century. Except for a few female-dominated vocations, such as nursing, teaching, and social work, women's representation in the professions generally remained under 5 percent until the 1960s. The underrepresentation of women of color was even more dramatic.[11]

At the lower reaches of the occupational hierarchy, gender discrimination was equally apparent, although its consequences were more double-edged. As in professional contexts, many women were disadvantaged in hiring, compensation, and promotion. However, they were also the beneficiaries of ostensibly favorable treatment in protective labor legislation. Controversies surrounding the wisdom of such legislation during the early twentieth century left an enduring legacy. The issue divided the women's movement for decades, sabotaged early efforts to secure a constitutional Equal Rights Amendment, and laid the foundations for contemporary disputes. Then, as now, gender-based protections were a means of mitigating gender-based disadvantages. Yet such safeguards also risked perpetuating the inequalities they sought to address.

This dilemma arose around the turn of the century as increasing numbers of state legislatures passed statutes that limited working hours, regulated labor conditions, and guaranteed minimum wages. Many of these statutes applied only to women, a limitation encouraged by the Supreme Court's celebrated 1908 decision in *Muller v. Oregon*. In *Muller,* a majority of justices upheld maximum-hour restrictions for women while adhering to a precedent that disallowed comparable restrictions for men. Underlying the Court's opinion was a "domesticity as destiny" argument only one step removed from that in *Bradwell v. State* a half-century earlier. History taught that "woman has always been dependent on man" for special protection and biology ensured that she always would be:

> That woman's physical structure and the performance of maternal functions place her at a disadvantage in the struggle for subsistence is obvious. This is especially true when the burdens of motherhood are upon her. . . . [T]he physical well-being of women becomes an object of public interest and care in order to preserve the strength and vigor of the race.[12]

Although approximately 80 percent of the female work force was then single, this maternal mission ideology dominated protective labor decisions for the next half-century. Women's differences rather than disadvantages remained the central focus. It was "known to all men," the Supreme Court announced in a subsequent case, that although a male worker could labor for more than ten hours a day without injury, a female could not.[13] Curiously oblivious to such universal male knowledge were the legislators who declined to extend hourly restrictions to some of the most grueling domestic service and agricultural occupations, as well as the husbands who declined to share the major household tasks that prolonged wives' working days.

What was "known to all men" was also uninformed by any systematic inquiry into the consequences for most women. In fact, those consequences pulled in different directions. As proponents noted, gender-based statutes were a means of responding to certain gender-linked hardships. Female employees faced competitive disadvantages in the public sphere and bore special burdens in the private sphere. Most women were crowded into low-paying, nonunionized jobs and assumed substantial household obligations in addition to the twelve- and fourteen-hour days that were common in unregulated industries. For many of the most vulnerable female employees, regulation of wages, hours, and working conditions made a substantial improvement in daily life.[14]

Yet that improvement came at a cost. By linking statutory protections to the sex of the worker rather than the nature of the work, courts and legislatures reinforced patterns of subordination that made special protection seem necessary. Regulations making women more expensive and less available for night shifts or overtime increased female unemployment, limited women's occupational choices, and further depressed their bargaining leverage. Even after the Supreme Court began upholding protective statutes that extended to both sexes, the pattern of gender-specific legislation continued. The result, throughout the first half of the twentieth century, was that women were "protected" out of many of the most desirable occupations.[15]

Moreover, the rationale underlying such legislation often spilled over into other contexts in which such protection was far less defensible. As late as 1961, the Supreme Court was still invoking woman's domestic destiny as a justification for her automatic exemption from jury service. Despite a certain measure of "enlightened emancipation," women remained at the center of home and family life, and their private duties could trump public responsibilities.[16]

The irony, however, was that courts talked most reverently of woman's preeminence in the home when restricting her activities outside it. When her domestic status was in fact at issue, the rhetoric suddenly shifted. Throughout the nineteenth and most of the twentieth centuries, men generally enjoyed exclusive power to manage marital property, determine domicile, and dictate their household's standard of living. Although women did receive certain preferences, including, for example, spousal support, such rights were unenforceable in the context of ongoing marriages; how heads of households provided for their families was not a fit subject for judicial scrutiny.[17]

Comparable attitudes characterized other areas of the law. Issues such as reproductive autonomy, sexual harassment, and domestic "chastisement" (the common law euphemism for wife beating) generally remained beyond the boundaries of legal concern. Nineteenth- and early twentieth-century jurisprudence dictated a circumscribed role for both women and the law. Females could be excluded from public pursuits and the courts from "private" disputes. For most of the nation's history, the sources of gender inequality went unacknowledged, unchallenged, and unchanged. Not until 1970, a full century after enactment of equal protection guarantees, did the Supreme Court extend protection to women. Even after that extension, many sources of gender subordination remained beyond the reach of conventional legal principles.

CONTEMPORARY DILEMMAS: THE SEARCH FOR STANDARDS

During the 1960s, a variety of demographic, socioeconomic, and ideological factors converged to challenge traditional legal doctrines affecting women. As was true a century earlier, women's increasing labor force participation, declining birthrates, and political activism in the civil rights movement encouraged an organized feminist movement. That movement in turn fueled initiatives against gender discrimination by federal, state, and local legislatures. Against this new legal and cultural backdrop, courts began reassessing conventional approaches. The result was a reformulation of the standards that should be applicable to sex-based discrimination and the forms of differential treatment that counted as discrimination. On the whole, this doctrinal development represented substantial progress toward gender equality. However, the unevenness of development also revealed limitations in standard legal strategies.

A critical threshold question facing the courts has been the appropriate constitutional standard for assessing sex-based discrimination. By the mid-twentieth century, equal protection analysis had crystallized into a two-tiered scheme of judicial review. The lower level of scrutiny, applicable for general economic regulation, required only that the distinctions at issue be "rationally related" to a legitimate state purpose. By contrast, in cases involving "fundamental interests" (such as freedom of speech or voting) or "suspect classifications" (race, alienage, or national origin), the reviewing court engaged in "strict scrutiny" and required that states establish a "compelling" interest that could not be more narrowly achieved. Since gender distinctions traditionally had triggered the more relaxed standard, women's rights groups in the 1970s directed much of their effort toward litigation and a constitutional Equal Rights Amendment that would mandate more exacting scrutiny.[18]

In the courts, much of the debate over standards took place on terms that obscured the central concerns at issue. In the first U.S. Supreme Court decision holding that gender discrimination violated equal protection principles, Chief Justice Warren Burger's opinion purported to apply a variation of the rational basis standard but failed to explain what was irrational about the statute at issue. The case, *Reed v. Reed* (1971), involved Idaho legislation preferring males as estate administrators. According to the state supreme court, that preference was a reasonable means of minimizing expense and controversy in administering decedents' affairs. Since males on the whole were likely to have more business experience than females, the statute was not self-evidently irrational, at least in the loose sense the Court had previously accepted. Yet none of those prior gender decisions were even mentioned, let alone distinguished, in the chief justice's opinion.[19]

Nor did the Court elaborate what was objectionable about the gender stereotypes underlying the Idaho scheme; that is, their tendency to perpetuate the inequalities they reflected. To presume by law that women are less qualified than men to manage business affairs validates a division of roles that is separate, but scarcely equal. Although abandoning such presumptions may entail some administrative costs, affirming their legitimacy carries a higher social price.

In its next case involving gender discrimination, the Supreme Court explicitly addressed the issue of standards but its members divided sharply on the result. *Frontiero v. Richardson* (1973) concerned a federal scheme that allowed male but not female members of the armed forces automatically to claim their spouses as dependents for purposes of gaining certain benefits. Eight justices voted to strike down the statute, but only four were willing to subject classifications based on sex to the same strict standard of scrutiny as those based on race. According to the other justices, the Court should not endorse a standard that would preempt the major function of a constitutional Equal Rights Amendment, an issue then pending before state legislatures.[20]

However, as subsequent cases and commentary suggested, judicial reluctance to treat sex like race has also rested on broader grounds. To Justice Lewis Powell, for example, the "perception of racial classifications as inherently odious stems from a lengthy and tragic history that gender-based classifications do not share."[21] Other theorists, building on the celebrated Footnote 4 in the Supreme Court's *Carolene Products* decision, have emphasized that women are not a discrete and insular minority. Since female voters can assert their interests through majoritarian political processes, heightened protection by the nonmajoritarian branch of government is allegedly unnecessary.[22]

Yet it logically follows from this analysis that all constitutional problems surrounding gender discrimination disappeared in 1920 with passage of the suffrage amendment. What this approach overlooks is that numerical majorities can—and in American culture sometimes do—assume the functional characteristics of minorities. Women, no less than racial or ethnic groups, have been singled out for subordinate treatment on the basis of involuntary attributes and have internalized many of the social values that perpetuate such subordination. As the preceding discussion has suggested, women no less than blacks or other minorities historically have been disempowered in the political process. Indeed, under a pluralist democratic system, status as a discrete and insular group is not an adequate indicator of vulnerability. It has, in part, been women's lack of self-identification and segregation that has impeded political mobilization around women's issues.[23]

To underscore the parallels between racial and sexual subordination is not, however, to endorse the kind of unqualified analogy drawn by the plurality opinion in *Frontiero,* or by other courts in similar contexts. Women as a group have not been subordinated and stigmatized in the same way as blacks. Most white females have lived on terms of intimacy with members of the dominant group, and many have enjoyed economic and social privileges traditionally denied to individuals of color. Racial discrimination has been perceived, on the whole, as degrading and disempowering. Gender discrimination, by contrast, has reflected a more complicated set of motives, including a desire to preserve privacy and protect women from the consequences of seemingly distinctive physical attributes. To take only the most obvious examples, sex-segregated schools or restrooms do not carry the same social meaning as racially segregated facilities. And while color blindness now commands societal consensus as an ultimate ideal, attitudes toward gender distinctions are more mixed.[24]

Part of the courts' and commentators' difficulties in constructing an adequate analytic framework for sex-based discrimination has stemmed from their weddedness to racial paradigms that fail adequately to capture the complexities of gender. One lesson of the feminist movement of the 1960s was that efforts to establish women's equal place in an oppression sweepstakes are rarely fruitful and often divisive. Comparisons that proceed as if race and sex were dichotomous categories ignore the experience of women of color and obscure relationships between the causes and consequences of various forms of subordination. What is needed is closer attention to the continuities and discontinuities in different patterns of discrimination. Ranking their severity or invoking the kind of selective analogies put forth in *Frontiero* is unlikely to assist in that endeavor.

By the mid-1970s, the perceived inadequacies of both rational basis and strict scrutiny standards led the Court to a new intermediate approach. Under that approach, sex-based classifications are permissible only if substantially related to important governmental objectives.[25] Although perceived inadequacies in that new standard have also provoked considerable scholarly criticism and political activism, the importance of the issue should not be overstated. Indeed, the most important consequence of the Court's doctrinal path may have been to fuel efforts for an Equal Rights Amendment.

Yet it is scarcely self-evident, as the Amendment's supporters and the Court's critics have often suggested, that a different standard would produce significantly different substantive results. To be sure, as constitutional scholars have often noted, the scrutiny of racial classifications has been "strict in theory and fatal in fact"; almost no nonremedial discrimination has passed muster. But that record indicates an attitude that is reflected in, rather than compelled by, the formal standard of review.[26] The indeterminacy of standards emphasized in much realist and critical legal scholarship has seldom been more apparent than in gender cases during the late 1970s and 1980s. A review of decisions under state equal rights amendments reinforces that point; no systematic relationship between result, rationale, and formal standard emerges. Some gender classifications have survived scrutiny under state equal rights amendments, and federal litigation could have generated comparable results even if sex had become a suspect classification.[27] It is the perspective from which courts have understood gender differences, rather than the formula such differences must satisfy, that impedes progressive legal change.

DEFINING DIFFERENCE

The decade and a half following the *Reed* decision witnessed substantial progress in discrimination doctrine. Legislative and judicial decision makers became increasingly sensitive to the harms of gender stereotypes and struck down a growing array of gender classifications in areas such as employment, education, credit, welfare, domestic relations, and criminal law. But the areas where such classifications survived reflected fundamental limitations in conventional legal paradigms.

American equal protection analysis has evolved largely within an Aristotelian framework that mandates similar treatment for those similarly situated. Under this approach, reflected in both statutory and constitutional interpretation, gender discrimination does not pose difficulties if the sexes are dissimilar in some sense related to valid regulatory objectives. This analytic paradigm has proven inadequate in both theory and practice. As a theoretical matter, it tends toward tautology. It permits different treatment for those who are different with respect to legitimate purposes, but provides no criteria for determining what differences matter and what counts as legitimate. As a practical matter, this approach has failed to generate coherent definitions of difference and has obscured the relationship between cultural and biological constructions of social roles. Gender distinctions have been both over- and undervalued. In some cases, such as those involving "bona fide occupational qualifications" and military service, courts have allowed biology to determine destiny. In other contexts, such as pregnancy discrimination, courts have failed to require accommodation of women's special reproductive needs. The search for "real differences" has deflected attention away from the process by which such differences are defined and from the groups that are underrepresented in that process. Too often, the focus has been on gender difference; too infrequently, on gender disadvantages.

To understand these limitations in conventional equal protection analysis, it is appropriate to focus on statutory as well as constitutional doctrines because their logic has been similar and their evolution has been intertwined. Many of the difficulties surrounding contemporary definitions of difference emerged in the wake of the 1964 Civil Rights Act. Title VII of that act bars sex-based employment discrimination but provides a defense for "bona fide occupational qualification[s] [BFOQs] reasonably necessary to the normal operation of [a] particular business or enterprise." Such a defense is available for discrimination based on sex, religion, or ethnicity but not race, and legislative history surrounding the provision is sparse and equivocal.[28]

Part of the problem in interpreting Title VII's gender provisions stems from the paradoxical way that they first crept into the statutory scheme. Early versions of Title VII did not prohibit sex-based discrimination. The sponsor of an amendment to include such a prohibition was a southern member of Congress who had long opposed civil rights legislation, including equal pay protections for women. The tenor of debate at "Ladies Day in the House" left little doubt that he intended the proposed ban on sex discrimination to encourage additional opposition to Title VII, not to secure greater equality for women.[29] However, the strategy fell short of his desired result, and the amendment passed with support from a curious coalition of women's rights supporters and civil rights opponents. From the legislative history it does not appear that either group gave a great deal of thought to the appropriate scope of gender-related prohibitions or to the BFOQ defense qualifying them.[30]

In light of this history, many judicial and administrative officials initially viewed the ban on sex discrimination with some reservations and limited its effect accordingly. Such attitudes were particularly apparent within the Equal Employment Opportunity Commission, which had authority to implement the legislation. Mixing his metaphors, the commission's first director labeled the gender provision a "statutory fluke," "conceived out of wedlock."[31] However, continuing political pressure and litigation challenges by women's rights organizations gradually succeeded in strengthening prohibitions on sex-based classifications and narrowing the scope of BFOQ defenses. By the late 1970s, most such classifications in protective labor statutes had been eliminated, extended to both sexes, or replaced by procedures for individual testing.[32]

That progress occurred without substantial assistance from the Supreme Court. Rather, the Court's two major decisions in the area left a troubling legacy. The first case, *Phillips v. Martin Marietta Corp.* (1970), involved an employment policy that barred job applications from women but not men with preschool children. In a brief per curiam opinion, the Supreme Court concluded that the policy constituted sex discrimination within the meaning of Title VII, but remanded for two determinations: whether conflicting family obligations were "demonstrably more relevant to job performance for a woman than for a man," and if so, whether that could constitute a BFOQ defense for the employer's policy.[33]

By declining to resolve those issues, the Court implied that employers might under some circumstances rely on gender stereotypes about parental roles. Denying women responsible job opportunities because of disproportionate family obligations imposes substantial hardships on female-headed households and encourages married couples to replicate stereotypical patterns. Families will benefit financially from assigning priority to the husband's career and allocating most domestic tasks to the wife. That allocation reinforces cultural assumptions about gender roles and the cycle perpetuates itself. By wedding itself to a theoretical framework that asked only if the sexes' different circumstances were relevant to their differential treatment, the Court ignored more fundamental questions about the legitimacy of that treatment: What were the social costs of penalizing individuals for their parental status and of visiting those penalties disproportionately on women?

Similar difficulties arose in the Supreme Court's second major BFOQ case, *Dothard v. Rawlinson* (1977). At issue were Alabama prison regulations that prevented women from serving as guards in positions requiring close physical contact with inmates. The Court began its analysis by suggesting that Congress intended the BFOQ to be an "extremely narrow exception" to general prohibitions on job discrimination, and that in the "usual case" whether a job was too dangerous was for each woman to determine for herself. However, the majority went on to sustain Alabama's restrictions in light of "substantial" trial testimony indicating that women would pose a "substantial" security problem because of their special vulnerability to sexual assault.[34]

The factual basis for that testimony, however, was somewhat less than substantial. It consisted largely of one administrator's speculations and two prior disturbances involving women, neither of whom were guards. Never did the state explain why sexual assaults, as opposed to assaults in general, posed a particular threat to prison safety. Nor did the Court explain its refusal to credit equally "substantial" evidence indicating that properly trained female guards had not presented risks in other states' maximum-security prisons. By adopting what Catharine MacKinnon has characterized as the "reasonable rapist" perspective, the *Dothard* decision ignored a range of countervailing social costs. Alabama's regulation perpetuated stereotypes of women's inability to protect themselves and penalized female job applicants for the "barbaric" prison conditions that allegedly placed them at particular risk.[35]

Dothard's conflicting signals—its rhetoric limiting BFOQs, and its rationale affirming them—complicated the development of discrimination doctrine in both statutory and constitutional contexts. The decision has served to justify gender restrictions in a variety of unrelated cases, including everything from bans on male nurses to disparate penalties in criminal sentencing statutes.[36] It has also served as a leading precedent in other occupational safety areas where discrimination is often permitted. For example, in the interest of maternal and fetal health, courts have sanctioned layoffs of pregnant employees and bans on employing fertile women in potentially toxic workplaces. Yet to preserve equal opportunity as well as to maximize occupational safety, analysis should focus on reducing dangers for both sexes and on providing equivalent employment opportunities to those at risk. A growing body of research suggests that working conditions that present reproductive hazards are generally threatening to men as well as women. Since some 20 million jobs may potentially present such hazards, it is crucial that legal decision makers demand responses that reduce workplace risks rather than limit women's employment.[37]

An adequate analytic framework would neither deny nor amplify gender differences but would take greater account of gender disadvantage. Under conventional approaches, courts have too often asked only whether gender is relevant to the job as currently structured, not whether the job could reasonably be restructured to make gender irrelevant. That sex, but not race, has constituted a permissible occupational qualification suggests a limitation both in our commitments to eradicating gender discrimination and our understandings of its origins. If, for example, a state were to demonstrate that black prison guards were more likely to provoke assaults by white prisoners than white guards, that finding would not provide legal justifications for racially based hiring. In such circumstances, we are prepared to pay the price of color blindness but not gender blindness. These different degrees of commitment may, in part, stem from a failure to identify the full countervailing costs of gender consciousness in employment decisions. No matter how "bona fide," sex-based hiring contributes to occupational stereotypes, segregation, and subordination.

Similar points are applicable to one other major occupational context in which gender classifications have survived scrutiny—that of military service. Throughout the nation's history, cultural expectations and formal restrictions have severely limited female involvement in the armed forces. Until the early 1970s, women constituted less than 2 percent of the U.S. military, and discrimination in placement and promotion, especially for racial minorities, was widespread.[38] Although female participation rose substantially over the next decade and a half, the increase occurred largely without judicial intervention, and entirely without assistance by the Supreme Court. In a 1984 decision, *Rostker v. Goldberg,* the Court rejected constitutional challenges to a draft registration system excluding women. Once again, the focus on difference obscured analysis. Speaking for the majority, Justice William Rehnquist reasoned that the purpose of the registration system was to prepare for a draft of combat-eligible troops. Since women were not permitted in combat, they were differently situated from men, and Congress was free to limit the registration system accordingly.[39]

This analysis presented a number of difficulties, not the least of which was its patent disregard of relevant precedents and legislative history. Under the prevailing intermediate standard for gender classifications, it was hard to see how women's exemption served substantial governmental interests that could not be more narrowly achieved. Even assuming the legitimacy of women's exclusion from combat, the legitimacy of their exclusion from registration did not follow. According to government estimates, about one-third of those drafted during a national mobilization would not need combat skills. The registration system at issue included noncombat-eligible males, and the joint chiefs of staff had unanimously recommended including females as well.[40]

Moreover, by analyzing the case purely in terms of asserted registration needs, the Court sidestepped the more fundamental values at issue. Much of the congressional opposition to female registration reflected precisely the kind of sex role stereotypes that the Court had increasingly rejected in other contexts. Legislative concerns were manifold: Women couldn't fight well and men wouldn't fight well in mixed units; the nation would be reluctant to mobilize if its daughters were at risk; sexual proximity would invite sexual promiscuity, and so forth.[41] Yet the evidence available about women's performance in combat and related military, police, and prison contexts afforded little support for such generalizations. Millions of women here and abroad have served with distinction in such positions, and serious problems of incapacity have yet to emerge. Technological developments have made physical strength unnecessary for many combat-related tasks, and gender-neutral guidelines have demonstrated their effectiveness in matching individual capabilities with job requirements.[42]

How actively to demand the benefits and burdens of military service has been a matter of considerable controversy within the women's movement. Among some constituencies, the objective is to end conscription for both sexes, not allocate its burdens equally. Many feminists have seen little to be gained from participation in a system so dominated by male values and male decision makers. Other feminists, while not necessarily disagreeing about the need for change in military structures and service requirements, view women's equal involvement as a means to the end of some opportunities and training. As they note, restrictions on women in combat have long served to limit women's access to desirable jobs and work experience, opportunities for promotion, and eligibility for veterans' benefits.[43]

However one assesses the practical effects of full female participation in the military, there remain powerful symbolic reasons to seek that objective. It is difficult for women to attain true equality of respect and treatment as citizens while exempt from one of citizenship's central responsibilities. The stereotypes that perpetuate such exemptions cannot readily be confined. Assumptions about women's physical incapacities and family obligations inevitably spill over to other areas of social life and reinforce expectations about gender roles and hierarchies. The issue in *Rostker* was more fundamental than the Court's analysis acknowledged. The result of its decision was to legitimate assumptions for which both men and women have paid a heavy price.

SPECIAL TREATMENT/EQUAL TREATMENT

A final area in which judicial definitions of difference have been highly problematic involves pregnancy. The difficulties have evolved against a cluster of cultural assumptions that discouraged accommodation of women's productive and reproductive roles. Until the mid-1970s, the prevailing and self-perpetuating view was that females were temporary workers who should suspend their employment during early child-rearing years. As a result, employers routinely dismissed pregnant women and failed to provide medical benefits or maternity leaves.[44]

By the mid-1970s, the disparity between traditional assumptions and labor force patterns had become increasingly apparent. About 85 percent of female employees could expect to become pregnant at some point in their working lives, and a growing percentage were returning to work within the year. Given these employment trends, the Supreme Court's initial decisions on maternity policies were of considerable practical importance. What enshrines these holdings as landmark sex discrimination cases was the Court's unwillingness to treat them as such.

Indeed, in its first pregnancy-related decision, *Geduldig v. Aiello* (1974), the majority opinion relegated its entire analysis of discrimination to a footnote. At issue was the constitutionality of an insurance program that excluded childbirth-related disabilities from coverage but included other disabilities affecting only men. In upholding the program, a majority of justices reached the somewhat novel conclusion that pregnancy discrimination did not involve "gender as such." Rather, as the Court explained in *Geduldig* and subsequent opinions, employers were simply distinguishing between "pregnant women and nonpregnant persons." Since males and females were not similarly situated, antidiscrimination principles were inapplicable; neither constitutional nor statutory mandates required coverage of women's "unique" and "additional" reproductive needs.[45]

By focusing on biological differences rather than societal disadvantages, the Court ended up with characterizations that were incoherent, inconsistent, and ultimately indefensible. To label pregnancy as "unique" both assumed what should have been at issue and made the assumption from a male reference point. The physiology of men set the standard against which women's claims appeared only "additional."

In the aftermath of these decisions, intense lobbying efforts prompted congressional initiatives. The 1978 Pregnancy Discrimination Act amended Title VII to provide that women affected by "childbirth [or] related medical conditions shall be treated the same . . . as other persons not so affected but similar in their ability or inability to work."[46] Although that amendment prompted significant improvements in maternity policies, it by no means solved the difficulties of reconciling women's productive and reproductive roles. Rather, in this context, equality in form has not yielded equality in fact. The act does not affirmatively require the provision of adequate disability programs, and in the absence of statutory requirements, such programs have been slow to develop. A decade after passage of the act, about a third of the female workforce still lacked job-protected maternity leaves and three-fifths were not entitled to wage replacement for the normal period of disability. America remained alone among the major industrialized countries in its failure to guarantee such benefits.[47]

Efforts to improve that situation have given new dimensions to long-standing dilemmas. In many respects, contemporary battles over maternity leaves have resembled the disputes over protective labor legislation earlier in the century. In the late 1980s, the issue came before the Supreme Court in a challenge to California legislation. Like analogous provisions in other states, the California statute required reasonable leaves of absence for pregnant workers but did not mandate comparable protection for other temporarily disabled workers. The defendant, a Los Angeles bank, claimed that the legislation was preempted by the federal Pregnancy Discrimination Act's requirement that pregnancy be treated the same as other temporary disabilities (e.g., sickness, injuries, etc.). In *California Federal Savings and Loan v. Guerra* (1987), the Supreme Court rejected that claim and sustained the state statute. Although acknowledging that the legislative history of the Pregnancy Discrimination Act was not entirely conclusive, the majority reasoned that policies such as California's were consistent with congressional intent, which was to guarantee women's right to "participate fully and equally in the workforce."[48]

Defenders of the Court's decision, and the "special treatment" for pregnant workers that it upheld, generally begin from the premise that women are unequally situated with respect to reproduction. While a no-leave policy poses common hardships for both sexes concerning the disabilities they share, it places an additional burden on female employees who wish to have children. Feminists who take this position generally distinguish between childbearing and childrearing and argue that gender-specific childbirth policies are appropriate but gender-specific parental policies are not.[49]

In supporting special benefits for pregnant workers, these feminists raise arguments of principle and prudence. As a matter of principle, women should not have to prove they are similarly situated to men in order to receive job security; childbirth should not have to seem "just like" the disabilities men suffer in order to gain adequate protection. From this perspective, the objective is not female assimilation to male norms but fair recognition of women's separate capacities and commitments. As a prudential matter, until legislatures mandate adequate protection for all workers, partial coverage is often a useful interim strategy. As was true with protective legislation in the early twentieth century, a "women-and-children-first" approach can lay the groundwork for broader gender-neutral regulations.

The danger, of course, is that settling for intervention on behalf of the most politically sympathetic constituency may erode impetus for more comprehensive approaches. Even with the benefit of hindsight, it is impossible to know whether protective labor regulation for all workers might have been possible sooner if proponents had avoided arguments based on gender difference. Predicting which strategy will be most effective in the current political climate is no less difficult.

Moreover, as feminists who advocate equal rather than special treatment have argued, sex-based protective legislation often carries other costs.

Pregnancy is in some important sense unique, but emphasizing that uniqueness in employment contexts has reinforced roles that are more separate than equal. By making women workers more expensive, much gender-based protective labor legislation "protected" them out of jobs desired by male competitors. Comparable results could follow from contemporary policies that emphasize differences rather than commonalities between male and female workers. Also, requiring that employers provide maternity but not parental policies may encourage, in fact and appearance, unequal allocations of family responsibilities.[50]

Yet one of the lessons we learn from history is that there are limits to what other lessons we can draw from it. Although one effect of gender-based protective statutes in the early twentieth century was to increase the costs and thus diminish the opportunities of women workers, those consequences occurred in a social context lacking significant legal and social sanctions against gender discrimination. In the current regulatory climate, the effects that adequate maternity policies may have is far less clear. Much will depend on how such policies are financed. Programs that do not require private employers to bear the full cost are an obvious way to mitigate the risk of discrimination against women of childbearing age. Without more careful empirical analysis, it is impossible to assess how many female workers at what income levels would benefit from preferential policies and how many would pay the price in terms of lower wages, fewer employment opportunities, or gender stereotyping.

The complexity of these concerns underscores the need to move beyond the framework in which they arise. Even the formulation of the "special treatment/equal treatment" debate is misconceived. To view childbirth-related policies as "special" assumes that male needs establish the norm. And to label only one camp "equal" assumes the conclusion. Feminists on both sides of the issue are seeking equality. They differ only on whether preferential policies are, in the short run, an effective means to attain it. The danger with the current controversy, like its predecessor a half-century earlier, is that women will spend too much of their energy fighting each other over the value of protection rather than challenging the conditions that make protection so valuable. What is crucial at this juncture is to foster less internal dispute and more focus on common objectives.

Those objectives should encompass a broad range of social policies. While the historical, ideological, and economic consequences of pregnancy should not be overlooked, neither should they be overemphasized. More employers provide job-protected childbirth leaves than other forms of assistance that are equally critical to workers and their families. Pregnancy-related policies affect most women workers for relatively brief intervals. The absence of broader disability, health, and child care programs remains a chronic problem for the vast majority of employees, male and female, throughout their working lives.

Responding to these inadequacies will require less dispute over the proper legal construction of existing statutes and increased political efforts to obtain better ones. Greater attention should focus on workplace organizing and collective bargaining and on policies that can unite the broadest range of constituencies. Whether to support or oppose preferential policies is a question that ought not to be resolved in the abstract. Rather, it should depend on a more contextual assessment of the most effective strategy in a given set of circumstances.

A comparable point is relevant to other issues that implicate equal protection values. Most legal questions of greatest significance to women do not find the sexes "similarly situated." Poverty, sexual violence, reproductive autonomy, divorce, child care, and occupational segregation all pose special concerns for women that conventional antidiscrimination strategies cannot adequately address. Although judicial decisions can play an important role in challenging gender subordination and the ideologies that sustain it, true equality between the sexes will require more fundamental public and private initiatives.

THE LIMITATIONS OF LAW

Despite recent changes in gender roles, the legacy of gender discrimination remains pronounced. All too often, equality in formal mandates has not translated into equality in actual status. For example, after a quarter-century's experience with equal pay legislation, women are still a considerable distance from equal pay. In the late 1980s, women working full-time were still earning only about 64 percent of the annual salaries of their male counterparts (70 percent of weekly wages).[51] Judicial and statutory reforms have promised "equal" or "equitable" treatment of divorcing spouses, but in practice most wives have received neither equality nor equity. Men's incomes generally have risen and women's have fallen in the aftermath of divorce, and the absence of adequate enforceable support awards has contributed to a growing feminization of poverty.[52] Other factors have further accelerated that trend, including the insufficiency of assistance for other economically vulnerable groups, such as adolescent mothers and women over sixty-five. Women head 90 percent of single-parent families, and half of these families are below the poverty line. Overall, about two-thirds of all indigent adults are female, and minorities face particular hardships.[53]

Although an adequate exploration of such inequalities is beyond the scope of this review, their persistence suggests a general point about legal doctrine. Law has been of critical importance in eliminating formal barriers to equal opportunity; it has been far less successful in challenging the informal structures, implicit assumptions, and social priorities that make such opportunities impossible to realize.

Illustrations are apparent in almost every area of gender discrimination law. For example, legislative reforms have secured gender neutrality in divorce statutes, but not in their application. Gone are provisions restricting alimony to women or giving preference to mothers in custody disputes. Still pervasive, however, are attitudes that perpetuate gender bias in fact if not in form. "Equal" division of assets has proven an inadequate response to women who are not equally situated to men in either home or workplace contexts. In the late 1980s, women were still receiving custody in 90 percent of divorce cases and were still unable to match their husbands' earning capacity. Despite formal guarantees of equal treatment, most divorcing wives have ended up with unequal family responsibilities and unequal resources to discharge them.[54]

Employment law reflects similar patterns. The recent proliferation of legislative, administrative, and judicial mandates against gender discrimination has played a critical role in breaking barriers to entry for those seeking nontraditional employment. Progress has been particularly dramatic in middle-managerial and professional contexts. However, the principal beneficiaries of such progress have been those willing and able to compete in environments structured by and for men. Most women remain in relatively low-paying, low-status, female-dominated occupations. Even those in more elite business and professional sectors have seldom risen to the highest positions. In this context, guaranteeing the sexes the same pay for the same work is of limited assistance since relatively few men and women in fact perform the same work.[55]

To make employment equity a serious national commitment, our strategies must extend beyond conventional equal protection frameworks. Women's subordinate status is a function of a broad variety of factors including sex role socialization, workplace structures, unconscious stereotypes, and competing family responsibilities. Changing that status will, in turn, require fundamental changes in our institutions and ideologies. Women must secure not simply access to, but alteration of, existing employment structures. At a minimum, our strategies must include ways of reducing occupational segregation, revaluing "women's work," and better accommodating vocational and family responsibilities. Pay equity, affirmative action, parental leaves, flexible work schedules, meaningful part-time employment, and adequate care for children and elderly dependents must be part of any coherent strategy for occupational equity.

Analogous points are relevant to a vast range of other legal contexts in which the sexes are not similarly situated. These contexts call for more than equal treatment in order to secure women's treatment as equals. Our legal frameworks must focus less on gender difference and more on the difference that it makes.[56] Yet our concern with differences between men and women must not obscure the differences among women and the way that race, class, age, ethnicity, and sexual orientation can amplify gender disadvantages.

What that implies is a reassessment both of doctrinal mandates and cultural priorities. If, as a nation, we are truly committed to equality between the sexes, we must translate our legal rhetoric into social resources. Such a commitment demands that we seek equality in practice as well as principle and begin again our struggle to achieve it.

NOTES

This chapter draws on other work, including Deborah L. Rhode, "Gender Equality and Constitutional Traditions," in L. Berlowitz, L. Merand, and Dennis Donoghue, eds., *America in Theory* (New York: Oxford University Press, 1988); "Justice, Gender and the Justices," in L. Crites and W. Hepperle, eds., *Women and the Courts* (Beverly Hills: Sage, 1988).

1. Declaration of Independence. Thomas Jefferson, author of that phrase, believed that in order to prevent "deprivation of morals and ambiguity of issues [women] should not mix promiscuously in gatherings of men." M. Gruberg, *Women in American Politics* (Oshkosh: Academy Press, 1968), p. 4. For a fuller exploration of the founders' views see Deborah Rhode, "Gender Equality and Constitutional Traditions," and Sylvia Law, "The Founders on Families," *University of Florida Law Review* 39 (1987), p. 583.
2. *United States v. Yazell,* 382 U.S. 341, 361 (Black, J., dissenting).
3. See generally W. Blackstone, *Commentaries on the Laws of England,* 11 ed., vol. 1 (1791; reprint, 1982), pp. 442–445; L. Kanowitz, *Women and the Law* (Albuquerque: University of New Mexico Press, 1969), pp. 35–37.
4. N. Basch, *In the Eyes of the Law* (Ithaca: Cornell University Press, 1982), pp. 30–35; L. Kerber, *Women of the Republic: Intellect and Ideology in Revolutionary America* (Chapel Hill: University of North Carolina Press, 1980), pp. 149–153; Salmon, "The Legal Status of Women in Early America: A Reappraisal," *Law and Historical Review* 1 (1983), p. 129.
5. See generally E. Flexner, *Century of Struggle: The Women's Rights Movement in the United States* (Cambridge, Mass.: Harvard University Press, 1959); C. Clinton, *The Other Civil War* (New York: Hill and Wang, 1984); N. Woloch, *Women and the American Experience* (New York: Alfred Knopf, 1984).
6. Elizabeth Cady Stanton, quoted in A. Lutz, *Created Equal: A Biography of Elizabeth Cady Stanton* (New York: John Day, 1940), p. 134.
7. Franklin Collins, "Statement on Woman Suffrage," Hearings Before the Senate Committee on Woman Suffrage, Senate Document No. 601, 62d Cong. 2d Session, ct. 27, 30; A. Kraditor, *The Ideas of the Woman Suffrage Movement, 1890–1920* (New York: Harper and Row, 1971); A. Sinclair, *The Better Half: The Emancipation of the American Woman* (Urbana: University of Illinois Press, 1965); M. Jo and P. Buhle, eds., *The Concise History of Woman Suffrage* (1978).
8. E. Bittenbender, "Woman in Law," in A. Meyer, ed., *Woman's Work in America* (New York: Henry Holt, 1891); K. Morello, *The Invisible Bar: The Woman Lawyer in America 1638 to the Present* (Berkeley: University of California Press, 1986); Barnes, "Women and Entrance to the Legal Profession," *Journal of Legal Education* 23 (1970).

9. *Bradwell v. State*, 83 U.S. (16 Wall.) 130, 141 (1872) (Bradley, J., concurring).
10. *In the Matter of Goodell*, 39 Wis. 232, 244 (1875). See also *In re Lockwood*, 9 Ct. Cl. 346, 348, 355 (1873); *In re Kilgore*, 17 Phil. 192, 193 (1884).
11. See sources cited in Morello, *The Invisible Bar;* B. Harris, *Beyond Her Sphere: Women and the Professions in American History* (Westport, Conn.: Greenwood Press, 1978); Rhode, "Perspectives on Professional Women," *Stanford Law Review* 40 (1987), p. 1163.
12. *Muller v. Oregon*, 208 U.S. 412, 422 (1908).
13. *W. C. Ritchie and Co. v. Wayman*, 244 Ill. 509 (1910).
14. E. Baker, *Protective Labor Legislation*, rev. ed. (1969), p. 207; S. Becker, *The Origins of the Equal Rights Amendment: American Feminism Between the Wars* (Westport, Conn.: Greenwood Press, 1981).
15. J. Baer, *The Chains of Protection* (Westport, Conn.: Greenwood Press, 1978); A. Kessler-Harris, *Out to Work* (1982); P. Foner, *Women and the American Labor Movement*, vol. 2 (New York: Free Press, 1980), pp. 94–96.
16. *Hoyt v. Florida*, 368 U.S. 57, 61–62 (1961).
17. *McGuire v. McGuire*, 157 Neb. 226, 59 N.W. 2d 336 (1953); *Miller v. Miller*, 78 Iowa 177, 182 (1889); Kanowitz, *Women and the Law;* J. Johnston and C. Knapp, "Sex Discrimination by Law: A Study in Judicial Perspective," *New York University Law Review* 46 (1971), p. 675.
18. See Gerald Gunther, "The Supreme Court 1971 Term, Forward: In Search of Evolving Doctrine on a Changing Court: A Model for a Newer Equal Protection," *Harvard Law Review* 86 (1972), p. 1.
19. *Reed v. Reed*, 404 U.S. 71 (1971).
20. *Frontiero v. Richardson*, 411 U.S. 677 (1973).
21. *Regents of the University of California v. Bakke*, 438 U.S. 265, 303 (1978) (Powell, J., concurring).
22. *United States v. Carolene Products*, 304 U.S. 144, 152 n. 4 (1938); J. Ely, *Democracy and Distrust* (Cambridge: Harvard University Press, 1980).
23. See generally Ackerman, "Beyond Carolene Products," *Harvard Law Review* 98 (1985), p. 713; W. Chafe, *Women and Equality: Changing Patterns in American Culture* (New York: Oxford University Press, 1977); Hacker, "Women as a Minority Group," *Soc. Forces* 30 (1951), p. 60.
24. See Richard Wasserstrom, "Racism, Sexism and Preferential Treatment: An Approach to the Topics," *UCLA Law Review* 24 (1977), p. 581; Deborah L. Rhode, "Association and Assimilation," *Northwestern Law Review* 81 (1986), p. 106.
25. *Craig v. Boren*, 429 U.S. 190, 197–199, 219 (1976).
26. Gunther, "Forward," p. 8.
27. P. Kurtz, "The State Equal Rights Amendments and Their Impact on Domestic Relations Law," *Family Law Quarterly* 13 (1977), p. 101; D. Driscoll and D. Rouse, "Through a Glass Darkly: A Look at State Equal Rights Amendments," *Suffolk University Law Review* 12 (1978), p. 1282; "Developments in the Law— The Interpretation of State Constitutional Rights," *Harvard Law Review* 95 (1982), p. 1324.
28. 42 U.S.C. §2000e-2(e) (1982). See M. Sirota, "Sex Discrimination: Title VII and the Bona Fide Occupational Qualifications," *Texas Law Review* 55 (1977), p. 1025.

29. See C. Bird, *Born Female,* rev. ed. (New York: McKays, 1970), pp. 13–18.
30. J. Itole and E. Levine, *The Rebirth of Feminism* (New York: Quadrangle, 1971), pp. 82–83.
31. C. Bird, *Born Female,* p. 3 (quoting D. Edlesberg).
32. See Sirota, "Sex Discrimination"; *Rosenfeld v. Southern Pacific Co.,* 293 F. Supp 1219 (C.D. Cal. 1968), aff'd, 444 F.2d 1219 (9th Cir. 1971).
33. *Phillips v. Martin Marietta Corp.,* 400 U.S. 542, 544 (1970).
34. *Dothard v. Rawlinson,* 433 U.S. 321, 334–336 (1977).
35. *Dothard v. Rawlinson,* at 321, 342 (Marshall, J., dissenting); C. MacKinnon, "Unthinking ERA Thinking," *University of Chicago Law Review* 54 (1987), p. 759.
36. See *Fesel v. Masonic Home of Delaware, Inc.,* 447 F. Supp 1346 (D. Del 1978) aff'd mem., 591 F.2d 1334 (3rd Cir. 1979); and sources cited in K. Powers, "The Shifting Parameters of Affirmative Action; Pragmatic Paternalism in Sex-based Employment Discrimination Cases," *Wayne Law Review* 26 (1980), pp. 1281, 1295, n. 81.
37. M. Becker, "From Muller v. Oregon to Fetal Vulnerability Policies," *University of Chicago Law Review* 53 (1986), p. 1219; W. Williams, "Firing the Woman to Protect the Fetus: The Reconciliation of Fetal Protection with Employment Opportunity Goals Under Title VII," *Georgetown Law Journal* 69 (1981), pp. 641, 655–665; see Equal Employment Opportunity Commission (EEOC) "Interpretative Guidelines on Employment Discrimination and Reproductive Hazards," Fed. Reg. 45 (February 1, 1980), p. 7514.
38. M. Binken and S. Bach, *Women and the Military* (1977), p. 1.
39. *Rostker v. Goldberg,* 453 U.S. 57, 78–79 (1984).
40. Ibid., at 97–99 (Marshall, J., dissenting).
41. For accounts of legislative testimony, see e.g., 126 Cong. Rec. 13876 (daily ed., June 10, 1980); S. Estrich and B. Kerr, "Sexual Justice," in N. Dorsen, ed., *Our Endangered Rights* (New York: ACLU, 1984), pp. 98, 113; S. Ruddick, "Women in the Military," *Report from the Center for Philosophy and Public Policy* 4 (1984), p. 4.
42. H. Rogan, *Mixed Company: Women in the Modern Army* (New York: Putnam, 1981), p. 258; J. Laffin, *Women in Battle* (New York: Abelard Schuman, 1967), pp. 10–16, 62–69; J. Stiehm, *Bring Me Men and Women: Mandated Changes at the U.S. Air Force Academy* (Berkeley: University of California Press, 1981), pp. 129–130, 167, 199, 250; L. Kornblum, "Women Warriors in a Men's World; The Combat Exclusion," *Law and Inequality* 2 (1984), pp. 351, 394–396, 407–417 (1984).
43. Binken and Bach, *Women and the Military,* pp. 31–38; and sources cited in note 41.
44. See S. Kamerman, A. Kahn, and P. Kingston, *Maternity Policies and Working Women* (New York: Columbia University Press, 1983), pp. 1–25; W. Williams, "Equality's Riddle: Pregnancy and the Equal Treatment/Special Treatment Debate," *N.Y.U. Review of Law and Social Change* 13 (1984–1985), pp. 325–335.
45. *Geduldig v. Aiello,* 417 U.S. 484, 496, n. 20 (1974); *General Electric Co. v. Gilbert,* 429 U.S. 125, 135–136 (1976).
46. 42 USC §2000 e(k) (1983).
47. Kamerman et al., *Maternity Policies;* Catalyst Inc., "Preliminary Report on a Na-

tionwide Survey of Maternity/Parental Leaves," *Perspective* (June 1984), p. 17; Congressional Caucus for Women's Issues, "Fact Sheet on Parental Leave Legislation" (1985); Family Policy Panel of the Economic Policy Council of UNA-USA, *Work and Family in the United States: A Policy Initiative* (1985); L. Finley, "Transcending Equality Theory: A Way Out of the Maternity and Workplace Debate," *Columbia Law Review* 86 (1986), pp. 1118, 1125.

48. *California Federal Savings & Loan Association v. Guerra,* 107 (S. Ct. 683 (1987).

49. H. Kay, "Equality and Difference: The Case of Pregnancy," *Berkeley Women's Law Journal* 1 (1985), pp. 33–35; S. Law, "Rethinking Sex and the Constitution," *University of Pennsylvania Law Review* 132 (1984), p. 132; Christine Littleton, "Reconstructing Sexual Equality," *California Law Review* 75 (1987), p. 279.

50. W. Williams, "Equality's Riddle," p. 371; N. Taub, "From Parental Leaves to Nurturing Leaves," *N.Y.U. Review of Law and Social Change* 13 (1985), pp. 381, 382.

51. Women's Research and Educational Institute, Congressional Caucus for Women, *The American Woman, A Report in Depth* (New York: Womens Research and Education Institute, 1987), pp. 27, 133; Congressional Caucus for Women, *Fact Sheet* 4 (1987); J. Peterson, "The Feminization of Poverty," *Journal of Economic Issues* 31 (1987), p. 329.

52. R. Sidel, *Women and Children Last* (New York: Viking, 1986); L. Weitzman, *The Divorce Revolution* (1985), pp. 323, 339; Congressional Caucus, *The American Woman,* pp. 85–90.

53. Congressional Caucus, *The American Woman; Fact Sheet,* p. 4; Peterson, "The Feminization of Poverty."

54. See Weitzman, *The Divorce Revolution;* Sidel, *Women and Children Last;* Fineman, "Implementing Equality: Ideology, Contradiction and Social Change," *Wisconsin Law Review* (1983), p. 789; New Jersey Supreme Court, *Task Force on Women and the Courts* (1984), pp. 60–80.

55. See e.g., H. Hartmann, D. Roos, and D. Treiman, "An Agenda for Basic Research on Comparable Worth," in H. Hartmann, ed., *Comparable Worth: New Directions for Research* (1985), pp. 3, 18–19; U.S. Commission on Civil Rights, "Comparable Worth: Issues for the '80s" (1984); B. Reskin and H. Hartmann, eds., *Women's Work, Men's Work: Sex Segregation on the Job* (1986); D. Rhode, "Perspectives on Professional Women," *Stanford Law Review* (1988).

56. See R. Dworkin, "DeFunis v. Sweatt," in M. Cohen, T. Nagel, and T. Scanlon, eds., *Equality and Preferential Treatment* (Cambridge, Mass.: Harvard University Press, 1977), pp. 63, 68; C. MacKinnon, *Feminism Unmodified* (1987).

11 ———·
Beyond the Liberal Idea of Privacy: Toward a Positive Right of Autonomy

RHONDA COPELON

Recognition by the Supreme Court in *Roe v. Wade*[1] that women have a qualified right to abortion has fueled a controversy that remains dangerously unresolved. At the center is the question of whether women are entitled to be self-determining, for to be denied control over reproduction or sexuality is to be reduced to dependence and servitude. The explosive response to *Roe* attests to the deeply radical nature of the demand, first by feminists and then by lesbians and gays, for a power so fundamental to our patriarchal liberal constitutional scheme as control over one's body.

The attack on *Roe v. Wade* has taken a number of forms. For about a decade following the 1973 decision, the "fetal personhood" campaign, spearheaded by the Catholic Church and later joined by Protestant New Right fundamentalists, held center stage. Right-to-life advocates argue for the subservience of woman to the fetus, pitting images of innocent and helpless souls against those of selfish, unnatural, and murderous femininity.[2] Their goal is not simply to save fetuses but to return woman to her "proper place"—to assure that motherhood remains her primary preoccupation. Their campaign has had some terrible successes in the Court, particularly in the decisions permitting legislatures to deny abortion funding to poor women[3] and to predicate a teenage girl's rights on parental approval or a judicial shaming ceremony.[4] In 1983, however, a number of fetal rights efforts—initiated at the outset of the Reagan administration to nullify or at least challenge the constitutional foundations of *Roe*—were defeated in Congress.[5] At the same time, the Court rejected the Reagan administration's effort to have the Court water down *Roe*.[6]

With the formal defeat of the fetal personhood claim,[7] a seemingly more neutral jurisprudential attack came to the fore. Drawing upon the work of conservative judges and scholars,[8] the Reagan administration fashioned a political program to delegitimize the more progressive civil rights decisions of the Court.[9] The banner of the campaign is "originalism"—the notion that the text of the Constitution and the particular historical meaning the framers would have given to that text define the outer limits of the judicial function.

As a method of interpretation, originalism is ahistorical, untenable, and hypocritical. That the revolutionaries who designed the Constitution or the republicans who led the fight for the Fourteenth Amendment intended to bind future generations by the literal limits of their own understanding of oppression is a dubious proposition at best.[10] There is ample evidence that in using such sweeping and indeterminate concepts as liberty, equality, and privileges and immunities, the framers envisioned constitutional interpretation as a process of evolving the concrete meaning of these values rather than freezing them.[11] The Court made a choice, widely seen as disingenuous, to uphold slavery in the *Dred Scott* case while wrapping itself in the flag of originalism.[12] The effort to resurrect the originalist position today is likewise a political choice, not a constitutional mandate.

Originalism obscures the critical value choices at issue; it cloaks the kind of society it would produce in a spurious debate about the usurpation of majoritarian preferences by a nonelected judiciary—as if legislative majorities invariably reflected either the people's preferences or democratic principles. Originalism creates a popular mythology that casts the "founding fathers" as the font of wisdom, the bearers of the true word, the secular gods.[13] It sets up the patriarchs against the pretenders in much the same way as religious fundamentalism attacks the legitimacy of secular humanism. The fact that the founders wrote implicit protections for slavery into the Constitution, and excluded women and the unpropertied from citizenship, is not often discussed in the new quasi-religious invocations of original authority.

A centerpiece of the originalist assault on the Constitution is the Court's decision in *Roe v. Wade* and its power to recognize unenumerated rights—those not explicitly articulated as such in the Constitution. The originalist attack underscores the absence of an explicit textual guarantee of a right to privacy embracing abortion or sexuality. Yet even this aspect of the originalist attack is highly selective, since a number of other unenumerated rights recognized by the Court are not under attack. The right to travel interstate or to send one's children to private school, for example, occasioned little consternation when identified by the Court and are rarely alluded to in the tirades against judicial usurpation today. In their opposition to *Roe,* neither Solicitor General Charles Fried nor Justice Byron White questioned the validity of an implied right of privacy covering contraception in the context of marital sexual intimacy. Not surprisingly, the unenumerated rights that draw the fire are those concerning the sphere of personal life and those challenging traditional views of sexuality, the role of women, and the hegemony of the heterosexual nuclear family.

Originalism in its most extreme form was tested in the Bork hearings before the Senate Judiciary Committee in 1987. The resignation of Justice Lewis Powell left the Court evenly divided on a number of critical civil rights and civil liberties issues, not the least of which was the existence and scope of constitutional protection for reproductive and sexual autonomy.[14] The nomination of Robert Bork was the Reagan administration's boldest effort to impress its right-wing agenda on the Court.[15] It resulted in exposing the originalist position to national scrutiny, which not only galvanized a broad grass-roots movement against Bork but also generated a repugnance for the rigid and dehumanizing methodology of the originalist approach.

The propriety of the Court's recognition of a substantive right of privacy against state interference in sexual or reproductive matters figured prominently in the Bork hearings and contributed significantly to his defeat. Bork's unswerving insistence that, contrary to *Griswold v. Connecticut,*[16] the Constitution provided no protection for a married couple to use contraception was a flame to which the senators repeatedly returned. Although the extremism of Bork's views in this regard elicited a clear consensus that a right of privacy does exist in the Constitution, the hearings provided little guidance on the scope of that protection. Some observers discount this ambiguity on the grounds that Bork's position made it unnecessary to take on his opposition to constitutional protection for abortion or gay rights, or more optimistically, that *Griswold* was a code word for a broader range of privacy rights encompassing, at least, abortion. But code words, though important, are not the equivalent of open discourse. The cautiousness of the senators on the propriety of protecting abortion, and their virtual silence on gay rights, signals greater discomfort about those aspects of privacy that reject the traditional gender-based views of sexuality, women, and family.

These issues were taken up, as was everything, half-heartedly in the subsequent hearings on the nomination of Anthony Kennedy. Given the general unwillingness of the liberal critics to challenge this nomination, it seems that Kennedy was confirmed not as a consequence of any searching examination of his substantive views on privacy and other critical civil rights issues, but because his repudiation of strict originalism permitted him to avoid clarifying his views.[17]

Thus, although the extreme originalist position has been repudiated, its influence on the jurisprudence of the Court and the values it espouses will continue to be substantial and may be decisive. If the new majority overrules or retreats from *Roe v. Wade,* it will most likely predicate its decision not on the fetal rights claim that has fueled the popular movement, nor on an explicit refusal to accede full personhood to women, but on the claim that, in recognizing a right of privacy encompassing abortion, or procreative and sexual autonomy, the Court overstepped the limits of its constitutional power to invalidate the acts of legislatures.

The influence of originalism on a nonexplicitly originalist formulation is outlined in the dissenting opinion of Justice White on abortion in *Thorn-*

burgh v. American College of Obstetricians and Gynecologists and in his majority opinion in *Bowers v. Hardwick* endorsing the criminalization of sodomy. In *Thornburgh,* the solicitor general pressed the Reagan administration's view that the Constitution provides no warrant for a right to abortion, characterizing it as the product of roaming judicial imagination rather than historical intention or permissible interpretation.[18] Justices White and William Rehnquist in dissent endorsed the solicitor general's call to overrule *Roe,* emphasizing the need for fidelity to the constitutional text and the traditions discernible therefrom.[19]

On the question of sexual self-determination, a bare majority of the Court has rejected, indeed denounced, a right to homosexual intimacy. In *Hardwick* the court rejected the challenge of a gay man arrested in his bedroom and upheld a Georgia statute that punishes heterosexual and homosexual sodomy by a term of one to twenty years in prison.[20] Justice White's majority opinion, echoing his dissent in *Thornburgh,* disdained a right of sexual intimacy for homosexuals and found no relation between gay intimacy and the interests of procreation and family protection recognized in earlier decisions. In reasoning that could as easily have been applied to sustain miscegenation laws twenty years ago, White reflected the originalist approach by uncritically relying on the history of criminal sodomy laws (originally designed to enforce the injunction to procreate) and on the long tradition of moralistic disapproval to trivialize the claim.

The opposition to this quasi-originalist, deeply hostile approach to women's and lesbian/gay rights was equally fervent. In *Thornburgh,* Justice Harry Blackmun asserted in a powerful opinion for the majority that if abortion was not held to be within the realm of constitutionally protected privacy, women would be denied equality in matters of the utmost significance to individual liberty, dignity, and autonomy. In *Hardwick,* he wrote a beautiful, indeed landmark, dissent recognizing that the right to choose one's intimate relationships is central to the authenticity of personal life and is protected for lesbians and gay men just as it is for those who conform to the heterosexual norm:

> Only the most willful blindness could obscure the fact that sexual intimacy is a "sensitive, key relationship of human existence, central to family life, community welfare, and the development of the personality." The fact that individuals define themselves in a significant way through their intimate sexual relationships with others suggests, in a Nation as diverse as ours, that there may be many "right" ways of conducting those relationships, and that much of the richness of a relationship will come from the freedom an individual has to choose the form and nature of these intensely personal bonds.[21]

Thus, at the very point when one faction of the Court is moving toward articulating the rights of reproductive and sexual autonomy in feminist terms, as an aspect of equality and not simply of privacy, the other is calling for the rejection of most or all constitutional protection of intimate matters. Justice Powell cast the deciding votes to make *Thornburgh* a victory and *Hardwick* a travesty. The division highlights, and the Kennedy hearings underscore, the fragile state of constitutional protection for reproductive autonomy and the depth of antagonism toward sexual freedom in the late 1980s.

In this chapter I will examine the progress in, as well as the inadequacy of, the development toward a right of reproductive and sexual autonomy. First, it is essential, particularly in light of the current debate on the role of the Court, to unpack the originalist critique of the right of privacy insofar as it protects reproductive and sexual decision making. By elucidating the gendered nature of the rights chosen by the framers for inclusion in the Bill of Rights, I want to go beyond the liberal critique of originalism to expose the patriarchal or gendered character of the original understanding and to highlight the necessity that the judiciary recognize reproductive and sexual rights in order fully to include those who were previously excluded.

Second, I will look at the influence of the original understanding on the Court's choice of the right of privacy as the vehicle for protection of intimate matters and on its elaboration. The creation of a right of privacy was a significant, albeit cautious, innovation that has resulted in an evolution toward recognizing the importance of personal autonomy with regard to reproduction and sexual self-definition. At the same time, the original gendered understanding has shaped and limited the development of the right of privacy. In particular, the right of privacy is, in the liberal tradition and in prevailing opinions, a qualified negative right that reinforces rather than fully challenges the traditional distinction between the public and private spheres.[22] This perspective results in a highly truncated and socially regressive concept of autonomy.

Finally, I will look at the relationship of privacy to a broader vision more consonant with a feminist understanding of rights and the social transformation feminism requires. Transcending the liberal origins of privacy, autonomy as a positive and socially supported right is a critical aspect of the feminist agenda.[23] I suggest that the concept of gender equality, coupled with a needs-oriented approach to equal opportunity, would provide a more encompassing framework for feminist goals. Rather than jettison the existing right of privacy or be constrained by it, it is essential to appreciate the dialectical relationship between privacy and equality that is part of the broader dialectic between social agitation, transformation, and legal change.

PATRIARCHY AND THE ORIGINAL UNDERSTANDING

THE GENDERED MATRIX OF THE CONSTITUTION

Consider the legal and ideological norms affecting women, reproduction, and sexuality that animated the framers of the original Constitution.[24] It is not insignificant that the framers accepted slavery and with it the objectification of slaves as property—that is, the denial to human beings of possession of themselves. Nonslave women, although privileged by comparison to slaves, were also treated in law as a species of property. They were destined to marry, and under the common law (which prevailed until the mid-nineteenth century), a married woman had no will of her own or identity separate from that of her husband. She was deemed to be in a state of coverture, which suspended her legal existence and thereby her ability to own property, to contract, to do business, to participate in political life, or to take a position at odds with those of her husband.[25]

A woman was also the sexual and reproductive property of her husband. He was entitled to beat her with a rod no wider than his thumb (the dubious origin of the "rule of thumb"). He could not possibly rape her because by her marriage "contract" she owed him sexual service—an exemption from the rape laws that persists in twenty-four states today.[26] A husband could sue his wife's sexual partners for damages (a tort claim called "criminal conversation") and the crime of adultery was defined as sexual relations with a married woman.[27] In a society that needed people, the purpose of sex was reproduction, although there is ample evidence of women's strategies for spacing childbearing. Interestingly, abortion was not illegal at least until quickening, but it was mainly the resort of single women. Thus, abortion laws, together with the panoply of other laws and customs, functioned to restrict legitimate propagation to marriage and inheritance to the husband's bloodline.[28]

Deviations from legitimate procreative sex, including adultery, sodomy (heterosexual as well as homosexual), and bestiality, were closely monitored by the community and severely sanctioned as the common law took over the functions of the canon law. Departures from procreative sex were viewed, however, as errant episodes rather than as a way of life.[29] Because the household was, until the Industrial Revolution, the unit for both production and reproduction, a homosexual identity or subculture—a different sexuality as a life-style—was impossible. The latter did not emerge until the nineteenth century when the growth of wage labor gave people, primarily men, the possibility of anonymity in the city and material independence from their biological families.[30] The legally sanctioned organization of private life was thus patriarchal and heterosexual, leavened only by the power of the equity courts to recognize property or commercial rights of women, by the discretion of religious and civil authorities to mitigate the severe punishments dictated for moral offenses, and by the need of husbands for the cooperation of a "helpmeet."[31]

This public ordering of personal life depended on maintaining the gender hierarchy and thus a gender dichotomy in all aspects of life. In the tenets of coverture as well as the predominant heritage of the Enlightenment, women were denied any role in public life. The education of women was not for intellectual pursuit but for interpersonal nurture. Although women and men worked interdependently in the household, the notion of men and women as having distinct roles was essential to justifying the system. Articulate or independent women who either were forced by or took the opportunity of the Revolutionary War to transcend dependency and the domestic sphere were commonly reviled as "masculine." At the same time, the keepers of republican virtue denounced bourgeois consumption as "effeminacy" in men.[32] Abigail Adams's private plea to her husband John to "Remember the Ladies" by eliminating from law the tyranny of husbands in the private realm and the exclusion of women from the public realm drew a revealing retort from him:

> As to your extraordinary code of laws, I cannot but laugh! . . . We know better than to repeal our masculine systems. Although they are in full force, you know they are little more than theory. . . . We have only the name of masters, and rather than give up this which would completely subject us to the despotism of the petticoat, I hope General Washington and all our brave heroes would fight.[33]

A GENDERED SET OF RIGHTS

Whereas the framers of the original Constitution were absorbed in a dispute over the abolition of slavery and the status of the slaves, there was no issue (Abigail Adams's private correspondence aside) as to status or rights of women. The Constitution was written by and for white propertied men; this was reflected not only by the fact that only white propertied men were deemed entitled to the rights of citizenship but also by the nature of the rights themselves. Women were not excluded by, but rather invisible to, the Constitution makers. It was, for example, not necessary to textually limit electors to males, so unquestioned was the assumption that states would render females ineligible to vote.

Equally important is the fact that the rights chosen to be included in the Bill of Rights protected what was then exclusively male activity in the realm of male authority. The predominant concern of the Bill of Rights was with activity in the public sphere. Freedom of speech and the press, the right to bear arms, freedom from self-incrimination as well as from cruel and unusual punishment, and the protections of due process emerged from the political processes of a revolution in which men, not women, were the recognized actors. Men were likewise the intended beneficiaries of the protection of private property, since women acquired control over property only as an exception (largely through widowhood) to the rule of coverture.

The Constitution protected the private realm by guarding the threshold of the home through the rules against search and seizure and the quartering of soldiers, thereby protecting the sphere in which culture and law gave authoritative predominance to men.[34] The recognition in recent court cases that woman is a separate autonomous adult in the household would have been completely inconsistent with the premise of coverture as well as with the procreative imperative.[35] Only the right of religious conscience—obedience to a higher patriarch—was permitted to women.

The silence of the Constitution on a right to bear children, or a right of bodily integrity explicit enough to embrace abortion or sexual self-determination, cannot be disconnected from the devalued status of women, from the preeminence awarded to the public sphere of male activity, or from the unquestioned hegemony of the heterosexual family and the prerogatives of the paterfamilias in the private sphere. My argument is not that the rights articulated in the Bill of Rights are quintessentially male or that they have no meaning for women, but rather that they reflected what was important to men—in particular, white, propertied men—and what maintained both their freedom and their power. The original Constitution's silence on, or its failure to enumerate, rights affecting woman in her person or activities thus reflected and reinforced the largely unquestioned gender hierarchy and heterosexual norm in both the public and private spheres.

The Fourteenth Amendment is likewise silent on reproduction[36] and sexuality because the basic patriarchal organization survived the first wave of the feminist movement, which increasingly focused on obtaining rights in the public rather than in the private sphere. Although the Married Women's Property Acts of the mid-nineteenth century gave women limited rights to hold and exchange property in their own names, the suffragist demand for political equality was defeated.[37] Industrialization led to the development—to which feminists contributed—of a bourgeois ideology of "separate spheres," which celebrated women's domesticity and elevated the status and authority of middle-class women within the home. Paradoxically, while the cult of domesticity provided a basis for women to get out of the home, to seek education, and to engage in social welfare agitation in the political sphere, it also heightened the ideological splits between male and female natures and between the public (male) and the private (female) spheres. The Supreme Court embraced the "separate spheres" ideology in a series of decisions that survived until 1971. These decisions constitutionalized the notion of women as properly being subject to different and subordinating treatment because they are suited for the domestic sphere.[38]

Thus the originalist insistence on the particular meaning of a Constitution structured by and for the eighteenth or nineteenth centuries is hardly value-free. Reverence for the original understanding is untenable in that it denies the personhood, if not the existence, of women by privileging a very limited set of rights drawn from and tailored to male experience. Equal citizenship for women thus requires the recognition of new rights.

The originalist would counter that the scope of protectible rights can be modified, but only by the super-majoritarian process of amending the Constitution. To so constrain the ability of the Constitution to evolve would, however, turn the Bill of Rights on its head—from a protection, however imperfect, of minoritarian rights into a protection of only those rights that majoritarian legislatures are unlikely to challenge. This constraint would pre-serve virtually in perpetuity the original hierarchies of privilege based on race, gender, and class that underlay the original Constitution and the Civil War amendments and that continue to affect contemporary laws and attitudes. If the Bill of Rights is to protect minoritarian rights, it is more appropriate to permit judicially recognized rights to stand unless a super-majority coalesces to eliminate them through amending the Constitution.[39]

To give constitutional protection to reproductive and sexual auton-omy is thus not an excess of the interpretive power of the Court but the necessary exercise of such power in a society where gender equality has emerged as a fundamental principle of justice. Recognition of rights not enu-merated or contemplated by the original framers is part of the process of making visible the previously invisible, of including the excluded, of filling in gaps that cannot be reconciled with equal justice.[40] The power to recog-nize rights must be grounded in a sense of justice derived from the interplay between original values, changed historical conditions, and evolving insights about liberty and equality. The women's and lesbian/gay movements have, like the abortion and civil rights movements before them, made new connec-tions between old promises and current oppressions. They have elucidated the connection between the new rights of sexual and reproductive autonomy and the textual guarantees of expression, association, bodily integrity, the privacy of the home, gender equality, and the rule against involuntary servi-tude.[41] The logic of these connections becomes accessible to those who, through experience, empathy, or ethical insight, understand the deep and systemic significance of their nonrecognition. The originalists would short-circuit the very effort to understand.

PRIVACY AND THE ORIGINAL UNDERSTANDING: DRIVING THE WEDGE, RECOGNIZING THE RESIDUE

The original understanding and the social matrix that created it shed impor-tant light on the resistance to, and limitations of, current doctrinal develop-ments. The fundamental paradox of constitutional change is that evolving conceptions of equality must be fit into a structure whose original premises have generated powerful institutional and ideological constraints. Scholars have demonstrated how protection of private property, the ideology of indi-vidual merit, and the presupposition of equality of opportunity have func-tioned to mask the class system that is central to maintaining institutional racism as well as class domination.[42]

The feminist project for the revision of the Constitution and society accepts and extends this critique. Feminism requires challenging a deeply ingrained ideology in which gender difference, heterosexism,[43] and the sepa-ration of the public and the private spheres are inextricably intertwined. Re-productive and sexual autonomy are a critical aspect of this challenge. But the articulation by the Court of a right of privacy as the vehicle for their protection is double-edged. On the one hand, it has constrained the ability of legislatures to maintain—through both intervention and nonintervention—the patriarchical order. On the other hand, it has reinforced the original distinction between the public and private spheres that has been essential to the patriarchal differentiation of male from female, the family from the state and market, the superior from the inferior, the standard measure from "the other."

FEMINIST ADVOCACY AND THE CONUNDRUM OF PRIVACY

In 1970, a collective of feminist lawyers and activists in the burgeoning abortion rights movement filed the first women's rights challenge to the criminal abortion laws.[44] Rather than envisioning abortion as a doctor's professional prerogative, as earlier cases and the major reform bills in the state legislatures had done, this case put women's right to control their bodies and lives at center stage. In the legislatures, women had to break into an ongoing dialogue between male legislators and experts, but in court women were better able to focus attention on their experience, need, and entitlement to control reproduction. The second wave of the feminist movement coalesced around the demand for legal abortion and the effort to win constitutional protection for women's decisions about reproduction, thus transforming a social reform movement for legal abortion led by doctors, family planners, and population controllers into a human rights struggle.[45]

The claim of privacy played a central role in early abortion rights advocacy. In large part, this trend flowed from the fact that the earliest cases involved doctors largely represented by nonfeminist attorneys who challenged the imposition of criminal sanctions as an interference with the privacy of the doctor-patient relationship. But it also reflected the more liberal orientation of some feminist abortion advocates as well as a more cautious approach to litigation.

The more radical feminist attorneys, echoing the movement's insistence on the right of women to control childbearing, sought abortion rights not simply as a matter of privacy but, more important, as a fundamental aspect of women's liberty.[46] The movement made the analogy between forced pregnancy and slavery, and attorneys have sought to elucidate the implications of the Thirteenth Amendment for criminal abortion laws.[47] Feminists have also elaborated the early idea that the choice whether to have an abortion is essential to sexual equality in terms of advancing both women's full personhood and their capacity to participate in society.[48] The disparate impact of the criminal abortion laws on rich and poor women has also been emphasized.

Feminist activists have also linked the right to terminate an unwanted pregnancy with the right of women to be sexual, free of either the patriarchal constraints of uncontrolled pregnancy or the mandate to be heterosexual.

With a few exceptions,[49] however, abortion rights advocates have been wary of the sexuality argument, even though antagonism to women's sexual freedom is the leitmotif of the attack on abortion.[50]

Against this array of available theories, it is significant that the Court chose privacy as the vehicle for protecting abortion.[51] The selection of privacy over some more affirmative notion of liberty or equality is the progeny of the original patriarchal dichotomy between the public and private spheres that has survived in liberal thought. Privacy was compatible with the common law tradition of noninterference in the marital home, a tradition that denied legal relief to women from economic and physical abuse by their husbands and therefore reinforced the dominance of men in the home. The notion of privacy reinforces the idea that the personal is separate from the political, which implies that the individual freedom to differ has no significant impact on the larger social structure, and that the larger social structure has no impact on the realm of private choice. The concept of privacy calls for toleration of otherness and thus perpetuates rather than dismantles the original hierarchy of norms. The liberal notion of privacy assumes that the individual is isolated and self-sufficient, not one to whom society bears affirmative responsibility.

This notion of privacy appealed to a broad constituency favoring contraception and abortion: the doctors who urged decriminalization on the basis of the privacy of the physician-patient relationship; the family planners who sought, among other things, to rationalize marriage; the population controllers who wanted only to discourage childbearing; and the libertarians who hold that in exchange for being left alone a person should ask nothing from society by the way of support.

The right of privacy, at least until *Hardwick,* figured prominently in gay rights litigation in part because the doctrine of privacy was well established and in part because the lesbian/gay movement, like the mainstream women's and abortion rights movement,[52] had given privacy center stage in its own advocacy. Advocates of lesbian/gay rights have also sought, largely unsuccessfully, to apply the constitutional guarantee of equal protection to discrimination based on sexual orientation.[53] There has, however, been very little attention to gender equality as an argument against this type of discrimination, and the few cases that have tried it have failed.[54] Privacy arguments, in part because of their success and in part because of their broad appeal, have until now been the predominant argument for reproductive and sexual rights.

In the twenty-three years since the right of privacy was first suggested by the Court, there has emerged a sharp tension between the liberal idea of privacy as the negative and qualified right to be left alone as long as nothing too significant is at stake and the more radical idea of privacy as the *positive* liberty of self-determination and an aspect of equal personhood. Before turning to the constraining application and implications of privacy doctrine, it is crucial to examine, both practically and theoretically, its progressive role in regard to reproductive rights as well as the role of feminist understanding in shaping the Court's formulation of the meaning of privacy in this sphere.

THE PROGRESSIVE IMPACT OF PRIVACY

Pragmatically, *Roe v. Wade* has had a profound impact on women's lives. Legalization of abortion transformed unwanted pregnancy from a potentially life-shattering event into one over which a woman could take rightful control. Abortion, though a significant and potentially painful decision, was no longer a life-endangering, desperate, and stigmatizing experience but rather a safe, legitimate health care option. By removing for many heterosexual women the duty or terror of unwanted pregnancy, legal abortion has also alleviated the repression and shame of female sexual desire.[55]

On the theoretical level, the right to abortion involves recognition of women's entitlement to be decision makers, agents of their destiny, and sexual beings. By permitting the separation of sexuality and reproduction, abortion indirectly affirmed the right of lesbians as well as heterosexual women to be sexually self-determining. Indeed, despite the rejection of sexual autonomy in *Hardwick*, Justice Blackmun's dissent for four members of the Court, which recognized the positive value of sexual self-definition, stands as a powerful challenge to the heterosexual norm. In a more broad sense, the right of privacy has undermined patriarchal control by men and the state over women's reproduction and ability to shape their lives.

Privacy doctrine, while still exceedingly limited, has evolved in several important respects. The notion of an independent right of privacy was first suggested in *Griswold v. Connecticut* to protect the use of contraceptives in marriage, which Justice William O. Douglas described as involving "a right of privacy older than the Bill of Rights."[56] Although a significant innovation in constitutional law, particularly at a time when Comstockery ran deep, marital privacy has operated historically to justify state nonintervention in the family and thus to reinforce patriarchal power over the resources and the person of the wife.[57]

The subsequent recognition in *Eisenstadt v. Baird*[58] that "the marital couple is an association of two individuals, each with a separate intellectual and emotional make-up," was far more radical. It marked the transformation of the family in constitutional law from a corporate body or unit, with privacy rights protecting the male-controlled entity, into an association of separate individuals, each of whom has a separate claim to constitutional protection.[59] The journey from familial privacy to individual autonomy was further advanced with the Court's rejection of the power of a husband or father to veto an abortion.[60] That a married woman has a right independently to decide significant questions affecting her life as well as the marriage relationship challenged the concept of merger at the heart of coverture.

A similar evolution occurred in relation to a woman's role in the abortion decision. Just as the caution or conservatism of the Court was expressed in the first contraception case by emphasizing the sacredness of marital intimacy, so when the Court first recognized the right to abortion it characterized the decision as belonging to the physician.[61] Because abortion is primarily a conscientious rather than a medical decision,[62] the women's movement interpreted *Roe* as announcing a woman's right to make the decision; the Court has since clarified that the woman is the source of the abortion decision.[63] Although doctors still exercise considerable control over the conditions under which abortion is performed,[64] the need for medical legitimation of the decision has diminished.

Interestingly, the Court's most forceful articulation of the right to abortion came in response to the most serious challenge to its legitimacy: the Reagan administration's request in *Thornburgh* that the Court overrule *Roe v. Wade*. In response, Justice Blackmun wrote:

> Few decisions are more personal and intimate, more properly private, or more basic to individual dignity and autonomy, than a woman's decision—with the guidance of her physician and with the limits specified in *Roe*—whether to end her pregnancy. A woman's right to make that choice freely is fundamental. Any other result, in our view, would protect inadequately a central part of the sphere of liberty that our law guarantees to all.[65]

This formulation of the abortion right is doubly significant because it situates the right to make autonomous decisions about childbearing in the context of equality. That women should have the right to abortion is not an instance of special treatment; it is instead an extension to women of the traditional liberal constitutional values of liberty, possession of the self, and opportunity to participate as producer and citizen. The opinion reflects, for the first time, a deeply feminist understanding of the necessity of the abortion right to women's full personhood.[66] It is significant that when the challenge to abortion rights intensifies, it is the affirmative feminist argument for self-determination,[67] rather than the negative liberal idea of being left alone, that comes to the fore.

This distinction is critical for the feminist critique of privacy. A mere right to be left alone reinforces the traditional liberal dichotomy between the public and private spheres, between the state and the family.[68] By contrast, privacy as a positive right of self-determination is a radical and deeply important idea for women, enabling women both to envision themselves as rightfully sovereign over themselves[69] and to demand that the state and market facilitate the conditions for autonomy.[70] The idea of women as decision makers regarding their reproductive capacity should have important implications for laws and policies, as it is inconsistent with the traditional view of women as objects of male need or state imperative.[71] As shall be seen in the next section, however, reproductive self-determination remains a sharply qualified principle.

Unfortunately, only four justices are willing even to extend the negative right of privacy to sexual autonomy. Indeed, apart from marital sexual intercourse, the Court has refused to recognize even heterosexual sexual expression as a positive right. Legalization of contraception was not based on a right to be sexual, but on the impermissibility of "prescrib[ing] pregnancy and the birth of an unwanted child as punishment for fornication."[72] By consistently refusing to question the validity of fornication and adultery statutes,[73] the Court preserved the foundation for upholding the criminalization of consensual sodomy between people of the same sex.

Nonetheless, Justice Blackmun's dissent in *Hardwick*, perhaps the most far-reaching decision of his career, elaborated further the positive meaning of privacy. Privacy, he suggested, means not simply that the state should not interfere with cloistered sexuality, but that the Constitution should protect sexual intimacy affirmatively and respect sexual difference because the process of sexual and familial self-definition is central to authenticity and self-realization.[74]

Despite the efforts of opponents of abortion and sexual freedom to trivialize these rights,[75] Justice Blackmun's decision in *Thornburgh* and his dissent in *Hardwick* have, for the first time, treated self-determination in intimate matters as an equality concern and as equivalent in importance to intellectual self-determination.[76] In so elevating the personal to constitutional importance as opposed to mere constitutional tolerance, Blackmun challenged the original understanding by integrating concerns traditionally associated with the female sphere into a Constitution designed exclusively to protect the male sphere.

PRIVACY AS RESIDUE OF THE ORIGINAL UNDERSTANDING

Notwithstanding the potential for transforming privacy into positive liberty, prevailing opinions have recognized privacy as no more than a very circumscribed right to be left alone. As a means of eliminating criminal sanctions, a negative right of privacy, when successful, provides a foothold from which to seek broader legitimacy. It is thus no small matter that the Court both legalized abortion and refused to invalidate the criminalization of homosexual sodomy. But the fact that the traditional idea of privacy is negative and defensive reinforces rather than undermines the power of the original patriarchal order in at least two ways: (1) it renders privacy a weak vehicle for challenging the hegemony of traditional norms of behavior, and (2) it denies the relationship of social conditions and public responsibility to the ability of the individual to exercise autonomy.

PRIVACY AND THE HEGEMONY OF TRADITIONAL NORMS

The liberal theory of privacy protects the right to differ from majoritarian norms where there is no deleterious impact on others. Private choices are tolerable because they are of little consequence to society, or as Justice White recently said of abortion, because "the evil does not justify the evils of forbidding it."[77] Moreover, while society must tolerate difference, it need not either encourage it or desist from discouraging it.

The negativity of privacy has consequences both for the development of constitutional protection and for the progress of a movement that relies too heavily upon it. The privacy argument seems at first blush easier to sell because it does not require a court to renounce society's prejudices. But the position that "Even though homosexuality is disgusting or abortion is murder, we must allow it," or "It's okay to be homosexual as long as it doesn't show in public," reinforces prejudice and shame. The notion of privacy as the protection of sexual difference reinforces the exclusion of a sexual minority from the mainstream society and thus reinforces the hierarchy of traditional norms as well as the fear of exclusion. Privacy, as it was argued before the Court in *Hardwick,* included the right to be an exception as long as it was within the home or duly cloistered. This concept of privacy does not, at least in common parlance, allow for the expression of one's difference in everyday life.[78] It carves out an exception to the norm; it preserves deviance at the same time that it permits it.

Privacy doctrine, like originalism, erroneously purports to be a value-free basis for decision. The result in *Hardwick* demonstrates, however, that the agnosticism of privacy as to the value of the protected activity does not survive where prejudice is deep. Justice Warren Burger made his hostility clear by quoting Sir William Blackstone's description of sodomy as "'the infamous crime against nature,' as an offense of 'deeper malignity' than rape."[79] Justice White's opinion for the majority was more sanitized but equally barbed. He compared sodomy to the possession of "drugs, firearms, or stolen goods" and dismissed the claim that there is a relationship between homosexuality and the protected realm of family, marriage, and procreation as "facetious."[80] Even Justice Powell, though disinclined to imprison gay people, was content to maintain the stigma of criminality.[81]

These opinions indicate indirectly that Hardwick lost because same-sex intimacy is seen as threatening—threatening to gender identity, the expectation of heterosexuality, and the power relations it embodies. A heterosexist culture will go to elaborate lengths to construct distinct gender identities as well as the propensity toward heterosexuality.[82] It may be that the very fragility of the channeled sexual self heightens the danger presented by crossing the line; that precisely because sexual identity and heterosexuality are not ordained but choosable,[83] those who deviate from the heterosexual norm must be stigmatized and excluded.[84]

Same-sex relationships also threaten the traditional hegemony of men in the sexual pecking order. Just as Justice Burger thinks homosexual sodomy worse than rape, the possibility of homosexual solicitation is treated more harshly than the sexual harassment of women.[85] Moreover, the potential for women to have sexual pleasure and to construct relationships and communities without men changes the balance of sexual power in familial relations, precisely the arena most resistant to equalitarian intervention.[86]

The sense in which the *Hardwick* majority is right highlights the shortsightedness of relying on a negative right of privacy. Sexual self-definition must cross the bounds of privacy, for autonomy cannot be realized apart from social interaction. While privacy implies secrecy and shame, the choice of sexual partners of the same sex is no more intrinsically private than the identity of a person's spouse. Nor is this choice easily confined to the private realm of the bed or the closet. It involves not only sexual but also familial and social identity—who one is in public as well as in private and what the legal norms are. To accept mere tolerance of sexual difference is not only degrading; it is ultimately self-defeating.

PRIVACY AND THE LEGITIMATION OF SOCIAL IRRESPONSIBILITY

Privacy is also deficient as a theory for reproduction and sexual self-determination because it perpetuates the liberal myth that the right to choose is inherent in the individual and a "given" of private life rather than acknowledging that choices are shaped, facilitated, or denied by social conditions. As Rosalind Petchesky reminds us, women exercise reproductive choice

> under the constraint of *material conditions* that set limits on "natural" reproductive processes—for example, existing birth control methods and technology and access to them; class divisions and the distribution of financing of health care; nutrition and employment, particularly of women; and the state of the economy generally. And she does so within a specific network of social relations and social arrangements involving herself, her sexual partners, her children and kin, neighbors, doctors, family planners, birth control providers, manufacturers, employers, the church and the state.[87]

The right of privacy not only disassociates the individual from this broader context; it also exempts the state from responsibility for contributing to material conditions and social relations that facilitate autonomous decision making.

Nowhere is this negative aspect of privacy theory more clearly or cruelly demonstrated than in the Court's decisions permitting the state to deny Medicaid funding for abortion.[88] The decisions recognize that by funding childbirth and not abortion, the state is seeking to influence private choice. They also recognize that the absence of funding will make it "difficult, if not impossible" for some poor women to implement their choice. But the Court treats both the intent and effect of this policy as constitutionally irrelevant because the inability to obtain an abortion flows not from an obstacle created by the state but rather from the fact of the woman's "indigency . . .[which] is neither created nor in any way affected by the . . .[Medicaid] regulation."[89] Not only does the negative right of privacy carry no corresponding state obligation to facilitate choice; the integrity of a woman's decision-making process is not even protected against purposeful manipulation through the selective provision of state resources, in this case, the funding of childbirth.

To treat a woman's poverty and her inability to exercise choice as a consequence not of market conditions and public policy but of private fault is a dangerous fiction built upon another aspect of the separation of the public and private spheres. It rests on the idea, central to capitalist patriarchy, that the family unit has the responsibility of being economically self-sufficient. Not only does this notion of privatization permit the state to escape responsibility for the tragic conditions of people's lives, but the ideology of private responsibility also makes it possible to blame the poor, who are overwhelmingly women, for their inability to be self-sufficient.

It is a small step, as the Medicaid cases indicate, from blame to control. The Court is explicit that where exercise of the right of privacy depends on public resources, moralistic disapproval or demographic considerations will justify its destruction.[90] Moreover, by attributing dependency to individual failure, the Court avoids the need to reexamine the feasibility and fairness of assigning responsibility for survival and caretaking exclusively to the family.

The gap between a private right of choice and the necessary conditions for autonomy widens when we consider the broad range of factors that influence and in many cases determine women's choices about reproduction. The prevalence of economically influenced abortions and the sterilization campaigns against poor, minority, and disabled women illustrate that autonomy is impossible without eradication of discrimination and poverty.[91] A viable conception of autonomy would presuppose a society in which both the workforce and the family were restructured to value the work and the gift of mothering and to encourage gender-neutral, same-sex, and communal participation therein. Autonomy would also require a positive, needs-oriented concept of rights that guarantees the preconditions for self-realization, including shelter, food, day care, health care, education, and the possibility of meaningful work, relationships, and engagement in political and social life.

Autonomy with regard to sexual self-determination is likewise inseparable from material and ideological conditions. It requires redistributing power between the sexes as well as dismantling heterosexism. The continuing economic and social realities of male power and female dependency, as well as their translation into male aggression and female passivity in the sexual realm, complicate the ability of women to make autonomous choices about their intimate sexual and familial relations. The possibility of choosing to live one's life as gay or lesbian did not emerge until social conditions permitted independence from the traditional family, and this choice will not be fully guaranteed until the right to express one's sexual identity is recognized and materially supported to the same extent as heterosexual intimacy.

Thus, to protect a "right to choose" without assuring the social conditions necessary to foster an autonomous choice provides equality of opportunity in form but not in fact. It creates an appearance of autonomy where it cannot exist. The full capacity for autonomy may not be magically achieved, even with the eradication of gender, sexual, race, and class oppression; but autonomy cannot be imagined short of major social transformation. The idea of privacy obscures the necessity of public responsibility to bring this transformation about.

CONCLUSION: THE POTENTIAL OF EQUALITY

The extensive social transformation required to guarantee autonomy cannot be accomplished through the mechanism of judicial recognition or enforcement of rights. Rather, it requires a multifaceted strategy involving litigation, legislation, collective bargaining, grass-roots activism, and, ultimately, cultural change in order to eradicate discrimination and change the nature of the family and the market as well as the relationship between them. Nonetheless, the ability, which the originalists deny, of our Constitution to embrace new insights about human rights is a critical component of the process of undoing oppression and empowering the excluded. Constitutionalization is important because it reflects not simply desirable social policy, but an ethical bottom line.

Just as the original Constitution arose from a particular social matrix, so does the evolving one. Material and ideological conditions underlie the demand for, and the acceptability of, new rights.[92] Activists and legal advocates in social liberation movements are an essential part of the forces that ultimately move the Court to take another tiny step forward.

Thus, how a movement and its advocates articulate its demands and its vision can make a difference to constitutional development as well as to the broader process of social change. While the notion of a right of privacy has substantively advanced reproductive and even sexual autonomy, it has also permitted these rights to be disconnected from the broader vision of equality that women's and lesbian/gay liberation requires. The danger is that the Court's mediated version of rights will become the measure of the movement's goals. The antidote is to recognize the dialectical character of the interaction between limited doctrine and broader visions as well as between social activism and legal reform.[93] By invoking principles of individual rights and equality, reserved by traditional liberal theory to white men, feminists have both challenged the patriarchal structure and contributed to the progressive revelation of the thoroughgoing transformation that feminist principles require.[94]

In both legal and political advocacy for reproductive and sexual rights, privacy need not be jettisoned but must be transformed into an affirmative right to self-determination and grounded in the broader principle of equality and in the concrete conditions of people's lives. In order to achieve gender equality, we must refute the intended conceptual division between the public and private spheres and demand an examination of the gendered assumptions that underlie this dichotomy. With regard to abortion, the equality principle requires us to recognize that forced pregnancy is involuntary servitude and that abortion is essential to women's full personhood and participation in all spheres of life. With regard to sexuality, equality does not simply carve an exception to the heterosexual model; it challenges the hegemony of the model itself. Moreover, a needs-based concept of equality requires us to attend to rather than ignore the social and material preconditions for the exercise of liberty. It forbids us to allow reproductive and sexual choices to hinge on socioeconomic status and requires us to guarantee, through an expanding concept of affirmative action, conditions such as day care and benefits to diverse familial arrangements that render affirmative choices possible. Rather than a society in which heterosexuality is programmed and presumed, equality counsels genuine acceptance of sexual diversity to protect the expression of sexual difference as well as the possibility of authentic self-definition and intimacy for everyone.

Although equality provides a capacious theory for the protection of autonomy and intimate association, equal protection doctrine (like that of privacy) is currently negative and truncated.[95] Equality should not be judged by the state of existing doctrine, but rather by its potential as an encompassing and ever-evolving vision for advancing social as well as constitutional change.

The originalists, of course, would have cut off constitutional evolution long ago and would preclude the Court from the task of trying to hear the cries of pain and new stirrings for liberation. It is critical to defend the Court's ability to do that. The fact that the Court will invariably be inadequate to the task argues not against rights advocacy but against acceding to the adequacy or legitimacy of limited judicial formulations.

NOTES

This chapter is a revision of a presentation delivered as part of the Rothstein/Dickenson Memorial Lectures of the Chicago Chapter of the National Lawyers' Guild and an article entitled "Unpacking Patriarchy: Reproduction, Sexuality, Originalism, and Constitutional Change," in J. Lobel, ed., *A Less Than Perfect Union* (New York: Monthly Review, 1988). I am immensely grateful for the encouragement and insightful comments of Susan Bryant, Sylvia Law, Howard Lesnick, Jules Lobel, Maureen McCafferty, Dorothy McCarrick, Rosalind Petchesky, Elizabeth Schneider, Nadine Taub, Sharon Thompson, Marilyn Young, and Patricia Williams.

1. *Roe v. Wade*, 410 U.S. 113 (1973).
2. Rosalind Petchesky, *Abortion and Woman's Choice: The State, Sexuality and Reproductive Freedom* (New York: Longman, 1984).
3. *Harris v. McRae*, 448 U.S. 297 (1980). The religious basis of the fetal rights

position is extensively documented in the District Court opinion and appendix. *McRae v. Califano,* 491 F. Supp. 630 (E.D.N.Y. 1980).

4. *Baird v. Bellotti,* 443 U.S. 622 (1979), upheld parental consent statutes so long as they provided for judicial review for minors who chose not to seek the consent of their parents. The trauma this produces for teen women is documented in *Hodgson v. State of Minnesota,* 648 F. Supp. 756 (D. Minn 1986).

5. The first attempt to enact a constitutional amendment died in the Senate Judiciary Committee in 1976. In 1980, Jesse Helms introduced the "Human Life Statute," a blatantly unconstitutional effort to overturn *Roe* by majoritarian vote. In the same period a number of constitutional amendments were under active consideration. Both efforts were defeated in the Senate in 1983.

6. Brief of the United States as Amicus Curiae, *City of Akron v. Akron Center for Reproductive Health,* 462 U.S. 416 (1983). The solicitor general's position was, however, substantially adopted by Justice Sandra Day O'Connor in her dissenting opinion.

7. That Congressional initiatives to overturn *Roe v. Wade* have been rejected does not obviate the impact of "fetal rights" claims on law, medicine, and society. Women are increasingly subject to involuntary procedures during pregnancy and childbirth. See Janet Gallagher, "Prenatal Invasions and Intervention: What's Wrong with Fetal Rights?" *Harvard Women's Law Review* (1987), p. 9. And the visualization of the fetus as an entity independent of the woman has affected cultural attitudes. See Rosalind Petchesky, "Fetal Images: The Power of Visual Culture in the Politics of Reproduction," *Feminist Studies* 13, no. 2 (1987), pp. 263–292.

8. See, e.g., Bork, "Neutral Principles and Some First Amendment Problems," *Indiana Law Journal* 47 (1971), p. 1; William Rehnquist, "The Notion of a Living Constitution," *Texas Law Review* 54 (1976), p. 693; R. Berger, *Government by Judiciary: The Transformation of the Fourteenth Amendment* (Cambridge, Mass.: Harvard University Press, 1977).

9. Address of Edwin Meese III, attorney general of the United States, before the American Bar Association, July 9, 1985; see also Meese, before the American Enterprise Institute, September 6, 1986.

10. Thomas Jefferson, for example, criticized "those who look at constitutions with sanctimonious reverence and deem them like the ark of the covenant too sacred to be touched. Let us not weakly believe that our generation is not as capable as another of taking care of itself and of ordering its own affairs." T. Jefferson, letter to Samuel Kercagual, July 12, 1816, in M. Peterson, ed., *The Portable Thomas Jefferson* (1973), pp. 1552, 1559–1560.

11. Scholars have strongly disputed that the framers' intent be so literally and woodenly applied. See, e.g., H. Jefferson Powell, "The Original Understanding of Intent," *Harvard Law Review* 98 (1985), p. 885 (examining cultural traditions that influenced the framers underscores the vision of constitutional interpretation as an evolutionary common law process); P. Brest, "The Misconceived Quest for the Original Understanding," B.U.L. 60 (1980), p. 204 (arguing the untenability of strict originalism and for a nonoriginalist perspective on the protection of fundamental values); A. Bickel, "The Original Understanding and the Segregation Decision," *Harvard Law Review* 69 (1955), p. 61 (suggesting that broad phrases in the Fourteenth Amendment—as in the original Constitution—

were chosen because they "were sufficiently elastic to permit reasonable future advances"). For a devastating critique of originalism generally, see Judith A. Baer's chapter "The Fruitless Search for Original Intent" in this volume.

12. "No one, we presume, supposes that any change in public opinion or feeling in relation to this unfortunate race, in the civilized nation of Europe or in this country, should induce the court to give to the words of the Constitution a more liberal construction in their favor than they were intended to bear when the instrument was framed and adopted." *Scott v. Sandford,* 60 U.S. (19 How.) 1393, 1426 (1856).

13. Peter Gabel, "Founding Father Knows Best: A Response to Tushnet," *Tikkun,* vol. 1, no. 2 (1986), pp. 41–45.

14. Two decisions in the 1986 term in which Powell had the deciding vote crystallized this split. In *Thornburgh v. American College of Obstetricians and Gynecologists* 106 S.Ct. 2169 (1986), the original 7–2 majority from *Roe v. Wade* had been whittled down by Reagan appointments to a bare majority, while in *Bowers v. Hardwick,* 106 S.Ct. 2841 (1986), a challenge to the criminalization of sodomy was rejected by a 5–4 vote.

15. The promotion of Rehnquist to chief justice and, more important, the confirmation of Antonin Scalia, escaped the opposition they deserved because of the reluctance of liberal senators and civil rights activists to challenge the ideological predisposition of a justice. Bork's nomination precipitated this confrontation because he would be the swing vote and had such extreme views.

16. *Griswold v. Connecticut,* 381 U.S. 479 (1965).

17. As to abortion, Kennedy was asked only how he would approach such a question, and he provided a thoroughly obfuscating response. To permit him to avoid direct questions about this position on *Roe v. Wade* in 1988 is like declining to ask a nominee in 1969 whether he supported the ruling in *Brown v. Board of Education,* 347 U.S. 483 (1954), that the ghettoization of black children into segregated schools denied equal protection.

18. See the brief for the United States as Amicus Curiae in *Thornburgh,* at 28, and Justice White's dissenting opinion in the case.

19. The White/Rehnquist dissent in *Thornburgh* is likely to draw the support of Justice Scalia. Justice O'Connor has so far declined to call for a total overruling of *Roe.* As a practical matter, she would, except in rare circumstances, sustain restrictions on legal abortion. See *City of Akron v. Akron Center for Reproductive Health,* at 452. Kennedy appears likely to take a position that would make abortion inaccessible particularly to young, poor, and working-class women.

Moreover, while some states will undoubtedly maintain abortion as legal, Congress, rid of the constitutional constraint of a fundamental right, may try to enact antiabortion legislation to override permissive state laws. In those states where abortion remains legal, it is predictable that unrestricted teen access and medical reimbursement will be jeopardized in the bargaining to maintain legal abortion.

20. Though the statute applies to both heterosexual and same-sex sodomy, the Court ruled on its constitutionality as to same-sex sodomy only.

21. *Bowers v. Hardwick,* at 2851.

22. In the literature of political theory, the public/private split refers to the difference between the state and the market. Feminists use the public/private dichotomy to

describe the distinction between the home or the personal sphere assigned to women and both the market and politics, or the public sphere assigned to men. See, e.g., Z. Eisenstein, *Feminism and Sexual Equality* (New York: Monthly Review, 1984), p. 97; F. Olsen, "The Family and the Market: A Study of Ideology and Legal Reform," *Harvard Law Review* 96 (1983), p. 1497; D. Polan,"Toward A Theory of Law and Patriarchy," in D. Kairys, ed., *The Politics of Law: A Progressive Critique* (New York: Pantheon Books, 1982), p. 301.

23. Eisenstein, *Feminism and Sexual Equality.*

24. Feminist and lesbian/gay historians have begun to demonstrate both the influence and the extent of deviation from the formal norms. For the purposes of constitutional construction, however, the rules, not the exceptions, are most significant. The history that follows has drawn from the following works: N. Cott, *The Bonds of Womanhood: "Women's Sphere" in New England 1780–1835* (New Haven: Yale University Press, 1977); C. Degler, *At Odds: Women and the Family from the Revolution to the Present* (London: Oxford, 1980); J. D'Emilio, "Capitalism and Gay Identity," in A. Snitow, C. Stansell, and S. Thompson, eds., *Powers of Desire: The Politics of Sexuality* (New York: Monthly Review, 1983); J. D'Emilio and E. Freedman, *Intimate Matters: A History of Sexuality in America* (New York: Harper & Row, 1988); L. Gordon, *Woman's Body, Woman's Right: A Social History of Birth Control in America* (New York: Grossman, 1976); J. N. Katz, *Gay/Lesbian American History* (New York: Crowell, 1976); J. N. Katz, *Almanac: A New Documentary* (New York: Crowell, 1983); L. Kerber, *Women of the Republic: Intellect and Ideology in Revolutionary America* (Chapel Hill: University of North Carolina Press, 1980); J. Mohr, *Abortion in America* (New York: Oxford University Press, 1978); M. B. Norton, *Liberty's Daughters: The Revolutionary Experience of American Women* (Boston: Little, Brown, 1980); Susan M. Okin, *Women in Western Political Thought* (Princeton, N.J.: Princeton University Press, 1979); Petchesky, *Abortion and Woman's Choice;* M. Ryan, *Womanhood in America: From Colonial Times to the Present,* 3rd ed. (New York: F. Watts, 1983); N. Taub and E. Schneider, "Perspectives on Women's Subordination and the Role of Law," in Kairys, ed., *The Politics of Law.*

25. Blackstone's *Commentaries on the Laws of England* (Chicago: Cooley, Callehan & Co., 1884); Kerber, *Women of the Republic,* discusses the question of whether to ascribe a husband's treason to the wife after the revolution.

26. Sir Matthew Hale, *History of the Pleas of the Crown* (1736), p. 629. Statistics provided by the Center for Women and Family Law, New York.

27. It was not until 1773 that women began to petition for and win divorce on the ground of their husband's adultery. Degler, *At Odds,* p. 17.

28. Mohr, *Abortion in America;* Gordon, *Woman's Body.*

29. D'Emilio and Freedman, *Intimate Matters.*

30. J. D'Emilio, "Capitalism and Gay Identity," in Snitow et al., eds., *Powers of Desire.*

31. Ryan, *Womanhood in America;* D'Emilio and Freedman, *Intimate Matters.*

32. Kerber, *Women of the Republic.*

33. M. Friedlander and M. Kline, *The Book of Abigail and John: Selected Letters of the Adams Family, 1762–1784* (Cambridge, Mass: Harvard University Press, 1975), p. 123.

34. Patrick Henry, for example, advocating the Bill of Rights, endorsed the liberty that allows a man to "enjoy the fruits of his labor, under his own fig tree, with

his wife and children around him, in peace and security." See J. Elliot, *Debates in the Several State Conventions on the Adoption of the Federal Constitution,* vol. 2, p. 268, and vol. 3 (New York: Franklin).

35. In *At Odds,* Carl Degler describes the state of women in the family: "[W]omen were not then thought of as anything other than supportive assistants—necessary to be sure, but not individuals in their own right. The individual as a conception in Western thought has always assumed that behind each man—this is each individual—was a family. But the members of that family were not individuals, except the man, who was by law and custom its head." See also, Heidi Hartmann, "Capitalism, Patriarchy, and Job Segregation by Sex," in Zillah Eisenstein, ed., *Capitalist Patriarchy and the Case for Socialist Feminism* (New York: Monthly Review Press, 1979), pp. 206–247.

36. As a practical matter, there was no need for constitutional protection of abortion because women had access to early abortion until the end of the nineteenth century, when a fledgling medical profession campaigned for the criminalization of abortion to establish its hegemony over midwives and lay healers. The significant rise of abortion, along with the aspirations of white Protestant middle- and upper-class women, was also a major factor fueling restriction. In other words, as abortion began to be chosen by women in order to control their lives rather than simply to avoid the desperation of illegitimacy, it became threatening to the patriarchal and class structure rather than supportive of it. Male supremacy in the family as well as the demographic and racial superiority of the white Anglo-Saxon Protestant middle class would be preserved by coercing procreation. L. Gordon, *Women's Body, Women's Right;* Mohr, *Abortion in America.* Despite women's resort to abortion, nineteenth-century feminists did not advocate birth control or oppose criminalization. Rather, they urged abstinence to assure "voluntary motherhood," heighten respect for women, and limit husbands' sexual access. L. Gordon, "Why Nineteenth-Century Feminists Did Not Support Birth Control and Twentieth-Century Feminists Do: Feminism, Reproduction, and the Family," in B. Thorne and M. Yalom, *Rethinking the Family: Some Feminist Questions* (New York: Longman, 1982).

37. The Fourteenth Amendment was not silent on the citizenship of women. Section 2 provided a remedy for denial of the franchise only to men and thereby wrote gender discrimination into the Constitution for the first time. On the struggle in this period, see E. Dubois, *Feminism and Suffrage: The Emergence of an Independent Women's Movement in America 1848–1869* (New York: Cornell University Press, 1978).

38. *Hoyt v. Florida,* 368 U.S. 57 (1961). *Reed v. Reed,* 404 U.S. 71 (1971) was the first case to reject this classic sex role stereotype. For an excellent discussion, see Taub and Schneider, "Perspectives on Women's Subordination."

39. By definition, to survive the political process, judicially recognized rights require very substantial, perhaps even more majoritarian support. For example, although approximately two-thirds to three-quarters of the people polled opposed a constitutional amendment on abortion, the effort to enact one was only narrowly defeated in 1983.

40. Understood in its historical context, the enumeration of rights in the Bill of Rights was itself animated by an equality principle, albeit a very truncated one. Thus, for example, the First Amendment envisioned free speech for the pam-

phleteer as well as for the powerful; the due process clause protected the property of anyone who could get it and not just those born into the landed class; and the establishment clause precluded unequal treatment of different religions.

41. For example, the due process clause was intended to protect one's body and liberty against unfair arrest and incarceration. More recently the Court held that pumping a suspect's stomach "shocks the conscience." *Rochin v. California*, 342 U.S. 165 (1952). But being dragged off to jail and having one's stomach pumped are not the only ways one can be seized. If women or gay people have an equal right to the possession of themselves, is not the state's seizure of control over the womb or the expression of sexual intimacy a comparable deprivation?

42. See, e.g., Alan D. Freeman, "Anti-Discrimination Law: A Critical Review," in Kairys, ed., *The Politics of Law;* McCann, Chapter 9 in this volume.

43. Heterosexism is the systematization of the ideology that treats the heterosexual organization and its concomitant gender differentiation of intimacy and family and social life as "natural" and superior. It is distinct from, although fed by, homophobia, the fear or loathing of gay men or lesbians.

44. The case, *Abramowicz v. Lefkowitz,* filed by 300 women plaintiffs in January 1970 in federal district court, was withdrawn after the New York state legislature, by a margin of one, voted on April 3, 1970, to repeal restrictions on abortion within the first twenty-four weeks of pregnancy. The work in this case provided the foundation for other feminist challenges to criminal abortion laws. The testimony is excerpted in D. Schulder and F. Kennedy, *Abortion Rap* (New York: McGraw-Hill, 1971).

45. Ellen Willis, *Village Voice*, March 3, 1980, p. 8. See also R. Petchesky, *Abortion and Woman's Choice*, pp. 125–129.

46. This was the primary argument in the Amicus Curiae Brief on behalf of New Women Lawyers filed in *Roe v. Wade.* (Hereinafter CCR Amicus.) Feminist attorney Nancy Stearns of the Center for Constitutional Rights, author of the brief and one of the architects of the constitutional theory of women's right to abortion, explained the difference between privacy and liberty: "The right to privacy is a passive right. The right to privacy says that the state can't interfere. The right to liberty . . . would seem to imply that the state has some kind of affirmative obligation to ensure that women exercise that right to liberty." J. Goodman, R. Schoenbrod and N. Stearns, "Doe and Roe: Where Do We Go From Here?" *Women's Rights Law Reporter* 1, no. 4 (Spring 1973), pp. 20, 27.

47. The CCR Amicus and the Amici Curiae Brief on behalf of Organizations and Named Women addressed the Thirteenth Amendment. The latter, written by Joan Bradford in *Roe v. Wade,* developed the argument that fetal life should not limit a woman's autonomy because the Thirteenth Amendment forbids the forced labor or subordination of one person to the needs or desires of another. The Thirteenth Amendment implications also have been suggested by L. Tribe, "The Abortion Funding Conundrum: Inalienable Rights, Affirmative Duties and the Dilemma of Dependence," *Harvard Law Review* 99 (1985), p. 330; D. Regan, "Rethinking *Roe v. Wade*," *Michigan Law Review* 77 (1977), p. 1569; J. Thomson, "A Defense of Abortion," *Philosophy and Public Affairs* 1 (1971), p. 1; and R. Copelon, "The Applicability of Section 241 of the Ku Klux Klan Acts to Private Conspiracies to Obstruct or Preclude Access to Abortion," *National Black Law Journal* 10 (1987), pp. 196–199.

48. In the *Roe v. Wade* amicus, Stearns also argued the centrality of abortion to women's equality, given that the law, and not nature, punished only women for "illicit" sex and that pregnancy operated broadly to exclude women from public life. The equal protection argument has since been developed in Appellees' Brief, in *Harris v. McRae*, in the Brief for Amici Curiae on behalf of New Jersey Coalition for Battered Women et al., and in *Right to Choose v. Byrne*, reprinted in *Women's Rights Law Reporter* 7 (1982), pp. 286–290, 296–299; see also S. Law, "Rethinking Sex and the Constitution," *University of Pennsylvania Law Review* 132 (1984), p. 955; Tribe, "The Abortion Funding Conundrum"; Regan, "Rethinking *Roe v. Wade*."

49. CCR Amicus; *Right to Choose v. Byrne*.

50. E. Willis, "Abortion: Is a Woman a Person?" in Snitow et al., eds., *Powers of Desire*; Petchesky, *Abortion and Woman's Choice*. Feminist theologian Beverly Harrison demonstrates that the early Christian opposition to abortion had to do more with sexual sin than the innate preciousness of fetal life, in *Our Right to Choose: Toward a New Ethic of Abortion* (Boston: Beacon, 1983).

51. The choices available to the Court at the time of *Griswold* are explored in T. Emerson, "Nine Justices in Search of a Doctrine," *Michigan Law Review* 64 (1965), p. 219.

52. The National Organization for Women (NOW) has excluded abortion and lesbian/gay rights from the ERA out of concern that these issues would be responsible for its defeat, while the mainstream abortion rights movements have tended to situate abortion in a libertarian as opposed to a feminist context. Although the groups are beginning to give more attention to the centrality of abortion to women's equality, NOW continues to separate reproduction and sexuality from its equality agenda.

53. This claim tends to falter on the need of the Court to recognize lesbians and gays as an impermissibly victimized class. But see *Watkins v. U.S. Army*, 847 F.2d 1362 (9th Cir. 1988).

54. See S. Law, "Homosexuality and the Social Meaning of Gender," *Wisconsin Law Review* (1988), p. 187.

55. One strand of late twentieth-century feminism rejects the contribution of contraception and abortion to a more liberated female sexuality based on the view that heterosexual sex, in a gender unequal society, is by definition oppressive. See C. MacKinnon, *Feminism Unmodified* (Cambridge, Mass.: Harvard University Press, 1987), pp. 93–102. This flat and dangerous stereotype precludes exploration of the complexity and wonder of sexual agency, power, and desire. Even if one accepts, as I do, that *some* women are coerced into sexual submission *some* of the time as a product of inequality, it still holds true that abortion does not increase their abuse. At the very least, abortion enables them to relieve further degrading and potentially life-destroying consequences. For many, it is an act of self-affirmation in the face of victimization and despair.

56. *Griswold v. Connecticut*, at 486.

57. See B. Babcock et al., *Sex Discrimination and the Law* (Boston: Little, Brown, 1975).

58. *Eisenstadt v. Baird*, 405 U.S. 438, 453 (1972) (striking a prohibition on the distribution of contraceptives to single people).

59. This change averted, on a doctrinal level, one of the major feminist concerns

about privacy doctrine—that it would be used offensively to shield familial abuse and rape from state intervention. See K. Powers, "Sex Segregation and the Ambivalent Directions of Sex Discrimination Law," *Wisconsin Law Review* (1979), p. 88. *Bruno v. Codd,* 419 N.Y.S. 2d 901 (1979); *People v. Liberta,* 64 N.Y. 2d 152 (1984); *People v. Stefano,* 121 Misc. 2d 113 (S. Ct. Supp. 1983); *State of Florida v. Rider,* 449 So. 2d 903 (Ct. App. 3d Dist. 1984). See Marcus, "Conjugal Violence: The Law of Force and Face of Violence," *California Law Review* 69 (1981), p. 1657. Nonetheless women continue to face multiple hurdles in obtaining effective state intervention.

60. *Planned Parenthood of Central Missouri v. Danforth,* 420 U.S. 918 (1975). *Scheinberg v. State* invalidated a spousal notification statute only after finding that abortion has no significant impact on a woman's reproductive capacity. 659 F.2d 476, rehearing denied 677 F.2d 931 (5th Cir), on remand 550 F. Supp. 1112. (D. Fla.).

61. See K. Glen, "Abortion in the Courts: A Lay Woman's Guide to the New Disaster Area," *Feminist Studies* 4 (1978), p. 1.

62. Medical indication, even of the gravest dimension, is never a basis for overriding a woman's decision to have a child. Conversely, when a woman's decision not to continue a pregnancy is thwarted, the stress of unwanted pregnancy can create or exacerbate life- and health-threatening risks. See *McRae v. Califano,* 491 F. Supp. 630, 664–690 (E.D.N.Y. 1980), *rev'd sub nom Harris v. McRae,* 448 U.S. 297.

63. *Whalen v. Roe,* 429 U.S. 589 (1977).

64. Although prevailing medical views now support limited regulation, for example, the Court's deference to the expertise of the medical establishment on the need for regulation is troubling. See *City of Akron v. Akron Center for Reproductive Health.*

65. *Thornburgh v. ACOG,* at 2185.

66. An Amicus Curiae Brief by Lynn Paltrow on behalf of the National Abortion Rights Action League (NARAL) filed in *Thornburgh* movingly explores the meaning of abortion in women's lives and suggests greater focus by mainstream abortion rights groups on the feminist arguments for abortion. Brief reprinted in *Women's Rights Law Reporter* 9 (1987), p. 3.

67. However, the Court's recognition of viable fetal life as a constraint upon a woman's decision threatens to subordinate women to medically determined needs of the fetus in abortion, procreation, and employment. See, e.g., authorities listed in note 48; N. Fost, D. Chudwin, and D. Wikler, "The Limited Moral Significance of Fetal Viability," *Hastings Center Report* (December 1980), p. 10; and *City of Akron v. Akron Center for Reproductive Health,* at 452 (O'Connor, dissenting); J. Gallagher, "Prenatal Invasions and Interventions: What's Wrong with Fetal Rights?" *Harvard Women's Law Journal* 10 (1987), p. 9; W. Williams, "Firing the Woman to Protect the Fetus: The Reconciliation of Fetal Protection with Employment Opportunity Goals Under Title VII," *Georgetown Law Journal* 69 (1981), p. 641.

68. See Mackinnon, *Feminism Unmodified;* Eisenstein, *Feminism and Sexual Equality.*

69. Although Carol Gilligan's work understates the significance of autonomy for women, her study of abortion decision making highlights the importance of the

transition from a traditional maternal morality that equates goodness with self-abnegation to a morality that encompasses the responsibility to care for both self and others, in *In a Different Voice* (Cambridge, Mass.: Harvard University Press, 1982), pp. 64–105. Robin West uses the term "individuation" to mean "the right *to be* the sort of creature who might have and then pursue one's 'own' ends," in "Jurisprudence and Gender," *University of Chicago Law Review* 55 (1988), pp. 1, 42.

70. Petchesky, *Abortion and Woman's Choice*, Chapter 1; Eisenstein, *Feminism and Sexual Equality.*
71. See A. Davis, *Race, Sex and Class* (1985); Gordon, *Woman's Body, Woman's Right;* Petchesky, *Abortion and Woman's Choice.*
72. *Eisenstadt v. Baird.*
73. *Carey v. Population Services, Intl.,* 431 U.S. 678, 688 n. 5 (1977).
74. Without detracting from Justice Blackmun's stirring recognition of sex as an aspect of intimate relationship, the protection of consensual sex as an aspect of bodily integrity, autonomy, and intimacy apart from relationship is likewise required.
75. For example, Justice Stewart's dissent in *Griswold* described the prohibition on contraception by describing it as an "uncommonly silly law." Robert Bork denounced that decision as constitutionalizing "gratification," a charge not leveled against economic liberty. Bork, "Neutral Principles." In the same vein, Justice White characterized abortion as a matter of "convenience, whim or caprice," in *Roe v. Wade*, at 221, and the claim to sexual self-determination in *Hardwick*, at 2846, as "facetious."
76. K. Karst, "The Right of Intimate Association," *Yale Law Journal* 89 (1980), p. 624.
77. *Thornburgh v. ACOG*, at 2196.
78. People have a lot less trouble with the idea of noninterference with a person's choice of sexual partners than they do with the idea of gay or lesbian marriage. See, e.g., *Singer v. Hara,* 11 Wn. App 247, 522 P.2d 118F (1974). Similarly, lesbian and gays are frequently accused of "flaunting it" simply because they are expressing affection in public in a way that would be considered sweet or heart-warming if they were heterosexual. The very choice of the descriptor "flaunting it" captures the degree to which the expression of gay or lesbian identity is felt as an attack.
79. *Bowers v. Hardwick,* at 2847 (Burger, concurring).
80. Ibid., at 2846.
81. Ibid., at 2847 (Powell, concurring).
82. See J. Money and A. Ehrhardt, *Man and Woman, Boy and Girl: The Differentiation and Dimorphism of Gender Identity from Conception to Maturity* (Baltimore: Johns Hopkins University Press, 1972); A. Rich, "Compulsory Heterosexuality and Lesbian Existence," Snitow et al., eds., *Powers of Desire,* p. 177; G. Rubin, "The Traffic in Women: Notes on the 'Political Economy' of Sex," in R. Reiter, ed., *Toward an Anthropology of Women* (New York: Monthly Review, 1975), p. 157.
83. Although some lesbians and gay men experience their sexual orientation as determined and immutable, others are very clear that it is a matter of choice. To reduce self-definition to biological, psychological, or cultural determinism as the

medical model does argues for tolerance of the pathetic, not respect for the courageous. Nor does it help people who don't identify as gay to examine sexual hypocrisy or desire in their own lives.

84. Likewise, Adrienne Asch has noted that discrimination against disabled people is fueled by fear of crossing the line into disability. (Private conversation.)

85. *Dronenburg v. Zech*, 741 F.2d 1388, rehearing denied 746 F.2d 1576 (D.C. Cir. 1984). Judge Bork wrote that the disruption from potential sexual solicitation justified the total exclusion of homosexuals from the military.

86. "Even women who had not the slightest inclination to cross the threshold of taboo reaped some benefits in their heterosexual negotiations from the general acknowledgement that lesbianism was not within the realm of the imaginable." Snitow et al., eds., *Powers of Desire*, p. 34.

87. Petchesky, *Abortion and Woman's Choice*.

88. Several state courts have invalidated the cut-off of abortion funds as an invasion of privacy protected under the state constitution and have thus rejected the wholly negative view of privacy adopted by the Supreme Court. See, e.g., *Roe v. Secretary of Administration and Finance*, 382 Mass 629 (1981); *Committee to Defend Reproductive Rights v. Myers*, 29 Cal. 3d 252 (1981); *Right to Choose v. Byrne*, 91 N.J. 287 (1982).

89. *Harris v. McRae*, at 315.

90. *Maher v. Roe*, 432 U.S. 464, at 478 n. 11.

91. Davis, *Race, Sex and Class*; Petchesky, *Abortion and Woman's Choice*.

92. Both *Brown v. Board of Education*, 347 U.S. 483 (1954), and *Roe v. Wade*, perhaps the most significant and controversial civil rights decisions of the current period, were preceded by significant economic and social changes, the exposure of inequities, and the coalescence of widespread acceptance of the need for change. The narrow margin in *Hardwick*, the breadth of the Blackmun dissent, and state court decisions favorable to lesbian/gay rights indicate that social change in regard to sexual self-determination is already under way.

93. For a provocative examination of this dialectic in feminist legal work, see E. Schneider, "The Dialectics of Rights and Politics: Perspectives From the Women's Movement," *N.Y.U. Law Review* 61 (1986), p. 589.

94. This point is nicely developed in Z. Eisenstein, *The Radical Future of Liberal Feminism* (New York: Monthly Review, 1981).

95. In regard to reproductive and sexual autonomy, for example, the Court has refused to recognize that pregnancy-based discrimination is within the constitutional prohibition on sex discrimination. *Geduldig v. Aiello*, 477 U.S. 484 (1974). The Medicaid abortion cases rejected the claims that the state was required to treat abortion and childbirth equally and ignored the argument that the exclusion of abortion is sex discriminatory. And the *Hardwick* majority made clear that moralistic disapproval is an acceptable basis for unequal treatment. While affirmative action is a positive aspect of equality doctrine, it is limited to opening access; it has not addressed the social conditions necessary to enable full equality.

Part 5 —————————————— .
Freedom of Speech and Belief

We conclude this collection with four chapters on the important First Amendment to the Constitution. First Amendment decisions regarding protection for political speech, press autonomy, and personal belief and religious practice have been so important in recent decades that we often forget that, like equal protection entitlements, they are almost entirely a product of the past half-century. During that time, the debate over constitutional protections for freedom has ranged less broadly than in some other areas, but the passions, values, and material impacts generating these debates nevertheless have been considerable. These four chapters not only cover a broad range of First Amendment issues but also represent an unusual mix of diverse and even antagonistic critical perspectives regarding the nature of these basic liberties.

The first chapter in this section, by Donald A. Downs, presents a brief historical overview of evolving constitutional protections for critical public discourse. He shows that the liberal doctrines emerging in the 1960s removed the exclusionary biases against leftist social critics that had prevailed in earlier decades but at the same time extended greater protection to symbolic assaults on women and members of racial, ethnic, and religious groups. Downs thus offers the provocative argument that traditional liberal concerns for personal dignity and equality justify a postmodern liberal doctrine excluding racist, sexist, and other forms of harmful speech from constitutional protection. Roger A. Simpson also begins from a critical unease with prevailing liberal constructions of protection for press freedom, but his argument advances in directions quite different from that of Downs. Focusing on the ways in which evolving Court doctrine has supported the antipluralistic biases of an oligopolistic, corporatized mass media industry, Simpson contends that prevailing libel doctrine is in need of reforms encouraging greater tolerance toward diverse forms of citizen participation and contentious public debate. John S. Shockley displays a parallel concern for expanding citizen participation in his critical analysis of Court decisions that have undone legislative reforms aiming to restrict the influence of money in public elections.

315

He combines philosophical argument and empirical evidence to support his plea for new judicial policies affirming restrictions on both campaign contributions and expenditures to assure a more level playing field in competition for public office. Finally, Ronald Kahn scrutinizes another highly controversial area of First Amendment rights—that concerning freedom of religious practice and separation of church and state. Building upon rigorous classification schemes for both doctrinal issues and voting blocs among justices on the Court, Kahn identifies a complex array of tensions between "rights" and "process" themes, which betray recent attempts to develop consistent and compelling understandings of these important issues in our modern interdependent society.

12 ——— ·
Beyond Modernist Liberalism: Toward a Reconstruction of Free Speech Doctrine

DONALD A. DOWNS

Most contemporary theorists have either propounded different "core values" of free speech (e.g., individual liberty, self-realization, the attainment of truth, political participation, self-government, and distrust of government) or have come to the conclusion that no single core value exists under the Constitution.[1] But it is fair to say that, in a general sense, the First Amendment now embraces an individualist liberal theory of the right to freedom of speech that reflects a more general liberal theory. In essence, modern liberal political theory stresses individualism and a concomitant state neutrality concerning individual choice, preference, and thought in civil society. Liberal theory also extols the value of "neutral principles" in adjudication.[2] Similarly, the modern doctrine of free speech (particularly pertaining to speech about public issues in the public forum) is based on the "content neutrality" and "anti–viewpoint discrimination" rules, which stipulate that speech may not be abridged on account of its viewpoint or out of a fear of its possible indirect communicative effects. In other words, government may not abridge speech either because it does not like the message or because it harbors an unsubstantiated fear that the message may lead to harmful actions if accepted by listeners.[3]

This chapter will deal with questions concerning these liberal notions of free speech that have arisen in recent years. The eruption of disputes in the 1980s about pornography and obscenity, extremist "hate-group" demonstrations, and even libel have challenged the contemporary regime of First Amendment law. I will argue that we should reconsider the excessively individualistic liberal doctrine of speech articulated today by the Supreme Court without forsaking certain important liberal principles that are part of a broader liberal tradition and that are conducive to a just polity. The liberal tradition is not encapsulated by the brand of individualism that underlies modern First Amendment law. As seen in some key Supreme Court cases and in the theories of such earlier liberals as Jeremy Bentham, John Stuart Mill, and John Dewey, the liberal tradition also includes room for such norms as community, pluralism, equal respect, civility, and state action to achieve the good life. If liberal free speech adjudication were to embrace these norms along with a more responsible notion of individualism, a more propitious balance of social interests could be achieved.[4] Such a balance would constitute a modified form of liberalism, as presently understood in First Amendment doctrines. I will argue, however, that this reform should be somewhat limited in regard to the First Amendment because speech is a special realm of social action in which state neutrality is presumptively more valid than in other areas of social life.

I will begin by outlining the evolution of modern liberal free speech doctrine in the direction of individualism and then briefly discussing major critiques of this liberal position from the Left and the Right. I will then develop and apply an alternative approach that constitutes a modified form of liberalism. I will presume the validity of a general liberal interpretation of free speech, but will argue that there are principled limits disallowed by the modern liberal approach that are nevertheless consistent with broader liberal principles and other forms of a just society.

THE EVOLUTION OF FREE SPEECH DOCTRINE

Historical perspective beckons one to be wary of proposing any reform to the modern doctrine of speech. This doctrine emerged only after a long struggle with censorious forces that were aimed primarily at the Left. It originated in the later World War I cases arising under the Espionage Act, which made it a crime to attempt to obstruct the nation's war effort. Before this time, free speech did not really enjoy a special constitutional status. The state's power to punish threatening and potentially disruptive speech was more or less taken for granted, as was the legitimacy of a predominant social consensus and morality.[5] For example, although criticism of the government is a core modern First Amendment value, federal courts (including circuit courts with Supreme Court judges presiding) consistently upheld the 1798 Sedition Act (the part of the Alien and Sedition Acts dealing with speech), which had been designed by federalists to stifle criticism of the federalist administration. The act made it a crime to "write, print, or publish . . . any false, scandalous and malicious writings against the government of the United States, or either House of Congress . . . or the President of the United States with the intent to defame . . . or to bring them into contempt or disrepute."[6] Furthermore, during the nineteenth century, abolitionists, critics of government policy concerning the Civil War, and immigrants and laborers who deviated from social norms all encountered discrimination and censorship, especially by private censors often acting as mobs.[7] Moreover, although the Constitution and the Bill of Rights were premised on the "rights of man," the modern notion of the individual replete with bundles of rights and a distinct personality (the modern "self") had not yet taken hold in the social, political, and legal worlds.[8] Legal authorities had not yet envisioned a special sphere of public speech that should enjoy substantially greater tolerance and forebearance than the realm of actions.

THE PRELIBERAL ERA: THE REIGN OF THE BAD-TENDENCY TEST

In the first stage of Supreme Court cases under the Espionage Act dealing with First Amendment defenses (1919), Justice Oliver Wendell Holmes treated mere advocacies of resistance to the draft as simple criminal attempts rather than as speech acts distinct from actions. Although Holmes stated that such speech must pose a "clear and present danger" to the state interest before it could be abridged, he found such danger despite the absence of specific evidence of imminent harm. The mere "tendency" of speech to lead to harmful results was enough, in his mind, to constitute clear and present danger.[9] This unprotective "bad-tendency" approach sanctioned widespread convictions under the Espionage Act, especially against criticisms couched in leftist terms. (The fear of bolshevism and similar movements augmented the incentive to censor, and more than one type of fear animated censorious efforts.) By the end of its reign in this period, the Espionage Act had generated over 2,000 convictions, including that of Socialist party leader Eugene Debs for delivering an antiwar speech to a large audience at a park.

Holmes was a transitional figure in the development of the modern doctrine of free speech. In his previous judicial decisions and in his first free speech decisions, he espoused an "assimilationist" approach to law, which holds that law should embody the standards and values of the dominant class and that citizens should be assimilated to these values.[10] But after these initial cases, in late 1919 Holmes began to develop a more liberal viewpoint in reaction to the growth of state repression of dissent from the Left. In key dissenting opinions he proposed a tighter doctrine of what constitutes a clear and present danger. Under the new doctrine, he emphasized the need to demonstrate immediate harm to the state, to distinguish speech from action, and to enlist a tolerance principle based on the marketplace-of-ideas principle (i.e., given the fallibility of judgment and knowledge, the best method of arriving at public policy is the unfettered exchange of ideas in the marketplace of opinion).[11] Holmes's maturation as a First Amendment theorist and his concomitant distrust of the "red scare" tactics of government in the 1920s (which included the infamous Palmer Raids against leftists suspected of Communist ties) drove him in a libertarian direction. It was also within this context that Justice Louis Brandeis further developed the modern doctrine of speech (usually from a dissenting position), culminating in his "concurrence" in *Whitney v. California* in 1927.

Whitney dealt with the constitutionality of California's criminal syndicalism law, which was designed to punish organizations—whether anarchist, political, or labor—that advocated overthrow of the government; many states had passed similar laws earlier in the twentieth century. Brandeis's opinion (which was really a de facto dissent) articulated an incitement test that was very close to the modern protective standard and presented theoretical rationales for bestowing a special tolerance upon political and public speech. Brandeis proclaimed that speech advocating social change and even disorder should be punished only if it intentionally threatened immediate and significant social harm (if it were a direct incitement).[12] He also tied the free speech right to the pursuit of truth, political participation by the citizenry, and the individual's self-development. This latter value laid the groundwork for the eventual emergence of the subjective, individualistic self as a basis of First Amendment rights. Holmes's and Brandeis's doctrines applied only to political speech, however; they did not question the validity of abridging such forms of expression as libel, obscenity, offensive speech, and fighting words, which had historically been considered outside of the First Amendment's parameters.

Brandeis's position on political speech gained limited adherence by the majority of the Court in several cases in the 1930s. But with the advent of McCarthyism and the fear of international communism in the early 1950s, the Court retreated to the bad-tendency logic in cases dealing with federal prosecutions of Communists. The Court upheld federal convictions of leaders of the Communist party under the Smith Act's provisions against advocating, or organizing to achieve, overthrow of the government (*Dennis v. U.S.,* 1951).[13] Although international communism was an organizational reality that the government was obligated to investigate, the government's case in *Dennis* lacked specific evidence of conspiracy, and no real clear and present danger existed. By the late 1950s, however, the Court modified its interpretation of the Smith Act and overturned convictions of low-level Communist party members under that act.[14] With the advent of the civil rights movement in the next decade, the Warren Court was poised to construct a more liberal doctrine in the area of advocacy of social change as well as in other domains of expression. Nonetheless, the history of the Court's movement toward the modern liberal doctrine reveals the potential precariousness of free political speech.

THE EMERGENCE OF LIBERALISM

The Early Stage

The cases involving the clear and present danger debate discussed above encompass the most important types of speech: speech about public and social issues and politics. In another line of constitutional development dealing with other types of speech, the Court traditionally afforded less constitutional protection. In a 1942 case, *Chaplinsky v. New Hampshire,* the

Court developed a two-level approach to free speech adjudication that has coexisted with the development of case law governing political speech and advocacy of action threatening the social and political order. According to this approach, although the state may not abridge such protected classes of speech as political speech unless it demonstrates the presence of a clear and present danger, it may abridge certain other forms of speech without this showing because not all classes of speech are covered by the First Amendment in the first place. *Chaplinsky* dealt specifically with punishment for "fighting words" (a Jehovah's Witness follower had been convicted for calling a policeman a "God damned racketeer" and a "damned Fascist"), but it also established a broader normative approach to speech that dealt with other forms of "excluded" expression. In *Chaplinsky* the Court held that:

> There are certain well-defined and narrowly limited classes of speech, the prevention and punishment of which have never been thought to raise any Constitutional problem. These include the lewd and obscene, the profane, the libelous, and the insulting or "fighting" words—those which by their very utterance inflict injury or tend to incite an immediate breach of the peace. Such utterances are no essential part of any exposition of ideas, and are of such slight social value as a step to truth that any benefit that may be derived from them is clearly outweighed by the social interest in order and morality.[15]

The two-level approach held that such forms of expression as obscenity (technically, later defined as sexually explicit material that offends community standards of decency by appealing to prurient interest, describes or depicts ultimate sex acts in a patently offensive way, and lacks serious scientific, literary, artistic, or political value),[16] fighting words (verbally assaultive speech), libel, and patently offensive speech are not protected by the First Amendment because they cause social harms, they are not part of the rational inquiry into truth, and they lack social value. *Chaplinsky* had two thrusts. While its moralistic underpinnings provided a basis for an assimilationist approach to free speech law, its emphasis on the value of civility also supported a more progressive approach to law—what Robert Post calls a "cultural pluralist" approach. The pluralist approach posits modest restraints on freedom of expression in order to promote the values of group and individual integrity, dignity, and respect. These values allegedly aim to foster less hostile group interaction in a pluralistic polity that is inherently subject to racial and ethnic strife and group conflict. Accordingly, limits on racial vilification in certain contexts may serve to reconcile free speech values with nonassimilationist, progressive, communitarian values. According to Post,

> If assimilationist law attempts to unify society around the cultural values of a single dominant group, pluralist law attempts to create ground rules by which diverse and potentially competitive groups can retain their distinct identities and yet continue to coexist. These

ground rules can range from the requirement of state neutrality respecting conflicting religions, to the enforcement of norms of mutual respect.[17]

In this sense, then, the understanding of civility and fighting words upheld in *Chaplinsky* may be construed in terms of pluralist communitarian values, not assimilationist law. By upholding norms of basic civility and equal respect in the otherwise wide-open public forum of speech, it is assumed that the polity may take at least modest affirmative steps to temper intergroup strife, thereby making it less difficult to achieve social justice. Thus, a progressive interpretation of the First Amendment would distinguish the assimilationist (closed community) and the pluralistic (open but civil community) possibilities of *Chaplinsky*.

During the first stage of free speech doctrine, from 1919 to the early 1960s, in which the political speech doctrine slowly emerged in cases that dealt with the clear-and-present-danger issue, few legal minds seriously questioned the traditional exceptions to free speech articulated in *Chaplinsky*. The key struggle involved carving out a realm of protection for robust political speech (although, as I have shown, this doctrine did not protect the Left when established authorities felt threatened by radicalism). But *Chaplinsky's* normative assumptions about restraints on other forms of speech—defamation, obscenity, fighting words, and so on—still prevailed.[18]

The Modern Liberal Stage: 1960s–1970s

The second stage of free speech jurisprudence emerged in the 1960s and 1970s. While thinkers and jurists in the first stage were preoccupied with the question of "how much" speech should be protected, theorists in the second stage (like many thinkers of that era) assumed that the more freedom from restraint, the better. In responding to the claims of civil rights activists, antiwar protesters, and other activists in this period, the Supreme Court went beyond anything envisioned by Holmes (or treated by Brandeis in only an embryonic fashion) and extended the liberal doctrine to the sphere of individual choice and morality. "From this secure core, arguments in the current phase of free speech theory have centered around the broadening of the first amendment."[19] The broadening emphasized stronger protection of speech impinging on politics and social issues,[20] as well as greater tolerance of other forms of expression never before considered protected by the First Amendment: the categories excluded by *Chaplinsky* as well as commercial advertising, campaign contributions, nude dancing, and pornography.[21]

This movement was predicated on two motives: (1) to fashion a more protective standard of speech (the content-neutrality and anti–viewpoint discrimination doctrines) in order to democratize the marketplace of ideas; and (2) to change the focus from a pluralistic notion of law to an individualistic concept in which the individual's right to express himself or herself is paramount to other social ends.[22] According to this concept, the rights of the speaker are paramount to the norms of civility and intergroup respect, and public standards of equal respect and value are downplayed in favor of the subjective individual's own personal construction of the good. (This principle reflects what philosophers call "emotivism," or "the doctrine that all evaluative judgments, and more specifically, all moral judgments are *nothing but* expressions of preference, expressions of attitude or feeling, insofar as they are moral or evaluative in character.")[23] One First Amendment case epitomizes this development from objective to subjective morality in the domain governed by *Chaplinsky*. In 1971, in *Cohen v. California,* the Supreme Court in one stroke undermined *Chaplinsky's* normative assumptions concerning civility and objective standards of conduct. The Court overturned Cohen's conviction (on charges of disturbing the peace) for walking in a courthouse wearing a jacket with the words "Fuck the Draft" written on its back. In so holding, the Court ruled that society no longer had a moral basis for punishing offensive speech and that the very notion of uncivil and fighting words was essentially meaningless except in very narrow face-to-face encounters. The Court's logic epitomizes the morality and epistemology of individualistic liberalism:

> That the air may at times seem filled with verbal cacophony is, in this sense, not a sign of weakness, but of strength. . . . How is one to distinguish this from any other offensive word [emblem]? . . . No readily ascertainable general principle exists [to so distinguish]. . . . *It is nevertheless often true that one man's vulgarity is another's lyric.* Indeed, we think it is largely because governmental officials cannot make principled distinctions in this area that the Constitution leaves matters of taste and style so largely to the individual.[24]

Although the specific result in *Cohen* is defensible on grounds of political speech, the broader implications of its emotivist underpinnings raise problems in other contexts, as we will see later in this chapter. In essence, *Cohen* undermined the tenets of a pluralistic communitarian concept of law in the public forum.

In the other line of constitutional development (the clear-and-present-danger line dealing with advocacy of disorder and illegal action), the Supreme Court also moved in a decidedly liberal direction in the 1960s, culminating in the establishment of the definitive-incitement test in 1969. In *Brandenburg v. Ohio,* a case dealing with racialist speech by a Ku Klux Klan group advocating race war, the Court propounded the new test: Speech about public issues may not be abridged unless it *directly incites imminent and significant social harm or violation of the law.*[25] The *Brandenburg* test is very protective of speech on both the Left and the Right. Only immediate danger specifically triggered by the speech at hand is punishable; since such demonstration is seldom possible, potentially dangerous speech enjoys unprecedented freedom under this standard.

Along with the decisions in *Brandenburg* and *Cohen*, the Court also developed other more liberal doctrines governing speech in the 1960s and 1970s. In a long series of cases dealing with public protest in *Cohen*'s wake, the Court virtually eliminated the concept of fighting words unless they involved a captive audience, and eliminated the notion of offensive speech except in special contexts.[26] The Court moved in this direction because it did not want "heckler's vetoes" (unjustified hostile crowd reactions) to abridge the freedom of protest speech during the civil rights movement. This protection is considered to be at its peak when the speech takes place in the "public forum," which is a specially designated area (a traditional arena such as a park, streetcorner, sidewalk, or similar public area) of uninhibited free speech.[27] The Court also granted unprecedented protection for the libel of public officials in political discussion; such libel must be made with "actual malice" in order to be held compensable.[28] And during the 1960s, the Court developed considerably more liberal obscenity standards that allowed the availability of pornography and sexual materials to proliferate. Ostensibly more restrictive decisions in the 1970s have not really changed the protected status of most sexually explicit material.[29] Finally, the Court began to protect forms of commercial expression, which it had previously placed outside of the First Amendment's protective umbrella.[30] Thus, by the end of the 1970s, the Court's overall First Amendment approach (the political public speech doctrine as well as *Chaplinsky*'s two-level doctrine) was predominantly liberal and individualistic: Individual choice prevailed unless a direct harm to society was posed.

Brandenburg's doctrine comports with Mill's libertarian doctrine of individual autonomy and Justice Holmes's doctrine of the marketplace of ideas. According to Holmes, in matters of speech (as opposed to actions) about public issues, decisions about the appropriateness of the message are to be left to individuals or groups in the marketplace. Only when speech triggers immediate illegal action or other harm can it be abridged.[31] The Supreme Court's approach to freedom of speech under the First Amendment is the most liberal and individualistic of all areas of constitutional law.[32] In many respects, this approach embodies a worthy ethic. According to Lee Bollinger, the liberal approach to speech has established a special, even extraordinary, realm of tolerance and liberty that contrasts with other realms in society. This realm contributes to a healthy polity because it fosters a more responsible civic character: "At this stage in our social history, then, free speech involves a special act of carving out one area of social interaction for extraordinary self-restraint, the purpose of which is to develop and demonstrate a social capacity to control feelings evoked by a host of social encounters."[33]

This liberal approach to political speech is based on principle as well as on practical historical experience. In terms of principle, it is based on a belief in individual and group liberty and a concomitant distrust of state paternalism. Bollinger offers a further theoretical basis: By restraining passion and the natural inclination to censor, the liberal tolerance principle engenders such republican virtues as self-control, a sense of personal enlargement, and the capacity for introspection and thought—in short, a "dialectic of tolerance."[34] These values correspond to the historical movement away from an assimilationist society governed by fixed standards and a mechanical morality. (Indeed, some argue that the capacity for philosophy arises in the context of the decline of social cohesion.)[35] In terms of practical experience, the liberal approach to free speech is based on a recognition that different, nonliberal approaches have resulted in unjustified government restrictions of speech in the name of conformity, repression, or undue apprehension of harm or disorder.

The Third Stage: Dispute and Postmodern Liberalism

Frederick Schauer posits a third stage of free speech development, which he calls the "reemergence of theory." In this stage, thinkers ask *why* speech should be broadened.[36] The first wave of theorists in the 1970s were predominantly libertarian. In matters of speech, they agreed with the logic of *Cohen.* They sought justifications for liberal interpretations of constitutional values in all areas of civil liberty, including speech. This form of legal theorizing constituted something new in the history of constitutional theory; it marked a merging of high-level deontological (pertaining to moral obligation), individualistic moral theory with constitutional theory.[37]

But the theoretical revolution has not been one-sided. The liberal interpretation of the Constitution and of the First Amendment triggered critical perspectives from both the Left and the Right questioning liberal (especially individualist) theory in general and liberal perspectives on free speech in particular.[38] These higher theoretical critiques have been accompanied by broader social movements in the 1980s.

Critiques from the Left emphasize equality, solidarity, power, and substantive justice over the abstract individualism and neutral principles of the modern liberal model of justice. Some leftist theorists (like the Critical Legal Studies scholars centered at Harvard Law School) argue that neutral principles are a sham, that at best they lack logical coherence, substance, and historical reality or, at worst, that they disguise the reality of social inequality and the lack of substantive justice.[39] Other leftists, such as Michael Sandel and Roberto Unger, have criticized the liberal emphasis on abstract individualism for not dealing adequately with the need for community, solidarity, and empowerment.[40] In a related yet different vein, "progressives," or Left liberal critics of neutral principles, have maintained that abstract liberal individualism and state neutrality doctrine should be abandoned in favor of an affirmative action approach to constitutional law (especially in the area of equal protection analysis) because of the reality of group-based inequality in American society. Owen Fiss, for example, has argued for a "group advantaging" principle in equal protection analysis.[41] These critiques (Left radical and Left liberal) of liberal individualism and neutral principles also apply to the First Amendment.

In 1969, Herbert Marcuse presented the most radical representative leftist critique of liberal legal neutrality and tolerance concerning speech to yet appear. Marcuse claimed that tolerance was actually "repressive" because it simply leaves the status quo intact and ignores the actual unequal distribution of power in society. Marcuse endorsed what he called "progressive censorship" in order to reorient society along progressive lines.[42] In the antipornography politics of the 1980s, radical feminist Catherine MacKinnon would pick up where Marcuse left off regarding the liberal doctrine of free speech.

Theorists on the Right have criticized liberalism in a surprisingly similar, if in a more moralistic, assimilationist fashion for lacking substantive values and standards, for comprising, in the words of Richard John Neuhaus, a "naked public square" that is devoid of moral meaning and guidance.[43] *Cohen v. California*'s logic embodies emotivism, which theorists like Alasdair MacIntyre claim cannot provide the basis for developing character and virtue; at its worst, emotivism is a hollow shell that cloaks nihilism.[44] Critics like Neuhaus and MacIntyre espouse a return to more traditional bases of moral judgment, community, and development of character. Neuhaus states that it is time to move from the "autonomous" self to the "authoritative" self linked to a community of character.[45]

Another recent critique of liberal public philosophy should be mentioned. In *The Closing of the American Mind,* Alan Bloom provides a counter to Bollinger's powerful tolerance thesis (even though he does not mention Bollinger at all).[46] Bloom's thesis is the antithesis of Bollinger's. According to Bloom, tolerance in America, ironically, is the sign of a *closed* mind, not an open mind, because we no longer tolerate authoritative standards. In sharp contrast to Bollinger, Bloom maintains that the contemporary context of thoughtless individualism has made tolerance a matter of conformity and ethical-intellectual complacency rather than the dynamic, virtuous self-restraint and pursuit of truth envisioned by champions of liberalism. Tolerance, he asserts, enhances individuals and society only within the context of a common good or cultural horizon that makes the act of tolerance an effort and that bestows qualitative standards upon judgment. Tolerance should be authoritative and discriminatory, not weak minded.[47]

These philosophical critiques were paralleled by social events in the late 1970s and early 1980s. In the late 1970s, a nationally prominent case arose that brought the liberal doctrine of political speech into question. In the *Skokie* controversy, a band of Nazis in the Chicago area wanted to hold a pro-Nazi, white power demonstration (replete with uniforms and swastika display) at the village hall of Skokie, a town in which many holocaust survivors lived. The village sought to keep the Nazi party out of town in order to protect the survivors from the significant emotional harm that such a rally might inflict. But the courts, relying strongly on the content neutrality doctrine, *Cohen v. California,* the doctrine of the public forum, and other liberal precedents in both the *Brandenburg* and *Chaplinsky* lines of cases, decided in favor of the Nazis' rights.[48] *Skokie* generated significant controversy and spawned a number of defenses and critiques of the liberal doctrine.[49] Bollinger's articulation of the tolerance principle centers on *Skokie* because of its importance as a symbol of the commitment to free political speech and tolerance.

The 1980s have also witnessed discontent with the modern liberal doctrine of justice. Certainly the rise of Ronald Reagan, the New Right, and a more aggressive American conservatism has signaled a move in this direction, at least concerning social issues.[50] The renewed mobilization by conservative forces against pornography and obscenity in the 1980s is also a major aspect of this shift in the social environment. And although the activist elements of the American Left sometimes seem to be in disarray, an influential feminist leftist critique of the liberal doctrine has emerged within the context of the pornography controversy. In liberal Minneapolis and conservative Indianapolis, city councils adopted an antipornography ordinance written by radical feminist activists Catherine MacKinnon and Andrea Dworkin. The ordinance defines pornography differently from obscenity (its authors held that obscenity law was ineffective and biased against women): Pornography is the sexually explicit subordination of women in pictures or in words.[51] This definition alleges a link between pornography and harmful actions against women (in particular, violence, subordination, and discrimination). The purpose of the ordinance was to limit pornography in order to gain respect for women and empower them in society. MacKinnon, whose social theory is based on a "dominance approach,"[52] understands her theory to be decidedly antiliberal in that it rejects modern liberalism's emphasis on individualism and state neutrality. She disdains the liberal approach to freedom of speech for largely Marcusan reasons—because it fails to deal with the unequal distributions of power along gender lines in society:

> The liberal view is that abstract categories—speech or equality—define systems. Every time you strengthen free speech in one place, you strengthen it elsewhere. . . .
>
> In this view, the problem with neutrality as the definition of principle in constitutional adjudication is its equation of substantive powerlessness with substantive power and treating these the same.[53]

THE QUESTION OF LIMITS: MODIFIED LIBERALISM

The *Skokie* case, the pornography controversy, and the theoretical critiques discussed above occasion a reconsideration of the liberal doctrine of speech as presently understood. A reconsideration should deal with the key *Branden-*

burg and *Chaplinsky* prongs of the First Amendment and should consider
how far Bollinger's tolerance principle should apply in the public forum. To
extrapolate from the critics, should we reject the tolerance principle altogether as a public philosophy, or should we seek to balance it with other
important values?

It would be irresponsible, on the one hand, to do away wholly with
the modernist liberal doctrine, at least in the area of public and political
speech. On the other hand, the liberal doctrine has been applied in such an
individualistic fashion that it disregards the broader communal context of
individualism as epitomized by *Cohen*. An orientation that preserves the standards of state neutrality and tolerance, while also acknowledging the less
individualistic values of the progressive community and civility, would provide a more propitious balance of social interests and values.[54] On the concrete level, the harms caused by targeted hate-group speech (as in *Skokie*) and
other forms of assaultive expression (perhaps including violent pornography)
can be substantial enough to outweigh the value of free speech. Liberals like
Bollinger make excellent arguments for a strong right to free speech, but they
do not deal adequately with concrete cases of delimitation.[55] On a more theoretical level, the extreme individualistic liberal approach does not adequately
account for the claims of civility and justice. As the doctrine's critics (on both
the Left and the Right) claim, it downplays certain valid substantive norms
that enhance social and individual life. As stated above, however, a liberal
approach need not be confined to purely individualistic dimensions (as expressed in *Cohen*). Thus, the problem is the particular form of liberalism
asserted in the modern doctrine of free speech.

Rather than accepting the more extreme critiques of the Left and the
Right, I propose a delimitation consistent with the polity of liberal cultural
pluralism discussed by Post and others. This approach would maintain the
norm of state neutrality concerning the viewpoint of speech but would allow
more concern for the civility of discourse in certain contexts. As long as the
norm of civility were applied to all viewpoints, viewpoint discrimination
would be avoided.

Rejecting liberalism in toto would be problematic in many respects.
One reason for accepting basic liberal assumptions in the area of free speech
is somewhat fatalistic: As long as we live in a society deeply ingrained in
liberalism and individualism, we have little realistic choice but to construct a
normative life that accommodates these values to some sufficient extent.[56]
This project entails making liberalism more consistent with its own admittedly problematic ideals of autonomy, dignity, and equality, given that
ideals in any regime possess negative potential. It also means resurrecting the
more communitarian values that historically accompanied liberalism but have
been downplayed by contemporary free speech doctrine. From this perspective, the polity has an obligation to establish at least minimal standards of
civility in the public forum in order to protect the basic integrity of individ-

uals and the interaction of groups. In addition, one of the basic purposes of the state and liberalism's social contract is to promote a sense of security in citizens so that they may pursue their ends and engage in speech and action without undue intimidation.[57] This sense of security may also contribute (however modestly) to equality in two ways. First, it would give legal authority to basic norms of civility that promote equal respect, as law is a teacher of values to some extent. Second, intimidation has been deployed throughout history to thwart egalitarian social change; people who feel threatened are less likely to enter the public arena and advocate change. Protecting citizens from malicious verbal assaults and emotional intimidation fosters the sense of trust that makes possible a more open politics.[58]

But this state purpose, in turn, should be limited in modern times for several reasons. To begin with, we cannot (and should not) return to the traditional notion of a unified (assimilationist) moral community in our relatively open society committed to essential governmental noninterference with the freedom of choice and the flow of knowledge. More important, there are positive reasons for accepting the basic liberal argument against viewpoint discrimination even as we seek to reconstruct liberalism. First, a special realm of freedom for speech (especially political speech) is essential to constitutional democracy. As Alexander Meiklejohn has shown, the very process of self-government requires that political discussion and debate be as wide open as is responsibly feasible.[59] Furthermore, Bollinger's thesis is persuasive up to a point. Learning to tolerate (legally, not morally) extremist speech and to distinguish speech from action can indeed engender self-control, maturity, enlargement, and political astuteness and understanding—qualities that nurture a responsible and active polity capable of responsible change in a complex world.[60] At Skokie, for example, the confrontation with the Nazis created a community of discourse and action based on renewed awareness of the evil of Nazis and political extremism.

In addition, there are more negative justifications for accepting a basic liberal doctrine governing public and political speech, especially its anti–viewpoint discrimination prong. Even if positive benefits do not always follow in the wake of free speech, it is a necessary if not sufficient condition for democratic freedom. Free speech may not guarantee justice, but a just democratic order is impossible without free speech about political issues.[61] In a related sense, free speech about political matters is necessary because we cannot trust the government to censor political speech in a principled manner.[62] The long experience with the repressive effects of the bad-tendency test counsels support of the liberal doctrine articulated in *Brandenburg*. In a related vein, those who wish to modify the liberal approach (especially the anti–viewpoint discrimination doctrine) assume a significant risk, for they cannot guarantee that forces sympathetic to them will assume the power to enforce free speech policy. This is especially the case with progressive movements if, as Marcuse maintains, society is nonprogressive in the first place. Thus, in

Indianapolis, overwhelmingly conservative forces would have implemented the putatively progressive antipornography ordinance had the federal courts not struck it down—a paradox that was not lost on some feminist critics of the ordinance.[63] This issue is analogous to the historical establishment of liberalism: Competing groups accepted a relatively neutral state based on consent of the governed because no single group possessed enough power to capture the state for its own purposes. In Roberto Unger's terms, they settled on liberalism's relatively neutral system of law and governance in order to salvage some benefit from a bad situation.[64]

Finally, the acceptance of liberalism in the area of free speech does not mean that we must accept it in other domains of society. Many other arenas of society and law are less than fully liberal today, including political economy (where state action is rampant); tort law (where a "fiduciary ethic" of care is more prominent than a liberal ethic of individual liberty, responsibility, and risk taking); and administrative law (which acknowledges the need to balance liberty with such social norms as efficiency and economic security).[65] As Bollinger stresses, free speech constitutes a special realm of "extraordinary" freedom and tolerance that does not prevail in other social realms. Thus, one may endorse the general liberal doctrine of content neutrality without being obliged to support state neutrality in other realms of society. Because modern society is characterized by a pluralism of realms, such a nonmonolithic approach may be congruent with social structure.[66]

Thus, we must accept the essential tenets of the liberal doctrine in the area of political speech, especially in terms of government neutrality. In fact, few serious thinkers endorse abandonment of the principle of free speech that is prevalent today. But these points merely justify accepting an essentially free speech in the domain of politics; they do not provide a basis for establishing the boundaries of that domain or for extending it to other realms of expression.

Thus, I am arguing for a modification of the liberal doctrine of free speech as it has been crafted by the Supreme Court. While accepting the importance of a special realm of freedom of speech in political life, I contend that this realm would be more responsible and ultimately more democratic if it were limited by a normative concern for basic civility. In essence, reform should focus on the excessive individualism of the contemporary doctrine, not the anti–viewpoint discrimination standard, as that emphasis has blinded the courts to certain harms perpetrated by uncivil speech. Patently uncivil and intimidating speech conflicts, in principle and in effect, with the democratic values of equal respect and opportunity and harms the integrity of individuals and groups in the political process of cultural pluralism. Constitutionally, this concern entails a return to *Chaplinsky*'s basic logic governing civility and rationality but tempers *Chaplinsky*'s assimilationist values with more progressive democratic principles. In terms of cases like *Skokie*, this approach would mean resurrecting the more traditional doctrine of fighting words. However, my proposal would not affect the *Brandenburg* doctrine. *Brandenburg* concerns the advocacy of unlawful or harmful action, not the direct infliction of verbal injury. Although such advocacy may be irrational in its content, the danger or harm it threatens is only a potential one, and its effects may be countered by other voices in the public forum.

Furthermore, a movement away from *Brandenburg* in the area of advocacy would amount to a return to the early bad-tendency test, which would offer no viable protection for free speech in controversial times. So we will have to distinguish cases of advocacy from cases of direct infliction of intimidation. This distinction would also prevent us from adopting a "group libel" logic in which speech that defamed groups (especially on grounds of race or ethnicity) is abridgeable. While group libel may indeed harm the corporate esteem of groups (and individuals in groups) as well as the integrity of the political process, it does not constitute a direct intimidation. Unfortunately, allowing its abridgement would pull us back to bad-tendency logic, which a free and open polity must reject. In this respect, my position differs from that of Robert Post, who favors laws against group libel in the name of pluralist values.[67] In terms of pornography, I propose another approach that would involve a new First Amendment exception for violent forms of pornography. In the area of libel of public officials, however, the Court's adoption of the malice test in 1964 (*New York Times v. Sullivan*)[68] should not be abandoned. *Sullivan* dealt directly with the most important form of political speech, speech that critically evaluates governmental actors and action. In the process of such speech and debate, honest error is a natural by-product. Thus, even though libel, per se, is not conducive to the normative and political ends asserted in *Chaplinsky*, libel of public officials must be allowed to some sufficient extent in the interests of ensuring freedom of political speech.[69] However, *Sullivan* draws a line that is consistent with minimal norms of civility as well as the free speech principle: Libel of public officials made *with actual malice* (i.e., libel made intentionally or with reckless disregard of the truth) is not protected. So *Sullivan*'s modification of *Chaplinsky* is consistent with a principled balance between liberty and such values as equal respect and opportunity, the integrity of cultural pluralism, and the integrity of individuals. But the evisceration of the fighting-words doctrine is a different story.

CIVILITY AND SPEECH IN A POSTLIBERAL POLITY

DEMOCRATIC THEORY

According to Bollinger, the act of tolerance engenders self-restraint at the same time as it broadens one's political horizon. This theory is similar to Meiklejohn's classic theory of free speech and self-government. But Meiklejohn's theory is more complex in its treatment of these values, for his argument encompasses self-control on the part of speakers as well as the government.[70] Bollinger's theory concerns the beneficial effects of tolerance on the recipients of the message (government and other listeners). These effects are very important, as restraint of unreflective impulses is a deep constitutional value.[71] But civility and restraint should be expected of speakers as well as of the government and listeners. Bollinger's thesis and the Supreme Court's evisceration of the fighting-words doctrine treat civil society and government too dichotomously: Government (and other targets of speech) must act with restraint, but speakers need not do so as long as they do not engage in or incite unlawful actions.[72] Yet if speakers are to be fit for the character of self-government that Bollinger celebrates (and if the system is to live up to its democratic promises), must not they, too, abide by at least minimal norms of self-restraint and civility? By treating speakers and nonspeakers too differently, the law ironically treats speakers as morally less responsible than others. To be sure, in a liberal democracy the government must be restrained by the norms of civility more fully than individuals in the private sphere. Government is all-powerful, and it is supposed to be the representative of the people. But even so, speakers should not be immune from at least minimal norms of civility that promote the integrity of democratic and pluralist values.

Civility entails both political and personal attributes, such as treating others with due respect; respecting manners (manners themselves being forms of self-control and involving the maintenance of a respectful distance from others in public life);[73] and engaging in political affairs as a form of responsible citizenship. From this perspective, civility contributes to the very virtues of self-control and enlargement that Bollinger places at the heart of tolerance. Rather than representing regressive "assimilationist" values, civility can promote the sense of respect and security that enables individuals and groups in a largely open society to pursue their ends and to engage in public life. Interestingly, by holding speakers in civil society more accountable to the norms of civility, the dialectic of tolerance that Bollinger espouses might be strengthened, for civility and tolerance depend upon similar virtues of character.[74]

HARM AND BASIC RESPECT

Bollinger is very cognizant of the emotional harms that extremist speech, as well as negative images of individuals and groups, can inflict, including oppression and psychological intimidation.[75] But he does not adequately heed the special significance of a particular context of extremist speech: the context of targeted intimidation or an extreme form of fighting words. When hate speech is directed at innocent targets, the speech can "inflict injury by its very utterance," to use words from *Chaplinsky*. In the next section I will explore this type of injury further. In addition, the very content of hate speech violates the basic norms or assumptions of a liberal order—that all citizens are entitled to at least equal respect in terms of their equality before the law.[76]

This understanding links and balances the ends of the First Amendment and the Fourteenth Amendment: freedom and equality. Entailed in this balance is the Kantian notion that individuals should be treated as ends in themselves, not as means, and a belief in individual dignity and responsibility. These norms are central to the historical development of constitutional law and liberalism.[77] But, as I have noted, the harm perpetrated by hate-group speech outside the context of direct targeting is indirect and less threatening; thus, it should be dealt with through the process of debate and counterargument, as Bollinger, Meiklejohn, and *Brandenburg* have asserted.[78] We must err on the side of freedom, or else state action may chip away at the doctrine of free speech. Consequently, any delimitation of the right to free speech must in turn be limited by a direct harms argument. In short, the conception of civility in political speech should be embodied in a limited version of the fighting-words doctrine (one which emphasizes intimidation), not in a broader group libel approach. In the next sections, I will show why this limited return to *Chaplinsky* in the area of intimidating speech is a responsible move and will suggest how it may be applied to pornography and other forms of expression.

HATE SPEECH AND FREE SPEECH

In *Skokie,* the courts ruled that a demonstration by a Nazi group, replete with uniform and swastika, was protected by the First Amendment despite the fact that the expression was targeted at a community of holocaust survivors. The courts held that the right to free speech outweighed the harms and that the doctrine of fighting words and assaultive speech, based on *Cohen,* required the targets of assaultive speech in the public forum to tolerate the expression unless they could not possibly avoid the expression.[79] On the concrete level, this position does not adequately account for the harms imposed by such speech on targeted individuals and discrete groups. Skokie holocaust survivors were indeed traumatized by the prospects of a Nazi rally in their community.[80] And on the more normative level, this position undervalues the interests of the community in protecting individuals from intentionally assaultive speech and in promoting civility in the public forum.

In order to grasp the meaning of assaultive speech, it is best to deal with real and hypothetical cases. Let us start with a Supreme Court case, *Organization for a Better Austin v. Keefe,* decided in 1971.[81] In *Keefe,* an Illinois circuit court had issued an injunction against the OBA, prohibiting it from distributing leaflets or similar literature in Westchester, a suburb near Chicago. The leaflets criticized Keefe, a real-estate broker, for engaging in "panic peddling" and "block busting" (practices in which agents spread rumors about impending change in the racial composition of the neighborhood in order to induce people to sell their homes, thus generating commissions for themselves). OBA had distributed leaflets at Keefe's church and in his neighborhood after previous efforts to stop Keefe had failed. The leaflets called for a "racially balanced" neighborhood (OBA consisted of both black and white members). The leaflets certainly "targeted" Keefe by invading his private sphere, and they were meant to be persuasive, even coercive. But Chief Justice Warren Burger of the Supreme Court set aside the injunction, proclaiming that

> The claim that the expressions were intended to exercise a coercive impact on respondent does not remove them from the reach of the First Amendment. . . . This is not fundamentally different from the function of a newspaper. . . . Petitioners were engaged openly and vigorously in making the public aware of respondent's real estate practices. . . . So long as the means are peaceful, the communication need not meet standards of acceptability.[82]

This decision embraces the liberal doctrine of free speech and demonstrates that the First Amendment should include intentional targeting and verbal "coercion" when the speech pertains to important public issues.[83] A free speech principle that encourages public debate and criticism must tolerate such forms of expression. But what about forms of expression that are threatening and assaultive? Let us modify the *Keefe* case in order to answer this question.

What if Keefe were Jewish and the leaflets read "Jew Greed Pockets Another Commission: Kike Keefe Cashes in on Families' Homes"? Should the same tolerance apply in this instance? No. Two major differences distinguish the two cases. First, the leaflets now focus on Keefe's ethnic origin rather than on his political positions, and in an intimidating fashion. Second, it is reasonable to assume that Keefe possesses a greater vulnerability in the second case than in the first. Why? The reference to race or ethnicity changes the very nature of the speech act from a criticism of Keefe's economic actions to a vilification of something over which Keefe has no control: his ethnicity. Furthermore, the leaflets in this case are unnecessarily emotionally assaultive. Even if Keefe's actions were selfish and troublesome, Keefe's ethnicity or race are morally irrelevant to his actions. The only reason for the ethnic slur would be to inflict emotional injury on Keefe (to "inflict injury by the very utterance," as in *Chaplinsky's* understanding of fighting words). The hypothetical leaflets, in effect, accuse Keefe of being Jewish, which echoes the ideology of racism responsible for extermination of the Jews under Hitler.[84] These factors would heighten the intimidating, inherently assaultive effects of the leaflets and would pollute the environment of cultural pluralism and political debate. The same conclusion, of course, would apply to other racial or ethnic slurs in this context.[85]

Angry references to race, ethnicity, and other unalterable traits are morally distinguishable from references (as in the actual *Keefe* case) to actions over which individuals are in some degree *morally* responsible. Compare, for example, an angry reference to a person's political affiliation to a reference to his or her race. Were Keefe a libertarian and had the leaflets read "Libertarian Pig Devours Homes for Profit," the link between party and action is not inherently absurd. It may be incorrect, but it does allege a link that is at least potentially logical, and it does not deny, in principle, the moral autonomy of the agent. In other words, the angry reference to ideology may be disturbing to our hypothetical Keefe, but it is not inherently absurd or unjustified. If the leaflet said "Libertarian Nigger Devours Homes for Profit," it would again slip into an inherently unjustified (and legally unprotected) reference to race.

These examples illustrate the following propositions: At the level of principle, the content of targeted racial vilification violates our most basic democratic norms; at the level of effects, it is inherently traumatic and assaultive and constitutes a form of direct intimidation. Such vilification denies the very humanity of targets, as the notion of humanity includes the notion of moral autonomy distinct from what Kant calls "necessitation," or the compulsions of passion and an unfree will.[86] Interviews with survivors in Skokie revealed that they felt violated by the proposed Nazi rally. They felt traumatized both as individuals and as members of a specific ethnic heritage.[87] Observers of racism in colonial settings and in totalitarian societies have also pointed out that the victims of racism in these contexts were especially oppressed by the prevalent allegation that race or ethnicity cause subhuman behavior.[88]

The *Skokie* decisions should have favored the community's interest in civility and protection against intentionally assaultive speech. Bollinger's tolerance principle concerning extremist and hate-group speech is valid as a basic concept but should not be applied to cases like *Skokie* that involve the direct, targeted, intentional infliction of emotional trauma on grounds of race or ethnicity. In terms of hate-group speech (the key expression for Bollinger and the type of speech at Skokie), I suggest the following proposition, which entails a partial return to the fighting-words and pluralist logics of *Chaplinsky*. I include such requirements as evidence of specific intent to vilify (i.e., malice) and the absence of provocation in order to single out those cases in which the intent is most malicious, as in *Sullivan*'s approach to libel of public officials. But I also include symbolic forms of expression: Targeting a swastika at our hypothetical Keefe would inflict the same harm as the hypothetical "Kike Keefe" leaflets.[89] Speech in the public forum involving race or ethnicity may be abridged:

1. When it is accompanied by the advocacy of death or violence perpetrated against a group; when it explicitly and maliciously demeans or vilifies through reference to race or ethnicity; or when it vilifies or demeans in a symbolic manner as understood by a reasonable person.
2. When such expression and harm are intended by the speaker and are unjustifiable owing to lack of significant provocation.

3. When such expression is directed at an individual, home, neighborhood, or discrete community in such a way as to single out an individual or specified group as the definite target of the expression.

This approach to racialist expression aims to delimit the domain of a special realm of tolerance (to delimit Bollinger) without forsaking the tolerance principle in general. It constitutes a balance of liberal, egalitarian, and communitarian principles. It also deals with the important public problem of hate-group speech without forsaking the significant interests in free speech and in civility. *Skokie* is only the most prominent instance of targeted hate speech. Other severe cases have arisen, often when a minority family moves into a white neighborhood, as happened recently in Philadelphia and in such places as Marquette Park and Cicero, near Chicago. Also, the Ku Klux Klan has engaged in campaigns of intimidation in recent years, including targeting individuals for symbolic intimidation.[90] A case in the early 1980s is illustrative. The Knights of the Ku Klux Klan began intimidating Vietnamese fishermen in Galveston Bay, Texas, because the fishermen were too successful to suit their more established white competitors. The Klan decided to promote "white" interests by taking a boat ride near the Vietnamese fishermen and engaging in symbolic intimidation. They wore full military regalia, brandished weapons, and hung an effigy of a Vietnamese fisherman—all within view of the fishermen. The Vietnamese sued for injunctive relief on the following grounds: intimidation and distress; contractual interferences; and violation of property and personal rights. The Klan responded by declaring that their actions were protected symbolic speech. The Vietnamese won, with the federal district court basing its decision largely on *Chaplinsky*'s notion of fighting words.[91] This case suggests that the doctrine of targeted hate speech or symbols is potentially reconcilable with First Amendment doctrine and that lower courts have been willing to consider a partial return to *Chaplinsky*.

THE APPROPRIATENESS OF THE DOCTRINE AND ITS EXTENSION TO OTHER TYPES OF EXPRESSION

This argument can be extended in two different directions. First, I will show why the proposed doctrine would not jeopardize free speech interests, especially in the crucial area of political speech. Second, I will suggest extensions of the doctrine to other areas of expression. This discussion is not definitive but rather suggests possible areas for further discussion.

DISTINGUISHING PROTECTED FROM UNPROTECTED DISPUTATIOUS SPEECH

The proposed doctrine on assaultive expression is limited in two key respects. First, it is limited to specific cases of direct targeting, thereby leaving the general speech rights of hate groups intact. Nazi and Klan groups, for example, would still be allowed to spew their views in most contexts, including appealing to sympathetic audiences. *Brandenburg*'s position concerning advocacy is not altered. Unless the speech were intentionally assaultive against a discrete target (e.g., a specific individual, group, neighborhood, or community cluster), it would merit First Amendment protection. Second, the heckler's veto doctrine would still be operative: Groups' or individuals' negative reactions to the speech in question could not support abridgement unless the speech was assaultive in an unjustified manner (e.g., including racial slurs or references to unalterable traits). This stipulation distinguishes disputatious or coercive speech criticizing someone's actions from speech that is malicious on grounds of unalterable traits such as race. It also distinguishes between targeted versus nontargeted speech. Martin Luther King, Jr.'s targeted criticisms of racism (as in the Selma March of 1965) would be protected regardless of the antipathy of whites because it criticized white actions, not whites for being white—and even this type of criticism would be protected if it were not threatening or patently vilifying (e.g., "whites are all morally insipid!").[92] The same position would apply to the civil rights march through the all-white Forsyth County in Georgia in early 1987 that met resistance from whites. Although white residents claimed that the march was an invasion of their communities and that it amounted to an attack on whites, the purpose of the march was to protest white actions to exclude blacks from the area. The proposed doctrine would also protect, say, targeted Communist criticisms of capitalist actions, capitalist criticisms of Communist violations of human rights, and Klan criticisms of Jewish interest group lobbying on behalf of Israel. Unless such expressions involved targeted intimidation and focused vilification on grounds of race (e.g., "Honkie Pigs," "Kikes Dominate Congress," etc.), it would be protected, even if it aroused the anger of the targets of criticism (recall Keefe's discomfort). The key distinguishing factors would be targeted intimidation and vilifying reference to racial or ethnic characteristics. All legal doctrines are subject to abuse; but as long as the governing standard is clear and containable and an important public interest is at stake, the risk may be worthwhile.

A final point is that the doctrine does not violate the anti–viewpoint discrimination doctrine, which is crucial to any liberal concept of speech, for the doctrine would be applied to all speech in a similar fashion regardless of the speech's content. Hate groups would be more likely to be subject to its strictures, but then pornographers are more likely to be subject to obscenity law and the critical press is more likely to be subject to libel law. The key is neutral enforcement not based on viewpoint discrimination. Analogously, obscenity law could not be enforced against only "radical" obscenity; such a policy would turn an erstwhile neutral restriction (in terms of viewpoint) into a restriction based on viewpoint. Discriminatory application would indeed invalidate the doctrine, but that rule would apply to all restrictions on speech.

RELATED APPLICATIONS

The doctrine is based on general principles concerning equality, individual responsibility and integrity, cultural pluralism, and the right to be protected against unjustified verbal intimidation or assault. On the basis of these principles, the doctrine could be applied to other contexts of expression as well. I suggest two areas for consideration: other forms of verbal intimidation and violent pornography. The application of the doctrine to race and ethnicity is perhaps the most obvious one because of the uniquely prominent role racial injustice has played in American history.[93] But the tenets of the argument might be extrapolative if done with care.

The most logical extensions of the proposed doctrine governing racialist speech would cover analogous forms of otherwise threatening speech—speech concerning unalterable traits and certain extreme forms of pornographic depiction. Targeted speech that directly threatens someone with death or violence (or is maliciously intended to cause significant emotional disturbance) would fit the category of unprotected speech along the lines developed above. For example, if a person maliciously targeted a rape victim with a sign that read "Free All Rapists: Rape Is a Political Crime," the speech would not be protected despite the ostensible political aspect of the message (even if committed in a public forum). Perhaps this type of speech would normally fall well outside the First Amendment anyway (as a form of harassment or a tortious intentional infliction of psychic injury), so we may not need to integrate it into the proposed doctrine.[94] But, as the *Skokie* case showed, such threatening speech conducted as political speech in the public forum would be protected by present First Amendment law. Consequently, our doctrine would recommend constitutional reconsideration of this type of speech as well.

What about targeted threats that are not serious, but rather rhetorical? It would depend on the degree of plausibility and the context, as determined by a reasonable person. At one extreme, purely rhetorical threats not targeted at a person or discrete group would clearly be protected. For example, in the late 1960s a man at an antiwar rally at the Washington Monument said "If they ever make me carry a rifle the first man I want to get in my sights is LBJ." He was arrested and convicted under a federal law punishing the threatening of the president. But the Supreme Court overturned the conviction on the grounds that the threat was merely rhetorical, and that it was political speech.[95] This decision is consistent with our doctrine, as no real or direct threat to an immediate target existed. Two other cases are more difficult. In one case decided just after *Cohen,* the Court gave First Amendment protection to a black person who shouted the following words at a police officer: "Whitie son of a bitch, I'll kill you; you son of a bitch, I'll choke you to death."[96] In another case, the Court protected the speech of an angry Black Panther who was arrested for calling people "mother fuckers" at a school board meeting several times.[97] The latter case does not involve a threat (though it is uncivil speech), and it was uttered in the context of a disputatious public meeting in which the arrestee was an invited speaker, so protection by the First Amendment in this case would not be undercut by our doctrine. But the former case could be discerned as threatening, and the use of the obviously negative reference to race was an unjustifiable racial slur. Thus, the content of this speech act would not be protected, according to our doctrine; however, the status of the target in this case (a police officer) perhaps should counsel discretion in favor of free speech, for officers (unlike average civilians) are trained to handle and to expect harsh encounters. The Court's differential treatment of "public officials" and "private figures" in the First Amendment law of libel is based on similar considerations; unlike public figures, private individuals have not voluntarily thrust themselves into the public arena replete with libelous discourse as a by-product of political discourse.[98]

Similarly, speech that directly reviles targeted people because of other unalterable traits could fall within our doctrine. Like race, such unalterable traits as gender, alienage, legitimacy, and handicapped status arguably are morally irrelevant to responsibility for actions, and hostile references to these qualities are inherently malicious. This application encapsulates the Fourteenth Amendment underpinnings of the doctrine, for Fourteenth Amendment jurisprudence grants higher judicial scrutiny to legal classifications based on some of these characteristics in the name of equality.[99] The doctrine could distinguish, say, speech that criticized a handicapped group's alleged lack of fiscal understanding in its support of massive subway access construction from a speech that pointed out this alleged lack but went on to say "are all Crips handicapped in the head as well?" Of course, an offense, according to our doctrine, would occur only if such ridicule were spoken directly at handicapped people and the vilification were not provoked. The same logic could apply to gender and other unalterable traits, such as illegitimacy (calling an illegitimate person a "bastard" to his face).[100] Again, such speech would have to be intentionally targeted at the subjects of the vilification in order to be unprotected.

Finally, we address the pornography issue, which has become so prominent in recent years.[101] The feminist critique of pornography raises issues we dealt with above: Pornography dehumanizes women by portraying them as sexual objects rather than as autonomous, responsible human beings, and it engenders disrespect for women as a group, thereby disadvantaging them in our pluralistic society.[102] But in order to fit into the doctrine developed above, pornography would have to constitute a form of assaultive vilification in order to be considered directly harmful. Our doctrine would certainly cover pornography targeted at or thrust upon an unwilling viewer, but the First Amendment already allows abridging this manner of expression (captive audience). What about other forms of display? As stated, our doctrine is both theoretical and empirical: It applies to expressions that vilify for unjustifiable reasons in the context of direct infliction of harm. Hence, this particular doctrine would not apply to pornography outside the context of targeting. Just as the doctrine would protect Nazi and hate-group vilifications outside of the context of malicious intentional targeting, so would it protect the general availability of pornography. Consequently, another approach would have to be adopted for pornography. But the fact that the First Amendment as understood by *Chaplinsky* does not protect all forms of expression (including obscenity) provides an opening for another approach. Below are some brief suggestions.

Rather than dealing with pornography using the doctrine developed in this chapter, a new exception to the First Amendment would have to be developed. Exceptions along the lines of those in *Chaplinsky* have not relied on the direct-harm requirement. Obscenity, for example, has not been shown to pose a direct harm to women or society, but it is nonetheless excluded from the First Amendment because it is said to pose long-range moral harm (it allegedly undermines family values and healthy sexuality) and because it is not a form of rational, ideational discourse, but rather a mere inducement to sexual arousal.[103] Though obscenity law has had its critics, it has managed to coexist with liberty fairly well and has not prevented liberty of political, social, scientific, and artistic expression from flourishing. A new compromise extending the obscenity exception to include certain types of pornography might be justifiable, especially if it were limited to those forms that are most dehumanizing and potentially harmful. Mere sexual depiction alone would not qualify for exclusion. Even though feminists may be correct about the way pornography eroticizes gender relations and makes women appear as mere sex objects, it would be unreasonable to conclude that all pornography should be censored on this basis. Sex and eroticization make up part of the fullness of life, and there are competing images of women in society that counter images of sexual reduction. Furthermore, as anticensorship activists stressed in the politics of the Minneapolis and Indianapolis feminist ordinances, antipornography measures could backfire on such groups as feminists and gays if they were implemented by forces unsympathetic to sexual depictions that these groups find suitable.[104] Consequently, caution is dictated in considering censorship in this area of expression.

But one type of pornography (which has, arguably, grown in recent years) is so dehumanizing and correlated with subsequent harms that excluding it from First Amendment protection is arguably appropriate: violent pornography.[105] Sexually explicit material that dwells on violence, especially if it shows (or intimates) that women victims are eventually sexually aroused by the violence, is dehumanizing in content. A consensus has emerged in the scientific community about the broader harmful effects of violent pornography on attitudes about women and the propensity to engage in violent behavior in laboratory settings (again, especially if combined with depictions of sexual arousal).[106] This type of pornography constitutes the most serious affront and threat to women as a group. The evidence is considerably less conclusive about nonviolent pornography, however. Thus, a new First Amendment exception restricted to violent pornography might be a responsible approach. In a recent piece, Cass Sunstein offered a potentially feasible new exception: "In short regulable pornography must (a) be sexually explicit, (b) depict women as enjoying or deserving some form of physical abuse, and (c) have the purpose and effect of producing sexual arousal."[107]

The Supreme Court fashioned a new exception for nonobscene "child pornography" as recently as 1982, in *New York v. Ferber*.[108] The Court allowed the abridgement of child pornography because of the overwhelming social interest in protecting children (who are unable to truly consent to participation) from obvious sexual exploitation in the production of such material. This rationale cannot be applied to adult pornography, however, as mature women can indeed give consent to being models in pornography. (If nonconsent is present, that is a different matter; but nonconsent cannot be presumed.) So a new exception would have to be based on the link between violent pornography and the negative attitudes about women and the propensity to violence that it may engender. The harms uncovered by psychological researchers are not direct (except in rare cases); but the correlation with indirect harms (the fostering of disrespect for women as a group), coupled with the fact that violent pornography is not conducive to the "exposition of ideas" articulated by *Chaplinsky,* might make such a new exception a feasible project. As in the discussion of hate-group speech above, this reform would entail a return to the original logic of *Chaplinsky;* this time what is emphasized is that case's logic concerning the difference between rational and nonrational discourse.

Unfortunately, two problems beset this approach. First, the creation of new exceptions could easily return us to the logic of group libel (that speech may be abridged because of its long-range damage to the self-respect of groups and their status in society), which I rejected above. Group libel laws deal with long-range effects, thereby challenging the core of the modern doctrine of speech that must be preserved (i.e., *Brandenburg*). This is one reason why the federal courts struck down Indianapolis's version of the feminist antipornography ordinance.[109] Second, as leading researchers have admitted, a large amount of nonobscene material (whether or not it is sexually explicit, including R-rated film material and even many television commercials and shows) generates negative attitudes about women and sexual aggression. The 1986 Commission, for example, alleged that the vast majority of sexual material available was harmful.[110] Consequently, censorship in this area would suffer from ineffectiveness and underinclusiveness unless it covered a very broad amount of material. But in gaining effectiveness in this manner, it would encounter severe problems of overbreadth that would certainly violate free speech values.[111] Given these intractable problems, the 1986 Commission's position may be a better approach: Restrict violent and degrading sexual material *that also fits the traditional obscenity exception to the First Amendment.* This approach would provide some basis for protecting women's claims to equal status through more vigorous enforcement of violent obscenity; but it would protect speech interests by restricting censorship to the traditional, well-established category of First Amendment exclusion, which has not jeopardized the flourishing of political, artistic, scientific, and literary discourse in modern times. Social activism in the form of boycotts, pickets, demonstrations, and educational efforts about pornography's effects are more advisable than a new inherently unlimited exception to the First Amendment, unless we are willing to abide the consequences for liberalism and the regime of free speech.[112]

CONCLUSIONS

In conclusion, a modified liberal approach that accepts the core assumptions of the modern doctrine of free speech is advisable for prudential and certain normative reasons. Alternative approaches that seek to incorporate distinctions based on particular viewpoints (progressive, conservative, or whatever) are very risky and jeopardize the special realm of relative tolerance that governs free speech in the public forum today. But the modern liberal doctrine is problematic in that it does not acknowledge the manner in which threats disguised as speech inflict concrete emotional harms and violate (in principle) the norms of equal respect and autonomy, which are central (even if imperfectly realized) to liberal justice. An approach that accounts for these harms without forsaking the direct-harms principle (unlike the new antipornography measures) would be consistent with a liberal regime of speech, especially when liberalism's more traditional embodiment of such supraindividualistic values as civility, pluralism, and progressive community is acknowledged. Such an approach would constitute a modest reform of present law and would serve to remind us that while individualism is important to liberalism, the liberal tradition is not encapsulated by this single value.

NOTES

1. See, for example, Steven Shiffrin, "The First Amendment and Economic Regulation: Away from a General Theory of the First Amendment," *Northwestern Law Review* 78 (1983).
2. The preeminent articulation of this doctrine in liberalism is Ronald Dworkin, "Liberalism," in Stuart Hampshire, ed., *Public and Private Morality* (Cambridge: Cambridge University Press, 1978), p. 113. See also Herbert Wechsler, "Toward Neutral Principles of Constitutional Law," *Harvard Law Review* 73 (1959), p. 1.
3. See Laurence Tribe, *American Constitutional Law* (Mineola, N.Y.: Foundation Press, 1978), Chapter 12.

4. On how the actual liberal tradition (as represented by Bentham, Mill, and Dewey) includes, *but is not limited to,* individualism and neutral principles, see Robin West, "Liberalism Rediscovered: A Pragmatic Definition of the Liberal Vision," *University of Pittsburgh Law Review* 46 (1985), p. 673.

5. See Thomas L. Tedford, *Freedom of Speech in the United States* (New York: Random House, 1985), Chapter 2.

6. Alien and Sedition Acts of June 25, 1798, 1 Stat. 570; July 14, 1798, 1 Stat. 596. For one authoritative view that the Alien and Sedition Acts were consistent with the original intent of the framers, see Leonard Levy, *Legacy of Suppression* (Cambridge, Mass.: Harvard University Press, 1961).

7. See David Kairys, "Freedom of Speech," in Kairys, ed., *The Politics of Law* (New York: Pantheon, 1982), pp. 146–149.

8. American society was in flux owing to industrialization and world commitment, but morality and mores were still largely traditional. The modern civil liberties movement as we know it (with an individualistic focus and a belief in the special value of free speech) did not develop until the debates over the Espionage Act in Congress in 1917 and subsequent court cases over its enforcements. See David M. Rabban, "The Emergence of Modern First Amendment Doctrine," *University of Chicago Law Review* 50 (1983), pp. 1213–1217.

9. *Schenck v. U.S.,* 249 U.S. 47 (1919) (sending letters to draftees advocating resistance to draft poses clear and present danger despite absence of effectiveness); *Debs v. U.S.,* 249 U.S. 211 (1919) (a speech to a large audience by a Socialist party leader advocating legal resistance to war poses a clear and present danger, despite no evidence of effectiveness).

10. On the nature of "assimilationist" law, see Robert Post, "Cultural Heterogeneity and the Law: Pornography, Blasphemy, and the First Amendment," working paper (forthcoming, 1988, *California Law Review*).

11. See Holmes' dissent in *Abrams v. U.S.,* 250 U.S. 616 (1919), at 624; and in *Gitlow v. New York,* 268 U.S. 652 (1925).

12. *Whitney v. California,* 274 U.S. 357 (1927). See Rabban, "The Emergence of Modern First Amendment Doctrine," pp. 1320–1345.

13. *Dennis v. U.S.,* 341 U.S. 494 (1951). On these developments (culminating in *Brandenburg* in 1969), see Rabban, "The Emergence of Modern First Amendment Doctrine," pp. 1345–1351.

14. See *Yates v. U.S.,* 354 U.S. 298 (1957).

15. *Chaplinsky v. New Hampshire,* 315 U.S. 568 (1942). In 1982, the Court added "child pornography" (pornography with children as models) to the exclusion list. "Pornography" is not the same thing as "obscenity," and is protected by the First Amendment (pornography is sexually lewd material, whereas obscenity has a more technical definition, as defined below). But in *New York v. Ferber* (458 U.S. 747 1982), the Court said the significant harms posed by child pornography justified adding it to the list of First Amendment exceptions.

16. See *Miller v. California,* 413 U.S. 15 (1973). *Miller* is the definitive contemporary obscenity test.

17. Post, "Cultural Heterogeneity and the Law," p. 5.

18. See Frederick Schauer, "Must Speech Be Special?" *Northwestern Law Review* 78 (1983), pp. 1284–1285.

19. Ibid., p. 1287.

20. See e.g., Harry Kalven, Jr., *The Negro and the First Amendment* (Chicago: University of Chicago Press, 1965).

21. See, for example, *Schad v. Mt. Ephraim,* 452 U.S. 61 (1981), in which the Supreme Court held that nude dancing at a bar can fall within the First Amendment's protection.

22. See Post, "Cultural Heterogeneity and the Law."

23. Alasdair MacIntyre, *After Virtue: A Study in Moral Theory* (Notre Dame, Ind.: University of Notre Dame Press, 1981), p. 11. Emphasis in original. See also Roberto Mangabiera Unger, *Knowledge and Politics* (New York: Free Press, 1973); Post, "Cultural Heterogeneity and the Law."

24. *Cohen v. California* 403 U.S. 15 (1971), at 25–25. Emphasis added.

25. *Brandenburg v. Ohio,* 395 U.S. 444 (1969), at 447. Emphasis added.

26. See, e.g., *Gooding, Warden v. Wilson,* 405 U.S. 518 (1972); *Lewis v. New Orleans,* 408 U.S. 913 (1972).

27. Key heckler's veto cases are *Edwards v. South Carolina,* 372 U.S. 229 (1963); *Cox v. Louisiana,* 379 U.S. 536 (1965); and *Gregory v. Chicago,* 379 U.S. 111 (1969). On the unique importance of the public forum and the heckler's veto doctrine, see Harry Kalven, Jr., "The Concept of the Public Forum: Cox v. Louisiana," *Supreme Court Review* (1965); Kalven, *The Negro and the First Amendment.*

28. *New York Times v. Sullivan,* 376 U.S. 254 (1964).

29. See, for example, *Memoirs v. Massachusetts,* 383 U.S. 413 (1966), the case in which the Supreme Court held that John Cleland's famous *Fanny Hill* was protected by the First Amendment. On the complex development of obscenity law liberalization in the 1960s, see N.Y.U. Obscenity Project, "An Empirical Inquiry into the Effects of *Miller v. California* on the Control of Obscenity," *N.Y.U. Law Review* 52 (1977), pp. 821–844.

30. See *Virginia State Board of Pharmacy v. Virginia Citizens Council, Inc.,* 425 U.S. 748 (1976). Commercial speech has not received the same level of protection as political and public speech, which has led to the development of three tiers or levels of First Amendment protection in place of the previous two. The same status pertains to "pornography" that is not quite "obscene." See *Young v. American Mini Theatres, Inc.,* 427 U.S. 50 (1976). However, this movement is really part of a broader liberalization.

31. John Stuart Mill, *On Liberty* (New York: Henry Holt, 1898). Mill's larger doctrine, of course, applies to all "self-regarding" *actions* as well as speech. But the First Amendment concerns speech, not action, and has normally held that invalid actions under the guise of speech are not protected by the First Amendment. See, e.g., *U.S. v. O'Brien,* 391 U.S. 367 (1968) (burning one's draft card is a form of illegal action, not expression). From this perspective, the marketplace rationale and the individual autonomy rationale for free speech are two sides of the same coin. More recent theorists, however, distinguish the two rationales. See, for example, C. Edwin Baker, "Scope of the First Amendment Freedom of Speech," *UCLA Law Review* 25 (1978), p. 964.

32. The constitutional realm of political economy, for example, no longer entails liberal state neutrality but rather encourages symbiosis between government and the private sector. See Theodore Lowi, *The End of Liberalism: The Second Republic of the United States* (New York: Norton, 1979).

33. Lee C. Bollinger, *The Tolerant Society: Freedom of Speech and Extremist Speech in America* (New York: Oxford University Press, 1986), p. 10.

34. Ibid., esp. Chapter 5, "The Internal Dialectic of Tolerance." Similar values also reflect underlying values of constitutionalism. See Cass Sunstein, "Naked Preferences and the Constitution," *Columbia Law Review* 84 (1984), p. 1689.

35. See Sheldon Wolin, *Politics and Vision: Continuity and Innovation in Western Political Thought* (Boston: Little, Brown, 1960), Chapters 1 and 2. Bollinger's theory presupposes a movement away from what Durkheim called "mechanical society" toward modern "organic" society.

36. Schauer, "Must Speech Be Special?" pp. 1288–1289.

37. See Laurence A. Wiseman, "The New Supreme Court Commentators: The Principled, the Political, and the Philosophical," *Hastings Law Quarterly* 10 (1983), p. 315. Moral philosophers such as John Rawls and Ronald Dworkin created individualistic moral philosophies with legal-constitutional import which were picked up by such constitutional commentators as Kenneth Karst, Paul Brest, Michael Perry, Owen Fiss, and Laurence Tribe.

38. Indeed, some of the liberals mentioned in the previous footnote (e.g., Tribe, Brest, and Fiss) have supported the feminist and/or "group-based" critiques of liberalism that I will discuss below.

39. See, e.g., Joseph Singer, "The Player and the Cards: Nihilism and Legal Theory," *Yale Law Journal* 94 (1984), p. 1; Roberto Unger, "The Critical Legal Studies Movement," *Harvard Law Review* 96 (1983), p. 561; Morton Horwitz, "The Jurisprudence of Brown and the Dilemmas of Liberalism," *Harvard Civil Rights–Civil Liberties Law Review* 14 (1979), p. 599; Catherine MacKinnon, *Feminism Unmodified: Discourses on Life and Law* (Cambridge, Mass.: Harvard University Press, 1987).

40. Michael Sandel, *Liberalism and the Limits of Justice* (Cambridge: Cambridge University Press, 1982); Roberto Unger, *Knowledge and Politics; Law in Modern Society* (New York: Free Press, 1976). Unger and Sandel comport with conservative critics like Bloom in criticizing the liberal theory of justice for having an impoverished notion of the self. John H. Scharr has criticized the liberal polity for lacking "authority," by which he means authoritative models and standards. Scharr's critique bridges leftist and rightist viewpoints. See *Legitimacy in the Modern State* (New Brunswick, N.J.: Transaction Books, 1981).

41. Owen Fiss, "Groups and the Equal Protection Clause," *Philosophy and Public Affairs* 5 (1976), p. 107. Catherine MacKinnon has drawn on Fiss's principle in her work on women's rights in a liberal regime. Horwitz has also argued for a similar approach in "Dilemmas of Liberalism."

42. Herbert Marcuse, "Repressive Tolerance," in Robert Paul Wolff, Barrington Moore, and Herbert Marcuse, *A Critique of Pure Tolerance* (Boston: Beacon Press, 1969).

43. Richard J. Neuhaus, *The Naked Public Square: Religion and Democracy in America* (Grand Rapids, Mich.: Eerdmans, 1984).

44. Alasdair MacIntyre, *After Virtue,* Chapter 3. MacIntyre's understanding of emotivism as the essential public philosophy of the age (a public philosophy of the private sphere, as it were, if there can be such a thing) corresponds to Roberto Unger's critique from the Left. Liberal epistemology and psychology, says Unger, are based on the postulates of subjective value and arbitrariness of de-

sire. *Knowledge and Politics,* pp. 31–53. "Given the postulate of arbitrary desire, there is no basis on which to prefer some ends to others." E.g., *Cohen v. California.*

45. Neuhaus, *The Naked Public Square,* p. 17. See also Stanley Hauerwas, *A Community of Character* (Notre Dame, Ind.: University of Notre Dame Press, 1981), esp. Chapter 4.

46. Alan Bloom, *The Closing of the American Mind* (New York: Simon and Schuster, 1987).

47. Bloom points out that Nietzsche, the nineteenth century's preeminent modernist philosopher, understood the importance of a common culture (what Nietzsche called a "horizon") to the development of character. Nietzsche's revolt and exaltation of the self made sense only in the context of a vibrant tension between the past and the future. See, for example, Nietzsche's *The Use and Abuse of History* (New York: Bobbs-Merrill, 1957).

48. *Village of Skokie v. Nat'l Socialists Party of America,* 373 N.E. 2d 21 (1978); *Collin v. Smith,* 578 F. 2d 1197 (7th Cir.) (1978).

49. Key defenses: Bollinger, *The Tolerant Society;* David Hamlin, *The Nazi/Skokie Conflict: A Civil Liberties Battle* (Boston: Beacon Press, 1980) (Hamlin served as the Illinois American Civil Liberties Union (ACLU) public relations agent during the *Skokie* battle; he was a veritable center of the storm); Aryeh Neier, *Defending My Enemy: American Nazis, the Skokie Case, and the Risks of Freedom* (New York: Dutton, 1979) (Neier was the national executive director of the ACLU during the *Skokie* conflict). Critiques: Hadley Arkes, *The Philosopher in the City* (Princeton: Princeton University Press, 1981), Part 1; Donald Alexander Downs, *Nazis in Skokie: Freedom, Community, and the First Amendment* (Notre Dame, Ind.: University of Notre Dame Press, 1985).

50. See Walter Dean Burnham, *The Current Crisis in American Politics* (New York: Oxford University Press, 1982), Introduction, and Part 4.

51. Proposed Minneapolis Ordinance Sec. 3, to add Minn. City. Ord. (MCO) Sec. 139.20 (gg). The definition is even longer, but this is its essence. For the fuller definition, see *American Booksellers Ass'n v. Hudnut,* 771 F. 2d 323 (7th Cir. 1985). The definition of pornography covers more sexual material than obscenity law. The ordinance was to be enforced by civil suits rather than criminal law (which covers obscenity law).

52. MacKinnon, *Feminism Unmodified,* Chapter 2.

53. MacKinnon, "Pornography, Civil Rights, and Speech," *Harvard Civil Rights– Civil Liberties Law Review* 20 (1985), pp. 4–5. See also *Feminism Unmodified,* Chapters 2 and 14.

54. On how such earlier thinkers as Bentham, Mill, and Dewey presented a less individualistic (and more progressive, communitarian) form of liberalism than more recent thinkers like Ronald Dworkin, see West, "Liberalism Rediscovered." On how the liberal tradition of law once recognized civility, equal respect, and pluralism as values in addition to individualism, see Post, "Cultural Heterogeneity and the Law."

55. Bollinger does deal with "drawing lines" in Chapter 6 of *The Tolerant Society,* but his treatment is very abstract and at times unclear.

56. To do otherwise would be utopian. One free speech theorist rejects both abstract communitarian and abstract libertarian approaches to free speech and

public philosophy as absolutist diversions from political and moral responsibility, preferring instead a more pragmatic "administrative" approach that balances these values and is based on the reality of modern government and society. See Edward L. Rubin, "Nazis, Skokie, and the First Amendment as Virtue," *California Law Review* 74 (1986), p. 260.

57. See Thomas Hobbes, *Leviathan* (New York: E. P. Dutton & Co., 1950); John Locke, *The Second Treatise of Government* (Cambridge: Cambridge University Press, 1960).

58. The German Nazi government's sanction of *Kristallnacht* in 1938, in which hordes of anti-Semites roamed Germany intimidating Jews and destroying their property (and also beating and killing some victims) epitomizes the breakdown of state protection of basic security. See Hadley Arkes, "Civility and the Restriction of Speech: Rediscovering the Defamation of Groups," in Philip B. Kurland, ed., *Free Speech and Association: The Supreme Court and the First Amendment* (Chicago: University of Chicago Press, 1975), p. 420.

59. Alexander Meiklejohn, *Political Freedom* (New York: Oxford University Press, 1965). Meiklejohn's position is not consequentialist, whereas Bollinger's is. Meiklejohn's theory is based on the logical necessity of free speech in a regime based on self-government. See also Hannah Arendt, *The Human Condition* (Chicago: University of Chicago Press, 1958).

60. The willingness to acknowledge and confront all political possibilities is a virtue in politics and life, as several political thinkers—including Mill, Machiavelli, and Ortega—have taught. Such awareness in Nazi Germany may have helped some Jews escape death. See Hannah Arendt, *Eichmann in Jerusalem* (New York: Penguin, 1963).

61. See Harry Kalven, Jr., "The New York Times Case: A Note on 'The Central Meaning of the First Amendment,'" *Supreme Court Review* (1964). See also Arendt, *The Human Condition; The Origins of Totalitarianism* (New York: Harcourt, Brace, Jovanovich, 1951).

62. See Vincent Blasi, "The Checking Value in First Amendment Theory," *American Bar Foundation Research Journal* (1977), p. 521; Frederick Schauer, *Free Speech: A Philosophical Enquiry* (Cambridge: Cambridge University Press, 1982).

63. See Varda Burstyn, ed., *Women Against Censorship* (Vancouver: Douglas and McIntyre, 1985).

64. Unger, *Law in Modern Society.* See also Philipe Nonet and Philip Selznick, *Law and Society in Transition: Toward Responsive Law* (New York: Harper, 1978), Chapter 3.

65. See, e.g., Jethro K. Lieberman, *The Litigious Society* (New York: Basic Books, 1983); Lawrence Friedman, *Total Justice* (New York: Russell Sage, 1985).

66. See Michael Walzer, *Spheres of Justice: A Defense of Pluralism and Equality* (New York: Basic Books, 1983); Daniel Bell, *The Cultural Contradictions of Capitalism* (New York: Basic Books, 1976).

67. Post, "Cultural Heterogeneity and the Law." Hadley Arkes, who also espouses civility as a norm, also embraces group libel. See "Civility and the Restriction of Speech."

68. *New York Times v. Sullivan*, 376 U.S. 255 (1964).

69. See Kalven, "Central Meaning." On how *Sullivan* pragmatically entails protect-

ing speech that, in principle, is not protected by the First Amendment (such as libel) in order to provide "breathing room" for speech that is central to the First Amendment's principles, see Lillian BeVier, "The First Amendment and Political Speech," *Stanford Law Review* 30 (1978), p. 299.

70. See Meiklejohn, *Political Freedom*, Chapters 1 and 4.

71. Sunstein, "Naked Preferences and the Constitution."

72. This dichotomization corresponds to the split between public and private spheres and norms that Unger says characterizes liberalism, in *Knowledge and Politics*. Thus, the more liberal the society, the greater the dichotomization. But a society that understood the social, as well as the individualist, basis of liberty would require more reciprocity between spheres. This is a central theme in José Ortega's classic *The Revolt of the Masses*, John Kerrigan, trans., (Notre Dame, Ind.: University of Notre Dame Press, 1985).

73. See Richard Sennett, *The Fall of Public Man* (New York: Knopf, 1974). On the link between manners and the "forms of liberty" that contribute to a healthy liberal polity, see Harvey Mansfield, Jr., "The Forms and Formalities of Liberty," *The Public Interest* (1983).

74. Glenn Tinder links the values of community, open inquiry, tolerance, and civility in *Community: Reflections on a Tragic Ideal*, Chapter 5.

75. Bollinger, *The Tolerant Society*, esp. Chapter 2.

76. See Dworkin, *Taking Rights Seriously*, Chapter 12.

77. Immanuel Kant, *Groundwork of the Metaphysic of Morals* (New York: Harper, 1964), esp. pp. 95–96. On Kantian norms and liberal principle, see John Rawls, *A Theory of Justice* (Cambridge, Mass.: Harvard University Press, 1971).

78. In *Whitney v. California*, at 377, Brandeis stressed that as long as there is the availability of counterspeech and thought, free speech should reign.

79. Of course, intentionally intimidating expression in the form of coercion, harassment, extortion, solicitation, and other forms of criminal actions are not protected by the First Amendment. See Franklyn Haiman, *Speech and Law in a Free Society* (Chicago: University of Chicago Press, 1981), Chapter 11. The type of speech I am concerned with is speech in the public forum about public issues that also involves direct infliction of intimidation.

80. See Downs, *Nazis in Skokie*, esp. Chapter 5, for an in-depth account of the psychological harms perpetrated at Skokie.

81. *Organization for a Better Austin v. Keefe*, 402 U.S. 415.

82. Ibid., at 419.

83. This type of "coercion" through speech is different from the type of coercion that is a criminal offense, of course. Criminal coercion occurs when someone forces or compels someone to commit a crime or engage in involuntary conduct (e.g., "Shoot at that cop or I will shoot you!"). Some form of threat must be present. This was not the case in *Keefe*.

84. See George L. Mosse, *The Crisis of German Ideology: Intellectual Origins of the Third Reich* (New York: Schocken Books, 1981).

85. The argument here parallels the Supreme Court's reasons in making certain classifications in the law "suspect classifications" meriting closer judicial scrutiny under the Fourteenth Amendment. Certain classifications are "suspect" because they deal with groups who have been discriminated against historically for morally illegitimate reasons, including their unalterable traits (e.g., race,

gender, legitimacy, or alienage). See John Hart Ely, *Democracy and Distrust: A Theory of Judicial Review* (Cambridge, Mass.: Harvard University Press, 1980), pp. 145–170. Religious classifications have also been treated as suspect under the First Amendment, largely for reasons of historical discrimination and because of the First Amendment's commands.

86. Kant, *Metaphysic of Morals*, pp. 80–81.
87. Downs, *Nazis in Skokie*, Chapters 5 and 6. Thus, their trauma had individualist and pluralist dimensions.
88. See Hannah Arendt, *The Origins of Totalitarianism*; Albert Memmi, *The Colonizer and the Colonized* (Boston: Beacon Press, 1965). Mosse, *Crisis of German Ideology*.
89. Arkes deals with cases of silent, symbolic intimidation in his work on hate speech, in *The Philosopher in the City*.
90. See *Southern Poverty Law Report*, May/June 1982; *Klan Watch Intelligence Report*.
91. *Vietnamese Fishermen's Ass'n v. Knights of the Ku Klux Klan*, 543 F. Supp. 198 (S.D. Tex. 1982). See also *Vietnamese Fishermen's Ass'n v. Knights of the Ku Klux Klan*, 518 F. Supp. 993 (S.D. Tex. 1981). Also, in January 1985 the U.S. District Court for the Eastern District of North Carolina issued an order pursuant to a consent decree that barred the Confederate (formerly Carolina) Knights of the KKK from marching in predominantly black neighborhoods, from harassing or intimidating North Carolina citizens, and from operating a paramilitary organization. See Order, *Person v. Carolina Knights of the Ku Klux Klan*, No. 84-534-CIV-5 (D.N.C. Jan. 18, 1985).
92. See the Selma decision, in which Judge Frank Johnson ruled in favor of the march on grounds of substantive racial justice. *Williams v. Wallace*, 240 F. Supp. 100 (M.D. Ala. 1965).
93. See Gunnar Myrdal, *An American Dilemma: The Negro Problem and Modern Democracy* (New York: Harper and Row, 1944).
94. See Haiman, *Speech and Law*, Chapters 7 and 11.
95. *Watts v. U.S.*, 394 U.S. 705 (1969). For a somewhat similar ruling in a different context, see *Rankin v. McPherson*, 107 S. Ct. 2891 (1987), in which the Supreme Court ruled that a clerical employee in a county constable's office could not be fired because she was overheard telling a friend over the telephone (upon hearing of John Hinckley's attempt on President Ronald Reagan's life) that "If they go for him again, I hope they get him."
96. *Gooding v. Wilson*, 405 U.S. 518 (1972).
97. *Rosenfeld v. New Jersey*, 408 U.S. 901.
98. See *Gertz v. Robert Welch*, 418 U.S. 323 (1974).
99. See William B. Lockhart, Yale Kamisar, Jesse H. Choper, and Steven H. Shiffrin, *Constitutional Rights and Liberties*, 6th ed. (St. Paul, Minn.: West Publishing Co., 1986), Chapter 6, Sec. 3, "Special Scrutiny for Other Classifications."
100. It should be noted that tort law over the years has recognized tort actions for the intentional infliction of emotional distress and for the intentional infliction of racial insults, epithets, and "name-calling." This development supports the doctrine I have developed in this chapter. See Richard Delgado, "Words that Wound: A Tort Action for Racial Insults, Epithets, and Name-Calling," *Harvard Civil Rights–Civil Liberties Law Review* 17 (1982), p. 133.

101. Recall that "pornography" and "obscenity" are different. Pornography is virtually any nonartistic sexual depiction, whereas obscenity, which has never received full First Amendment protection, is sexual depiction that patently offends community standards and appeals to the prurient interest. Thus, the term "pornography" covers more material than "obscenity."

102. See, for example, Eric Hoffman, "Feminism, Pornography, and the Law," *University of Pennsylvania Law Review* 133 (1985), p. 497.

103. See Frederick Schauer, "Speech and 'Speech'—Obscenity and 'Obscenity': An Exercise in the Interpretation of Constitutional Language," *Georgetown Law Journal* 67 (1979), pp. 922–928.

104. See, e.g., Varda Burstyn, ed., *Women Against Censorship.*

105. The 1986 Attorney General's Commission on Pornography concluded that violent pornography constituted the most harmful type of pornography. The commission also concluded that nonviolent but "degrading" pornography was harmful, but the commission was much less convincing about this proposition, especially given the very broad way it defined "degrading." *Attorney General's Report* (Washington, D.C.: U.S. Justice Dept., 1986), Part 2, Chapter 5.

106. See Edward Donnerstein, Daniel Linz, and Steven Penrod, *The Question of Pornography: Research Findings and Policy Implications* (New York: Free Press, 1987), esp. Chapter 5. The evidence on violent pornography suggests only correlational, not causal relationships with harm, however.

107. Cass Sunstein, "Pornography and the First Amendment," *Duke Law Journal* (1986), p. 592.

108. *New York v. Ferber,* 458 U.S. 747 (1982).

109. *American Booksellers Ass'n v. Hudnut.* The ordinance attempted to distinguish forms of sexual depiction according to their effects on the status of women in society.

110. *Attorney General's Report,* Part 2, Chapter 5, "The Question of Harm." The commission put sexual material into four classes and maintained that two classes—Class I (violent pornography) and Class II ("degrading" pornography, which contains most pornography)—were harmful.

111. Edward Donnerstein, perhaps the leading psychological researcher on the effects of pornography in laboratory settings, stressed this point in an interview. Donnerstein interview with Donald A. Downs, Madison, Wisconsin, July 1985.

112. Three leading researchers on pornography's effects have recently endorsed noncensorious alternatives to alleviating pornography's effects. See Daniel Linz, Steven D. Penrod, and Edward Donnerstein, "The Attorney General's Commission on Pornography: The Gaps Between 'Findings' and 'Facts," *American Bar Foundation Research Journal* (1987), pp. 731–736.

13 ———·
Freedom of the Press: The Press and the Court Write a New First Amendment

ROGER A. SIMPSON

The free press, wrote Karl Marx in 1842, "is the ruthless confession of a people to itself, and it is well known that the power of confession is redeeming." Marx wrote those words in a newspaper that was fighting the stranglehold of government censorship.[1] A century later, a member of the Commission on Freedom of the Press in the United States offered a rationale for a functional alliance between the press and government. Neither confession nor redemption were any longer pertinent. Indeed, even the "people" appeared to be tangential to the postwar theory of a free press:

> Today there is reason to suppose that this self-correcting process, although commonly considered to function fully, does not in fact function, to our danger. . . . [T]here are no such natural harmonies and balances in a community as democratic theory used to assume. . . . Our people have put too much trust in the automatic tendencies of our society to right itself. We have found that we cannot depend on unmanaged processes, whether in economics or in communications. We need more effective methods of self-correction.[2]

Any theory of the role of a free press in a democracy must have as its foundation a conception of individual conscience and the right of a person or group to communicate their convictions. Moreover, there must be tolerance for the various ways in which people communicate to others, for the diversity of forms in which ideas are expressed. Individual conscience must have a function in governance as well. Our liberal faith holds that freedom enriches and strengthens the community—each individual member as well as the aggregate. That trust rests on the valuing of each person's intellectual, moral, and emotional confrontation with the test of being. Our best evidence thus far is that given fair means to do so, people will make government serve them. They do so when governing is essentially part of their lives. But what are these "fair means" of governing?

One is the instrument that allows the products of individual conscience to be shared. The press Marx described was such an instrument, as is the press enshrined in much of our political rhetoric. However, since World War II, political theory, economic change, and judicial interpretation have weakened the potential of the American press to provide that "ruthless confession of a people to itself."

This chapter examines this pivotal change in our understanding of press freedom and shows that it has led to two distinct and contradictory definitions of freedom of the press: One definition elevates the products of the printing press to a special and protected place in our scheme of democracy; the other places the mass media of information—newspapers, radio, television, magazines, and books—under the trusteeship of the courts. The legal system's increasing preoccupation with that latter definition is robbing the historic idea of press freedom of its vitality.

HISTORY OF THE IDEA OF FREEDOM OF THE PRESS: FROM MADISON TO MEIKLEJOHN

Two English Whig writers, John Trenchard and Thomas Gordon, outlined the idea of popular government in one of the "Cato" letters widely printed in the American colonies after 1730: "The Administration of Government, is nothing else but the Attendance of the Trustees of the People upon the Interest, and Affairs of the People. And it is the Part and Business of the People, for whose sake alone all Publick Matters are or ought to be transacted, to see whether they be well or ill transacted."[3]

The received theory of the British experience gained authority in the crucible of the American Revolution and during the federalist period of the new nation. By 1800, the Jeffersonian theorist Tunis Wortman described a sophisticated theory of society in which sovereignty rested with the people. "The general will, which is the necessary result of Public Opinion, being superior to Political Institution, must of consequence remain independent of its control. Governments are entrusted with the exercise of the ordinary powers of sovereignty: but Society is, nevertheless, the real and substantial sovereign."[4]

Wortman and others of his time placed the individual intellect at the core of their model of government. The individual's milieu was robust discourse on public matters. The individual's opinion was offered in discussion with other persons of diverse views, and the whole process led toward the "general opinion" that functioned as the control on government. The value of the free press in this system was inescapable: "While Society is furnished with so powerful a vehicle of Political Information, the conduct of administration will be more cautious and deliberate: it will be inspired with respect towards a Censor whose influence is universal."[5] Although Wortman, Jefferson, and their confederates were hardly paradigms of progressive thought in many respects, they did embrace a notion of active citizenship that has been eclipsed by the discourses of modern corporate-dominated, consumer-oriented society.[6] The idea of the linkage of the activist, informed citizen with the moral limits and duties of government needs to survive in the modern discourse. The arguments about the meaning of freedom of the press have become burdened by a wicked debate about the founders' intentions and tolerances; the quality of the idea is not itself at issue, only whether the frequent references to it truly reflected the practices of the day.[7]

Thus, the language of the First Amendment provided for a clear governance role of the citizen by protecting religion, speech, assembly, and printing and implicitly acknowledged the value of newspapers in political action. Early American newspaper editors read the constitutional pledge as a license to practice politics with printed communication that stretched the boundaries of vehemence and virulence.

"The more I consider the independence of the press in its principal consequences," wrote Alexis de Tocqueville, "the more am I convinced that in the modern world it is the chief and, so to speak, the constitutive element of liberty."[8] The robust Jacksonian press exceeded the fondest hopes of Enlightenment theory; partisan editors thoughtfully juxtaposed their opinions to the contrary views so that every newspaper, no matter what its bias, served as a functional forum for political debate. Moreover, the newspaper and its editor served as party organizers, thereby expanding the political importance of the medium. The Jacksonian era, spanning from the late 1820s to 1837, was the zenith of the political newspaper in America.[9] A commercial press, already flourishing in the 1830s, eclipsed and replaced the partisan newspaper and then rapidly became the dominant form of newspaper throughout the country.

By the middle of the twentieth century, the house of self-government, with its core of press freedom, had been badly battered. The theory had been undermined in two central respects. First, theorists abandoned the "individual intellect" as the linchpin of a democratic system and replaced it with a notion of corporate authority in the marketplace of ideas. Second, the press evolved into a significantly different institution than that which had flourished in the nation's first half-century.

THE DEMISE OF THE VALUED INDIVIDUAL

Sigmund Freud and Karl Marx, to name only two iconoclasts of a democratic social order, helped to undermine the American intellectuals' optimism about the functional role of the press in self-government. Marx, by showing that the protection of free speech in a capitalist economy was likely to result only in a defense of the ideas of those in power, left liberal democracy and the hallowed "free marketplace of ideas" in disarray. Freud, by illuminating barriers to self-awareness, essentially challenged the liberals' confidence that citizens could mold some degree of truth about public issues from spontaneous and unregulated discourse.

By the 1920s, the benefits of a free press were doubted by intellectuals. Walter Lippmann wrote that newspapers "inevitably reflect, and therefore, in greater or lesser measure, intensify the defective organization of public opinion."[10] In the 1930s, Harold Lasswell, a political scientist, directly attacked the assumed positive relationship between "social harmony" and free discussion. Letters to editors and opinion columns by diverse writers, which had justified the newspaper's claim to be a political forum, were implicated by the attack. "Discussion frequently complicates social difficulties, for the discussion by farflung interests arouses a psychology of conflict which produces obstructive, fictitious and irrelevant values."[11] The extraordinary effects of both Fascist and allied-nations propaganda simply affirmed for Lasswell and others the need to abandon any theory that posited more than a nominal role for the citizen in governance.

By 1947, press theorists who had lived through two world wars and a global depression had little stomach for Enlightenment optimism. The Commission on Freedom of the Press assembled by Henry Luce, a magazine publisher, showed from 1943 to 1947 how libertarian theory had been undermined. Twelve highly respected scholars and the chairman of the Federal Reserve Bank of New York met every few months for three years and ultimately provided thousands of pages of transcripts and manuscript drafts focused on the ideal role of the press in the postwar world.[12]

Disenchantment with the idealized rational citizen was apparent in the several publications of the commission. William Hocking, a Harvard University philosopher, wrote: "The democracy of mental participation by the people in the main lines of public action runs shallow."[13] In part, the citizen was seen simply as being lazy; the apathy also reflected failures of family, school, church, and press to give individuals training and encouragement in citizenship. "When these free authorities are weak or absent, the weaker truth-seekers may so far flounder as to set up a prima facie case for a reversion to authoritarian control, to the loss of that mental power on which social progress depends."[14]

These were arguments of men full of the ascendancy of the attitudes of social science. In one sense, scientific rationalism reflected the aspirations of the Enlightenment as it focused the academics' interest on other human beings; however, the methods by which the scholars separated themselves from those whom they studied emphasized a loss of faith in social equality and diversity.

THE NEW ROLE OF THE NEWSPAPER

The new theory rested on the recognition that the newspaper had assumed a new political role. The newspaper of Jefferson's day thrived on personal and partisan opinion, often so casually laced with fact that Jefferson, in a dark moment, ranted that "Truth itself becomes suspicious by being put into that polluted vehicle."[15] But throughout the nineteenth century, the rapidly growing newspaper publishing industry steadily pulled that medium away from its roots in political discourse. Whereas the colonial newspaper had been the instrument of rebellion and the Jacksonian papers had been agents of the party, the twentieth-century press was a bifurcated institution. The commercial newspaper was allegedly factual, yet it was also adept at the arcane techniques of entertainment and diversion. It was an observer whose reports filled leisure time, whose advertisements, reflecting the logic of commodity exchange, provided the new vocabulary for the language of political discourse. Opinion—at least, passionate, critical opinion of the sort in which Marx saw the conscience of a people—was the province of a variety of modest magazines and a ragtag collection of pamphlets and newsletters. Theories of press freedom had to take this split into account.

Revisionist thinking about press freedom was not solely a product of American intellectuals. In the late 1940s, in a United Nations forum on the role of the press, a French delegate summarized the new view precisely:

> In the 18th and 19th centuries, the press was used as a vehicle of personal opinion; it was not a vehicle of information. The immediate consequence of that change was that at present the "subject of right" was the public, whose freedom of information had to be guaranteed, rather than the individual's liberty of expression. [Thus, freedom of information is the universal concept.] Then should come the right of expressing an opinion, which involved the individual's responsibility and necessarily entailed numerous limitations.[16]

The words were echoed by delegates from all parts of the world—the Soviet bloc, the neutral nations of the Third World, and even France and other European allies. In the UN, debates on conventions of gathering and transmitting news, a right of correction and freedom of information helped freeze bloc and national positions on the role of the press.[17] The press increasingly was viewed as a pipeline for information to be consumed by citizens.

The arguments had little to say about the value of opinion; it was concern about facts, and their role in government information programs, that dominated debate. Many nations, the United States included, had used information to build and sustain war efforts. The integral roles of both propaganda and intelligence gathering during the war inspired government information programs geared to domestic rebuilding and international relations.

The emerging theory was built on a view that a citizen requires certain information in order to serve as a voter. Desirable in itself, voting unfortunately was the only patch saved by theorists from the tattered quilt of self-governance. The voters' needs were elevated consciously above the rights of individuals to express their convictions. The American Commission on Freedom of the Press pointedly had distinguished the phrase "freedom from," with its implications of government suppression, from "freedom for," which implied not only opportunity but also responsibility. Libertarians had often talked about responsibility, but never with the chop-licking fervor with which postwar theorists embraced the array of ideas that came to be called "social responsibility."

"Social responsibility" reflected the growing corporate role in American life while excusing its abuses of economic power with faith prescriptions. In terms of the press, the theory institutionalized the private interest of the newspaper publisher while arguing, with amazing naivete, that a press that satisfied "the needs" of the voters would be socially responsible. What the people had a right to know proved to be remarkably consistent with what the press corporations had a bent to provide.[18]

The Commission on Freedom of the Press resolved its queasiness about the power and frivolous interests of commercial newspapers by linking the freedom to publish to the obligation to provide useful information to the public. No longer a forum for speakers or a voice worthy of protection in its own right, the newspaper needed to be subject to independent standards. The standards for performance had to originate outside the press, and by default, these standards were as likely to be rooted in government needs as in any other institutional needs. In their final report, the commissioners agreed: "Freedom of the press for the coming period can only continue as an accountable freedom. Its moral right will be conditioned on the acceptance of this accountability. Its legal right will stand unaltered as its moral duty is performed."[19]

The commission hinted wistfully that there might be a loss of legal freedom if the press did not mend its ways; however, the power of government was to be used as a "last resort." (Though the commission tried to stay clear of speculation about how that power might be used, the mere idea was enough to infuriate American publishers.) The American formulation of the theory was a marvelous hybrid: freedom from some government penalties; freedom for responsible performance.

The commission had specified five requirements for the press in a healthy society—only one of these touched upon the most controversial realm of opinion and debate; the others listed necessary utilities for press content:

> A truthful, comprehensive, and intelligent account of the day's events
> in a context which gives them meaning;
> A forum for the exchange of comment and criticism;
> The projection of a representative picture of the constituent groups
> in the society;
> The presentation and clarification of the goals and values of the society;
> Full access to the day's intelligence.[20]

The role of the press, this list makes clear, was to feed to its audience that information necessary for an understanding of "the broad outlines of reality." The model on which these shapers of postwar communication appeared to act was the successful wartime propaganda campaigns. Yet the prescription for the postwar period suggested a far more sweeping indoctrination. In Lasswell's words, "It is by no means fantastic to imagine that the controllers of mass media of communication will take the lead in bringing about a high degree of equivalence throughout society between the layman's picture of significant relationships, and the picture of the expert and the leader."[21] The comment is deceptive: The layman is mentioned first, but it is the expert's picture that is created first; the layman would be provided "equivalent enlightenment." Lasswell provided the engineering for an alternative to the incomplete "pictures in our heads" described by Lippmann two decades earlier. There was no apology for making the layman accept the view of the expert or politician. The expert's "enlightenment" was, of course, also an ideology, and in this way of thinking, the layman's own capacity for forming and expressing opinion was simply irrelevant. The commission's investment in a science of information production and distribution, a foundation for public opinion formation, was supported and reinforced in the international arena first, and then in the changing nature of the American press.

The idea of media responsibility had been wedded to the political issue of "false news" in the League of Nations since at least the early 1930s. "News," in this debate, originated in another country; it was false because it described one's own country unfavorably. From the beginning, the "false news" cry served to justify barriers to international commerce in information.[22] The debate over false news illustrated the extent of the fear of many nations about control over news by the English and American news corporations, which were viewed as working hand in glove with their governments. The largely rhetorical UN debates about the press show the basis for calls for responsibility: Standards of performance were necessary if the international market for information was to be at all free of Anglo-American domination.

Thus, the postwar crucible formed a new theory of the press. Its emotional antecedents were the European Fascist experience, and in a more subtle way, the Russian Revolution. The techniques for information management were learned during the war in the intelligence and propaganda campaigns geared to raising domestic morale while manipulating news sent abroad. According to the new theory, the citizen was a passive individual, highly susceptible to certain kinds of information. Cynicism had replaced Enlightenment optimism; the evidence was the awkward juxtaposition of democratic rhetoric with extraordinary faith in technical manipulation of information.

Hocking had described the new role of the press: "With the rights of editors and publishers to express themselves there must be associated a right of the public to be served with a substantial and honest basis of fact for its judgments of public affairs."[23] The rational authority for that public right to fact was provided by the philosopher Alexander Meiklejohn, whose ideas on free speech appeared in an influential book in 1948, only a year after publication of the several volumes of the Commission on Freedom of the Press.[24]

Meiklejohn salvaged the commitment to self-governance from what remained of the Enlightenment dream by the middle of the twentieth century. He called passionately for the protection of political speech as a necessary condition for self-governance. He derided the Holmesian notion that the marketplace of ideas was a test of truth. Faith in the "competition of the market" relieved individuals of intellectual responsibility and replaced a commitment to self-governance with a zeal to promote one's own interests.

> Our aim is to "make a case," to win a fight, to make our plea plausible, to keep the pressure on. And the intellectual degradation which that interpretation of truth-testing has brought upon the minds of our people is almost unbelievable. Under its influence, there are no standards for determining the difference between the true and the false. The truth is what a man or an interest or a nation can get away with. That dependence upon intellectual laissez-faire, more than any other single factor, has destroyed the foundations of our national education, has robbed of their meaning such terms as "reasonableness" and "intelligence," and "devotion to the general welfare." It has made intellectual freedom indistinguishable from intellectual license.[25]

Meiklejohn declined to examine that "intellectual degradation," though there was no doubt of his growing fear that information could be packaged for selfish purposes and then handed to the public by an irresponsible media. The citizen would be unprepared, indeed unwilling to question the information.[26] He concentrated on the form of communication between government and citizen that would make informed voting possible. There was no guarantee that votes would be cast wisely. Still, voting was the essential act of self-governance reserved to citizens under the Constitution. The First Amendment, he said, was a "device" to facilitate governance. It barred government from denying the voter any information that might affect the vote. In one area of press content—political information—there should be no curb on content, whatsoever. (Other information might be regulated, subject to due process requirements.)

> Shall we give a hearing to those who hate and despise freedom, to those who, if they had the power, would destroy our institutions? Certainly, yes! Our action must be guided, not by their principles, but by ours. We listen, not because they desire to speak, but because we need to hear. If there are arguments against our theory of government, our policies in war or in peace, we the citizens, the rulers, must hear and consider them for ourselves. That is the way of public safety. It is the program of self-government.[27]

Meiklejohn gave a new reading to the view that the people should control their government. The state was to intervene in the political system to assure a steady flow of information to a voter with apparently modest interest in the task. The citizen was no longer at the heart of a robust political system. It was now the voter who stood at the center of the scheme, waiting for a bombardment of information that, it was hoped, would inspire a trip to the polls.

The cynicism of the view is best revealed by what it omits. Citizens, in Meiklejohn's scheme, listened and read but only rarely spoke and thought; when they did speak, it was in only the most superficial manner. Action was restricted to voting, not to debate and initiative. Meiklejohn was far less interested in the reasons for people speaking than in the need of listeners to know what was being said. Reason and the individual were subjugated to new concerns about public opinion and the community; the change was radical. Opinions themselves were viewed as "facts," units in a universe of information of which a voter should be aware.

> Just so far as, at any point, the citizens who are to decide an issue are denied acquaintance with information or opinion or doubt or disbelief or criticism which is relevant to that issue, just so far the result must be ill-considered, ill-balanced planning for the general good. *It is that mutilation of the thinking process of the community against which the First Amendment to the Constitution is directed.*[28]

One imagines a radar screen on which the citizen monitors the public issue "skies." An attack on a public official created a blip as important in the monitoring process as the action of the public official. Self-governance had taken on the nature of a parlor game in which one stockpiled facts toward a monopoly of information. The game, however, was not as much about education as it was about consumption, and the rules dealt with improving the consumption of information through the mass media.

Meiklejohn's advocacy of absolute freedom in political matters thus was not a reiteration of confidence in human reason. Nor was his enthusiasm for the model of a controlled town meeting simply an updating of the venerable "marketplace of ideas." Meiklejohn argued for a functional moderator in political discussion—one person in a town meeting, the government in the process of building a national consensus. The "moderator" abridges speech simply by enforcing rules of order (in the way the courts have upheld time, place, and manner restrictions on speech activities). He or she also regulates or abridges speech by recognizing speakers, declaring speakers out of order, moving discussion toward a decision, and preventing redundant comments. The distance Meiklejohn traveled from his Enlightenment heritage is shown vividly in two short sentences: "It is not a dialectical free-for-all. It is self-government."[29]

The town meeting was certainly an appropriate democratic symbol, but it was one that could not be applied to the nation without provision for the federal government's role in fostering voting decisions. The trap into which Meiklejohn stumbled almost at once was determining what information directly fueled the "voting of wise decisions." The philosopher would have banished nonpolitical opinion and many other kinds of speech from the protection of the First Amendment. "It has no concern about the 'needs of many men to express their opinions.' It provides, not for many men, but for all men."[30] Indeed, Meiklejohn's First Amendment appeared to have no concern about many matters that always had been considered fully protected. He stumbled about, trying to create categories of speech content, each with its own degree of protection. The exercise so confounded the issue that it should have served to forewarn any agency, including the Supreme Court of the United States, that would attempt a similar classification.

"The constitutional status of a merchant advertising his wares, of a paid lobbyist fighting for the advantage of his client, is utterly different from that of a citizen who is planning for the general welfare," Meiklejohn wrote.[31] The idea appealed to others. Harry Kalven wrote in 1961 that "novels, or dramas or paintings or poems" had nothing to do with the matter of governance, but Meiklejohn retorted: "The people do need novels and dramas and paintings and poems, 'because they will be called upon to vote.'"[32] The dialogue had a curious echo in the failed nomination of Circuit Judge Robert Bork to the Supreme Court in 1987. That Bork had written that discussion of the arts might be beyond the scope of the First Amendment prompted critics from that realm to join the attack on his nomination.

It is perhaps less useful today to muse on the classificatory quagmire Meiklejohn entered than to understand how deep was his despair about the repair of democracy. He and his contemporaries had been thrust into the role of communications engineers by a pervasive sense of the failure of the premise of democratic government. The extent of Meiklejohn's fear is illustrated in his view of American radio. Rather than serving governance, it had become the province of selfish private owners. Its fare was entertainment and advertising; it scarcely deserved consideration in the context of the First Amendment. "We have used it [the First Amendment] for the protection of private, possessive interests with which it has no concern."[33]

Meiklejohn's book, reissued in 1960, continues to influence thinking about freedom of the press. In one sense, the book has done injustice to its author, who dedicated his life to strengthening the freedom of academic and political speech. Its unfortunate legacy is the proposition that information can be managed in ways that will yield productive citizenship. Unintentionally, the book has encouraged the belief that the historic humanistic concern about individual freedom could be replaced with an orchestrated collective wisdom. The theorists of the postwar years were not recasting their models of a free press in intellectual isolation. Indeed, the press industries were in perfect harmony with the new view of the First Amendment.

THE NEWSPAPER INDUSTRY'S ROLE
IN BUILDING A THEORY

The American Newspaper Publishers Association fought from the time of its founding against all threats to the economic autonomy of its members. In the 1930s, the ANPA and its chief legal counsel, Elisha Hanson, argued in case after case that freedom of the press protected the business practices of the newspaper industry from government regulation. The argument won the favor of the Supreme Court only once, in a case involving a Louisiana tax on the largest of the state's newspapers, most of which were critics of Senator Huey Long.[34] Nevertheless, Hanson's arguments had a life of their own and were repeated in the briefs for numerous press cases in the 1930s and 1940s. The First Amendment, Hanson argued, protected the business of publishing as well as the act of publishing.[35]

The argument rested on a claim of a special political value in newspapers. The newspaper was not simply a voice, but part of an institution with a special role in a democracy. The argument was a reiteration of dicta by Justice George Sutherland in *Grosjean v. American Press* in 1936. "A free press stands as one of the great interpreters between government and the people," Sutherland wrote, suggesting a role quite different from that in which the newspaper spoke for the government or for the people (i.e., the party) in Jacksonian America.[36]

In 1936, a federal appeals court upheld a National Labor Relations Board ruling that the Associated Press had illegally fired an employee because of his membership in a union, the American Newspaper Guild. In its appeal, the AP, supported by the ANPA, tried to stretch the concept of the newspaper as a neutral or objective interpreter even further. The news organizations argued that news objectivity justified firing employees who were members of voluntary associations, including unions, because such affiliation would compromise their reporting. (A surprising number of American newspapers still deny their reporters the freedom to join nonprofessional associations.) The argument was self-serving; there never was a doubt that the publishers were primarily interested in stopping the fledgling reporters' union. The Supreme Court endorsed the NLRB position, thus stopping the pernicious extension of a legal foundation for the argument of special privilege for the press.[37]

The publishers' objectivity argument, however, concealed much about the nature of the American newspaper in the 1930s. News dominated its front pages; syndicated features filled its back pages, along with sports, theater, films, cooking, and other kinds of information. Opinion was typically exiled to a sterile "editorial" page or two, duller in both appearance and content than any other part of the newspaper. In fact, ideology, hiding behind the veil of objectivity, flourished in the newspaper. Objective news rationalized things as they were, demeaned and discounted those who wanted change, and found its authority in the voices of corporate capitalism. Publishers convinced themselves, and tried to convince the public, that objectivity was the price they paid for the privilege of serving the public welfare. Yet, as Michael Schudson has argued:

> Objectivity in journalism, regarded as an antidote to bias, came to be looked upon as the most insidious bias of all. For "objective" reporting reproduced a vision of social reality which refused to examine the basic structures of power and privilege. It was not just incomplete, as critics of the thirties had contended, it was distorted. It represented collusion with institutions whose legitimacy was in dispute.[38]

The publishers' promotion of the ideal of objectivity, as well as the newspaper's "interpreter" and information roles, was concurrent with the newspaper industry's rapid evolution as the most influential element of a national mass media information system. That system was built on the principles of monopoly profits, chain ownership, and linkages through syndicates, wire services, and other purveyors of information. Government and industry were inextricably bonded.

Most American daily newspapers (98 percent of 1,676) enjoy either a monopoly of their markets or unchallenged domination.[39] The nature of the daily newspaper monopoly assures that most operators face no direct competition (that is, from another daily newspaper published in the same geographic market). The profit potential of the monopoly situation is substantially greater than that of a competitive newspaper. Occasionally, the profits are returned to the news departments; often, however, the profits go to new machinery, new buildings, or straight to the bank. What results from the high profitability of the daily newspaper monopoly is not an expanding interest in news but an increasingly efficient handling of the flow of news. (Incidentally, the competition of television has not seriously threatened the economic power of the daily newspaper industry; where television has diminished the appeal of afternoon newspapers, they either have been shifted to morning publication or have disappeared, leaving the market to a morning publication. As a source of news, television at its best only echoes the commercial newspaper—too few ideas are designed for passive viewers and given over to selling products.)

The history of the newspapers in any American city shows how the trend toward the local monopoly has paralleled changes in content from opinion to fact. In the late nineteenth century, any major city might have counted several competing daily newspapers; in the following decades, it would have recorded a steady reduction in that number. Economists sometimes suggest an inexorable process of elimination of competition, but the unseen hand was often less of a factor than conspiracies of advertisers bent on getting the most punch for their sales messages. Moreover, the paralyzed hand of federal and state government contributed to the deaths of hundreds of newspapers. Antitrust laws, among others which might have been used against unfair competition, were rarely applied to newspapers that simply gave their weakened competitors an extra-legal shove to speed their departure from the marketplace.

A city with several newspapers enjoyed a robust competition of ideas. Being noticed in that shouting fray meant having viewpoints and opinions, even if information did fill up most of the pages. When a newspaper finally emerged as the sole newspaper, the survivor of the competition, it could settle down to the comfortable task of managing information. A newspaper whose last competitor has just died would invariably raise its prices to subscribers and advertisers in order to reap the most profits possible. Moreover, the monopoly newspaper's destiny for profitability made it a desirable property for a corporation with a chain of newspapers. Indeed, the chaining of newspapers has flourished, encouraged by federal tax policy and ignored by federal antitrust policy.

The financial and political muscle of the newspaper industry, and particularly of its chain-owning corporations, gives it extraordinary access to agencies of the federal government. In the twentieth century, publishers have persuaded Congress to keep the borders open for Canadian newsprint, fought against work standards under the National Recovery Administration, cajoled the State Department to push for increased overseas access to news for American news media, and most recently, pushed President Richard Nixon and the Congress to exempt independently owned competing newspapers that use common printing and business facilities from the antitrust laws. The Newspaper Preservation Act of 1970 saved forty-four newspapers in twenty-two cities from antitrust prosecution. The beneficiaries of the law, all of whom were enjoying the unusual profits flowing from the joint operations arrangement, included some of the largest newspaper chains in the country, including the Hearst Corporation, the Gannett Company, and the Knight-Ridder Corporation.

The newspaper is a product whose makers almost invariably reap a profit, face only modest competition, and enjoy conspicuous political and economic standing in the nation. This highly successful industry claims a privileged institutional position, as "interpreter" between government and the people, by virtue of a supposed relationship between the citizen's consumption of news and the act of voting. The newspaper evolved—that is, progressed—from its nineteenth-century roots in ideology and partisanship to its present role of social service, the publishers say. They are reluctant to concede that their news is itself filtered through the ideology of the corporate political and economic system and that such a bias, by virtue of its supposition of corporate authority over the consumer, is far more dangerous than the populist partisanship of newspapers of the past.

The intricate relationship of the newspaper industry to freedom of the press is germane to this change in content. Each campaign by publishers for government assistance has rested on a claim of the newspaper's special benefit to the public. The intense cooperation of the news industry with the U.S. State Department in developing communication policy after World War II grew out of a concern for accurate war information. American wire services, principally the Associated Press and United Press International, worked with the government to undermine territorial domination by foreign services as well as to gain international agreement on principles of access for all journalists.[40]

By 1964, then, the American media—radio, television, and newspapers—constituted a national system of information distribution. The newspaper industry dominated the system, setting news agendas for federal, state, and local governments in ways no other medium could match. Spokespersons for the industry described its benefits to the public in terms reserved for institutions of much more formal standing—the church, the law, education. The industry had evolved to process and publish information, and particularly that information flowing from the hub in Washington, D.C.

The thinking of the postwar years suggested that information fueled the citizen's participation in a democratic government. Any doubt about the initiative of the citizens shifted attention to the way information was handled. The citizen was increasingly viewed as a consumer of information, especially as television became a major partner with the newspaper in information production. In a time marked by official sensitivity to the ignorance and naivete of product consumers, it was easy for officials to think of the citizen or voter in the same light. The consumer-voter-citizen needed accurate information. But if the government had tried to compel the media to publish any specific information, it would have been confronted by the news industry's own rhetoric about the independent "watchdog" role of the press. The First Amendment to the Constitution forbade either suppression or forced disclosure of information. And it was naive to preach to journalists who fervently believed in their independence from government. Only the Supreme Court, in its rapidly enlarging authority over civil liberties, could embark on the remarkably novel adventure of specifying how newspapers should collect and publish information.

THE COURT'S ADVENTURE WITH FREEDOM OF THE PRESS

The Supreme Court waited until 1925, in *Gitlow v. New York,* to affirm that liberty of the press was among the cluster of liberties protected from state action by the Fourteenth Amendment.[41] Beginning in 1919, with *Schenck v. United States,* the Court had examined radical speech cases arising from the federal Espionage Act of 1917 and from similar state statutes.[42] Whether they were reacting to the society's repressive character or to their own lack of faith in unbridled free expression, the justices subjected free speech to limiting tests, notably the clear-and-present-danger test. Although libertarians admired the test because it at least posited a line that the state could not cross in political speech cases, the courts frequently drew the line in ways that gave governments ample opportunity to punish their opponents.

Gitlow v. New York involved publication in a Socialist party newspaper of a manifesto urging a Communist revolution in the United States. In upholding Gitlow's conviction under a New York law, the Court even set aside the clear-and-present-danger test, reasoning that the State of New York was entitled to legislate that certain utterances "are so inimical to the general welfare and involve such danger of substantive evil that they may be penalized."[43] It appeared that if state legislatures could prohibit publication of certain political ideas, press freedom was a terribly insubstantial reed, even if it was incorporated into the Fourteenth Amendment.

However, in 1931, the Supreme Court under Chief Justice Charles Evans Hughes began to build a framework for protecting freedom of the press. Government restraint before publication was deemed unconstitutional. The freedom to print, the Court said, included the freedom to distribute the printed material. Moreover, the constitutional protection of the press included leaflets and pamphlets, the medium typical of political protest.[44] The legacy of the Hughes Court was a broad protection for the content of printed material, a protection that did not ask—in theory, at least—who had prepared the publication, how carefully it had been done, or for what purposes.

The turnabout in Court posture toward the press obviously depended on test cases that moved the focus on content away from revolutionary agitation to other kinds of expression. Even so, the anti-Semitic, government-badgering tactics of the *Saturday Press* of Minneapolis must have appeared at least as harmful to the officials of Minnesota who tried to close it down as the Socialist newspaper prosecuted in New York in the *Gitlow* case had been. In *Near v. Minnesota,* however, the Supreme Court rejected Minnesota's effort at prior restraint, although it took pains to leave the state common-law rules of libel intact (along with the notion of postpublication punishment of offensive material). Chief Justice Hughes borrowed James Madison's imagery to explain the constitutional protection:

> Some degree of abuse is inseparable from the proper use of everything, and in no instance is this more true than in that of the press. It has accordingly been decided by the practice of the states, that it is better to leave a few of its noxious branches to their luxuriant growth, than, by pruning them away, to injure the vigour of those yielding the proper fruits.[45]

The case involved a scandalous "rag"; assistance was given in its defense by Col. Robert R. McCormick, the Chicago newspaper baron who used his newspaper consistently to voice his own prejudices. The significance of the case is, in part, its ringing rebuke of state efforts at prior restraint of the press; the case is also significant as the first formal intervention by an established commercial newspaper publisher in the Court's deliberations about the limits of freedom of the press. McCormick, with the support of the ANPA, deliberately appealed to the high Court for a conclusive reading of the prior restraint issue.[46]

The glorious revolution of the Hughes Court ended with the decade of the 1930s, and for the next two decades the Supreme Court did little to define or expand the definition of press freedom. Issues that would affect the definition, such as libel and invasion of privacy, remained in the hands of state courts. In the civil rights tempest of the 1960s, the Court changed course, imposed its jurisdiction over the state courts in libel matters, and struck a Faustian bargain with the press of the United States. In 1964, in *New York Times v. Sullivan,* the justices offered to spare the press from libel suits by public officials angered by aggressive reporting of the civil rights movement.

For their part, newspapers and other press organizations simply needed to come into court when challenged by one of those offended officials for a review of how they had done their work. At first, the deal delighted the press. Alexander Meiklejohn, the advocate of regulating information in the interests of the public, praised the Supreme Court's decision in *New York Times v. Sullivan* as "an occasion for dancing in the streets."[47] Yet Meiklejohn of all people should have seen the trap; he had repeatedly called for absolute protection for printed advocacy related to the voting decision, and this decision clearly provided only a very qualified sort of immunity for the press.

In that moment, the newspaper's capacity to be the conscience of the people was at stake. The case raised an issue of similarity between the repugnant state repression of the press under the federal Sedition Act of 1798 and a southern state's tolerance of the use of its civil courts by state officials to exact libel awards from the press. The "court of history" declared the Sedition Act inconsistent with the First Amendment, Justice William Brennan wrote. "What a State may not constitutionally bring about by means of a criminal statute is likewise beyond the reach of its civil law of libel," he added. The Court was at the threshold of a declaration that our society could tolerate free—completely free—criticism of public officials.

Instead of outlawing the punishment of the press for investigating and commenting on public officials—the very essence of self-governance—it created a test merely to discourage officials seeking revenge against the press by the libel route. This so-called "actual-malice" test was to be used by state and federal courts to determine whether those who published the libel knew of its falsity or had recklessly disregarded the truth.

The case involved an advertisement in the *New York Times* that described the harassment of the Rev. Dr. Martin Luther King, Jr., because of his crusade for black civil rights. A number of southern officials sued the newspaper for libel, and one Montgomery, Alabama, city commissioner won a $500,000 judgment against the *Times* in a verdict upheld by the Alabama Supreme Court.[48]

Brennan's opinion contained so many generous compliments to the press that it is easy to understand media euphoria at the time. The Court affirmed the protection of political content in advertising, recognized the value in "vehement, caustic, and sometimes unpleasantly sharp attacks on government and public officials," and acknowledged that the ease with which public officials could sue the press for libel amounted to a de facto law of seditious libel. That public officials used the libel tort as a way to punish critics was beyond question. The crime of criticizing public officials disappeared in theory with the repeal of the Alien and Sedition Acts in 1800, but a shadow of seditious libel survived even longer in such latter-day repressive laws as the Espionage Act of 1917 and the Smith Act of 1940. Libertarians always had cheered the demise of seditious libel; Americans should be free, it was insisted, from penalties for criticizing their officials. Thus, as it became clear how extensively public officials were using libel suits against the press, the stage was set for the Court to eradicate the latest insidious form of seditious libel.[49]

The actual-malice test was not a complete shield against the officials' libel suits, despite all the rhetoric about seditious libel and the importance of "uninhibited, robust, and wide-open" debate on public issues. In fact, this test opened the door to the possibility of fairly severe restrictions on press freedoms. Justice Hugo Black wrote, "The requirement that malice be proved provides at best an evanescent protection for the right critically to discuss public affairs and certainly does not measure up to the sturdy safeguard embodied in the First Amendment."[50]

The landmark decision deceived proponents of an expanding press freedom. Brennan's eloquent applause for the ideal of freedom was widely taken as evidence of a grand expansion of press freedom to comment on public officials. The opinion outlined a theory of self-government in which the press plays a significant role. There was no explanation for the element that essentially contradicted the whole argument—the troublesome actual-malice test. Indeed, it appears that the justices were so affected by the tension between the Alabama courts and the federal system that much of their discussion related to how far the opinion should go toward preventing a retrial of the suit in Alabama. A recent study of the justices' memoranda in the case also shows little interest in giving the press immunity in matters relating to governance.[51]

Three years later, Hugo Black, in a remarkable dissent in a case extending the new rules to libel suits by prominent persons, described the result of the Court's use of the actual-malice test.

> If this precedent is followed, it means that we must in all libel cases hereafter weigh the facts and hold that all papers and magazines guilty of gross writing or reporting are constitutionally liable, while they are not if the quality of the reporting is approved by a majority of us. . . .
> In fact, the Court is suggesting various experimental expedients in libel cases, all of which boil down to a determination of how offensive to this Court a particular libel judgment may be, either because of its

immense size or because the Court does not like the way an alleged libelee was treated.[52]

In order to appreciate *New York Times v. Sullivan* and its progeny, one must take its intellectual heritage into account. In many ways, it was a mechanistic experiment to prove Meiklejohn's argument that self-government depended on a regulated flow of appropriate information. Reckless journalism rendered public discussion inefficient and left the voter, whose interests were at the heart of the case, hampered in the duties of citizenship. Yet Meiklejohn had argued in the abstract; the Court, through its actual-malice test, provided a practical instrument by which state and federal courts could manage the content of the news media.

Defenders of the Court, including many newspaper publishers, like to invoke a fearsome picture of American politics should it be "freed" from judicial news management. According to this view, the press lies about public officials, indulges in unwarranted personal attacks on public servants, and disdains facts in its frenzy to smash enemies or elevate favored figures. The assumption of such abuses is a red herring, which can be countered by two other arguments: First, in the period of American history in which the press was most extreme in its pursuit of political ends—the time of the party-supported press early in the nineteenth century—the net result was a marvelously rich public discourse on political matters. Second, the vision of an "evil" press is an opportunistic argument. The established press is likely to maintain its own cautiousness about political matters for commercial reasons; the imagined recklessness patently identifies the marginal publications that take risks, shout louder at government abuses, and disdain commercial considerations. For those publications to be forced into the high-rent environment of the libel court amounts to a substantial chill on press freedom. For all the neutrality implied by the judicial scrutiny of journalistic methods and the invocation of the rhetoric of responsibility, the courts finally can be seen as anything but neutral; their decisions affirm corporate hegemony because they use the journalism standards of the corporate giants to define "responsible journalism" for everything issuing from a printing press.

Despite its rhetoric, the case had little to do with protecting political opinion. Printed opinions—if clearly understood to be conclusions based on facts widely shared—were protected under common law as well as under the First Amendment. But this case was about facts rather than about conclusions that might be drawn from facts, so its direct effect on expanding freedom of opinion was negligible. Moreover, adjudication of libel suits has afforded judges the opportunity to blur the lines between fact and opinion to the point that determining categories of content is a growing preoccupation of the courts. Some statements, it seems, are so ambiguous that only the judicial mind is bold enough to conclude with even temporary certainty that they are fact or opinion.

As a result of its decision in *New York Times v. Sullivan,* the Court has made the federal and state judiciary manager of the political information provided by the news industries. To be sure, news organizations always had been subject to review of their work in the state courts. But from 1964 on, the standards for review were dictated by the Supreme Court. It was a brand new responsibility, and one for which the Court had little useful precedent or experience. Justice Louis D. Brandeis had argued reasonably nearly fifty years earlier that "courts are ill equipped to make the investigations which should precede a determination . . . of the circumstances under which news gathered by a private agency should be deemed affected with a public interest."[53]

Nevertheless, the Court quickly expanded the reach of its *Times* decision to apply the same test to libel suits by prominent persons with no connection to government. The wider umbrella for protection for the press was, at the same time, a wider umbrella of Supreme Court jurisdiction over the news process. It didn't take long for the Court to find reason to respect, if not to heed, the warning of Justice Brandeis.

For more than two decades, *New York Times v. Sullivan,* and those subsequent cases that fine-tuned its application, have guided court review of libel suits by public officials and persons who involve themselves in controversial public issues. The news industry has complied, if not conspired, with the new judicial oversight, turning to its own corporate lawyers to serve as the ultimate in-house editors. Lawyer-editors do a good deal more than read news copy on a video terminal; throughout the industry, reporting and editing methods are being changed dramatically as attorneys translate Supreme Court actions in libel into guidelines for news personnel. Whereas reporters thirty years ago may have undertaken an investigation with a vague sense of a potential for a libel suit, today's reporters can read the corporate guidelines for every step of a comparable investigation, including such matters as how to take and dispose of notes, what to put in internal memoranda, and what to do with unused information. The enhanced care in routine reporting is accompanied by an increased emphasis on the risks of investigative journalism. Better not to investigate at all, reporters have come to assume.

The Court has compounded the problem with a brief flirtation with a relatively expansive, if not truly faithful, version of Meiklejohn's theory. In *Rosenbloom v. Metromedia,* in 1971, a plurality of the Court would have expanded the use of the actual-malice test by applying it to libel suits involving issues of great concern or controversy.[54] But three years later, the justices narrowed the definition of "public figure" substantially from the Meiklejohn ideal:

> For the most part those who attain this [public figure] status have assumed roles of especial prominence in the affairs of society. Some occupy positions of such persuasive power and influence that they are deemed public figures for all purposes. More commonly, those classed as public figures have thrust themselves to the forefront of particular

public controversies in order to influence the resolution of the issues involved. In either event, they invite attention and comment.[55]

The "public-figure" test served to limit the range of protected press reporting about "private" persons; it had no effect on the courts' authority to examine in intricate detail how the news had been gathered and written. In fact, in the late 1970s, the Court affirmed that judicial examination of the news process was a fair price to pay for the limited constitutional protection afforded by the High Court. The state of mind of journalists and other aspects of newsgathering had to be examined as a way of establishing a standard of good journalistic behavior.

In *Herbert v. Lando,* a majority of the Court rejected the argument that the process of gathering news was protected from invasion by the Constitution.[56] The case involved the efforts of Lt. Col. Anthony Herbert to conduct extensive prelibel trial discovery about the news procedures of CBS. States of mind of reporters and editors and how they went about collecting information and shaping it into media news formats all were related to the fault standard of *New York Times v. Sullivan,* the majority affirmed. The majority delighted in pointing out the salutary effects of court-supervised reviews of newsgathering; reporters would have clearer standards of good and bad behavior. The idea that the federal courts are overseers of the news business had gained so much ground in the previous decade that *Herbert v. Lando* stirred little reaction.

The Court's management of news might be more appealing if beneficial results were more apparent either in the press or among the libel plaintiffs. To the contrary, the history of Court intervention in news has not markedly improved the commercial press; yet it has roughly paralleled and contributed to a growing national awareness of the ethical flaws of the press. A surge of books highlighting journalistic caprice in coverage of all manner of persons and a growing attention to journalistic ethics in the industry and in education thrives in part on the abundance of disclosure of the subtle inner workings of news organizations.

The courts have been bringing into public view a news system prone to error and excess. Renata Adler offered an illuminating conclusion after her study of two sensational libel trials in the 1980s, those brought by General William Westmoreland against CBS and Israeli Defense Minister Ariel Sharon against *Time* magazine:

> Received ideas, as so often upon examination in detail, happened to be wrong. The received, the right-minded, the liberal position in both cases was that the press defendants were protecting some valued and fragile Constitutional right against the assaults of whatever ideology was personified by two former military men. The reality had to do, rather, with the fragility, under the combined assault of modern newsgathering and contemporary litigation, of the shared sense of historic fact.[57]

The lesson of those two troublesome cases is that the Supreme Court's foray into libel oversight has not invested the news giants with ethical saintliness. A penchant for moral abuse is possible in any publication; the conventions of news are products of the marketing of a commodity. The power of the media conglomerate enables it to mount an awesome defense that need not, if the spirit is unwilling, include evidence of humility.

If the social benefits of plaintiff recourse to the courts to restore wounded reputations were more clear, a case might be made for the Court's approach. However, a recent study concludes that the plaintiffs' dominant interest in setting the record straight is rarely satisfied in litigation because the essential matter of truth or falsity is infrequently resolved by the suit.[58] Indeed, the social effect of defamation litigation has been, in one critic's view, a judicial invitation to compensate for injuries to the psyche.[59]

The press has appeared to read this era of court scrutiny as endorsement of its political value rather than as a recognition of its political power. Indeed, the corporate press has lobbied and litigated zealously to gain new rights as the supplier of the nation's political information. But as the dust has settled in the 1980s, it is clear that the courts have not enlarged the political role of the mass news media.

First, the Supreme Court has eschewed rulings that encourage any fundamental change in the process of producing news. The most radical attempt grew out of 1960s community and the consumer activism movement. Jerome Barron and others argued for a constitutional right of public access to the news media, but when a modest version of the idea—a state statute granting limited public access to newspapers—reached the Court, it was declared void with a firmness deeply appreciated throughout the newspaper industry. The government cannot compel publication, wrote Chief Justice Warren Burger in an opinion that purposely viewed the right of access in a very narrow way. Yet, the chief justice used the opinion to express his fears about press power:

> The result of these vast changes has been to place in a few hands the power to inform the American people and shape public opinion. Much of the editorial opinion and commentary that is printed is that of syndicated columnists distributed nationwide and, as a result, we are told, on national and world issues there tends to be a homogeneity of editorial opinion, commentary, and interpretative analysis. The abuses of bias and manipulative reportage are, likewise, said to be the result of the vast accumulations of unreviewable power in the modern media empires. In effect, it is claimed, the public has lost any ability to respond or to contribute in a meaningful way to the debate on issues.[60]

But the Court had invested too much in its scheme for managing news to let it be undermined by a solution as wonderfully democratic as setting aside some space in a newspaper for public use without the paper's own editorial interference.

Second, it became clear that the Court did not mean to expand the constitutional rights of the press when reporter organizations asked for access to government facilities, such as courts and prisons. Although the Court typically has framed such issues in terms of a public right to know rather than a right of the press to gather news, that reasoning has opened relatively few locked doors. The right of reporters, as members of the public, to attend trials and pretrial hearings has been affirmed, but in troublesome cases judges still are authorized to bar observers. Even more certainly, the press's claim to be gathering information for the public benefit has had little effect in expanding the tightly controlled access to prisons.

Third, in the protection of news sources from identification in court, the press has gained at best a legal shield placing the burden on prosecutors to show the need for the names to be revealed or for the testimony of persons who have given information to reporters confidentially to be subpoenaed. Again, explaining its intervention in the news process as a condition of a "limited" First Amendment protection of confidential sources, the Court said the government could breach the constitutional protection and require reporters to testify about sources in a trial by showing:

1. That there is probable cause to believe that the reporter has information clearly relevant to a specific probable violation of the law.
2. That the information sought cannot be obtained by alternative means less destructive of First Amendment rights and
3. That a compelling and overriding interest in the information can be shown.[61]

Moreover, testimony is generally required before grand juries and in civil suits. Courts often have refused to recognize the privilege when reporters have been plaintiffs in civil suits. Protection of sources has been high on the agenda of news organizations seeking an expansion in the meaning of freedom of the press. Use of secret sources is a newsgathering tradition with a history of many centuries. Yet only in the past century have there been claims that freedom of the press included the relationship of reporters with the people who gave them sensitive information. The modest acknowledgment by the Supreme Court of the value to the public of such sources has not been translated into any substantial gain in the political freedom of the press.

Thus, after a generation of lobbying on the part of the corporate press for a greater role in the American political system, little success can be claimed. The courts and other institutions have effectively limited the institutional claims of the press. That result is not at issue here; indeed, courts and prisons may have good reasons for imposing restraints on public and media access. The threat in all this is that judicial guidance of the press restrains it to do government work rather than the people's work.

This fear is reinforced by growing evidence of a press retreat from investigative journalism in the nation's daily newspapers during the 1970s.

Caution replaced dedication to the watchdog ideal of journalism even for newspapers whose legal costs could be borne by well-cushioned newspaper-chain corporations.[62] For the small shoestring political journal, a libel suit filed by a public figure—no matter what the outcome in court—has become a virtual death sentence. That potential plaintiffs frequently pass up such piddling targets because of their obvious poverty will be of little comfort on the day that an angered official takes aim at a publication that has accused him or her of wrongdoing.

CONCLUSION: THE FREEING OF THE FREEDOM OF THE PRESS

The courts are so deeply involved in the management of newsgathering that an argument for their withdrawal from that unwarranted field of interest seems both futile and irrelevant. The news media have grown ever more concentrated, powerful, and narrow since the Commission on Freedom of the Press turned much more modest evidence of that trend into a call for a new approach to press freedom in 1947.

One can see some wisdom in having a consumer protection agency for news—in this case, the Supreme Court. After all, news, contrary to the views of some theorists, is not what *is* happening; it appears, rather, to be what journalists *say* is happening. It is the tightly defined pinpoint of light that emerges from the focusing power of the market-oriented news media. That the pinpoint of law bears little resemblance to a "ruthless confession of a people to itself" is obscured by the news industry's self-serving rhetoric about freedom of the press. The newspaper industry, in particular, promotes the idea that it remains as independent of governmental authority as ever. It also courts public support by extolling the democratic benefits of responsible journalism. Freedom of the press, it is implied, is a sufficient condition for democracy; it is rarely acknowledged that freedom of the press also fosters a highly concentrated media system driven by the need for growth and profitability. The First Amendment has excused the government from thinking about media policy.

The Supreme Court is largely to blame for failing to state clearly that in regulating the press it is essentially allowing the newspaper industry and other news media industries to go their own way. The difficulty is that it is not well understood in this country that the Court has played such a role. A recent analysis of the Burger Court's work in press law commented:

> Yet journalists have continued to believe that freedom of the press has been seriously compromised and that the Burger Court was largely responsible. Such feelings are not unreasonable, for each decision that laid out a new sector of freedom also placed a fence around it. . . . These and many other decisions provide a truly ambiguous legacy, not least because the parsing and hairsplitting of the Burger Court

have not left a set of principles that can be readily explained or widely understood. The tangle that is First Amendment libel law is the prime example.[63]

The problem is even more serious. The Court has gone so far toward conditioning press rights on the imagined rights of the hypothetical citizen that it is incapable of accurately describing its own efforts. Thus, the great deception advanced in *New York Times v. Sullivan* that the Court was enlarging the freedom of the press continues to serve as a model for new rhetorical deception in subsequent cases.[64]

If honest advertising were required of the Court, it would have to say that it has fashioned out of the freedom-of-the-press clause of the First Amendment a new area of law that requires that the news media serve the citizenry "responsibly," which implies maintaining the status quo, preserving establishment biases, perpetuating social and nationalistic myths, and barring challenges to this role from the media forum. Candor also requires that the Court admit that it has not been careful to respect the idea that a healthy political system reflects diverse ideas, eccentric forms of expression, and impassioned argument. Indeed, the Burger Court, in its zeal to regulate the information media, has greatly blurred the lines between journalism of opinion and journalism of fact. The confusion is manifest in the numerous lower-court decisions in which judges have strained to find a test to distinguish fact from opinion once and for all. It is highly doubtful, for example, that the *Saturday Press* of Minneapolis, whose scathing and sometimes incorrect attacks on corrupt public officials won the Hughes Court's marvelous ringing endorsement of press freedom in 1931, would today survive the mandatory inquisition required in a libel suit involving a public official. Saying this is not meant to imply anything but disrespect for false accusation. The sad thing is that there is little room today for an opinionated, abrasive newspaper like the *Saturday Press,* and that fact alone is enough to intimidate all but the most courageous of the political publications. Given the narrow terms of political discourse in America, we should be reluctant to deter publications at the margins.

If the justices truly believe in serving the principle and the system of self-government in the United States, they need to go back to *New York Times v. Sullivan,* reread Brennan's stirring language about a commitment to "uninhibited, robust and wide-open debate," and then declare simply that the First Amendment protects that debate without qualification. They should jettison the actual-malice test and let Americans debate freely and openly. The alternative to an industry of libel litigation is apparent—some means of mediation which provides for prompt correction of false information. For the Court, this move would be a diplomatic retreat from an activist experiment of a quarter-century's duration.

To move in this direction requires that the Court recognize honestly that news reflects ideology as much as does the cry of the political dissident.

It should avoid the trap into which Meiklejohn stepped by ceasing its efforts to define categories of political speech. All of our public discourse deserves protection "because [we] will be called upon to vote." The Court would need to let go of artificial distinctions between the ideas of the corporate news media and the ideas of political debate. It will have to reject the intellectually flawed assumption that a person's opinions and their expression in print or through voting should be directly affected by a regulated flow of information. And this approach, of course, is unlikely to come from so conservative an institution. Moreover, the Court cannot be expected to change the social conditions that have increasingly reduced citizens to consumers, but it at least can work to preserve the ideal of citizens as actors in law and politics. Otherwise, if these legacies of America's twentieth century experience are not renounced, freedom of the press simply will remain the shield behind which corporate media grow stronger. Whether freedom of the press also will be the shield behind which Americans form and express their opinions will remain in doubt.

NOTES

1. Karl Marx, *On Freedom of the Press and Censorship,* Saul K. Padover, trans., *The Karl Marx Library,* vol. 4 (New York: McGraw-Hill, 1974), p. 31.
2. Quoted in Zechariah Chafee, Jr., *Government and Mass Communications* (Chicago: University of Chicago Press, 1947), I, pp. 26–27. Chafee did not identify the member.
3. Leonard W. Levy, ed., *Freedom of the Press from Zenger to Jefferson* (Indianapolis: Bobbs-Merrill, 1966), p. 12.
4. Tunis Wortman, *A Treatise Concerning Political Enquiry, and the Liberty of the Press* (New York: George Forman, 1800; reprint, New York: De Capo Press, 1970), p. 118.
5. Ibid., pp. 245–246.
6. Russell L. Hanson, *The Democratic Imagination in America* (Princeton: Princeton University Press, 1985), particularly pp. 257–292.
7. See, for example, Leonard W. Levy, *Emergence of a Free Press* (New York: Oxford University Press, 1985).
8. Alexis de Tocqueville, *Democracy in America* (New York: Alfred A. Knopf, 1980), vol. 1, p. 193.
9. Gerald J. Baldasty, "The Press and Politics in the Age of Jackson," *Journalism Monographs,* no. 89 (August 1984).
10. Walter Lippmann, *Public Opinion* (New York: Macmillan, 1922), p. 32.
11. Harold Lasswell, *Psychopathology and Politics* (Chicago: University of Chicago Press, 1930), pp. 196–197.
12. The principal publication of the Commission on Freedom of the Press was *A Free and Responsible Press* (Chicago: University of Chicago Press, 1947).
13. William Hocking, *Freedom of the Press: A Framework of Principle* (Chicago: University of Chicago Press, 1947), p. 18.
14. Ibid., p. 96.

15. Thomas Jefferson to John Norvell, June 11, 1807, in Andrew A. Lipscomb and Albert Ellery Bergh, eds., *The Writings of Thomas Jefferson* (Washington, D.C.: Thomas Jefferson Memorial Association of the United States, 1904–1905), vol. 11, p. 224.

16. United Nations, Economic and Social Council, Records of the Sub-Commission on Freedom of Information and of the Press (E/CN.4/Sub.1/SR 27, January 20, 1948).

17. Margaret A. Blanchard, *Exporting the First Amendment: The Press-Government Crusade of 1945–1952* (New York: Longman, 1986).

18. See R. Jeffrey Lustig, *Corporate Liberalism: The Origins of Modern American Political Theory, 1890–1920* (Berkeley: University of California Press, 1982); J. Herbert Altschull, *Agents of Power* (New York: Longman, 1984), pp. 301–305.

19. *A Free and Responsible Press*, p. 19.

20. Ibid., pp. 20–29.

21. Harold Lasswell, "The Structure and Function of Communication in Society," in Lyman Bryson, ed., *The Communication of Ideas* (New York: Institute for Religious and Social Studies, 1948), p. 51.

22. Blanchard, *Exporting the First Amendment*, pp. 133–139.

23. Hocking, *Freedom of the Press*, p. 169.

24. Alexander Meiklejohn, *Free Speech and Its Relation to Self-Government* (New York: Harper & Brothers, 1948); reprinted in Meiklejohn, *Political Freedom* (New York: Harper & Brothers, 1960).

25. Meiklejohn, *Free Speech*, p. 87.

26. Ibid., p. 4.

27. Ibid., pp. 65–66.

28. Ibid., p. 26. Emphasis added.

29. Ibid., p. 23.

30. Ibid., p. 63.

31. Ibid., p. 39.

32. Harry Kalven, "Metaphysics of the Law of Obscenity," *Supreme Court Review* (1960), pp. 1, 15–16; Alexander Meiklejohn, "The First Amendment Is an Absolute," *Supreme Court Review* (1961), pp. 245, 263.

33. Meiklejohn, *Free Speech*, pp. 104–105.

34. *Grosjean v. American Press Co.*, 297 U.S. 233 (1936).

35. I am indebted to Timothy W. Gleason, School of Journalism, University of Oregon, for this observation.

36. *Grosjean v. American Press Co.*, at 250.

37. Timothy Wilson Gleason, "Freedom of the Press in the 1930s: The Supreme Court's Interpretation of Liberty in a Changing Political Climate," unpublished master's thesis, University of Washington, 1983, pp. 138–140; *Associated Press v. National Labor Relations Board*, 301 U.S. 103 (1937).

38. Michael Schudson, *Discovering the News* (New York: Basic Books, 1978), p. 160.

39. Ben H. Bagdikian, *The Media Monopoly*, 2nd ed. (Boston: Beacon Press, 1987), p. 124.

40. Blanchard, *Exporting the First Amendment*; Kent Cooper, *Barriers Down* (New York: Farrar and Rinehart, 1942).

41. *Gitlow v. New York*, 268 U.S. 652 (1925).

42. *Schenck v. U.S.*, 249 U.S. 47 (1919).

43. *Gitlow v. New York,* at 668.
44. *Lovell v. Griffin,* 303 U.S. 444, 450–451 (1938).
45. *Near v. Minnesota,* 283 U.S. 697, 718 (1931).
46. Fred W. Friendly, *Minnesota Rag* (New York: Random House, 1981).
47. William J. Brennan, "The Supreme Court and the Meiklejohn Interpretation of the First Amendment," *Harvard Law Review* 79 (1965), pp. 1, 17, citing Kalven, "The New York Times Case: A Note on 'The Central Meaning of the First Amendment,'" *Supreme Court Review* (1964), p. 221.
48. *New York Times Co. v. Sullivan,* 376 U.S. 254 (1964).
49. Harold L. Nelson, ed., *Freedom of the Press from Hamilton to the Warren Court* (Indianapolis: Bobbs-Merrill, 1967), p. 98.
50. *New York Times Co. v. Sullivan,* at 293.
51. Bernard Schwartz, *Super Chief: Earl Warren and His Supreme Court: A Judicial Biography* (New York: New York University Press, 1983), pp. 531–541.
52. *Curtis Publishing Co. v. Butts,* 388 U.S. 130, 171–172.
53. *International News Service v. Associated Press,* 248 U.S. 215, 267 (1918).
54. *Rosenbloom v. Metromedia,* 403 U.S. 29 (1971).
55. *Gertz v. Robert Welch, Inc.,* 418 U.S. 323 (1974).
56. *Herbert v. Lando,* 441 U.S. 153 (1979).
57. Renata Adler, *Reckless Disregard* (New York: Alfred A. Knopf, 1986), p. 225.
58. Randall P. Bezanson, Gilbert Cranberg, and John Soloski, *Libel Law and the Press: Myth and Reality* (New York: The Free Press, 1987).
59. Rodney A. Smolla, *Suing the Press: Libel, the Media and Power* (New York: Oxford University Press, 1986).
60. *Miami Herald Publishing Co. v. Tornillo,* 418 U.S. 241 (1974).
61. *Branzburg v. Hayes,* 408 U.S. 665 (1972).
62. Bezanson et al., *Libel Law;* Richard Labunski, *Libel and the First Amendment* (New Brunswick, N.J.: Transaction, Inc., 1987).
63. James Boylan, "How Free is the Press?" *Columbia Journalism Review* (September/October 1987), p. 32.
64. Gerald J. Baldasty and Roger A. Simpson, "The Deceptive 'Right to Know': How Pessimism Rewrote the First Amendment," *Washington Law Review* (1981), p. 365; reprinted in Bill F. Chamberlin and Charlene J. Brown, eds., *The First Amendment Reconsidered* (New York: Longman, 1982), p. 62.

14 ——·
All the Free Speech That Money Can Buy?
The Supreme Court Constricts
Campaign Finance Reform

JOHN S. SHOCKLEY

"The First Amendment is not a vehicle for turning this country into a plutocracy," wrote Joseph Rauh, civil rights lawyer and former chairman of the
Americans for Democratic Action, in 1975.[1] Responding to the Supreme
Court's major campaign finance reform case of the modern era, *Buckley v.
Valeo*,[2] Rauh was stating a hope rather than a fact. In this chapter, I will
attempt to explain how and why the Court has in fact used the First Amendment to protect the influence of the wealthy in American politics, reshaping
a constitutional amendment that has usually been thought of as a "vehicle by
which otherwise powerless people can gain power"[3] into a means to afford
both fundamental and exclusive protection to the wealthy in the political
process. This First Amendment transformation echoes the nineteenth-
century Court's conversion of the Fourteenth Amendment's concern for protecting the rights of newly freed slaves into protection for the business corporation. In each case a laissez-faire liberal ideology praising a free political
marketplace has dominated constitutional construction to the clear benefit of
established powerful interests. In neither case did this turn of events occur
without a struggle. For the First Amendment, the final result has not been
inevitable, but it has also not been surprising.

I will first examine why the U.S. Supreme Court has viewed campaign
finance reform more skeptically than other process-oriented political movements that have also sought to broaden access to politics and to create greater
political equality. In doing this, I will also discuss why the Court therefore
refused to respond sympathetically to efforts to bring greater monetary
equality to political campaigns. I will then explore central tendencies and
ironies in Supreme Court reasoning on campaign finance reform, especially
their view that First Amendment monetary rights can be both fundamental

and exclusive. In the final sections of the chapter, I will discuss what the political impact of their decisions seems to have been and will focus on alternative yet difficult routes to limit the impact of money in politics and thereby enhance democracy.

EARLY JUDICIAL REACTION TO CAMPAIGN FINANCE ISSUES

The battle over campaign finance reform is a revealing example of how competing views can differ on the question of what democracy in the liberal state should mean. The aim of democracy is, after all, to make people more politically equal. But how far should equality be taken, and what is its relationship to liberty? Historically, the argument for liberal democracy has stressed that the right to vote and to have one's vote counted equally with others has democratized the political process, even though inequalities still exist in private (and economic) spheres. Because the millionaire's vote counts no more than that of the landless tenant, we can call our nation a democracy; we can claim that at a fundamental level, we have political equality and equality before the law. But evidence that the admitted inequalities in the private economic sphere have intruded into the political process undermines this claim. Campaign finance reform has attempted to protect democratic practice against this intrusion and thus has always been controversial.

Beginning with the Progressive era's reaction to corporate domination of politics at the turn of the century, the policing of money in electoral campaigns has been an item of concern to the reformer. As early as 1907, President Theodore Roosevelt proposed that government subsidize campaign expenses, limit the amount a person could contribute, and require full disclosure of campaign funding. The nation would have to wait until 1974 for such laws to pass, although laws were passed banning corporate contributions, requiring expenditure limitations for House and Senate campaigns, and setting up some disclosure requirements.[4] But loopholes and lack of enforcement rendered many of the laws from the Progressive era ineffective. At times, the Supreme Court took a broad and sympathetic view of the need to protect the political process from the corruption of money. In *Burroughs v. United States* (1934), the Supreme Court gave solid grounds for the regulation of campaign finance. In upholding the power of Congress to require certain political committees involved in presidential elections to issue financial reports, the Court concluded: "To say that Congress is without power to pass appropriate legislation to safeguard such an election from the improper use of money to influence the result is to deny the nation . . . the power of self-protection."[5]

After decades of sporadic interest, campaign finance issues again reached center stage in the early 1970s and have been with us ever since. Three factors seem to account for the renewed salience of this issue. Technological changes, including the growth and power of television, have seemingly required an enormous increase in the amount of money being spent on campaigns. Together with the weakening of political party ties that could have served as an alternative mediator in place of money, voter sentiment has become more volatile and therefore more susceptible to the influence of money. With these two factors was added the sensational disclosures of corruption surrounding the Nixon administration. Not only were bribery and extortion practices common in the Nixon reelection effort of 1971–1972, but secret cash contributions were used to finance the Watergate burglary of the Democratic National Committee and then to pay hush money to the burglars. All of this brought a revulsion against then-current campaign finance practices. This reaction culminated in the 1974 Amendments to the Federal Election Campaign Act, the most comprehensive campaign finance law ever passed.

The act contained a number of interrelated features, the most important of which were as follows:

1. Public Funding. For the first time ever, presidential campaigns became publicly funded (financed by money from income tax check-offs). For the primaries, matching grants for individual contributions up to $250 were instituted, and in the general election there was full public funding and a prohibition on contributions to the official campaigns of the major party candidates.

2. Limits on Contributions. Individual contributions to federal candidates (presidential and congressional) could not exceed $1,000 per candidate for the primaries and again for the general election. There was also an overall contribution limitation per person of $25,000 per year for federal candidates. Each multicandidate committee (political action committee) was limited to contributing no more than $5,000 per candidate for the primaries and $5,000 for the general election, and party committees also faced limits on how much they could contribute or spend on behalf of candidates.[6]

3. Limits on Expenditures. All federal candidates and their campaign committees were limited to a specific overall dollar amount, indexed to inflation, that could be spent on their campaigns. The amount that individuals and groups spend independently (that is, not in cooperation with or with the consent of the candidate or his campaign) were also limited.

4. Disclosure and Enforcement. Disclosure requirements for contributions and spending were strengthened, and since all previous campaign finance reform acts had suffered from loopholes and lack of enforcement, Congress for the first time created a special agency, the Federal Election Commission (FEC), to receive disclosure materials, publicize the data, and enforce and interpret the statutes.

These comprehensive reforms clearly tried to address a variety of monetary abuses in election campaigns, which by now were widely viewed as undermining the health of American democracy.

Before examining how the Supreme Court reacted to this act, we should place their response in context. In the decades leading up to the 1970s the Supreme Court had worked to remove impediments to equality in voting on a series of fronts. In areas of voting rights, reapportionment, poll taxes, and high filing fees, the Supreme Court actively and often courageously intervened to ban discriminatory practices. Yet in its work to expand and protect the right to vote against forces of blockage and dilution, the Court had not moved in advance of other governmental branches to protect the vote against campaign finance abuses. This inaction occurred even though campaign finance practices allowed wealthy people much greater access and influence and prevented poor people from being able to run credible campaigns for office. This inaction helps explain why campaign finance legislative reform, when it did occur, became the "stepchild" of the movement for protection of the right to vote.

As money in politics reemerged as an issue in the 1970s, legal scholars began to posit that recent precedents in Supreme Court equal protection cases might be interpreted as *requiring* affirmative judicial action in order to prevent the political process from being dominated by monied interests.[7] In guaranteeing all Americans the "equal protection of the laws," could the Fourteenth Amendment be used to protect the First Amendment rights of the nonwealthy, whether or not legislatures were addressing the problem? *Harper v. Virginia Board of Elections, Reynolds v. Sims,* and *Bullock v. Carter* all contained language expressing concern over economic discrimination in voting.[8] In *Bullock* a unanimous Court criticized high filing fees for candidates, declaring that "we would ignore reality were we not to recognize that this system falls with unequal weight on voters, as well as candidates, according to their economic status."[9] On the basis of this precedent, Professor Marlene Arnold Nicholson noted that if candidate registration fees bar candidates of modest means from running for office, "then surely the huge sums necessary to wage an effective campaign . . . place much more formidable roadblocks in the paths of such candidates."[10]

Yet there were problems with such a bold constitutional move ahead of legislative action. The Fourteenth Amendment says that "no state" shall "deny to any person within its jurisdiction the equal protection of the laws." Because of that wording, only inequalities involving "state action" have been held to be actual violations. Although governments had passed laws requiring poll taxes and expensive filing fees and had set malapportioned district boundaries, they had not passed laws requiring or supporting large private expenditures. They were thus not directly responsible for the inequalities at stake; they had merely acquiesced in the practice. In order for the courts to have moved in advance of legislatures to reform campaign finance practices, they would have had to move into an area of great sensitivity within liberal theory: the curtailment of what had historically been viewed as private rights beyond the reach of governmental power. Although this approach had precedents, most notably within the civil rights movement, it would not have been an easy, obvious step for the courts to take.

At least as important in such a move, the courts would also have had to challenge the powerful belief that the First Amendment should be modeled on the economic marketplace metaphor, which implied that tampering with the economic resources for free expression should be suspect. One First Amendment scholar has recently summarized this dominant view, which inhibited preemptive judicial action in the area of campaign finance reform, by commenting that "problems occasioned by physical scarcity or governmental monopoly must be distinguished from those caused by economic scarcity. The system of freedom of expression is by definition a laissez-faire system and must tolerate differences in the economic capacity of the various participants."[11] While there is, in fact, no "definition" of freedom of expression in the Constitution that says it must be a laissez-faire system—any more than any part of the Constitution prohibits the Sherman Anti-Trust Act—such a statement emphasizes the influence of the dominant ideology in First Amendment interpretation.

In addition to the problems of having to find state action and of impinging on an important component of liberal laissez-faire economic ideology, arguments for High Court rulings advancing campaign finance reform also encountered the difficulty of finding easy remedies to the problem. Simply banning the poll tax, or instituting the one-person, one-vote standard had no comparable remedy in campaign finance reform. Prohibiting contributions or expenditures above a certain amount had historically been the solution most in use around the country since the turn of the century, but this remedy had always derived from the legislative rather than the judicial branch. It required setting specific dollar limits and trying to plug loopholes, a task traditionally considered more legislative or administrative than judicial in nature. Other remedies would have entailed government revenues to replace newly prohibited funds or to supplement the efforts of those with little or no funds. Setting standards for prohibiting expenditures above a certain amount or requiring government subsidies would have demanded enormous judicial effort sure to arouse serious controversy. Thus, although related precedents would not have made the development of doctrine or remedies impossible, aggressive judicial action based on constitutional obligations to limit campaign finance inequalities involved problems of greater proportion and complexity than did reapportionment, poll taxes, filing fees, or voting rights.

THE 1974 LEGISLATION AND THE JUDICIAL RESPONSE

All areas of campaign finance reform, from disclosure of funding sources to government subsidies, involve sensitive issues within a democracy because they regulate the manner in which elections are conducted. But those regulations limiting the prerogatives of some citizens so that others can have a more equal voice are the most controversial. The campaign for equalization in areas where inequality traditionally has been tolerated is likely to evoke the greatest protest. Such protests have arisen in regard to campaign finance laws only because the economic inequality inherent in our society has become entrenched in aspects of our politics as well. Campaign contribution and spending limitations infringe upon what powerful interests have grown to view as part of their constitutional rights to political expression.

When the Supreme Court faced the issue of economic laissez faire as a prerogative in the political arena, it became clear how differently the Court was treating campaign finance legislation from other political process issues. Rather than supporting legislative measures promoting greater equality in the political process, as it did on reapportionment, high filing fees, and the right to vote, the Court elevated "liberty" to a far more important goal than "equality"; these values were seen as competing rather than complementary.[12] Engaging in aggressive judicial review, the Court overturned or modified crucial parts of the broad federal legislation passed in the wake of the Watergate scandal in 1974. Acting decisively to prohibit certain practices viewed as infringements upon the constitutional rights of the wealthy, the Court not only overruled Congress but also overruled much of the District of Columbia Court of Appeals decision, which had used quite different arguments and standards to find the legislation constitutional.

The clash over equalizing access to politics or protecting the liberties of wealthy candidates and individuals was met head-on in the approaches taken by these two courts. The lower court viewed the federal statutes sympathetically, as designed to implement the one-person, one-vote principle and to safeguard the integrity of elections. Summing up their philosophy, the Court of Appeals stated, "It would be strange indeed if, by extrapolation outward from the basic rights of individuals, the wealthy few could claim a constitutional guarantee to a stronger political voice than the unwealthy many because they are able to give and spend more money, and because the amounts they give and spend cannot be limited."[13] Limiting the intrusion of private inequalities into the political process, then, was a perfectly legitimate constitutional goal, in the opinion of the lower court.

But the U.S. Supreme Court expressed far less commitment to the goal of equalization. The majority first held that money was a form of speech, not merely speech-related conduct. This fascinating ideological leap allowed them to apply strict scrutiny to legislation in the campaign finance reform area, since political speech is a protected right. With this leap they then found that "The concept that government may restrict the speech [meaning money] of some elements of our society in order to enhance the relative voice of others is wholly foreign to the First Amendment."[14] They were now able to strike down or modify a number of aspects of the law which went against this philosophy:

1. Public financing was allowed, but the Court insisted that the provisions (together with their expenditure limits) must be voluntary.

2. Limits on contributions were allowed to stand, on grounds that this legislation deterred corruption and the appearance of corruption. However, the Court struck down limits on what candidates could spend on their own races, arguing that candidates cannot corrupt themselves.

3. All expenditure limits were struck down, including the overall expenditure limits on congressional campaigns and the amount anyone could spend independently to promote or attack candidates. The only exception the Court allowed was to uphold spending limits when tied to public funding in the presidential race, where this spending was clearly part of or coordinated with the candidate's campaign. In a later opinion, *Federal Election Commission v. National Conservative Political Action Committee* (1985), limits on independent expenditures by individuals and PACs in publicly funded races (which were never enforced after *Buckley v. Valeo*) were also struck down. To the majority on the Court, spending in support of a candidate that occurs independently of the candidate's campaign does not arouse the same danger of corruption that a contribution does.

4. Basic provisions of disclosure and enforcement were allowed, on grounds that these requirements were necessary to dampen corruption and the appearance of corruption. The Court expressed potential concern for disclosure of contributions to unpopular minor parties and required that appointment procedures of FEC commissioners be changed.

How are we to view this outstanding example of activism in terms of what it says about the justices' understanding of the meaning of the First Amendment? All members seem to have viewed the deterrence of quid pro quo corruption (that is, simple bribery or extortion) among politicians as an entirely constitutional goal. But a majority of justices expressed much less sympathy, or indeed distaste, for introducing greater equality of access to influence campaigns by closing off all monetary avenues for the wealthier strata to exercise their "freedom of speech."[15] The Court generally seemed to view too much equality as a threat to liberty rather than seeing equality and liberty as necessary supports for each other. Narrowing the legitimate goal of campaign finance reform to merely quid pro quo corruption effectively struck down those aspects of the laws that tried to introduce greater equality of access. To reformers it was also a peculiarly cramped goal, since narrow quid pro quo corruption occurs far less often than other forms of corruption.[16] What about the "corruption" that exudes from the need for massive amounts of money in order to run credible campaigns for office? What about preserving the integrity of the electoral process, a goal that an earlier Court in *Burroughs* had considered constitutional? The expenditure limits were supposed to solve this problem by freeing candidates from the need to spend so much time and energy raising funds and by preventing money from determining the outcome of elections and subsequent policy decisions. The broad goals of restricting the "undue influence" or "excessive influence" of money on political campaigns aim to protect democracy, prevent the cynicism and apathy that result from the belief that "money talks," and address the issue of inequality in the funding process. But these goals were not given constitutional legitimacy. The majority preferred to constrict the focus of campaign finance reform to the simpler issues of bribery and extortion, i.e., quid pro quo corruption of the straight-out dollars for political favors sort.

This overall conclusion about the goals of *Buckley* is derived from an examination of what was allowed and disallowed by the decision as well as the reasons given for so ruling. In four ways the Court decision had the effect of protecting the wealthy from the congressional reforms: (1) The majority struck down limits on the amount a candidate could spend on his or her own race and (2) reallowed the wealthy (both individuals and political action committees) to spend unlimited amounts on elections so long as it was done "independently" of the candidate.[17] The judges' intervention also (3) protected the candidate's right to raise unlimited funds from the stratum of society that can contribute money to campaigns by striking down candidate expenditure limits and (4) allowed a candidate to reject public funds if a more effective campaign could be waged through increased private spending. In all these ways, the Court preserved important prerogatives for the wealthy. The justices may even have been trying to "clean up" and legitimize this power by separating it from the more discredited individualized corruption of outright bribery and extortion.

By upholding disclosure and contribution limitations, as well as the public financing of elections, *Buckley* was a compromise decision: A majority on the Court felt it important to uphold the restraints upon those forms of financial activity most clearly connected with corrupt practices. The Court was no doubt sensitive both to the Watergate scandal and to the shaken public confidence in government and the electoral process. Yet the aggressive judicial review in *Buckley* allowed the wealthy to keep their options open in a manner that middle-class and poor citizens, and candidates with only middle-class or poor supporters, simply could not.[18]

To protect the differential impact of wealth by striking down campaign finance laws on grounds of a violation of "free speech" has been imitated by no other Western democracy. Surely a more accurate justification for striking down these laws can be seen in a sympathetic defense of the opinion by Brice Clagett and John Bolton, who were cocounsels for the plaintiffs in the case. To them, "our social system is based on the premise that inequalities of wealth serve valid and useful purposes," and "the wealthy need means to exercise their financial power to defend themselves politically against the greater numbers who may believe that their economic interests militate toward leveling."[19] Since money can be considered a countervailing force to a natural majority or to a large aggregate of voters, and such a countervailing force is *needed*,[20] the wealthy should be allowed, or indeed should be considered to have earned, special political privileges not given to the majority of citizens. These beliefs are alive today in the idea that the wealthy have more at stake in the political system and that their activity is particularly necessary to the overall health of the economic, social, and political structure of the society.[21]

The Supreme Court majority did not explicitly use this argument in protecting the rights of the wealthy, however. As we noted, they relied upon the more noble concept of the protection of the right to freedom of expression. But analysis of the Court decision leads to the conclusion that an ideologically cramped view of the First Amendment must have been the motivating force behind their opinion.[22] In a revealing passage, the majority stated that limiting a candidate and his family to personal expenditures of $25,000, $35,000, or $50,000 *annually* (depending upon the office), "imposes a *substantial restraint* on the ability of persons to engage in protected First Amendment expression."[23] If being able to spend only $25,000 to $50,000 annually on federal campaigns is, in fact, a substantial restraint upon constitutional expression, what does this say about the rights of the 99 percent of the American electorate who cannot expend even this "substantially restrained" amount?[24] Since those who are not wealthy find their ability to speak is restrained even more, where are they to look for the protection of their First Amendment rights?[25] Without even realizing it, the Court acknowledged that ordinary Americans' First Amendment rights are greatly restrained by the fact of economic inequality, a restraint about which the Court did nothing. The greatest revelation of the Court's perspective on the unequally enjoyed rights of "free speech" is the Court's own *lack* of concern for the basic rights of those without wealth. The right to spend tens of thousands of dollars annually to influence political campaigns is simultaneously fundamental and exclusive. It belongs only to those few who have the resources.

In an equally revealing quotation, the Court majority stated that the $1,000 ceiling on spending for a clearly identified candidate "would appear to exclude all citizens . . . from *any* significant use of the most effective modes of communication."[26] And elsewhere in *Buckley* the Court noted that virtually every means of communicating ideas in today's mass society requires considerable expenditures of money and that the "electorate's increasing dependence on television, radio, and other mass media for news and information has made these expensive modes of communication *indispensable instruments* of effective political speech."[27] My point here is not that the Supreme Court is wrong; indeed, they are correct.[28] What is so revealing is that these premises were used to protect the wealthy's right to continued dominance rather than to limit this dominance or to support the rights of those without large sums of money to have a chance to use these "indispensable instruments." Through the Court's own words, they have unwittingly acknowledged that the great majority of the American people are excluded from the chance to effectively communicate their political ideas. From a reading of the Court's most important campaign finance reform decision, the unmistakable conclusion is that the exercise of our constitutional rights of free speech *requires* the amount of money that only a few in our society have.

This interpretation is supported by the fact that most of those who defend the Court argue for the permissibility or necessity of inequality in politics, or defend laissez-faire capitalism as an appropriate standard for First Amendment protection. U.S. Circuit Judge Ralph Winter, for years a respected conservative writer on campaign finance reform, followed a path of defense similar to that employed by the Court and by Clagett and Bolton. After noting that "It is simply beyond argument that effective communication in modern society pervasively requires large expenditures," he conceded that "no one denies that some persons and groups have advantages—indeed, enormous advantages—in political communication." This conclusion did not lead him down the path to equality, however. Instead, because "these inequalities are so ubiquitous throughout our polity" that it is impossible to bring about equalities, he concluded that efforts to promote equalities "will merely create new inequalities."[29]

This is a startling admission, one that the Supreme Court itself has not been so provocative as to repeat. Instead, the Court has said that the government is under no constitutional obligation to create greater equality of access in campaign finance. If the legislature wants to subsidize the rights of the majority via the fairness doctrine, tax credits, or matching funds, it may do so. The Court majority is not blocking *all* means of democratization of campaign finance, although they show little sympathy with the goal. Instead, they view campaign finance to be basically a private, voluntary matter that should reflect the wills of individual citizens rather than artificial government involvement. The liberty of people to support whomever they want is more important than government intervention to ensure more equal access. The Court majority does view policing the system (as with disclosure and the creation of the FEC) and protecting it from clear illegalities of bribery and extortion to be entirely proper goals of campaign finance legislation. They also are not against all forms of improving access so long as the means do not go too far in curtailing individual voluntarism. Again, the Court seems to be implicitly using the free-market model, where the government may serve as umpire to the system but should not upset its basically private, voluntary nature.[30] To the Court majority, the philosophical battle is over the proper realm of private activity versus public control and whether equality should be allowed to threaten basic private liberties. The *results* of their decisions may produce protections to the wealthy few over the unwealthy many, but their mode of justification rests on the protection of private liberties for "all."

The fear of government using the goal of equality in campaign finance as a means to trample liberty perhaps was best expressed by Daniel Polsby when he concluded that "speech is not 'free' in any important sense if it is protected only when and to the extent that such protection is consistent with a congressionally defined notion of political equality."[31] Polsby's eloquence loses some of its force unless one accepts his premise that *money* is speech, rather than speech-related conduct, and forgets that these regulations do not suppress the *content* of speech. In fact, under the reforms, all rights of direct political expression and advocacy are retained. Polsby's argument loses further power if one agrees that money is speech but believes that, as a result, we need to share the wealth and dismantle economic inequality. Those who believe the latter want to move beyond a society with "all the free speech that money can buy" to greater equality in free speech of the sort that a democratic society would seem to require.

Those who share the preference for liberty over government intervention are also less convincing if one believes that, as with the maintenance and regulation of the free-market system itself, the government is already deeply implicated in the creation and destruction of wealth. Since taxation, subsidies, tariffs, and procurement policies profoundly affect who wins and who loses in the game of wealth, critics of the dominant view on the Court argue that government cannot be neutral regarding who has money to spend on "speech." It can only pretend to be neutral.

It is interesting that all these arguments have been made from within the Court. Justice Byron White, never reconciled to the *Buckley* decision, repeated his fundamental critique of both the premises and conclusions of the Court majority nine years later, in *FEC v. NCPAC* (1985):

> The First Amendment protects the right to speak, not the right to spend, and limitations on the amount of money that can be spent are not the same as restrictions on speaking. I agree with the majority that the expenditures in this case "produce" core First Amendment speech. But that is precisely the point: they produce such speech; they are not speech itself. At least in these circumstances, I cannot accept the identification of speech with its antecedents. Such a house-that-Jack-built approach could equally be used to find a First Amendment right to a job or to a minimum wage to "produce" the money to "produce" the speech.[32]

Given the premises and conclusions the majority continues to adhere to, is there more we can say about what seem to be the deeper justifications for the particular choices they have made and rejected? To justify supporting principles that result in such fundamental and exclusive rights to monetary speech in a democracy, the Court presumably must believe that such rights should not be hereditary or discriminatory. To put the matter in constitutional language, these rights should not be exercised in a manner that violates the due process or equal protection rights of others seeking the opportunity to become so wealthy that spending only $25,000 to $50,000 a year would be a "substantial restraint" upon their First Amendment rights.[33] How can one reconcile the concepts of due process and equal protection of the laws with the philosophy expressed in *Buckley*? It seems that one must believe that the American economic system is open and fair enough to allow each citizen an equal opportunity to gain enough monetary resources. According to this reasoning, if the unequal distribution of goods is just and fair, then laws limiting citizens to spending only tens of thousands of dollars a year on campaigns actually *violate* their First Amendment rights. Exactly how the Supreme Court endorses this notion is unclear, since such reasoning about the fundamentals of democracy, justice, equality, and liberty is not explicitly expressed and must be inferred from the Court's opinion. Yet, without such a perspective, is there any other way the Court could have reached the conclusions in *Buckley* from the premise that money is speech?

Actually, a majority on the Court at times seems to have gone even further. When the results lead in a direction the Court does not like, the Court can be surprisingly cognizant of the "dangers" of wealth. In *CBS v. Democratic National Committee,* Chief Justice Warren Burger agreed to allow CBS to refuse to run a paid political advertisement against the Vietnam War. The public interest in providing access to the marketplace of ideas, he said, "would scarcely be served" by compelling broadcasters to accept paid political advertisements, because this procedure would be "so heavily weighted in favor of the financially affluent, or those with access to wealth."[34] Similarly, when they prohibit involuntary union contributions by members while allowing corporations to spend directly, regardless of individual shareholder views, in all ballot proposition campaigns and where not prohibited by law, the justices seem more skeptical of the use of labor union wealth than business wealth in campaigns.[35]

An examination both of what they strike down and what they allow indicates that the Supreme Court's theory of the First Amendment and campaign finance reform rests upon extreme deference to certain kinds of wealth and unexamined assumptions of liberty that parallel free-market capitalism. To be viable as a form of democratic theory, these free-market assumptions must include such basics as a belief in relatively equal bargainers in the marketplace, true competition, and adequate knowledge. But none of these points is carefully examined by the Court.[36] In truth, whatever its logic of liberty and antistatism, the Supreme Court is protecting money *over* the actual speech and ideas of all Americans. Through declaring money to be a form of speech, the Court loses the ability to distinguish between money and speech and therefore allows the First Amendment to undercut that which it was designed to protect. This distorted view of American economic and political reality is a very narrow base for a theory of free speech—and certainly goes against some of the basic ideas of the meaning of the First Amendment and the concept of democracy in Western political thought.[37]

Many have protested this distorted view. An angry Judge Skelly Wright of the D.C. Circuit Court of Appeals has explained the Supreme Court's philosophy as follows: "A latter-day Anatole France might well write, after observing American election campaigns, 'the law, in its majestic equality, allows the poor as well as the rich to form political action committees, to purchase the most sophisticated polling, media, and direct mail techniques, and to drown out each other's voices by overwhelming expenditures in political campaigns.'"[38] From a courageous amendment protecting the unpopular pamphleteer, publisher, and powerless against the mighty, the First Amendment thus has been transformed into a means to protect those who turn economic power into political power against the powerless.[39]

In response to the Court's elevation of liberty over equality in First Amendment interpretation, a number of scholars have propounded a constitutional principle of equal liberty, rather than of liberty in conflict with equality. One especially prominent attempt comes from Kenneth Karst, who notes that although some say that First Amendment interests involve not equality but liberty, "This line of argument is misleading. . . . The principle of equality, when understood to mean equal liberty, is not just a peripheral support for the freedom of expression, but rather part of the 'central meaning of the First Amendment.'"[40] The philosopher John Rawls has also defended the constitutional principle of equal liberty. In arguing for governmental obligations to "underwrite a fair opportunity to take part in and influence the political process . . . irrespective of their economic and social class," Rawls notes that "The liberties protected by the principle of participation lose much of their value whenever those who have greater private means are permitted to use their advantages to control the course of public debate."[41] In his Tanner lecture of 1981, Rawls continued developing the idea of equal liberty:

> The First Amendment no more enjoins [requires] a system of representation according to influence effectively exerted in free political rivalry between unequals than the Fourteenth Amendment enjoins [requires] a system of liberty of contract and free competition between unequals in the economy, as the Court thought in the Lochner era. In both cases the results of the free play of the electoral process and of economic competition are acceptable only if the necessary conditions of background justice are fulfilled. . . . The danger of *Buckley* is that it risks repeating the mistake of the Lochner era, this time in the political sphere where, for reasons the Court itself has stated [in *Wesberry* and *Reynolds*], the mistake could be much more grievous.[42]

As these and other critics note, the greatest danger from the Supreme Court's hostility to the goal of equality in First Amendment protection is that in their eagerness to protect liberty, but not equal liberty, they are denying liberty to those who are not equal.

CASES AFTER *BUCKLEY V. VALEO*

Much of the Court's reasoning in *Buckley* was amplified and extended in *First National Bank of Boston v. Bellotti,* a case decided two years later by a 5–4 majority.[43] In *Bellotti,* the Court protected from state interference the right of corporations to spend unlimited funds on ballot propositions. The case arose in Massachusetts, a state that has had a long history of litigation over legislative attempts to limit corporate spending on ballot proposals. The law challenged by corporations in *Bellotti* was a moderate reform measure: It did not prohibit corporations from spending unlimited treasury funds on issues affecting any of the property, business, or assets of the corporation; it merely prohibited corporate spending on ballot proposals in which corporations were not "materially affected" by the outcome. Corporations, however, feared that if this prohibition were upheld, later regulations might try to limit campaign contributions on ballot issues that "materially affected" corporations. The Massachusetts law stipulated that a personal income tax (as opposed to a corporate income tax) did not materially affect corporations. As a result, corporations were forbidden from spending corporate treasury funds to oppose a referendum instituting a progressive personal income tax, even though a number of them wanted to do so.[44]

The Supreme Court side-stepped the historically thorny question of whether a corporation could be considered a "person" entitled to First Amendment rights of free speech. Writing for the majority, Justice Lewis Powell couched the matter in terms of the citizen's right to hear all sides of an issue, including a corporation's speech. In this way, he deflected the bitter dissent by Justice Byron White, who, in contending that the Massachusetts law was a reasonable exercise of state power in the campaign finance area, argued that "The state need not permit its own creation to consume it."[45] In holding that ballot propositions involve ideas, not candidates for office, and therefore could not be bought or corrupted, the Court majority tightened the grip of narrow quid pro quo corruption as the legitimate concern of campaign finance reform.[46]

When the City of Berkeley tried to work around the *Bellotti* strictures by enacting a contribution limitation (not a ban on expenditures) that applied to corporations in local ballot proposition campaigns, the Court struck even this down. A majority ruled the law unconstitutional even though the Berkeley statute allowed corporations to spend unlimited amounts so long as they did so directly under their own name and not through contributions.[47]

The Court seems sensitive to the changes it has rendered, and in order to emphasize continuity rather than highlight the mutation, they have often couched the changes in the rhetoric of popular egalitarianism, concealing the reality behind the rhetoric. For example, writing for the majority in the Berkeley case, Chief Justice Warren Burger tried to frame the decision in a way that suggested that the Court was actually acting to protect the rights of the nonwealthy. He stated that under the Berkeley ordinance, "an affluent person can, acting alone, spend without limit to advocate individual views on a ballot measure. It is only when contributions are made in concert with one or more others in the exercise of the right of association that they are restricted."[48]

Burger did not mention that the original Berkeley ordinance did in fact restrict expenditures as well as contributions. The statute had been modified to restrict contributions but not expenditures in response to the Court's decision in *Buckley v. Valeo.* The city of Berkeley was thus trapped in a "Catch-22" situation with the Court: If it tried to effectively limit the power of the affluent through expenditure restrictions, the ordinance would be struck down as a violation of the First Amendment under *Buckley;* if it decided to selectively restrict the power of the affluent by requiring direct expenditures once the contribution limit had been reached, it would be accused of showing favoritism to the rich by allowing them an alternative (unlimited spending) unavailable to the less affluent. The Court in *Citizens Against Rent Control v. City of Berkeley* followed this line of reasoning, suddenly caring about alternatives for the nonwealthy, and could thus appear to be courageously striking a victory for the nonwealthy.[49]

The Court made the same misleading argument in *FEC v. NCPAC* (1985), contending that contribution limitations with no limitations on direct expenditures (to meet the *Buckley* requirement) would "subordinate the voices of those of modest means as opposed to those sufficiently wealthy to be able to buy expensive media ads with their own resources."[50] But once again, those of modest means would not have been subordinated if the Court had not previously struck down the restrictions on large expenditures.

Not all aspects of the Court's decisions in campaign finance fit neatly into a simple view emphasizing its protection of the prerogatives of the wealthy. The refusal to allow the California Medical Association to contribute unlimited funds to a political action committee, *CMA v. FEC,* served to limit the raising of PAC funds. Writing for the plurality in the opinion, Justice Thurgood Marshall reiterated that "speech by proxy [which is what contributions are] . . . is not the sort of political advocacy that this Court in *Buckley* found entitled to full First Amendment protection."[51] The refusal to hear the case brought by the Republican National Committee challenging the constitutionality of expenditure limitations for candidates who accept public funds, *RNC v. FEC,* is also an example of the Court ruling against monied interests.[52] And in the recent case of *FEC v. Massachusetts Citizens for Life,* Justice William Brennan's majority opinion distinguished nonprofit, nonstock corporations, such as "Massachusetts Citizens for Life," from corporations falling under the federal prohibitions on direct corporate expenditures in connection with the election of candidates to public office. In making this distinction, Brennan acknowledged "the legitimacy of Congress' concern that organizations that amass great wealth in the economic marketplace not gain unfair advantage in the political marketplace."[53] Similarly, the Court has not overturned federal statutes prohibiting corporations from spending directly on candidates, although PACs have provided an effective alternative outlet for political influence.

These cases emphasize that the Court is not composed of five or more justices who consistently back the antistatist, libertarian view on all campaign finance reform issues, which would leave no room for bargaining. The *Buckley* case itself of course indicated a degree of flexibility, as that opinion itself was clearly a compromise decision. But the fact that the Court has not applied its restrictive, *Lochner*-like position to every campaign finance issue does not negate the fact that its most important cases have twisted the impact of attempted campaign finance reform away from the goal of equality. The goal of most members of the Supreme Court, despite occasional inconsistencies or the necessity of compromise, still seems to be to prevent narrowly defined quid pro quo corruption of politicians while protecting liberty over equality in campaign finance, which results in protecting the prerogatives of the wealthy to continue exercising greater political influence.[54]

THE IMPACT OF THE COURT ON CAMPAIGN FINANCE PRACTICES

Given the admitted inequalities rampant in campaign finance, what impact has the Supreme Court had by modifying or striking down laws that aimed to promote greater equality in this sphere? Wealth is unlike other political resources in that it is easily convertible into other political resources. Because of this, it is difficult to isolate its exact influence on elections. Few would deny that the Court's campaign finance decisions have affected who has won and who has lost elections, the nature of the campaign process, and public policy. But the extent of the influence has been the subject of continued debate. The main difficulty is that of assessing causation where many possible causes are surely at work. Certainly money is not the only or always the most important factor in who wins and who loses. Because factors besides money are influential in how a potential voter behaves or what an elected official will do, the relative impact of money and of campaign finance reform laws obviously varies, depending upon the particular situation. And because the Supreme Court is only one participant in the regulation of money, not all developments related to the impact of money on politics can be attributed to the Court. What the Congress, the Federal Election Commission, the Federal Communications Commission, and state and local governments have done and not done all relate to the impact of money in campaigns.

Frank Sorauf is correct in noting that "concern about campaign finance far outstrips knowledge about it" and, "Money will not translate into enough votes if the persuasion it buys cannot overcome the opposing means and resources of persuasion."[55] Yet in the face of the difficulty of assessing discrete impact, we should not forget that both campaign finance laws and the judicial response to these laws are premised on the idea that money makes a difference in the electoral and governing process. If money were not seen by challengers, incumbents, Republicans, Democrats, minor parties, political consultants, and the court system as important to political campaigns and government, there would be little need for regulation and little controversy on the subject.

The best evidence from political scientists and journalists on the impact of money on elections indicates that partisanship and incumbency are the most powerful antidotes to money.[56] A candidate with vast amounts of money running in a district heavily populated by members of the opposition party is likely to lose. An incumbent will usually be able to generate enough free publicity (and favors) to be able to counteract the challenger's money. But to complicate matters, neither partisanship nor incumbency are totally unrelated to the ability to attract funds. An incumbent has perquisites of office (a paid staff, free mailings, etc.) that are the equivalent of considerable sums of money, and partisanship (and issue positions) affects how easy it is for a person to raise funds. Because of this intermingling of causes, isolating the effect of one discrete cause is not easy. Interestingly, no study has yet found that money makes no difference in voting behavior or in candidate and officeholder behavior. Thus, the status quo is not a neutral ground on the issue of regulations on money. What most studies have found is that challengers and members of the minority party (usually Republicans), who often need to engage in more persuasion during a campaign, generally find money to have a greater impact.[57]

Because money tends to make races more competitive, some scholars have opposed restrictions on money (especially expenditure ceilings) on grounds that money can be an "equalizer" in campaigns, overcoming the advantages of incumbency and partisanship.[58] If so, however, it is a strange kind of equalizer, one that can equalize only those who already have money. Those without funds to contribute remain on the periphery, more likely than ever to have their voices "drowned out," and more likely than ever to believe that politics is for those with wealth. Surely there are better ways to equalize the playing field of politics than through unlimited spending.

A series of complementary trends, including the decline of partisan identification and increasingly sophisticated campaign techniques, indicate that money is becoming more important in our political process. The aggregate level of campaign spending is rising with each election, and at a rate far above inflation. By the 1983–1984 election cycle, $1.8 billion was being spent on campaigns, an amount almost unimaginable a decade ago.[59] If we consider the areas of judicial activism in *Buckley* and examine how striking down aspects of the 1974 law affected behavior, we find the following:

1. So far all presidential candidates except John Connally in 1980 have accepted public funding, although candidates from Ronald Reagan to Pat Robertson have criticized the public financing system.

2. A number of congressional candidates have been able to spend parts of their personal fortunes, now that the Supreme Court has disallowed the law's ceiling for candidates' spending in their own races. The record so far has been set by Jay Rockefeller of West Virginia, who spent $10.3 million of his own fortune in his successful race for the Senate in 1984. In a number of cases, the personal spending did not result in victory.[60] In a few cases, however, such as John Heinz's narrow Senate victory over William Green in 1976, most observers thought the extra money made the difference. It is also true that the number of millionaires in the Senate is now at an all-time high, at roughly half the Senate.

3. The striking down of expenditure limits has probably had the most dramatic effect, as most races for the House and Senate now involve money above what the limits would have been. For the 1985–1986 election cycle, Senate candidates who won their races averaged more than $3 million dollars on their own election efforts, and spending officially reported by all congressional candidates reached a record-breaking $450 million, a 20 percent increase over the previous two-year cycle.[61] This amount is far above what would have been allowed under the 1974 law. Lack of expenditure limits has also facilitated the growing contributions of PACs, because under the original expenditure ceilings most candidates would not have been able to accept so much money.

4. The use of the independent-spending loophole has been escalating, for when the Court struck down the stringent limits on independent spending, it offered PACs another viable, unregulated way to spend money in campaigns. In 1980 NCPAC (the National Conservative Political Action Committee) created a furor by spending millions in targeting a number of liberal Democratic senators for defeat, primarily through negative television advertising. Most of the targeted candidates were in fact defeated, but to attribute their losses solely to NCPAC's spending would be to ignore other factors which had made these Democratic senators vulnerable. By 1986 independent spending reached more than $4 million in House races and $5 million on Senate races. These figures were almost as much as the amount spent by the political parties in support of House candidates and nearly half the amount spent by parties in support of Senate candidates—a disturbing result for those who favor stronger parties.[62]

Independent spending in presidential campaigns also involved millions of dollars. In 1980 more than $13 million was spent in support of the Republican candidates, but only $170,000 was spent independently for the Democrats. By 1984 independent presidential spending for the Republicans increased to more than $16 million, while the Democrats spent just slightly more than $1 million, which was still less than 10 percent of the total of independent funds.[63]

5. If we add the impact of *First National Bank of Boston v. Bellotti,* which opened the floodgates to direct corporate contributions and spending on state and local ballot propositions, we find that in the 1983–1984 election cycle more than $70 million was spent on these campaigns.[64] Since most of this money was likely from corporate funds, the Court ensured a greater role for money in initiative and referenda campaigns as well and undoubtedly

determined the outcome of some of the contests.[65] In a world with this amount of money, it is not entirely clear how ordinary citizens, or those with the support of only ordinary people, can compete.

Modern fund-raising techniques, especially mass mail appeals, and provisions of the Federal Election Campaign Act that legitimated political action committee involvement in the political process have also greatly added to the amount of money raised and spent in campaigns. From 1974 to 1984, PAC spending mushroomed from $21 million to $265 million, a more than ten-fold increase. While labor unions had disbursed 52 percent of the PAC total in 1974, they could not keep up with the explosion of corporate, health-care related, and nonconnected (that is, independent, usually ideological) PAC growth. By 1984, labor PACs were contributing less than 18 percent of all PAC funds, less than all three of the other sources of PAC funds.[66] While the Court was only partly responsible for the growth of PAC spending, judicial action certainly facilitated their vast growth.

Political parties, especially the Republican party, have also increased their fund-raising capabilities. By the 1983–1984 election cycle, national, state, and local political party committees spent almost $400 million, of which the Republicans spent more than three-fourths of the total. But PACs have become major institutional competitors to parties, and the link between parties and candidates has in general weakened. More important, many fear that the "commodification" of politics, as money assumes a more important role than ever before, has weakened the ordinary voter's link to campaigns and governance. Politics is becoming more professionalized into permanent campaign technologies and detached from ordinary voter concerns. Money obviously is not the only cause of these changes in American elections, but it seems to be an essential ingredient in allowing these technologies to transform the system. While campaign finance reform could not have suppressed the technologies of a high consumptive society, it could have provided barriers to inhibit turning politics into advertising and citizens into either spectators or consumers. Reform could have reinforced and protected the distinction between the inequality inherent in an entrepreneurial mass consumptive economy and the equality necessary to that society's democratic political life, retaining some semblance of autonomy between these two spheres.

The Supreme Court, however, greatly weakened the barriers. The impact of this trend on the Democratic Party, both in weakening and transforming the party as it either loses out in the fund-raising game or is forced to become more dependent upon corporate and wealthy contributors, is profound. As the party that has historically attracted and mobilized the common man and the disadvantaged in American society, the Democratic party is now trapped between its financial needs and its electoral constituency. If there is no obvious resolution of this dilemma, record-low voter turnout, together with cynicism and confusion among the bottom half of the electorate, should continue if not worsen.[67]

Even the perception that money "buys" elections influences our polity. It discourages or prevents many potential candidates who are unable or unwilling to compete on such terrain from running for office. The number of voters who have dropped out of the system or never become involved because of what they see as a deck stacked in favor of the rich probably is equally significant. Multiple causes are no doubt involved, but no one disputes the fact that voter turnout in American elections is at near record lows, and that the poor and less educated are now voting at a rate far below that of other groups.[68]

AVENUES TO REFORM

Given the Supreme Court's activism in modifying and striking down laws that worked for greater equality in campaign finance, what options are left for supporters who still harbor the goals of the original reforms? Such goals will not be easy to implement, but it is important to remember that the Court has never closed off all avenues to reform. The following alternatives are still open, even if the political will to pursue them is not there:

1. Public funding of campaigns, which could include either expenditure ceilings, as with the presidential system now, or floors, which would provide a minimum amount from public funds over which private contributions could still be made.

2. Changes in the privileges of incumbency so as to benefit non-incumbents, as with limiting the franking privilege or extending it to challengers.

3. Closing loopholes on "soft" (unreported) money, which now is usually funneled into states with no contribution limitations and usually goes unreported.

4. A series of moves to make money a less important factor, the most effective of which would probably be government funding of television time, perhaps combined with the prohibition of paid political advertising on television and radio.[69]

5. More effective disclosure requirements, as the evidence now being accumulated indicates that voters are often unaware of the principal donors to campaigns. If states and the federal government required more adequate disclosure with the necessary publicity (such as disclosure of the primary funding sources on the ads themselves), voters might be able to associate campaign arguments with their financial sponsors in a way that rarely happens now.[70]

6. Changing laws so as to try to strengthen party control over candidates and party influence relative to PACs, such as by lifting limits on party expenditures while tightening them on PACs.

These and other solutions have been offered by a wide variety of scholars.[71] Some reform attempts have tried to counteract the loopholes created by Supreme Court rulings. Senate Bill S2, the campaign finance reform measure that had majority support in Congress but was killed by Republican filibusters in 1987 and 1988, stipulated that if a candidate refused voluntary public funding and exceeded the expenditure ceilings, his opponent would receive additional public funds and could raise additional funds through private contributions. The bill also provided that if an individual or group made independent expenditures against a candidate participating in public funding, the candidate would receive additional public funds.[72]

The fact that a majority in the Senate supported this wide-ranging bill attests to the unpopularity of the current system, but the filibuster indicates the partisanship of the issue. Most Republicans feel that extra money is a crucial component of their ability to compete "equally" with Democrats and fear that expenditure ceilings will benefit incumbents (more likely to be Democrats) more than challengers.

A danger of reform efforts stems from the fact that all measures at the federal level must be passed by incumbent officeholders. This leads to the fear that reforms may end up being "incumbent protection" acts, especially if a system of expenditure ceilings were set so low as to make it difficult for challengers to overcome incumbents' built-in advantages.[73] Yet incumbents are already so advantaged by our current system of limitless private spending that it is hard to imagine a reform making incumbents more advantaged. In the 1986 elections to the House of Representatives, for example, 98 percent of those members who sought reelection won. Senate races are more competitive, but even here a solid majority of incumbents usually wins reelection.

States with the initiative process have the option of by-passing legislatures to enact campaign finance measures more favorable to challengers, but at the federal level there is no such possibility. Because of the difficulties or inadequacies of adhering to Supreme Court doctrine while trying to solve the problems of a system with "all the free speech that money can buy," some have gone so far as to suggest a constitutional amendment to overturn *Buckley*. After noting that the constitutional loopholes for the wealthy are great, former Congressman Jonathon Bingham (D, New York) has suggested an amendment reading, "Congress, having due regard for the need to facilitate full and free discussion and debate, may enact laws regulating the amounts of contributions and expenditures intended to affect elections to federal office."[74] Although several members of Congress have endorsed the idea, the possibility of mustering the political force to pass such an amendment appears slim.[75] Without some new scandal that would further discredit the current system, without several more senators supporting reforms, or without considerable change in Supreme Court personnel, the importance of money seems likely to grow in our political process. Technology seems to have combined with ideology to increase our dependence upon money in campaigns.

As long as wealth is as unequally distributed as it now is in American society, and as long as political interests are organized around private rather than public rewards, American politics generally will reflect the power of the best organized and wealthiest groups in society. The expense of television, our growing dependence upon this medium for information, the rise of more sophisticated and more expensive political consultants, and the growth of computers in direct-mail targeting for fund-raising will all ensure that candidates will need greater and greater supplies of money.[76] When these trends are combined with the constitutional legitimacy that the Supreme Court has given to monied interests, we seem in danger of heading for an "elective oligarchy."[77]

Certainly not all developments in American politics in the middle and late twentieth century have pushed toward greater inequality. The civil rights movement (with its voting rights component) and reapportionment battles are obvious examples of movements toward greater equality that have been implemented with the encouragement of the Supreme Court. But campaign finance reform involves higher stakes that threaten more powerful interests and encroach upon the privileges of economic inequality in a way that the other reforms do not. These powerful forces have felt threatened and have, to a large extent, been rescued by a free-market capitalist interpretation of the First Amendment. The Court's interpretation gave the defenders of money ideological legitimacy and has made campaign finance reform a "stepchild" more abandoned than embraced by the Supreme Court. In becoming this stepchild, campaign finance battles have exposed tensions between the ideas and practices of democracy and capitalism. While these tensions do not appear to be a matter the Supreme Court is interested in resolving, in truth the Court cannot on its own resolve the inherent conflict between a system of private economic inequality and a public ideology of democracy. The Court has neither the expertise, the authority, nor the will to tackle the fundamental cause of the need for campaign finance reform: the degree of economic inequality in our society. For, lest it be forgotten, there would be much less need for campaign finance measures if all citizens had more equal resources to use in campaigns for office and in participating in public life.

NOTES

I would like to thank Michael McCann for his comments on an earlier draft of this chapter and Debbie Wiley at Western Illinois University for her typing skills.

1. Quoted in Jonathon Bingham, "Democracy or Plutocracy? The Case for a Constitutional Amendment to Overturn *Buckley v. Valeo*," *The Annals of the American Academy of Political and Social Science* 486 (July 1986), pp. 103, 104.
2. *Buckley v. Valeo*, 424 U.S. 1 (1976).
3. Mark Tushnet, "Corporations and Free Speech," *The Politics of Law: A Progressive Critique*, David Kairys, ed. (New York: Pantheon, 1982), pp. 253, 257. Tushnet has gone so far as to claim recently that "The First Amendment has replaced the due process clause as the primary guarantor of the privileged. Indeed, it protects

the privileged more perniciously than the due process clause ever did." "An Essay on Rights," *Texas Law Review* 62 (1984), pp. 1363, 1387.

4. For a review of the modern era and of the first era of campaign finance reform, see Herbert Alexander, *Financing Politics,* Chapter 2, 2nd ed. (Washington, D.C.: Congressional Quarterly, 1980); *United States v. UAW-CIO,* 352 U.S. 567 (1957); *Buckley v. Valeo,* 519 F. 2d 821 (D.C. Cir. 1975).

5. *Burroughs v. United States,* 290 U.S. 534, 545. In *Newberry v. U.S.,* 256 U.S. 232 (1921), however, the Supreme Court had thrown out the conviction of a U.S. Senator from Michigan for exceeding the legal spending limit in winning the Republican nomination. In a split decision, the Court held that primaries were not "elections," and that therefore expenditure limitations could not apply to primaries. The Court reversed itself on primaries as elections in the civil rights case of *Smith v. Allright,* 321 U.S. 649 (1944).

6. Ironically, in both regulating and loosening crucial restrictions on PACs, the law legitimized PAC activity and allowed PACs to fill some of the void created by the law's other restrictions on money. The dramatic increase in PACs (from 608 in 1974 to over 4,200 in 1987) and in PAC funding (from $12.5 million in 1974 to $139.4 million in 1987) can be partly attributable to the act. For more on the history of PACs and how the law, Federal Election Commission opinions, and Court opinions combined with general trends in American politics to facilitate PAC growth, see Edwin Epstein, "Business and Labor Under the Federal Election Campaign Act of 1971," in Michael Malbin, ed., *Parties, Interest Groups, and Campaign Finance Laws* (Washington, D.C.: American Enterprise Institute, 1980), pp. 107–151; and Frank Sorauf, *Money in American Elections* (Glenview, Ill.: Scott, Foresman, 1988), Chapter 4.

7. Professors Joel Fleishman and Marlene Arnold Nicholson have both examined this question in some detail. See generally Fleishman, "Public Financing of Election Campaigns: Constitutional Constraints on Steps Toward Equality of Political Influence of Citizens," *North Carolina Law Review* 52 (1973), p. 349; and Nicholson, "Campaign Financing and Equal Protection," *Stanford Law Review* 26 (1974), p. 815.

8. *Harper v. Virginia Board of Elections,* 383 U.S. 663 (1966); *Reynolds v. Sims,* 377 U.S. 533 (1964); *Bullock v. Carter,* 405 U.S. 134 (1972).

9. *Bullock v. Carter,* at 144.

10. Nicholson, "Campaign Financing," p. 816.

11. Thomas Emerson, "The Affirmative Side of the First Amendment," *Georgia Law Review* 15 (1981), pp. 795, 823. Emerson is more sympathetic to campaign finance reform than many, and he does add that "Some government intervention to assist those further down the economic ladder is often desirable, as the government-subsidy programs demonstrate."

12. Among many who have discussed the fact that liberal (pluralist) democracy tends to pit liberty against equality and elevate the first to prominence over the latter is John Manley, "Neo-Pluralism: A Class Analysis of Pluralism I and Pluralism II," *American Political Science Review* 77 (1983), pp. 368, 375–376. Says Manley, "True liberty is impossible without equality; to be truly free, individuals in society must be roughly equal in the means necessary to exercise freedom. Far from being opposed to liberty, equality is its necessary condition."

13. *Buckley v. Valeo* (1975), at 841.

14. *Buckley v. Valeo* (1976), at 48–49.
15. Assessing motives among Supreme Court justices is never easy or beyond dispute, nor is it the same as assessing consequences. In *Buckley* (and some other campaign finance reform cases) an uneasy coalition engaged in considerable compromise. Only Chief Justice Burger would have virtually struck down the entire law (including public funding of presidential campaigns and contribution limitations) as "an impermissible intrusion by the Government into the traditionally private political process" (at 235). Only Justice White would have allowed almost all of the law, on grounds of "the undoubted power of Congress to vindicate the strong public interest in controlling corruption and other undesirable uses of money in connection with election campaigns" (at 258). Both White and Burger, together with Blackmun, were unconvinced of the crucial distinction between contributions and expenditures the Court was making. The majority allowed far more restrictions on contributions than on expenditures, arguing that the first was more closely tied to corruption than the second.
16. Political scientist Frank Sorauf has noted that by the time of *FEC v. NCPAC* (1985) the Court had narrowed the corruption issue so greatly as to reach irrelevance: "There may be instances of legislators or would-be legislators accepting campaign contributions in return for promised votes on bills or promised pressure on public agencies—but no one thinks that such transactions are in any sense common, at least in the Congress." "Caught in a Political Thicket: The Supreme Court and Campaign Finance," *Constitutional Commentary* 3 (1986), pp. 97, 104. Sorauf notes that they "framed a jurisprudence that was strangely, even quaintly, at odds with contemporary political realities" (p. 119). This chapter argues, however, that the framing is *not* that strange given the ideological goals of a majority of the justices.
17. Since *Buckley* the Court has been remarkably tolerant of whether "independent" expenditures are really independent of the candidate's campaign. See *FEC v. NCPAC, U.S. Law Week* 53 (1985), p. 4293, especially Byron White's dissent on pp. 4301–4302, wherein he states, "'Independent' PAC expenditures function as contributions. Indeed, a significant portion of them no doubt would be direct contributions to campaigns had the FECA [the Federal Election Campaign Act] not limited such contributions to $5,000. . . . The PACs do not operate in an anonymous vacuum. There are significant contacts between an organization like NCPAC [the National Conservative Political Action Committee] and candidates for, and holders of, public office. In addition, personnel may move between the staffs of candidates or officeholders and those of PACs."
18. The best, although hardly perfect, survey data we have on contributions to campaigns indicates that at least 90 percent of the electorate do not contribute to campaigns. The 10 percent who said they did contribute in 1984 were far wealthier, better educated, and more Republican than the electorate as a whole, although not necessarily more conservative on all issues. These data are with the Center for Political Studies, University of Michigan, most of which are reported in Sorauf, *Money in American Elections,* pp. 44–48.
19. Brice Clagett and John Bolton, *"Buckley v. Valeo,* Its Aftermath and Its Prospects: The Constitutionality of Government Restraints on Political Campaign Financing," *Vanderbilt Law Review* 29 (1976), pp. 1327, 1335.
20. Although this need is never explicitly stated in the Constitution, James Madison

probably gave the most famous defense of the necessity for barriers to popular rule in the Constitution. *Federalist* 10, in J. Cooke, ed. (New York: B. Blackwell, 1987).

21. Of course Reaganomics, either as "supply-side" or "trickle-down" theory, would fit well with this view of the First Amendment. The political concept, however, is broader than either of these economic theories. See William Greider, "The Education of David Stockman," *Atlantic* 248 (December 1981), p. 27.

22. In striking down laws that resulted in rescuing the rich, the Supreme Court had to ignore or avoid powerful reasons for governmental action. See Laurence Tribe, *American Constitutional Law* (Mineola, N.Y.: Foundation, 1978), p. 802, n. 9. In noting that Court decisions in this broad area of "the right to what money can buy" are not insupportable, Tribe has said that "the confidence with which the Court espoused conclusions that were at best debatable leads one to wonder whether unarticulated premises must not have been strongly guiding the Court's hand" (p. 1132, n. 12).

23. *Buckley v. Valeo* (1976), at 52 (emphasis added). These ideas are contrary to the reasoning behind *Reynolds v. Sims*, 377 U.S. 565, wherein the Warren Court stated that "each and every citizen has an inalienable right to *full and effective participation* in the political process. . . . [This] requires . . . that each citizen have an *equally effective voice* in the election" (emphasis added).

24. While numerous scholars have discussed income and wealth inequality in American society, Lester Thurow's analysis is one of the most persuasive. See his *The Zero-Sum Society: Distribution and the Possibilities for Economic Change* (New York: Basic Books, 1980). In addition to noting that the United States has the second-highest inequality of all Western democracies, Thurow states that "the top quintile of all households has almost 80 percent of total wealth" (pp. 7–8, 168).

25. With roughly 15 percent of our workforce unemployed, underemployed, or too discouraged to look for work, and with many others in minimum-wage jobs, it hardly needs pointing out that many Americans may not be able to contribute or spend any money on campaigns. See note 18.

26. *Buckley v. Valeo* (1976), at 19–20 (emphasis added). The complete quotation reads: "The $1,000 ceiling on spending 'relative to a clearly identified candidate' [citation omitted] would appear to exclude all citizens and groups except candidates, political parties, and the institutional press from any significant use of the most effective modes of communication."

27. Ibid., at 19 (emphasis added).

28. For a recent work agreeing and elaborating on this point, see Neil Postman, *Amusing Ourselves to Death: Public Discourse in the Age of Show Business* (New York: Penguin, 1985).

29. Ralph Winter, "Political Financing and the Constitution," *The Annals* 486 (1986), pp. 34, 36, 38. Perhaps the most straightforward defense of the marketplace metaphor has come from Stephen Harder, "Political Finance in the Liberal Republic: Representation, Equality, and Deregulation," *The Annals* 486 (July 1986), pp. 49, 56, who has said, "The existing market for political finance is almost a textbook example of a perfectly competitive market." This claim allows him to conclude that the setup is fair even if there is not equality. Yet critics of the marketplace argue, of course, that the metaphor itself suggests a vital need for government regulation.

30. The Court's agreeing to full public funding of general election campaigns (that is, after voluntarism has played its important role in the selection of the party nominees), makes more sense when one remembers that the Court insisted that the decision to accept full public funding of general election campaigns must itself be a voluntary decision made by the candidate.

31. Daniel Polsby, "Buckley v. Valeo: The Special Nature of Political Speech," *The Supreme Court Review 1976*, pp. 42–43. Polsby, it should be noted, does not take the libertarian view on campaign finance. He supports public financing as long as it does not contain overall spending limitations. Along with many others, he favors "floors" rather than "ceilings." For more on these proposals, see the final section of this chapter.

32. *FEC v. NCPAC, U.S. Law Week*, p. 4301. The decision struck down limits on independent PAC spending in campaigns where the candidates have accepted full public funding of their campaigns. Disallowing this portion of the 1974 Campaign Amendments had allowed NCPAC to spend millions for the election and reelection of President Reagan.

33. Many have discussed the degree of social mobility in American society. In *The Zero-Sum Society*, p. 172, Thurow notes that 50 percent of the very rich received their fortunes through inheritance.

34. *CBS v. Democratic National Committee*, 412 U.S. 94, 123 (1973).

35. Compare *Pipefitters v. United States*, 407 U.S. 385 (1972), with *First National Bank of Boston v. Bellotti*, 435 U.S. 765 (1978), and see Shockley, "Money in Politics: Judicial Roadblocks to Campaign Finance Reform," *Hastings Constitutional Law Quarterly* 10 (1983), p. 679; William Patton and Randall Bartlett, "Corporate 'Persons' and Freedom of Speech: The Political Impact of Legal Mythology," *Wisconsin Law Review* (1981), p. 494. This differential treatment of union dissent and corporate shareholder dissent was noted and attacked by Justice White in his *First National Bank of Boston v. Bellotti* dissent, 435 U.S. 802.

36. Among the many who have examined the assumptions behind the belief in a laissez-faire marketplace are Michael Best and William Connolly, *The Politicized Economy*, 2nd ed. (Lexington, Mass.: D. C. Heath, 1982), pp. 20–27. Stanley Ingber has attacked in detail the marketplace metaphor in "The Marketplace of Ideas: A Legitimizing Myth," *Duke Law Journal* (1984), p. 1.

37. See generally Laurence Tribe, "Toward a Metatheory of Free Speech," in R. Collins, ed., *Constitutional Government in America* (Durham, N.C.: Carolina Academic Press, 1980), p. 1. Many others have noted the unarticulated conservative premises and class biases of the Court. Edwin Firmage and Kay Christensen speak of the "canonization" of Adam Smith in "Speech and Campaign Reform: Congress, the Courts and Community," *Georgia Law Review* 14 (1980), pp. 195, 198, 218, and argue that "the Court should play a decisive role in assuring that the various checks and balances and interest groups within our governmental and economic systems do not become so disparate as to render any metaphor of the 'marketplace' completely unrealistic."

38. Skelly Wright, "Money and the Pollution of Politics: Is the First Amendment an Obstacle to Political Equality?" *Columbia Law Review* 82 (1982), pp. 609, 631. See also Geoffrey Stone, "The Burger Court and the Political Process: Whose First Amendment?" *Harvard Journal of Law and Public Policy* 10 (1986), pp. 21, 22, who notes that the Court's "highly selective form of judicial activism" has

produced a "highly elitist perspective" on political communication, because the Court "seems oblivious to the reality that many participants in the political process . . . do not have large amounts of cash to spend . . . and therefore cannot have access to . . . mainstream means of political communication."

39. For further development of this analysis, see Wright, "Money and the Pollution of Politics": "By equating political spending with political speech and according both the same constitutional protection, the Court placed the First Amendment squarely in opposition to the democratic ideal of political equality" (pp. 631–632). "The core notion of the First Amendment remains the protection of diverse, antagonistic, and unpopular speech from restriction based on substance. To invoke the First Amendment, not to protect diversity but to prevent society from defending itself against the stifling influence of money in politics, is to betray the historical development and philosophical underpinnings of the First Amendment" (p. 636).

40. Kenneth Karst, "Equality as a Central Principle in the First Amendment," *University of Chicago Law Review* 43 (1975), pp. 20, 21.

41. John Rawls, *A Theory of Justice* (Cambridge, Mass.: Harvard University Press, 1971), pp. 224–225. Rawls also observed at this time, as campaign finance was just about to reemerge as a central issue in American politics: "Historically one of the main defects of constitutional government has been the failure to insure the fair value of political liberty. The necessary corrective steps have not been taken, indeed, they never seem to have been seriously entertained" (p. 226).

42. John Rawls, "The Basic Liberties and Their Priority," *The Tanner Lectures on Human Values* 3 (Salt Lake City: University of Utah Press, 1982), pp. 78–79 (delivered at the University of Michigan, April 10, 1981).

43. *First National Bank of Boston v. Bellotti,* at 765. The critique of aspects of the Court's reasoning set forth here is not meant to imply that the Massachusetts law was without fault. The purpose here is rather to show that the reasoning the Court employed continues certain unarticulated, ideological premises. For more discussion of *Bellotti* see my "Money in Politics"; Francis Fox, "Corporate Political Speech: The Effect of *First National Bank of Boston v. Bellotti* Upon Statutory Limitations on Corporate Referendum Spending," *Kentucky Law Journal* 67 (1978–1979), p. 75; and Thomas R. Kiley, "PACing the Burger Court: The Corporate Right to Speak and the Public Right to Hear After *First National Bank v. Bellotti,*" *Arizona Law Review* 22 (1980), p. 427.

44. Mass. Ann. Laws, ch. 55, §§8-88a (Michle/Law. Co-op. 1978). "No corporation . . . shall . . . expend or contribute . . . any money or other valuable thing for the purpose of . . . influencing or affecting the vote on any question submitted to the voters, other than one materially affecting any of the property, business or assets of the corporation. . . . No question submitted to the voters solely concerning the taxation of the income property or transactions of individuals shall be deemed materially to affect the property, business or assets of the corporation."

45. *First National Bank of Boston v. Bellotti,* at 809.

46. They did hedge slightly, saying that if it could be proven that corporations were dominating the process or undermining citizen confidence in the electoral process, then such proof "would merit our consideration" (Ibid., at 789). However,

what would constitute proof was left so unclear as to allow the Court to ignore any social science evidence of domination if it wanted to.

47. *Citizens Against Rent Control v. City of Berkeley,* 454 U.S. 290 (1981). For more on this case see Shockley, "Money in Politics."

48. *Citizens Against Rent Control v. City of Berkeley,* at 296. While elsewhere in this article I try to note the possible distinction between intentions and results, in this particular line of argument the Court majority does seem to be sensitive to the consequences of its decisions and to therefore try to shift the view of the consequences via the misleading argument Burger makes.

49. Requiring direct expenditures under an individual's or corporation's own name is in fact a politically sound regulation, because misleading, seductive names for political committees are often chosen to hide the true identity of sponsors in advertising. Berkeley, like California and many other areas of the country, has suffered from this deception. One example cited by Berkeley City Attorney Natalie West in oral argument before the U.S. Supreme Court on October 13, 1981, concerned a measure allowing for municipal ownership of electrical facilities for the city. A "Southwest Berkeley No No No on W Committee" was formed to oppose the measure, but *all* of its contributions came from one source, Pacific Gas and Electric Company! The title was even more deceptive than it at first appears in that southwest Berkeley is the minority section of the city.

50. *FEC v. NCPAC, U.S. Law Week* 53, pp. 4293, 4297.

51. *CMA v. FEC,* 453 U.S. 182, 196 (1981).

52. *RNC v. FEC,* 445 U.S. 182 (1981).

53. *FEC v. NCPAC, U.S. Law Week* 55, pp. 4067, 4074.

54. For a response that argues that the Court's actions have been "meandering" rather than coherent in defense of a particular ideology, see Marlene Arnold Nicholson, "The Supreme Court's Meandering Path in Campaign Finance Regulation and What it Portends for Future Reform," *Journal of Law and Politics* 3 (1987), pp. 509, 542–546. Nicholson seems correct in concluding that "regardless of the Court's views on equalization, it has not been sufficiently hostile to that interest to thwart the equalization which occurs as a byproduct of attempts to prevent [what it considers to be] corruption" (p. 541).

55. Sorauf, *Money in American Elections,* pp. 297, 301. See his Chapter 10 for a review and summary of evidence on the impact of money on elections and public policy.

56. Note that money is therefore more likely to be determinative in primary elections and in contests with no incumbent. Note also that examining the impact of money in elections is not the same as studying the impact of money in the entire political process. Long ago, Cornelius Vanderbilt knew the difference. He refused to contribute to election campaigns, believing it was cheaper to buy legislators after they were elected. See Susan Welch et al., *American Government,* 2nd ed. (St. Paul, Minn.: West Publishing Co., 1988), p. 254.

57. Gary Jacobson has carefully examined the differential impact of campaign spending for challengers and incumbents. While finding a point of diminishing returns for money, he also finds that the point tends to be high enough so that it still makes sense for candidates to raise as much as they can. Although Jacobson does not put the matter in quite these terms, he in effect finds that money and the lack

of it is determining who wins in dozens, but not hundreds, of U.S. House races every election. See, for example, his "The Effects of Campaign Spending on Voting Intentions: New Evidence from a Panel Study of the 1986 House Elections," paper prepared for delivery at the 1988 annual meeting of the Midwest Political Science Association, Chicago. Other Jacobson sources are noted in Sorauf, *Money in American Elections*.

58. Gary Jacobson's work implies this point, and Joel Fleishman and Pope McCorkle, in "Level-Up Rather Than Level-Down: Toward a New Theory of Campaign Finance Reform," *Journal of Law and Politics* 1 (1984), p. 211, make one of the best cases for public financing floors without the ceiling of overall expenditure limits, in the hopes that these would make races more competitive. The difficulty with this proposal is that it would do nothing to stop the escalating costs of campaigns, the "arms race mentality" that infects campaigns, and the perceived problem of too much special interest money pouring into campaigns. See text accompanying note 73.

59. The $1.8 billion figure comes from Herbert Alexander, *Spending in the 1984 Elections* (Lexington, Mass.: Lexington Books, 1987). Of this total more than $300 million was spent each on presidential and congressional campaigns.

60. See Federal Election Commission, *Record,* June 1988, vol. 14, no. 6, pp. 11–12; and Sorauf, *Money in American Elections,* p. 166. Independent spending data given by the FEC and by Sorauf differ. I am considering the most recent FEC data (June 1988) to be the most complete.

61. The figures for 1985–1986 are from the Federal Election Commission press release, "1986 Congressional Spending Tops $450 Million," May 10, 1987. PAC and other nonparty committees contributed a record $132 million of the $450 million total.

62. Sorauf, *Money in American Elections,* p. 166.

63. Ibid., pp. 208–209. Sorauf notes (p. 211), however, that Michael Malbin's research indicates that much of this money was actually spent on fund-raising costs.

64. Herb Alexander, *Spending in the 1984 Elections,* p. 124. For more on the impact of money in ballot proposition campaigns, see John S. Shockley, "Direct Democracy, Campaign Finance, and the Courts: Can Corruption, Undue Influence, and Declining Voter Confidence Be Found?" *University of Miami Law Review* 39 (1985), p. 377, and Daniel Lowenstein, "Campaign Spending and Ballot Propositions: Recent Experience, Public Choice Theory, and the First Amendment," *U.C.L.A. Law Review* 29 (1982), p. 505.

65. See Shockley, "Direct Democracy"; Lowenstein, "Campaign Spending"; and Shockley, *The Initiative Process in Colorado Politics: An Assessment* (Boulder, Colo.: Bureau of Governmental Research and Service, University of Colorado, 1980). Two distinctive features of money in ballot proposition campaigns are that the imbalance is often far greater than in candidate campaigns and that with the absence of partisan labels voters seem all the more susceptible to the appeals that money can buy.

66. The terminology used on PACs is that of the Federal Election Commission, which compiles the best records we have of campaign funds in federal elections. For a good discussion of the growing role of money in American politics and its relationship to the forces of technology, see David Adamany, "The New Faces of

American Politics," *The Annals* 486 (July 1986), p. 12; Neil Postman, *Amusing Ourselves to Death*.

67. The two best-known works to make this case are Thomas Edsall, *The New Politics of Inequality* (New York: Norton, 1984) and Thomas Ferguson and Joel Rogers, *Right Turn* (New York: Hill and Wang, 1986).

68. For one of the best examinations of voter demobilization in American elections, see Walter Dean Burnham, "The Turnout Problem," in James Reichley, ed., *Elections American Style* (Washington, D.C.: Brookings, 1987), pp. 97–133, who calls the increase in vote abstention in the non-South since 1960 "the largest mass movement of our time" (p. 128), involving tens of millions of Americans.

69. Elizabeth Drew, *Money and Politics: The New Road to Corruption* (New York: Macmillan, 1983) exclaims that no other Western democracy allows the buying of television time for election campaigning.

70. The best evidence on lack of knowledge comes from ballot proposition campaigns, but it is a general phenomenon in an electorate that does not pay much attention to campaigns. See D. Hensler and C. Hensler, *Evaluating Nuclear Power: Voter Choice on the California Nuclear Initiative* (Santa Monica, Calif.: Rand, 1979), p. 128. This study reports that in a postelection poll by the Rand Corporation only 37 percent of those who said they voted on the nuclear issue knew that there was more advertising against the initiative than in favor of it. Yet the opposition had spent roughly $3 million more than proponents (or nearly four times as much), and supporters had tried to make this a major issue of the campaign.

71. Among many who discuss possible reforms, see Nicholson, "The Supreme Court's Meandering Path," especially pp. 555–565, and Sorauf, *Money in American Elections*, Chapter 12. Among other proposals, many in Congress (and in Common Cause, the public interest group active on campaign finance reform issues) also favor limiting the overall amount candidates can accept from PACs. To supporters of the idea, these limits would alleviate the public's suspicion of special interest money corrupting the process and would lessen the candidates' need to engage in the demeaning or controversial practice of constantly asking for PAC funds. But many fear that PACs would simply increase their "independent" spending for or against candidates. Given the Supreme Court's views on independent spending, this move would be impossible to stop. But for ways around Supreme Court prohibitions, see text accompanying note 72.

72. For more on S2, see Carol Matlock, "Frayed Finance Law," *National Journal* (March 5, 1988), p. 593. For the battle in the Senate, see "Stalemated Senate Shelves Campaign Measure," *Congressional Quarterly* (Feb. 27, 1988), pp. 485–490.

73. Minor parties can also be placed at a disadvantage. Publicly funded floors would more likely benefit challengers, who may have difficulty raising "seed money." The weakness of enacting floors but not ceilings, however, is that the rat race for more funding just continues, with all its possible demeaning compromises, only at a higher level.

74. Bingham, "Democracy or Plutocracy," p. 113.

75. By a vote of 53–37 in April 1988, the U.S. Senate supported a constitutional amendment to allow Congress and state governments to impose limits on cam-

paign spending. However, a two-thirds vote is necessary for passage. A weakness of this approach is the lengthy approval process required for constitutional amendments. In addition, Congress would still have to enact legislation imposing limits (which is precisely what was thwarted with the defeat of S2). This vote, however, offers continued evidence of the dissatisfaction with the current system of campaign finance. For more on the vote see "Senate Declines New Approach to Limiting Campaign Finances," *Congressional Quarterly,* April 23, 1988, p. 1108.

76. On technologies rendering "the fruits of the free speech struggle somewhat obsolete," see David Kairys, "Freedom of Speech," *The Politics of Law,* pp. 140, 166. Also see Postman, *Amusing Ourselves to Death.* On the importance of political consultants, see Larry Sabato, *The Rise of Political Consultants* (New York: Basic Books, 1981).

77. The term is Philip Green's in *Retrieving Democracy: In Search of Civic Equality* (Totowa, N.J.: Rowman and Allanheld, 1985), p. 256. While Green favors a ban on paid TV ads, he is pessimistic about most other reform proposals.

15 ——— ·
Ideology, Religion, and the First Amendment

RONALD KAHN

Some scholars challenge advocates of either a substantive rights or a process-based normative theory in favor of an emphasis on "pragmatism."[1] Vincent Blasi, for example, has stressed the continuity of Burger Court jurisprudence with that of the Warren Court in regard to the overall level of judicial *activity*. Such activity is responsive to the respect for precedent in the legal culture; to the need for federal courts to protect citizens from a growing, complex bureaucracy and single-issue legislative politics; and to an impoverished parochial/public debate in which self-interest rather than collective norms and general values predominate. But in trying to show that no counter-revolution to a liberal Warren Court took place, he understates the role of values in Burger Court jurisprudence. Blasi sees pragmatic and moderate justices in the center as keys to the Court's success as an active institution with an eye for continuity. This "pragmatic middle"—Blasi named Justices Potter Stewart, Harry Blackmun, Lewis Powell, Byron White, and John P. Stevens on the Burger Court—countered the ideological excesses of justices at the right and left extremes on the Court and was the primary guiding force behind Burger Court doctrine. Blasi states that

> [Burger Court] activism has been inspired not by a commitment to fundamental constitutional principles or noble political ideas, but rather by the belief that modest injections of logic and compassion by disinterested, sensible judges can serve as a counterforce to some of the excesses and irrationalities of contemporary government decision-making. In other words, in the hands of the Burger Court, judicial activism has become a centrist philosophy—dominant, transcending most ideological divisions, but essentially pragmatic in nature, lacking a central theme or agenda.[2]

Conversely, confusion over the role of values in constitutional law-making by Supreme Court justices has plagued even the most sympathetic of modern scholars. Alexander Bickel, for example, searched fruitlessly for a core consensus based on traditional values that are determinative in judicial choice.[3] Michael Perry, in an equally ambitious search, has striven to conform judicial noninterpretivism to a more functional model, based not on consensus but on a more elevated plane of shared, moral values.[4] While these scholars have sought to transcend the subjective value orientations of individual judges and cases, others seek not to define them so much as to influence and channel their development. Laurence Tribe, Frank Michelman, and Richard Parker recognize that substantive values inform even the most process-based and interpretive views of the Constitution and are the genuine staple of Supreme Court decision making. These values cannot be presumed to always fit neat theoretical models of Court actions; they are problematic and defy analytical permanence through time. But their trends can be pinpointed to process-oriented or substantive rights ends and can be shaped to particular scholarly schema.[5]

In opposition to Blasi's thesis, this chapter analyzes church and state cases in the Burger era to show that Supreme Court justices make constitutional choices on process and rights values rather than in terms of outcomes alone. This more complex view of judicial activity reflects a diminishing consensus on the controlling principles of political and legal theory, including, among other trends, the tendency of constitutional scholarship to fragment into either process-based or substantive rights–based theories. It is also a product of the increasing dilemma facing legal theory in a liberal democracy: that is, how to achieve equity without undermining the autonomy of law from "politics," a goal that repeatedly has been called into question by critical scholars and activists alike.[6]

Unfortunately, scholars of rights or process orientations often fail to recognize the central *interrelationship* of process and rights values in the development of constitutional principles. Because some persons view values as irrelevant or arbitrary, it is not surprising that the values that inform judicial choice should themselves come under attack as an inadequate measure of judicial perspective in this era. Although such values admittedly are difficult to categorize and next to impossible to quantify, recent scholarship has carried the point too far in abandoning the study of values. Rather, we must *qualify* in a positive sense, using qualitative and quantitative data in the Establishment Clause cases, the statement, "A jurisprudence of values is a poor one if the proper function of commentators and justices is to rationalize the case law . . . [or] to organize the Court's decisions into consistent patterns. For in the contemporary world, individual value systems are both internally inconsistent and inconsistent with those held by others."[7]

Rooting scholarly analysis of constitutional law once again in a debate over values might also serve as a response to what might be labeled a rebirth of the relativism and empiricism of postwar scholarship. The scholarly debate that pits pluralist theories of access and participation against theories emphasizing structural inequalities and elite rule in our polity cannot have been lost on the Court, which has the capability to enforce and enact such positions in law.[8] Blasi does not choose to address the question he begs: Certainly the Court is active—but to what end? It is at this level of values that critical analysis must take place. By refusing to make prescriptive statements about the nature of judicial choices in Burger era activity, Blasi refuses to analyze those theoretical elements of political theory that serve as the reservoir of values upon which justices inevitably rely.

In addition, this chapter will explore and counter the familiar argument that the Burger Court simply chose not to resist the activism of its predecessor and thus responded to practical imperatives of the judicial process in disinterested, detached, nonideological ways.[9] We will see that Burger Court pragmatism is at hopeless odds with the principles, norms, and conventions that underlie constitutional choices in an *institutional* sense. Considerations of complex polity relationships guide, and are affected by, the Supreme Court's capacity for political change. In fact, judicial policy is influenced by institutional requirements such as honoring past precedent, respecting the institutional momentum that the Warren era created as status quo, and simply accepting the role of the Court as an activist institution. These considerations must be taken into account in any analysis of the Court and in practice help to temper, in any case, the ideological fervor of individual justices who may oppose such institutional constraints. Even so, the Burger era witnessed significant innovation in the area of civil liberties, indicating that the Court, in tune with its ideology in this area, was more than simply reactive to the doctrine of the Warren era.[10]

Ultimately, the core value of Blasi's work—nonideological political compromise—is antithetical to the fundamental presence of a constitutional legacy in society, particularly as a benchmark for Establishment Clause principles and for understanding the institutional roles of the court system and judicial review in our polity. There is, in John Brigham's terms, an entire range of ideologies that political scientists have lost track of—a range that I argue can be delineated into either process or rights principles—above and beyond the "cult" of institutional characteristics that mark an obsession with empirical analyses. Such "intersubjective" dimensions of the legal environment bring justices into common ideological ground, away from predictable responses based on expectations of what Court policy outcomes should be.[11] In sum, we need to understand that Supreme Court justices are moved by ideological interests just as are other political officials in the policy processes.[12]

IDENTIFYING IDEOLOGIES ON THE BURGER COURT

Throughout this book the concept of ideology is used in macrolevel ways to refer to Hartzian culture-wide hegemonic values. Some authors suggest that these values fit with, even in an imperfect way, neo-Marxian structural analyses in societies. For others the objective is to show the discontinuities between liberal legal values and equality principles in American society. Unlike the equal protection jurisprudence explored by McCann, my objective in analyzing separation of church and state issues is not (directly) to show that the Court has an elitist bias or to show that church and state cases reflect, even in an imperfect way, the capitalist structure of society.

Rather, I will be focusing on various disputes among justices and factions *within* the broader liberal ideological framework of law, at the micro- rather than the macrolevel of ideology. These factions are contending variations within the Hartzian liberal discourse. Liberal ideology contains a tension between elements of process values (institutional autonomy) and rights values (free-exercise values to secure individual autonomy from government). Ideological factions on the Supreme Court hold different mixes of process and substantive rights values informing their constitutional choices. My objective is to analyze how the justices define church and state issues. Do they view them primarily as questions of: (1) how to mediate between secular government and sectarian institutions in process terms, with an objective of securing institutional autonomy; (2) how to protect the individual rights of believers in parochial institutions and/or nonbelievers; or (3) how to protect both process and rights values?

The religion clauses ask the Court to look at both process (institutional separation) and substantive rights (free-exercise) values. Justices' choices of process or substantive rights definitions of constitutional problems result in both a bounded discipline in Supreme Court decision making and a movement to process-based choices, with a resulting breakdown of the separation between law and politics. Thus politics and law are not completely autonomous of each other. An analysis of the interplay of process and substantive rights values, and of the justices' ideological interests in support of different concepts of process and rights values, indicates that under our liberal tradition rights are precarious because of their linkage to process values, which are subject to the justices' views of institutional relationships in society. Thus, the liberal legal tradition, with its concern for religious freedom and the separation of law and politics, also contains the seeds of decline in these values. This microlevel analysis of ideological conflict will help us understand the process of change in this tradition and thus will inform the process of the larger hegemonic change reported in the other chapters.

Justices decide cases by fitting them into their continuing process and substantive rights values rather than by deciding outcomes and then making any argument they can in support of the outcome. Justices are ideological, in that these process and rights principles provide *definable limits* on the range of values that individual justices can use in development of more innovative Court doctrine.[13] The volatility of such principles indicates, in my view, not a tendency on behalf of the Court to engage in simplistic bargaining as the hallmark of its activity; but rather, an "ideological jurisprudence" that is highly motivated and highly competitive, with certain ends clearly in sight for all justices who hold such principles as key elements of their informed knowledge about an increasingly complex polity.

To delve a little deeper, a cue for ideological interests can be seen when justices attempt to pattern case merits along systematic, nonrandom outlines and make them conform to particularized philosophies. For example, the fact that individual justices have advocated widely varying interpretations of the standard established in *Lemon v. Kurtzman* (1971)[14] for deciding whether a government action violates the separation of church and state results in dif- fering prohibitions on state intervention in religious affairs. This patterning of cases to principles is a more flexible positivism for Justices Harry Black- mun, Lewis Powell, Sandra Day O'Connor, William Brennan, and Thurgood Marshall, as distinguished from that of former Chief Justice Warren Burger, and Justices Byron White and William Rehnquist, who are ideological in the strictest, most rigid sense. A flexible ideology consists of process and rights principles serving to inform the structural logic of judicial *choices,* not just guaranteed or expected outcomes. For example, Justice Stevens has a striking fixation with rule of law ideals—notions of impartiality and equality— whereas Justices Brennan and Marshall are more concerned with questions of moral right or wrong and come to each case with specific, more particu- larized questions to ask. In this area of Burger Court jurisprudence at least, these justices can vote for the "wall of separation" between church and state, their personal perspectives congruent with the issues at hand. Ideological commitments involve case-by-case issue *definition* rather than just *determina- tion.*

If I am correct about the different ideological currents on the Burger Court, the differences among the justices displayed in the religion clauses should manifest themselves in the following ways: (1) at crucial times justices would make clear statements as to past and future directions of the Court and trigger turning points where a continuation of doctrine would undercut long-held process and rights values (for example, Blackmun in the *Regan* case);[15] (2) groups of justices would differ consistently as to whether process and rights values are to be considered in each case, although the actual deci- sion may be variable; (3) similarly, justices would differ as to whether strong notions of individual freedom of religious conscience or free exercise through institutional autonomy are the best guiding norms for Establishment Clause doctrine (for example, the individual autonomy notions of Justice O'Connor in the *Jaffree* and *Grand Rapids* cases).[16] Therefore, consistency alone proves unsatisfactory as the sole or primary benchmark for determining whether ideology informs judicial choices, given the complexity of process and rights values inherent in the religion clauses as abstracted from outcomes; internal questions of value (process and rights) are posed, rather than an exclusive structure being imposed by desires for consistency in *policy* questions. The benefits of this "Gutman" scale type of ideology analysis is that it does not place an undue quantitative weight on case outcomes as the best indicator of a justice's personal views.

THE PROCESS AND RIGHTS PARADIGM

Historically, the clash between process and substantive rights principles extends all the way back to the founding period, when the Article VII structural credo necessary for ratification of the Constitution at the Philadelphia Convention was countered by the first ten amendments. The federalist/antifederalist debate is most informative in tracing the arguments for and against strict adherence to the most fundamental of constitutional doctrines, such as separation of powers, federalism, and characteristics of constituencies, and the nature of and the need for rights to be stated in the Constitution.[17] With only slight contextual modification, these arguments resound with unsettling poignancy today. It is important to note, however, that owing to their close proximity to the founders in the constitutional debate, Establishment Clause questions tend to have a stronger constructionist basis than is found in modern innovations, such as the creation of privacy rights or procedural guarantees such as the expanded right to vote. The nature and scope of the controversy today about what is fundamental to us in the religious guarantees of the First Amendment are similar to the debates that involved the founders.[18] The founders had no conception of publicly funded education; even so, there has been little dilution up until recent times of Establishment Clause guarantees, despite substantial judicial review taking place in this century since the *Everson v. Board of Education* decision.[19] The question before the justices has not been whether to sanction such rights or guarantees, but rather how to best integrate and accommodate the general logic of the doctrine regarding separation of church and state and free-exercise rights within modern society, given the problem that original intent is not uniform or clear.

Generally speaking, polity or "process" principles include justices' beliefs about the jurisdictional question of where constitutionally authorized decisions should be made. Such values include questions about whether federal courts or electorally accountable institutions should make choices; the *degree* of autonomy granted to state and local authority in our federal system; a somewhat related question, how much of a role interest groups should play in our polity; and finally, whether such polity principles are given greater weight when balanced against rights arguments—to be enumerated momentarily—of a less defined, and potentially more substantive nature. At best, judicial choices based on process values are grounded *structurally,* relying on the enumerated powers in the Constitution, which imply for some of the justices judicial self-restraint, reliance on existing political power structures, and a firm faith in participational and access norms—as the main legacy of the past—to ensure a normally functioning democratic system.[20]

Substantive rights principles are those views held by justices about claims individual citizens may make for legally enforceable privileges or immunities under the Constitution, statutes, and law. Thus, polity concerns divide up authority within government; substantive rights divide up citizen prerogatives and protections against government. Many rights relate to "cocoons" that shield citizens from government intrusion; these rights are the "positive libertarian" interests embodied in the Bill of Rights, which have been articulated most recently in work by Frank Michelman.[21] Other rights principles, such as those in modern equal protection law, may include *affirmative* responsibilities on behalf of government to citizen access to legal and political institutions or to impartial treatment under the law in the distribution of goods. For example, the Supreme Court outlawed state residency requirements for welfare as a violation of citizens' rights to travel. Such rights do not generally involve questions of relations *among* distributional sites or agencies, or "of jurisdictional boundaries on decision-making authority"—for example, among branches of majoritarian political processes—so much as the nature of entitlements that individuals deserve as citizens and human beings within such arenas.[22]

The Establishment Clause involves both a general (public) process value, that the state must not establish religion, and a (private) rights imperative, that the individual be allowed free exercise of religion uninhibited by state action. Both depend on a contrived public/private split in liberal thought that has caused an enduring dilemma.[23] This tension has allowed for much leeway in judicial policy making and has generated a surprisingly wide spectrum of ideological disputes in modern judicial interpretations of church and state doctrine. Absolute state neutrality toward any religion—the "wall-of-separation" judicial view—has had prominent adherents on the Court, and the Court abides mainly on a strict adherence to the prohibitions imposed on the government by the Establishment Clause. This principle of hermetically sealed, exclusive spheres belonging either to church or state is a process norm that some justices have seen as unrealistic in the light of modern-day complexity, on the one hand, or as the only means of maintaining the integrity of religious practice and principled adjudication by the Supreme Court in protection of such rights, on the other. The establishment/separation principle works to restrict government; it is negative, limiting the state vis à vis religion. The Burger Court era witnessed severe cracks in the foundation of the wall-of-separation argument as a result of decisions upholding state patronage of carefully weighed religious functions.

Process arguments in church and state cases are balanced against the substantive rights interests of individuals, religious minorities, or nonbelievers who cannot count on the institutional support of process-oriented outcomes for protection. Rights protection requires the courts to take a more positive, interventionist role, at least potentially. Hence, conflicts over dual obligations are at the heart of the First Amendment religion clauses. This conflict is apparent when scholars and jurists argue over whether the equal protection clause of the Fourteenth Amendment is meant to protect groups denied access to the political system or the substantive rights of individuals.

Finally, the free-exercise rights central to deciding questions of government establishment of religion may be conceived of as either external or internal to a religious institution or activity. The religious atmosphere of society and government *external* to the institutions in question is at issue; free exercise in a generally hospitable political and cultural environment is the ideal for all believers. Nonbelievers also have external free-exercise rights, since the state should not signal its support of specific religious values. The question remains, however, as to what degree the state can encourage such an environment and how it should go about doing so without invoking the clear prohibitions of the Establishment Clause. Similarly, the rights principles in church and state cases involve an *internal* right to free exercise within particular institutions—dissidents possess rights to have beliefs opposed to the majority, and autonomy-regarding rights of religious belief compel state respect. Justices will differ as to the external free-exercise rights of believers and nonbelievers and the degree to which internal free-exercise rights need protection from government intrusion.

BURGER COURT VOTING IN AID TO RELIGIOUS EDUCATION CASES

Given these guidelines, we are in a position to trace the expected relationship between competing ideologies and outcomes. First, however, we must present the voting patterns themselves. This data, and the analyses of the process and rights values in Establishment Clause cases that follow, raise serious questions about the validity of Blasi's "pragmatic center" thesis and, more broadly, about the conventional wisdom among scholars and the public that the Burger Court merely reacted to doctrinal innovations of the Warren Court (see Tables 15.1 through 15.4).

The statistics shown in the tables suggest that the bloc of justices in the pragmatic middle (Blackmun, Powell, White, Stevens, and Stewart) is not definite in composition over a period of time and is vague enough by nature to defy easy generalization or analysis. Justices listed by Blasi as members of the moderate and pragmatic middle appear at *all* points when the justices are listed by percentage of dissenting votes from majority opinions.

Table 15.1
Burger Court Aid to Religious Schools, 1970–1985

Case Number	Date Decided	Name
1	May 4, 1970	Walz v. Tax Commission of New York (397 U.S. 664)
2	June 28, 1971	Lemon v. Kurtzman (403 U.S. 602)
3	June 28, 1971	Tilton v. Richardson (403 U.S. 672)
4	June 25, 1973	Comm. for Public Ed. & Rel. Lib. v. Nyquist (413 U.S. 756)
5	June 25, 1973	Levitt v. Comm. for Public Ed. & Rel. Lib. (413 U.S. 472)
6	June 25, 1973	Sloan v. Lemon (413 U.S. 825)
7	June 25, 1973	Hunt v. McNair (413 U.S. 734)
8	May 19, 1975	Meek v. Pittenger (421 U.S. 349)
9	June 21, 1976	Roemer v. Board of Public Works of Maryland (426 U.S. 736)
10	June 24, 1977	Wolman v. Walter (433 U.S. 229)
11	February 20, 1980	Comm. for Public Ed. & Rel. Lib v. Regan (444 U.S. 646)
12	June 29, 1983	Mueller v. Allen (463 U.S. 388)
13	July 1, 1985	Grand Rapids School District v. Ball (473 U.S. 373)
14	July 1, 1985	Aguilar v. Felton (473 U.S. 402)

Note: Important post-1980 cases involving spheres of state and religious authority but not involving state aid as such include: Wallace v. Jaffree, 472 U.S. 38 (1985), a case overturning a moment of silence statute passed in Alabama when it was ascertained that the legislature was not content-neutral in its religious choice; Lynch v. Donnelly, 465 U.S. 668 (1984), a case upholding the constitutionality of a crèche display in a state-sponsored display at Christmas; and Marsh v. Chambers, 463 U.S. 783 (1983), a case upholding the right of prayer in state legislative chambers.

Between 1970 and 1985 the justices can be grouped into those voting against the majority less than 10 percent of the time (Harlan, Powell, Stewart, and Blackmun); 25 to 36 percent (Black, Douglas, Stevens, Brennan, Marshall, and Burger), and 50 percent and over (O'Connor, Rehnquist, and White). Moderate "middle" justices appear in all three groupings. Justice White has the highest percentage of dissents of any justice on the Burger Court. Justice Stevens represents a median. Justices Powell, Stewart, and Blackmun did tend to vote with the majority position of the Court most of the time.

To argue, however, that three members of the Burger Court can impose a coherent and overriding influence on Court jurisprudence oversimplifies the reality of the judicial choices on church and state issues. It is especially difficult to talk about a coherent middle after 1980, with the retirement of Justice Stewart, because according to these statistics only two justices, Powell and Blackmun, could have been considered to be in the middle. Finally, after

Table 15.2
Burger Court Voting on Aid to Religious Schools

												Case Number											
	1	2		3		4			5	6	7	8		9	10				11	12	13		14
Justice	A	A	B	A	B	A	B	C	A	A	A	A	B	A	A	B	C	D	A	A	A	B	A
Harlan	M																						
Powell		M*	M*	M	M	M	M*	M*	M	M	M	M	M	D	M	M	M	M	M	M	M	M	M
Stewart	M	M	M	M	M	M	M	M	M	D	M	M	M	M	M	M*	M	M	M	M	M	M	M
Blackmun	M	M	M	M	M	M	M*	M*	M	M	M	M	M	M*	M	M*	M*	M*	D	M	M	M	M
Black	M	M	M	D																			
Douglas	D	M	M	D	M	M	M	M	D	M													
Stevens										D	D	D	M	D	D	D	M	M	M	M	M	M	M
Marshall	M	M	M	D	M	M	M	M	M	M	D	D	D	D	D	D	D	D	D	M	M	M	M
Brennan	M	M	M	D	M	M*	M	M	M	M	D	D	D	D	D	D	D	D	D	M	M*	M*	M*
Burger	M*	M*	M*	M	M	M*	M	M	M	M	M	M	M	M	M	M	M	M	M	M	D	D	D
O'Connor																			M	M*	M	M*	M
Rehnquist				M	M	M	M*	M	M*	M	M	M	M	D	M	M	M	D	D	D	D	D	D
White	M	D	D	M	M	M	D	M	D	D	M	M	M	M	M	M	M	M	M*	M	D	D	D

Note: A, B, C, and D column headings refer to the substance of the opinions listed in Table 15.3.
* Justice writing the majority opinion.
M represents a majority vote.
D represents a dissent.

418

Table 15.3
Substance of Parochial School Aid Majority Opinions (by case number)

1. Permits property tax exemption for church property.
2. A. No reimbursement to nonpublic schools for teacher salaries and instruction materials.
   B. No 15 percent state salary reimbursement directly to church school teachers for teaching secular subjects.
3. Permits federal aid for secular buildings at parochial universities.
4. A. No aid for maintenance and repair of nonpublic schools, including parochial grammar and secondary schools.
   B. No tuition reimbursement for low-income parents of parochial school children.
   C. No income-tax benefits to parents of children attending nonpublic, including parochial, schools.
5. No aid for direct payment to parochial schools for test grading, including teacher-prepared tests.
6. No reimbursement for tuition to parents of children attending nonpublic, including parochial, schools.
7. Permits states to secure less expensive financing of parochial college buildings, through allowing use of the state bonding power.
8. A. Provides aid to parochial school children through the loan of secular textbooks.
   B. No direct aid to parochial schools for instructional materials/remedial teaching.
9. Allows annual state fiscal subsidy to nonpublic, including parochial, colleges and universities.
10. A. Permits state aid for textbook loans and testing/scoring of state-provided tests.
    B. Permits aid for out-of-parochial-school (off-premise) remedial, guidance, therapeutic services by staff hired by public school officials.
    C. No aid for instructional materials (maps, projectors) even if loaned to students and parents.
    D. No aid for field trips.
11. Allows direct payment to parochial schools for paying salaries of teachers for attendance recordkeeping, state standardized tests, including tests that have subjective element in grading.
12. Allows parents of children in all nonprofit public and nonpublic schools, including parochial schools, to deduct expenses for tuition, textbooks, and transportation.
13. A. Forbids a shared-time program: state-provided secular classes and guidance services in parochial schools to parochial school children.
    B. Forbids a community education program: state-provided classes after school for students and adults in parochial schools.
14. Forbids use of federal funds to pay for public school teachers to teach in parochial school buildings remedial reading and math courses to economically disadvantaged children attending parochial schools, even when a close state supervision of content is provided.

Table 15.4
Dissents from Majority Opinions

Justice	Number of Choices	Dissents from Majority	Percentage of Dissents
Harlan	4	0	0.00
Powell	18	1	5.55
Stewart	18	1	5.55
Blackmun	21	2	9.52
Black	4	1	25.00
Douglas	12	4	33.33
Stevens	9	3	33.33
Brennan	22	8	36.36
Marshall	22	8	36.36
Burger	22	8	36.36
O'Connor	4	2	50.00
Rehnquist	18	9	50.00
White	22	13	59.09

1980, Powell and Blackmun voted in opposite ways from each other in two of the four cases concerning aid to education decided by the Court, *Mueller* and *Regan*. They disagreed on two of the five policy choices they could make in these cases.

The data in Table 15.4 also suggests that it is incorrect to argue that the right and left wings of the Court take similarly extreme positions on church and state issues. Simply put, Blasi's liberal justices (Brennan and Marshall) seemed more likely to go along with the majority position than those he labels conservative (Rehnquist, Burger, O'Connor). White, whom Blasi called a pragmatic centrist justice, took the most extreme positions on these cases. Moreover, coherence among the middle justices, Blackmun and Powell, declined after 1980. Also, Blackmun's voting with the majority may be a thing of the past; since 1980 he has voted with the majority in only two of four cases involving aid to parochial schools.

Since 1980 there has been a trend toward bloc voting. Blackmun has voted most often with Marshall, Stevens, and Brennan. White, Rehnquist, and Burger have usually voted together. O'Connor has voted with conservatives Burger, Rehnquist, and White in three of the four aid to parochial education choices since 1980 and in two of the three major nonaid Establishment Clause cases, *Marsh v. Chambers* and *Lynch v. Donnelly*.[24] She voted against her bloc, however, in *Wallace v. Jaffree*, Alabama's moment-of-silence law, and in *Grand Rapids v. Ball*, a case involving parochial school personnel teaching secular subjects after school hours. Only Justice Powell voted with the majority opinion in all aid to education cases after 1980. This data suggests that the Burger Court after 1980 had a "pragmatic middle" of *one* justice, who is now gone from the Rehnquist Court.[25]

These statistics raise serious questions about the Blasi thesis, especially the notion that "modest injections of logic and compassion by disinterested, sensible judges [in the middle] can serve as a counterforce to some of the excesses and irrationalities of contemporary government decision-making," or that judicial excesses came solely from the extreme right and left of the Burger Court. Rather, all justices manifest *nonrandom* ideological interests in their jurisprudence. Such interests are informed by a tension between fundamental process and rights principles in their choices, and this trend is likely to continue in the future.[26]

IDEOLOGY AND OUTCOMES

The Burger Court, as the data suggests, reacted to the Establishment Clause in a variety of ways. As we predicted, inconsistency in specific policy outcomes does not necessarily indicate inconsistency in judicial perspective. In fact, we can identify a markedly ideological bent, with at least one notable exception, Justice Powell, whose process and rights values are present but seem less controlling. More specifically, the Burger Court expressed a variety of judicial outlooks, ranging from process-emphasis absolutism on the part of Justices Rehnquist, White, and Burger; process and rights tension on the part of Justices O'Connor and Powell; and substantive rights emphasis (with clearly defined process underpinnings) by Justices Blackmun, Brennan, and Marshall. All of these perspectives are ideologically informed and reflect greater or lesser degrees of tension between process and rights values. It is useful to chart, in a preliminary sense, some of these perspectives.

Justice Powell has voted with the majority in all cases since he took the bench. This record implies that he takes each case on the merits and is swayed by particular contexts and by the opinions of both his process- and rights-oriented colleagues on the Court. This style can lead to contradictory outcomes. For example, in 1973 Powell wrote the *Nyquist* opinion disallowing aid for facility maintenance and tuition reimbursement and tax benefits for parents of children attending parochial schools. Ten years later, he voted with the majority in *Mueller,* which allowed parents of parochial school children virtually the same thing—tax deduction benefits for tuition, textbooks, and transportation. Justice Powell was, at base, willing to honor legislative determinations before his own consistency of rulings. He also resurrected in *Aguilar v. Felton* (1985) the "political divisiveness" prong he declared obsolete in *Wolman v. Walter.* We can expect Justice Powell to base his judicial view on process norms requiring that legislative outcomes are to be respected in all cases and that parochial schools have a right to be helped, or to have "benevolent neutrality" extended to them by the state.

For conservative Justices Rehnquist, White, and Burger there is no such tension. These justices feel it is within state authority or prerogative to extend paternalistic aid to religious institutions and, despite more insular rights of such institutions and their members to be left undisturbed, nevertheless support most legislative action in the Establishment Clause area, short of state religion. Burger, after 1973, no longer displayed concern for a stringent entanglement standard.

Justice O'Connor shares the initial presumption of good faith on the part of the state to get in and then out of church affairs (or to keep the scope of the interaction constitutional in even longer relationships, as in *Mueller*). She does, however, uphold individual rights of free exercise more strongly than her process-oriented colleagues.

Justice Blackmun's voting record in the Establishment Clause cases perhaps reveals the most abrupt change, with the exception of Burger. Like Powell, Blackmun voted with the majority in every one of these cases prior to *Mueller v. Allen* and with the process-oriented bloc prior to and including *Wolman v. Walter*. Fearful that he had gone too far in subscribing to the majority's flexible reading of the *Lemon* standard (a three-part test involving political divisiveness, effects, and entanglement, to be further explored in the next section of this chapter), and wondering about the future implications of such choices, he dramatically joined the rights-oriented bloc in dissent in *Regan*. Although his past voting record clearly indicates his capacity for supporting process determinations about the church-state relationship, Blackmun has consistently refused to accept *direct* aid to parochial schools. Since 1983 he has voted to stop direct state and Court support of the religious enterprise and to return to a more forceful application of the *Lemon* standard.

Perhaps Blackmun finally heeded Justice Stevens who, as in other areas of constitutional law, has embarked on a crusade to reintroduce watertight principles in Establishment Clause adjudication. For Justice Stevens there is no tension involved in guaranteeing religious rights and practices for citizens. Since he came on the Court in 1976, Stevens has written typically terse (even austere) opinions advocating the reintroduction of an inviolable wall of separation and lamenting the decline of the *Lemon* standard as a guide for stringent scrutiny. One problematic area does exist for Stevens, however. In *Wolman v. Walter,* he ruled against a "package plan" of aid to parochial schools in all provisions *except* that which would afford parochial school children remedial, guidance, and therapeutic services off school premises implemented by employees who were not parochial school teachers. For Stevens, the exception to his rigid rule could be justified on the grounds that it furthered universal state and private (or religious) goals of better health and adjustment for society's children.

On the "liberal" bloc, Justice Brennan has relied to a greater extent than Justice Marshall on process guides to achieve his rights aims. Relying most often on process violations of the *Lemon* standard, Brennan abides more by a criticism of current process practice than an explicit rights protection, as he might in other areas of First Amendment doctrine. We see this tendency most clearly in his opinion in the *Aguilar v. Felton* case—in which process norms served to bolster rights protection. But this approach is not overtly instrumentalist; the *Lemon* standard itself is a tool designed to achieve the same end, through an overlay of both process and rights guarantees. Brennan reflects the process weight of that standard but brings internal and external rights to it, whereas many of the other justices do not. He would like to make the *Lemon* standard something more than operable; he would, ironically, give Establishment Clause doctrine a push in a substantive direction by building a wall around it. He would not even allow legislatures the right to determine the degree and nature of mutual jurisdiction with the parochial institutions in their boundaries. In a twist of logic, Brennan and Marshall assert that religious institutions are best helped by not helping them at all, a position seemingly close to that of Madison and many of the federalists.

PROCESS VALUE TENSIONS IN THE *LEMON* STANDARD

Given the shifting nature of rights guarantees in a structurally oriented Constitution, it makes sense that the Supreme Court should come up with schema to accommodate its many views of church and state issues and even that it would have overestimated its ability to make consistent decisions in these areas by forging loosely defined scrutiny guides like the *Lemon* standard.[27] For a statute that has raised Establishment Clause questions to pass muster under this standard it must meet the following three-part test: (1) it must have a secular legislative purpose; (2) its principal or primary effect must be one that neither advances nor inhibits religion; (3) it must not foster an excessive government entanglement with religion. Rather than focus on the well-documented decline of those judicial guidelines, I will use its internal structure to guide the argument made here about the relevance of process principles found in Establishment Clause choices. Tension presupposes conflicting values and ideology; with these guidelines in hand, we are in a position to explore some of the more subtle, underlying processes at work in the justices' logic.

ENTANGLEMENT

The prong of the *Lemon* standard most debated in Establishment Clause cases is the entanglement of political and religious pursuits through state involvement in sectarian affairs. General sharing and reimbursement of secular textbooks in religious elementary schools was upheld by the Court in the *Board of Education v. Allen Commissioner* (1968)[28] and *Meek v. Pittenger* (1975) cases, but not the establishing of church/state financial relationships of a somewhat more intricate and durational complexity. In *Lemon v. Kurtzman,* Chief Justice Burger articulated the fears that had prompted his subscription to this prong of the *Lemon* test, warning against the "self-perpetuating" and "self-expanding" tendencies of annual government appropriations, which had the effect of entrenching the state in religious affairs—a sort of institutional and fiscal momentum.[29] Questions of political divisiveness—itself a process norm—were instrumental in this argument, but the case further concerned the degree of state supervision that would be conferred upon the church/state relationship by teachers' salary supplements and general subsidies for instructional materials. Burger would only allow that so much state monitoring of such a relationship could occur before the "variable barrier" would be breached and state intrusion would occur. If fiscal arrangements of a direct nature made him uneasy in *Lemon,* he made no indication of it in *Committee for Public Education and Religious Liberty v. Regan,* when a bare plurality vote endorsed direct payment to parochial schools for teachers' time in the administration of standardized tests and routine state-required attendance and recordkeeping.

In *Meek,* the Court split its decision on entanglement grounds, arguing that the loan of secular textbooks was acceptable in the *Allen* tradition, but not the loan of instructional materials and equipment directly to the schools. Given the religious mission of the schools, the latter could only be constitutionally permissible if it relied on an *unconstitutional* policing process. Justice Stewart wrote: "It would simply ignore reality to attempt to separate secular educational functions from the predominantly religious role performed by many of Pennsylvania's schools. Such aid cannot be considered as beneficial to the secular without providing direct aid to the sectarian." [30]

In this case, Justices Brennan, Marshall, and Douglas opposed even the loan of the textbooks to parochial schools on entanglement grounds, a conflict that would eventually lead Justice Marshall, in *Wolman,* to call for the overruling of *Allen.* [31]

Process entanglement has been referred to as a "tightrope," and indeed it presents a difficult problem for state legislatures. Justice White described it in *Lemon* as "an insoluble paradox. . . . The State cannot finance secular instruction if it permits religion to be taught in the same classroom; but if it exacts a promise that religion not be so taught . . . and enforces it, it is then entangled in the 'no entanglement' aspect of the Court's Establishment Clause jurisprudence." [32] Nevertheless, in every case involving elementary and secondary parochial schools—as opposed to the collegiate institutions awarded aid in *Tilton, Hunt,* and *Roemer*—the Court applied strict scrutiny for political entanglement with important political divisiveness, religious permeability, and rights principle considerations serving as the key elements.

The most recent example of the Court's reevaluation of entanglement occurred in *Lynch v. Donnelly* (1984), a case in which the Court allowed a crèche as part of a city's holiday display. Justice O'Connor advocated a more stringent entanglement test in response to increasing dissatisfaction on the Court with the *Lemon* standard after *Regan.* This test relied on proof of entanglement rather than the potential for political divisiveness—a measure that she believes is too difficult to gauge. In her view, a prohibitive Court stance in protection of free-exercise rights was not as necessary in entanglement questions as an after-the-fact policing of abuse of such rights by the Court. A strict reading of the entanglement provision better ensures that the institutional strength afforded to religious institutions by state participation in their affairs will not tip the balance against similar process rights shared by nonadherents.[33]

POLITICAL DIVISIVENESS

This process argument, first articulated by Justice Harlan in *Walz* (1970), has become the focus of rights-oriented justices on the liberal wing of the Court in their effort to bolster the *Lemon* standard against unprecedented state encouragement to religious institutions. With a strict assertion of the potentials of political divisiveness resulting from various religious bodies vying with each other over state funds, Justices Brennan, Marshall, Stevens, and Blackmun hoped to reintroduce some of the prohibitive aspects into the Establishment Clause that they felt the loose application of the *Lemon* standard in the Burger era helped to erode.

As mentioned earlier, direct subsidies to parochial institutions, like those afforded in *Regan,* tend to promote an unhealthy competition among religious groups for state funds, particularly when the religious institutions are the sole beneficiaries. For example, in *Nyquist* (1973), the Court feared that direct aid to parents would result in political strife over maintaining levels of aid in the future and the growth of constituencies for and against such aid, resulting in conflict within the interest-group structure. In that case, polity principles weighed heavily against direct state aid.[34]

In the *Wolman* case, we see Justice Powell's views concerning the political divisiveness prong of the *Lemon* standard fully articulated for the first time. There he stated outright that in the modern era we need not fear religious control over democratic processes or deep religious divisions in politics.[35] As such, Powell does not demand a neat and analytic tidiness from the Establishment Clause cases, but rather he supported aid to parochial education as sound judicial policy when there were not serious intrusions of the state in parochial schools or specific evidence of political divisiveness. Accordingly, Powell concurred with the majority in favor of the aid.

However, in a dramatic reversal eight years later in *Aguilar v. Felton* (1985), Justice Powell reasserted the "political divisiveness" standard of the *Lemon* test in a move that indicated a reevaluation of his traditional position in these areas and countered his earlier voting record. Concerning a New York system whereby public school teachers taught secular subjects in parochial school classrooms, Powell stated:

> The risk of entanglement is compounded by the additional risk of political divisiveness stemming from the aid to religion at issue. . . . I do not suggest that at this point in our history the Title I program or similar parochial aid programs could result in the establishment of a state religion. There likewise is small chance that these programs would result in significant religious or denominational control over our democratic processes. . . . Nevertheless, there remains a consid-

erable risk of continuing political strife over the propriety of direct aid to religious schools and the proper allocation of governmental resources.[36]

Powell still accepted *indirect* aid to parochial schools through even-handed programs to the parents of both public and parochial school children, in contrast to the other members of the *Aguilar* majority. However, he had clearly reconsidered his position in reaching the conclusion with Brennan that these programs do not constitute the "indirect and incidental effect beneficial to [the] religious institutions that we suggested in *Nyquist* would survive Establishment Clause scrutiny."[37]

The process value of deterring political divisiveness has, with the *Grand Rapids* and *Aguilar* cases, received at least a temporary lease on life, even if Chief Justice Burger's use of the *Lemon* standard in *Lynch* was revealed as consequentialist enough to render any state government action toward religion legitimate. Under Burger's application of the watered-down *Lemon* standard in *Lynch,* states were guaranteed the presumption of secular purpose and good faith in *all* actions directed at religious institutions, short of establishing a state religion as the framers would understand it.[38] In a concurrence in *Lynch* displaying a more subtle analytical twist, we have seen how Justice O'Connor abandoned the political divisiveness prong of the *Lemon* standard in favor of a more stringent "no entanglement" test. In *Lynch,* she found that the state crèche display did not violate any of her modified *Lemon* criteria, and she voted with the Burger majority. Justice Brennan, however, dissenting in the *Lynch* case, warned about the perils of "religious chauvinism" because political antagonism might come from minority dissident religious groups,[39] and as of 1985 he seems to have been heeded. Just how much of a recovery the *Lemon* standard can make, in process terms, based on the perhaps unexpected concurrence of Justice Powell in the 1985 cases, remains to be seen. What can be pinpointed, however, is that ideological tensions are rife on the Court at this time and are being reflected in the reshaping of Court coalitions in Establishment Clause cases, not merely in process terms but on rights and free-exercise grounds as well (to be examined in the next section). The *Lemon* standard, for so long an overly flexible tool, may at least provide for its own resurrection.

SECULAR PURPOSE AND DEFERENCE TO STATE AUTHORITY

All justices acknowledge that state legislatures have a legitimate secular interest in assuring a hospitable environment for religious institutions in society. Broadly defined, this interest involves the services that sectarian schools provide as educational alternatives for many schoolchildren with the resulting alleviation of tax burdens on society; wholesome competition with public schools resulting in the overall betterment of a pluralistic society; and a general state interest in seeing that its children are properly educated to cope in a complex and modern society.[40] The scope of that interest, however, is the source of much heated debate.

The secular interest, and its effective implementation through statute, lies somewhere between the two poles of judicial deference to process determinations on the one hand (as advocated by conservatives Rehnquist, White, Burger, and to a lesser degree O'Connor), and outright distrust of those same processes on the other (with liberals Brennan, Marshall, and to a lesser degree Stevens and Blackmun as the main proponents), with an eye for context thrown in. Polity principles of the most fundamental sort come into play when the justices are asked to what extent governments should be trusted to intrude into the religious enterprise, even when benefiting from such intrusion. The question of state neutrality is in turn reflected back on the Court's role in determining such neutrality, and views about the Court's role in the polity must inevitably underlie any choices made by justices about who has authority to intervene in which situations.

These questions of decision-making authority—that is, whether state legislatures, federal courts, or school systems are to be trusted to make choices about aid to parochial education—are crucial to the substantive outcomes of the choices themselves. It is a polity-oriented question; incumbent biases in the political system range from pluralist interpretations of the "open" American political system to theories that argue that a main function of broad-based political institutions like the presidency and the Supreme Court is to remain vigilant against such entrenched values.[41] Justices Brennan and Marshall lean toward the prohibitive constraints on state action found in the Establishment Clause. Their bloc emphasizes a hermetically sealed church and state relationship of the most limited variety, with the Court as a proscriptive body policing the integrity of that relationship *preventively*. Justices Burger and O'Connor, on the other hand, emphasize an initial presumption of good faith on the part of agents of the state in dealing in church affairs. Evidence of the latter position is provided in O'Connor's dissent in *Aguilar v. Felton*, in which she declared her support for the ability of public school teachers to keep the *potentials* of indoctrination out of the sectarian classroom, relying on the record in the case to support the assertion.[42]

Justices White and Rehnquist—one from the center and one on the ideological extreme, in Blasi's view—share the same process value of Court deference to legislatures in these cases as a matter of course. Characteristically to the point, Justice White said in *Lemon v. Kurtzman*, "It is enough for me that the States and the Federal Government are financing a separable secular function of overriding importance in order to sustain the legislation here challenged. That religion and private interests other than education may substantially benefit does not convert these laws into impermissible establishments of religion."[43] Justice White has consistently subscribed to this view and has favored dismantling the *Lemon* standard in favor of such a deferential outlook.[44] Justice White should be credited for acknowledging his predispositions outright, but he implicates himself as well when he accuses the majority in *Lemon v. Kurtzman* for banning the Rhode Island and Pennsylvania statutory aid schemes, saying that they substitute "presumption for proof" of potential state abuse.[45] The majority may be overly proscriptive of state action in expectation of state abuse, but Justice White fails to see that he is equally presumptuous in *denial* of the potential for such abuse. The consensus that the state has a secular interest in acknowledging religious institutions breaks down once we try to define that interest. The Court balances standards of state neutrality toward religious institutions, on the one hand, and the process principle—separation of powers—of the Court stance toward majoritarian political processes, on the other.

The most crucial views on the Court concerning church/state relations and the institutional role of the Court in the polity are found at the center. In this regard, Blasi is right, but for the wrong reasons. Justice Blackmun has seriously reevaluated the views in contention in church and state cases since he wrote for the majority in *Roemer v. Board of Public Works* that, "It has not been the Court's practice, in considering facial challenges to statutes of this kind, to strike them down *in anticipation* that particular applications may result in unconstitutional use of funds."[46] He has retreated to more principled, if less flexible, grounds in Establishment Clause cases since *Regan.* The general trend is leaning toward less fixed ideas about key process principles in church and state cases; thus, Justices Powell and O'Connor have also cast crucial votes against the conservative coalition with whom they are usually associated.

THE "EFFECTS" TEST: ACCOMMODATIVE VERSUS PROSCRIPTIVE JURISPRUDENCE

The justices' views vary a great deal on the question of what actually constitutes or causes a detrimental effect upon the religious enterprise. Questions of process entanglement, political divisiveness, and religious pervasiveness are figured in to the extent that the "no entanglement" tier of the *Lemon* test is a redundancy of the "effects" test. In his concurrence in *Roemer,* Justice White stated:

> Today's plurality leaves the impression that the [*Lemon*] criterion really may not be "separate" at all. . . . In affirming the District Court's conclusion that the legislation here does not create "excessive entanglement" of church and state, the plurality emphasizes with approval that "the District Court [found that the religious institution is] capable of separating secular and religious functions." Yet these are the same factors upon which the plurality focuses in concluding that the Maryland legislation satisfies the second ["effects"] part of the Lemon I test.[47]

The internal redundancies of the *Lemon* standard give justices sympathetic to aid to parochial schools a great degree of leeway in determining how far any authority can be entrusted. In the *Tilton, Hunt* and *Roemer* cases, and in the parochial school cases after *Meek,* we see that the *Lemon* standard ceased to be a tool for constraints on legislative action. On the contrary, *Lemon* has been invoked loosely to accommodate ideologically conservative process norms of deference to legislative bodies.

The saving grace of the property tax exemption permitted churches in *Walz v. Tax Commission of New York* was that it was not *directly* provided by state government, but rather was only passively endorsed as part of a general tax exemption for nonprofit institutions and that, historically, such an exemption had been allowed. As a rule, in the early Establishment Clause cases of the Burger era, direct grants—be they salary supplements, provision for instructional materials, test grading, tuition reimbursement, or tax-deduction schemes—were disallowed (*Nyquist, Lemon, Levitt*). But state legislatures responded to Court prohibitions with increasing persistence and ingenuity, forcing the Court to both inject their tests with a greater amount of broad applicability to the new legislative schemes and, for individual justices, to reevaluate the limits they were willing to impose on what several of them perceived as clearly legitimate and justifiable state action.

For former Chief Justice Burger, the limit was reached in *Tilton v. Richardson* (1971), decided the same day the *Lemon* ruling came down. In this case concerning the effects of state subsidization of building construction on sectarian college campuses, we see a sudden weight given to *context* by the Burger Court. The *character* of the institution that benefited and the *nature* of the individual recipients were appended to the *Lemon* standard as evaluated criteria. This consideration became the first of what would end up being a large number of exceptions to the supposedly principled *Lemon* rule. The collegiate atmosphere, coupled with the essentially inanimate (and therefore unproselytizing) nature of the services provided, such as building grants, were enough, with strict warnings, to diffuse the fears of the majorities in the earlier cases.

Perhaps the criterion that served to qualify the process guarantees of the *Lemon* standard to the fullest degree was the *breadth* of the aid offered by state legislatures and the federal government. In *Walz,* an instance where the property tax exemptions were offered to all nonprofit institutions, the Court found it difficult to reject aid on narrow, Establishment Clause grounds. Conversely, the statutory schemes in *Lemon, Nyquist,* and *Sloan v. Lemon* were all invalidated because of the exclusive advantages offered solely to sectarian schools or to the parents of children attending them. The Court was most amenable to aid in those instances when it could look to past precedent—in particular, the *Everson* and *Allen* cases, which allowed for general state subsidies of bus rides and secular textbooks for parochial school children—in support for state subsidization of any one of a broad number of nonprofit needs.

Another widely disputed aspect of government aid to religious institutions has concerned the incorporation of secular values into parochial schools as a by-product of state aid. The dilution of religious atmosphere as a consequence of "benevolent neutrality" on the part of state legislatures is connected in kind, but not in scope, to the free-exercise religious rights of *individuals,* to be discussed at length in the next section. Justices on the rights-oriented bloc have used institutional integrity arguments as process violations to bolster individual rights of conscience against state aid and interference. The permeability problem has been elevated since *Walz,* resulting, along with other reasons, in the different string of rulings marked by the *Lemon* and *Tilton* progression of cases. In *Walz,* Justice Douglas warned of the importance of severing the private and public domains of the church and state relationship, keeping within strict adherence to the distinct spheres of activity that both church and state represented to him.[48] Similarly, in a concurring statement in *Lemon v. Kurtzman,* Douglas, joined by Justice Black, termed the religious enterprise as a whole entity within itself—an "organism" that could suffer irreparable damage if its internal equilibrium were altered. For example, entanglement arguably might serve to dilute both religious environment and controlling sectarian purpose. As he put it: "The intrusion of government into religious schools through grants, supervision, or surveillance may result in establishment of religion in the constitutional sense when what the state does enthrones a particular sect for overt or subtle propagation of its faith."[49]

Many of these process and rights distinctions turn on the differences between individual and institutional forums of rights protection. As in other aspects of the *Lemon* standard process formulation, the justices carry predispositions toward state efforts to disentangle active intervention and guarantee the integrity of religious pursuit. In a related concern, we see that statistical determinants of adverse effects on parochial schools are given more or less credence by justices depending upon the desired ideological result. White mentions in an important footnote that, "Our prior cases demonstrate that the question of whether aid programs satisfy the 'excessive entanglement' test [like the broader 'effects' test] depends at least to some extent on the degree to which the Court accepts lower courts' findings of fact."[50]

In sum, the effect standard of the *Lemon* test has been construed to justify as much as to prevent expansion of state aid to parochial institutions, depending on the nature of the aid itself: whether it is indirect or direct; whether it involves buildings or whether the immediate recipients are individual parents rather than the institution per se; and finally, the diffusive nature and broad applicability of the aid that was offered. The Burger/*Lemon* effects approach was geared toward policy outcomes and a flexibility toward majoritarian process determinations by legislatures rather than toward principles focused on rights. Furthermore, within the framework of a limited effects test that allows for content-specific applications by some of the Court's members—Burger, O'Connor, and formerly Powell on the conservative bloc seem most susceptible to statistical arguments—we are faced with fertile ground for the manipulation of the *Lemon* standard to ideological ends. Wall-of-separation theories as well as benevolent-neutrality and flexibility norms that prompt the coalitions on the Court have been appended by the appropriate justices onto the *Lemon* standard in specific cases to further these process and rights ideologies. Pragmatism premised "more on experience and history than on logic" in Establishment Clause cases[51] certainly has been fueled by a readily perceptible ideology.

PROCESS VALUE DOMINANCE IN THE *LEMON* STANDARD

In conclusion, the prevailing *Lemon* standard is a process-oriented and process-accommodating measure of judicial scrutiny that relies upon constituency arguments about the safeguarding of religious minorities; questions of institutional entanglement; political divisiveness, which can occur as a result of asserted state favoritism; and the nature of the institutional benefit that churches can or should receive under state auspices. It has tended—the 1985 cases excepted—to vary with the legislatures that challenge it, resulting in a flexible Establishment Clause case jurisprudence that has characterized late Burger era church and state activity. This coupling of deference to legislative bodies with a concern for the institutional or policy implications of aid to parochial education in Court decision making has served to unite and divide different members of the Court in the process of bloc formation and group voting.

That these developments are attributed to ideological considerations rather than a disinterested pragmatism should be clear by now. In fact, those genuinely centrist justices, Powell and O'Connor—as opposed to Blackmun, Stevens, and White who are at ideological extremes—displayed the most innovative and adaptive responses in their changing balancing of process and rights values. In *Lynch*, O'Connor redefined the *Lemon* standard so as to put added bite into the entanglement prong and revealed, as we shall see, considerable sympathy for the free-exercise rights of both believers and nonbelievers in the *Grand Rapids* and *Wallace v. Jaffree* cases. Similarly, Justice Powell displayed a willingness to reevaluate the process principle of political divisiveness in the *Aguilar* case. His retirement has cut short any subsequent development of his ideology in these cases. However, that justices have displayed clear ideological closure in their choices; that process-oriented justices on the conservative wing have used the flexibility afforded through loose application of the *Lemon* standard to further ideological ends; and that a center in ideological flux and development, rather than in an accord of disinterested pragmatism, exists to spur Rehnquist Court doctrinal development, and therefore change in society—all indicate a profound refutation of the Blasi "pragmatic-middle" thesis.

RIGHTS PRINCIPLES: THE WALL OF SEPARATION

We now turn from process values to those substantive rights principles embedded in the structural guarantees of the First Amendment religious provisions. As might be expected, these considerations center on rights of individuals and groups more readily than on broader institutional arguments.

Although never downplaying the process value protections afforded by the Establishment Clause, the liberal wing of the Court has consistently relied on rights arguments to bolster their position for a "high and impregnable" barrier between church and state. That the early work of Justices Douglas, Brennan, and Marshall has paid off in this regard is indicated not by the abandonment or renewed strength of the *Lemon* standard as it has consistently been applied by the process-oriented Court majority, but rather by the recent addition of new adherents to the rights-oriented camp, namely, Justices Blackmun and Stevens, and by the acknowledgment by Justice O'Connor that free-exercise rights constitute limitations on state and church involvement.

Compared to process principles at work in the Establishment Clause cases, rights-based principles allow for more rigidity in the Supreme Court stance toward state aid to religious institutions; in fact, a denial of all aid to religious institutions is seen as preferable in the long run to benevolent neutrality toward such institutions generally. The prohibitive aspects of the Establishment Clause therefore are invoked to supersede any aid that the Court might wish to offer on the basis of a magnanimous reading of the free-exercise clause (a reading to which those justices on the process-oriented bloc primarily subscribe). Relying upon principled separation arguments, the liberal justices have sought to use the strong process orientation of the Establishment Clause to their best advantage in protection of free-exercise clause values. Accordingly, unprincipled adjudication—as indicative of a general Court leniency toward political bodies—does not fit their stance well.

In sketching the rights principles at work in these cases, it is useful to abide by the contours of free-exercise guarantees as outlined by the Court along what I have divided into *external* and *internal* free-exercise categories. Discussion of such questions assumes the relationship of state and church to some small degree and presupposes a means of removing the adverse effects of such a relationship by keeping the religious atmosphere of sectarian institutions inviolate. The result is to guarantee a bare minimum of entanglement and political divisiveness within the context of a modern society. These process and rights predispositions of the liberal bloc on the Court are again determinative in answering the many subtle choices of degree that must be made in exploring what constitutes an "effect" in this prong of the *Lemon* test. In fact, the liberal justices hope to keep those flexible choices at a minimum by creating a principled separation that will allow fewer questions to be asked of the church and state relationship in the first place. The external and internal components of the free-exercise clause are best articulated by Justice Brennan in his majority opinion in *Aguilar v. Felton:*

> The principle that the state should not become too closely entangled with the church in the administration of assistance is rooted in two concerns. When the state becomes enmeshed with a given denomination in matters of religious significance, the freedom of religious belief of those who are not adherents of that denomination suffers, even when the governmental purpose underlying the involvement is

largely secular. In addition, the freedom of even the adherents of the denomination is limited by the government intrusion into sacred matters.[52]

The external free-exercise rights of sectarian institutions and non-adherents in society are best articulated by Justice Brennan's "symbolic union" thesis described in his majority opinion in the *Grand Rapids* case. The symbolic union premise is based on a concern that state and federal programs not be perceived by adherents of the controlling denominations as an endorsement of their religious beliefs *or* by nonadherents as a disapproval of their individual religious choices. In *Grand Rapids,* Brennan wrote:

> Government promotes religion as effectively when it fosters a close identification of its powers and responsibilities with those of any—or all—religious denominations as when it attempts to inculcate specific religious doctrines. If this identification conveys a message of government endorsement or disapproval of religion, a core purpose of the Establishment Clause is violated.[53]

Questions concerning the integrity of religious atmosphere for denominations and their individual members also touch on the free-exercise rights of individual nonbelievers to *not* support particular religions, or of atheists to support none at all. In a passionate defense of the external rights of nonbelievers, Justice Douglas, in dissent in *Walz,* argued that these people should not be asked to support churches with their tax dollars.[54] He argued that if the dictates of pluralism applauded by the majority of the Court in this case are to be properly followed, then nonbelievers deserve just as much financial support as believers. In short, independence for religious institutions is the price of liberty, and state aid is the sacrifice.[55] Implicit in Brennan's argument in both the 1985 *Aguilar* and *Grand Rapids* majority opinions is also a concern for the individual child's *internal* free-exercise rights. Faced with state support of schooling in any regard, a child could very easily be passively indoctrinated into believing his particular sect was superior to those of his friends across the block, or perhaps even the views of his agnostic relatives.

Justice O'Connor concurred in the outlawing of the community program taught after school by parochial school teachers, in *Grand Rapids,* relying on the substance of the "symbolic union" thesis and using the strengthened entanglement prong she advocated in *Lynch.* She determined that in this program, as distinguished from the shared-time program, there was a likelihood that entanglement could occur in monitoring the activities of parochial school teachers who taught in a public capacity after school hours in the same classrooms with many of the same pupils. In addition, state involvement infringed substantially on the right of children not to have religious and secular messages mixed. It seems that, for O'Connor, children have the right not to be confused about the neutrality of the state concerning religious issues. It is this emphasis, rather than a broader notion of the inability of the state to separate the secular and religious spheres, that distinguishes her position from that of Brennan.

Free-exercise rights for sectarians and nonsectarians, and their internal and external rights, pervade the wall-of-separation arguments of the liberal bloc on the Court. The preceding section showed how the conservative wing of the Court—Rehnquist, Burger, White, Powell, and O'Connor—tried to transform the process guarantees in the same cases from a prescriptive separation of church and state to a *positivistic* one in which all state and church interactions are considered constitutional unless they are shown *by the facts* to result in unconstitutional state indoctrination. But just as Powell exerted independence from his bloc in process terms over the issue of political divisiveness, indicating a process and rights value relationship in flux, so O'Connor portrays some nonpragmatic innovation in her depiction of free-exercise rights principles in another post-1980 case, *Wallace v. Jaffree.*

In *Wallace,* the Court decided that an Alabama law authorizing a period of silence for "meditation or voluntary prayer" in public schools respected the establishment of religion and should be struck down. O'Connor, in a concurrence, strongly supported a free-exercise internal right that would find general moment-of-silence laws, without implicit state encouragement or favoritism, constitutional. She disagreed that free-exercise principles should be evaluated solely on the basis of the framers' preference for prayer in the schools, as asserted by Rehnquist in the case, and found the secular purpose and "effects" tests of the *Lemon* standard not to be ahistorical in this regard. Content choices by states warrant Court vigilance, as opposed to wholesale support of state aid to religion, as Burger and Rehnquist urge, or wholesale removal of the question from Court scrutiny by erecting the "wall" that her liberal colleagues urge. State objectives need not be exclusively secular, but they must not be content-based—a requirement that the record confirmed could not be met in the case of Alabama. It is clear, however, that Justice O'Connor supports a consequentialist case-by-case *Lemon* test in the interest of free exercise, and this flexibility is more characteristic of the conservative bloc with whom she is usually associated. She seems to trust in the Court's ability to differentiate between sham secular purposes and actual ones in state laws and, as shown in her concurring opinion in *Lynch,* she favors a scrupulously monitored system of state support for religion that has respect for both believers and nonbelievers. Justice O'Connor will continue to play a crucial role in church and state cases. With these significant exceptions, however, the coalitions on the Supreme Court remain intact.

CONCLUSION

In this chapter, I have aimed to demonstrate three points: (1) that the "pragmatic-middle" thesis is not borne out by the evidence from Establishment Clause cases prior to 1980, and is clearly not a useful way to describe post-

1980 Burger Court decision making; (2) that the substantive basis of judicial choice—the polity and rights principles on which the Establishment Clause cases were decided prior to 1980—informed the bloc voting in the post-1980 cases; and (3) that an "ideological jurisprudence" methodology is particularly suited for analysis of Supreme Court decision making in general.

The pragmatic middle that Blasi claims was central to a disinterested and balanced Burger Court jurisprudence never acted in the way he describes. If one were to identify such a center, it consisted only of Justices Stewart, Powell, and Blackmun, those justices who had relatively few dissenting positions from the majority opinions prior to 1980. One-third of the Court does not make a coherent center that can perform the tasks and inculcate the values described by Blasi. The other members of the pragmatic middle, White and Stevens, had high percentages of dissents from the majority opinions: They were ranked higher in dissents than many of the justices labeled as extreme by Blasi. As the principled basis for judicial choice in cases involving aid to parochial education declined in the late 1970s, these middle justices on the Court could no longer support the movement toward wholesale deference to process rather than rights determinations of Establishment Clause issues. Thus Blackmun, and to a certain degree O'Connor and Powell, have refused support for the unprincipled, narrowly policy-oriented choices made by the Court's right wing. The only justice in the years after 1980 who consistently voted with the majority opinion on the Court was Powell.

In church and state cases, the Court has split primarily into two groups. Justices Brennan, Marshall, Stevens, and more recently, Justice Blackmun sought to reintroduce a wall of separation between church and state; that is, to secure a more principled basis of choice than is now in vogue with the decline of the forceful application of the *Lemon* test in Establishment Clause cases. They sought to reintroduce a strong free-exercise component for nonbelievers as well as for believers into Establishment Clause jurisprudence, and accordingly relied upon strong process proscriptions of state entanglement and political divisiveness in government aid to sectarian institutions.

The process-oriented bloc, consisting of Justices White, Rehnquist, and Burger, and to a lesser degree, Justices O'Connor and formerly Powell, have worked to do away with the old *Lemon* test, especially that part which seeks to assure that the primary effect of government aid is not to advance or inhibit religion. They reject the notion that parochial schools have a pervasive religious atmosphere and have determined that almost all effects of government aid are incidental when considered within the broader context of a complex society in which religion plays an integral role. They are conservative in several senses. They view aid to education in instrumental policy rather than principled constitutional terms. They do not fear entanglement—that the state might corrupt the church and vice versa. Nor do they fear there will be a denial of the free-exercise rights of parochial school children or of believers and nonbelievers in the wider society. As such, they have been sensitive to Reagan administration and New Right followers.

Justices O'Connor and Powell share a similar view to White, Rehnquist, and Burger, who do not want to inhibit state action through a strict reading of the free-exercise or process components in the Establishment Clause. However, it is significant that O'Connor and Powell see a special role for the Supreme Court in protecting the rights of believers and nonbelievers in (internal) institutions from external incursion. Ultimately, O'Connor admits that the Court must ensure that government is not putting its stamp of approval on religion, as in the *Jaffree* case, or allowing the same parochial school teachers to teach religious classes in the day and secular classes after school, as in the *Grand Rapids* case. Similarly, Justice Powell seems to have reinvigorated his concern for the separation of church and state in the 1985 cases, particularly in the prohibition of state subsidization of secular teaching programs in religious schools, which he saw as the responsibility of the schools themselves.

The appointment of Justice Scalia, who is supportive of government accommodation to religion, and Justice Kennedy to replace Powell, coupled with the independent jurisprudence advocated by Justice O'Connor, has decreased the likelihood that a pragmatic middle will coalesce in the near future. Doctrinal development and conflict in church and state cases will remain dependent upon the degree to which Kennedy and O'Connor accept a greater free-exercise component for believers (internal) and nonbelievers (external) in their mix of process and rights values. It appears that Justice Scalia has not accepted free-exercise components. The insertion of new personalized ideologies on the Court could dramatically affect the church and state coalitions. A reciprocal relationship exists between individual justices' values and their expectations of the general Court stance toward the polity. With changes in Court personnel, particularly in the case of crucial deciding votes, the Court stance could certainly change. No centrist structure exists on the Rehnquist Court for Kennedy to step into. Also, it is unlikely that Kennedy's views on church and state matters will conform to those of O'Connor to form an embryonic centrist bloc, especially with Scalia on the Supreme Court. Therefore, we can expect the Rehnquist Court to be marginally more accommodating to religion than the Burger Court.

The new Burger Court majority, which persists into the Rehnquist era, generally assumes that the polity will respect everyone's religious rights. However, having established no principled basis in determining *how much* religious speech is desirable, (or how much aid to parents of students in parochial schools is or is not permissible), the new majority essentially has turned such choices over to allegedly more accountable "political" branches of government. We see a system of judicial choice that has flexibility, pragmatism, and an understandable context. We can expect government-endorsed religious speech or subsidies in various forms to the religious enterprise, given the emphasis on process rather than rights values. This trend will favor churches that are organized, funded, and zealous. The ideology behind such process rather than substantive rights values is one of "trusting the political collective," which in turn leaves the power of zealous religious minorities unchecked.

This analysis demonstrates that the Burger Court, through its reliance on a tension between long-standing process and rights values in the religion clauses of the First Amendment, has not given in doctrinally to the movement by religious fundamentalists to place schools and government in a position of advocating or directly accommodating their religious beliefs. However, the nose of the camel is under the tent a bit, so to speak, with regard to the crèche case and cases involving general programs of aid to parents of schoolchildren. In short, the Court in essence has endorsed religion as part of our more general societal values and religious education as part of a general system of public, tax-supported education. However, the Burger Court has stopped short of allowing schools and legislatures to affirmatively support religious fundamentalism as a right of children in secular schools. In so doing, the Burger Court has said that religion is an important value in our liberal society, but not one that will replace the objectives of our schools to educate in a secular, rather than a sectarian, manner. The creationism cases confirm these findings.

Inevitably, the pragmatic-middle thesis leads one to view the Supreme Court and its process of decision making as similar to electorally accountable institutions to a degree unwarranted by the legal constraints on federal courts. By contrast, the analysis of process and rights values helps to document tensions among such values in the jurisprudence of justices and blocs of justices in key doctrinal areas of Court policy making over time and elucidates differences in constitutional principles in different Court eras. Finally, we are able to consider normative issues concerning the role of law, courts, and rights in our society—questions that at present are clouded both by the assumption of valueless pragmatism and by constitutional theorists who emphasize either process or rights values exclusively in their work.[56]

Underlying ideology and values provide the key to each judicial era, as we have seen in the case of the Burger Court.[57] The reconstitution of doctrine, rather than merely a reaction to past precedent, continues into the Rehnquist era of the Supreme Court. Court decision making reflects justices' continuing process and rights values as they decide cases that arise out of modern political tensions in society. In the 1980s, tensions on church and state questions have been spawned by the political emergence of fundamentalist religions. Hence, law is neither above politics nor merely mimetic with power relationships in society: Process and rights principles act as a filter for Court decision making and ensure that the Court's choices reflect longstanding constitutional values as it meets political tensions in society. Thus the swing to the right in the Reagan years has been reflected in church and state cases, both through the influence of new members of the Court and in the cases brought to the Court. However, these cases have been decided without denuding church and state jurisprudence of the discipline of process and rights values, which continue to protect the citizen and the state from the most devastating effects of government establishment of religion.

NOTES

I would like to express my appreciation to the Research and Development Committee of Oberlin College for financial support. I am also indebted to my three Dana Foundation Research Assistants, Stuart Christie, Jeffrey Auerbach, and William Hirshorn, who ably assisted me at various stages of this project, and to the editors of this volume for their very helpful suggestions.

1. See Vincent Blasi, "The Rootless Activism of the Burger Court," in Vincent Blasi, ed., *The Burger Court: The Counter-Revolution That Wasn't* (New Haven: Yale University Press, 1983).
2. Ibid., p. 211.
3. See John Hart Ely, *Democracy and Distrust* (Cambridge: Harvard University Press, 1980), pp. 71–72.
4. See Michael Perry, *The Constitution, the Courts, and Human Rights* (New Haven: Yale University Press, 1982), pp. 91–146.
5. See Laurence H. Tribe, "Unraveling National League of Cities: The New Federalism and Affirmative Rights to Essential Government Services," *Harvard Law Review* 90 (1977), pp. 1065–1104; Frank I. Michelman, "States' Rights and States' Roles: Permutations of 'Sovereignty' in National League of Cities v. Usery," *Yale Law Journal* 86 (1977), pp. 1165–1195; and Richard Davies Parker, "The Past of Constitutional Theory—and Its Future," *Ohio State Law Journal* 42 (1981), pp. 223–259. Also, see Ronald Kahn, "Process and Rights Principles in Modern Constitutional Theory," *Stanford Law Review* 36 (1984), pp. 253–269, for a discussion of the consequences of viewing the Constitution in *either* process or rights terms, as John Hart Ely and Laurence Tribe are prone to do.
6. See Roberto Unger, *Law in Modern Society* (New York: The Free Press, 1976), pp. 203–214, for a discussion of the basic dilemma of modern liberal jurisprudence: how to meet objectives of formality, equity, and substantive justice. Bright-line distinctions between church and state achieve formality and equity to a degree but may undermine free-exercise values; securing substantive justice for free-exercise rights in *some* cases undermines formality and equity. For example, in *Wisconsin v. Yoder*, 406 U.S. 205 (1972), the Supreme Court allowed Amish children to leave school prior to the end of the year mandated by state law because the Court viewed the Amish as a traditional religious community unlike that of other unnamed sects.
7. Martin Shapiro, "Fathers and Sons: The Court, the Commentators, and the Search for Values," in Vincent Blasi, ed., *The Burger Court: The Counter-Revolution That Wasn't*, p. 238.
8. See Ronald Kahn, "The Burger Court, Boundary Setting, and State and Local

Power," in *Proteus* 4 (Autumn 1987), for a detailed description of the pluralist/ critical pluralist debate in modern political and legal theory.

9. Blasi, "Rootless Activism," pp. 198–199.
10. Lawrence Baum, "Explaining the Burger Court's Support for Civil Liberties," *PS* 20 (Winter 1987), pp. 25–26.
11. John Brigham, *The Cult of the Court* (Philadelphia: Temple University Press, 1987), pp. 21–22.
12. See David Greenstone and Paul E. Peterson, *Race and Authority in Urban Politics* (New York: Russell Sage Foundation, 1973), pp. 125–126; and Paul E. Peterson, *School Politics Chicago Style* (Chicago: University of Chicago Press, 1976), Chapter 2, for explanations of how the "ideological interests" of big city mayors for or against citizen participation led to choices that were not, in pragmatic terms, in their electoral and organizational interests.
13. See Brigham, *Cult of the Court*, Chapters 1 and 2, for how behavioralism as a tenet practiced by political scientists is undercut by ideologies of authority upon which the Supreme Court relies within its institutional framework. These ideologies impose constitutive characteristics on the values that motivate judicial action. Also, see R. Jeffrey Lustig, *Corporate Liberalism* (Berkeley: University of California Press, 1982), Chapters 6 and 8, for an excellent analysis of "pragmatism" and ideology.
14. *Lemon v. Kurtzman*, 403 U.S. 602 (1971).
15. *Committee for Public Education and Religious Liberty v. Regan*, 444 U.S. 646 (1980).
16. *Wallace v. Jaffree*, 472 U.S. 38 (1985); *Grand Rapids School District v. Ball*, 473 U.S. 373 (1985).
17. Herbert Storing, *What the Anti-Federalists Were For: The Political Thought of the Opponents of the Constitution* (Chicago: University of Chicago Press, 1981).
18. For a different view see Justice Rehnquist's dissent in *Wallace v. Jaffree*, in which he claims that current Establishment Clause jurisprudence is without any historical basis. For an interpretation of the founders in *support* of a strong application of the Establishment Clause, see the Douglas dissenting opinion in *Walz v. Tax Commission of New York*, 397 U.S. 664 (1970).
19. *Everson v. Board of Education*, 330 U.S. 1 (1947), was the Court's first full-scale examination of Establishment Clause's constitutional guidelines. The case involved the permissibility of state-subsidized busing for children attending private schools. The aid was allowed in a 5–4 decision with Black and Douglas in the majority. Some twenty years later, Justice Douglas would admit to regretting his vote in that case, preferring instead to abide by a more rigid wall-of-separation stance (*Walz v. Tax Commission of New York*, at 703).
20. For an analysis of process and polity principles extending back to the founding period, see Ronald Kahn, "The Intersection of Polity and Rights Principles on the Burger Court: Towards a Social Science of Jurisprudence," *Legal Studies Forum* 11 (1987), pp. 5–28.
21. See Frank I. Michelman, "Forward: Traces of Self-Government," *Harvard Law Review* 100 (1986), pp. 4–77, for a discussion of the judicial role as imperial in the polity enumerating "positive" and "negative" libertarian interests in the republican juridical tradition. In scope these interests rely on similar assumptions by justices about process and rights values in the polity.

22. As defined, process and rights principles are analytically distinct. These separate definitions, however, serve as heuristic tools only for understanding the nature of judicial choices. Theories based on process or rights principles, but not both, undervalue the connectedness of the two bases of judicial choice (see note 5). Even the most ideological and monolithic of judicial views has little meaning unless there is some opposite to give it an adversarial substance.

23. See Karl Marx, "On the Jewish Question," in Robert C. Tucker, *The Marx Engel Reader,* 2nd ed. (New York: W. W. Norton, 1978), pp. 26–52, for an analysis of how under liberalism in a bourgeois society religious liberty and the separation of church and state, like property, is part of a broader separation of thought and reality into public/political and private/civil spheres, with law as mediation protecting individual rights in the civil sphere and thus allowing self-interest rather than collective equalitarian values to dominate.

24. See David M. O'Brien, *Storm Center: The Supreme Court in American Politics* (New York: W. W. Norton, 1986), p. 183; and "The Supreme Court: From Warren to Burger to Rehnquist," *PS* 20 (Winter 1987), p. 17, for reasons why there are more plurality, concurring, and dissenting opinions and less obeisance to collective decisions. Process and rights constitutional theory adds to the institutional reasons suggested by O'Brien.

25. See O'Brien, "The Supreme Court: From Warren to Burger to Rehnquist," p. 16. Justice Powell has voted against prevailing opinion in case selection least often—seventy times (O'Brien, *Storm Center,* p. 194).

26. See Ronald Kahn, "The Intersection of Polity and Rights Principles" for an analysis of the relationship of process and rights values in selected First Amendment, due process of law, and equal protection cases.

27. See *Lemon v. Kurtzman,* 403 U.S. 602, 623–624 (1971).

28. *Board of Education v. Allen, Commissioner,* 392 U.S. 236 (1968).

29. *Lemon v. Kurtzman,* at 623–624.

30. *Meek v. Pittenger,* 421 U.S. 349, 365 (1975).

31. *Wolman v. Walter,* 433 U.S. 229, 259 (1977).

32. *Lemon v. Kurtzman,* at 668.

33. *Lynch v. Donnelly,* 465 U.S. 668, 689 (1984).

34. *Committee for Public Education and Religious Liberty v. Nyquist,* 413 U.S. 756, 797 (1973).

35. *Wolman v. Walter,* at 263.

36. *Aguilar v. Felton,* 473 U.S. 402, 416 (1985).

37. Ibid., at 417.

38. *Lynch v. Donnelly,* at 680, 686.

39. Ibid., at 701.

40. *Wolman v. Walter,* at 262.

41. See Grant McConnell, *Private Power in American Democracy* (New York: Alfred A. Knopf, 1966); Theodore J. Lowi, *The End of Liberalism: The Second Republic of the United States,* 2nd ed. (New York: W. W. Norton, 1979), pp. 295–313.

42. *Aguilar v. Felton,* at 424–425.

43. *Lemon v. Kurtzman,* at 664.

44. *Roemer v. Board of Public Works of Maryland,* 426 U.S. 736, 768 (1976).

45. *Lemon v. Kurtzman,* at 670.

46. *Roemer v. Board of Public Works of Maryland,* at 761.

47. Ibid., at 769.
48. *Walz v. Tax Commission of New York,* at 714.
49. *Lemon v. Kurtzman,* at 634.
50. *Roemer v. Board of Public Works of Maryland,* at 769. Justices White and Rehnquist reflect, by and large, a more principled stance toward reliance upon statistical data as determination of case outcomes than their process-deferential colleagues on the Court (particularly O'Connor and Powell).
51. *Committee for Public Education and Religious Liberty v. Nyquist,* at 802.
52. *Aguilar v. Felton,* at 409–410.
53. *Grand Rapids School District v. Ball,* at 389.
54. *Walz v. Tax Commission of New York,* at 700.
55. Ibid., at 716.
56. See Martin Shapiro, "The Supreme Court's 'Return' to Economic Regulation," *Studies in American Political Development* 1 (1986), pp. 91–141, for an analysis of noninterpretivism as it is at work on the Court in substantive economic due process and administrative law.
57. See Kahn, "The Burger Court," *Proteus* 4 (Autumn 1987), for the argument that process-based norms have steered the Burger Court toward an advocacy of pluralist values and deference to legislative bodies and federalism in equal protection, fundamental rights and interest, First Amendment, and standing to sue jurisprudence.

About the Contributors

David Gray Adler received his Ph.D. from the University of Utah and is presently Assistant Professor of Political Science at Idaho State University. He has written a book, *The Constitution and the Termination of Treaties,* and several articles on constitutional issues. His current research includes a book project addressing the changing conceptions of constitutional authority in foreign affairs.

Judith A. Baer received her M.A. and Ph.D. from the University of Chicago and is currently Professor of Political Science at Texas A & M University. She is the author of two books, *The Chains of Protection* and *Equality Under the Constitution: Reclaiming the Fourteenth Amendment,* and several articles on constitutional issues.

John Brigham is Professor of Political Science at the University of Massachusetts at Amherst. He is the author of many articles and several books on the Supreme Court and the politics of constitutional lawmaking, including *Constitutional Language, Civil Liberties and American Democracy,* and *The Cult of the Court.*

Lief H. Carter, who received a Ph.D. from the University of California at Berkeley and a J.D. from Harvard University, is now Professor of Political Science at the University of Georgia. He is the author of several books, including *Reason in Law* and *Contemporary Constitutional Lawmaking: The Supreme Court and the Art of Politics,* and numerous essays on the nature of judicial decision making.

Rhonda Copelon is a scholar and legal activist who has been affiliated with the Center for Constitutional Rights since 1971. She has participated in litigation on a wide variety of civil rights issues generally and on sexual and reproductive rights issues specifically, arguing before the Supreme Court in the controversial *Harris v. McRae* case. She is also Associate Professor at CUNY Law School, Queens College, and the author of several articles on sexuality, gender, and constitutional rights.

Donald A. Downs received his Ph.D. from the University of California at Berkeley and is now Assistant Professor of Political Science at the University of Wisconsin at Madison. His research specializes in the theoretical analysis of conflicts over constitutional protection for free speech. He is the author of *Nazis in Skokie: Freedom, Community, and the First Amendment,* several articles, and a forthcoming book on pornography and the First Amendment.

John Gilliom has worked as a political activist and is currently a doctoral candidate in political science at the University of Washington, where he focuses on public law, political theory, and mass communications. His dissertation research is exploring changing technologies and policies of surveillance and their impact on traditional discourses of rights.

William Haltom received his Ph.D. in political science from the University of Washington and is currently Assistant Professor at the University of Puget Sound. He has published articles on constitutional and judicial issues. His current work examines the relationship between the Supreme Court and the mass media.

Gerald L. Houseman has taught at the University of California at Irvine and at the University of Illinois, and is presently Professor of Political Science at Indiana University–Fort Wayne. He has written over a dozen articles and five books, including *The Right of Mobility, City of the Right,* and *G.D.H. Cole,* on various political and legal issues. His most recent research is in corporate law and comparative law.

Ronald C. Kahn received his Ph.D. in political science from the University of Chicago and is currently Professor and Chairman of the Department of Government at Oberlin College. He has written extensively on constitutional law and public policy. He is currently at work on a book that compares the Warren and Burger/Rehnquist eras of the Supreme Court.

Michael W. McCann received his Ph.D. in political science from the University of California at Berkeley and is presently Associate Professor at the University of Washington. He is the author of *Taking Reform Seriously: Perspectives on Public Interest Liberalism* and several articles on constitutional equality. He is now working on a book analyzing the development of rights claims and legal strategies in political battles over comparable worth wage policies.

Margaret Jane Radin has been a Visiting Professor of Law at both Harvard University and the University of California at Los Angeles, and is presently Carolyn Craig Franklin Professor of Law at the University of Southern California School of Law. She has published numerous articles in law reviews and philosophical journals, as well as a recent book, *Property and Parenthood,* that analyze the tradition of property rights discourse and law-making in America.

Deborah L. Rhode received her J.D. from Yale Law School and is presently Professor of Law and Director of the Institute for Research on Women and Gender at Stanford University. She has published over a dozen articles and several books on professional ethics, legal representation, and constitutional gender issues, including *The Legal Profession: Responsibility and Regulation* and, most recently, *Justice and Gender.*

Stuart A. Scheingold is Professor of Political Science at the University of Washington. He is the author of numerous articles and books, including *The Politics of Rights: Lawyers, Public Policy, and Political Change* and *The Politics of Law and Order.* His most recent research includes a multicultural study of political activity and attitudes among radical lawyers.

John S. Shockley received his B.A. from the University of Texas and his Ph.D. in political science from the University of Wisconsin at Madison. He is currently Professor of Political Science at Western Illinois University. His publications include *Chicago Revolt in a Texas Town*, a monograph on the initiative process, and several articles on campaign reform law.

Roger A. Simpson was formerly a journalist and is now Associate Professor in the School of Communications at the University of Washington, where he teaches journalism and the history, law, and economics of mass media. His research has focused on labor relations in the media (*Unionism or Hearst: The Seattle-Post Intelligencer Strike of 1936*) and, most recently, on legal protection for press freedom in modern corporate society.

Rogers M. Smith received his Ph.D. from Harvard University and is presently Associate Professor of Political Science at Yale University. He is the author of *Liberalism and American Constitutional Law* and a variety of articles on the American legal tradition. He is currently working on a book on the evolution of citizenship ideals in America.

Case Index

447